STARTING OUT WITH

Games & Graphics

in C++

STARTING OUT WITH

Games & Graphics
in C++

Tony Gaddis
Haywood Community College

Addison-Wesley

Boston   San Francisco   New York
London   Toronto   Sydney   Tokyo   Singapore   Madrid
Mexico City   Munich   Paris   Cape Town   Hong Kong   Montreal

Editor-in-Chief	*Michael Hirsch*
Editorial Assistant	*Stephanie Sellinger*
Managing Editor	*Jeffrey Holcomb*
Senior Production Supervisor	*Meredith Gertz*
Senior Media Producer	*Bethany Tidd*
Marketing Manager	*Erin Davis*
Marketing Coordinator	*Kathryn Ferranti*
Senior Manufacturing Buyer	*Carol Melville*
Senior Media Buyer	*Ginny Michaud*
Text Design	*Joyce Cosentino Wells and Gillian Hall*
Project Management, Production Coordination, Composition, and Illustrations	*Gillian Hall, The Aardvark Group*
Copyeditor	*Kathleen Cantwell, C4 Technologies*
Proofreader	*Holly McLean-Aldis*
Indexer	*Jack Lewis*
Cover Art Direction	*Linda Knowles*
Cover Designer	*Elena Sidorova*
Cover Image	*©2009 BLOOMimage/Getty Images*

Many of the designations used by manufacturers and sellers to distinguish their products are claimed as trademarks. Where those designations appear in this book, and Addison-Wesley was aware of a trademark claim, the designations have been printed in initial caps or all caps.

The programs and applications presented in this book have been included for their instructional value. They have been tested with care, but are not guaranteed for any particular purpose. The publisher does not offer any warranties or representations, nor does it accept any liabilities with respect to the programs or applications.

Library of Congress Cataloging-in-Publication Data

Gaddis, Tony.
  Starting out with games & graphics / Tony Gaddis.
     p. cm.
  Includes index.
  ISBN 978-0-321-51291-8
  1. Computer programming. 2. Computer games--Programming. 3. Computer graphics. I. Title.
  QA76.6.G3148 2009
  005.1--dc22
                                                                                     2009008074

Addison-Wesley
is an imprint of

www.pearsonhighered.com

ISBN-13: 978-0-321-51291-8
ISBN-10: 0-321-51291-X

2 3 4 5 6 7 8 9 10—EB—13 12 11 10 09

Brief Contents

Preface   xi

Chapter 1   **Introduction to Computers and Programming**   1

Chapter 2   **Graphics Programming with C++ and the Dark GDK Library**   37

Chapter 3   **Variables, Calculations, and Colors**   81

Chapter 4   `void` **Functions**   139

Chapter 5   **Working with Images**   179

Chapter 6   **Control Structures**   213

Chapter 7   **The Game Loop and Animation**   281

Chapter 8   **The Vulture Trouble Game: Introducing Audio, Physics, and Text Effects**   345

Chapter 9   **Value-Returning Functions and Mouse Input**   409

Chapter 10   **Arrays and Tile Mapping**   473

Chapter 11   **Strings and Files**   559

Chapter 12   **Object-Oriented Programming**   611

Appendix A   **Downloading and Installing the Required Software**   681

Appendix B   **The ASCII Character Set**   687

Index   689

Contents

Preface   xi

Chapter 1   Introduction to Computers and Programming   1

1.1   Introduction 1
1.2   Hardware 2
1.3   How Computers Store Data 6
1.4   How a Program Works 11
1.5   C++ and the Dark GDK Library 19
IN THE SPOTLIGHT: Writing Your First Program with Visual C++ 2008
        Express Edition and the Dark GDK 20
IN THE SPOTLIGHT: Opening and Executing an Example Program 27
Review Questions 30
Programming Exercises 33

**Chapter 2   Graphics Programming
with C++ and the Dark GDK Library   37**

2.1   Getting Your Feet Wet with C++ and the Dark GDK Library 37
2.2   The Screen Coordinate System 43
2.3   Basic 2D Shapes 48
2.4   Displaying Text 61
IN THE SPOTLIGHT: The Orion Constellation Program 67
2.5   The Program Development Cycle 74
Review Questions 75
Programming Exercises 79

Chapter 3   Variables, Calculations, and Colors   81

3.1   Introduction 81
3.2   Literal Data 81
3.3   Variables 84
3.4   Calculations 92
IN THE SPOTLIGHT: Drawing Simple Bar Charts 103
3.5   Getting Values from Functions 108

3.6   Reading Numeric Input from the Keyboard 117
3.7   Colors 122
IN THE SPOTLIGHT: Drawing the Italian Flag 126
3.8   Named Constants 129
3.9   Changing the Size of the Program Window 131
Review Questions 133
Programming Exercises 137

Chapter 4   `void` Functions   139

4.1   Modularizing a Program with Functions 139
4.2   Defining and Calling a `void` Function 141
4.3   Designing a Program to Use Functions 148
4.4   Local Variables 151
4.5   Passing Arguments to Functions 155
4.6   Global Variables and Constants 169
Review Questions 173
Programming Exercises 176

Chapter 5   Working with Images   179

5.1   Introduction 179
5.2   Bitmaps 179
IN THE SPOTLIGHT: Using a Bitmap as a Background Image 182
IN THE SPOTLIGHT: Creating a Slide Show Program 188
5.3   Color Key Transparency 195
IN THE SPOTLIGHT: Using Microsoft Paint to Create Images 199
IN THE SPOTLIGHT: Adding a Key Color to Digital Photos
                   and Other Images 204
Review Questions 208
Programming Exercises 210

Chapter 6   Control Structures   213

6.1   Introduction 213
6.2   Writing a Decision Structure with the `if` Statement 215
6.3   The `if-else` Statement 223
IN THE SPOTLIGHT: A Number Guessing Game 226
6.4   Nested Decision Structures and the `if-else-if` Statement 228
IN THE SPOTLIGHT: Enhancing the Number Guessing Game with Feedback . . 232
6.5   Repetition Structures: The `while` Loop and the `do-while` Loop . . . 237
IN THE SPOTLIGHT: Enhancing the Number Guessing Game
                   with a `while` Loop 240

6.6   The Increment and Decrement Operators 248
6.7   Repetition Structures: The for Loop 249
6.8   Using the for Loop to Process Pixels in an Image 255
6.9   Logical Operators 260
6.10 The switch Statement 266
6.11 Numeric Truth, Flags, and bool Variables 271
      Review Questions 273
      Programming Exercises 278

Chapter 7   The Game Loop and Animation   281

7.1   The Game Loop 281
7.2   Simple Animation 286
7.3   Controlling Objects with the Keyboard 289
7.4   Sprites 296
7.5   Cel Animation and Sprite Sheets 323
7.6   Sprite Collision Detection 329
      IN THE SPOTLIGHT: The PizzaBot Game 333
      Review Questions 340
      Programming Exercises 342

Chapter 8   The Vulture Trouble Game: Introducing Audio, Physics, and Text Effects   345

8.1   Introduction 345
8.2   Playing Sound Effects and Music 345
8.3   Simulating Falling Objects 364
8.4   Text Effects 374
8.5   The Vulture Trouble Game 382
      Review Questions 404
      Programming Exercises 406

Chapter 9   Value-Returning Functions and Mouse Input   409

9.1   Writing a Value-Returning Function 409
      IN THE SPOTLIGHT: Returning a Color from a Function 417
      IN THE SPOTLIGHT: Constraining a Sprite to the Screen's Visible Area 422
9.2   Working with the Mouse 439
      IN THE SPOTLIGHT: Processing Full Mouse Clicks 444
      IN THE SPOTLIGHT: Clicking Sprites 448
      IN THE SPOTLIGHT: Creating a Custom Mouse Pointer 452
9.3   The Bug Zapper Game 454
      Review Questions 466
      Programming Exercises 469

Chapter 10   **Arrays and Tile Mapping   473**

10.1 Array Basics 473
IN THE SPOTLIGHT: Drawing Polylines 487
IN THE SPOTLIGHT: The Memory Match Game 490
IN THE SPOTLIGHT: Shuffling an Array 498
IN THE SPOTLIGHT: Dealing Cards with Partially Filled Arrays 504
10.2 Sorting Arrays 511
10.3 Two-Dimensional Arrays 521
10.4 Tile Maps 529
Review Questions 552
Programming Exercises 556

Chapter 11   **Strings and Files   559**

11.1 Working with Strings 559
IN THE SPOTLIGHT: Getting a File Name and Testing
       for the File's Existence 569
IN THE SPOTLIGHT: Mad Libs Word Games 571
11.2 Introduction to File Input and Output 578
11.3 Saving a Game's High Score 595
Review Questions 605
Programming Exercises 609

Chapter 12   **Object-Oriented Programming   611**

12.1 Procedural and Object-Oriented Programming 611
12.2 Classes and Objects 614
IN THE SPOTLIGHT: A Sprite Class 645
12.3 Inheritance 652
IN THE SPOTLIGHT: The `MoveableSprite` Class 661
12.4 An Object-Oriented Game: Balloon Target 667
Review Questions 676
Programming Exercises 678

Appendix A   **Downloading and Installing
               the Required Software   681**

Appendix B   **The ASCII Character Set   687**

Index   689

Preface

Welcome to *Starting Out with Games & Graphics in C++*. This book teaches the traditional topics of an introductory programming course—but it does so unconventionally. Instead of working in a console environment, students using this book will write programs that produce graphics, manipulate images, work with audio, and play games. The examples and assignments are designed to excite and motivate students, and engage them throughout the semester.

This book covers fundamental topics such as data types, variables, input, output, control structures, functions, arrays, files, classes, and objects. Alongside these topics, students learn to draw with primitive graphics, load and manipulate images, create sprites and animations, play music and sound effects, and detect collisions between the graphical elements of a program. Students also learn to combine these skills to create their own interactive video games!

Because this book's primary purpose is to teach programming fundamentals, it does not overwhelm students with game theory or the intricacies of a graphics library such as DirectX or OpenGL. Instead, it uses the Dark GDK (Game Development Kit)—a free library that makes graphics programming simple enough for beginners, and handles the complexities of game programming. This means that students can focus on the fundamentals while creating interesting graphics and game programs.

Required Software

To use this book, you will need the following software and files:

- **Microsoft® Visual C++® 2008**

  When purchased new, this book includes a DVD containing Microsoft® Visual C++® 2008 Express Edition. If your book does not have the DVD, you can download this software. See Appendix A for instructions.

- **The Dark GDK (Game Development Kit)**

  The Dark GDK must be downloaded and installed. See Appendix A for instructions.

- **Sample Source Code and Media Files**

  The source code for the book's example programs, as well as graphics, audio files, and game case studies, are available for download from the publisher's Web site at www.aw.com/gaddis. See Appendix A for instructions.

Brief Overview of Each Chapter

Chapter 1: Introduction to Computers and Programming

This chapter begins by giving a concrete and comprehensive explanation of how computers work, how data is stored and manipulated, and why we write programs in high-level languages. Step-by-step tutorials introduce students to using Visual C++ with the Dark GDK.

Chapter 2: Graphics Programming with C++ and the Dark GDK Library

This chapter begins by showing students how to write simple programs. The importance of comments and programming style are discussed. Then, the screen coordinate system that is used by the Dark GDK to map the locations of pixels is introduced. Next, students learn to draw with primitive shapes and display text in a graphical environment. The program development cycle is also discussed.

Chapter 3: Variables, Calculations, and Colors

In this chapter, students learn to work with numerical data. Variables, data types, literals, and named constants are introduced. Students learn to perform mathematical operations, get values from predefined value-returning functions, and read numeric input from the keyboard. Students also learn how the RGB color system is used to produce colors.

Chapter 4: `void` Functions

This chapter shows the benefits of modularizing programs and using the top-down design approach. Students learn to define and call `void` functions, pass arguments to functions, and use local variables. Hierarchy charts are introduced as a design tool.

Chapter 5: Working with Images

This chapter takes students beyond simple primitive shapes. Students learn to load images such as those taken with a digital camera, or created with graphics programs such as Microsoft Paint. The chapter covers various special effects that can be done with images, and demonstrates how to use color key technology to create transparent pixels. Students learn how to take multiple images, using color key technology, and combine them to produce a single image.

Chapter 6: Control Structures

This chapter explores the various control structures available in C++. Students learn to write decision structures using the `if`, `if-else`, `if-else-if`, and `switch` statements. Additionally, students learn to write repetition structures using the `while`, `do-while`, and `for` loops. Relational operators, the increment/decrement operators, and logical operators are covered. Interesting applications, such as scanning the pixels in an image, drawing patterns, and programming a number guessing game, are demonstrated.

Chapter 7: The Game Loop and Animation

This chapter introduces the game loop, which is common in game programming. The game loop is a special loop that constantly runs, controlling the game's action. The game loop also controls the rate at which the screen is updated. First, students learn to write game loops that produce simple animations with primitive shapes. Then, students advance to create sprites and animated sprites. Students learn to write code that reads keystrokes (such as the arrow keys) and allows the user to control objects on the screen. The chapter concludes by discussing collision detection, and demonstrates a simple game named PizzaBot.

Chapter 8: The Vulture Trouble Game: Introducing Audio, Physics, and Text Effects

This chapter begins by discussing audio files and how they can be used for sound effects in a game. First, students learn to load and play audio files, and manipulate them in various ways. Next, students learn how to perform the calculations necessary to simulate the motion of an object falling toward Earth. Then, the chapter discusses how to change the appearance of text by setting the font, style, and point size. All of this is finally brought together in the Vulture Trouble game, a high-quality video game that incorporates all of the programming skills that students have learned to this point.

Chapter 9: Value-Returning Functions and Mouse Input

In this chapter, students learn to write their own value-returning function. Value-returning functions are demonstrated in various applications, such as generating random colors, determining whether a pixel is of a certain color, and constraining a sprite to the visible part of the screen. Then, students learn to perform operations with the mouse, such as reading the mouse position and determining whether the mouse buttons are being clicked. The chapter concludes with the Bug Zapper game, in which the user attempts to click randomly appearing bugs as fast as possible.

Chapter 10: Arrays and Tile Mapping

In this chapter, students learn to create and work with one-dimensional and two-dimensional arrays. Several interesting game-related array applications are discussed. For example, students learn to create an array of images, and then create algorithms to shuffle and sort the array. These techniques are perfect for creating card games. Students also learn to use two-dimensional arrays to map tiles (small rectangular images) to the screen in order to construct the background for a game.

Chapter 11: Strings and Files

This chapter shows students how to store strings in memory and perform various operations with them. The Mad Libs word game is introduced as a string manipulation example. Sequential file input and output is also covered, using the Dark GDK file functions. Examples include storing a set of random colors in a file and saving a game's high score.

Chapter 12: Object-Oriented Programming

This chapter compares procedural and object-oriented programming practices. It covers the fundamental concepts of classes and objects. Member variables, member functions, access specification, constructors, accessors, and mutators are discussed. The chapter also introduces inheritance. An object-oriented game named Balloon Target is presented.

Appendix A: Downloading and Installing the Required Software

This appendix guides students through downloading and installing the software and files that are necessary to use this book.

Appendix B: The ASCII Character Set

This appendix lists the characters and codes in the ASCII character set.

The following materials are available for download from the publisher's Web site at www.aw.com/gaddis. Appendix A provides instructions for downloading them.

Scones McNabb: A Game Case Study (available online)

In the game, the user helps Scones McNabb save his family bakery from the clutches of Baron Von Reek. The case study provides complete source code, media files, and an in-depth explanation of how the program works.

Object-Oriented Vulture Trouble (available online)

This case study presents an object-oriented version of the Vulture Trouble game that is discussed in Chapter 8. It provides complete source code, media files, and an in-depth explanation of how the program works.

Answers to Checkpoints (available online)

This file gives the answers to Checkpoints that appear throughout the text.

Features of the Text

Concept Statements. Each major section of the text starts with a concept statement. This statement concisely summarizes the main point of the section.

Example Programs. Each chapter has an abundant number of complete and partial example programs, each designed to highlight the current topic.

In the Spotlight. Numerous *In the Spotlight* sections appear throughout the book. They provide detailed discussions and examples of how certain programming techniques can be applied to specific applications.

NOTE: Notes are short explanations of interesting or often misunderstood points relevant to the topic at hand. They appear at several places throughout the text.

TIP: Tips advise students on the best techniques for approaching different programming or animation problems.

 WARNING: Warnings caution students about programming techniques or practices that can lead to malfunctioning programs or lost data.

 Checkpoint. Checkpoints, placed at intervals throughout each chapter, are designed to test the student's knowledge soon after learning a new topic.

Review Questions. Each chapter presents a thorough and diverse set of Review Questions, including Multiple Choice, True-or-False, Short Answer, and Algorithm Workbench.

Programming Exercises. Each chapter offers a pool of Programming Exercises designed to solidify the student's knowledge of the topics currently being studied.

Supplements

Microsoft Visual Studio 2008 Express Edition

When purchased new, this book comes with Visual Studio 2008 Express Edition on an accompanying DVD. This DVD provides a suite of software development tools, including Visual C++ 2008 Express Edition. If your book does not have the DVD, you can download the software. See Appendix A for more information.

Online Resources

This book's online resource page contains numerous student supplements. To access these supplements, go to `www.aw.com/gaddis` and click the image of this book's cover. You will be able to download the following items:

- Source code for the book's example programs
- Graphics and audio files that can be used in student projects
- The Scones McNabb game case study
- The Object-Oriented Vulture Trouble game case study
- Answers to Checkpoints

Instructor Resources

The following supplements are available to qualified instructors:

- Answers to the Review Questions
- Solutions for the Programming Exercises
- PowerPoint presentation slides for each chapter

Visit the Addison-Wesley Instructor Resource Center (`www.pearsonhighered.com/irc`) or send an e-mail to `computing@aw.com` for information on how to access the supplements.

Acknowledgments

I want to thank The Game Creators for developing the Dark GDK, a powerful game development kit that is simple enough for beginning students. I also want to thank Christopher Rich for his invaluable contributions to this book. His original artwork, audio, knowledge of the Dark GDK, and his work on the Vulture Trouble and Scones McNabb games helped make this book what it is. Thanks, Chris!

I would also like to thank everyone at Addison-Wesley for making the *Starting Out with* series very successful. I have worked so closely with the team at Addison-Wesley that I consider them among my closest friends. I am extremely grateful that Michael Hirsch is my editor. He and Stephanie Sellinger, editorial assistant, have guided me through the process of writing this book. I am also thankful to have Erin Davis as marketing manager. Her energy and creativity are inspiring. The production team, including Meredith Gertz, Jeff Holcomb, Gillian Hall, Bethany Tidd, Carol Melville, and Linda Knowles, worked tirelessly to make this book a reality. Thanks to all!

Last, but not least, I want to thank my family for the patience, love, and support they have shown me throughout this and my many other projects.

About the Author

Tony Gaddis is the principal author of the *Starting Out with* series of textbooks. Tony has nearly 20 years of experience teaching computer science courses, primarily at Haywood Community College. He is a highly acclaimed instructor who was previously selected as the North Carolina Community College *Teacher of the Year*, and has received the *Teaching Excellence* award from the National Institute for Staff and Organizational Development. The *Starting Out with* series includes introductory books covering C++, Java™, Microsoft® Visual Basic®, Microsoft® C#®, Python, Programming Logic and Design, and Alice, all published by Addison-Wesley.

1 Introduction to Computers and Programming

TOPICS

1.1 Introduction

1.2 Hardware

1.3 How Computers Store Data

1.4 How a Program Works

1.5 C++ and the Dark GDK Library

1.1 Introduction

The goal of this book is to teach computer programming. We assume that you are a beginner, with little or no programming experience. As you work through the book you will write some very interesting programs. You will start by writing programs that display graphics, and you will quickly advance to programs that produce special effects with images, such as those taken with a digital camera. Then, you will learn about game programming. The games that you will create will be graphical, interactive, and fun to play! Along the journey you will be learning the fundamentals of computer programming.

A *program* is a set of instructions that a computer follows to perform a task. Programs are commonly referred to as *software*. Software is essential to a computer because without software, a computer can do nothing. All of the software that we use to make our computers useful (and entertaining) is created by individuals known as programmers or software developers. A *programmer*, or *software developer*, is a person with the training and skills necessary to design, create, and test computer programs. Computer programming is an exciting and rewarding career. In addition to creating computer games, you will find programmers working in business, medicine, government, law enforcement, agriculture, academics, telecommunications, and almost every other field.

Before we begin to explore the concepts of programming, you need to understand a few basic things about computers and how they work. This chapter will build a solid foundation of knowledge that you will continually rely on as you study computer science. First, we will discuss the physical components of computers. Next, we will look at how computers store data and how programs work. Finally, we will discuss the specific tools that you will use in this book to create games and graphical programs: the C++ language and the Dark GDK library.

1.2 Hardware

CONCEPT: The physical devices that a computer is made of are referred to as the computer's hardware. Most computer systems are made of similar hardware devices.

The term *hardware* refers to all of the physical devices, or *components*, that a computer is made of. A computer is not one single device, but a system of devices that work together. Like the different instruments in a symphony orchestra, each device in a computer plays its own part.

If you have ever shopped for a computer, you've probably seen sales literature listing components such as microprocessors, memory, disk drives, video displays, graphics cards, and so forth. Unless you already know a lot about computers, or at least have a friend who does, understanding what these different components do might be challenging. As shown in Figure 1-1, a typical computer system consists of the following major components:

- The central processing unit (CPU)
- Main memory
- Secondary storage devices
- Input devices
- Output devices

Let's take a closer look at each of these components.

Figure 1-1 Typical components of a computer system

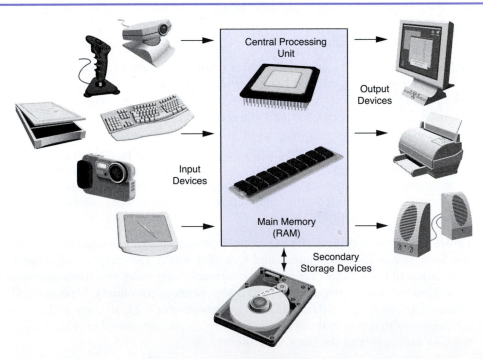

The CPU

When a computer is performing the tasks that a program tells it to do, we say that the computer is *running* or *executing* the program. The *central processing unit*, or *CPU*, is the part of a computer that actually runs programs. The CPU is the most important component in a computer because without it, the computer could not run software.

In the earliest computers, CPUs were huge devices made of electrical and mechanical components such as vacuum tubes and switches. Figure 1-2 shows such a device. The two women in the photo are working with the historic ENIAC computer. The *ENIAC* is considered by many as the world's first programmable electronic computer, and was built in 1945 to calculate artillery ballistic tables for the U.S. Army. This machine, which was primarily one big CPU, was 8 feet tall, 100 feet long, and weighed 30 tons.

Figure 1-2 The ENIAC computer (U.S. Army photo)

Today, CPUs are small chips known as *microprocessors*. Figure 1-3 shows a photo of a lab technician holding a modern-day microprocessor. In addition to being much smaller than the old electro-mechanical CPUs in early computers, microprocessors are also much more powerful.

Main Memory

You can think of *main memory* as the computer's work area. This is where the computer stores a program while the program is running, as well as the data that the program is working with. For example, suppose you are using a word processing program to write an essay for one of your classes. While you do this, both the word processing program and the essay are stored in main memory.

Figure 1-3 A lab technician holds a modern microprocessor
(photo courtesy of Intel Corporation)

Main memory is commonly known as *random-access memory*, or *RAM*. It is called this because the CPU is able to access data stored at any random location in RAM quickly. RAM is usually a *volatile* type of memory that is used only for temporary storage while a program is running. When the computer is turned off, the contents of RAM are erased. Inside your computer, RAM is stored in chips, similar to the ones shown in Figure 1-4.

Figure 1-4 Memory chips (photo courtesy of IBM Corporation)

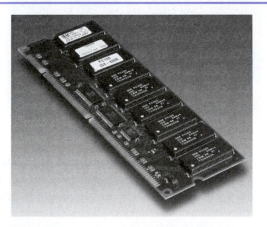

Secondary Storage Devices

Secondary storage is a type of memory that can hold data for long periods of time, even when there is no power to the computer. Programs are normally stored in secondary memory and loaded into main memory as needed. Important data, such as word processing documents, payroll data, and inventory records is saved to secondary storage as well.

The most common type of secondary storage device is the disk drive. A *disk drive* stores data by magnetically encoding it onto a circular disk. Most computers have a disk drive mounted inside their case. External disk drives, which connect to one of the computer's communication ports, are also available. External disk drives can be used to create backup copies of important data or to move data to another computer.

In addition to external disk drives, many types of devices have been created for copying data, and for moving it to other computers. For many years floppy disk drives were popular. A *floppy disk drive* records data onto a small floppy disk, which can be removed from the drive. Floppy disks have many disadvantages, however. They hold only a small amount of data, are slow to access data, and are sometimes unreliable. The use of floppy disk drives has declined dramatically in recent years, in favor of superior devices such as USB drives. *USB drives* are small devices that plug into a computer's USB (universal serial bus) port, and appear to the system as a disk drive. These drives do not actually contain a disk, however. They store data in a special type of memory known as *flash memory*. USB drives, which are also known as *memory sticks* and *flash drives*, are inexpensive, reliable, and small enough to be carried in your pocket.

Optical devices such as the *CD* (compact disc) and the *DVD* (digital versatile disc) are also popular for data storage. Data is not recorded magnetically on an optical disc, but is encoded as a series of pits on the disc surface. CD and DVD drives use a laser to detect the pits and thus read the encoded data. Optical discs hold large amounts of data, and because recordable CD and DVD drives are now common, they are good mediums for creating backup copies of data.

Input Devices

Input is any data the computer collects from people and from other devices. The component that collects the data and sends it to the computer is called an *input device*. Common input devices are the keyboard, mouse, joystick, scanner, microphone, and digital camera. Disk drives and optical drives can also be considered input devices because programs and data are retrieved from them and loaded into the computer's memory.

Output Devices

Output is any data the computer produces for people or for other devices. It might be a sales report, a list of names, or a graphic image. The data is sent to an *output device*, which formats and presents it. Common output devices are video displays and printers. Disk drives and CD recorders can also be considered output devices because the system sends data to them in order to be saved.

 Checkpoint

    1.1. What is a program?

    1.2. What is hardware?

    1.3. List the five major components of a computer system.

    1.4. What part of the computer actually runs programs?

1.5. What part of the computer serves as a work area to store a program and its data while the program is running?

1.6. What part of the computer holds data for long periods of time, even when there is no power to the computer?

1.7. What part of the computer collects data from people or other devices?

1.8. What part of the computer formats and presents data for people or other devices?

1.3   How Computers Store Data

CONCEPT: All data that is stored in a computer is converted to sequences of 0s and 1s.

A computer's memory is made of tiny storage locations known as *bytes*. One byte is only enough memory to store a letter of the alphabet or a small number. In order to do anything meaningful, a computer has to have lots of bytes. Most computers today have millions, or even billions, of bytes of memory.

Each byte is made of eight smaller storage locations known as bits. The term *bit* stands for *binary digit*. Computer scientists usually think of bits as tiny switches that can be either on or off. Bits aren't actual "switches," however, at least not in the conventional sense. In most computer systems, bits are tiny electrical components that can hold either a positive or a negative charge. Computer scientists think of a positive charge as a switch in the *on* position, and a negative charge as a switch in the *off* position. Figure 1-5 shows the way that a computer scientist might think of a byte of memory: as a collection of switches that are each flipped to either the on or off position.

Figure 1-5 Think of a byte as eight switches

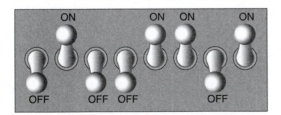

When a piece of data is stored in a byte, the computer sets the eight bits to an on/off pattern that represents the data. For example, the pattern shown on the left in Figure 1-6 shows how the number 77 would be stored in a byte, and the pattern on the right shows how the letter A would be stored in a byte. In a moment you will see how these patterns are determined.

Figure 1-6 Bit patterns for the number 77 and the letter A

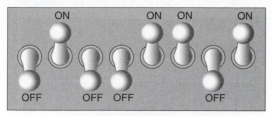

The number 77 stored in a byte.

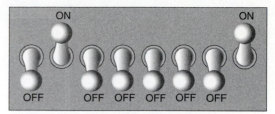

The letter A stored in a byte.

Storing Numbers

A bit can be used in a very limited way to represent numbers. Depending on whether the bit is turned on or off, it can represent one of two different values. In computer systems, a bit that is turned off represents the number 0 and a bit that is turned on represents the number 1. This corresponds perfectly to the *binary numbering system*. In the binary numbering system (or *binary*, as it is usually called) all numeric values are written as sequences of 0s and 1s. Here is an example of a number that is written in binary:

```
10011101
```

The position of each digit in a binary number has a value assigned to it. Starting with the rightmost digit and moving left, the position values are 2^0, 2^1, 2^2, 2^3, and so forth, as shown in Figure 1-7. Figure 1-8 shows the same diagram with the position values calculated. Starting with the rightmost digit and moving left, the position values are 1, 2, 4, 8, and so forth.

Figure 1-7 The values of binary digits as powers of 2

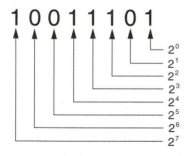

Figure 1-8 The values of binary digits

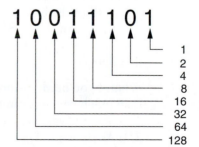

To determine the value of a binary number you simply add up the position values of all the 1s. For example, in the binary number 10011101, the position values of the 1s are 1, 4, 8, 16, and 128. This is shown in Figure 1-9. The sum of all of these position values is 157. So, the value of the binary number 10011101 is 157.

Figure 1-9 Determining the value of 10011101

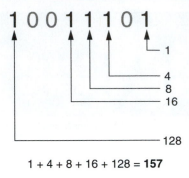

$$1 + 4 + 8 + 16 + 128 = \textbf{157}$$

Figure 1-10 shows how you can picture the number 157 stored in a byte of memory. Each 1 is represented by a bit in the on position, and each 0 is represented by a bit in the off position.

Figure 1-10 The bit pattern for 157

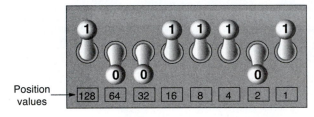

$$128 + 16 + 8 + 4 + 1 = \textbf{157}$$

When all of the bits in a byte are set to 0 (turned off), then the value of the byte is 0. When all of the bits in a byte are set to 1 (turned on), then the byte holds the largest value that can be stored in it. The largest value that can be stored in a byte is 1 + 2 + 4 + 8 + 16 + 32 + 64 + 128 = 255. This limit exists because there are only eight bits in a byte.

What if you need to store a number larger than 255? The answer is simple: Use more than one byte. For example, suppose we put two bytes together. That gives us 16 bits. The position values of those 16 bits would be 2^0, 2^1, 2^2, 2^3, and so forth, up through 2^{15}. As shown in Figure 1-11, the maximum value that can be stored in two bytes is 65,535. If you need to store a number larger than this, then more bytes are necessary.

TIP: If you are feeling overwhelmed by all this, relax! You will not actually have to convert numbers to binary while programming. Knowing that this process is taking place inside the computer will help you as you learn, and in the long term this knowledge will make you a better programmer.

Figure 1-11 Two bytes used for a large number

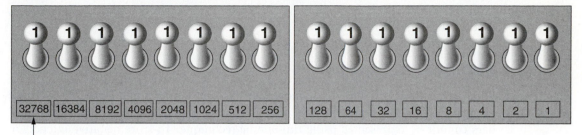

| 32768 | 16384 | 8192 | 4096 | 2048 | 1024 | 512 | 256 | | 128 | 64 | 32 | 16 | 8 | 4 | 2 | 1 |

32768 + 16384 + 8192 + 4096 + 2048 + 1024 + 512 + 256 + 128 + 64 + 32 + 16 + 8 + 4 + 2 + 1 = **65535**

Position values

Storing Characters

Any piece of data that is stored in a computer's memory must be stored as a binary number. This includes characters, such as letters and punctuation marks. When a character is stored in memory, it is first converted to a numeric code. The numeric code is then stored in memory as a binary number.

Over the years, different coding schemes have been developed to represent characters in computer memory. Historically, the most important of these coding schemes is *ASCII*, which stands for the *American Standard Code for Information Interchange*. ASCII is a set of 128 numeric codes that represent the English letters, various punctuation marks, and other characters. For example, the ASCII code for the uppercase letter A is 65. When you type an uppercase A on your computer keyboard, the number 65 is stored in memory (as a binary number, of course). This is shown in Figure 1-12.

Figure 1-12 The letter A is stored in memory as the number 65

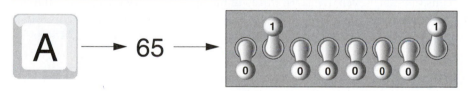

 TIP: The acronym ASCII is pronounced "askee."

In case you are curious, the ASCII code for uppercase B is 66, for uppercase C is 67, and so forth. Appendix B shows all of the ASCII codes and the characters they represent.

The ASCII character set was developed in the early 1960s, and eventually was adopted by all computer manufacturers. ASCII is limited however, because it defines codes for only 128 characters. To remedy this, the Unicode character set was developed in the early 1990s. *Unicode* is an extensive encoding scheme that not only is compatible with ASCII, but also can represent all the characters of most of the languages in the world. Today, Unicode is quickly becoming the standard character set used in the computer industry.

Negative Integers

Perhaps it has occurred to you by now that the binary numbering technique we have been discussing can represent only integer values, beginning with 0. Negative numbers cannot be represented using this simple technique. To store negative integers in memory, computers use *two*'s complement arithmetic. In *twos complement arithmetic* a negative integer is encoded so it can be represented as a binary number.

Real Numbers

You might also have realized that the binary numbering technique we have been discussing cannot be used to store real numbers with a fractional part (such as 3.14159). To store a number with a fractional part in memory, computers typically use floating-point notation. In *floating-point* notation, a real number is encoded so it can be represented as a binary number. They are called floating-point numbers because there is no fixed number of digits before or after the decimal point. Floating-point notation can be used to represent real numbers such as 2176.6 or 1.3783652.

Real numbers sometimes have many digits, or even an infinite number of digits, appearing after the decimal point. For example, when we convert the fraction $^1/_3$ to decimal we get 1.333333..., with an infinite number of 3s after the decimal point. Storing a value such as $^1/_3$ in memory is problematic because there is no exact way to represent such values using binary numbers. So, floating-point numbers are stored in memory with a specified precision. The *precision* is the total number of digits (both before and after the decimal point) that are stored in memory.

For example, if we use seven digits of precision when storing a floating-point number, it means that only seven digits are stored in memory. If we try to store a real number that has more than seven digits, it will be rounded to seven digits. For example, the number 1.23456789 (which has nine digits) would be rounded to 1.234568.

Other Types of Data

Computers are often referred to as digital devices. The term *digital* can be used to describe anything that uses binary numbers. *Digital data* is data that is stored in binary, and a *digital device* is any device that works with binary data. In this section, we have discussed how numbers and characters are stored in binary, but computers also work with many other types of digital data.

For example, consider the pictures that you take with your digital camera. These images are composed of tiny dots of color known as *pixels*. (The term pixel stands for *picture element*.) As shown in Figure 1-13, each pixel in an image is converted to a numeric code that represents the pixel's color. The numeric code is stored in memory as a binary number.

Figure 1-13 A digital image is stored in binary format

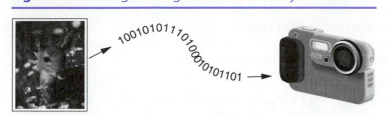

The music that you play on your CD player, iPod, or MP3 player is also digital. A digital song is broken into small pieces known as *samples*. Each sample is converted to a binary number, which can be stored in memory. The more samples that a song is divided into, the more it sounds like the original music when it is played back. A CD quality song is divided into more than 44,000 samples per second!

 Checkpoint

   1.9. What amount of memory is enough to store a letter of the alphabet or a small number?

   1.10. What do you call a tiny "switch" that can be set to either on or off?

   1.11. In what numbering system are all numeric values written as sequences of 0s and 1s?

   1.12. What is the purpose of ASCII?

   1.13. What encoding scheme is extensive and represents all the characters of all the languages in the world?

   1.14. What do the terms "digital data" and "digital device" mean?

1.4 How a Program Works

> **CONCEPT:** A computer's CPU only understands instructions that are written in machine language. Because people find it very difficult to write entire programs in machine language, other programming languages have been invented.

Earlier, we stated that the CPU is the most important component in a computer because it is the part of the computer that runs programs. Sometimes the CPU is called the "computer's brain," and is described as being "smart." Although these are common metaphors, you should understand that the CPU is not a brain, and it is not smart. The CPU is an electronic device that is designed to do specific things. In particular, the CPU is designed to perform operations such as the following:

  • Reading a piece of data from main memory
  • Adding two numbers

- Subtracting one number from another number
- Multiplying two numbers
- Dividing one number by another number
- Moving a piece of data from one memory location to another location
- Determining whether one value is equal to another value
- And so forth...

As you can see from this list, the CPU performs simple operations on pieces of data. The CPU does nothing on its own, however. It has to be told what to do, and that's the purpose of a program. A program is nothing more than a list of instructions that cause the CPU to perform operations.

Each instruction in a program is a command that tells the CPU to perform a specific operation. Here's an example of an instruction that might appear in a program:

```
10110000
```

To you and me, this is only a series of 0s and 1s. To a CPU, however, this is an instruction to perform an operation.[1] It is written in 0s and 1s because CPUs only understand instructions that are written in *machine language*, and machine language instructions are always written in binary.

A machine language instruction exists for each operation that a CPU is capable of performing. For example, there is an instruction for adding numbers; there is an instruction for subtracting one number from another; and so forth. The entire set of instructions that a CPU can execute is known as the CPU's *instruction set*.

NOTE: There are several microprocessor companies today that manufacture CPUs. Some of the more well-known microprocessor companies are Intel, AMD, and Motorola. If you look carefully at your computer, you might find a tag showing the logo of its microprocessor company.

Each brand of microprocessor has its own unique instruction set, which is typically understood only by microprocessors of the same brand. For example, Intel microprocessors understand the same instructions, but they do not understand instructions for Motorola microprocessors.

The machine language instruction that was previously shown is an example of only one instruction. It takes a lot more than one instruction, however, for the computer to do anything meaningful. The operations that a CPU knows how to perform are very basic in nature; therefore, a meaningful task can be accomplished only if the CPU performs many operations. For example, if you want your computer to calculate the amount of interest that you will earn from your savings account this year, the CPU will have to perform a large number of instructions, carried out in the proper sequence. It is not unusual for a program to contain thousands, or even a million or more machine language instructions.

Programs are usually stored on a secondary storage device such as a disk drive. When you install a program on your computer, typically the program is copied to your computer's disk drive from a CD-ROM, or perhaps downloaded from a Web site.

---

[1]The example shown is an actual instruction for an Intel microprocessor. It tells the microprocessor to move a value into the CPU.

Although a program can be stored on a secondary storage device such as a disk drive, it has to be copied into main memory, or RAM, each time the CPU executes it. For example, suppose you have a word processing program on your computer's disk. To execute the program you use the mouse to double-click the program's icon. This causes the program to be copied from the disk into main memory. Then, the computer's CPU executes the copy of the program that is in main memory. This process is illustrated in Figure 1-14.

Figure 1-14 A program is copied into main memory and then executed

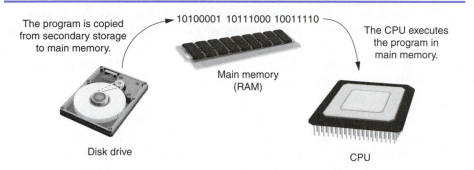

The program is copied from secondary storage to main memory.

10100001 10111000 10011110

The CPU executes the program in main memory.

Main memory (RAM)

Disk drive

CPU

When a CPU executes the instructions in a program, it is engaged in a process that is known as the *fetch-decode-execute cycle*. This cycle, which consists of three steps, is repeated for each instruction in the program, as follows:

1. **Fetch**   A program is a long sequence of machine language instructions. The first step of the cycle is to fetch, or read, the next instruction from memory into the CPU.

2. **Decode**   A machine language instruction is a binary number that represents a command that tells the CPU to perform an operation. In this step, the CPU decodes the instruction that was just fetched from memory, to determine which operation it should perform.

3. **Execute**   The last step in the cycle is to execute, or perform, the operation.

Figure 1-15 illustrates these steps.

Figure 1-15 The fetch-decode-execute cycle

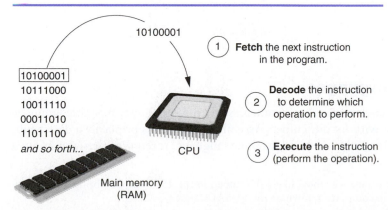

10100001

① **Fetch** the next instruction in the program.

10100001
10111000
10011110
00011010
11011100
and so forth...

② **Decode** the instruction to determine which operation to perform.

CPU

③ **Execute** the instruction (perform the operation).

Main memory (RAM)

From Machine Language to Assembly Language

Computers can only execute programs that are written in machine language. As previously mentioned, a program can have thousands, or even a million or more binary instructions, and writing such a program would be very tedious and time consuming. Programming in machine language would also be very difficult because putting a 0 or a 1 in the wrong place will cause an error.

Although a computer's CPU only understands machine language, it is impractical for people to write programs in machine language. For this reason, in the early days of computing[2] *assembly language* was created as an alternative to machine language. Instead of using binary numbers for instructions, assembly language uses short words that are known as *mnemonics*. For example, in assembly language, the mnemonic add typically means to add numbers, mul typically means to multiply numbers, and mov typically means to move a value to a location in memory. When a programmer uses assembly language to write a program, he or she can write short mnemonics instead of binary numbers.

NOTE: There are many different versions of assembly language. It was mentioned earlier that each brand of CPU has its own machine language instruction set. Each brand of CPU typically has its own assembly language as well.

Assembly language programs cannot be executed by the CPU, however. The CPU only understands machine language, so a special program known as an *assembler* is used to translate an assembly language program into a machine language program. This process is shown in Figure 1-16. The machine language program that is created by the assembler can then be executed by the CPU.

Figure 1-16 An assembler translates an assembly language
program into a machine language program

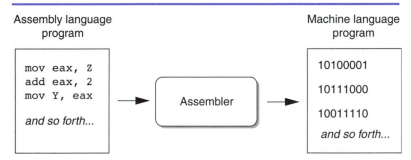

High-Level Languages

Although assembly language makes it unnecessary to write binary machine language instructions, it is not without difficulties. Assembly language is primarily a direct substitute for machine language, and like machine language, it requires that you know a

---

[2]The first assembly language was most likely developed in the 1940s at Cambridge University for use with an historic computer known as the EDSAC.

lot about the CPU. Assembly language also requires that you write a large number of instructions for even the simplest program. Because assembly language is so close in nature to machine language, it is referred to as a *low-level language*.

In the 1950s, a new generation of programming languages known as *high-level languages* appeared. A high-level language allows you to create powerful and complex programs without knowing how the CPU works, and without writing large numbers of low-level instructions. In addition, most high-level languages use words that are easy to understand. For example, if a programmer were using COBOL (which was one of the early high-level languages created in the 1950s), he or she would write the following instruction to display the message *Hello world* on the computer screen:

```
DISPLAY "Hello world"
```

Doing the same thing in assembly language would require several instructions, and an intimate knowledge of how the CPU interacts with the computer's video circuitry. As you can see from this example, high-level languages allow programmers to concentrate on the tasks they want to perform with their programs rather than on the details of how the CPU will execute those programs.

Since the 1950s, thousands of high-level languages have been created. Table 1-1 lists several of the more well-known languages.

Table 1-1 Programming languages

Language	Description
Ada	Ada was created in the 1970s, primarily for applications used by the U.S. Department of Defense. The language is named in honor of Countess Ada Lovelace, an influential and historic figure in the field of computing.
BASIC	**B**eginners **A**ll-purpose **S**ymbolic **I**nstruction **C**ode is a general-purpose language that was originally designed in the early 1960s to be simple enough for beginners to learn. Today, there are many different versions of BASIC.
FORTRAN	**FOR**mula **TRAN**slator was the first high-level programming language. It was designed in the 1950s for performing complex mathematical calculations.
COBOL	**C**ommon **B**usiness-**O**riented **L**anguage was created in the 1950s, and was designed for business applications.
Pascal	Pascal was created in 1970, and was originally designed for teaching programming. The language was named in honor of the mathematician, physicist, and philosopher Blaise Pascal.
C and C++	C and C++ (pronounced "c plus plus") are powerful, general-purpose languages developed at Bell Laboratories. The C language was created in 1972. The C++ language, which was based on the C language, was created in 1983.
C#	Pronounced "c sharp." This language was created by Microsoft around the year 2000 for developing applications based on the Microsoft .NET platform.

(continues next page)

Table 1-1 Programming languages (*continued*)

Language	Description
Java	Java was created by Sun Microsystems in the early 1990s. It can be used to develop programs that run on a single computer or over the Internet from a Web server.
JavaScript	JavaScript, created in the 1990s, can be used in Web pages. Despite its name, JavaScript is not related to Java.
Python	Python is a general-purpose language created in the early 1990s. It has become popular in business and academic applications.
Ruby	Ruby is a general-purpose language that was created in the 1990s. It is increasingly becoming a popular language for programs that run on Web servers.
Visual Basic	Visual Basic (commonly known as VB) is a Microsoft programming language and software development environment that allows programmers to create Windows-based applications quickly. VB was originally created in the early 1990s.

Key Words, Operators, and Syntax: An Overview

Each high-level language has its own set of predefined words that the programmer must use to write a program. The words that make up a high-level programming language are known as *key words* or *reserved words*. Each key word has a specific meaning, and cannot be used for any other purpose. In this book we use the C++ programming language. Table 1-2 shows the C++ key words.

Table 1-2 The C++ key words

and	continue	goto	public	try
and_eq	default	if	register	typedef
asm	delete	inline	reinterpret_cast	typeid
auto	do	int	return	typename
bitand	double	long	short	union
bitor	dynamic_cast	mutable	signed	unsigned
bool	else	namespace	sizeof	using
break	enum	new	static	virtual
case	explicit	not	static_cast	void
catch	export	not_eq	struct	volatile
char	extern	operator	switch	wchar_t
class	false	or	template	while
compl	float	or_eq	this	xor
const	for	private	throw	xor_eq
const_cast	friend	protected	true	

NOTE: As you look at Table 1-2, you might be wondering if you will have to memorize these key words, or learn what all of them are used for. The answer is no! As you learn to program in C++, you will find that you frequently use a handful of these key words, and you will quickly learn what they do. Even experienced programmers occasionally have to look up the proper usage of a key word that they do not use often.

In addition to key words, programming languages have *operators* that perform various operations on data. For example, all programming languages have math operators that perform arithmetic. In C++, as well as in most other languages, the + sign is an operator that adds two numbers. The following adds 12 and 75:

```
12 + 75
```

There are numerous other operators in the C++ language, many of which you will learn about as you progress through this book.

In addition to key words and operators, each language also has its own *syntax*, which is a set of rules that must be strictly followed when writing a program. The syntax rules dictate how key words, operators, and various punctuation characters must be used in a program. When you are learning a programming language, you must learn the syntax rules for that particular language.

The individual instructions that you use to write a program in a high-level programming language are called *statements*. A programming statement can consist of key words, operators, punctuation, and other allowable programming elements, arranged in the proper sequence to perform an operation.

Compilers and Interpreters

Because the CPU understands only machine language instructions, programs that are written in a high-level language must be translated into machine language. Depending on the language that a program has been written in, the programmer will use either a compiler or an interpreter to make the translation.

A *compiler* is a program that translates a high-level language program into a separate machine language program. The machine language program can then be executed any time it is needed. This is shown in Figure 1-17. As shown in the figure, compiling and executing are two different processes.

Some languages use an *interpreter*, which is a program that both translates and executes the instructions in a high-level language program. As the interpreter reads each individual instruction in the program, it converts it to a machine language instruction and then immediately executes it. This process repeats for every instruction in the program. This process is illustrated in Figure 1-18. Because interpreters combine translation and execution, they typically do not create separate machine language programs.

NOTE: The C++ language uses a compiler to make the translation from C++ to machine language.

Figure 1-17 Compiling a high-level program and executing it

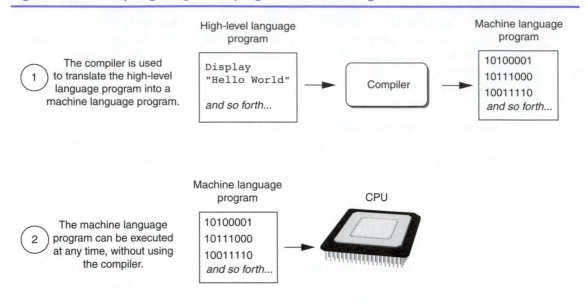

Figure 1-18 Executing a high-level program with an interpreter

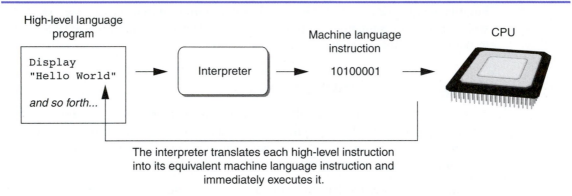

The interpreter translates each high-level instruction into its equivalent machine language instruction and immediately executes it.

This process is repeated for each high-level instruction.

The statements that a programmer writes in a high-level language are called *source code*, or simply *code*. Typically, the programmer types a program's code into a text editor and then saves the code in a file on the computer's disk. Next, the programmer uses a compiler to translate the code into a machine language program, or an interpreter to translate and execute the code. If the code contains a syntax error, however, it cannot be translated. A *syntax error* is a mistake such as a misspelled key word, a missing punctuation character, or the incorrect use of an operator. If this happens, the compiler or interpreter displays an error message indicating that the program contains a syntax error. The programmer corrects the error and then attempts again to translate the program.

> **NOTE:** Human languages also have syntax rules. Do you remember when you took your first English class, and you learned all those rules about commas, apostrophes, capitalization, and so forth? You were learning the syntax of the English language.
>
> Although people commonly violate the syntax rules of their native language when speaking and writing, other people usually understand what they mean. Unfortunately, compilers and interpreters do not have this ability. If even a single syntax error appears in a program, the program cannot be compiled or executed.

 ## Checkpoint

1.15. A CPU understands instructions that are written only in what language?

1.16. A program has to be copied into what type of memory each time the CPU executes it?

1.17. When a CPU executes the instructions in a program, it is engaged in what process?

1.18. What is assembly language?

1.19. What type of programming language allows you to create powerful and complex programs without knowing how the CPU works?

1.20. Each language has a set of rules that must be strictly followed when writing a program. What is this set of rules called?

1.21. What do you call a program that translates a high-level language program into a separate machine language program?

1.22. What do you call a program that both translates and executes the instructions in a high-level language program?

1.23. What type of mistake is usually caused by a misspelled key word, a missing punctuation character, or the incorrect use of an operator?

 ## 1.5 C++ and the Dark GDK Library

CONCEPT: C++ is a high-level programming language, and the Dark GDK is a library of prewritten code that can be used in C++ to write games and graphical programs.

As previously mentioned, we will be using the C++ programming language in this book. C++ is one of the most popular programming languages used by professional programmers, and is widely used by game developers.

The C++ programming language was based on the C programming language. C was created in 1972 by Dennis Ritchie at Bell Laboratories for writing system software. *System software* controls the operation of a computer. For example, an operating system like Windows, Linux, or Mac OS X is system software. Because system software must be efficient and fast, the C programming language was designed as a high-performance language.

The C++ language was created by Bjarne Stroustrup at Bell Laboratories in the early 1980s, as an extension of the C language. C++ retains the speed and efficiency of C, and adds numerous modern features that make it a good choice for developing large applications. Today, many commercial software applications are written in C++. Game programmers especially like C++ because speed and performance are critical in game programming.

Although C++ is a fast and efficient programming language, it does not have built-in features for writing graphical programs or games. For this reason, we also use the Dark GDK library in this book. A *library* is a collection of code that has already been written for some specific purpose. The Dark GDK library is a collection of code that can be used with C++ for handling graphics and writing game programs. The Dark GDK library was developed by The Game Creators, a software company based in the United Kingdom. (GDK stands for Game Development Kit. In this book, we will sometimes refer to the Dark GDK library simply as the Dark GDK.)

The Software You Will Need

To use this book you will need to install the following software and files:

- **Microsoft Visual C++ 2008.** When purchased new, this book comes with Visual C++ 2008 Express Edition on an accompanying DVD. If your book does not have the DVD, you can download and install Visual C++ 2008 Express Edition from Microsoft's Web site. See Appendix A for instructions.
- **The Dark GDK.** The Dark GDK must be downloaded from the Game Creators Web site. Appendix A provides instructions for downloading and installing the Dark GDK
- **Sample Source Code and Media Files.** These files comprise all of the example programs in the book, as well as graphics and audio files that you can use in your projects. Appendix A provides instructions for downloading the files from the publisher's Web site. The Web site also provides case studies detailing games written with the Dark GDK.

Before going any further, you should make sure that you have downloaded and installed the necessary software and files on your computer. Once you have done that, go through the following tutorials. In the following *In the Spotlight*, you will write your first C++/Dark GDK program and execute it. The steps that you will follow in the tutorial will be the same for most of the programs that you will write as you work through this book. In the second *In the Spotlight*, you will open and execute one of the book's example programs.

In the Spotlight:
Writing Your First Program with Visual C++
2008 Express Edition and the Dark GDK

Step 1:   Start Visual C++ 2008 Express Edition. (You can find it by clicking the *Start* button, then selecting *All Programs*, then selecting *Visual C++ 9.0 Express Edition*.)

Visual C++ 2008 Express Edition appears similar to Figure 1-19 when it first starts up. The screen shown in the figure is the *Start Page*, which typically displays information about new software releases, upcoming conferences and training events, links to recent articles, and so forth.

Figure 1-19 The Visual C++ *Start Page*

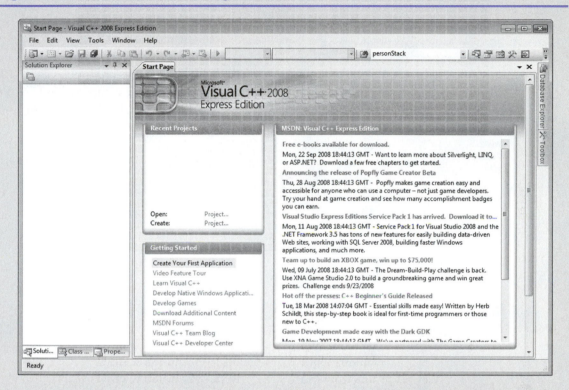

Step 2: To write a program in Visual C++ you need to create a project. A *project* is a group of one or more files that make up a software application. (Even if your program consists of no more than a single source code file, it still must belong to a project.)

To start a new project, click *File* on the menu bar, then *New*, then *Project*. The *New Project* dialog box appears, as shown in Figure 1-20. Under *Project types:* (the left pane), select *Wizards*. Then, under *Templates:* (the right pane), select *Dark GDK - 2D Game*.

Each project must have a name. Notice that an entry field for the project's name appears at the bottom of the dialog box. As shown in Figure 1-20, the project's default name is *Dark GDK - 2D Game1* (or something similar to that on your system). Change this name to `MyFirstProgram`, and then click the *OK* button to continue.

TIP: When your instructor gives you a programming assignment, you will want to give the project a name that identifies the assignment, such as `Lab6`, or `Assignment7`. Enter the name of the project in the *Name* text box, and then click the *OK* button to continue.

NOTE: When you create a project, Visual C++ creates a folder where all the project files are stored. This folder is referred to as the *project folder* and it has the same name as the project. The *Location:* entry field lets you specify a location on your system where the project folder will be created. You will probably want to keep the default location, but if not, click the *Browse...* button to select a different one.

Figure 1-20 The *New Project* dialog box

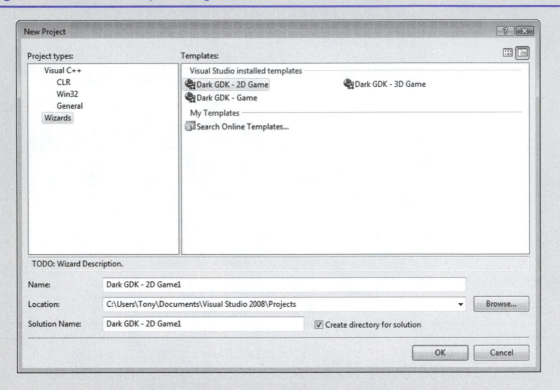

Step 3: Visual C++ has a *Solution Explorer* window that shows a list of all the files in your project. Figure 1-21 shows the *Solution Explorer*, which should be visible. If you do not see the *Solution Explorer*, click *View* on the menu bar, and then click *Solution Explorer*.

When you start a new *Dark GDK* project, an example program is automatically created, and several files are added to the project. Specifically, you see the following files listed in the *Solution Explorer*:

```
Main.cpp
ReadMe.txt
Backdrop.bmp
Sprite.bmp
```

We will not be using any of these files, so we will remove them from the project. Simply right-click each file name, and then select *Remove* from the menu that pops up. A confirmation dialog box will appear next. Click the *Delete* button to permanently delete the file. Do this for each of the four

Figure 1-21 The *Solution Explorer*

The *Solution Explorer* —
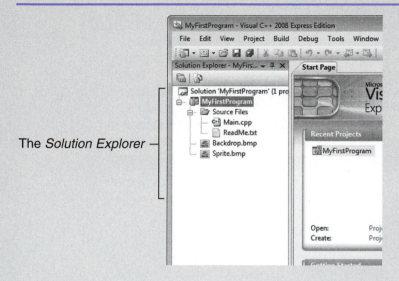

files. After the files have been removed, the *Solution Explorer* should appear as shown in Figure 1-22.

Step 4:   Now you will create an empty C++ source code file that you can type code into. Click *Project* on the menu bar, then click *Add New Item*. The *Add New Item* dialog box appears, as shown in Figure 1-23. Under *Templates:* (the right pane), make sure C++ *file (.cpp)* is selected. At the bottom of the dialog box you see an entry field for the file's name. As shown in the figure, the field reads `<Enter_name>`. Change this to `MyFirstProgram.cpp` and

Figure 1-22 The *Solution Explorer* with all files removed

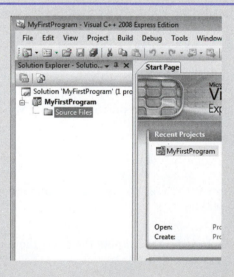

Figure 1-23 The *Add New Item* dialog box

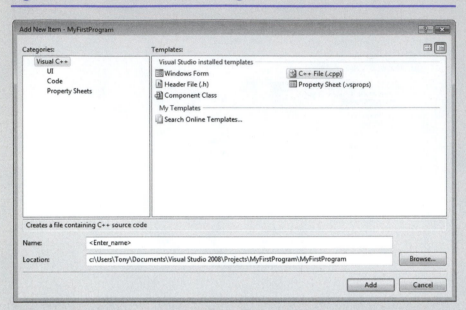

then click the *Add* button. (You can name the file anything that you wish, as long as the name ends with the the `.cpp` extension. The extension indicates that the file is a C++ source code file. We will follow the convention of giving the source code file the same name as the project.)

Step 5: In the *Solution Explorer*, you should now see the file `MyFirstProgram.cpp` listed, as shown in Figure 1-24. A text editing window should also be opened, as shown in the figure. This text editing window is where you will type the C++ code for the file.

 TIP: If the text editing window is not opened, you can double-click `MyFirstProgram.cpp` in the *Solution Explorer*. This will open the text editing window.

Type the following C++ code, exactly as it appears, in the text editing window. (For now, do not worry about what the code does. This exercise is merely meant to give you practice working with Visual C++.)

```
#include "DarkGDK.h"

void DarkGDK()
{
    dbPrint("This is my first program!");
    dbWaitKey();
}
```

When you have finished typing the code, the text editing window should appear as shown in Figure 1-25.

Figure 1-24 The `MyFirstProgram.cpp` file added to the project

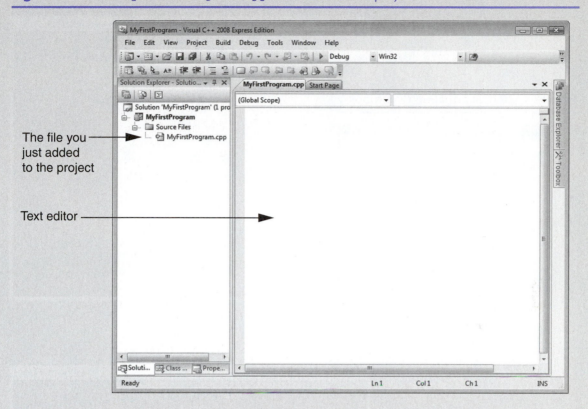

The file you just added to the project

Text editor

Figure 1-25 Code typed into the text editing window

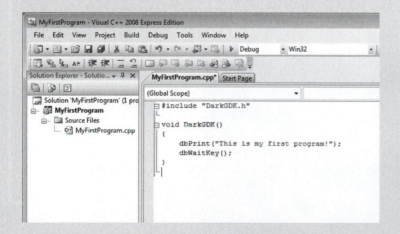

Step 6: Click *File* on the menu bar, then click *Save All* to save the project. (Anytime you are writing a program, it is a good idea to save the project often.)

Step 7: Now you will compile and execute the program. Earlier in this chapter, you read that compiling and executing are two separate processes. Visual C++, however, can compile a program and immediately execute it, as long as there are no errors in the program. That is what you will do in this step.

Click *Debug* on the menu bar, and then click *Start without debugging*. (Alternatively you can press Ctrl+F5 on the keyboard.) Next, you will see the dialog box, as shown in Figure 1-26. Click the *Yes* button.

Figure 1-26 Confirmation dialog box

Step 8: If you typed the program with no mistakes, you should see the program execute, as shown in Figure 1-27. The program simply prints the following message: *This is my first program!* Press any key on the keyboard to end the program.

Figure 1-27 MyFirstprogram.cpp running

If you did not type the program exactly as it was shown, you will probably see the following error message: *There were build errors. Would you like to continue and run the last successful build?* If you see this, click the *No* button, then compare the code that you typed with the code shown in Step 5. Make sure your code is exactly like the code we have given you. After correcting any mistakes, repeat Steps 7 and 8.

Step 9:   To exit Visual C++, click *File* on the menu bar, then click *Exit*.

In the Spotlight:
Opening and Executing an Example Program

As you work through this book you will see many example programs. Program 1-1 shows how an example program will appear. (For now, do not worry about what the program does. We are merely using it for demonstration purposes.)

Program 1-1   **(Circles.cpp)**

```
1   // This is an example Dark GDK program.
2   #include "DarkGDK.h"
3
4   void DarkGDK()
5   {
6       // Variables for the center points.
7       int x = 319, y = 239;
8
9       // Draw concentric circles.
10      for (int radius = 50; radius <= 200; radius += 50)
11          dbCircle(x, y, radius);
12
13      // Wait for the user to press a key.
14      dbWaitKey();
15  }
```

Notice that the program's name, `Circles.cpp`, is shown at the top of the program listing. Assuming you have downloaded and unzipped the student source code files from the publisher's Web site (www.aw.com/gaddis), you can follow these steps to open, compile, and execute the program.

Step 1:   Start Visual C++ 2008 Express Edition.

Step 2:   Click *File* on the menu bar, then select *Open*, then select *Project/Solution*. The *Open Project* dialog box will appear. Navigate to the location on your system where you unzipped the student source code files, and locate the source code folder for Chapter 1. Inside that folder you will see another folder named *Circles*. Open that folder and you will see a file named *Circles.sln*, as shown in Figure 1-28. Select the *Circles.sln* file and click *Open*.

Figure 1-28 The *Open Project* dialog box

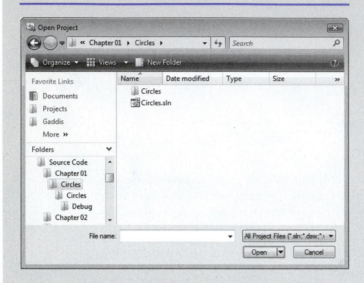

Step 3:   You have just opened the project that contains the `Circles.cpp` program. Locate the entry for the *Circles.cpp* file in the *Solution Explorer* window, as shown in Figure 1-29. (If the *Solution Explorer* window is not visible, click *View* on the menu bar, then click *Solution Explorer*.) Double-click the entry for the *Circles.cpp* file to open it in the text editing window, as shown in Figure 1-30.

Figure 1-29 The *Circles.cpp* file's entry in the *Solution Explorer*

Double-click the entry for *Circles.cpp* in the *Solution Explorer*.

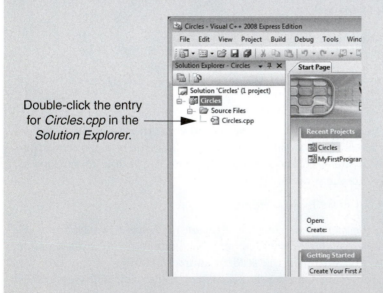

Figure 1-30 The *Circles.cpp* file opened in the text editing window

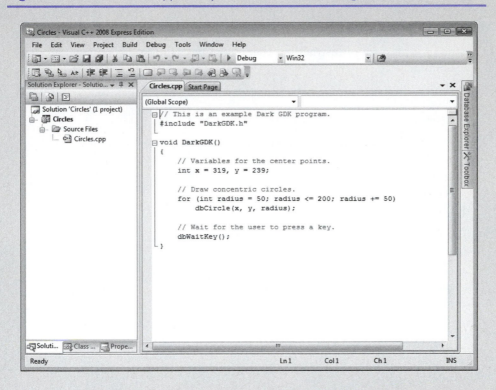

Step 4: Now you will compile and execute the program. Click *Debug* on the menu bar, and then click *Start without debugging*. (Alternatively you can press Ctrl+F5 on the keyboard.) If the dialog box that was shown in Figure 1-26 appears, click the *Yes* button. You should see the program execute, as shown in Figure 1-31. Pressing any key on the keyboard will end the program.

Figure 1-31 The `Circles.cpp` program executing

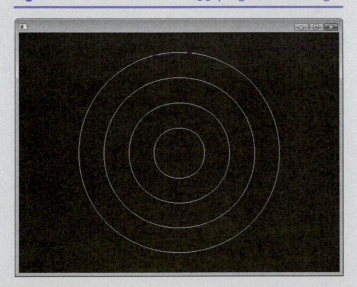

Review Questions

Multiple Choice

1. A(n) _____ is a set of instructions that a computer follows to perform a task.
   a. compiler
   b. program
   c. interpreter
   d. programming language

2. The physical devices that a computer is made of are referred to as _____.
   a. hardware
   b. software
   c. the operating system
   d. tools

3. The part of a computer that runs programs is called _____.
   a. RAM
   b. secondary storage
   c. main memory
   d. the CPU

4. Today, CPUs are small chips known as _____.
   a. ENIACs
   b. microprocessors
   c. memory chips
   d. operating systems

5. The computer stores a program while the program is running, as well as the data that the program is working with, in _____.
   a. secondary storage
   b. the CPU
   c. main memory
   d. the microprocessor

6. This is a volatile type of memory that is used only for temporary storage while a program is running.
   a. RAM
   b. secondary storage
   c. the disk drive
   d. the USB drive

7. A type of memory that can hold data for long periods of time—even when there is no power to the computer is called _____.
   a. RAM
   b. main memory
   c. secondary storage
   d. CPU storage

8. A component that collects data from people or other devices and sends it to the computer is called _____.
   a. an output device
   b. an input device

  c. a secondary storage device

  d. main memory

9. A video display is a(n) _____ device.

  a. output device

  b. input device

  c. secondary storage device

  d. main memory

10. A _____ is enough memory to store a letter of the alphabet or a small number.

  a. byte

  b. bit

  c. switch

  d. transistor

11. A byte is made up of eight _____.

  a. CPUs

  b. instructions

  c. variables

  d. bits

12. In a(n) _____ numbering system, all numeric values are written as sequences of 0s and 1s.

  a. hexadecimal

  b. binary

  c. octal

  d. decimal

13. A bit that is turned off represents the following value: _____.

  a. 1

  b. −1

  c. 0

  d. "no"

14. A set of 128 numeric codes that represent the English letters, various punctuation marks, and other characters is _____.

  a. binary numbering

  b. ASCII

  c. Unicode

  d. ENIAC

15. An extensive encoding scheme that can also represent all the characters of most of the languages in the world is _____.

  a. binary numbering

  b. ASCII

  c. Unicode

  d. ENIAC

16. Negative numbers are encoded using the _____ technique.

  a. two's complement

  b. floating-point

  c. ASCII

  d. Unicode

17. Real numbers are encoded using the _____ technique.
    a. two's complement
    b. floating-point
    c. ASCII
    d. Unicode

18. The tiny dots of color that digital images are composed of are called _____.
    a. bits
    b. bytes
    c. color packets
    d. pixels

19. If you look at a machine language program, you will see _____.
    a. C++ code
    b. a stream of binary numbers
    c. English words
    d. circuits

20. In the _____ part of the fetch-decode-execute cycle, the CPU determines which operation it should perform.
    a. fetch
    b. decode
    c. execute
    d. immediately after the instruction is executed

21. Computers can only execute programs that are written in _____.
    a. Java
    b. assembly language
    c. machine language
    d. C++

22. The _____ translates an assembly language program to a machine language program.
    a. assembler
    b. compiler
    c. translator
    d. interpreter

23. The words that make up a high-level programming language are called _____.
    a. binary instructions
    b. mnemonics
    c. commands
    d. key words

24. The rules that must be followed when writing a program are called _____.
    a. syntax
    b. punctuation
    c. key words
    d. operators

25. A(n) _____ program translates a high-level language program into a separate machine language program.
    a. assembler
    b. compiler
    c. translator
    d. utility

True or False

1. Today, CPUs are huge devices made of electrical and mechanical components such as vacuum tubes and switches.

2. Main memory is also known as RAM.

3. Any piece of data that is stored in a computer's memory must be stored as a binary number.

4. Images, like the ones you make with your digital camera, cannot be stored as binary numbers.

5. Machine language is the only language that a CPU understands.

6. Assembly language is considered a high-level language.

7. An interpreter is a program that both translates and executes the instructions in a high-level language program.

8. A syntax error does not prevent a program from being compiled and executed.

9. The C++ language has built-in features for writing games and graphical programs.

10. C++ is a good language for game programming because it is fast and efficient.

Short Answer

1. Why is the CPU the most important component in a computer?

2. What number does a bit that is turned on represent? What number does a bit that is turned off represent?

3. What would you call a device that works with binary data?

4. What are the words that make up a high-level programming language called?

5. What are the short words that are used in assembly language called?

6. What is the difference between a compiler and an interpreter?

7. What language was the C++ language based on?

Programming Exercises

1. This exercise will give you additional practice using Visual C++ to create a Dark GDK project. Before attempting this exercise you should complete the first *In the Spotlight* in this chapter.

Use the steps that you followed in the first *In the Spotlight* in this chapter to create a new project named Lines. When you add a C++ source code file to the project (as you did in Step 4 of the first *In the Spotlight*), name it `Lines.cpp`. Then, type the following code into the file. (Be sure to type the code exactly as it appears here.)

```cpp
#include "DarkGDK.h"

void DarkGDK ()
{
    // Draw some lines.
    dbLine(0, 239, 639, 239);
    dbLine(319, 0, 319, 479);
    dbLine(0, 0, 639, 479);
    dbLine(639, 0, 0, 479);

    // Wait for the user to press a key.
    dbWaitKey();
}
```

Save the project, then compile and execute it. If you typed the code exactly as shown, the window shown in Figure 1-32 should appear. Press any key on the keyboard to exit the program.

Figure 1-32 Output of the `Lines.cpp` program

If you did not type the program exactly as shown, you will probably see the following error message: *There were build errors. Would you like to continue and run the last successful build?* If you see this, click the *No* button, then compare the code that you typed with the code shown in the book. Make sure your code is exactly like the code we have given you. After correcting any mistakes, save the project, then try to compile and execute it again.

2. Use what you've learned about the binary numbering system in this chapter to convert the following decimal numbers to binary:

    11
    65
    100
    255

3. Use what you've learned about the binary numbering system in this chapter to convert the following binary numbers to decimal:

    ```
    1101
    1000
    101011
    ```

4. Use the Web to research the history of computer games, and answer the following questions:

    • From your research, what was the first computer game?
    • Have computer games that do not use graphics ever been created?
    • What is a serious game?

2 Graphics Programming with C++ and the Dark GDK Library

TOPICS

2.1 Getting Your Feet Wet with C++ and the Dark GDK Library

2.2 The Screen Coordinate System

2.3 Basic 2D Shapes

2.4 Displaying Text

2.5 The Program Development Cycle

2.1 Getting Your Feet Wet with C++ and the Dark GDK Library

CONCEPT: All C++ programs that use the Dark GDK library start out with the same code. The first step in learning to write a graphics program is to learn how to start a Dark GDK program in C++.

You've probably heard of the sink or swim approach to learning. The phrase "sink or swim" comes from the idea that you can learn to swim by jumping right into the deep water. If this approach works, then you learn to swim very quickly. Otherwise, you discover just as quickly that the consequences can be disastrous.

The sink or swim approach can also be used to learn programming. You can jump right into the "deep water," and try to learn the topics and concepts as quickly as possible. For most students, however, this approach simply doesn't work. A better way to learn programming is first to get your feet wet by learning the simplest concepts. Then you can wade in a bit deeper and learn some more advanced concepts. As you gradually wade in, deeper and deeper, you learn more and more. Before you know it, you're on your way!

That's the approach we take in this book. Rather than throwing you in over your head, we want to start gently. Let's get your feet wet by looking at the smallest, simplest program that we can write in C++ using the Dark GDK library:

```
#include "DarkGDK.h"

void DarkGDK()
{

}
```

This program does absolutely nothing, but the code that you see must appear in every program that uses the Dark GDK library. In fact, we can call it a "skeleton" program because it is the minimum framework of a C++/Dark GDK program. Soon we will show you how to flesh out this program by adding more code to it. But now let's take a closer look at the parts of the skeleton program.

The first line, which reads `#include "DarkGDK.h"`, is called an *include directive*. It causes the contents of a file named `DarkGDK.h` to be included in the program. There is a lot of setup code that has to be written into a C++ program in order for it to work with the Dark GDK library. Fortunately, all of that setup code has already been written for us, and stored in the file `DarkGDK.h`. The include directive causes that code to be included in the program, just as if we had written it.

 NOTE: You won't actually see the contents of the `DarkGDK.h` file appear in a program as a result of the include directive. The contents of `DarkGDK.h` are included only temporarily, while the program is being compiled.

Following the include directive is a blank line. The blank line is not required, but it makes the program easier for humans to read. Programmers commonly insert blank lines at various places to make the code easier to read.

The following code appears next:

```
void DarkGDK()
{

}
```

This is called a *function*. You will learn a great deal about functions later in this book, but for now, you simply need to know that a function is a group of programming statements that collectively has a name. The name of this function is `DarkGDK`, and it is required in any program that uses the Dark GDK library. For now, don't be concerned about the word `void`, or the parentheses that appear after the name of the function. You will learn what they mean in Chapter 4.

 NOTE: C++ is a case-sensitive language, which means it regards uppercase letters as being entirely different characters than their lowercase counterparts. The name of the function `DarkGDK` must be written as uppercase `D`, followed by lowercase `ark`, followed by uppercase `GDK`. C++ doesn't see `darkgdk` the same as `DarkGDK`, or `VOID` the same as `void`.

Notice that a set of curly braces appears below the line that reads `void DarkGDK()`. The purpose of these braces is to enclose the statements that are in the `DarkGDK` function. In this particular program, the `DarkGDK` function is empty. If any programming statements were written in the function, they would appear between the curly braces. When a Dark GDK program runs, the statements that are written inside the `DarkGDK` function will execute. Figure 2-1 summarizes the parts of the skeleton program.

Figure 2-1 Summary of the skeleton program

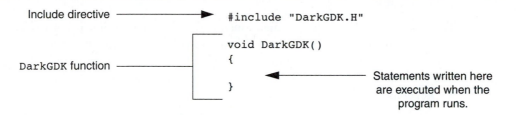

Include directive ⟶ `#include "DarkGDK.H"`

DarkGDK function ⟶
```
void DarkGDK()
{

}
```
⟵ Statements written here are executed when the program runs.

Now look at the code shown in Program 2-1. In this program, we've added a statement to the `DarkGDK` function and created a program that actually does something. If you compile and execute this code as a Dark GDK project in Microsoft Visual C++, the empty window shown in Figure 2-2 will appear.

Program 2-1   **(EmptyWindow.cpp)**

```
1   #include "DarkGDK.h"
2
3   void DarkGDK()
4   {
5       dbWaitKey();
6   }
```

Figure 2-2 Window displayed by Program 2-1

The program pauses with this window displayed until you press a key on the keyboard. Then the window closes and the program ends.

The line numbers that are shown in Program 2-1 are *not* part of the program. From this point forward, we will include line numbers in the program listings so we can easily refer to various lines. However, you should not type the line numbers when you write your own programs. Doing so will cause an error.

Let's take a closer look at Program 2-1. The following statement appears in line 5:

```
dbWaitKey();
```

This is a *function call*. It was mentioned earlier that a function is a set of programming statements that has a name. When you *call* a function, the statements in that function will execute. The statement in line 5 calls a function named dbWaitKey. When the dbWaitKey function executes, the program pauses until a key is pressed on the keyboard.

Notice the parentheses after the name of the function. In a function call, a set of parentheses always appears after the name of the function. Also, notice that the statement ends with a semicolon. In C++, a semicolon marks the end of a statement.

The statement in line 5 calls the dbWaitKey function (causes it to execute), but the code for that function is written elsewhere. It is part of the Dark GDK library, and any C++ program that is set up properly to use the Dark GDK library can call the function. In addition to dbWaitKey, the Dark GDK library contains numerous other functions. As you progress through this book you will learn about many of them, and how to execute them.

Comments

Comments are short notes that are placed in different parts of a program, explaining how those parts of the program work. Comments are not intended for the compiler. They are intended for anyone who is reading the code.

In C++ there are two types of comments: line comments and block comments. You begin a *line comment* with two forward slashes (//). Everything written after the slashes, to the end of the line, is ignored by the compiler. Program 2-2 shows an example of a program that contains line comments.

The comment in line 1 describes what the program does—it displays an empty window. The comment in line 6 explains what the dbWaitKey function call in line 7 does—it pauses the program until the user presses a key.

Program 2-2   (EmptyWindow2.cpp)

```
1   // This program displays an empty window.
2   #include "DarkGDK.h"
3
4   void DarkGDK ()
5   {
6       // Pause the program until the user presses a key.
7       dbWaitKey();
8   }
```

Block comments can occupy more than one line. A block comment starts with /* (a forward slash followed by an asterisk) and ends with */ (an asterisk followed by a forward slash). Everything between these markers is ignored. Program 2-3 demonstrates how block comments may be used. Notice that a block comment starts in line 1 with the /* symbol, and it ends in line 4 with the */ symbol.

Program 2-3   **(EmptyWindow3.cpp)**

```
 1   /*   Filename: EmptyWindow3.cpp
 2        Written by Gaddis
 3        This program displays an empty window.
 4   */
 5
 6   #include "DarkGDK.h"
 7
 8   void DarkGDK ()
 9   {
10       // Pause the program until the user presses a key.
11       dbWaitKey();
12   }
```

Block comments make it easier to write long explanations because you do not have to mark every line with a comment symbol.

Remember the following advice when using multiline comments:

- Be careful not to reverse the beginning symbol (/*) with the ending symbol (*/).
- Do not forget the ending symbol.

Each of these mistakes can be difficult to track down, and will prevent the program from compiling correctly.

As a beginning programmer, you might resist the idea of writing a lot of comments in your programs. After all, it's a lot more fun to write code that actually does something! However, it's crucial that you take the extra time to write comments. They will almost certainly save you time in the future when you have to modify or debug the program. Even large and complex programs can be made easy to read and understand if they are properly commented.

NOTE: When reading about computer programming you will often see the user mentioned. For example, the comment in line 10 of Program 2-3 mentions the user pressing a key. The *user* is any person who is using the program while it is running. When you are running one of your programs, you are the user. When your instructor runs one of your programs for grading purposes, he or she is the user.

Programming Style: Making Your Code Easier to Read

Programmers commonly use blank lines and indentations in their code to create a sense of visual organization. This is similar to the way that authors visually arrange the text on the pages of a book. Instead of writing each chapter as one long series of sentences, they break it into paragraphs. This does not change the information in the book; but it makes it easier to read.

For example, we have already mentioned the blank line that appears between the include directive and the beginning of the DarkGDK function (see line 7 in Program 2-3). This visually separates these code elements and makes the program easier for people to read. Also notice in Programs 2-1, 2-2, and 2-3 that the statements inside the DarkGDK function are indented. Indenting the statements inside a function is not required, but it makes your code much easier to read. By indenting the statements inside a function, you visually set them apart. As a result, you can tell at a glance which statements are inside the function. This practice is a convention that virtually all programmers follow.

Although you are generally free to place blank lines and indentations anywhere in your code, you should not do this haphazardly. Programmers follow certain conventions when it comes to this. For example, you have just learned that one convention is to indent the statements inside a function. These conventions are known as *programming style*. As you progress through this book you will see many other programming style conventions.

 Checkpoint

2.1. The following program will not compile because the statements are mixed up:

```
{
void DarkGDK()
}
// This is a mixed up program.
dbWaitKey();

#include "DarkGDK.h"
```

When the lines are properly arranged the program should display an empty window and wait for the user to press a key. Rearrange the lines in the correct order. Test the program by entering it on the computer, compiling it, and running it.

2.2. What does the directive #include "DarkGDK.h" do?

2.3. What is a function? What function is required in any C++ program that uses the Dark GDK library?

2.4. In C++, is the name DarkGDK considered the same as the name darkGDK?

2.5. In C++, how do you write a line comment?

2.6. In C++, how do you write a block comment?

2.2 The Screen Coordinate System

CONCEPT: A system of *X* and *Y* coordinates is used to identify the locations of pixels in a window.

The images that are displayed on a computer screen are made up of tiny dots called pixels. The default window that is displayed by a Dark GDK program is 640 pixels wide and 480 pixels high. This is shown in Figure 2-3. We say that the window has a *resolution* of 640 by 480.

Figure 2-3 The width and height of the default window

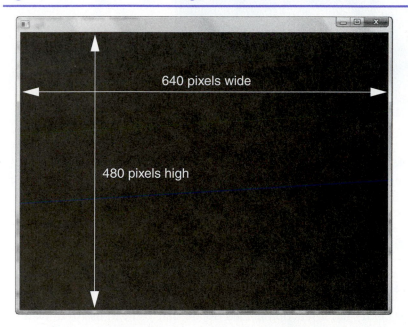

A *screen coordinate system* is used to identify the position of each pixel in the window. Each pixel has an *X* coordinate and a *Y* coordinate. The *X* coordinate identifies the pixel's horizontal position, and the *Y* coordinate identifies its vertical position. The coordinates are usually written in the form (*X, Y*). For example, the coordinates of the pixel in the upper-left corner of the screen are (0, 0). This means that its *X* coordinate is 0 and its *Y* coordinate is 0.

The *X* coordinates increase from left to right, and the *Y* coordinates increase from top to bottom. In a window that is 640 pixels wide by 480 pixels high, the coordinates of the pixel at the bottom right corner of the window are (639, 479). In the same window, the coordinates of the pixel in the center of the window are (319, 239). Figure 2-4 shows the coordinates of various pixels in the window.

Notice that the pixels at the far right edge of the window have an *X* coordinate of 639, not 640. This is because coordinate numbering begins at 0 in the upper-left corner. Likewise, the pixels at the bottom edge of the window have a *Y* coordinate of 479, not 480.

Figure 2-4 Various pixel locations in a 640 by 480 window

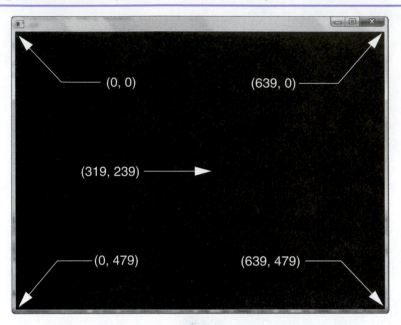

 NOTE: The screen coordinate system differs from the Cartesian coordinate system that you learned about in mathematics. In the Cartesian coordinate system, the Y coordinates decrease as you move downward. In the screen coordinate system, the Y coordinates increase as you move downward, toward the bottom of the screen.

Drawing Dots with the dbDot Function

The Dark GDK library has a function named dbDot that you can use to draw a dot at a specific pixel location. Here is the general format of how you call the dbDot function:

```
dbDot(x, y);
```

The values that you write inside the function's parentheses are known as arguments. *Arguments* are pieces of data that you send to a function when you call it. In the general format, the *x* argument is an *X* coordinate and the *y* argument is a *Y* coordinate. When the function executes it will draw a tiny dot in the window at the specified coordinates. For example, the following statement will draw a dot at the *X* coordinate 319 and the *Y* coordinate 239:

```
dbDot(319, 239);
```

When an argument is sent to a function, we say that we are *passing* the argument to the function. In this statement we are passing two arguments to the dbDot function.

 NOTE: Make sure you place a comma between the function arguments.

Program 2-4 demonstrates the dbDot function by drawing five dots in a horizonal line. When the program runs it displays a window similar to the one shown in Figure 2-5. (If you run this program on your system, the dots will appear smaller than those shown in the figure. We've made the dots slightly larger in the figure so they are easier to see.)

Program 2-4   **(Dots.cpp)**

```
 1   // This program demonstrates the dbDot function.
 2   #include "DarkGDK.h"
 3
 4   void DarkGDK ()
 5   {
 6       // Draw five dots in a horizontal line.
 7       dbDot(310, 239);
 8       dbDot(315, 239);
 9       dbDot(320, 239);
10       dbDot(325, 239);
11       dbDot(330, 239);
12
13       // Pause the program until the user presses a key.
14       dbWaitKey();
15   }
```

Figure 2-5 The dots displayed by Program 2-4

NOTE: In the screen coordinate system, *X* and *Y* coordinates are always integers. If you call a Dark GDK function such as dbDot and pass a fractional number as a coordinate, the function will drop the fractional part of the number. For example, look at the following statement:

```
dbDot(99.9, 77.6);
```

In this statement we are passing 99.9 as the *X* coordinate and 77.6 as the *Y* coordinate. The dbDot function will drop the fractional parts of the coordinates, and the dot will be drawn at the location (99, 77). The process of dropping a number's fractional part is known as *truncation*.

The dbWait Function

Students who are new to programming are sometimes surprised at how quickly the statements execute in a program. For example, look at the statements that appear in lines 7 though 11 in Program 2-4. These statements execute one at a time, in the order that they appear in the program. When the program runs, the statements execute so quickly that the five dots seem to appear simultaneously.

If we want the program to appear to execute more slowly, we can call the dbWait function at various places in the code. The dbWait function causes the program to wait for a specified amount of time before continuing. Here is the general format of how you call the function:

```
dbWait(time);
```

The value that you provide for the *time* argument is the number of milliseconds that you want the program to wait. There are 1000 milliseconds in a second, so the following statement will cause the program to wait for one second:

```
dbWait(1000);
```

Program 2-5 shows how we can modify the Dots.cpp program with the dbWait function. In this version of the program, the dbDot function is called in line 9 to draw the first dot, and then the dbWait function is called in line 10 to make the program wait before going any further. Notice that we pass 2000 as the argument to the dbWait function. This causes the program to wait for two seconds before continuing. Then, in line 13 we call the dbDot function to draw the second dot. In line 14 the dbWait function is called again to make the program wait for two seconds. This

NOTE: So far, you have learned about three Dark GDK library functions: dbDot, dbWaitKey, and dbWait. You've probably noticed that each of the function names begins with the letters db. The software company that created the Dark GDK library has also created a programming language named Dark BASIC. Most of the functions in the Dark GDK library are the C++ equivalents of commands found in the Dark BASIC language. For this reason, the Dark GDK function names start with the letters db, meaning Dark BASIC.

Program 2-5   **(Dots2.cpp)**

```
1    // This program demonstrates the dbWait function.
2    // It draws five dots, pausing for two seconds between
3    // drawing each dot.
4    #include "DarkGDK.h"
5
6    void DarkGDK ()
7    {
8       // Draw the first dot, then wait two seconds.
9       dbDot(310, 239);
10      dbWait(2000);
11
12      // Draw the second dot, then wait two seconds.
13      dbDot(315, 239);
14      dbWait(2000);
15
16      // Draw the third dot, then wait two seconds.
17      dbDot(320, 239);
18      dbWait(2000);
19
20      // Draw the fourth dot, then wait two seconds.
21      dbDot(325, 239);
22      dbWait(2000);
23
24      // Draw the last dot, then wait for the user
25      // to press a key.
26      dbDot(330, 239);
27      dbWaitKey();
28   }
```

process continues with the third and fourth dots. After the fifth dot is displayed by the statement in line 26 the user presses a key to end the program.

 Checkpoint

2.7. What is the resolution of the default window created by a Dark GDK program?

2.8. What are the coordinates of the pixel in the upper-left corner of the window?

2.9. In a window that is 640 pixels wide by 480 pixels high, what are the coordinates of the pixel in the lower-right corner?

2.10. How is the screen coordinate system different from the Cartesian coordinate system?

2.11. Write a statement that displays a dot at the coordinates (150, 210).

2.12. Write a statement that causes the program to wait for five seconds before continuing.

2.3 Basic 2D Shapes

CONCEPT: The Dark GDK library contains several functions for drawing basic 2D shapes.

If you've ever played a simple arcade-style video game, then you are probably familiar with *two-dimensional (2D)* graphics. The objects that appear in 2D graphics have only two dimensions: height and width. Figure 2-6 shows an example of a two-dimensional game character that exists with only height and width.

The Dark GDK library provides several functions for drawing simple 2D shapes. In this section, we will discuss functions for drawing lines, circles, ellipses, and rectangles.

Figure 2-6 A two-dimensional game character

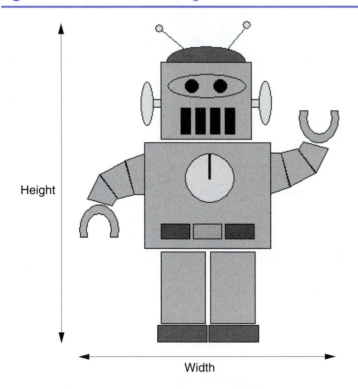

Drawing Lines: The `dbLine` Function

The `dbLine` function draws a line between two points in the Dark GDK window. Here is the general format of how you call the function:

```
dbLine(x1, y1, x2, y2);
```

You pass four arguments to the function. The `x1` and `y1` arguments are the *X* and *Y* coordinates for the line's starting point. The `x2` and `y2` arguments are the *X* and *Y* coordinates for the line's ending point. For example, the following statement draws a line between the points (80, 120) and (400, 520):

```
dbLine(80, 120, 400, 520);
```

The diagram in Figure 2-7 shows how the arguments in this example designate the endpoints of a line.

Figure 2-7 A line drawn from (80, 120) to (400, 520)

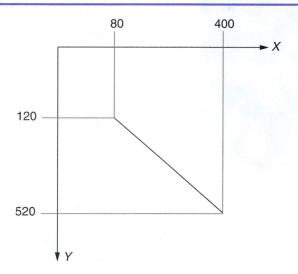

Program 2-6 demonstrates the dbLine function. The program draws three lines to form a triangle. The program's output is shown in Figure 2-8. Figure 2-9 shows the coordinates of the triangle's corners.

Program 2-6   **(Triangle.cpp)**

```
1   // This program uses the dbLine function
2   // to draw three lines that form a triangle.
3   #include "DarkGDK.h"
4
5   void DarkGDK()
6   {
7       // Draw the first line from (320,180) to (240,300).
8       dbLine(320, 180, 240, 300);
9
10      // Draw the second line from (320,180) to (400,300).
11      dbLine(320, 180, 400, 300);
12
13      // Draw the third line from (240,300) to (400,300).
14      dbLine(240, 300, 400, 300);
15
16      // Pause the program until the user presses a key.
17      dbWaitKey();
18  }
```

Figure 2-8 Output of Program 2-6

Figure 2-9 Coordinates of the triangle's corners

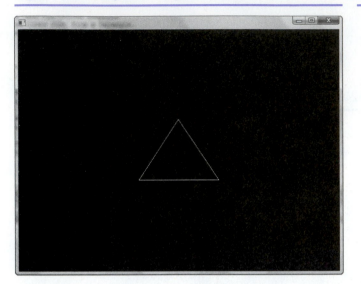

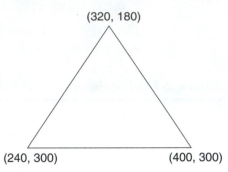

Let's look at another example. Program 2-7 uses the dbLine function to draw a city skyline. The outline of the buildings is made of 13 lines. For that reason, the dbLine function is called 13 times, in lines 7 through 19. Then, in lines 22 through 27 we call the dbDot function six times to draw some stars in the sky. Figure 2-10 shows the program's output.

Program 2-7   (CitySkyline.cpp)

```
1   // This program draws a city skyline.
2   #include "DarkGDK.h"
3
4   void DarkGDK ()
5   {
6       // Draw the outline of the buildings.
7       dbLine(  0, 339, 59,  339);
8       dbLine( 59, 339, 59,  239);
9       dbLine( 59, 239, 159, 239);
10      dbLine(159, 239, 159,  59);
11      dbLine(159, 59,  299,  59);
12      dbLine(299, 59,  299, 279);
13      dbLine(299, 279, 399, 279);
14      dbLine(399, 279, 399, 139);
15      dbLine(399, 139, 519, 139);
16      dbLine(519, 139, 519, 239);
17      dbLine(519, 239, 599, 239);
18      dbLine(599, 239, 599, 339);
19      dbLine(599, 339, 639, 339);
20
21      // Draw some stars.
22      dbDot(59,    59);
```

```
23          dbDot(119, 179);
24          dbDot(239,  19);
25          dbDot(359,  79);
26          dbDot(559,  39);
27          dbDot(599, 179);
28
29          // Pause the program until the user presses a key.
30          dbWaitKey();
31    }
```

Figure 2-10 Output of Program 2-7

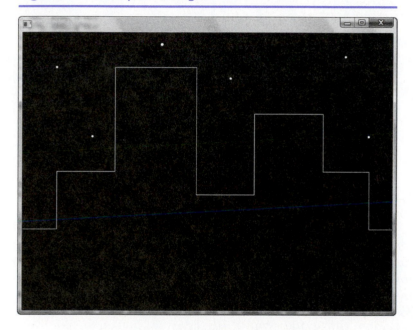

Before going any further, let's discuss the process of writing Program 2-7. First, we sketched the outline of the buildings on a piece of graph paper, as shown in Figure 2-11. We used the grid on the graph paper to determine the coordinates of each line's endpoints. Then, we used the grid to determine the coordinates of the stars.

After making the sketch and determining the necessary coordinates, we did not immediately start writing C++ code. Because small mistakes like misspelled words and forgotten semicolons can cause syntax errors, we must remember such small details when writing actual code. For this reason, it is helpful to write a program in pseudocode (pronounced "sue doe code") before writing it in the actual code of a programming language such as C++.

The word "pseudo" means fake, so *pseudocode* is fake code. It is an informal language that has no syntax rules, and is not meant to be compiled or executed. Instead, programmers use pseudocode to create models, or "mock-ups" of programs. Because you don't have to worry about syntax errors while writing pseudocode, you can focus all of your attention on the program's design. Once a satisfactory design has been created with pseudocode, the pseudocode can be translated directly to actual code.

Figure 2-11 Sketch of the skyline

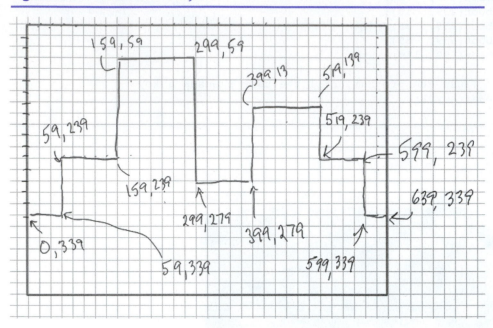

Here is the pseudocode that we wrote for displaying the city skyline:

Draw a line from (0, 339) to (59, 339)
Draw a line from (59, 339) to (59, 239)
Draw a line from (59, 239) to (159, 239)
Draw a line from (159, 239) to (159, 59)
Draw a line from (159, 59) to (299, 59)
Draw a line from (299, 59) to (299, 279)
Draw a line from (299, 279) to (399, 279)   This is how we draw the
Draw a line from (399, 279) to (399, 139)   outline of the buildings.
Draw a line from (399, 139) to (519, 139)
Draw a line from (519, 139) to (519, 239)
Draw a line from (519, 239) to (599, 239)
Draw a line from (599, 239) to (599, 339)
Draw a line from (599, 339) to (639, 339)

Draw a dot at (59, 59)
Draw a dot at (119, 179)
Draw a dot at (239, 19)   These dots make the stars.
Draw a dot at (359, 79)
Draw a dot at (559, 39)
Draw a dot at (599, 179)

Wait for the user to press a key.

As you can see, the pseudocode simply lists the steps that must be taken in the program. These steps are known as an algorithm. An *algorithm* is a set of well-defined logical steps that must be taken to perform a task.

Of course, in a C++/DarkGDK program, we can't write statements like "Draw a line. . ." or "Draw a dot. . ." Instead, we have to call the `dbLine` and `dbDot` functions. Once we are satisfied that the pesudocode has listed all of the steps that must be taken by the program, we translate it into actual C++ code.

Drawing Rectangles: The `dbBox` Function

The `dbBox` function draws a filled rectangle. By "filled" we mean that it is filled with a color. (For now, we will draw rectangles that are filled with white. In Chapter 3, you will learn how to change the color.)

Here is the general format of how you call the `dbBox` function:

```
dbBox(x1, y1, x2, y2);
```

You pass four arguments to the function. The *x1* and *y1* arguments are the X and Y coordinates for the rectangle's upper-left corner. The *x2* and *y2* arguments are the X and Y coordinates for the rectangle's lower-right corner. For example, look at the following statement:

```
dbBox(100, 80, 540, 380);
```

As illustrated in Figure 2-12, this statement draws a rectangle with its upper-left corner located at (100, 80) and its lower-right corner located at (540, 380).

Figure 2-12 A rectangle with corners at (100, 80) and (540, 380)

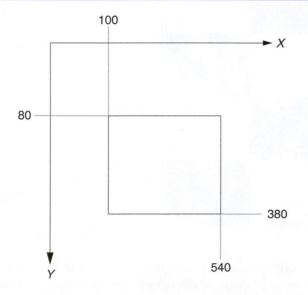

Program 2-8 demonstrates how the dbBox function can be used to create a checker-board pattern. The program's output is shown in Figure 2-13.

Program 2-8 (CheckerBoard.cpp)

```
1   // This program draws a checkerboard pattern.
2   #include "DarkGDK.h"
3
4   void DarkGDK()
5   {
6       // Draw eight filled rectangles to create
7       // a checkerboard pattern.
8       dbBox(160,   0, 320, 120);      // Box #1
9       dbBox(479,   0, 639, 120);      // Box #2
10      dbBox(  0, 120, 160, 240);      // Box #3
11      dbBox(320, 120, 479, 240);      // Box #4
12      dbBox(160, 240, 320, 360);      // Box #5
13      dbBox(479, 240, 639, 360);      // Box #6
14      dbBox(  0, 360, 160, 639);      // Box #7
15      dbBox(320, 360, 479, 639);      // Box #8
16
17      // Pause the program until the user presses a key.
18      dbWaitKey();
19  }
```

Figure 2-13 Output of Program 2-8

The comments in the program indicate that line 8 draws box #1, line 9 draws box #2, and so forth. Figure 2-14 shows the program's output with each box labeled so you can see which line of code draws each box.

Figure 2-14 Output of Program 2-8 with each box labeled

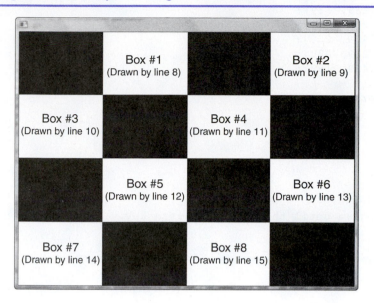

Program 2-9 shows another example. This is a modified version of Program 2-7, which draws a city skyline. In this version of the program the statements in lines 22 through 28 have been added. The dbBox statements in these lines draw six windows on the buildings. Figure 2-15 shows the program's output.

Program 2-9   **(CitySkyline2.cpp)**

```
 1   // This program draws a city skyline
 2   // with some windows showing.
 3   #include "DarkGDK.h"
 4
 5   void DarkGDK ()
 6   {
 7       // Draw the outline of the buildings.
 8       dbLine(  0, 339, 59,  339);
 9       dbLine( 59, 339, 59,  239);
10       dbLine( 59, 239, 159, 239);
11       dbLine(159, 239, 159,  59);
12       dbLine(159, 59,  299,  59);
13       dbLine(299, 59,  299, 279);
14       dbLine(299, 279, 399, 279);
15       dbLine(399, 279, 399, 139);
16       dbLine(399, 139, 519, 139);
17       dbLine(519, 139, 519, 239);
18       dbLine(519, 239, 599, 239);
19       dbLine(599, 239, 599, 339);
20       dbLine(599, 339, 639, 339);
21
22       // Draw six lit windows on the buildings.
```

```
23        dbBox(179,  99, 189, 109);
24        dbBox(179, 129, 189, 139);
25        dbBox(259, 179, 269, 189);
26        dbBox( 99, 259, 109, 269);
27        dbBox(239, 319, 249, 329);
28        dbBox(419, 179, 429, 189);
29
30        // Draw some stars.
31        dbDot(59,   59);
32        dbDot(119, 179);
33        dbDot(239,  19);
34        dbDot(359,  79);
35        dbDot(559,  39);
36        dbDot(599, 179);
37
38        // Pause the program until the user presses a key.
39        dbWaitKey();
40    }
```

Figure 2-15 Output of Program 2-9

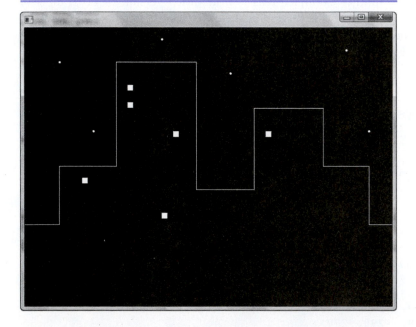

Drawing Circles: The dbCircle Function

The dbCircle function draws a circle. Here is the general format of how you call the function:

```
dbCircle(x, y, radius);
```

The *x* and *y* arguments are the coordinates of the circle's center point. The *radius* argument specifies the circle's radius. The circle's radius is the distance, in pixels, from the center point to the outer edge of the circle. Here is an example:

```
dbCircle(320, 240, 100);
```

Figure 2-16 shows how the values from this example are used to draw a circle.

Figure 2-16 A circle with its center at (320, 240) and a radius of 100

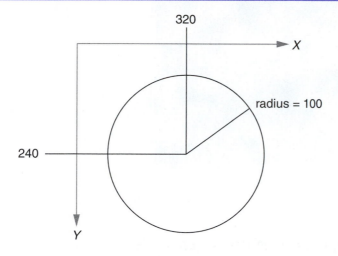

Program 2-10 demonstrates the dbCircle function by drawing three concentric circles to form a bull's eye. Figure 2-17 shows the program's output.

Program 2-10   **(BullsEye.cpp)**

```
 1   // This program demonstrates the dbCircle function
 2   // by drawing three circles to form a bull's eye.
 3   #include "DarkGDK.h"
 4
 5   void DarkGDK()
 6   {
 7       // Draw three concentric circles.
 8       dbCircle(320, 240, 150);
 9       dbCircle(320, 240,  75);
10       dbCircle(320, 240,  25);
11
12       // Pause the program until the user presses a key.
13       dbWaitKey();
14   }
```

Figure 2-17 Output of Program 2-10

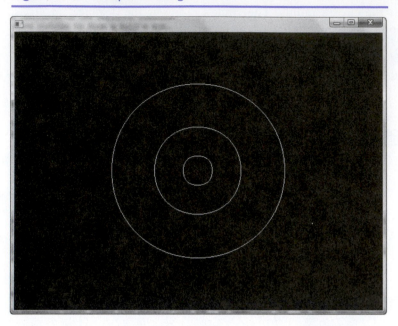

Drawing Ellipses: The `dbEllipse` Function

The `dbEllipse` function draws an ellipse, which is an oval shape. Here is the general format of how you call the function:

```
dbEllipse(x, y, xrad, yrad);
```

The *x* and *y* arguments are the coordinates of the ellipse's center point. The *xrad* argument specifies the ellipse's radius along the *X* axis. The *yrad* argument specifies the ellipse's radius along the *Y* axis. Here is an example:

```
dbEllipse(320, 240, 140, 100);
```

As shown in Figure 2-18, the ellipse drawn by this statement will have its center located at (320, 240), an x-radius of 140 pixels, and a y-radius of 100. The use of two different radii, one for the *X* axis and one for the *Y* axis, gives the ellipse its shape.

Program 2-11 demonstrates the `dbEllipse` function. The program draws a flower pattern using four ellipses and a circle. Figure 2-19 shows the program's output.

 NOTE: If an ellipse's x-radius and y-radius have the same value, then the ellipse will be a circle.

Figure 2-18 An ellipse's center point, x-radius, and y-radius

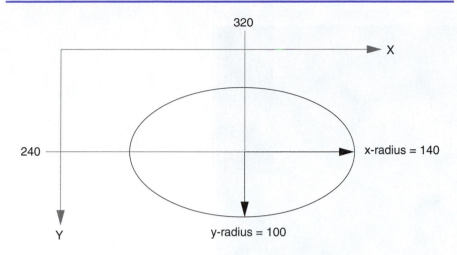

Program 2-11   **(Flower.cpp)**

```
1   // This program draws a flower pattern.
2   #include "DarkGDK.h"
3
4   void DarkGDK ()
5   {
6       // Ellipse #1: center = (319,119)
7       // x radius = 40, y radius = 80
8       dbEllipse(319, 119, 40, 80);
9
10      // Ellipse #2: center = (439,239)
11      // x radius = 80, y radius = 40
12      dbEllipse(439, 239, 80, 40);
13
14      // Ellipse #3: center = (199,239)
15      // x radius = 80, y radius = 40
16      dbEllipse(199, 239, 80, 40);
17
18      // Ellipse #4: center = (319,359)
19      // x radius = 40, y radius = 80
20      dbEllipse(319, 359, 40, 80);
21
22      // Circle: center = (319,239)
23      // radius = 40
24      dbCircle(319, 239, 40);
25
26      // Pause the program until the user presses a key.
27      dbWaitKey();
28  }
```

Figure 2-19 Output of Program 2-11

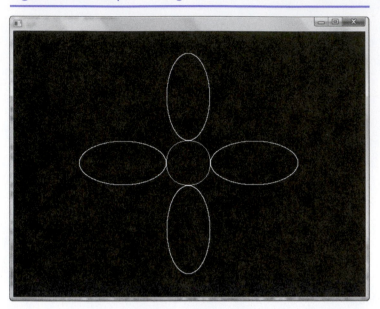

Drawing Outside the Dark GDK Window

Any point that has an X coordinate from 0 through 639, and a Y coordinate from 0 through 479 is visible in the Dark GDK window. You can use points that have coordinates outside these ranges, but they are not visible in the window.

For example, the following statement draws a dot at the coordinates (800, 600), but because that location is outside the Dark GDK window, it will not be visible.

```
dbDot(800, 600);
```

The points that are above the top row of pixels in the window have a negative Y coordinate, and the points that are to the left of the leftmost column of pixels have a negative X coordinate. This is shown in Figure 2-20. The following statement draws a circle with its center point located at (–50, –20) and with a radius of 200. Figure 2-21 shows how the circle will appear partially in the window.

```
dbCircle(-50, -20, 200);
```

Figure 2-20 Negative coordinates

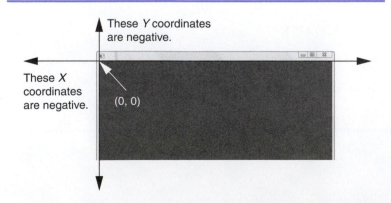

Figure 2-21 Circle drawn partially offscreen

 Checkpoint

2.13. Write a statement that will draw a line from (100, 75) to (150, 200).

2.14. What is pseudocode?

2.15. Write a statement that will draw a rectangle. The rectangle's upper-left corner should be at (0, 0) and its lower-right corner should be at (100, 80).

2.16. Write a statement that will draw a circle. The circle's center point should be at (300, 200) and its radius should be 50 pixels.

2.17. Write a statement that will draw an ellipse. The ellipse's center point should be at (120, 100). Its x-radius should be 100 pixels and its y-radius should be 60 pixels.

2.18. What happens when an ellipse's x-radius is the same as its y-radius?

2.4 Displaying Text

CONCEPT: You can use the **dbprint**, **dbText**, or **dbCenterText** functions to display text in the Dark GDK window. You can use the **dbSetWindowTitle** function to display text in the window's title bar.

Displaying Text Inside the Dark GDK Window

You can use the dbPrint function, the dbText function, or the dbCenterText function to display text in the Dark GDK window. First, let's look at the dbPrint function. The purpose of the dbPrint function is to display a string of characters. (In programming, we use the term *string* to mean "string of characters.") Here is the general format of how you call the dbPrint function:

```
dbPrint(string);
```

The *string* argument is the string that you want to display. The dbPrint function prints the string as a line of output in the Dark GDK window. The first time you call dbPrint, its output is printed at the top of the window, justified along the left side. Each subsequent time that you call dbPrint, it prints a line of output below the previous line of output. Program 2-12 shows an example. The program's output is shown in Figure 2-22. Notice that in line 14 we call the dbPrint function with no argument being passed. This causes a blank line to be displayed.

Program 2-12   (PrintLines.cpp)

```
1    // This program uses the dbPrint function
2    // to display lines of output.
3    #include "DarkGDK.h"
4
5    void DarkGDK()
6    {
7        // Display Hello in different languages.
8        dbPrint("Hello");
9        dbPrint("Hola");
10        dbPrint("Guten Tag");
11        dbPrint("Bonjour");
12
13        // Print a blank line.
14        dbPrint();
15
16        // Prompt the user to press a key.
17        dbPrint("Press any key to exit the program.");
18
19        // Wait for the user to press a key.
20        dbWaitKey();
21    }
```

Figure 2-22 Output of Program 2-12

Here is the general format of how you call the `dbText` function:

```
dbText(x, y, string);
```

The purpose of the function is to display a string of characters at a specific location in the window. The *x* and *y* arguments are a set of coordinates, and the *string* argument is the string that is to be displayed. When the string is displayed, the upper-left corner of the first character will be positioned at the *X* and *Y* coordinates.

Let's look at an example. The following statement displays the string "Hello World" in the window. As shown in Figure 2-23, the upper-left corner of the first character ("H") will be located at the coordinates (10, 10):

```
dbText(10, 10, "Hello World");
```

Figure 2-23 Results of the `dbText` function

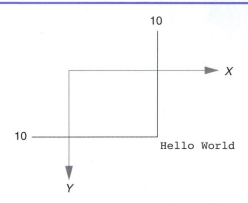

Notice that the string is enclosed in double quotes. The double quotes are required, but they will not appear on the screen.

Program 2-13 demonstrates how the `dbText` function can be used to display a message on the screen. Figure 2-24 shows the program's output.

Program 2-13   (`HelloWorld.cpp`)

```
 1  // This program uses the dbText function to display a
 2  // message on the screen.
 3  #include "DarkGDK.h"
 4
 5  void DarkGDK()
 6  {
 7      // Display the string "Hello World" at
 8      // the coordinates (10, 10).
 9      dbText(10, 10, "Hello World!");
10
11      // Wait for the user to press a key.
12      dbWaitKey();
13  }
```

Figure 2-24 Output of Program 2-13

Text can be centered horizontally by specifying a single point and a string of characters. Here is the general format of how you call the function:

```
dbCenterText(x, y, string);
```

The *x* and *y* arguments are a set of coordinates, and the *string* argument is the string that is to be displayed. When the string is displayed, it will be horizontally centered just below the point at the specified coordinates. Here is an example:

```
dbCenterText(319, 239, "Game Over");
```

Figure 2-25 illustrates how the dbCenterText function works using the arguments from this example.

Figure 2-25 A string centered just below the point at (319, 239)

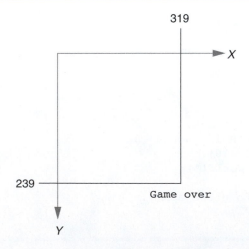

Program 2-14 further demonstrates the dbCenterText function by displaying a knock-knock joke. The program displays the joke line-by-line, waiting for the user to press a key between each line. Figure 2-26 shows the interaction that takes place when the program runs.

Program 2-14   (KnockKnock.cpp)

```
1   // This program tells a corny knock-knock joke.
2   #include "DarkGDK.h"
3
4   void DarkGDK ()
5   {
6      // Display the first line of the joke and then
7      // wait for the user to press a key.
8      dbCenterText(319, 10, "Knock Knock");
9      dbWaitKey();
10
11     // Display the second line and wait for the
12     // user to press a key.
13     dbCenterText(319, 40, "Who's there?");
14     dbWaitKey();
15
16     // Display the third line and wait for the
17     // user to press a key.
18     dbCenterText(319, 70, "Boo");
19     dbWaitKey();
20
21     // Display the fourth line and wait for the
22     // user to press a key.
23     dbCenterText(319, 100, "Boo who?");
24     dbWaitKey();
25
26     // Display the punch line and wait for the
27     // user to press a key.
28     dbCenterText(319, 130, "Don't cry!");
29     dbCenterText(319, 160, "I promise to stop telling");
30     dbCenterText(319, 190, "corny jokes!");
31     dbWaitKey();
32  }
```

Displaying Text in the Window's Title Bar

In a Dark GDK program, the dbSetWindowTitle function displays text in the window's title bar, which appears at the top of the window. This helps you to customize the appearance of the window. Here is the general format of how you call the function:

dbSetWindowTitle(*string*)

In the general format, *string* is the string that you want to appear in the window's title bar. (Don't forget to enclose the string in quotation marks!) For example,

Figure 2-26 Output of Program 2-14

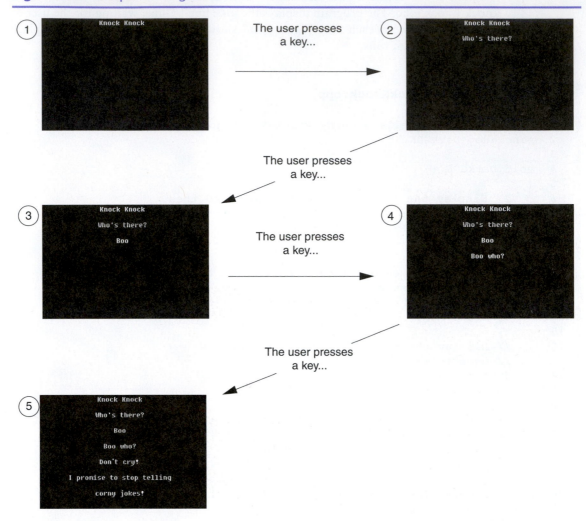

Program 2-15 draws a circle. When the program runs, the title bar at the top of the window will read **Circle Demonstration**. Figure 2-27 shows an enlarged view of the upper-left corner of the window, where the title appears.

Program 2-15   **(WindowTitle.cpp)**

```
1  // This program displays text in the window's
2  // title bar.
3  #include "DarkGDK.h"
4
5  void DarkGDK()
6  {
7      // Display a title.
8      dbSetWindowTitle("Circle Demonstration");
```

```
 9
10      // Draw a circle.
11      dbCircle(100, 100, 80);
12
13      // Wait for the user to press a key.
14      dbWaitKey();
15   }
```

Figure 2-27 Output of Program 2-15

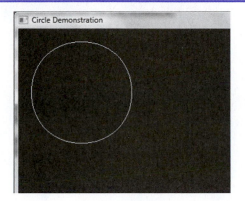

In the Spotlight:
The Orion Constellation Program

Orion is one of the most famous constellations in the night sky. The diagram in Figure 2-28 shows the approximate positions of several stars in the constellation. The topmost stars are Orion's shoulders, the row of three stars in the middle are Orion's belt, and the bottom two stars are Orion's knees. The diagram in Figure 2-29 shows the names of each of these stars, and Figure 2-30 shows the lines that are typically used to connect the stars.

In this section, we will develop a program that first displays the stars shown in Figure 2-28. When the user presses a key, the program will display the star names shown in Figure 2-29. When the user presses a key next, the program will display the constellation lines shown in Figure 2-30. After that, when the user presses a key the program will end.

When the program executes initially it will display dots to represent the stars. We will use a piece of graph paper, as shown in Figure 2-31, to sketch the positions of the dots and determine their coordinates.

Using the coordinates that we identified on the graph paper, we write pseudocode for displaying the program's initial screen. Notice in the following pseudocode that we will also display a title in the window's title bar, and a caption at the top of the screen.

Figure 2-28 Stars in the
Orion constellation

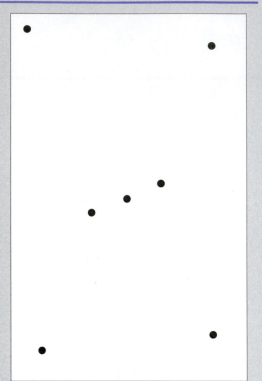

Figure 2-29 Names of the stars

Figure 2-30 Constellation lines

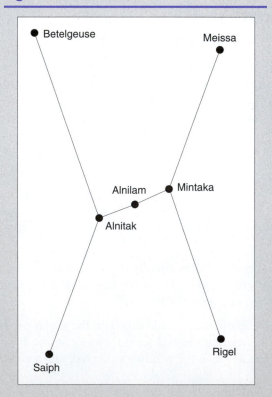

Figure 2-31 Hand sketch of the Orion constellation

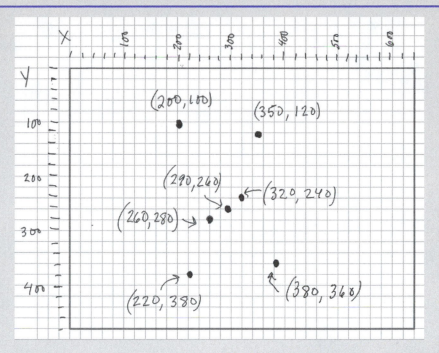

Set the window's title to "The Orion Constellation"
Display the text "Stars of the Constellation" centered at the top of the window
Draw a dot at (200,100)   *// Left shoulder*
Draw a dot at (350,120)   *// Right shoulder*
Draw a dot at (260,280)   *// Leftmost star in the belt*
Draw a dot at (290,260)   *// Middle star in the belt*
Draw a dot at (320,240)   *// Rightmost star in the belt*
Draw a dot at (220,380)   *// Left knee*
Draw a dot at (380,360)   *// Right knee*
Display a message telling the user to press a key to continue.
Wait for the user to press a key.

After the user presses a key, we want to display the names of each star, as sketched in Figure 2-32. The pseudocode for displaying these names follows. Notice that we will display an additional title near the top of the screen.

Display the text "Star Names" centered near the top of the window
Display the text "Betelgeuse" near (200, 100)   *// Left shoulder*
Display the text "Meissa" near (350, 120)   *// Right shoulder*
Display the text "Alnitak" near (260, 280)   *// Belt-left star*
Display the text "Alnilam" near (290, 260)   *// Belt-middle star*
Display the text "Mintaka" near (320, 240)   *// Belt-right star*
Display the text "Saiph" near (220, 380)   *// Left knee*
Display the text "Rigel" near (380, 360)   *// Right knee*
Wait for the user to press a key.

Figure 2-32 Orion sketch with the names of the stars

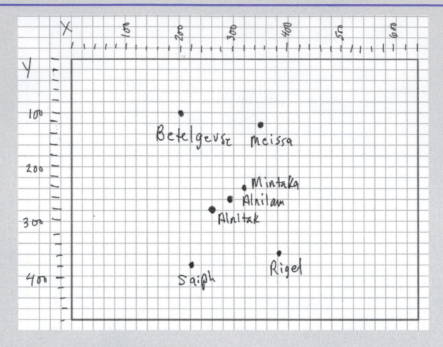

Next, when the user presses a key, we want to display the lines that connect the stars, as sketched in Figure 2-33.

Figure 2-33 Orion sketch with the names of the stars and constellation lines

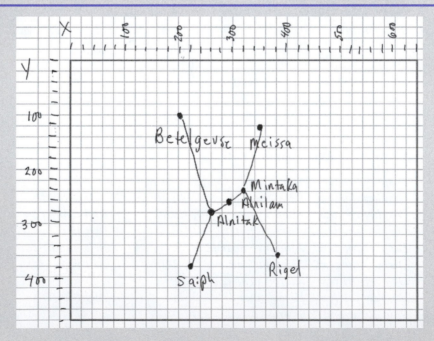

The pseudocode for displaying these lines follows. Notice that we will display an additional title near the top of the screen.

Display the text "Constellation Lines" centered near the top of the window
Draw a line from (200, 100) to (260, 280)   // Left shoulder to left belt star
Draw a line from (350, 120) to (320, 240)   // Right shoulder to right belt star
Draw a line from (260, 280) to (290, 260)   // Left belt star to middle belt star
Draw a line from (290, 260) to (320, 240)   // Middle belt star to right belt star
Draw a line from (260, 280) to (220, 380)   // Left belt star to left knee
Draw a line from (320, 240) to (380, 360)   // Right belt star to right knee
Wait for the user to press a key, then exit.

Now that we know the logical steps that the program must perform, we are ready to start writing code. Program 2-16 shows the entire program.

Program 2-16   (`Orion.cpp`)

```
1   // This program draws the stars of the constellation Orion,
2   // the names of the stars, and the constellation lines.
3   #include "DarkGDK.h"
4
5   void DarkGDK()
6   {
7       // Set the window's title.
8       dbSetWindowTitle("The Orion Constellation");
9
10      // Display a caption.
11      dbCenterText(319, 20, "Stars of the Constellation");
12
13      // Draw the stars.
14      dbDot(200, 100);        // Left shoulder
15      dbDot(350, 120);        // Right shoulder
16      dbDot(260, 280);        // Leftmost star in the belt
17      dbDot(290, 260);        // Middle star in the belt
18      dbDot(320, 240);        // Rightmost star in the belt
19      dbDot(220, 380);        // Left knee
20      dbDot(380, 360);        // Right knee
21
22      // Prompt the user to press a key.
23      dbCenterText(319, 450, "Press any key to continue.");
24      dbWaitKey();
25
26      // Next display the star names.
27      dbCenterText(319, 40, "Star Names");
28      dbCenterText(200, 100, "Betelgeuse");        // Left shoulder
29      dbCenterText(350, 120, "Meissa");            // Right shoulder
30      dbText(260, 280, "Alnitak");                 // Belt-left star
31      dbText(290, 260, "Alnilam");                 // Belt-middle star
32      dbText(320, 240, "Mintaka");                 // Belt-right star
33      dbCenterText(220, 380, "Saiph");             // Left knee
```

```
34        dbCenterText(380, 360, "Rigel");     // Right knee
35
36        // Wait for the user to press a key.
37        dbWaitKey();
38
39        // Next display the constellation lines.
40        dbCenterText(319, 60, "Constellation Lines");
41        dbLine(200, 100, 260, 280);          // Left shoulder to belt
42        dbLine(350, 120, 320, 240);          // Right shoulder to belt
43        dbLine(260, 280, 290, 260);          // Left belt to middle belt
44        dbLine(290, 260, 320, 240);          // Middle belt to right belt
45        dbLine(260, 280, 220, 380);          // Left belt to left knee
46        dbLine(320, 240, 380, 360);          // Right belt to right knee
47
48        // Wait for the user to press a key, then exit.
49        dbWaitKey();
50    }
```

When the program runs, it initially displays the window shown in Figure 2-34. After the user presses a key, the window is updated with the names of the stars, as shown in Figure 2-35. After the next keypress, the window is updated with the constellation lines as shown in Figure 2-36. (Note that we have slightly enlarged the size of the dots in each figure, to ensure that they are visible on the printed page.)

Figure 2-34 The initial screen showing the stars

Figure 2-35 The screen showing the star names

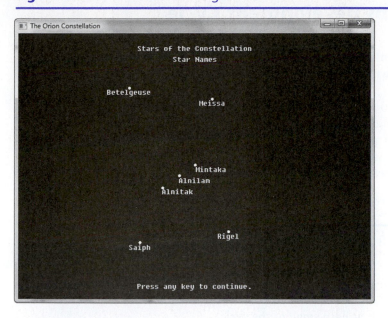

Figure 2-36 The screen showing the constellation lines

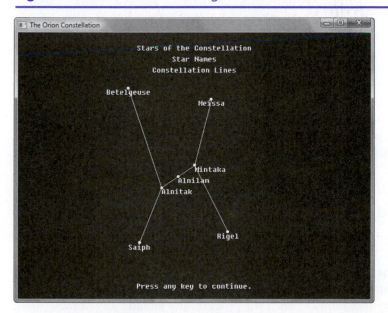

 **Checkpoint**

2.19. Write a statement that displays the text *Four score and seven years ago*. The upper-left corner of the first character should be located at (100, 50).

2.20. Write a statement that displays the text *To be, or not to be*. The text should be centered just below (100, 50).

2.5 The Program Development Cycle

CONCEPT: When creating programs, programmers typically follow a process known as the program development cycle.

As you progress through this text, you will use the C++ language and the Dark GDK library to create programs. There is much more to creating a program than writing code, however. The process of creating a program that works correctly typically requires the five phases shown in Figure 2-37. The entire process is known as the *program development cycle*.

Figure 2-37 The program development cycle

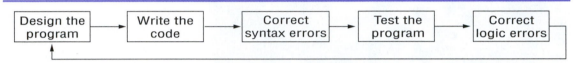

Let's take a closer look at each stage of the cycle.

Design the Program

All professional programmers will tell you that a program should be carefully designed before the code is actually written. When programmers begin a new project, they never jump right in and start writing code as the first step. They start by creating a design of the program. In this chapter, you learned about two design techniques that can be used when creating a graphics program. The first technique is to sketch on graph paper the images that the program will display. You can use the sketch to lay out the positions of graphic items and determine their screen coordinates. The second technique is to write pseudocode that lists the logical steps that the program must take.

Write the Code

After designing the program, the programmer begins writing code in a high-level language such as C++. Recall from Chapter 1 that each language has its own rules, known as syntax, that must be followed when writing a program. A language's syntax rules dictate things such as how key words, operators, and punctuation characters can be used. A *syntax error* occurs if the programmer violates any of these rules.

Correct Syntax Errors

If the program contains a syntax error, or even a simple mistake such as a misspelled key word, the compiler will display an error message indicating what the error is. Virtually all code contains syntax errors when it is first written, so typically the programmer will spend some time correcting these. Once all of the syntax errors and simple typing mistakes have been corrected, the program can be compiled.

Test the Program

Once the code has been successfully compiled, it is tested to determine whether any logic errors exist. A *logic error* is a mistake that does not prevent the program from being compiled or running, but causes it to produce incorrect results. (Mathematical mistakes are common causes of logic errors. We cover mathematical operations in Chapter 3.)

Correct Logic Errors

If the program produces incorrect results, the programmer *debugs* the code. This means that the programmer finds and corrects logic errors in the program. Sometimes during this process, the programmer discovers that the program's original design must be changed. In this event, the program development cycle starts over, and continues until no errors can be found.

 Checkpoint

2.21. What is a syntax error?

2.22. What is a logic error?

2.23. What does the term "debug" mean?

Review Questions

Multiple Choice

1. When a(n) _____ appears in a C++ program it causes the contents of another file to be included in the program.
   a. copy directive
   b. include directive
   c. setup command
   d. initialize command

2. A _____ is a group of programming statements that collectively has a name.
   a. language
   b. library
   c. function
   d. program skeleton

3. The _____ function call causes the program to wait until the user presses a key.
   a. waitKey();
   b. dbWaitKey();
   c. dbGetKeyPress();
   d. dbWait();

4. A(n) _____ is a short note that is intended for a person reading a program's code.
   a. comment
   b. directive
   c. function call
   d. invisible statement

5. _____ refers to the conventions used in placing blank lines and indentations in a program's code.
   a. Code dressing
   b. Paragraphing
   c. Block commenting
   d. Programming style

6. _____ refers to the number of pixels in a display.
   a. Pixelation
   b. Resolution
   c. Texture
   d. Grain count

7. The _____ identifies the position of each pixel in the Dark GDK window.
   a. pixel detector
   b. pixel location device
   c. screen coordinate system
   d. *A,B* coordinate system

8. A(n) _____ is a piece of data that is sent into a function.
   a. argument
   b. constraint
   c. directive
   d. packet

9. The _____ function draws a tiny dot in the Dark GDK window.
   a. `dbDrawDot`
   b. `dbDot`
   c. `dbPixel`
   d. `dbPoint`

10. The _____ function causes a program to wait for a specified amount of time before continuing.
    a. `dbPause`
    b. `dbStop`
    c. `dbHalt`
    d. `dbWait`

11. An informal language that has no syntax rules and is not meant to be compiled or executed is known as _____.
    a. machine language
    b. faux code
    c. pseudocode
    d. C++

12. A(n) _____ is a set of well-defined logical steps that must be taken to perform a task.
    a. algorithm
    b. logarithm
    c. plan of attack
    d. logic schedule

13. The _____ function draws a rectangle in the Dark GDK window.
    a. `dbRectangle`
    b. `dbBox`
    c. `dbDrawRectangle`
    d. `dbDrawBox`

14. The _____ function draws a circle in the Dark GDK window.
    a. `dbDrawCircle`
    b. `dbCircle`
    c. `dbRound`
    d. `dbRadius`

15. The _____ function can be used to draw an oval in the Dark GDK window.
    a. `dbDrawOval`
    b. `dbOval`
    c. `dbOblong`
    d. `dbEllipse`

16. The term "string" refers to _____.
    a. a string of errors
    b. a section of memory
    c. a sequence of dots displayed on the screen
    d. text, or a string of characters

17. The _____ function displays text with the upper-left corner of the first character positioned under a specified point.
    a. `dbText`
    b. `dbDisplayText`
    c. `dbCenterText`
    d. `dbTextLeft`

18. The _____ function displays text centered under a specified point.
    a. `dbText`
    b. `dbDisplayText`
    c. `dbCenterText`
    d. `dbTextMid`

19. A _____ error occurs when the programmer violates the rules of a programming language.
    a. logic
    b. grammatical
    c. syntax
    d. legal

20. A _____ error does not prevent the program from running, but produces incorrect results.
    a. logic
    b. grammatical
    c. syntax
    d. legal

True or False

1. In C++, the name `DarkGDK` is the same as the name `darkgdk`.

2. The `//` characters mark the beginning of a line comment.

3. The screen coordinate system works exactly like the Cartesian coordinate system.

4. In a 640 by 480 window, the coordinates of the pixel that is visible in the upper-left corner are (0, 0).

5. In a 640 by 480 window, the coordinates of the pixel that is visible in the lower-right corner are (640, 480).

6. The `dbCircle` function accepts the circle's diameter as an argument.

7. An ellipse is a circle if its x-radius and y-radius are the same.

8. The `dbCenterText` function always displays text in the center of the Dark GDK window.

9. It is impossible to change the text that is displayed in a Dark GDK window.

10. A logic error prevents a program from being compiled or running.

Short Answer

1. Why is the `#include "DarkGDK.h"` statement needed in a program that uses the Dark GDK library?

2. What does a function call do?

3. How do you write a line comment in C++? How do you write a block comment?

4. What is the resolution of the default Dark GDK window?

5. In a 640 by 480 window, what are the coordinates of the pixel that is visible in the upper-right corner of the window?

6. What are the arguments that you pass to the `dbLine` function?

7. What are the arguments that you pass to the `dbBox` function?

8. What are the two radii that are passed as arguments to the `dbEllipse` function?

9. Describe the two functions that were presented in this chapter for displaying text.

10. What are the steps in the program development cycle, as described in this chapter?

Algorithm Workbench

1. Write the code for a program that opens an empty Dark GDK window and waits for the user to press a key.

2. Write a statement that draws a dot at the coordinates (100, 25).

3. Write a short program that will display five dots in a vertical line.

4. Write a statement that causes a program to wait for five seconds before continuing.

5. Assume that a program opens a Dark GDK window with a resolution of 640 by 480 pixels. Write a statement that draws a line from the upper-left corner to the lower-right corner.

6. Write a statement that draws a rectangle. The upper-left corner of the rectangle should be at (20, 30) and the lower-right corner should be at (99, 74).

7. Write a statement that draws a rectangle. The upper-right corner of the rectangle should be at (120, 50) and the lower-left corner should be at (20, 200).

8. Write a statement that draws a circle. The circle's center point should be at (100, 150) and its radius should be 100 pixels.

9. Write a statement that draws an ellipse. The ellipse's center point should be at (300, 200). Its x-radius should be 100 pixels and its y-radius should be 50 pixels.

10. Write a statement that calls the `dbEllipse` function to draw a circle. The circle's center point should be at (100, 150) and its radius should be 100 pixels.

11. Write a statement that displays the text *Hello World* in the Dark GDK window. The upper-left corner of the first character should appear just under the location (50, 100).

12. Write a statement that displays the text *Hello World* in the Dark GDK window. The text should be centered just under the location (100, 100).

Programming Exercises

1. **This Old House**
   Use the basic 2D shapes you learned in this chapter to draw a house. Be sure to include at least two windows and a door. Feel free to draw other objects as well, such as the sky, sun, and even clouds.

2. **Tree Age**
   Counting the growth rings of a tree is a good way to tell the age of a tree. Each growth ring counts as one year. Use either the `dbCircle` or `dbEllipse` function to draw how the growth rings of a 5-year-old tree might look. Then, using the `dbText` function, number each growth ring starting from the center and working outward with the age in years associated with that ring.

3. **Hollywood Star**
   Make your own star on the Hollywood Walk of Fame. Write a program that displays a star similar to the one shown in Figure 2-38, with your name displayed in the star.

4. **Vehicle Outline**
   Using the 2D shapes you learned about in this chapter draw the outline of the vehicle of your choice (car, truck, airplane, and so forth).

5. **Secret Cipher**
   Using basic 2D shapes, create a unique symbol for each letter of your initials. Display the symbols in the center of the screen, and use the `dbText` function to display the letter each symbol represents below the symbol.

Figure 2-38 Hollywood star

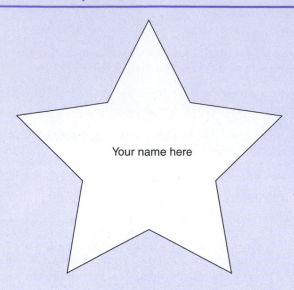

Your name here

6. **Solar System**
   Use the `dbCircle` function to draw each of the planets of our solar system. Draw the sun first, and then each planet according to distance from the sun. (Mercury, Venus, Earth, Mars, Jupiter Saturn, Uranus, Neptune). Label each planet using the `dbText` function.

7. **Mr. Robotic**
   Use basic 2D shapes to construct an image of a robot. Then, use the `dbText` function to display the phrase *Greetings Human!*

8. **Flower Power**
   Draw a flower using the basic 2D shapes you learned in this chapter. Try to use each type of shape at least once.

9. **Create a Logo**
   Most commercial game studios have their own company logo. Using the basic 2D shapes you learned in this chapter, design a prototype of your own logo.

Group Project

10. **Connect the Dots**
    Use the `dbDot` function to arrange pixels on the screen so that they will make a design. Use the `dbText` function to number the dots in the order you would like them connected. Then switch programs with a lab partner and use the `dbLine` function to connect the dots on each other's programs.

CHAPTER

3

Variables, Calculations, and Colors

TOPICS

3.1 Introduction
3.2 Literal Data
3.3 Variables
3.4 Calculations
3.5 Getting Values from Functions

3.6 Reading Numeric Input from the Keyboard
3.7 Colors
3.8 Named Constants
3.9 Changing the Size of the Program Window

3.1 Introduction

Programs almost always work with data of some type. For example, in Chapter 2 you saw programs that work extensively with *XY* coordinates. We used the *XY* coordinate data to draw shapes on the screen. You also saw programs that use strings of characters to display text on the screen.

In this chapter, we will take a closer look at how numerical data can be used in a program. We will discuss how a program can store data in memory, perform calculations, and retrieve data from functions in the Dark GDK library. We will also go beyond the simple world of black and white and discuss how to draw in color.

3.2 Literal Data

CONCEPT: A literal is an item of data that is typed into a program's code.

The simplest form of data that a program can use is data that has been typed into the program's code. This type of data is known as *literal* data. For example, look at Program 3-1. This program draws the circle shown in Figure 3-1.

Program 3-1 (`DrawCircle.cpp`)

```
1   // This program draws a circle.
2   #include "DarkGDK.h"
3
4   void DarkGDK()
5   {
6        dbCircle(319, 239, 150);
7        dbWaitKey();
8   }
```

Figure 3-1 Output of Program 3-1

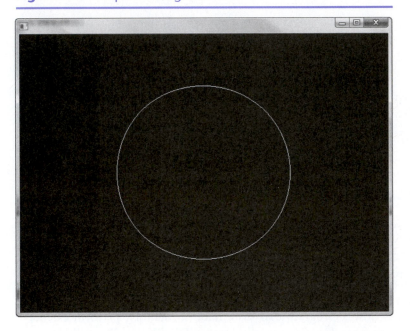

As shown in Figure 3-2, the program uses the following literal data in line 6:

- 319 is the X coordinate of the circle's center point
- 239 is the Y coordinate of the circle's center point
- 150 is the circle's radius

These data items are *integer literals* because they are integers that we typed directly into the code when we wrote the program. (Recall that in Chapter 2 you saw some programs that used many sets of XY coordinates. As a result, these programs had a lot of literal data.)

Programs can also have *string literals*, which is string data that has been typed into the program. In C++, a string literal must be enclosed in double quote marks. Program 3-2 shows an example. Figure 3-3 points out the string literals in the program.

Figure 3-2 Literal data in Program 3-1

```
// This program draws a circle.
#include "DarkGDK.h"


void DarkGDK()
{
    dbCircle(319, 239, 150);
    dbWaitKey();
}
```

This integer literal is the
X coordinate of the circle's center

This integer literal is the circle's radius

This integer literal is the Y coordinate
of the circle's center

Program 3-2

```
1   // This program has numeric and string literal data.
2   #include "DarkGDK.h"
3
4   void DarkGDK()
5   {
6       dbSetWindowTitle("A Simple Program");
7       dbText(10, 10, "Hello World!");
8       dbWaitKey();
9   }
```

Figure 3-3 String literals in Program 3-2

```
// This program has numeric and string literal data.
#include "DarkGDK.h"
```
String literal

```
void DarkGDK()
{
    dbSetWindowTitle("A Simple Program");
    dbText(10, 10, "Hello World!");
    dbWaitKey();
}
```
String literal

String literal

You use literal data to represent known values in a program. For example, if you know that you want to draw a line from (100, 50) to (400, 200) you can pass the integer literals 100, 50, 400, and 200 as arguments to the dbLine function. However, there are many times when the values that you need in a program are unknown at the time that you are writing the program. For example, suppose you are programming a hockey game and you want to draw a circle on the screen to simulate the puck. As the program runs, the puck will move to different locations on the screen, in response to the user's input. Each time the program makes the puck move, it has to calculate the coordinates of the circle's midpoint. Instead of using literal values for these coordinates, you will have to use variables, which we discuss next.

Checkpoint

3.1. What are the numeric literals in the following program?

```
#include "DarkGDK.h"

void DarkGDK()
{
        dbCenterText(300, 200, "Demo");
        dbLine(50, 75, 100, 120);
}
```

3.2. What are the string literals in the program shown in Checkpoint 3.1?

 ## 3.3 Variables

CONCEPT: A variable is a storage location in memory that is represented by a name.

Most programs store data in the computer's memory and perform operations on that data. For example, consider the typical online shopping experience: you browse a Web site and add the items that you want to purchase to the shopping cart. As you add items to the shopping cart, data about those items is stored in memory. Then, when you click the *checkout* button, a program running on the Web site's computer calculates the cost of all the items you have in your shopping cart, applicable sales taxes, shipping costs, and the total of all these charges. When the program performs these calculations, it stores the results in the computer's memory.

Programs use variables to store data in memory. A *variable* is a storage location in memory that is represented by a name. For example, a program that calculates the sales tax on a purchase might use a variable named tax to hold that value in memory. And a program that calculates the distance from Earth to a distant star might use a variable named distance to hold that value in memory.

In C++, you must *declare* a variable in a program before you can use it to store data. You do this with a variable declaration, which is a statement that specifies two things about the variable:

1. the variable's data type
2. the variable's name

Let's take a closer look at each of these variable characteristics.

Data Types

When you declare a variable, you must specify its *data type*, which is simply the type of data that the variable will hold. For the next several chapters we will be working extensively with numbers (such as *XY* coordinates) so we will discuss only numeric data types in this chapter.

Table 3-1 lists the four numeric data types that you will use most often in this book.

Table 3-1 The numeric data types that you will use most often

Data Type	Description
int	A variable of the int data type can hold whole numbers only. For example, an int variable can hold values such as 42, 0, and –99. An int variable cannot hold numbers with a fractional part, such as 22.1 or –4.9.
	You will use variables of the int data type to hold data such as *X* and *Y* coordinates, the lengths of lines, the radii of circles, and so forth. An int variable uses 32 bits of memory, and can hold an integer number in the range of –2,147,483,648 through 2,147,483,647.
float	A variable of the float data type can hold floating-point numbers such as 3.5, –87.95, and 3.0. A number that is stored in a float variable is stored in memory with seven digits of precision.
	In memory a float variable uses 32 bits of memory. The Dark GDK uses the float data type extensively when working with three-dimensional graphics.
double	A variable of the double data type can hold either whole numbers or floating-point numbers. A number that is stored in a double variable is stored in memory with 15 digits of precision.
	Because double variables use twice the precision of float variables, you will want to use them to store the results of some mathematical calculations. In memory a double variable uses 64 bits of memory.
DWORD	This is a special data type that the Dark GDK library uses extensively when working with colors. A variable of the DWORD data type can hold non-negative integers. Because the DWORD data type is *unsigned*, it cannot hold negative values. (Note that this data type is spelled with all uppercase letters.)
	A DWORD variable can hold integer values in the range of 0 through 4,294,967,295. In memory a DWORD variable uses 32 bits.

Variable Names

When writing a program, you make up names for the variables that you want to use. In C++, these are the rules that you must follow when naming variables:

- Variable names must be one word. They cannot contain spaces.
- The first character must be one of the letters a through z, A through Z, or an underscore character (_).
- After the first character you may use the letters a through z, A through Z, the digits 0 through 9, or underscores.
- Uppercase and lowercase characters are distinct. This means `LineLength` is not the same as `linelength`.

In addition to following the C++ rules, you should always choose names for your variables that give an indication of what they are used for. For example, a variable that holds the temperature might be named `temperature`, and a variable that holds a car's speed might be named `speed`. You may be tempted to give variables names like `a` and `b2`, but names like these give no clue about the variable's purpose.

Because a variable's name should reflect the variable's purpose, programmers often find themselves creating names that are made of multiple words. For example, consider the following variable names:

```
centerpointx
lengthofline
xradiuslength
```

Unfortunately, these names are not easily read by the human eye because the words aren't separated. Because we can't have spaces in variable names, we must find another way to separate the words in a multiword variable name, and make it more readable to the human eye.

One way to do this is to use the underscore character to represent a space. For example, the following variable names are easier to read than those previously shown:

```
center_point_x
length_of_line
x_radius_length
```

Another way to address this problem is to use the *camelCase* naming convention. camelCase names are written in the following manner:

- You begin writing the variable name with lowercase letters.
- The first character of the second and subsequent words is written in uppercase.

For example, the following variable names are written in camelCase:

```
centerPointX
lengthOfLine
xRadiusLength
```

Because the camelCase convention is very popular with programmers, we will use it in this book.

NOTE: This style of naming is called camelCase because the uppercase characters that appear in a name sometimes suggest a camel's humps.

Declaring a Variable

As previously mentioned, a variable declaration specifies a variable's data type and its name. Here is an example:

```
int centerX;
```

This statement declares a variable named `centerX`. The name suggests that perhaps the variable will hold the *X* coordinate of a center point, maybe that of a circle. The variable's data type is `int`, so it can be used to hold integer values. Notice that the statement ends with a semicolon. Here is another example:

```
float distance;
```

This statement declares a variable named `distance`. The variable's data type is `float`, so it can be used to hold floating-point values.

You can declare multiple variables of the same data type with one declaration statement. Here is an example:

```
int centerX, centerY, radius;
```

This statement declares three variables named `centerX`, `centerY`, and `radius`. Each one is an `int` variable, so it can hold integers. Notice that commas separate the variable names.

Assigning Values to Variables

You use the equal sign (=) to store a value in a variable. Here is an example (assume `centerX` is an `int` variable):

```
centerX = 319;
```

The equal sign is known as the *assignment operator*. When we store a value in a variable we say that we are assigning the value to the variable. The value that appears on the right side of the assignment operator is stored in the variable that is named to the left of the operator. When this statement executes, the value 319 will be stored in the `centerX` variable. Notice that a semicolon appears at the end of the statement.

Here is another example (assume `distance` is a `float` variable):

```
distance = 159.9;
```

When this statement executes, the value 159.9 will be stored in the `distance` variable.

The name of the variable receiving the assignment must appear on the left side of the = sign. For example, the following statement is incorrect:

```
319 = centerX;    // ERROR!
```

This is a syntax error. Writing a statement like this in a program will cause an error when you compile the program.

Initializing Variables

You can also use the = operator to assign an initial value to a variable in the declaration statement. This is called *initializing* a variable. Here is an example:

```
int centerX = 319;
```

This statement declares an `int` variable named `centerX` and initializes it with the value 319. Here is an example that initializes three variables:

```
int centerX = 319, centerY = 239, radius = 150;
```

This statement does the following:

- It declares an `int` variable named `centerX` and initializes it with the value 319.
- It declares an `int` variable named `centerY` and initializes it with the value 239.
- It declares an `int` variable named `radius` and initializes it with the value 150.

You've learned enough about variables that we can now look at a program that uses them. Program 3-3 shows a complete program that uses the `centerX`, `centerY`, and `radius` variables that we have used as examples. Figure 3-4 shows the program's output.

Program 3-3 (`DrawCircle2.cpp`)

```
1   // This program draws a circle.
2   #include "DarkGDK.h"
3
4   void DarkGDK()
5   {
6       // Declare variables for a circle's
7       // center point and radius.
8       int centerX = 319;
9       int centerY = 239;
10      int radius = 150;
11
12      // Draw a circle.
13      dbCircle(centerX, centerY, radius);
14
15      // Wait for the user to press a key.
16      dbWaitKey();
17  }
```

The statements in lines 8 through 10 declare and initialize the `centerX`, `centerY`, and `radius` variables. Then the statement in line 13 calls the `dbCircle` function to draw a circle. Notice that the `centerX`, `centerY`, and `radius` variables are passed as arguments. When a variable is passed as an argument to a function, it is the value that is stored in the variable that is actually passed. That means that line 13 passes the values 319, 239, and 150 as arguments to the `dbCircle` function.

When you assign a value to a variable, any value that was previously stored in the variable will be replaced by the new value, as demonstrated by Program 3-4. The statements in lines 8 through 10 declare and initialize the `centerX`, `centerY`, and `radius` variables. The statement in line 13 uses these variables as arguments to the `dbCircle` function. Then, the statements in lines 16 through 18 assign different values to the `centerX`, `centerY`, and `radius` variables. When the `dbCircle` function is called in line 22, the variables are once again passed as arguments. As a result a different circle is drawn, using the new values of the variables. The program's output is shown in Figure 3-5.

Figure 3-4 Output of Program 3-3

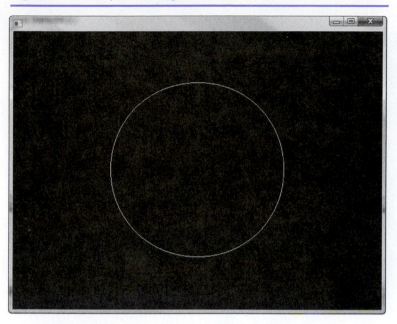

Program 3-4   **(DrawCircle3.cpp)**

```
 1   // This program draws two circles.
 2   #include "DarkGDK.h"
 3
 4   void DarkGDK()
 5   {
 6       // Declare variables for a circle's
 7       // center point and radius.
 8       int centerX = 319;
 9       int centerY = 239;
10       int radius = 150;
11
12       // Draw a circle.
13       dbCircle(centerX, centerY, radius);
14
15       // Assign new values to the variables.
16       centerX = 479;
17       centerY = 359;
18       radius = 75;
19
20       // Draw another circle, using the new
21       // values as arguments.
22       dbCircle(centerX, centerY, radius);
23
24       // Wait for the user to press a key.
25       dbWaitKey();
26   }
```

Figure 3-5 Output of Program 3-4

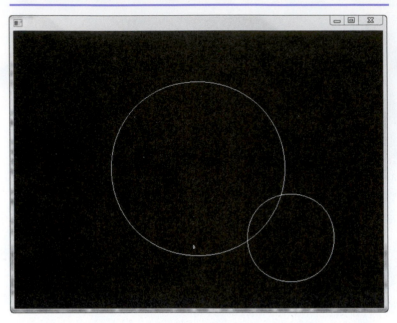

Where to Declare Variables

Notice that the variables in Program 3-3 are declared inside the DarkGDK function. Variables that are declared inside of a function are known as *local variables*. In Chapter 4, we will discuss other places to declare variables, but for now you will declare all of your variables inside the DarkGDK function.

You must also write a variable's declaration above any statement that uses the variable. Notice that in Program 3-3 all of the variables are declared at the top of the DarkGDK function, in lines 7 through 9. This is above the statement in line 13 that uses the variables.

TIP: When you compile a program, the compiler reads the source code from the top of the program to the bottom. With this in mind, it makes sense that a variable's declaration must appear above any statement that uses that variable. The compiler must read the declaration statement before it can process any statement that performs an operation with the variable.

Uninitialized Variables

An *uninitialized variable* is a variable that has been declared, but has not been initialized or assigned a value. Uninitialized variables are a common cause of logic errors in programs. For example, look at the following code:

```
int x, y, radius;
dbCircle(x, y, radius);
```

Here we have declared the x, y, and radius variables, but we have not initialized them or assigned values to them. Therefore, we do not know what values these variables hold. Nevertheless, we have passed them as arguments to the dbCircle function.

You're probably wondering what would happen if this code were executed. An honest answer would be "I don't know." This is because uninitialized local variables hold unpredictable values. When an uninitialized local variable is declared, a place in memory is set aside for the variable, but the contents of that memory location are not altered. As a result, an uninitialized local variable holds the value that happens to already be stored in its memory location. Programmers typically refer to unpredictable values such as this as "garbage."

Uninitialized variables can cause logic errors that are hard to find in a program. You should always make sure that a variable is either initialized with a value when it is declared, or is assigned a value before the variable is used in any operation.

Floating-Point Truncation

When you declare a variable to be of an integer data type, such as int, you can only store integer values in the variable. If you assign a floating-point number to an integer variable, C++ will convert the floating-point number to an integer by dropping the part of the number that appears after the decimal point. Recall from Chapter 2 that the process of dropping a floating-point number's fractional part is known as *truncation*. For example, look at the following code:

```
int width;
width = 7.9;
```

In the first statement, the width variable is declared as an int. In the second statement, the floating-point value 7.9 is assigned to the width variable. When C++ converts 7.9 to an int, the part of the number after the decimal point is dropped. As a result, the value 7 will be assigned to the width variable. The following code shows another example, where the value of a double variable is being assigned to an int variable:

```
double magnitude;
int lineLength;
magnitude = 98.7;
lineLength = magnitude;
```

In the last statement, the value of the magnitude variable, 98.7, is being assigned to the lineLength variable, which is an int. After the code executes, the value 98 will be assigned to lineLength.

NOTE: Normally it is safe to assign an integer value to a float or double variable. Here is an example:

```
double score;
score = 14;
```

In this code, the score variable is declared as a double in the first statement. In the second statement, the integer value 14 is converted to the double value 14.0 and assigned to the score variable.

 **Checkpoint**

3.3. What is a variable?

3.4. What two items do you specify with a variable declaration?

3.5. Summarize the rules for naming variables in C++.

3.6. What variable naming convention do we follow in this book?

3.7. Does it matter where you write the variable declarations inside a function?

3.8. What is variable initialization?

3.9. What is an uninitialized variable?

3.10. Do uninitialized variables pose any danger in a program?

3.11. What happens when you assign a floating-point number to an integer variable?

 3.4 **Calculations**

CONCEPT: You can use math operators to perform simple calculations. Math expressions can be written using the math operators and parentheses as grouping symbols. The result of a math expression can be assigned to a variable.

Most programs require calculations of some sort to be performed. A programmer's tools for performing calculations are *math operators*. C++ provides the math operators shown in Table 3-2.

Programmers use the operators shown in Table 3-2 to create math expressions. A *math expression* performs a calculation and gives a value. The following is an example of a simple math expression:

```
12 * 2
```

The values on the right and left of the + operator are called *operands*. These are values that the * operator multiplies together. The value that is given by this expression is 24.

Table 3-2 Math operators

Operator	Name of the Operator	Description
+	Addition	Adds two numbers
−	Subtraction	Subtracts one number from another
*	Multiplication	Multiplies one number by another
/	Division	Divides one number by another and gives the quotient
%	Modulus	Divides one integer by another and gives the remainder

Variables may also be used in a math expression. For example, suppose we have two `int` variables named `startingX` and `length`, and we have assigned values to each of the variables. The following math expression uses the + operator to add the value of the `startingX` variable to the value of the `length` variable:

```
startingX + length
```

When we use a math expression to calculate a value, normally we want to save that value in memory so we can use it again in the program. We do this with an assignment statement. For example, suppose we have another `int` variable named `endingX`. The following statement assigns the value of `startingX` plus `length` to the `endingX` variable:

```
endingX = startingX + length
```

In many of your programs you will have to perform calculations to determine the XY coordinates for a shape. For example, recall that the `dbBox` function accepts as arguments the coordinates of the box's upper-left corner and lower-right corner. Suppose we want to draw a box and we know the coordinates of the upper-left corner, but we do not know the coordinates of the lower-right corner. If we know the desired width and height of the box, then we can calculate the coordinates of the lower-right corner. The X coordinate of the lower-right corner will be the X coordinate of the upper-left corner plus the box's width. The Y coordinate of the lower-right corner will be the Y coordinate of the upper-left corner plus the box's height. Or, to express it in pseudocode:

lowerRightX = upperLeftX + width
lowerRightY = upperLeftY + height

This is shown in Figure 3-6.

Figure 3-6 Calculating the coordinates of a box's lower-right corner

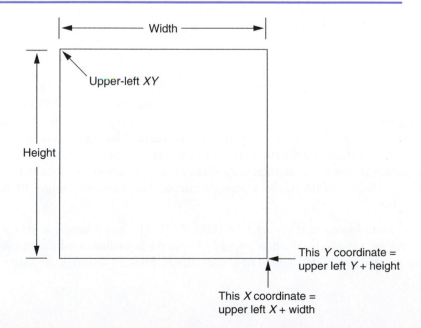

Suppose that in another case we know the coordinates of the box's lower-right corner, but we do not know the coordinates of the upper-left corner. If we know the desired width and height of the box, then we can calculate the coordinates of the upper-left corner. The *X* coordinate of the upper-left corner will be the *X* coordinate of the lower-right corner minus the box's width. The *Y* coordinate of the upper-left corner will be the *Y* coordinate of the lower-right corner minus the box's height. Or, we can express it this way in pseudocode:

upperLeftX = *lowerRightX* − *width*
upperLeftY = *lowerRightY* − *height*

This is shown in Figure 3-7.

Figure 3-7 Calculating the coordinates of a box's upper-left corner

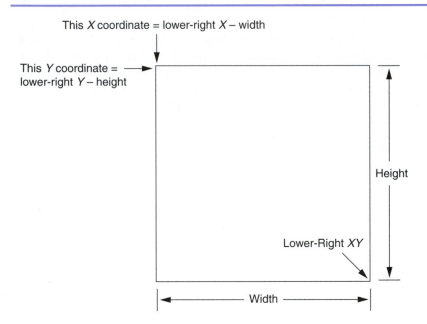

This *X* coordinate = lower-right *X* − width

This *Y* coordinate = lower-right *Y* − height

Height

Lower-Right *XY*

Width

Program 3-5 shows how we might perform these calculations in code. The program draws two boxes. The first box's height is 330 pixels and its width is 250 pixels. Its upper-left corner is at the coordinates (50, 20). We don't readily know the coordinates of the lower-right corner, so we will calculate them. The statements in lines 19 through 22 assign the known values to the `upperLeftX`, `upperLeftY`, `boxHeight`, and `boxWidth` variables. The statements in lines 26 and 27 use these variables to calculate the coordinates of the box's lower-right corner. The statement in line 30 draws the box.

The second box's lower-right corner is at (600, 450). The box's height is 400 pixels and its width is 200 pixels. We don't readily know the coordinates of the upper-left corner, so we will calculate them. The statements in lines 34 through 37 assign the

Program 3-5   (`CalculatePoints.cpp`)

```
 1   // This program draws two boxes. The height and width of
 2   // each box is known. The coordinates of only one corner
 3   // of each box is known. The coordinates of each box's
 4   // other corner are calculated.
 5   #include "DarkGDK.h"
 6
 7   void DarkGDK()
 8   {
 9       // Variable declarations
10       int boxHeight;          // To hold a box's height
11       int boxWidth;           // To hold a box's width
12       int upperLeftX;         // To hold an upper-left X coordinate
13       int upperLeftY;         // To hold an upper-left Y coordinate
14       int lowerRightX;        // To hold a lower-right X coordinate
15       int lowerRightY;        // To hold a lower-right Y coordinate
16
17       // The first box's upper-left coordinates are (50, 20).
18       // Its height is 330 pixels and its width is 250 pixels.
19       upperLeftX = 50;
20       upperLeftY = 20;
21       boxHeight = 330;
22       boxWidth = 250;
23
24       // Calculate the first box's lower-right
25       // corner coordinates.
26       lowerRightX = upperLeftX + boxWidth;
27       lowerRightY = upperLeftY + boxHeight;
28
29       // Draw the first box.
30       dbBox(upperLeftX, upperLeftY, lowerRightX, lowerRightY);
31
32       // The second box's lower-right coordinates are (600, 450).
33       // Its height is 400 pixels and its width is 200 pixels.
34       lowerRightX = 600;
35       lowerRightY = 450;
36       boxHeight = 400;
37       boxWidth = 200;
38
39       // Calculate the second box's upper-left
40       // corner coordinates.
41       upperLeftX = lowerRightX — boxWidth;
42       upperLeftY = lowerRightY — boxHeight;
43
44       // Draw the second box.
45       dbBox(upperLeftX, upperLeftY, lowerRightX, lowerRightY);
46
47       // Wait for the user to press a key.
48       dbWaitKey();
49   }
```

known values to the `lowerRightX`, `lowerRightY`, `boxHeight`, and `boxWidth` variables. The statements in lines 41 and 42 use these variables to calculate the coordinates of the box's lower-right corner. The statement in line 45 draws the box. The program's output is shown in Figure 3-8.

Figure 3-8 Output of Program 3-5

The Order of Operations

You can write mathematical expressions with several operators. The following statement assigns the sum of 17, the variable x, 21, and the variable y to the variable `answer`.

```
answer = 17 + x + 21 + y;
```

Some expressions are not that straightforward, however. Consider the following statement:

```
outcome = 12 + 6 / 3;
```

What value will be stored in `outcome`? The number 6 is used as an operand for both the addition and division operators. The outcome variable could be assigned either 6 or 14, depending on when the division takes place. The answer is 14 because the *order of operations* dictates that the division operator works before the addition operator does.

The order of operations can be summarized as follows:

1. Perform any operations that are enclosed in parentheses.
2. Perform any multiplications, divisions, or modulus operations as they appear from left to right.
3. Perform any additions or subtractions as they appear from left to right.

Mathematical expressions are evaluated from left to right. Multiplication and division are always performed before addition and subtraction, so the statement

```
outcome = 12 + 6 / 3;
```

works like this:

1. 6 is divided by 3, yielding a result of 2
2. 12 is added to 2, yielding a result of 14

It could be diagrammed as shown in Figure 3-9.

Figure 3-9 The order of operations at work

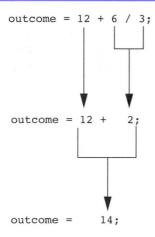

Table 3-3 shows some other sample expressions with their values.

Table 3-3 Some math expressions and their values

Expression	Value
5 + 2 * 4	13
10 / 2 − 3	2
8 + 12 * 2 − 4	28
6 − 3 * 2 + 7 − 1	6

Grouping with Parentheses

Parts of a mathematical expression may be grouped with parentheses to force some operations to be performed before others. In the following statement, the variables a and b are added together, and their sum is divided by 4:

```
result = (a + b) / 4;
```

But what if we left the parentheses out, as shown here?

```
result = a + b / 4;
```

We would get a different result. Without the parentheses b would be divided by 4 and the result added to a. Table 3-4 shows some math expressions that use parentheses, and their values.

Table 3-4 More expressions and their values

Expression	Value
(5 + 2) * 4	28
10 / (5 − 3)	5
8 + 12 * (6 − 2)	56
(6 − 3) * (2 + 7) / 3	9

Suppose we want to write a program that draws a horizontal line, and we want to show where the line's midpoint is located by drawing a small circle around it. The program's output would look something like Figure 3-10.

Figure 3-10 A line with its midpoint circled

We can calculate the coordinates of a horizontal line's midpoint as follows: calculate half of the line's length, and then add that value to the line's starting X coordinate. Let's assume that the variables `startX` and `startY` hold the lines starting XY coordinates, and the variables `endX` and `endY` hold the line's ending XY coordinates. Here is an example of code that calculates the coordinates of the line's midpoint:

```
halfLength = (endX − startX) / 2;
midX = startX + halfLength;
midY = startY;
```

The first statement calculates half of the line's length and assigns that value to the `halfLength` variable. The second statement adds the line's starting X coordinate to the half-length, and assigns the resulting value to the `midX` variable. This is the X coordinate of the line's midpoint. The third statement assigns the line's starting Y coordinate to the `midY` variable. (Because the line is horizontal, all of the points in the line have the same Y coordinate.) After this code executes, the variables `midX` and `midY` will hold the coordinates of the line's midpoint.

Now that we have calculated the coordinates of the line's midpoint, we can draw a circle using those coordinates as the circle's center. Assuming a variable named `radius` holds the desired radius, we would call the `dbCircle` function as follows:

```
dbCircle(midX, midY, radius);
```

Now let's look at Program 3-6, a complete program that demonstrates these calculations. The program draws a line from the coordinates (50, 200) to (590, 200). The program's output is shown in Figure 3-11.

Program 3-6   (`LineMidpoint.cpp`)

```
 1   // This program draws a line and circles its midpoint.
 2   #include "DarkGDK.h"
 3
 4   void DarkGDK()
 5   {
 6       // These variables hold known values
 7       int startX = 50;        // The line's starting X coordinate
 8       int startY = 200;       // The line's starting Y coordinate
 9       int endX = 590;         // The line's ending X coordinate
10       int endY = 200;         // The line's ending Y coordinate
11       int radius = 5;         // Radius of circle at midpoint
12
13       // These variables will hold calculated values
14       int halfLength;         // To hold half the line's length
15       int midX;               // To hold the midpoint's X coordinate
16       int midY;               // To hold the midpoint's Y coordinate
17
18       // Draw a line.
19       dbLine(startX, startY, endX, endY);
20
21       // Calculate half of the line's length.
22       // This will be used to find the line's
23       // midpoint.
24       halfLength = (endX - startX) / 2;
25
26       // Determine the line's midpoint.
27       midX = startX + halfLength;
28       midY = startY;
29
30       // Draw a circle at the line's midpoint.
31       dbCircle(midX, midY, radius);
32
33       // Wait for the user to press a key.
34       dbWaitKey();
35   }
```

Figure 3-11 Output of Program 3-6

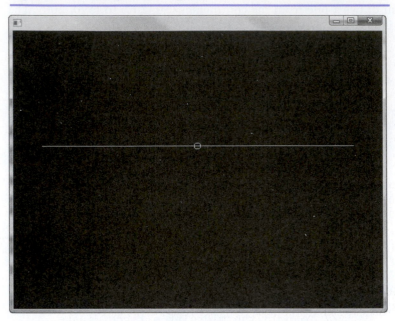

Integer Division

When you divide an integer by an integer in C++, the result is always given as an integer. If the result has a fractional part, it will be truncated. For example, look at the following code:

```
int length;          // Declare length as an int
double half;         // Declare half as a double
length = 75;         // Assign 75 to length
half = length / 2;   // Calculate half the length
```

The last statement divides the value of `length` by 2 and assigns the result to `half`. Mathematically, the result of 75 divided by 2 is 37.5. However, that is not the result that we get from the math expression. The `length` variable is an `int`, and it is being divided by the numeric literal 2, which is also an integer. (Any numeric literal that is written without a decimal point is treated as an integer.) The result of the division will be truncated, giving the value 37. This is the value that will be assigned to the `half` variable. It doesn't matter that the `half` variable is declared as a `double`. The fractional part of the result is truncated before the assignment takes place.

Combined Assignment Operators

Sometimes you want to increase a variable's value by a certain amount. For example, suppose you have a variable named `number` and you want to increase its value by 1. You can accomplish that with the following statement:

```
number = number + 1;
```

The expression on the right side of the assignment operator calculates the value of `number` plus 1. The result is then assigned to `number`, replacing the value that was previously stored there. Effectively, this statement adds 1 to number. For example, if number is equal to 6 before this statement executes, it will be equal to 7 after the statement executes.

Similarly, the following statement subtracts 5 from number:

```
number = number - 5;
```

If number is equal to 15 before this statement executes, it will be equal to 10 after the statement executes. Here's another example. The following statement doubles the value of the number variable:

```
number = number * 2;
```

If number is equal to 4 before this statement executes, it will be equal to 8 after the statement executes.

These types of operations are very common in programming. For convenience, C++ offers a special set of operators known as *combined assignment operators* that are designed specifically for these jobs. Table 3-5 shows the combined assignment operators.

Table 3-5 Combined assignment operators

Operator	Example Usage	Equivalence
+=	x += 5;	x = x + 5;
-=	y -= 2;	y = y - 2;
*=	z *= 10;	z = z * 10;
/=	a /= b;	a = a / b;
%=	c %= 3;	c = c % 3;

As you can see, the combined assignment operators do not require the programmer to type the variable name twice. Also, they give a clear indication of what is happening in the statement. Program 3-7 uses the += combined assignment operator to draw concentric circles. The program's output is shown in Figure 3-12.

Program 3-7   (Concentric.cpp)

```
1   // This program draws concentric circles.
2   #include "DarkGDK.h"
3
4   void DarkGDK()
5   {
6       // Declare variables for the circle's center
7       // point and radius.
8       int x = 319, y = 239, radius = 50;
9
10      // Draw the first circle.
11      dbCircle(x, y, radius);
```

```
12
13       // Add 20 to radius and draw another circle.
14       radius += 20;
15       dbCircle(x, y, radius);
16
17       // Add 20 to radius and draw another circle.
18       radius += 20;
19       dbCircle(x, y, radius);
20
21       // Add 20 to radius and draw another circle.
22       radius += 20;
23       dbCircle(x, y, radius);
24
25       // Wait for the user to press a key.
26       dbWaitKey();
27   }
```

Figure 3-12 Output of Program 3-7

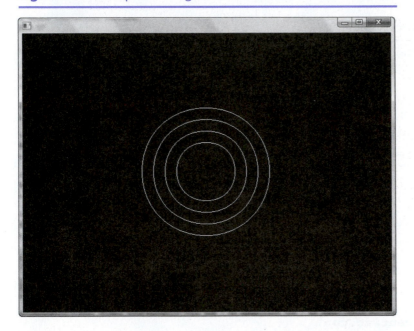

In line 8 the radius variable is declared and initialized with the value 50. So, the statement in line 11 draws a circle with a radius of 50 pixels. Then, the statement in line 14 adds 20 to the radius variable. After this statement executes, the radius variable will equal 70. The statement in line 15 draws a circle with a radius of 70 pixels. This process is repeated in lines 18 and 19 to draw a circle with a radius of 90 pixels, and then again in lines 22 and 23 to draw a circle with a radius of 110 pixels.

In the Spotlight:
Drawing Simple Bar Charts

You are probably familiar with bar charts, which give a graphical comparison of a set of values. In a bar chart each value is represented by a rectangular bar. The height of each bar is proportional to the value it represents. For example, suppose five students earn the following scores on an exam: 85, 98, 70, 62, and 100. We could write a program that displays a bar chart with each of the exam scores represented by a bar. For the first score, 85, we would draw a bar that is 85 pixels high. For the second score, 98, we would draw a bar that is 98 pixels high. This would continue for each score, giving us a bar chart similar to the one shown in Figure 3-13.

Figure 3-13 Bar chart comparing exam scores

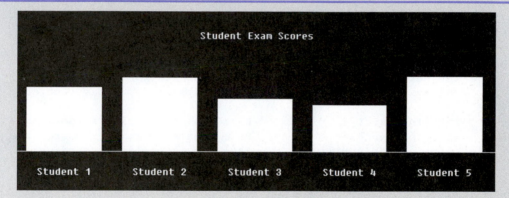

In many cases, the heights of the bars in a bar chart must be scaled to fit on the screen. For example, suppose three video game players have the following scores:

- Player 1: 1850 points
- Player 2: 2930 points
- Player 3: 960 points

If you want to display a bar chart comparing these three scores, you can't use the scores as the bar heights. This is because you can't fit rectangles that are 1850 pixels high, 2930 pixels high, and 960 pixels high in a window that is only 480 pixels high. If you want to display a bar chart comparing these scores you will have to scale the bars so they will fit in the Dark GDK window. You can do this by dividing each of the scores by some value. For example, if we divide each score by 10, we get the values 185, 293, and 960. These "scaled" values can then be used as the bar heights. The code in Program 3-8 shows how this is done. Figure 3-14 shows the program's output.

Program 3-8   (BarChart.cpp)

```
1    // This program draws a bar chart comparing three
2    // game players' scores.
3    #include "DarkGDK.h"
4
5    void DarkGDK()
6    {
7       // Variable declarations
8       int playerOneScore = 1850;    // Player 1's score
9       int playerTwoScore = 2930;    // Player 2's score
10      int playerThreeScore = 960;   // Player 3's score
11
12      int pointsPerPixel = 10;  // Each pixel = 10 points in bar height
13      int barWidth = 150;       // Each bar is 150 pixels wide
14      int barHeight;            // To hold a bar's height
15
16      int lowerRightX;          // To hold a bar's lower-right X
17      int lowerRightY;          // To hold a bar's lower-right Y
18      int upperLeftX;           // To hold a bar's upper-left X
19      int upperLeftY;           // To hold a bar's upper-left Y
20
21      int textX;     // To hold the X coordinate for a bar caption
22      int textY;     // To hold the X coordinate for a bar caption
23
24      int lineStartX = 0;       // Base line's starting X coordinate
25      int lineStartY = 400;     // Base line's starting Y coordinate
26      int lineEndX = 639;       // Base line's ending X coordinate
27      int lineEndY = 400;       // Base line's ending Y coordinate
28
29      // Set the window's title.
30      dbSetWindowTitle("Player Score Bar Chart");
31
32      // Draw a base line for the bars.
33      dbLine(lineStartX, lineStartY, lineEndX, lineEndY);
34
35      // DRAW PLAYER 1'S BAR
36      //************************************************
37      // The lower-right corner will be at (200, 400).
38      lowerRightX = 200;
39      lowerRightY = 400;
40
41      // Calculate the upper-left X coordinate.
42      upperLeftX = lowerRightX – barWidth;
43
44      // Calculate the upper-left Y coordinate.
45      barHeight = playerOneScore / pointsPerPixel;
46      upperLeftY = lowerRightY – barHeight;
47
48      // Draw the bar.
49      dbBox(upperLeftX, upperLeftY, lowerRightX, lowerRightY);
50
51      // Set the Y coordinate for the bar's text to 420.
52      textY = 420;
```

```
53
54       // Calculate the X coordinate of the bar's text.
55       textX = upperLeftX + ( (lowerRightX - upperLeftX) / 2);
56
57       // Display a caption centered under the bar.
58       dbCenterText(textX, textY, "Player 1");
59
60       // DRAW PLAYER 2'S BAR
61       //************************************************
62       // This bar's lower-right corner will be 200 pixels to
63       // the right of the previous bar's lower-right corner.
64       // That will leave a space of 50 pixels between the bars.
65       // To calculate the X coordinate we add 200 to the value
66       // already stored in the lowerRightX variable.
67       lowerRightX += 200;
68
69       // Note: We will use the same Y coordinate for each bar's,
70       // lower-right corner, so we will not change the value of
71       // the lowerRightY variable.
72
73       // Calculate the upper-left X coordinate.
74       upperLeftX = lowerRightX - barWidth;
75
76       // Calculate the upper-left Y coordinate.
77       barHeight = playerTwoScore / pointsPerPixel;
78       upperLeftY = lowerRightY - barHeight;
79
80       // Draw the bar.
81       dbBox(upperLeftX, upperLeftY, lowerRightX, lowerRightY);
82
83       // Calculate the X coordinate of the bar's text.
84       // Note: We will use the same Y coordinate for each bar
85       // caption, so we will not change the value of textY.
86       textX = upperLeftX + ( (lowerRightX - upperLeftX) / 2);
87
88       // Display a caption centered under the bar.
89       dbCenterText(textX, textY, "Player 2");
90
91       // DRAW PLAYER 3'S BAR
92       //************************************************
93       // This bar's lower-right corner will be 200 pixels to
94       // the right of the previous bar's lower-right corner.
95       // That will leave a space of 50 pixels between the bars.
96       // To calculate the X coordinate we add 200 to the value
97       // already stored in the lowerRightX variable.
98       lowerRightX += 200;
99
100      // Note: Since we are using the same Y coordinate for each
101      // bar's lower-right corner, so we will not change the value
102      // of the lowerRightY variable.
103
104      // Calculate the upper-left X coordinate.
105      upperLeftX = lowerRightX - barWidth;
106
107      // Calculate the upper-left Y coordinate.
```

```
108        barHeight = playerThreeScore / pointsPerPixel;
109        upperLeftY = lowerRightY — barHeight;
110
111        // Draw the bar.
112        dbBox(upperLeftX, upperLeftY, lowerRightX, lowerRightY);
113
114        // Calculate the X coordinate of the bar's text.
115        // Note: We will use the same Y coordinate for each bar
116        // caption, so we will not change the value of textY.
117        textX = upperLeftX + ( (lowerRightX — upperLeftX) / 2 );
118
119        // Display a caption centered under the bar.
120        dbCenterText(textX, textY, "Player 3");
121
122        // Wait for the user to press a key.
123        dbWaitKey();
124    }
```

Figure 3-14 Output of Program 3-8

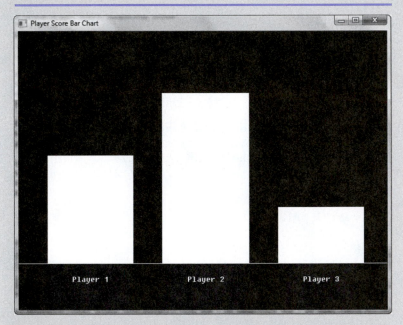

Here is a summary of the variable declarations:

- The variables declared in lines 8 through 10 hold the three player scores.
- The variables in lines 12 through 14 hold values that determine the size of each bar. We will divide each score by pointsPerPixel to get the bar height. The barWidth variable holds the width of each bar, in pixels. The barHeight variable will hold the height of each bar.
- The variables declared in lines 16 through 19 will hold the X and Y coordinates of each bar's upper-left and lower-right corners.

- The `textX` and `textY` variables declared in lines 21 and 22 will hold the *X* and *Y* coordinates used in displaying a caption below each bar.
- The variables declared in lines 24 through 27 hold the starting and ending *X* and *Y* coordinates of the base line. This is a line that we will draw across the window, at the bottom of the bars.

Line 30 sets the text for the window's title bar and line 33 draws the base line across the window.

Lines 35 through 58 draw the bar for player 1's score. Here is a summary of the code:

- Lines 38 and 39 assign the *X* and *Y* coordinates for the bar's lower-right corner to the `lowerRightX` and `lowerRightY` variables.
- Line 42 calculates the *X* coordinate of the bar's upper-left corner. This is done by subtracting the bar's width from the *X* coordinate of the bar's lower-right corner.
- Lines 45 and 46 calculate the *Y* coordinate of the bar's upper-left corner. This is done in two steps: line 45 calculates the bar's height (by scaling the player's score) and line 46 subtracts the height from the *Y* coordinate of the lower-right corner.
- Line 49 draws the bar.
- Line 52 sets the *Y* coordinate for the bar's caption to 420, and line 55 calculates the *X* coordinate for the bar's caption.
- Line 58 displays a caption centered below the bar.

Lines 60 through 89 follow a similar set of steps to display the bar for player 2, and lines 91 through 120 display the bar for player 3.

 Checkpoint

3.12. Summarize the mathematical order of operations.

3.13. When the following statement executes, what value will be stored in `result`?

```
result = 4 + 10 / 2;
```

3.14. When the following statement executes, what value will be stored in `result`?

```
result = (2 + 5) * 10;
```

3.15. When the following statement executes, what value will be stored in `result`?

```
result = 5 / 2;
```

3.16. Rewrite the following statements using combined assignment operators:
  a. `x = x + 1;`
  b. `lowerY = lowerY - 5;`
  c. `radius = radius * 10;`
  d. `length = length / 2;`

3.5   Getting Values from Functions

CONCEPT: A value-returning function returns a value back to the statement that called it.

In Chapter 2, you learned about several Dark GDK functions, such as `dbLine`, `dbCircle`, `dbBox`, and others. When you want to execute these functions, you call them. Calling a function causes the program to jump to the code for that function and execute the statements inside it. When the function is finished, the program jumps back to the point in the program at which the function was called and resumes execution.

In this section, we will look at a special type of function known as a *value-returning function*. When you call a value-returning function, it performs some operation and then returns a value back to the statement that called it. The value that is returned from the function can be used like any other value: it can be assigned to a variable, used in a mathematical expression, and so forth.

The Dark GDK library has numerous value-returning functions. For example, the `dbScreenWidth` function returns the width of the Dark GDK window, in pixels. The value that is returned from the function is an integer. For example, suppose we have declared an `int` variable named `width`, as shown here:

```
int width;
```

The following statement shows how we can call the `dbScreenWidth` function and assign the function's return value to the `width` variable:

```
width = dbScreenWidth();
```

The part of the statement that reads `dbScreenWidth()` is the function call. The value that is returned from the function will be assigned to the `width` variable. So, after this statement executes, the `width` variable will hold the current width of the Dark GDK window.

Recall that the default width of the Dark GDK window is 640 pixels. If this code is in a program that uses the default window size, the `dbScreenWidth` function will return the value 640, as shown in Figure 3-15.

The Dark GDK also provides a function named `dbScreenHeight`, which returns the current height of the Dark GDK window. The following code demonstrates how you can call the function to get the window height, and assign that value to a variable:

```
int height;
height = dbScreenHeight();
```

Figure 3-15 The `dbScreenWidth` function returns a value

After this code executes, the height variable will be assigned the current height, in pixels, of the Dark GDK window.

 NOTE: Since we already know that the default Dark GDK window is 640 pixels wide by 480 pixels high, you might be wondering why we would ever need to call these functions. Later in this chapter, you will learn how to change the size of the Dark GDK window. Rather than using literal numbers for the window's width and height in your program code, it is better to call the `dbScreenWidth` and `dbScreenHeight` functions to get the current width and height. This way, you will always be able to determine the window's width and height, even after changing its size.

Program 3-9 demonstrates how you can get the window's current width and height and use those values to calculate the window's center point. The program's output is shown in Figure 3-16.

Program 3-9   (`WindowCenter.cpp`)

```
1   // This program calculates the window's center point.
2   #include "DarkGDK.h"
3
4   void DarkGDK()
5   {
6       int width;     // To hold the screen width
7       int height;    // To hold the screen height
8       int centerX;   // To hold the center X coordinate
9       int centerY;   // To hold the center Y coordinate
10
11      // Get the window's width and assign it to the
12      // width variable.
13      width = dbScreenWidth();
14
15      // Get the window's height and assign it to the
16      // height variable.
17      height = dbScreenHeight();
18
19      // Calculate the X coordinate of the window's center.
20      centerX = width / 2;
21
22      // Calculate the Y coordinate of the window's center.
23      centerY = height / 2;
24
25      // Display a dot at the window's center.
26      dbDot(centerX, centerY);
27
28      // Display some text centered below the dot.
29      dbCenterText(centerX, centerY, "This is the center");
30
31      // Wait for the user to press a key.
32      dbWaitKey();
33  }
```

Figure 3-16 Output of Program 3-9

Getting a Random Number

The Dark GDK library provides a function named dbRND that generates random numbers. Random numbers are useful for lots of different programming tasks. The following are a few examples:

- Random numbers are commonly used in games. For example, computer games that let the player roll dice use random numbers to represent the values of the dice. Games that show cards being drawn from a shuffled deck use random numbers to represent the face values of the cards.
- Random numbers are useful in simulation programs. In some simulations, the computer must randomly decide how a person, animal, insect, or other living being will behave. Formulas can be constructed in which a random number is used to determine various actions and events that take place in the program.
- Random numbers are useful in statistical programs that must randomly select data for analysis.
- Random numbers are commonly used in computer security to encrypt sensitive data.

The following statement shows an example of how you might call the dbRND function. Assume that we have already declared number as an int variable.

```
number = dbRND(100);
```

The dbRND function returns a random integer number from 0 to an upper limit that you specify as an argument. In this example, the argument 100 is being passed to the function as the upper limit. When this statement executes, the number variable will be assigned a random number in the range of 0 through 100.

Program 3-10 demonstrates the dbRND function by drawing three circles that are randomly positioned on the screen, each with a random radius. The program's output is shown in Figure 3-17.

Program 3-10   **(RandomCircles1.cpp)**

```
1   // This program draws three randomly positioned circles,
2   // each with a random radius.
3   #include "DarkGDK.h"
4
5   void DarkGDK()
6   {
7       int centerX;            // X coord of a circle's center
8       int centerY;            // Y coord of a circle's center
9       int radius;             // To hold the circle's radius
10      int maxRadius = 100;    // A circle's maximum radius
11      int screenWidth;        // To hold the screen width
12      int screenHeight;       // To hold the screen height
13
14      // Get the screen width.
15      screenWidth = dbScreenWidth();
16
17      // Get the screen height.
18      screenHeight = dbScreenHeight();
19
20      // Draw the first circle.
21      centerX = dbRND(screenWidth);
22      centerY = dbRND(screenHeight);
23      radius = dbRND(maxRadius);
24      dbCircle(centerX, centerY, radius);
25
26      // Draw the second circle.
27      centerX = dbRND(screenWidth);
28      centerY = dbRND(screenHeight);
29      radius = dbRND(maxRadius);
30      dbCircle(centerX, centerY, radius);
31
32      // Draw the third circle.
33      centerX = dbRND(screenWidth);
34      centerY = dbRND(screenHeight);
35      radius = dbRND(maxRadius);
36      dbCircle(centerX, centerY, radius);
37
38      // Wait for the user to press a key.
39      dbWaitKey();
40  }
```

Figure 3-17 Output of Program 3-10

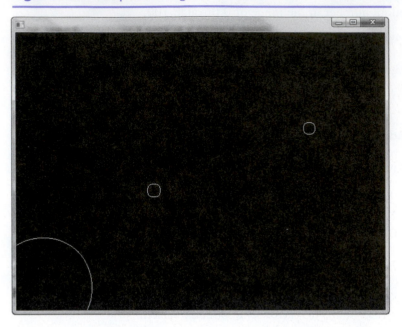

Lines 15 and 18 get the Dark GDK window's width and height. Those values are stored in the screenWidth and screenHeight variables. The code in lines 21 though 24 draws the first circle. Here is a summary of those statements:

- Line 21 generates a random number for the X coordinate of the circle's center point. The window's width is used as the upper limit for the number, to make sure that the circle's center is somewhere inside the window along the X axis.
- Line 22 generates a random number for the Y coordinate of the circle's center point. The window's height is used as the upper limit for the number, to make sure that the circle's center is somewhere inside the window along the Y axis.
- Line 23 generates a random number for the circle's radius, using maxRadius as the upper limit. (Notice that in line 10 maxRadius is initialized with the value 100. This keeps the circle's radius in the range of 0 through 100.)
- Line 24 draws the circle.

Lines 27 through 30 repeat these same steps to draw the second circle, and lines 33 through 36 repeat the steps to draw the third circle.

Seeding the Random Number Generator

The positions and radii of the three circles displayed by Program 3-10 appear to be random, but if you run the program repeatedly you will find that the circles appear exactly the same each time. This is because the numbers that are returned from dbRND are not truly random, but *pseudorandom* numbers. Pseudorandom numbers are generated by a formula that must be initialized with a starting value. This starting value is known as the *seed value*. If the formula always uses the same seed value, it will always produce the same sequence of numbers. To change the sequence of numbers (and make them appear more random), you must provide a different seed value each time you use it.

You can use the `dbRandomize` function to change the seed value that is used by the `dbRND` function. The `dbRandomize` function accepts an `int` argument which is used as the new seed value for `dbRND`. A common practice for getting unique seed values is to call the `dbTimer` function. The `dbTimer` function returns the computer's internal system time in milliseconds. (A millisecond is 1/1000th of a second.) Once you get a value from the `dbTimer` function, you pass that value as an argument to the `dbRandomize` function, as shown here:

```
int seed;
seed = dbTimer();
dbRandomize(seed);
```

Program 3-11 is a modified version of Program 3-10. This version of the program uses the `dbTimer` and `dbRandomize` functions (in lines 22 and 23) to reseed the random number generator. As a result, the program will display different output each time it is executed, as shown in Figure 3-18. The figure shows four different outputs of the program.

Program 3-11   **(RandomCircles2.cpp)**

```
 1   // This program draws three randomly positioned circles,
 2   // each with a random radius.
 3   #include "DarkGDK.h"
 4
 5   void DarkGDK()
 6   {
 7       int centerX;         // X coord of a circle's center
 8       int centerY;         // Y coord of a circle's center
 9       int radius;          // To hold the circle's radius
10       int maxRadius = 100; // A circle's maximum radius
11       int screenWidth;     // To hold the screen width
12       int screenHeight;    // To hold the screen height
13       int seed;            // To hold a seed value
14
15       // Get the screen width.
16       screenWidth = dbScreenWidth();
17
18       // Get the screen height.
19       screenHeight = dbScreenHeight();
20
21       // Reseed the random number generator.
22       seed = dbTimer();
23       dbRandomize(seed);
24
25       // Draw the first circle.
26       centerX = dbRND(screenWidth);
27       centerY = dbRND(screenHeight);
28       radius = dbRND(maxRadius);
29       dbCircle(centerX, centerY, radius);
```

```
30
31      // Draw the second circle.
32      centerX = dbRND(screenWidth);
33      centerY = dbRND(screenHeight);
34      radius = dbRND(maxRadius);
35      dbCircle(centerX, centerY, radius);
36
37      // Draw the third circle.
38      centerX = dbRND(screenWidth);
39      centerY = dbRND(screenHeight);
40      radius = dbRND(maxRadius);
41      dbCircle(centerX, centerY, radius);
42
43      // Wait for the user to press a key.
44      dbWaitKey();
45  }
```

Figure 3-18 Four outputs of Program 3-11

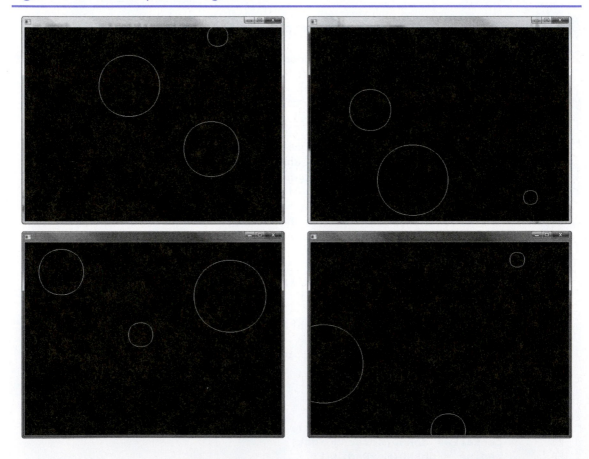

Nesting Function Calls

Take a look at the following code, which seeds the random-number generator:

```
seed = dbTimer();
dbRandomize(seed);
```

This code performs two steps: (1) it gets the internal system time, and (2) it sends that value to the dbRandomize function. A seasoned programmer would look at this code and recognize that this could all be done in one step. This can be accomplished by nesting function calls, as shown here:

```
dbRandomize( dbTimer() );
```

In this statement we are calling the dbRandomize function. Notice that inside the parentheses, where we write the argument that we are passing to the function, we have called the dbTimer function. This causes the dbTimer function to be called first, and the value that it returns is passed as an argument to dbRandomize. In one line of code we have accomplished what previously took two lines of code.

We've also eliminated the seed variable. Because we are immediately sending the dbTimer function's return value as an argument to dbRandomize, there is no need to store it in a variable. Because nested function calls are commonly used by programmers, you will frequently see code like this as you progress through the book.

Math Functions

C++ and the Dark GDK library provide numerous functions for performing mathematical operations. For example, C++ provides a function named pow that raises a number to a power. Here is the function's general format:

```
pow(Base, Exponent)
```

When this function executes, it returns the value of *Base* raised to the power of *Exponent*. Here is an example of how the function works:

```
float result;
float base = 2.0;
float exponent = 10.0;
result = pow(base, exponent);
```

The first statement declares a float variable named result. The second statement declares a float variable named base, initialized with the value 2.0. The third statement declares a float variable named exponent, initialized with the value 10.0. The last statement calls the pow function, passing base and exponent as arguments. The function returns the value of base raised to the power of exponent. The value that is returned from the function is assigned to the result variable.

NOTE: When you call the pow function, the arguments that you pass for *Base* and *Exponent* can be either floats or doubles. If you pass float arguments, the function returns a float. If you pass double arguments, the function returns a double.

The Dark GDK library provides several mathematical functions of its own. Table 3-6 lists many of them. These functions accept an argument, perform a mathematical operation using the argument, and return the result. For example, one of the functions is named dbSQRT. The dbSQRT function accepts an argument and returns the square root of the argument. Here is an example of how it is used:

```
float number = 16.0;
float result = dbSQRT(number);
```

This statement calls the dbSQRT function, passing the number variable as an argument. The function returns the square root of number, which is then assigned to the result variable.

Table 3-6 Many of the Dark GDK math functions

Function	Description
dbCOS(*angle*)	Returns, as a float, the cosine of angle in radians. The argument angle is a float specifying an angle between 0 and 360 degrees.
dbSIN(*angle*)	Returns, as a float, the sine of angle in radians. The argument angle is a float specifying an angle between 0 and 360 degrees.
dbTAN(*angle*)	Returns, as a float, the tangent of angle in radians. The argument angle is a float specifying an angle between 0 and 360 degrees.
dbACOS(*angle*)	Returns, as a float, the arccosine of angle in radians. The argument angle is a float specifying an angle between 0 and 360 degrees.
dbASIN(*angle*)	Returns, as a float, the arcsine of angle in radians. The argument angle is a float specifying an angle between 0 and 360 degrees.
dbATAN(*angle*)	Returns, as a float, the arctangent of angle in radians. The argument angle is a float specifying an angle between 0 and 360 degrees.
dbSQRT(*value*)	Returns, as a float, the square root of value, which is a float argument.
dbABS(*value*)	Returns, as a float, the absolute value of value, which is a float argument.

Other Value-Returning Functions

When it comes to value-returning functions, we have really just scratched the surface in this section. As you progress through the book, you will learn about many other value-returning functions in the Dark GDK library, and in Chapter 9 you will learn to write your own value-returning functions.

Checkpoint

3.17. What value does the dbScreenWidth function return? What value does the dbScreenHeight function return?

3.18. Write code that does the following:
- Declares two int variables named width and height
- Calls the appropriate functions to assign the Dark GDK window's width and height to the two variables

3.19. What is the purpose of the dbRND function?

3.20. Describe the value that will be stored in the number variable after the following statement executes:

```
number = dbRND(25);
```

3.21. What does the dbRandomize function do?

3.22. What does the dbTimer function return? How is this value used in the generation of random numbers?

3.6 Reading Numeric Input from the Keyboard

CONCEPT: Programs commonly need the user to enter data at the keyboard. We will use the Dark GDK library's **dbInput** function to do this.

Most programs rely on the user to input data of some sort. In this section, we will discuss a simple technique for reading data that the user has typed on the keyboard. The Dark GDK library provides a function named dbInput that does the following:

- It waits for the user to type something on the keyboard and then press the Enter key.
- It returns the data that the user typed as a string.

Sometimes you might want the user to enter string data. For example, you might be developing a game in which the user enters commands like turn right and look down. However, we will not discuss string processing until Chapter 11. In this chapter, we will cover reading numeric input—integers and floating-point numbers—from the keyboard.

Suppose you need the user to enter a number that will be used as an *X* coordinate, and you need to store this value in an int variable. Because the dbInput function always returns the user's input as a string, you will need another function to convert the string to a number. In C++, you can use the atoi function to convert a string to an int, or the atof function to convert a string to a double.

The following code shows an example of getting input from the user and converting that input to an integer:

```
int x;
dbPrint("Enter an X coordinate.");
x = atoi( dbInput() );
```

The first statement declares an `int` variable named x. The second statement displays the message `"Enter an X coordinate"`. The third statement uses nested function calls to do the following:

- It calls the `dbInput` function, which returns the data entered by the user.
- The data returned by `dbInput` is passed as an argument to the `atoi` function. The `atoi` function returns that data converted to an `int`.
- The `int` value returned from `atoi` is assigned to the x variable.

After this code executes, the x variable will contain the value entered by the user.

The following shows another example. Here, we are getting input from the user and converting that input to a floating-point number:

```
double temperature;
dbPrint("What is the temperature?");
temperature = atof( dbInput() );
```

The first statement declares a `double` variable named `temperature`. The second statement displays the question `"What is the temperature?"` The third statement uses `dbInput` to get the user's input, uses `atof` to convert that input to a `double`, and assigns the number to the `temperature` variable.

Program 3-12 is a complete program that gets data from the user and uses that data to draw a circle. Figure 3-19 shows an example of the program's output.

Program 3-12   (GetData.cpp)

```
1   // This program gets data from the user and draws a circle.
2   #include "DarkGDK.h"
3
4   void DarkGDK ()
5   {
6       // Declare variables for the circle's center point
7       // coordinates and radius.
8       int centerX, centerY, radius;
9
10      // Display an introduction.
11      dbPrint("This program will get some information from you");
12      dbPrint("and then draw a circle.");
13      dbPrint();
14
15      // Get the X coordinate of the circle's center.
16      dbPrint("Enter the X coordinate of the center point.");
17      centerX = atoi( dbInput() );
18
19      // Get the Y coordinate of the circle's center.
20      dbPrint("Enter the Y coordinate of the center point.");
```

```
21        centerY = atoi( dbInput() );
22
23        // Get the circle's radius.
24        dbPrint("Enter the circle's radius.");
25        radius = atoi( dbInput() );
26
27        // Draw the circle.
28        dbCircle(centerX, centerY, radius);
29
30        // Pause the program until the user presses a key.
31        dbWaitKey();
32   }
```

Figure 3-19 Example output of Program 3-12

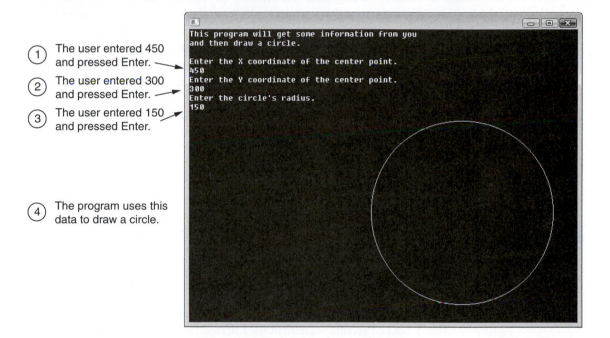

① The user entered 450 and pressed Enter.

② The user entered 300 and pressed Enter.

③ The user entered 150 and pressed Enter.

④ The program uses this data to draw a circle.

In line 8, we declare three int variables. The centerX variable will hold the X coordinate of the circle's center point, the centerY variable will hold the Y coordinate of the circle's center point, and the radius variable will hold the circle's radius.

Lines 11 through 13 display an introduction, explaining what the program does. Then, line 16 tells the user to enter the X coordinate of the circle's center point. The statement in line 17 uses dbInput to get the user's input, atoi to convert that input to an int, and then assigns that value to the centerX variable.

Line 20 tells the user to enter the Y coordinate of the circle's center point. The statement in line 21 uses dbInput to get the user's input, atoi to convert that input to an int, and then assigns that value to the centerY variable.

Line 24 tells the user to enter the circle's radius. The statement in line 25 uses `dbInput` to get the user's input, `atoi` to convert that input to an `int`, and then assigns that value to the `radius` variable.

Line 28 calls the `dbCircle` function, passing the `centerX`, `centerY`, and `radius` variables as arguments. Then, line 31 waits for the user to press a key.

How `atoi` and `atof` Handle Invalid Characters

When you need the user to input data, you should always display a message telling the user what to enter. This message is known as a *prompt*. However, there is nothing preventing the user from entering data that contains invalid characters, which therefore, cannot be converted to a number. Here is a summary of how the `atoi` and `atof` functions convert strings to numbers, and what they do when the strings contain invalid characters:

- The `atoi` and `atof` functions both ignore any spaces that might appear at the beginning of the string. For example, `atoi` would convert "   2" to the value 2, and `atof` would convert the string "   1.5" to the value 1.5.
- If the string contains any invalid characters, these functions will perform the conversion process until an invalid character is encountered. For example, `atoi` would convert "34abc" to the value 34, and `atof` would convert the string "6.3#" to the value 6.3.
- If the string is empty (contains no characters), these functions return 0.
- If the string cannot be converted to a number, these functions return 0.

Converting Numeric Values to Strings

If you have a numeric value, such as the contents of an `int` or `float` variable, and you want to display that value with `dbPrint`, `dbText`, or `dbCenterText`, you will need to convert it to a string. This can be done with the `dbStr` function, which is part of the Dark GDK library. Here is an example:

```
int score = 550;
dbPrint( dbStr(score) );
```

The first statement declares an `int` variable named `score` and initializes the variable with the value 550. The second statement uses nested function calls to do the following:

- The `dbStr` function is called and the value of the `score` variable is passed as an argument. The function returns a string representation of the value.
- The string that is returned from `dbStr` is passed as an argument to the `dbPrint` function.

After this code executes, the value 550 will be printed in the window. Program 3-13 shows a complete program that uses the `dbStr` function along with the `dbText` function to display the window's width and height. Figure 3-20 shows the program's output.

Program 3-13   `(DisplayWidthAndHeight.cpp)`

```
 1   // This program displays the window's width and height.
 2   #include "DarkGDK.h"
 3
 4   void DarkGDK ()
 5   {
 6       // Get the window's width and height.
 7       int width = dbScreenWidth();
 8       int height = dbScreenHeight();
 9
10       // Display the width.
11       dbText(20, 20, "Width:");
12       dbText(90, 20, dbStr(width));
13
14       // Display the height.
15       dbText(20, 40, "Height");
16       dbText(90, 40, dbStr(height));
17
18       // Pause the program until the user presses a key.
19       dbWaitKey();
20   }
```

Figure 3-20 Output of Program 3-13

✓ Checkpoint

3.23. The `dbInput` function always returns the user's input as what type of data?

3.24. What C++ function do you use to convert a string to an integer?

3.25. What C++ function do you use to convert a string to a floating-point value?

3.26. Write a statement that reads data from the keyboard, converts it to an integer, and assigns the integer to a variable named x.

3.7 Colors

CONCEPT: The Dark GDK uses the RGB color system to generate colors. In the RGB system, you define a color by specifying values for its red, green, and blue components.

Until now our programs have produced graphics only in black and white. In this section, we will discuss colors and demonstrate how to use them in your programs.

The Dark GDK uses the *RGB color system* to define colors. In the RGB color system, all colors are created by mixing various shades of red, green, and blue. For example, in the RGB system, if you mix bright red, bright green, and no blue you get yellow. If you mix bright red, bright blue, and no green you get purple. White is created when you mix all three colors at their maximum brightness, and black is created when there is no red, green, or blue.

In programming, we commonly refer to the red, green, and blue components of a color as *color channels*. When you define a color, you specify a value in the range of 0 through 255 for each of the color channels. The higher the number for a channel, the brighter that color component will be. For a quick demonstration of how these channels work, we can use the dbClear function. The dbClear function clears the Dark GDK window and fills it with a specified color. Here is the general format of how you call the function:

```
dbClear(red, green, blue);
```

In the general format, the red, green, and blue arguments are values for the red, green, and blue color channels. For example, the following statement calls the function and specifies 255 for the red channel, 0 for the green channel, and 127 for the blue channel:

```
dbClear(255, 0, 127);
```

The color that is created by these channel values will be the combination of bright red, no green, and medium intensity blue. The result will be a color in the purple or magenta family. Here is another example:

```
dbClear(255, 0, 0);
```

This statement specifies 255 for red, 0 for green, and 0 for blue. As a result, the window will be filled with bright red. Here is another example:

```
dbClear(255, 255, 255);
```

This statement specifies 255 for red, 255 for green, and 255 for blue. As a result, the window will be filled with white. Figure 3-21 (which is located in this book's color insert) shows how various red, green, and blue channel values create cyan, magenta, white, and black.

Program 3-14 shows a program that you can run on your system to demonstrate the dbClear function. When you run this program you will first see the window cleared to red, then to white, then to blue, and finally to black.

Program 3-14   **(ClearColors.cpp)**

```
 1   // This program demonstrates the RGB color system
 2   // by using the dbClear function to clear the screen
 3   // to several different colors.
 4   #include "DarkGDK.h"
 5
 6   void DarkGDK()
 7   {
 8       // Clear the screen to red.
 9       dbClear(255, 0, 0);
10
11       // Wait for 1 second.
12       dbWait(1000);
13
14       // Clear the screen to white.
15       dbClear(255, 255, 255);
16
17       // Wait for 1 second.
18       dbWait(1000);
19
20       // Clear the screen to blue.
21       dbClear(0, 0, 255);
22
23       // Wait for 1 second.
24       dbWait(1000);
25
26       // Clear the screen to black.
27       dbClear(0, 0, 0);
28
29       // Wait until a key is pressed.
30       dbWaitKey();
31   }
```

Storing RGB Colors in Memory

You might be surprised to find out that colors can be stored in variables! Well, you can't store an actual color in a variable, but you can store a color's RGB channel values in a variable. Doing so requires a 32-bit integer variable. Figure 3-22 shows how the first set of 8 bits is used to store the red channel value, the second set of 8 bits is

Figure 3-22 Memory format for storing an RGB color

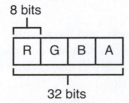

used to store the green channel value, and the third set of 8 bits is used to store the blue channel value. The fourth set of 8 bits is used to store the *alpha channel* value, which is used to make the color transparent. We will not be using the alpha channel in this book, but it is required any time you are storing an RGB color in memory.

The DWORD data type is typically used to store RGB colors. Recall from our discussion on data types earlier in this chapter that a DWORD variable uses 32 bits of memory, and can hold unsigned integers. Fortunately, you don't have to worry about formatting the individual bits in a DWORD variable if you want to store an RGB color. The Dark GDK library provides a function named dbRGB that does this for you. The following code sample shows how to use the function:

```
DWORD brightRed;
brightRed = dbRGB(255, 0, 0);
```

The first statement declares a DWORD variable named brightRed. The second statement calls the dbRGB function, passing the argument 255 for the red, 0 for the green channel, and 0 for the blue channel. The function returns a 32-bit value, formatted as shown in Figure 3-22. This value is then assigned to the brightRed variable. Here is another example:

```
DWORD magenta;
magenta = dbRGB(255, 0, 255);
```

The first statement declares a DWORD variable named magenta. The second statement calls the dbRGB function, passing the argument 255 for the red channel, 0 for the green channel, and 255 for the blue channel. The function returns a 32-bit value which is assigned to the magenta variable.

You can also declare a DWORD variable and initialize it with a color value in one statement. Here is an example:

```
DWORD brightRed = dbRGB(255, 0, 0);
```

Drawing in Color

By default, shapes and text are drawn in white on a black background. However, once you have created and stored some colors in DWORD variables, you can use those variables to draw colored shapes. The Dark GDK library provides a function named dbInk, which changes the current drawing colors. You call the function using this general format:

```
dbInk(foreground, background);
```

The *foreground* argument is a DWORD value specifying the foreground color, and the *background* argument is a DWORD value specifying the background color. After calling the dbInk function, all subsequent shapes and text will be drawn in the foreground color.

The *background* argument only applies to text, and has no affect on shapes like lines, circles, and boxes. For drawing shapes, you can pass any color you like as the second argument and see no change on the screen. (We will discuss changing the background color of text in more detail later in this section.)

The following code sample shows how to draw a blue circle:

```
// Declare variables for the colors blue and black.
DWORD blue = dbRGB(0, 0, 255);
DWORD black = dbRGB(0, 0, 0);

// Change the current drawing colors.
dbInk(blue, black);

// Draw a circle at (100, 100) with a radius of 50.
dbCircle(100, 100, 50);
```

First, we declare two DWORD variables, blue and black, and we call the dbRGB function to initialize them. Then, we call the dbInk function to change the foreground color to blue and the background color to black. As previously mentioned, the background color has no affect on shapes, but we must pass a value anyway. Then, we draw a circle with the dbCircle function. Because the current foreground color is set to blue, the circle will be drawn in blue.

 NOTE: The circle that is drawn by the previous code sample will not be filled, but it will appear as a blue outline. In the Dark GDK, rectangles drawn with the dbBox function are the only shapes that are filled with a color.

Program 3-15 shows a complete demonstration. The program clears the window to blue, then draws a magenta box, and then draws a white circle on top of the box. The program's output is shown in Figure 3-23 (which is located in this book's color insert).

Program 3-15 (ColorDemo.cpp)

```
 1   // This program demonstrates color.
 2   #include "DarkGDK.h"
 3
 4   void DarkGDK()
 5   {
 6       // Declare variables for blue, magenta, white, and black.
 7       DWORD blue    = dbRGB(0, 0, 255);
 8       DWORD magenta = dbRGB(255, 0, 255);
 9       DWORD white   = dbRGB(255, 255, 255);
10       DWORD black   = dbRGB(0, 0, 0);
11
12       // Clear the window to a blue background.
13       dbClear(0, 0, 255);
14
15       // Change the current drawing color to magenta.
16       dbInk(magenta, black);
17
18       // Draw a box.
19       dbBox(50, 50, 590, 430);
20
```

```
21        // Change the current drawing color to white.
22        dbInk(white, black);
23
24        // Draw a circle.
25        dbCircle(320, 240, 100);
26
27        // Wait until a key is pressed.
28        dbWaitKey();
29   }
```

In the Spotlight:
Drawing the Italian Flag

In this section, we will discuss a program that displays the Italian flag, which is shown in Figure 3-24 (located in this book's color insert). The flag consists of three colored bars, each of which is one-third the width of the flag. The leftmost bar is green, the middle bar is white, and the rightmost bar is red.

We could use a piece of graph paper to sketch the colored bars, and then determine their coordinates, assuming the flag will be displayed in a window that is 640 by 480 pixels. This was the approach we took for several programs in Chapter 2. However, later in this chapter you will learn how to resize the Dark GDK window, and we want this program to always display the flag with each bar occupying one-third of the window. So, we will calculate the coordinates of the bars as follows:

To determine the coordinates of the leftmost bar (green):

- The upper-left corner's X coordinate is 0.
- The upper-left corner's Y coordinate is also 0.
- To calculate the lower-right corner's X coordinate, add one-third of the window's width to the upper-left corner's X coordinate.
- The lower-right corner's Y coordinate is the window's height.

To determine the coordinates of the middle bar (white):

- The upper-left corner's X coordinate is one-third the window's width.
- The upper-left corner's Y coordinate is 0.
- To calculate the lower-right corner's X coordinate, add one-third of the window's width to the upper-left corner's X coordinate.
- The lower-right corner's Y coordinate is the window's height.

To determine the coordinates of the rightmost bar (red):

- The upper-left corner's X coordinate is two-thirds the window's width.
- The upper-left corner's Y coordinate is 0.
- To calculate the lower-right corner's X coordinate, add one-third of the window's width to the upper-left corner's X coordinate.
- The lower-right corner's Y coordinate is the window's height.

Program 3-16 shows the code, which displays the flag shown in Figure 3-24 (located in this book's color insert).

Program 3-16   (`ItalianFlag.cpp`)

```cpp
1   // This program draws an Italian flag.
2   #include "DarkGDK.h"
3
4   void DarkGDK()
5   {
6       // Declare variables for the colors.
7       DWORD green = dbRGB(0, 255, 0);
8       DWORD white = dbRGB(255, 255, 255);
9       DWORD red   = dbRGB(255, 0, 0);
10      DWORD black = dbRGB(0, 0, 0);
11
12      // Declare variables for the window width and height.
13      int width  = dbScreenWidth();
14      int height = dbScreenHeight();
15
16      // Calculate 1/3 of the window's width.
17      int oneThird = width / 3;
18
19      // Declare variables for the rectangle's coordinates.
20      int upperX, upperY, lowerX, lowerY;
21
22      // Set the text in the window's title bar.
23      dbSetWindowTitle("The Italian Flag");
24
25      // Draw a green bar in the left 1/3 of the window.
26      // ********************************************
27      // First, set the bar's coordinates.
28      upperX = 0;
29      upperY = 0;
30      lowerX = upperX + oneThird;
31      lowerY = height;
32
33      // Next, set the drawing color to green.
34      dbInk(green, black);
35
36      // Next, draw the bar.
37      dbBox(upperX, upperY, lowerX, lowerY);
38
39      // Draw a white bar in the middle 1/3 of the window.
40      // **********************************************
41      // First, set the bar's coordinates.
42      upperX = oneThird;
43      upperY = 0;
44      lowerX = upperX + oneThird;
45      lowerY = height;
46
47      // Next, set the drawing color to white.
48      dbInk(white, black);
49
50      // Next, draw the bar.
51      dbBox(upperX, upperY, lowerX, lowerY);
52
53      // Draw a red bar in the right 1/3 of the window.
```

```
54        // ************************************************
55        // First, set the bar's coordinates.
56        upperX = oneThird * 2;
57        upperY = 0;
58        lowerX = upperX + oneThird;
59        lowerY = height;
60
61        // Next, set the drawing color to red.
62        dbInk(red, black);
63
64        // Next, draw the bar.
65        dbBox(upperX, upperY, lowerX, lowerY);
66
67        // Wait until a key is pressed.
68        dbWaitKey();
69    }
```

More about Clearing the Window

The Dark GDK library provides two functions for clearing the window: dbClear and dbCLS. As you have seen, the dbClear function clears the window with a specific background color. When you call the function, you pass arguments for the background color's red, green, and blue components.

The dbCLS function can be called with no arguments, as shown here:

```
dbCLS();
```

When the function is called this way, it clears the window with a black background. To clear the window with another color, you pass a DWORD argument specifying the color. Here is an example:

```
DWORD blue = dbRGB(0, 0, 255);
dbCLS(blue);
```

When this code executes, it clears the window with a blue background.

 Checkpoint

3.27. What three color channels does the RGB system use to generate colors?

3.28. To what color does each of the following statements clear the Dark GDK window?

```
dbClear(0, 0, 255);
dbClear(255, 0, 0);
dbClear(0, 255, 0);
dbClear(255, 255, 255);
dbClear(0, 0, 0);
```

3.29. What type of variable do you use to store an RGB color?

3.30. Show an example of how you would store the RGB values for the color green in a variable.

3.8 Named Constants

CONCEPT: A named constant represents a value that cannot change while the program is running. You use the C++ key word `const` in a variable declaration to create a named constant.

Sometimes you want to be sure that a variable's value does not change while the program is running. For example, suppose you have determined that the particular shade of blue you are interested in using is obtained with the RGB values (0, 0, 75). In your program, you have the following variable declaration, which stores the RGB values for this color in a variable:

```
DWORD myBlue = dbRGB(0, 0, 75);
```

Although you might not mean to write a statement that changes the value of this variable, you might do so unintentionally. To make sure that the variable's value is not changed by any statement in the program, you can prefix the declaration with the word `const`, as shown here:

```
const DWORD myBlue = dbRGB(0, 0, 75);
```

By writing the C++ key word `const` at the beginning of the declaration, you are making the variable a *named constant*. If the compiler encounters any statement in the program that attempts to change the variable's contents (such as an assignment statement), an error will occur. You will not be able to compile the program until you fix the statement that caused the error.

Most programmers use the convention of writing a named constant's name in all uppercase letters. This is not required, but it helps to distinguish named constants from regular variables in a program's code. Here is an example:

```
const DWORD MY_BLUE = dbRGB(0, 0, 75);
```

Because the constant is named `MY_BLUE` instead of `myBlue`, you will immediately recognize that it is a named constant when you see its name in the program code. This is the practice that we will follow in this book.

When you declare a named constant, you must provide an initialization value. For example, the following code will cause an error:

```
const int UPPER_LEFT;      // ERROR! Missing initialization
UPPER_LEFT = 0;
```

Program 3-17 shows a modified version of the Italian Flag program. In this version, we have used `const` in the declarations of each variable that should not be changed while the program is running. (The output of the program is the same as Program 3-16, which is shown in Figure 3-24 located in this book's color insert.)

Program 3-17 (ItalianFlag2.cpp)

```cpp
1   // This program draws an Italian flag.
2   #include "DarkGDK.h"
3
4   void DarkGDK()
5   {
6       // Declare constants for the colors.
7       const DWORD GREEN = dbRGB(0, 255, 0);
8       const DWORD WHITE = dbRGB(255, 255, 255);
9       const DWORD RED   = dbRGB(255, 0, 0);
10      const DWORD BLACK = dbRGB(0, 0, 0);
11
12      // Declare constants for the window width and height.
13      const int WIDTH  = dbScreenWidth();
14      const int HEIGHT = dbScreenHeight();
15
16      // Calculate 1/3 of the window's width.
17      const int ONE_THIRD = WIDTH / 3;
18
19      // Declare variables for the rectangle's coordinates.
20      int upperX, upperY, lowerX, lowerY;
21
22      // Set the text in the window's title bar.
23      dbSetWindowTitle("The Italian Flag");
24
25      // Draw a green bar in the left 1/3 of the window.
26      // ***********************************************
27      // First, set the bar's coordinates.
28      upperX = 0;
29      upperY = 0;
30      lowerX = upperX + ONE_THIRD;
31      lowerY = HEIGHT;
32
33      // Next, set the drawing color to green.
34      dbInk(GREEN, BLACK);
35
36      // Next, draw the bar.
37      dbBox(upperX, upperY, lowerX, lowerY);
38
39      // Draw a white bar in the middle 1/3 of the window.
40      // ***********************************************
41      // First, set the bar's coordinates.
42      upperX = ONE_THIRD;
43      upperY = 0;
44      lowerX = upperX + ONE_THIRD;
45      lowerY = HEIGHT;
46
47      // Next, set the drawing color to white.
48      dbInk(WHITE, BLACK);
49
50      // Next, draw the bar.
51      dbBox(upperX, upperY, lowerX, lowerY);
52
53      // Draw a red bar in the right 1/3 of the window.
```

```
54        // *************************************************
55        // First, set the bar's coordinates.
56        upperX = ONE_THIRD * 2;
57        upperY = 0;
58        lowerX = upperX + ONE_THIRD;
59        lowerY = HEIGHT;
60
61        // Next, set the drawing color to red.
62        dbInk(RED, BLACK);
63
64        // Next, draw the bar.
65        dbBox(upperX, upperY, lowerX, lowerY);
66
67        // Wait until a key is pressed.
68        dbWaitKey();
69    }
```

 Checkpoint

3.31. What is the purpose of the key word const in a variable declaration?

3.32. Is it possible to execute a program even if it has a statement that tries to change the value of a named constant?

 3.9 ## Changing the Size of the Program Window

CONCEPT: You can use the dbSetDisplayMode function to set the size of the program's window.

By default, the Dark GDK window is 640 pixels wide by 480 pixels high. This is adequate for many of the programs that you will write, but in some cases you might want a bigger or smaller window. To change the window size you call the dbSetDisplayMode function. This is the general format of how you call the function:

    dbSetDisplayMode(*Width*, *Height*, *ColorDepth*);

In the general format, *Width* is an integer specifying the window's width, *Height* is an integer specifying the window's height, and *ColorDepth* is an integer specifying the number of bits that will be used to store the colors that are displayed in the window. Here is an example:

    dbSetDisplayMode(150,   100,   32);

This statement sets the window size at 150 pixels wide by 100 pixels high, and sets the color depth at 32 bits.

When changing the display mode, be sure to specify a size and color depth that your system can accommodate. For example, if your system's screen has a resolution of

1024 pixels by 768 pixels, you cannot display a window that is larger than those dimensions. If you specify a window size or color depth that your system cannot accommodate, you will see an error message and then the program will resume execution using the default Dark GDK window.

In Windows you can find your system's current screen resolution and color depth by right-clicking on the desktop, then selecting *Properties*, then selecting *Display Settings*. You can also call the dbScreenDepth function in your program to get the screen's color depth. Here is an example:

```
int colorDepth = dbScreenDepth();
dbSetDisplayMode(150, 100, colorDepth);
```

This code calls the dbScreenDepth function to get the screen's current color depth setting, and assigns that value to the colorDepth variable. Then the dbSetDisplayMode function is called to set the window size to 150 by 100, using the current color depth.

Program 3-18 demonstrates how to use these functions to set the program's window size to 100 by 100, using the system's current color depth setting. The program's output is shown in Figure 3-25.

Program 3-18   (ChangeWindowSize.cpp)

```
1  // This program changes the window size to 100 by 100.
2  #include "DarkGDK.h"
3
4  void DarkGDK()
5  {
6      // Use variables to hold the window's
7      // width, height, and color depth
8      int width = 100;
9      int height = 100;
10     int colorDepth = dbScreenDepth();
11
12     // Set the window size and color depth.
13     dbSetDisplayMode(width, height, colorDepth);
14
15     // The centerX and centerY variables will hold
16     // the coordinates of the window's center point.
17     int centerX = dbScreenWidth() / 2;
18     int centerY = dbScreenHeight() / 2;
19
20     // Draw a circle around the window's center
21     // point, with a radius of 25.
22     dbCircle(centerX, centerY, 25);
23
24     // Wait for the user to press a key.
25     dbWaitKey();
26  }
```

Figure 3-25 Output of Program 3-18

Review Questions

Multiple Choice

1. A string literal must be enclosed in _____.
   a. parentheses
   b. single quotes
   c. double quotes
   d. either single quotes or double quotes

2. The _____ data type can be used to hold whole numbers only.
   a. `double`
   b. `float`
   c. `int`
   d. `whole`

3. _____ is a special data type that the Dark GDK library uses extensively when working with colors.
   a. `DWORD`
   b. `float`
   c. `int`
   d. `color`

4. Which of the following variable names is illegal in C++?
   a. `aLongVariableName`
   b. `_value`
   c. `year1492`
   d. `99bottles`

5. A(n) _____ stores a value in a variable.
   a. variable declaration
   b. assignment statement
   c. math expression
   d. string literal

6. The _____ when a floating-point value is assigned to an integer variable.
   a. immediate termination of the program happens
   b. variable automatically becomes a `double`
   c. value is rounded up
   d. value is truncated

7. Assuming `x` is an `int` variable, which of the following statements will cause an error?
   a. `x = 17;`
   b. `17 = x;`
   c. `x = 99999;`
   d. `x = 0;`

8. _____ performs division, but instead of returning the quotient it returns the remainder.
   a. `%`
   b. `*`
   c. `**`
   d. `/`

9. The `+=` operator is an example of a(n)_____ operator.
   a. simple assignment
   b. combined assignment
   c. complex assignment
   d. reverse assignment

10. The _____ function returns the width of the program's window, in pixels.
    a. `dbWindowWidth`
    b. `dbWidth`
    c. `dbScreenWidth`
    d. `dbPixelWidth`

11. The _____ function returns the height of the program's window, in pixels.
    a. `dbScreenHeight`
    b. `dbHeight`
    c. `dbWindowHeight`
    d. `dbPixelHeight`

12. The _____function returns a random number.
    a. `dbRandom`
    b. `dbGetRandom`
    c. `dbRandomNumber`
    d. `dbRND`

13. The _____function seeds the random number generator.
    a. `dbSeed`
    b. `dbGetRandom`
    c. `dbRandomize`
    d. `dbRNDSeed`

14. The _____function returns the internal system time in milliseconds.
    a. `dbSystemTime`
    b. `dbTimer`
    c. `dbInternal`
    d. `dbMilliTime`

15. The _____function returns an RGB color formatted as a `DWORD` value.
    a. `dbRGB`
    b. `dbFormattedRGB`
    c. `dbColor`
    d. `dbRGBtoDWORD`

True or False

1. In C++ the first character of a variable name cannot be a number.

2. Variable names can have spaces in them.

3. In C++, variables do not have to be declared before they are used.

4. In C++, uninitialized variables always hold the value 0.

5. The following statement subtracts 1 from x: `x = x - 1;`

6. In a math expression, multiplication and division takes place before addition and subtraction.

7. The Dark GDK's random number generator automatically reseeds itself with a unique value each time it is executed.

8. You can specify a value in the range of 0 through 255 for an RGB color channel.

9. You use variables of the `float` data type to store colors.

10. A named constant's value can be altered by the program during the program's execution.

Short Answer

1. What two things do you specify in a variable declaration?

2. How is a camelCase name written?

3. What are variables that are declared inside a function known as?

4. What is an uninitialized variable? What value does an uninitialized variable start with?

5. What would happen if you assigned the value 7.9 to an `int` variable?

6. What happens when you divide an integer by another integer?

7. What would cause the random numbers that are generated in a program to be the same every time that the program runs?

8. What are the three color channels in an RGB color?

9. The `dbInput` function always returns data as what type?

10. What C++ function do you use to convert a string to an integer? What C++ function do you use to convert a string to a floating-point value?

Algorithm Workbench

1. Assume the variables `result`, `w`, `x`, `y`, and `z` are all integers, and that w = 5, x = 4, y = 8, and z = 2. What value will be stored in `result` after each of the following statements execute?
   a. `result = x + y;`
   b. `result = z * 2;`
   c. `result = y / x;`
   d. `result = y − z;`

2. Write a statement that assigns the sum of 10 and 14 to the variable `total`.

3. Write a statement that divides the variable `length` by 2 and assigns the result to the variable `midpoint`.

4. Write a statement that gets the width of the program's window and stores that value in a variable named `width`.

5. Write a statement that gets the height of the program's window and stores that value in a variable named `height`.

6. Write the code that you would use to calculate the coordinates of the center point of the program's window. Store the X coordinate in a variable named `centerX` and store the Y coordinate in a variable named `centerY`.

7. Write the code that you would use to seed the Dark GDK's random number generator.

8. Write a statement that generates a random number in the range of 0 through 1000 and stores the number in a variable named `randomNum`.

9. Write a statement that clears the Dark GDK window and fills it with the color blue.

10. The color yellow can be generated with the RGB channel values (255, 255, 0). Write a variable declaration for a variable named `yellow`. Initialize the variable with these RGB color values.

11. Write code that prompts the user to enter an integer, reads a value from the keyboard, converts that value to an integer, and assigns it to the variable `number`.

12. Write a statement that gets the screen's current color depth and assigns that value to a variable named `colorDepth`. Then, write another statement that sets the window size to 250 by 200, using the `colorDepth` variable to specify the window's color depth.

Programming Exercises

1. **Bar Chart**

    Write a program that displays a bar chart comparing the following sales amounts:

    January: $5,000
    February: $2,500
    March: $7,000

    Use a different color for each bar in the chart. Display the name of the month just below its bar in the chart.

2. **Bar Chart Modification**

    Modify the Bar Chart program that you wrote for Exercise 1 so it asks the user to enter the sales amounts.

3. **Picket Fence**

    Write a program that draws the picket fence shown in Figure 3-26. Your program should calculate the coordinates for each rectangle that makes up the fence.

Figure 3-26 Picket fence output

4. **Random Line Midpoint**

    Write a program that draws a horizontal line on the screen. Use random numbers for the starting X and ending X coordinates. Then, draw a small colored 10 pixel by 10 pixel square centered over the line's midpoint.

5. **Random Xs**
Write a program that generates five random sets of XY coordinates. Then draw a small x centered over each point in the window.

6. **World Flags**
Figure 3-27 (located in this book's color insert) shows three flags: The flag of France, the flag of England, and the flag of Norway. Write programs that display each of these flags.

7. **Color Tester**
Write a program that asks the user to enter the numeric values for a color's red, green, and blue components. Then, draw a box in the center of the window that is filled with the resulting color.

8. **Random Color**
Write a program that generates random numbers for a color's red, green, and blue components. Then, clear the screen to the resulting color.

4 void Functions

TOPICS

4.1 Modularizing a Program with Functions

4.2 Defining and Calling a void Function

4.3 Designing a Program to Use Functions

4.4 Local Variables

4.5 Passing Arguments to Functions

4.6 Global Variables and Constants

4.1 Modularizing a Program with Functions

CONCEPT: A large program can be broken up into manageable functions that each performs a major task.

In Chapter 2, you learned that a function is a group of programming statements that has a name. Every program that you have written so far has a function named DarkGDK, which is executed when you run the program. You have also called (or executed) many of the functions that are in the Dark GDK library.

There are two general types of functions: those that return a value, and those that do not. When you call a value-returning function, it performs some operation and then returns a value back to the statement that called it. For example, in Chapter 3, we discussed the function dbRND, which generates a random number, and returns that number back to the statement that called it.

In C++, a function that does not return a value is known as a void function. For example, dbDot, dbLine, dbBox, and dbCircle are all void functions. When you call a void function, the program jumps to the code for that function and executes the statements inside it. When the function is finished, the program jumps back to the point in the program at which the function was called and resumes execution.

In this chapter, we will demonstrate how void functions can be used to break down a long program into smaller, manageable pieces. Instead of writing one long DarkGDK function that contains all of the program's statements, several small functions that each perform a specific task within the program can be written. These small functions can then be executed in the desired order.

139

This approach is sometimes called *divide and conquer* because a large problem is divided into several smaller problems that are easily solved. Figure 4-1 illustrates this idea by comparing two programs: one that uses a long complex function containing all of the statements necessary to solve a problem, and another that divides a problem into smaller problems, each of which is handled by a separate function.

Figure 4-1 Using functions to divide and conquer a large task

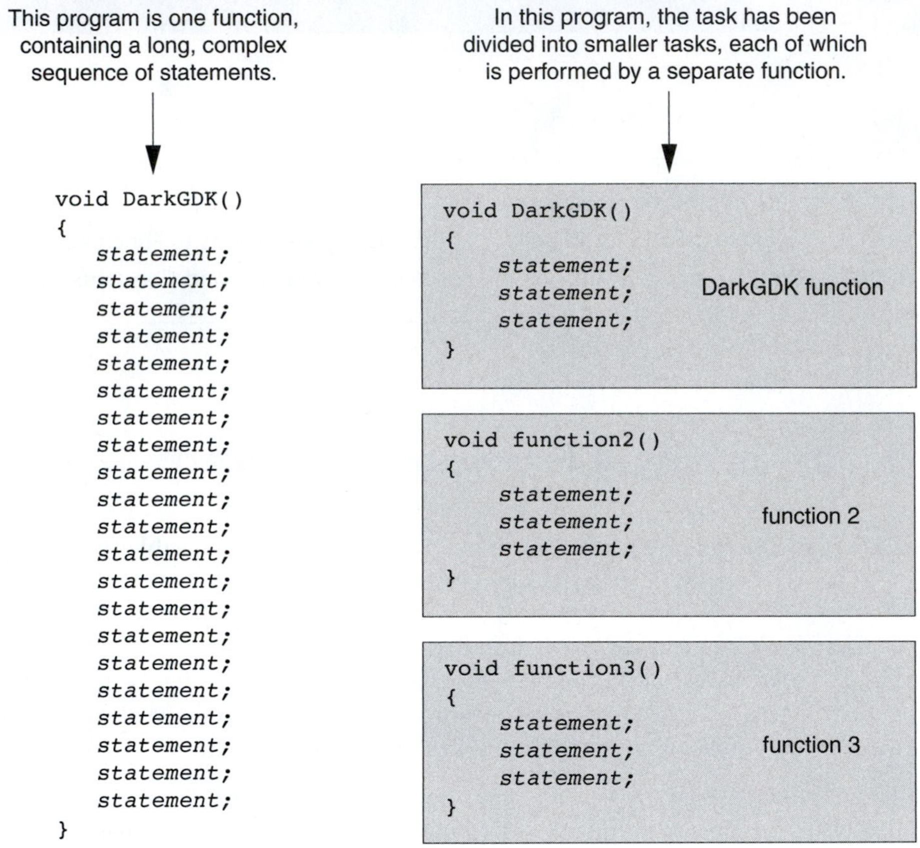

This program is one function, containing a long, complex sequence of statements.

In this program, the task has been divided into smaller tasks, each of which is performed by a separate function.

```
void DarkGDK()
{
    statement;
    statement;
    statement;
    statement;
    statement;
    statement;
    statement;
    statement;
    statement;
    statement;
    statement;
    statement;
    statement;
    statement;
    statement;
    statement;
    statement;
    statement;
    statement;
    statement;
}
```

```
void DarkGDK()
{
    statement;
    statement;           DarkGDK function
    statement;
}
```

```
void function2()
{
    statement;
    statement;           function 2
    statement;
}
```

```
void function3()
{
    statement;
    statement;           function 3
    statement;
}
```

Benefits of Using Functions

A program benefits in the following ways when it is broken down into functions.

Simpler Code

A program's code tends to be simpler and easier to understand when it is broken down into functions. Several small functions are much easier to read than one long sequence of statements.

Code Reuse

Functions also reduce the duplication of code within a program. If a specific operation is performed in several places in a program, a function can be written once to perform that operation, and then be executed any time it is needed. This benefit of using functions is known as *code reuse* because you are writing the code to perform a task once and then reusing it each time you need to perform the task.

Better Testing

When each task within a program is contained in its own function, testing and debugging becomes simpler. Programmers can test each function in a program individually, to determine whether it correctly performs its operation. This makes it easier to isolate and fix errors.

Faster Development

Suppose a programmer or a team of programmers is developing multiple programs. They discover that each of the programs performs several common tasks, such as asking for a username and a password, displaying the current time, and so forth. It doesn't make sense to write the code for these tasks multiple times. Instead, functions can be written for the commonly needed tasks, and those functions can be incorporated into each program that needs them.

Easier Facilitation of Teamwork

Functions also make it easier for programmers to work in teams. When a program is developed as a set of functions that each performs an individual task, then different programmers can be assigned the job of writing different functions.

 ## Checkpoint

4.1. What is meant by the phrase "divide and conquer?"

4.2. How do functions help you reuse code in a program?

4.3. How can functions make the development of multiple programs faster?

4.4. How can functions make it easier for programs to be developed by teams of programmers?

 # 4.2 Defining and Calling a `void` Function

> **CONCEPT:** The code for a function is known as a function definition. To execute a function you write a statement that calls it.

Function Names

Before we discuss the process of defining and calling functions, we should mention a few things about function names. Just as you name the variables that you use in a program, you also name the functions. A function's name should be descriptive enough so that anyone reading your code can reasonably guess what the function does.

When naming a function, C++ requires that you follow the same rules for naming variables, which we recap here:

- Function names must be one word. They cannot contain spaces.
- The first character must be one of the letters a through z, A through Z, or an underscore character (_).
- After the first character you may use the letters a through z or A through Z, the digits 0 through 9, or underscores.
- Uppercase and lowercase characters are distinct. This means the name DrawLines is not the same as the name drawLines.

Because functions perform actions, programmers commonly use verbs in function names. For example, a function that draws a smiley face might be named drawSmileyFace. This name would make it evident to anyone reading the code that the function draws a smiley face. Other examples of good function names would be setDrawingColor, displayCaption, clearScreen, and so forth. Each function name describes what the function does.

Defining a void Function

To create a function you write its *definition*. This is the general format of a void function definition:

```
void functionName()
{
    statement;
    statement;
    statement;
}
```

The first line is known as the *function header*. It marks the beginning of the function definition. The header for a void function begins with the key word void, followed by the name of the function, followed by a set of parentheses. (Notice that the function header does *not* end with a semicolon. Writing a semicolon at the end of the function header will cause an error.)

After the function header, a set of statements that are enclosed in curly braces appears. This set of statements is known as the *body* of the function. These are the statements that execute when the function is called.

Let's look at an example of a void function definition. Keep in mind that this is not a complete program. We will show the entire program in a moment.

```
void displayMessage()
{
    dbPrint("I am Arthur,");
    dbPrint("King of the Britons.");
}
```

This code defines a void function named displayMessage. The body of the function contains two statements, which are executed any time the function is called.

Notice in the previous example that the statements in the body of the function are indented. The indentation is not required, but it makes the code easier for people to read. By indenting the statements in a function, you visually set them apart. As a result, you can tell at a glance which statements are inside the function. Virtually all programmers follow this practice.

Calling a Function

A function definition specifies what a function does, but it does not cause the function to execute. To execute a function, you must *call* it. This is how we would call the displayMessage function:

```
displayMessage();
```

To call a function, you write its name, followed by a set of parentheses, followed by a semicolon. Notice that you do *not* write the word void in the function call statement.

When a function is called, the program jumps to that function and executes the statements inside it. Then, when the end of the function is reached, the program jumps back to the statement that called the function, and execution resumes with the very next statement. When this happens, we say that the function *returns*. To demonstrate how function calling works, we will look at Program 4-1. The program's output is shown in Figure 4-2.

Program 4-1 (FunctionDemo.cpp)

```
1   // This program demonstrates void functions.
2   #include "DarkGDK.h"
3
4   // Below is the displayMessage function.
5   void displayMessage()
6   {
7       dbPrint("I am Arthur,");
8       dbPrint("King of the Britons.");
9   }
10
11  // Below is the pauseProgram function.
12  void pauseProgram()
13  {
14      dbPrint();
15      dbPrint("Press any key to exit...");
16      dbWaitKey();
17  }
18
19  // Below is the DarkGDK function. This is where
20  // the program begins execution
21  void DarkGDK ()
22  {
23      // Display a message.
24      displayMessage();
25
26      // Pause the program until the user presses a key.
27      pauseProgram();
28  }
```

Figure 4-2 Output of Program 4-1

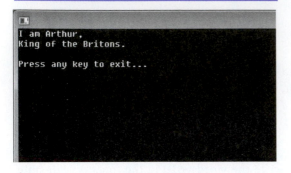

This program has three functions:

- `displayMessage`, which is defined in lines 5 through 9
- `pauseProgram`, which is defined in lines 12 through 17
- `DarkGDK`, which is defined in lines 21 through 28

Let's examine what happens when the program runs. First, execution begins at the `DarkGDK` function in line 21. (A Dark GDK program always begins execution at the `DarkGDK` function.) Inside the `DarkGDK` function, the first statement that executes is in line 24. This is a call to the `displayMessage` function. This causes the program to jump to the `displayMessage` function, as shown in Figure 4-3, and execute the statements inside it.

Figure 4-3 Calling the `displayMessage` function

```
// This program demonstrates a simple function.
#include "DarkGDK.h"

// Below is the displayMessage function.
void displayMessage()
{
    dbPrint("I am Arthur,");
    dbPrint("King of the Britons.");
}

// Below is the pauseProgram function.
void pauseProgram()
{
    dbPrint();
    dbPrint("Press any key to exit...");
    dbWaitKey();
}

// Below is the DarkGDK function. This is where
// the program begins execution
void DarkGDK ()
{
    // Display a message.
    displayMessage();

    // Pause the program until the user presses a key.
    pauseProgram();
}
```

The program jumps to the displayMessage function and begins executing the statements inside it.

After the statements in the `displayMessage` function have executed, the program returns to the statement that called it and resumes execution with the very next statement. This is shown in Figure 4-4. The next executable statement is in line 27, and it is a call to the `pauseProgram` function. As shown in Figure 4-5, the program jumps to the `pauseProgram` function and executes the statements inside it.

After the statements in the `pauseProgram` function have executed, the program returns to the statement that called it and resumes execution at that point. As shown in Figure 4-6, there are no more statements in the `DarkGDK` function, so the program ends.

> **NOTE:** When a program calls a function, programmers commonly say that the *control* of the program transfers to that function. This simply means that the function takes control of the program's execution.

Function Prototypes

In Program 4-1, notice that the function definitions for the `displayMessage` and `pauseProgram` functions appear before the function definition for the `DarkGDK` function. In C++, a function's definition must appear in the file before any statements that call that function. Otherwise, a compiler error will occur. The only exception is when you use function prototypes. A *function prototype* is a statement that declares the

Figure 4-4 The `displayMessage` function returns

When the `displayMessage` function ends, the program returns to the statement that called it, and resumes execution from that point.

```
// This program demonstrates a simple function.
#include "DarkGDK.h"

// Below is the displayMessage function.
void displayMessage()
{
    dbPrint("I am Arthur,");
    dbPrint("King of the Britons.");
}

// Below is the pauseProgram function.
void pauseProgram()
{
    dbPrint();
    dbPrint("Press any key to exit...");
    dbWaitKey();
}

// Below is the DarkGDK function. This is where
// the program begins execution
void DarkGDK ()
{
    // Display a message.
    displayMessage();

    // Pause the program until the user presses a
    pauseProgram();
}
```

Figure 4-5 Calling the pauseProgram function

```
// This program demonstrates a simple function.
#include "DarkGDK.h"

// Below is the displayMessage function.
void displayMessage()
{
    dbPrint("I am Arthur,");
    dbPrint("King of the Britons.");
}

// Below is the pauseProgram function.
void pauseProgram()
{
    dbPrint();
    dbPrint("Press any key to exit...");
    dbWaitKey();
}

// Below is the DarkGDK function. This is where
// the program begins execution
void DarkGDK ()
{
    // Display a message.
    displayMessage();

    // Pause the program until the user presses
    a key. pauseProgram();
}
```

The program jumps to the pauseProgram function and begins executing the statements inside it.

Figure 4-6 The pauseProgram function returns

```
// This program demonstrates a simple function.
#include "DarkGDK.h"

// Below is the displayMessage function.
void displayMessage()
{
    dbPrint("I am Arthur,");
    dbPrint("King of the Britons.");
}

// Below is the pauseProgram function.
void pauseProgram()
{
    dbPrint();
    dbPrint("Press any key to exit...");
    dbWaitKey();
}

// Below is the DarkGDK function. This is where
// the program begins execution
void DarkGDK ()
{
    // Display a message.
    displayMessage();

    // Pause the program until the user presses a key.
    pauseProgram();
}
```

When the pauseProgram function ends, the program returns to the statement that called it, and resumes execution from that point.

existence of a function, but does not define the function. It is merely a way of telling the compiler that a particular function exists in the program, and its definition appears at a later point.

This is how function prototypes for the displayMessage and pauseProgram functions would look:

```
void displayMessage();
void pauseProgram();
```

The prototypes look like the function headers, except a semicolon appears at the end of each. Function prototypes are usually placed near the top of a program so the compiler will encounter them before any function calls. Program 4-2 is a modification of Program 4-1. The definitions of the displayMessage and pauseProgram functions have been placed after the DarkGDK function, and function prototypes have been placed near the top of the program. The program's output is identical to that of Program 4-1.

Program 4-2   **(Prototypes.cpp)**

```
 1  // This program demonstrates function prototypes
 2  #include "DarkGDK.h"
 3
 4  // Function prototypes
 5  void displayMessage();
 6  void pauseProgram();
 7
 8  // Below is the DarkGDK function. This is where
 9  // the program begins execution
10  void DarkGDK ()
11  {
12      // Display a message.
13      displayMessage();
14
15      // Pause the program until the user presses a key.
16      pauseProgram();
17  }
18
19  // Below is the displayMessage function.
20  void displayMessage()
21  {
22      dbPrint("I am Arthur,");
23      dbPrint("King of the Britons.");
24  }
25
26  // Below is the pauseProgram function.
27  void pauseProgram()
28  {
29      dbPrint();
30      dbPrint("Press any key to exit...");
31      dbWaitKey();
32  }
```

Most C++ programmers use function prototypes. Using function prototypes in a Dark GDK program allows you to write the DarkGDK function, which is the program's starting point, at the top of your source code file. This is the approach we will use in this book.

 Checkpoint

4.5. What is the first line of a function definition?

4.6. What is the body of a function?

4.7. Why do programmers usually indent the lines in the body of a function?

4.8. You are reading the code for a program that has a void function named drawMap, and you see the following statement. Is this statement a function header or a function call? How can you tell?

```
drawMap();
```

4.9. You are reading the code for a program that has a void function named clearScreen, and you see the following statement. Is this statement a function header or a function call? How can you tell?

```
void clearScreen()
```

4.10. When a function is executing, what happens when the end of the function is reached?

4.11. What is a function prototype?

 4.3 **Designing a Program to Use Functions**

CONCEPT: Programmers commonly use a technique known as top-down design to break down a program into functions that each performs a single task.

In this chapter, we have discussed and demonstrated how void functions work. You've seen how control of a program is transferred to a function when it is called, and then returns to the statement that called it when the function ends. It is important that you understand these mechanical aspects of functions.

Just as important as understanding how functions work, is understanding how to design a program that uses functions. Programmers commonly use a technique known as *top-down design* to break down a program into functions. The process of top-down design is performed in the following manner:

- The overall task that the program is to perform is broken down into a series of subtasks.
- Each of the subtasks is examined to determine whether it can be further broken down into more subtasks. This step is repeated until no more subtasks can be identified.
- Once all of the subtasks have been identified, they are written in code.

This process is called top-down design because the programmer begins by looking at the topmost level of tasks that must be performed, and then breaks down those tasks into lower levels of subtasks.

For example, in Chapter 2, you saw a program that draws a city skyline. (See `CitySkyline2.cpp`, shown in Program 2-9.) The program's overall task is to draw an outline of some city buildings against a night sky. We can break down that task into the following three subtasks:

- Draw the outline of buildings
- Use boxes to draw some windows on the buildings
- Use dots to draw some stars in the sky above the buildings

In the original version of the program, all three of these tasks were performed in the `DarkGDK` function. A better design is to separate these tasks into their own functions, and then call those functions when needed. This is demonstrated by the revised version of the program, shown in Program 4-3. The program's output is shown in Figure 4-7.

Program 4-3   (`ModularCitySkyline.cpp`)

```
1   // This program draws a city skyline.
2   #include "DarkGDK.h"
3
4   // Function prototypes
5   void drawBuildings();
6   void drawWindows();
7   void drawStars();
8
9   //*********************************************
10  // The DarkGDK function                       *
11  //*********************************************
12  void DarkGDK ()
13  {
14      // Draw the outline of the buildings.
15      drawBuildings();
16
17      // Draw some lit windows on the buildings.
18      drawWindows();
19
20      // Draw some stars.
21      drawStars();
22
23      // Pause the program until the user presses a key.
24      dbWaitKey();
25  }
26
27  //*********************************************
28  // The drawBuildings function draws the outline *
29  // of the buildings.                          *
30  //*********************************************
31  void drawBuildings()
32  {
33      dbLine(  0, 339, 59,  339);
```

```
34        dbLine( 59, 339,  59,  239);
35        dbLine( 59, 239, 159,  239);
36        dbLine(159, 239, 159,   59);
37        dbLine(159,  59, 299,   59);
38        dbLine(299,  59, 299,  279);
39        dbLine(299, 279, 399,  279);
40        dbLine(399, 279, 399,  139);
41        dbLine(399, 139, 519,  139);
42        dbLine(519, 139, 519,  239);
43        dbLine(519, 239, 599,  239);
44        dbLine(599, 239, 599,  339);
45        dbLine(599, 339, 639,  339);
46    }
47
48    //**********************************************
49    // The drawWindows function draws the windows  *
50    // on the buildings.                           *
51    //**********************************************
52    void drawWindows()
53    {
54        dbBox(179,  99, 189, 109);
55        dbBox(179, 129, 189, 139);
56        dbBox(259, 179, 269, 189);
57        dbBox( 99, 259, 109, 269);
58        dbBox(239, 319, 249, 329);
59        dbBox(419, 179, 429, 189);
60    }
61
62    //**********************************************
63    // The drawStars function draws the stars.     *
64    //**********************************************
65    void drawStars()
66    {
67        dbDot(59,    59);
68        dbDot(119, 179);
69        dbDot(239,  19);
70        dbDot(359,  79);
71        dbDot(559,  39);
72        dbDot(599, 179);
73    }
```

Hierarchy Charts

When designing a program, programmers commonly use *hierarchy charts* to represent the relationships between the functions visually. A hierarchy chart, which is also known as a *structure chart*, shows boxes that represent each function in a program. The boxes are connected in a way that illustrates the functions called by each function. Figure 4-8 shows a hierarchy chart for Program 4-3.

The chart shows the DarkGDK function as the topmost function in the hierarchy. It calls the drawBuildings, drawWindows, drawStars, and dbWaitKey functions. The drawBuildings function calls the dbLine function, the drawWindows function calls the dbBox function, and the drawStars function calls the dbDot function.

Figure 4-7 Output of Program 4-3

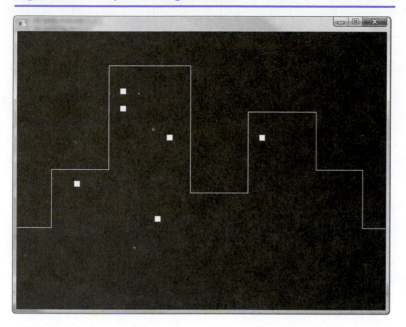

Figure 4-8 Hierarchy chart

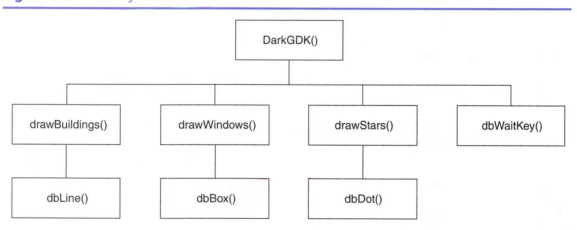

4.4 Local Variables

CONCEPT: A local variable is declared inside a function and cannot be accessed by statements that are outside the function. Different functions can have local variables with the same names because the functions cannot see each other's local variables.

A variable that is declared inside a function is called a *local variable*. A local variable belongs to the function in which it is declared, and only statements inside that function can access the variable. (The term *local* is meant to indicate that the variable can be used only locally, within the function in which it is declared.)

An error will occur if a statement in one function tries to access a local variable that belongs to another function. For example, look at Program 4-4. (Note that this program will not compile because of the errors.)

Program 4-4   (`ErrorLocalVars.cpp`)

```
1    // This program has errors and will not compile!
2    #include "DarkGDK.h"
3
4    // Function prototypes
5    void drawBlueBox();
6    void drawRedBox();
7
8    //***********************************************
9    // The DarkGDK function                        *
10   //***********************************************
11   void DarkGDK ()
12   {
13       // Create some color variables.
14       DWORD blue  = dbRGB(0,   0, 255);
15       DWORD red   = dbRGB(255, 0, 0);
16       DWORD black = dbRGB(0,   0, 0);
17
18       // Draw a blue box.
19       drawBlueBox();
20
21       // Draw a red box.
22       drawRedBox();
23
24       // Pause the program until the user presses a key.
25       dbWaitKey();
26   }
27
28   //***********************************************
29   // The drawBlueBox function draws a blue box.  *
30   //***********************************************
31   void drawBlueBox()
32   {
33       // Try to set the foreground drawing color to blue.
34       dbInk(blue, black);    // This causes an error!
35
36       // Draw a box.
37       dbBox(0, 0, 319, 239);
38   }
39
40   //***********************************************
41   // The drawRedBox function draws a red box.    *
42   //***********************************************
43   void drawRedBox()
44   {
```

```
45        // Try to set the foreground drawing color to red.
46        dbInk(red, black);      // This causes an error!
47
48        // Draw a box.
49        dbBox(320, 240, 639, 479);
50  }
```

Notice that three variables, `blue`, `red`, and `black` are declared in lines 14 through 16. These variables are declared inside the `DarkGDK` function, so they are local variables belonging to that function. Inside the `drawBlueBox` function, line 34 attempts to use both the `blue` and `black` variables. This results in a compiler error because these variables are not visible in the `drawBlueBox` function. The same type of compiler error also occurs at line 46. The `drawRedBox` function attempts to use the `red` and `black` variables, which are not visible in the `drawRedBox` function.

NOTE: If you compile Program 4-4 with Visual C++, you will get error messages indicating that lines 34 and 46 have "undeclared identifiers." This is because the variables used in those lines have not been declared in the `drawBlueBox` and `drawRedBox` functions.

The code in Program 4-5 shows how we can correct Program 4-4. Notice that in this version of the program, the variables used by the `drawBlueBox` and `drawRedBox` functions are declared inside those functions.

Program 4-5   (`LocalVars.cpp`)

```
1   // This program demonstrates local variables.
2   #include "DarkGDK.h"
3
4   // Function prototypes
5   void drawBlueBox();
6   void drawRedBox();
7
8   //**********************************************
9   // The DarkGDK function                        *
10  //**********************************************
11  void DarkGDK ()
12  {
13      // Draw a blue box.
14      drawBlueBox();
15
16      // Draw a red box.
17      drawRedBox();
18
19      // Pause the program until the user presses a key.
20      dbWaitKey();
21  }
22
```

```
23   //**********************************************
24   // The drawBlueBox function draws a blue box.   *
25   //**********************************************
26   void drawBlueBox()
27   {
28       // Declare color variables for blue and black.
29       DWORD blue  = dbRGB(0, 0, 255);
30       DWORD black = dbRGB(0, 0, 0);
31
32       // Set the drawing color to blue.
33       dbInk(blue, black);
34
35       // Draw a box.
36       dbBox(0, 0, 319, 239);
37   }
38
39   //**********************************************
40   // The drawRedBox function draws a red box.      *
41   //**********************************************
42   void drawRedBox()
43   {
44       // Declare color variables for red and black.
45       DWORD red   = dbRGB(255, 0, 0);
46       DWORD black = dbRGB(0,   0, 0);
47
48       // Set the drawing color to red.
49       dbInk(red, black);
50
51       // Draw a box.
52       dbBox(320, 240, 639, 479);
53   }
```

Scope and Local Variables

Programmers commonly use the term *scope* to describe the part of a program in which a variable may be accessed. A variable is visible only to statements inside the variable's scope.

A local variable's scope begins at the variable's declaration and ends at the end of the function in which the variable is declared. The variable cannot be accessed by statements that are outside this region. This means that a local variable cannot be accessed by code that is outside the function, or inside the module but before the variable's declaration.

Duplicate Variable Names

You cannot have two variables with the same name in the same scope, because the compiler would not know which variable to use when a statement tries to access one of them. This means that a function cannot have two local variables with the same name.

Because local variables are visible only to statements in the same function, it is permissible to have local variables with the same name declared in separate functions.

This happened in Program 4-5. Both the `drawBlueBox` and `drawRedBox` functions declare a local variable named `black`.

 Checkpoint

4.12. What is a local variable? How is access to a local variable restricted?

4.13. What does the term "scope" mean?

4.14. Is it permissible to have more than one variable with the same name in the same scope?

4.15. Is it permissible for a local variable in one function to have the same name as a local variable in another function?

 # 4.5 Passing Arguments to Functions

CONCEPT: An argument is a piece of data that is passed into a function when the function is called. When an argument is passed into a function, a special variable in the function known as a parameter receives the argument.

Sometimes it is useful not only to call a function, but also to send one or more pieces of data into the function. Pieces of data that are sent into a function are known as *arguments*. The function can use its arguments in calculations or other operations.

If you want a function to receive arguments when it is called, you must equip the function with one or more parameter variables. A *parameter variable*, often simply called a *parameter*, is a special variable that is assigned the value of an argument when a function is called. Let's look at an example of a function that uses a parameter variable to accept an argument. The following function is named `drawCircle`. The function calculates the coordinates of the window's center point and draws a circle around it. When you call the function, you pass an argument indicating the circle's radius.

```
void drawCircle(int radius)
{
    // Get the width and height of the window.
    int width = dbScreenWidth();
    int height = dbScreenHeight();

    // Calculate the coordinates of the center.
    int x = width / 2;
    int y = height / 2;

    // Draw the circle.
    dbCircle(x, y, radius);
}
```

Look at the function header and notice that the words `int radius` appear inside the parentheses. This is the declaration of a parameter variable. The parameter variable's name is `radius`, and its data type is `int`. The purpose of the parameter variable is to receive an integer argument when the function is called. Program 4-6 demonstrates the function. Figure 4-9 shows the program's output.

Program 4-6   **(CenterCircle.cpp)**

```
 1   // This program has a function that accepts an argument.
 2   #include "DarkGDK.h"
 3
 4   // Function prototype
 5   void drawCircle(int);
 6
 7   //**********************************************
 8   // The DarkGDK function                        *
 9   //**********************************************
10   void DarkGDK ()
11   {
12      // Draw a circle with a radius of 100 pixels.
13      drawCircle(100);
14
15      // Pause the program until the user presses a key.
16      dbWaitKey();
17   }
18
19   //***********************************************
20   // The drawCircle function draws a circle around *
21   // the window's center point. The circle's radius *
22   // is passed as an argument.                      *
23   //***********************************************
24   void drawCircle(int radius)
25   {
26      // Get the width and height of the window.
27      int width = dbScreenWidth();
28      int height = dbScreenHeight();
29
30      // Calculate the coordinates of the center.
31      int x = width / 2;
32      int y = height / 2;
33
34      // Draw the circle.
35      dbCircle(x, y, radius);
36   }
```

First, notice the function prototype for the drawCircle function in line 5:

```
void drawCircle(int);
```

It is not necessary to list the name of the parameter variable inside the parentheses. Only its data type is required. (You will not cause an error if you write the names of parameters in a function prototype. Since they are not required, the compiler merely ignores them.)

When this program runs, the DarkGDK function begins executing. The statement in line 13 calls the drawCircle function. Notice that the number 100 appears inside the

Figure 4-9 Output of Program 4-6

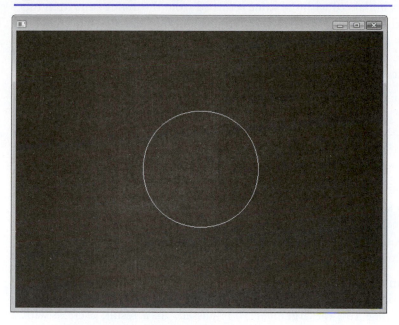

parentheses. This is an argument that is being passed to the function. When the
`drawCircle` function executes, the value 100 will be assigned to the `radius` parameter. This is shown in Figure 4-10.

Figure 4-10 The argument 100 is assigned to the `radius` parameter

```
drawCircle(100);


                                    The argument 100 is assigned
                                    to the radius parameter.



     void drawCircle(int radius)
     {
         // Get the width and height of the window.
         int width = dbScreenWidth();
         int height = dbScreenHeight();

         // Calculate the coordinates of the center.
         int x = width / 2;
         int y = height / 2;

         // Draw the circle.
         dbCircle(x, y, radius);
     }
```

Let's step through the drawCircle function. Line 27 declares a local int variable named width. It is initialized with the value returned from the dbScreenWidth function. As a result, the width variable will contain the width of the program's window. Line 28 declares a local int variable named height, initialized with the value returned from the dbScreenHeight function. As a result, the height variable will contain the height of the program's window.

Line 31 declares a local int variable named x, and initializes the variable with the value of width / 2. As a result, the variable x will contain the X coordinate of the window's center point. Line 32 declares a local int variable named y, and initializes the variable with the value of height / 2. As a result, the variable y will contain the Y coordinate of the window's center point.

Line 35 calls the dbCircle function to draw the circle. We want the circle's center to be at the window's center point, so the x and y variables are passed as the first two arguments. The radius parameter variable is passed as the third argument. As a result, the circle's radius will be whatever value was passed as an argument to the drawCircle function. In this program, that value is 100.

Let's look at one more program that uses the drawCircle function. Program 4-7 calls the function four times (in lines 13 through 16) to draw four concentric circles. In the first function call (line 13), the argument 50 is passed. As a result, a circle with a radius of 50 pixels is drawn. In the second function call (line 14), the argument 100 is passed. This causes a circle with a radius of 100 to be drawn. The third function call (line 15) passes 150 as an argument, resulting in a circle with a radius of 150. The fourth function call (line 16) passes 200 as an argument, resulting in a circle with a radius of 200. The program's output is shown in Figure 4-11.

Program 4-7   (ConcentricCircles.cpp)

```
 1   // This program calls the drawCircle function four times.
 2   #include "DarkGDK.h"
 3
 4   // Function prototype
 5   void drawCircle(int);
 6
 7   //*********************************************
 8   // The DarkGDK function                       *
 9   //*********************************************
10   void DarkGDK ()
11   {
12       // Draw four concentric circles.
13       drawCircle(50);
14       drawCircle(100);
15       drawCircle(150);
16       drawCircle(200);
17
18       // Pause the program until the user presses a key.
19       dbWaitKey();
20   }
21
```

```
22  //**************************************************
23  // The drawCircle function draws a circle around    *
24  // the window's center point. The circle's radius    *
25  // is passed as an argument.                          *
26  //**************************************************
27  void drawCircle(int radius)
28  {
29      // Get the width and height of the window.
30      int width = dbScreenWidth();
31      int height = dbScreenHeight();
32
33      // Calculate the coordinates of the center.
34      int x = width / 2;
35      int y = height / 2;
36
37      // Draw the circle.
38      dbCircle(x, y, radius);
39  }
```

Figure 4-11 Output of Program 4-7

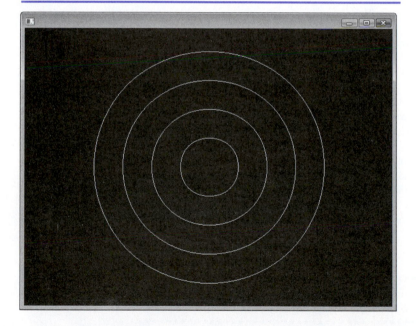

Parameter Variable Scope

Earlier in this section, you learned that a variable's scope is the part of the program in which the variable may be accessed. A variable is visible only to statements inside the variable's scope. A parameter variable's scope is the entire function in which the parameter is declared. It is visible only to statements inside the function.

Passing Multiple Arguments

If a function needs multiple arguments, you can equip it with multiple parameter variables. For example, Program 4-8 has a function named printSum that accepts two int arguments. The function adds the two arguments and displays their sum. Figure 4-12 shows an example of the program's output.

Program 4-8   (Sum.cpp)

```
1   // This program demonstrates a function that accepts
2   // two arguments.
3   #include "DarkGDK.h"
4
5   // Function prototype
6   void printSum(int, int);
7
8   //*******************************************************
9   // DarkGDK function                                     *
10  //*******************************************************
11  void DarkGDK ()
12  {
13     // Variables to hold two numbers
14     int firstNum, secondNum;
15
16     // Get the first number from the user.
17     dbPrint("Enter a number:");
18     firstNum = atoi( dbInput() );
19
20     // Get the second number from the user.
21     dbPrint("Enter another number:");
22     secondNum = atoi( dbInput() );
23
24     // Print the sum of the numbers.
25     dbPrint("The sum of those numbers is");
26     printSum(firstNum, secondNum);
27
28     // Pause the program until the user presses a key.
29     dbWaitKey();
30  }
31
32  //*******************************************************
33  // The printSum function accepts two integer arguments  *
34  // and displays their sum.                              *
35  //*******************************************************
36  void printSum(int num1, int num2)
37  {
38     // Store the sum of num1 and num2 in
39     // the sum variable.
40     int sum = num1 + num2;
41
42     // Display the sum.
43     dbPrint( dbStr(sum) );
44  }
```

Figure 4-12 Example output of Program 4-8

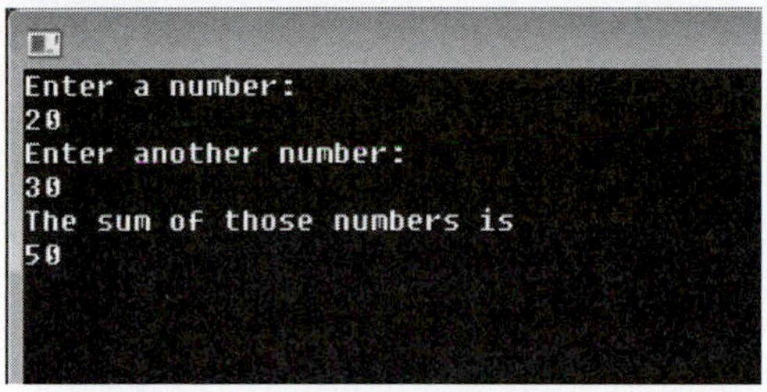

Notice that in line 36, two parameter variables, num1 and num2 are declared inside the parentheses in the function header. This is often referred to as a *parameter list*. Also notice that a comma separates the declarations.

Lines 17 and 18 prompt the user to enter a number, which is assigned to the firstNum variable. Lines 21 and 22 prompt the user to enter another number, which is assigned to the secondNum variable. The statement in line 26 calls the printSum function and passes firstNum and secondNum as arguments. The arguments are passed into the parameter variables in the order that they appear in the function call. In other words, the first argument is passed into the first parameter variable, and the second argument is passed into the second parameter variable. So, this statement causes the value of firstNum to be passed into the num1 parameter and the value of secondNum to be passed into the num2 parameter, as shown in Figure 4-13.

Figure 4-13 Two arguments passed into two parameters

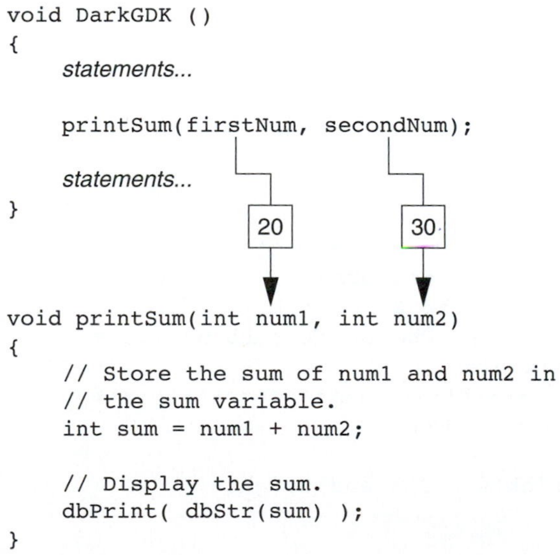

```
void DarkGDK ()
{
    statements...

    printSum(firstNum, secondNum);

    statements...
}
                          20        30

void printSum(int num1, int num2)
{
    // Store the sum of num1 and num2 in
    // the sum variable.
    int sum = num1 + num2;

    // Display the sum.
    dbPrint( dbStr(sum) );
}
```

Program 4-9 shows another example of a program with a function that accepts multiple arguments. The drawBrick function, in lines 43 through 59, draws a red box that is 40 pixels wide by 20 pixels high. The function accepts two arguments: the *X* and *Y* coordinates of the brick's lower-left corner.

Program 4-9   (RandomBricks.cpp)

```
 1   // This program draws random bricks.
 2   #include "DarkGDK.h"
 3
 4   // Function prototype
 5   void drawBrick(int, int);
 6
 7   //**********************************************************
 8   // DarkGDK function                                        *
 9   //**********************************************************
10   void DarkGDK ()
11   {
12       // Variables to hold XY coordinates.
13       int x, y;
14
15       // Seed the random number generator.
16       dbRandomize( dbTimer() );
17
18       // Draw a brick at a random location.
19       x = dbRND(600);
20       y = dbRND(460);
21       drawBrick(x, y);
22
23       // Draw a second brick at a random location.
24       x = dbRND(600);
25       y = dbRND(460);
26       drawBrick(x, y);
27
28       // Draw a third brick at a random location.
29       x = dbRND(600);
30       y = dbRND(460);
31       drawBrick(x, y);
32
33       // Pause the program until the user presses a key.
34       dbWaitKey();
35   }
36
37   //**********************************************************
38   // The drawBrick function draws a red brick. The leftX     *
39   // and leftY parameters specify the XY coordinates of      *
40   // the brick's lower left corner. The brick will be 40     *
41   // pixels wide and 20 pixels high.                         *
42   //**********************************************************
43   void drawBrick(int leftX, int leftY)
44   {
45       // Constants for the brick's width and height
46       const int WIDTH = 40;
47       const int HEIGHT = 20;
48
49       // Color constants
50       const DWORD RED = dbRGB(255, 0, 0);
51       const DWORD BLACK = dbRGB(0, 0, 0);
52
53       // Set the drawing color to red.
```

```
54        dbInk(RED, BLACK);
55
56        // Draw a brick at the specified coordinates.
57        // The brick is 40 pixels wide by 20 pixels high.
58        dbBox(leftX, leftY, leftX+WIDTH, leftY+HEIGHT);
59   }
```

In the DarkGDK function, line 13 declares two local variables, x and y. Line 16 seeds the random number generator, and then lines 19 and 20 generate random values for the x and y variables. Then, line 21 calls the drawBrick function, passing x and y as arguments. As a result, a brick will be drawn, with its lower-left corner at the coordinates specified by the x and y variables.

Lines 24 through 26 repeat these steps to draw another brick at a random location, and lines 29 through 31 draw a third random brick. Figure 4-14 shows an example of the program's output.

Figure 4-14 Example output of Program 4-9

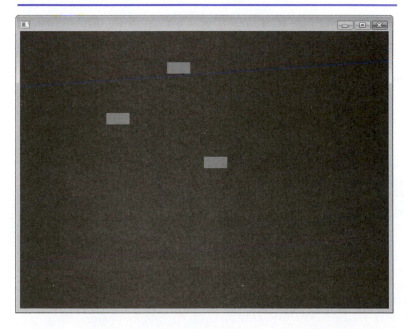

Passing Arguments by Value

All of the example programs that we have looked at so far pass arguments by value. Arguments and parameter variables are separate items in memory. Passing an argument *by value* means that only a copy of the argument's value is passed into the parameter variable. If the contents of the parameter variable are changed inside the function, it has no effect on the argument in the calling part of the program. For example, look at Program 4-10. The program's output is shown in Figure 4-15.

Program 4-10   (PassByValue.cpp)

```cpp
1   // This program demonstrates pass by value.
2   #include "DarkGDK.h"
3
4   // Function prototype
5   void changeMe(int);
6
7   //*******************************************************
8   // DarkGDK function                                     *
9   //*******************************************************
10  void DarkGDK ()
11  {
12      // Initialize a variable with 99.
13      int number = 99;
14
15      // Display the value stored in number.
16      dbPrint("In the DarkGDK function, number is:");
17      dbPrint( dbStr(number) );
18      dbPrint();
19
20      // Call the changeMe function, passing number
21      // as an argument.
22      changeMe(number);
23
24      // Display the value of number again.
25      dbPrint("Back in the DarkGDK function, number is:");
26      dbPrint( dbStr(number) );
27
28      // Pause the program until the user presses a key.
29      dbWaitKey();
30  }
31
32  //*******************************************************
33  // changeMe function                                    *
34  //*******************************************************
35  void changeMe(int myValue)
36  {
37      // Display the myValue parameter.
38      dbPrint("In the changeMe function, myValue is:");
39      dbPrint( dbStr(myValue) );
40
41      // Set the myValue parameter variable to 0.
42      dbPrint("I am changing the value.");
43      myValue = 0;
44
45      // Display the value in myValue.
46      dbPrint("The value is now:");
47      dbPrint( dbStr(myValue) );
48      dbPrint();
49  }
```

Figure 4-15 Example output of Program 4-10

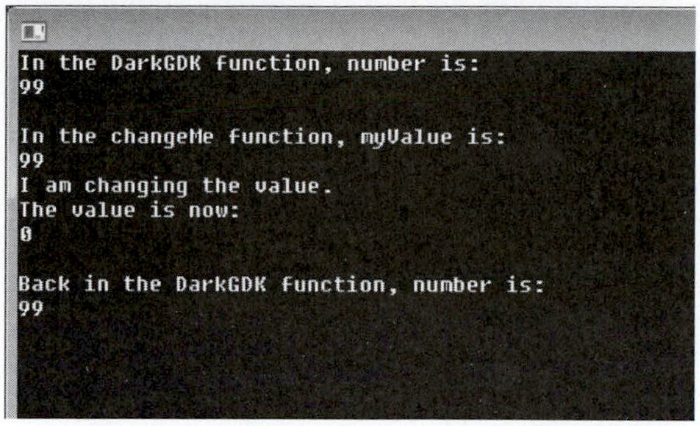

```
In the DarkGDK function, number is:
99

In the changeMe function, myValue is:
99
I am changing the value.
The value is now:
0

Back in the DarkGDK function, number is:
99
```

The DarkGDK function declares a local variable named number in line 13, and initializes it with the value 99. As a result, the statement in line 17 displays 99. The number variable's value is then passed as an argument to the changeMe function in line 22. This means that in the changeMe function, the value 99 will be assigned to the myValue parameter variable.

Inside the changeMe function, in line 39, the value of the myValue parameter variable is displayed. When this statement executes, myValue contains the value 99. But, line 43 sets myValue to 0. As a result, the statement in line 47 displays 0.

After the changeMe function finishes, control of the program returns to the DarkGDK function. When the statement in line 26 executes, the value 99 will be displayed. Even though the parameter variable myValue was changed in the changeMe function, the argument (the number variable in the DarkGDK function) was not modified.

Passing an argument is a way that one function can communicate with another function. When the argument is passed by value, the communication channel works in only one direction: The calling function can communicate with the called function. The called function, however, cannot use the argument to communicate with the calling function.

Passing Arguments by Reference

Passing an argument *by reference* means that the argument is passed into a special type of parameter known as a *reference variable*. When a reference variable is used as a parameter in a function, it allows the function to modify the argument in the calling part of the program.

A reference variable acts as an alias for the variable that was passed into it as an argument. It is called a reference variable because it references the other variable. Anything that you do to the reference variable is actually done to the variable it references.

Reference variables are useful for establishing two-way communication between functions. When a function calls another function and passes a variable by reference, communication between the functions can take place in the following ways:

- The calling function can communicate with the called function by passing an argument.
- The called function can communicate with the calling function by modifying the value of the argument via the reference variable.

In C++, you declare a reference variable by placing an ampersand (&) before the variable's name. For example, look at the following function:

```
void setToZero(int &value)
{
    value = 0;
}
```

Inside the parentheses, the & indicates that value is a reference variable. The function assigns 0 to the value parameter. Because value is a reference variable, this action is actually performed on the variable that was passed to the function as an argument.

When using a reference parameter variable, be sure to include the ampersand after the data type in the function prototype. Here is the prototype for the setToZero function:

```
void setToZero(int &);
```

Program 4-11 demonstrates this function and Figure 4-16 shows the program's output.

Program 4-11   (PassByReference.cpp)

```
 1   // This program demonstrates pass by reference.
 2   #include "DarkGDK.h"
 3
 4   // Function prototype
 5   void setToZero(int &);
 6
 7   //*********************************************
 8   // DarkGDK function                           *
 9   //*********************************************
10   void DarkGDK ()
11   {
12      // Declare some variables.
13      int a = 99;
14      int b = 99;
15      int c = 99;
16
17      // Display the values in those variables.
18      dbPrint("The variables a, b, and c are:");
19      dbPrint( dbStr(a) );
20      dbPrint( dbStr(b) );
21      dbPrint( dbStr(c) );
22      dbPrint();
23
24      // Pass each variable to setToZero.
25      setToZero(a);
```

```
26        setToZero(b);
27        setToZero(c);
28
29        // Display the values now.
30        dbPrint("Now the variables a, b, and c are:");
31        dbPrint( dbStr(a) );
32        dbPrint( dbStr(b) );
33        dbPrint( dbStr(c) );
34
35        // Pause the program until the user presses a key.
36        dbWaitKey();
37    }
38
39    //**********************************************
40    // setToZero function                         *
41    //**********************************************
42    void setToZero(int &value)
43    {
44        value = 0;
45    }
```

Figure 4-16 Output of Program 4-11

```
The variables a, b, and c are:
99
99
99

Now the variables a, b, and c are:
0
0
0
```

In the DarkGDK function, the variable a, b, and c are each initialized with the value 99. Then, in lines 25 through 27 those variables are passed as arguments to the setToZero function. Each time setToZero is called, the variable that is passed as an argument is set to 0. This is shown when the values of the variables are displayed in lines 31 through 33.

NOTE: Only variables may be passed by reference. If you attempt to pass a non-variable argument, such as a literal, a constant, or an expression into a reference parameter, an error will result. Using the setToZero function as an example, the following statements will cause an error when the program is compiled:

```
setToZero(5);          // Error!
setToZero(a + 10);     // Error!
```

Program 4-11 demonstrates how passing by reference works, but Program 4-12 shows a more practical example. This program has a function named getWindowSize, which accepts two int arguments. The arguments are passed into reference parameter variables. The function gets the width and height of the Dark GDK window and stores those values in the parameters. Because the parameters are reference variables, these values are actually stored in the variables that were passed as arguments to the function.

Figure 4-17 shows the output of Program 4-12.

Program 4-12   (WindowSizes.cpp)

```cpp
1   // This program uses reference parameter variables.
2   #include "DarkGDK.h"
3
4   // Function prototype
5   void getWindowSize(int &, int &);
6
7   //*******************************************************
8   // DarkGDK function                                     *
9   //*******************************************************
10  void DarkGDK ()
11  {
12     // Declare variables for the window sizes.
13     int windowWidth, windowHeight;
14
15     // Get the window sizes.
16     getWindowSize(windowWidth, windowHeight);
17
18     // Display the window sizes.
19     dbPrint("Window width:");
20     dbPrint( dbStr(windowWidth) );
21     dbPrint();
22     dbPrint("Window height:");
23     dbPrint( dbStr(windowHeight) );
24
25     // Pause the program until the user presses a key.
26     dbWaitKey();
27  }
28
29  //*******************************************************
30  // The getWindowSize function accepts two arguments,    *
31  // passed by reference. The window width is assigned    *
32  // to the width parameter, and the window height is     *
33  // assigned to the height parameter.                    *
34  //*******************************************************
35  void getWindowSize(int &width, int &height)
36  {
37     width = dbScreenWidth();
38     height = dbScreenHeight();
39  }
```

Figure 4-17 Output of Program 4-12

 Checkpoint

4.16. What are the pieces of data that are passed into a function called?

4.17. What are the variables that receive pieces of data in a function called?

4.18. What is a parameter variable's scope?

4.19. Explain the difference between passing by value and passing by reference.

4.6 Global Variables and Constants

CONCEPT: A global variable is accessible to all the functions in a program.

A *global variable* is declared outside of all the functions in a program. A global variable's scope begins at the variable's declaration and ends at the end of the program file. This means that a global variable can be accessed by all functions that are defined after the global variable is declared. Program 4-13 shows how you can declare a global variable. Figure 4-18 shows the program's output.

Program 4-13   **(GlobalVar.cpp)**

```
 1  // This program demonstrates a global variable.
 2  #include "DarkGDK.h"
 3
 4  // Global variable declaration
 5  int number;
 6
 7  // Function prototype
 8  void getNumber();
 9  void showNumber();
10
11  //*****************************************************
12  // DarkGDK function                                  *
13  //*****************************************************
14  void DarkGDK ()
```

```
15  {
16      // Get a number from the user.
17      getNumber();
18
19      // Display the number.
20      showNumber();
21
22      // Pause the program until the user presses a key.
23      dbWaitKey();
24  }
25
26  //*****************************************************
27  // getNumber function                                 *
28  //*****************************************************
29  void getNumber()
30  {
31      dbPrint("Enter a number:");
32      number = atoi( dbInput() );
33  }
34
35  //*****************************************************
36  // showNumber function                                *
37  //*****************************************************
38  void showNumber()
39  {
40      dbPrint("The number is:");
41      dbPrint( dbStr(number) );
42  }
```

Figure 4-18 Example output of Program 4-13

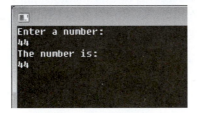

Line 5 declares an int variable named number. Because the declaration does not appear inside a function, the number variable is a global variable. All of the functions that are defined in the program have access to the variable. When the statement in line 32 (inside the getNumber function) executes, the value entered by the user is stored in the global variable number. When the statement in line 41 (inside the showNumber function) executes, it is the value of the same global variable that is displayed.

You should be careful when using global variables. The reasons are as follows:

- Global variables make debugging difficult. Any statement in a program can change the value of a global variable. If you find that the wrong value is being stored in a global variable, you have to track down every statement that accesses it to determine where the bad value is coming from. This can be difficult in a program with thousands of lines of code.

- Functions that use global variables are usually dependent on those variables. If you want to use such a function in a different program, most likely you will have to redesign it so it does not rely on the global variable.
- Global variables make a program hard to understand. A global variable can be modified by any statement in the program. If you are to understand any part of the program that uses a global variable, you have to be aware of all the other parts of the program that access the global variable.

When it is possible, you should declare variables locally and pass them as arguments to the functions that need to access them.

Global Constants

A *global constant* is a named constant that is available to every function in the program. Because a global constant's value cannot be changed during the program's execution, you do not have to worry about many of the potential hazards that are associated with the use of global variables.

Global constants are typically used to represent unchanging values that are needed throughout a program. For example, in a Dark GDK program you might create global constants for all of the colors you need to use in the program. Program 4-14 shows a modularized version of the Italian Flag program that you saw in Chapter 3. In addition to being modularized, this version of the program uses global constants for colors, which are declared in lines 5 through 8. The program's output is shown in Color Figure 3.

Program 4-14   (`ItalianFlag3.cpp`)

```
1   // This program draws an Italian flag.
2   #include "DarkGDK.h"
3
4   // Global color constants
5   const DWORD GREEN = dbRGB(  0, 255,   0);
6   const DWORD WHITE = dbRGB(255, 255, 255);
7   const DWORD RED   = dbRGB(255,   0,   0);
8   const DWORD BLACK = dbRGB(  0,   0,   0);
9
10  // Function prototypes
11  void drawGreenBar();
12  void drawWhiteBar();
13  void drawRedBar();
14
15  void DarkGDK()
16  {
17      // Set the text in the window's title bar.
18      dbSetWindowTitle("The Italian Flag");
19
20      // Draw the green, white, and red bars.
```

```
21      drawGreenBar();
22      drawWhiteBar();
23      drawRedBar();
24
25      // Wait until a key is pressed.
26      dbWaitKey();
27  }
28
29  //**********************************************
30  // The drawGreenBar function draws a green bar  *
31  // in the left 1/3 portion of the window.       *
32  //**********************************************
33  void drawGreenBar()
34  {
35      // Variables for the rectangle's coordinates.
36      int upperX, upperY, lowerX, lowerY;
37
38      // Set the bar's coordinates.
39      upperX = 0;
40      upperY = 0;
41      lowerX = upperX + (dbScreenWidth() / 3);
42      lowerY = dbScreenHeight();
43
44      // Set the drawing color to green.
45      dbInk(GREEN, BLACK);
46
47      // Draw the bar.
48      dbBox(upperX, upperY, lowerX, lowerY);
49  }
50
51  //**********************************************
52  // The drawWhiteBar function draws a white bar  *
53  // in the middle 1/3 portion of the window.     *
54  //**********************************************
55  void drawWhiteBar()
56  {
57      // Variables for the rectangle's coordinates.
58      int upperX, upperY, lowerX, lowerY;
59
60      // Set the bar's coordinates.
61      upperX = dbScreenWidth() / 3;
62      upperY = 0;
63      lowerX = upperX + (dbScreenWidth() / 3);
64      lowerY = dbScreenHeight();
65
66      // Set the drawing color to white.
67      dbInk(WHITE, BLACK);
68
69      // Draw the bar.
70      dbBox(upperX, upperY, lowerX, lowerY);
71  }
72
73  //**********************************************
74  // The drawRedBar function draws a white bar    *
75  // in the right 1/3 portion of the window.      *
```

```
76   //**********************************************
77   void drawRedBar()
78   {
79       // Variables for the rectangle's coordinates.
80       int upperX, upperY, lowerX, lowerY;
81
82       // Set the bar's coordinates.
83       upperX = (dbScreenWidth() / 3) * 2;
84       upperY = 0;
85       lowerX = upperX + (dbScreenWidth() / 3);
86       lowerY = dbScreenHeight();
87
88       // Set the drawing color to red.
89       dbInk(RED, BLACK);
91       // Draw the bar.
92       dbBox(upperX, upperY, lowerX, lowerY);
93   }
```

 Checkpoint

4.20. What is the scope of a global variable?

4.21. Give one reason that you should restrict the use global variables in a program.

4.22. What is a global constant? Is it permissible to use global constants in a program?

Review Questions

Multiple Choice

1. To help reduce the duplication of code within a program you use _____.
   a. code reuse
   b. divide and conquer
   c. unit testing
   d. facilitation of teamwork

2. The first line of a function definition is known as the _____.
   a. body
   b. introduction
   c. initialization
   d. header

3. You _____ to execute a function.
   a. define the function
   b. call the function
   c. import the function
   d. export the function

4. A statement, usually appearing near the top of the program, which declares the existence of a function, but does not define the function is a _____.
   a. function predefinition
   b. function prototype
   c. function initialization
   d. function disclosure

5. A design technique that programmers use to break down an algorithm into functions is _____.
   a. top-down design
   b. code simplification
   c. code refactoring
   d. hierarchical subtasking

6. A diagram that gives a visual representation of the relationships between functions in a program is a _____.
   a. flowchart
   b. function relationship chart
   c. symbol chart
   d. hierarchy chart

7. A variable that is declared inside a function is _____.
   a. a global variable
   b. a local variable
   c. a hidden variable
   d. none of the above because you cannot declare a variable inside a function.

8. A variable's _____ is the part of a program in which the variable may be accessed.
   a. declaration space
   b. area of visibility
   c. scope
   d. mode

9. A(n) _____ is a piece of data that is sent into a function.
   a. argument
   b. parameter
   c. header
   d. packet

10. A(n) _____ is a special variable that receives a piece of data when a function is called.
    a. argument
    b. parameter
    c. header
    d. packet

11. With _____, only a copy of the argument's value is passed into the parameter variable.
    a. passing by reference
    b. passing by name
    c. passing by value
    d. passing by data type

12. With _____, the function can modify the argument in the calling part of the program.
    a. passing by reference
    b. passing by name
    c. passing by value
    d. passing by data type

13. A special type of variable that acts as an alias for the variable that was passed into a function as an argument is a(n) _____.
    a. shadow variable
    b. value variable
    c. alias variable
    d. reference variable

14. A _____ is visible to every function in the program.
    a. local variable
    b. universal variable
    c. program-wide variable
    d. global variable

15. You should exercise caution when using a _____ variable in a program.
    a. local
    b. global
    c. reference
    d. parameter

True or False

1. The phrase "divide and conquer" means that all of the programmers on a team should be divided and work in isolation.

2. Functions make it easier for programmers to work in teams.

3. Function names should be as short as possible.

4. Calling a function and defining a function mean the same thing.

5. A function prototype declares the existence of a function, but does not define the function.

6. A hierarchy chart shows boxes representing the functions in a program.

7. A statement in one function can access a local variable in another function.

8. You cannot have two variables with the same name in the same scope.

9. It is permissible to have local variables with the same name declared in separate functions.

10. Functions are not allowed to accept multiple arguments.

11. When an argument is passed by reference, the function can modify the argument in the calling part of the program.

12. Passing an argument by value is a means of establishing two-way communication between functions.

Short Answer

1. How do functions help you to reuse code in a program?

2. Name and describe the two parts of a function definition.

3. When a function is executing, what happens when the end of the function is reached?

4. What is a local variable? What statements are able to access a local variable?

5. Where does a local variable's scope begin and end?

6. What is the difference between passing an argument by value and passing it by reference?

Algorithm Workbench

1. Write the definition of a function named `diagonal`. The function should draw a line from the upper-left corner of the window to the lower-right corner of the window.

2. Write the definition of a function named `showName`. It should accept an *X* coordinate and a *Y* coordinate as arguments. The function should display your name centered just below these coordinates. (Use the `dbCenterText` function to display your name.)

3. Write the definition of a function named `getCoordinates`. It should have two reference variable parameters, one for an *X* coordinate and one for a *Y* coordinate. The function should ask the user to enter an *X* coordinate and a *Y* coordinate, and store those values in the parameter variables.

4. Write the definition of a function named `drawTriangle`. It should accept an *X* coordinate and a *Y* coordinate as arguments. The function should draw a triangle, with the top of the triangle located at the coordinates passed as arguments. The height of the triangle should be 50 pixels.

Programming Exercises

1. **Modular Snowman**
Write a program that displays a snowman, similar to the one shown in Figure 4-19. In addition to the required `DarkGDK` function, the program should also have the following functions:

   - `drawBase`—This function should draw the base of the snowman, which is the large snowball at the bottom.
   - `drawMidSection`—This function should draw the middle snowball.
   - `drawArms`—This function should draw the snowman's arms.
   - `drawHead`—This function should draw the snowman's head, with eyes, mouth, and other facial features you desire.
   - `drawHat`—This function should draw the snowman's hat.

Figure 4-19 Snowman

2. **Rectangular Pattern**

In a program, write a function named `drawPattern` that draws the rectangular pattern shown in Figure 4-20. The `drawPattern` function should accept two arguments: one that specifies the pattern's width and another that specifies the pattern's height. (The example shown in Figure 4-20 shows how the pattern would appear when the width and the height are the same.)

When the program runs, the `DarkGDK` function should ask the user for the width and height of the pattern, and then pass these values as arguments to the `drawPattern` function.

Figure 4-20 Rectangular pattern

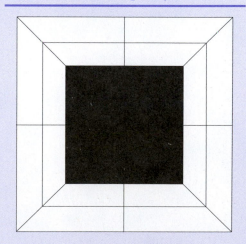

3. **Octagon**

   In a program, write a function named `drawOctagon` that draws the octagon shown in Figure 4-21. The `drawOctagon` function should accept arguments for the *X* and *Y* coordinates of the octagon's center point. When the function executes, it should draw the octagon with its center point located at these coordinates. The octagon should be 40 pixels high and 40 pixels wide.

   To demonstrate the function, the program should determine the coordinates of the window's center point. These values should be passed to the `drawOctagon` function as arguments.

Figure 4-21 Octagon

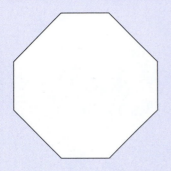

4. **Octagon Pattern**

   Modify the program that you wrote for Programming Exercise 3 so that it calls the `drawOctagon` function four times to draw the pattern shown in Figure 4-22.

Figure 4-22 Octagon pattern

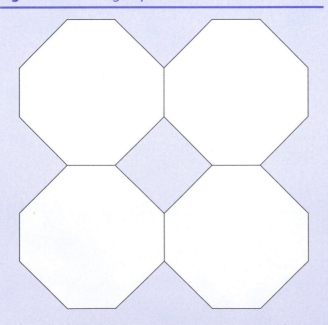

5 Working with Images

TOPICS

5.1 Introduction   5.3 Color Key Transparency
5.2 Bitmaps

5.1 Introduction

So far in this text, you have written programs that draw primitive shapes using functions such as `dbLine`, `dbCircle`, and `dbBox`. These functions are limited, however, and can be used to draw basic images only. In this chapter, you will learn how to display images that have been created with graphics programs such as Microsoft Paint, or captured with a digital camera. We will cover various special effects that can be done with images, and demonstrate how to use color key technology to create transparent pixels.

5.2 Bitmaps

CONCEPT: Images are commonly saved to disk as bitmaps. The Dark GDK library provides functions for loading, displaying, and modifying bitmaps.

When graphic images are stored on a computer's disk, they are commonly stored as bitmaps. The term *bitmap* refers to a set of data that describes every pixel in an image. When an image is saved on the computer's disk as a bitmap, it is saved in a file that contains data describing every pixel in the image.

If you use a digital camera, a scanner, or a graphics program like Microsoft Paint, you have probably created image files that end with extensions such as `.jpg`, `.bmp`, and `.gif`. These are all different formats for saving a bitmap image in a file.

179

Loading a Bitmap Image

The Dark GDK library provides a function named `dbLoadBitmap` that loads a bitmap file into memory. You call the function, passing the name of the bitmap file as an argument. (You can use the function to open files that have been saved in the `.bmp`, `.jpg`, `.tga`, `.dds`, `.dib` or `.png` formats.) The image is loaded from the file into memory and displayed in the Dark GDK window. Here is an example:

```
dbLoadBitmap("MyPhoto.jpg");
```

When this statement executes, the image stored in the file `MyPhoto.jpg` is loaded into memory and displayed on the screen. Program 5-1 shows a complete example. The statement in line 8 loads a bitmap image from the file `Boston.jpg` and displays it in the window. The program's output is shown in Figure 5-1.

Program 5-1 (BitmapDemo.cpp)

```
 1   // This program displays a bitmap image.
 2   #include "DarkGDK.h"
 3
 4   void DarkGDK()
 5   {
 6       // Load and display the image stored in
 7       // the Boston.jpg file.
 8       dbLoadBitmap("Boston.jpg");
 9
10       // Wait for the user to press a key.
11       dbWaitKey();
12   }
```

Figure 5-1 Output of Program 5-1

NOTE: The program window shown in Figure 5-1 has a resolution of 640 by 480. The `Boston.jpg` bitmap image that is displayed in the window also has a resolution of 640 by 480. When a bitmap is loaded, it will *not* be scaled to fit the size of the program's window. If an image is smaller than the program's window, it will occupy only part of the window. If an image is larger than the program's window, only part of the image will be displayed.

Bitmap File Locations

When you pass the name of a bitmap file to the `dbLoadBitmap` function, the function must be able to locate the file on your system's disk. If the function cannot locate the file, you will see nothing displayed.

In the Visual C++ environment, there are two ways you can make sure the function locates the bitmap file. One is to copy the bitmap file to the program's project folder. This is the approach we took when we created Program 5-1. The other approach is to specify the file's path, as well as its name. Let's look at each technique.

Copying Bitmap Files to the Project Folder

In line 8 of Program 5-1, we specified only the bitmap's file name, without specifying a path. When we compile and execute the program with Visual C++, the program will look for the file in the project folder. In order for the program to work, we have to make sure that the bitmap file has been copied to the project folder.

You specify the location of the project folder when you create the project. For example, suppose you want to create a project named `BitmapDemo` to test the code shown in Program 5-1. In Visual C++, you would click *File*, then *New*, then *Project*. This brings up the *New Project* dialog box, as shown in Figure 5-2.

Figure 5-2 Visual C++ *New Project* dialog box

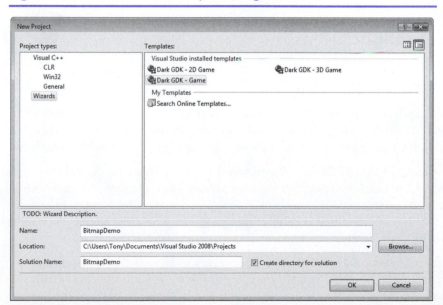

Notice that in the figure we have entered `BitmapDemo` as the project name. Also notice that the location has already been set to `C:\Users\Tony\Documents\Visual Studio 2008\Projects`. When we click *OK*, a project folder will be created at the following location:

`C:\Users\Tony\Documents\Visual Studio 2008\Projects\BitmapDemo\BitmapDemo`

This is the location where you would copy the `Boston.jpg` image file.

> **NOTE:** You might be wondering why two folders named `BitmapDemo` are created in the previous example. When you create a project in Visual C++, the project is stored in a solution folder with the same name. The first `BitmapDemo` folder listed in the path is the solution folder, and the second `BitmapDemo` folder is the project folder. The second (innermost) `BitmapDemo` folder is the location where we need to copy any bitmap files that we want the program to display.

Specifying a Bitmap File's Path

Another technique is to specify the file's path, as well as its name, when you call the `dbLoadBitmap` function. This eliminates the need to copy the bitmap file to the program's project folder. For example, suppose the `Boston.jpg` file is stored in the folder `C:\Images`. The file's name, including path, would be as follows:

`C:\Images\Boston.jpg`

There is an important detail you must remember, however: when you write a Windows path as a string literal in a C++ program, each backslash character must be written as *two* backslashes. Here is an example:

`dbLoadBitmap("C:\\Images\\Boston.jpg");`

When this statement executes, the program will load and display the bitmap file `C:\Images\Boston.jpg`.

In the Spotlight:
Using a Bitmap as a Background Image

After a bitmap has been loaded, you can use functions such as `dbLine`, `dbCircle`, `dbBox`, and so forth to draw primitive graphics on top of the bitmap image. This gives you the ability to use a bitmap image as a background for your primitive graphics.

For example, recall that in Chapter 2 you saw a program that first displays the stars of the constellation Orion, then, after the user presses a key, displays the names of the stars, and then, after the user presses a key again, displays the constellation lines. Program 5-2 shows a modified version of that program. The program has been modified in the following ways:

- A bitmap image named `OrionBackground.bmp` is loaded and displayed as a background. The image is a simple *color gradient*, which smoothly blends two colors. The image is blue at the top and gradually blends to black at the bottom.

- The code has been modularized into functions, with each function performing the following major tasks:
  - The `DarkDK` function, which appears in lines 14 through 33 calls all of the other functions.
  - The `displayBackground` function in lines 39 through 42 displays the background image. The image is stored in a file named `OrionBackground.bmp`.
  - The `drawStars` function in lines 48 through 65 displays the stars and waits for the user to press a key.
  - The `displayStarNames` function in lines 71 through 87 displays the names of the stars and waits for the user to press a key.
  - The `drawLines` function in lines 93 through 105 draws the constellation lines and waits for the user to press a key.

The program's final output, after the user has pressed keys twice, is shown in Figure 5-3. A color version of Figure 5-3, which shows the gradient more clearly, appears in the color insert.

Program 5-2   **(ModularOrion.cpp)**

```
1   // This program draws the stars of the constellation Orion,
2   // the names of the stars, and the constellation lines.
3   #include "DarkGDK.h"
4
5   // Function prototypes
6   void displayBackground();
7   void drawStars();
8   void displayStarNames();
9   void drawLines();
10
11  //*********************************************
12  // The DarkGDK function                       *
13  //*********************************************
14  void DarkGDK()
15  {
16      // Set the window's title.
17      dbSetWindowTitle("The Orion Constellation");
18
19      // Display the background image.
20      displayBackground();
21
22      // Draw the stars.
23      drawStars();
24
25      // Next display the star names.
26      displayStarNames();
27
28      // Next display the constellation lines.
29      drawLines();
30
31      // Wait for the user to press a key, then exit.
32      dbWaitKey();
33  }
```

```
34
35   //***********************************************
36   // The displayBackground function loads and    *
37   // displays a bitmap image for the background. *
38   //***********************************************
39   void displayBackground()
40   {
41       dbLoadBitmap("OrionBackground.bmp");
42   }
43
44   //***********************************************
45   // The drawStars function draws the stars       *
46   // in the constellation.                        *
47   //***********************************************
48   void drawStars()
49   {
50       // Display a caption.
51       dbCenterText(319, 20, "Stars of the Constellation");
52
53       // Draw the stars.
54       dbDot(200, 100);                      // Left shoulder
55       dbDot(350, 120);                      // Right shoulder
56       dbDot(260, 280);                      // Leftmost star in the belt
57       dbDot(290, 260);                      // Middle star in the belt
58       dbDot(320, 240);                      // Rightmost star in the belt
59       dbDot(220, 380);                      // Left knee
60       dbDot(380, 360);                      // Right knee
61
62       // Prompt the user to press a key.
63       dbCenterText(319, 450, "Press any key to continue.");
64       dbWaitKey();
65   }
66
67   //***********************************************
68   // The displayStarNames function displays the  *
69   // names of each star.                          *
70   //***********************************************
71   void displayStarNames()
72   {
73       // Display a caption.
74       dbCenterText(319, 40, "Star Names");
75
76       // Display the name of each star.
77       dbCenterText(200, 100, "Betelgeuse");    // Left shoulder
78       dbCenterText(350, 120, "Meissa");        // Right shoulder
79       dbText(260, 280, "Alnitak");             // Belt-left star
80       dbText(290, 260, "Alnilam");             // Belt-middle star
81       dbText(320, 240, "Mintaka");             // Belt-right star
82       dbCenterText(220, 380, "Saiph");         // Left knee
83       dbCenterText(380, 360, "Rigel");         // Right knee
84
85       // Wait for the user to press a key.
86       dbWaitKey();
87   }
88
```

```
89   //***********************************************
90   // The drawLines function draws the          *
91   // constellation lines.                       *
92   //***********************************************
93   void drawLines()
94   {
95       // Display a caption.
96       dbCenterText(319, 60, "Constellation Lines");
97
98       // Draw the constellation lines.
99       dbLine(200, 100, 260, 280);        // Left shoulder to belt
100      dbLine(350, 120, 320, 240);        // Right shoulder to belt
101      dbLine(260, 280, 290, 260);        // Left belt to middle belt
102      dbLine(290, 260, 320, 240);        // Middle belt to right belt
103      dbLine(260, 280, 220, 380);        // Left belt to left knee
104      dbLine(320, 240, 380, 360);        // Right belt to right knee
105  }
```

Figure 5-3 Final output of Program 5-2

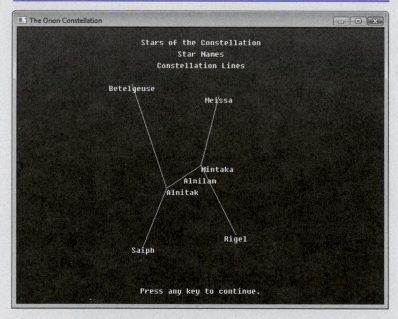

This figure also appears in this book's full-color insert.

Getting a File Name from the User

Recall from Chapter 3 that the dbInput function reads string input from the keyboard. Because the dbInput function returns a string, you can use it to get a file name from the user. The following code shows an example:

```
dbPrint("Enter the name of the bitmap file to display.");
dbLoadBitmap( dbInput() );
```

The first statement uses dbPrint to prompt the user for a bitmap file name. The second statement uses nested function calls. The dbInput function is called to get a string from the keyboard. The string that is returned from dbInput is passed as an argument to the dbLoadBitmap function. Program 5-3 demonstrates this. The program's output is shown in Figure 5-4.

Program 5-3   **(ShowBitmap.cpp)**

```
1    // This program lets the user enter the name of the
2    // bitmap file to display.
3    #include "DarkGDK.h"
4
5    void DarkGDK()
6    {
7        // Prompt the user to enter a file name.
8        dbPrint("Enter the name of the bitmap file to display.");
9
10       // Open the specified bitmap file.
11       dbLoadBitmap( dbInput() );
12
13       // Wait for the user to press a key.
14       dbWaitKey();
15   }
```

Figure 5-4 Example output of Program 5-3

① The user enters a file name and presses Enter. ⟶

② The specified bitmap file is loaded and displayed.

Earlier you learned that when you write a Windows path as a string literal in a C++ program, each backslash character must be written as two backslashes. The double backslash rule applies only to paths that have been written as string literals in a program's code. It does *not* apply to paths that are entered as input by the user. For example, suppose the user of Program 5-3 wants to display the bitmap file `C:\Images\Beach.jpg`. He or she would enter the path with single backslashes, as shown in Figure 5-5.

Figure 5-5 A path entered by the user

Loading Multiple Bitmaps

With the `dbLoadBitmap` function, you can load up to 32 bitmap images into memory at a time. Only one bitmap can be displayed at a time, but others can be held in memory until they are ready to be displayed.

Each bitmap is assigned a number in the range of 0 through 31. This *bitmap number* is how the Dark GDK keeps track of the bitmaps that are in memory. Previously, we called the `dbLoadBitmap` function, providing only the bitmap file name as an argument as shown here:

```
dbLoadBitmap("MyPhoto.jpg");
```

This statement causes the bitmap file `MyPhoto.jpg` to be loaded as bitmap number 0. Bitmap number 0 is a special bitmap because it is the only one that is displayed on the screen. As a result, when this statement executes, the bitmap `MyPhoto.jpg` is also displayed. You can also specify a bitmap number as a second argument when you call the `dbLoadBitmap` function. Here is an example:

```
dbLoadBitmap("MyPhoto.jpg", 1);
```

This statement loads the bitmap file `MyPhoto.jpg` as bitmap number 1. Although the bitmap will not be displayed, it will be held in memory. The following code shows an example of loading multiple bitmap images:

```
dbLoadBitmap("Kim.jpg", 1);
dbLoadBitmap("Chris.jpg", 2);
dbLoadBitmap("Paul.jpg", 3);
```

After this code executes, the bitmap `Kim.jpg` will be loaded as bitmap 1, `Chris.jpg` will be loaded as bitmap 2, and `Paul.jpg` will be loaded as bitmap 3. None of these bitmaps will be displayed, however, because none of them is bitmap 0.

NOTE: Only the values 0 through 31 are valid bitmap numbers. If you pass any other value to the `dbLoadBitmap` function as a bitmap number, the bitmap will not be loaded.

If a bitmap has a number other than 0, you display the bitmap by copying it to bitmap 0. This is done with the dbCopyBitmap function. When you call the function, you pass two arguments: The first is the number of the bitmap you are copying, and the second is the bitmap number you are copying it to. The following is an example. This statement will copy bitmap 1 to bitmap 0. As a result, bitmap will be displayed.

```
dbCopyBitmap(1, 0);
```

The following code shows how we can load multiple bitmap images and then display them one at a time:

```
// Load three bitmaps.
dbLoadBitmap("Kim.jpg", 1);
dbLoadBitmap("Chris.jpg", 2);
dbLoadBitmap("Paul.jpg", 3);

// Display bitmap 1 and wait for a key press.
dbCopyBitmap(1, 0);
dbWaitKey();

// Display bitmap 2 and wait for a key press.
dbCopyBitmap(2, 0);
dbWaitKey();

// Display bitmap 3 and wait for a key press.
dbCopyBitmap(3, 0);
dbWaitKey();
```

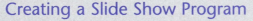

In the Spotlight:
Creating a Slide Show Program

A slideshow program displays a series of images, usually with a short time delay between each image. Program 5-4 shows an example. When this program executes, it displays the images shown in Figure 5-6, with a three-second pause between each image.

Program 5-4   **(SlideShow.cpp)**

```
 1   // This program displays a slide show of photos.
 2   #include "DarkGDK.h"
 3
 4   // Global constant for the time to wait after
 5   // each image is displayed. (3000 = 3 seconds)
 6   const int WAIT_TIME = 3000;
 7
 8   // Function prototypes
 9   void loadBitmaps();
10   void runSlideShow();
11   void displayPrompt();
12
13   //*********************************************
14   // The DarkGDK function                      *
```

```
15    //**********************************************
16    void DarkGDK()
17    {
18        // Set the window's title.
19        dbSetWindowTitle("Slide Show");
20
21        // Load the bitmap images.
22        loadBitmaps();
23
24        // Run the slide show, then end the program.
25        runSlideShow();
26    }
27
28    //**********************************************
29    // The loadBitmaps function loads the bitmap   *
30    // images into memory.                         *
31    //**********************************************
32    void loadBitmaps()
33    {
34        dbLoadBitmap("Boston01.jpg", 1);          // Bitmap #1
35        dbLoadBitmap("Boston02.jpg", 2);          // Bitmap #2
36        dbLoadBitmap("Boston03.jpg", 3);          // Bitmap #3
37        dbLoadBitmap("Boston04.jpg", 4);          // Bitmap #4
38    }
39
40    //**********************************************
41    // The runSlideShow function displays each of  *
42    // the bitmaps, with a pause between them.      *
43    //**********************************************
44    void runSlideShow()
45    {
46        // Display bitmap #1.
47        dbCopyBitmap(1, 0);
48        dbWait(WAIT_TIME);
49
50        // Display bitmap #2.
51        dbCopyBitmap(2, 0);
52        dbWait(WAIT_TIME);
53
54        // Display bitmap #3.
55        dbCopyBitmap(3, 0);
56        dbWait(WAIT_TIME);
57
58        // Display bitmap #4.
59        dbCopyBitmap(4, 0);
60        dbWait(WAIT_TIME);
61    }
```

Let's take a closer look at the program. First, notice that a global constant named WAIT_TIME is created in line 6, and given the value 3000. This value will be used later in the program to control the pause that occurs after each image is displayed.

The DarkGDK function appears in lines 16 through 26. It displays a caption in the window's title bar in line 19. Then, in line 22 it calls the loadBitmaps function. This

Figure 5-6 Bitmap images displayed by Program 5-4

function loads the bitmaps into memory. Then, in line 25 it calls the runSlideShow function. This function displays the loaded bitmaps with a pause after each one.

The loadBitmaps function appears in lines 32 through 38. This function loads the file Boston01.jpg as bitmap 1, the file Boston02.jpg as bitmap 2, the file Boston03.jpg as bitmap 3, and the file Boston04.jpg as bitmap 4.

The runSlideShow function appears in lines 44 through 61. This function performs the following steps:

- Line 47 copies bitmap 1 to bitmap 0. This causes bitmap 1 to be displayed. Line 48 then calls the dbWait function passing WAIT_TIME as an argument. This causes the program to pause for 3000 milliseconds (3 seconds).
- Line 51 copies bitmap 2 to bitmap 0. This causes bitmap 2 to be displayed. Line 52 pauses the program for 3 seconds.
- Line 55 copies bitmap 3 to bitmap 0. This causes bitmap 3 to be displayed. Line 56 pauses the program for 3 seconds.
- Line 59 copies bitmap 4 to bitmap 0. This causes bitmap 4 to be displayed. Line 60 pauses the program for 3 seconds.

Getting a Bitmap's Size and Color Depth

The Dark GDK library provides the following functions for getting a bitmap's width, height, and color depth: dbBitmapWidth, dbBitmapHeight, and dbBitmapDepth.

When you call the dbBitmapWidth function, you pass a bitmap number as an argument. The function returns the bitmap's width (in pixels), as an integer. The following statement shows an example:

```
width = dbBitmapWidth(1);
```

After this statement executes, the width variable will contain the width of bitmap 1. The dbBitmapHeight function works similarly. You pass a bitmap number as an argument, and the function returns the bitmap's height (in pixels) as an integer. The following statement shows an example:

```
height = dbBitmapHeight(1);
```

After this statement executes, the height variable will contain the height of bitmap 1. The dbBitmapDepth function follows this same general format. You pass a bitmap number as an argument, and the function returns the bitmap's color depth as an integer. The bitmap's color depth is the maximum number of colors that the bitmap can display. Here is an example:

```
depth = dbBitmapDepth(1);
```

After this statement executes, the depth variable will contain the color depth of bitmap 1.

Deleting Bitmaps from Memory

After a program is finished using the bitmaps it has loaded into memory, it can remove them with the dbDeleteBitmap function. You pass a bitmap number as an argument to the function and it removes that bitmap from memory. Here is an example:

```
dbDeleteBitmap(10);
```

This statement removes bitmap number 10 from memory. In many programs it's a good idea to remove bitmaps once the program has finished using them. Some bitmap images are very large, so removing them after they are no longer needed frees memory and can improve the program's performance.

 NOTE: The dbDeleteBitmap function removes a bitmap from memory only. It does not delete the bitmap file from your disk.

Flipping, Mirroring, Fading, and Blurring Bitmaps

The Dark GDK library provides several functions for performing "special effects" with bitmap images. These functions allow you to flip, mirror, fade, and blur bitmaps.

The `dbFlipBitmap` Function

The `dbFlipBitmap` function flips a bitmap vertically. Here is the general format of how you call the function:

```
dbFlipBitmap(BitMapNumber);
```

The argument that you pass as the `BitMapNumber` is the number of the bitmap that you want to flip. Figure 5-7 shows an example of a bitmap before and after it is flipped.

Figure 5-7 Original and flipped bitmaps

Original bitmap   Flipped bitmap

The `dbMirrorBitmap` Function

The `dbMirrorBitmap` function mirrors a bitmap horizontally. Here is the general format of how you call the function:

```
dbMirrorBitmap(BitMapNumber);
```

The argument that you pass as the `BitMapNumber` is the number of the bitmap that you want to mirror. Figure 5-8 shows an example of a bitmap before and after it is mirrored.

The `dbFadeBitmap` Function

The `dbFadeBitmap` function fades a bitmap. Here is the general format of how you call the function:

```
dbFadeBitmap(BitMapNumber, FadeValue);
```

The argument that you pass as the `BitMapNumber` is the number of the bitmap that you want to fade. The argument that you pass as the `FadeValue` is an integer that indicates the level of fading. This value must be in the range of 0 through 100. A value of 0 fades the bitmap completely to black, while a value of 100 performs no fading.

Figure 5-8 Original and mirrored bitmaps

Original bitmap   Mirrored bitmap

Figure 5-9 shows an example of a bitmap before and after it is faded with a fade value of 40.

Figure 5-9 Original and faded bitmaps

Original bitmap   Faded bitmap

The `dbBlurBitmap` Function

The `dbBlurBitmap` function blurs a bitmap. Here is the general format of how you call the function:

```
dbBlurBitmap(BitMapNumber, BlurValue);
```

The argument that you pass as the `BitMapNumber` is the number of the bitmap that you want to blur. The argument that you pass as the `BlurValue` is an integer that indicates the intensity of blurring. This value must be in the range of 1 through 9. A value of 1 only slightly blurs the bitmap, while a value of 9 greatly blurs it.

Figure 5-10 shows an example of a bitmap before and after it is blurred with a blur value of 9.

Figure 5-10 Original and blurred bitmaps

Original bitmap   Blurred bitmap

 NOTE: The larger the bitmap is, the longer it takes the `dbFadeBitmap` and `dbBlurBitmap` functions to work. When you call these functions, you might notice a delay while the program performs the necessary calculations.

 NOTE: The `dbFlipBitmap`, `dbMirrorBitmap`, `dbFadeBitmap`, and `dbBlurBitmap` functions only affect bitmaps in memory. They do not affect the bitmap files that the images are loaded from.

 Checkpoint

5.1. How many bitmaps can you load into memory using the `dbLoadBitmap` function?

5.2. What are the valid bitmap numbers?

5.3. Which bitmap is always the one that is displayed?

5.4. How do you display a bitmap that is not currently displayed?

5.5. How do you get a bitmap's size?

5.6. How do you get the maximum number of colors that can be displayed in a particular bitmap?

5.7. Why is it a good idea for a program to delete a bitmap from memory once the bitmap is no longer needed?

5.8. The `dbFadeBitmap` function accepts an argument as the fade value. Describe how the fade value determines the way the bitmap is faded.

5.9. The `dbBlurBitmap` function accepts an argument as the blur value. Describe how the fade value determines the way the bitmap is faded.

5.3 Color Key Transparency

CONCEPT: Color key technology is used to make some pixels in an image transparent. This allows you to display an image on top of a background image. The background image will show through the transparent pixels in the foreground image.

Color key technology, also known as *chroma key*, is widely used for special effects in movies and television. The technology allows filmmakers to blend two images, making them appear as one. For example, take the typical sword fighting scene from a pirate movie. While the actors might appear to be carrying out their conflict on the deck of a pirate ship, they were probably filmed in a studio. The background imagery of the ship's deck was inserted later, making it appear that the actors were actually there.

To create this scene, the filmmaker will shoot two videos: one of the actors engaged in a sword fight in the studio (let's call this the primary video), and another showing the ship's deck (let's call this the background video). When the actors in the primary video are filmed in the studio, they are standing in front of a large screen that is a specific color. This color is known as the *key color*. The primary video, containing the actors, is then placed on top of the background video of the ship's deck. However, the pixels in the primary video that contain the key color are not shown. As a result, they become transparent, allowing the background video to show through. In the resulting video, it appears that the actors are on the ship!

Color key technology is also used in television weather forecasts. To the TV viewer, it appears that the weather person is standing in front of a giant weather map. In the studio, however, the weather person is actually standing in front of a key-colored background. Before the image of the weather person is transmitted, a computer removes the pixels containing the key color and places it on top of the weather map image.

 NOTE: Color key technology is often referred to as *blue screen technology* or *green screen technology* because blue and green are commonly used as key colors.

You can also use color keying in your Dark GDK programs to blend multiple images. However, you have to use a different set of functions than the bitmap functions that we discussed in the previous section to display your images.

The `dbLoadImage` Function

The `dbLoadImage` function loads an image from a file. Here is the general format of how you call the function:

```
dbLoadImage(Filename, ImageNumber);
```

`Filename` is the name of the file containing the image. The function can load images that have been saved in the `.bmp`, `.jpg`, `.tga`, `.dds`, `.dib`, or `.png` formats. `ImageNumber` is a number that you assign to the image. The image number must be an integer in the range of 1 through 65,535. After the image is loaded into memory, you will use its image number to identify it in subsequent operations. Here is an example:

```
dbLoadImage("MyPicture.bmp", 1);
```

This statement loads the image stored in `MyPicture.bmp` and assigns it the image number 1.

> **NOTE:** The `dbLoadImage` function loads an image into memory, but it does not display the image.

Displaying Images with the `dbPasteImage` Function

After you have loaded an image, you can display it in the program's window with the `dbPasteImage` function. Here is the general format of how you call the function:

```
dbPasteImage(ImageNumber, X, Y, Transparency);
```

`ImageNumber` is the number of the image that you want to display. `X` and `Y` are integers specifying the screen coordinates where the image's upper-left corner will be positioned. `Transparency` is either 0 or 1. If `Transparency` is 0, then no pixels in the image will be treated as transparent. If `Transparency` is 1, then all pixels in the image that contain the key color will be treated as transparent. By default, the key color is black (red = 0, green = 0, and blue = 0). Here is an example:

```
dbPasteImage(1, 0, 0, 1);
```

This statement will display image 1 at the coordinates (0, 0), and all key color pixels will become transparent. As a result, any image that appears under this image will show through the transparent pixels.

Changing the Key Color with the `dbSetImageColorKey` Function

As previously mentioned, the key color is black by default. However, you can use the `dbSetImageColorKey` function to change the key color to anything you wish. This is the general format of how you call the function:

```
dbSetImageColorKey(Red, Green, Blue);
```

The arguments that you pass for `Red`, `Green`, and `Blue` are the key color's red, green, and blue component values. For example, the following statement will set the key color to red:

```
dbSetImageColorKey(255, 0, 0);
```

You have to call the `dbSetImageColorKey` function before loading an image with `dbLoadImage`. If you execute the statement shown above, and then load an image with `dbLoadImage`, all of the pixels in the image that have RGB values of 255, 0, 0 will be transparent when the image is displayed.

For example, suppose we have the images `Web.bmp` and `Spider.bmp`, as shown in Figure 5-11, and we want to combine the two images so the spider appears to be on the web. (See Figure 5-12 located in the color insert for an example of the combined images.) The `Web.bmp` image shows a white spider web drawn on a gray background. The `Spider.bmp` image shows an orange and black spider drawn on a green background.

Figure 5-11 The `Web.bmp` and `Spider.bmp` images

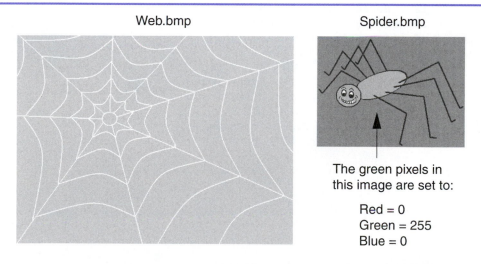

When the `Spider.bmp` image was drawn, the background color was set to the RGB values 0, 255, 0. We want the spider's green background to disappear when we display the spider on top of the web, so we will need to set the key color to 0, 255, 0. Here are the general steps that we will perform to combine the two images:

- Set the key color to the RGB values 0, 255, 0.
- Load the `Web.bmp` image.
- Load the `Spider.bmp` image.
- Display the `Web.bmp` image. There is no need to use transparency when we display this image because it is the background image.
- Display the `Spider.bmp` image at the desired coordinates. We will use transparency when we display this image so the green pixels will not appear.

Program 5-5 shows the actual code. The program's output is shown in Figure 5-13. (See Figure 5-12 located in the color insert for a color version.)

Program 5-5   `(FriendlySpider.cpp)`

```
1    // This program demonstrates color key transparency.
2    #include "DarkGDK.h"
3
4    void DarkGDK()
5    {
6        // Set the key color to green.
7        // (Red = 0, Green = 255, Blue = 0)
8        dbSetImageColorKey(0, 255, 0);
9
10       // Open the Web.bmp file as image #1.
11       dbLoadImage("Web.bmp", 1);
12
13       // Open the Spider.bmp file as image #2.
14       dbLoadImage("Spider.bmp", 2);
15
16       // Display image #1 (the web) at the
17       // coordinates (0,0). The last argument
18       // is 0 because this is the background
19       // image, and we don't need to treat any
20       // of its pixels as transparent.
21       dbPasteImage(1, 0, 0, 0);
22
23       // Display image #2 (the spider) at the
24       // coordinates (300, 150). The last
25       // argument is 1, indicating that all key
26       // color pixels should be transparent.
27       dbPasteImage(2, 300, 150, 1);
28
29       // Wait for the user to press a key.
30       dbWaitKey();
31   }
```

Let's take a closer look at the program:

- Line 8 sets the key color to green, using the RGB values 0, 255, 0.
- Line 11 loads the `Web.bmp` file as image #1.
- Line 14 loads the `Spider.bmp` file as image #2.
- Line 21 uses the `dbPasteImage` function to display image #1. The image is displayed at the screen coordinates (0, 0). Notice that the last argument is set to 0, indicating that we do not want to use transparency with this image.
- Line 27 uses the `dbPasteImage` function to display image #2. The image is displayed at the screen coordinates (300, 150). The last argument in this function call is 1, indicating that we want to use transparency. As a result, all of the pixels containing the key color will not be displayed.
- Line 30 waits for the user to press a key.

Figure 5-13 Output of Program 5-5

In the Spotlight:
Using Microsoft Paint
to Create Images

If you want to create your own images to use in your programs, you will need a graphics program. There are numerous programs available, including Microsoft Paint, which comes with the Windows operating system. In this section, we will lead you through the process of using Microsoft Paint to create a companion for the spider in Figure 5-13. The image we will create, which is shown in Figure 5-14, is a spider drawn on a green background. The green background color will be our key color. Then we will demonstrate a program that displays both spiders, perched on their spider web.

Figure 5-14 `Spider2.bmp`

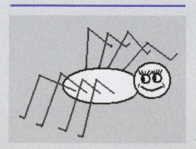

Step1:   In Windows Vista or Windows XP, you run the Paint program by clicking the *Start* button, then selecting *All Programs*, then selecting *Accessories*, then *Paint*. Figure 5-15 shows the *Paint* program. The drawing tools are located on the left edge of the window, and the color palette is located at the top.

Figure 5-15 Microsoft Paint

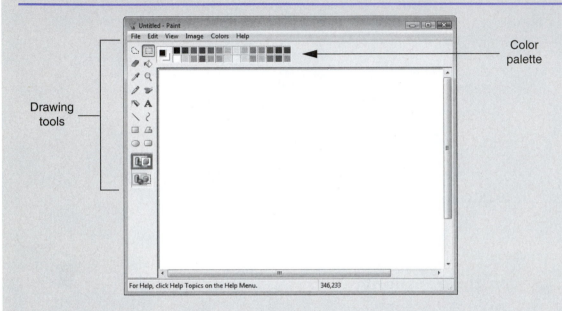

Step 2:   Now we will change the size of the image to 220 by 160 pixels. Click *Image* on the menu bar, then click *Attributes*. You will see the *Attributes* dialog box shown in Figure 5-16. In the dialog box, change the width to 220 and the height to 160. Make sure *Pixels* is selected as the units. Click *OK*.

Figure 5-16 *Attributes* dialog box

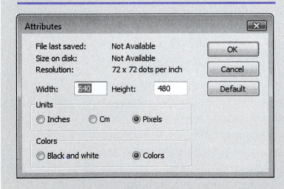

Step 3:   Now we will set the image's background color to green, with an RGB value of 0, 255, 0. This will be the key color. There are many shades of green, so we need to make sure that the color we select has the correct RGB values.

On the menu bar, select *Colors*, then select *Edit Colors...* You will see the *Edit Colors* dialog box shown on the left of Figure 5-17. Click the *Define Custom Colors >>* button. This will expand the *Edit Colors* dialog box as shown on the right of Figure 5-16.

Figure 5-17 The *Edit Colors* and the expanded *Edit Colors* dialog box

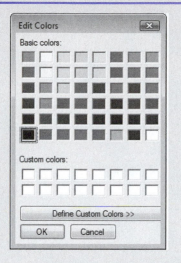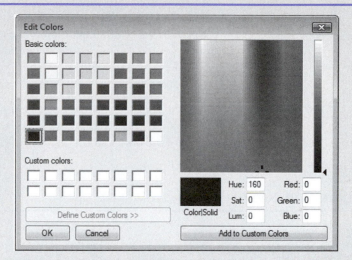

Step 4: In the lower-right corner of the dialog box you will see fields labeled *Red*, *Green*, and *Blue*. These allow you to enter specific RGB values. Enter 0 for Red, 255 for Green, and 0 for blue. Click *OK* to select this color and dismiss the dialog box.

Step 5: Click the *Fill with Color* tool (shown in Figure 5-18) and then click inside the image. This fills the image with the green color that we defined in Step 4.

Figure 5-18 The *Fill with Color* tool

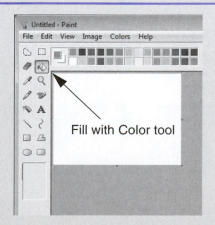

Step 6: Now it's time to use your creativity, along with the drawing tools, to create a spider similar to the one shown in Figure 5-13. Don't worry if your spider doesn't look exactly like the one in the figure. Here are some tips:

- You can use the ellipse tool to make the spider's body, head, and eyes. Don't forget to use the *Fill with Color* tool to fill the spider's body and head with the color of your choice. We used a shade of yellow in our example. Be sure not to use the green key color, though! If you do, the spider will be transparent when we display it in our program.
- You can use the line tool to draw the spider's legs.
- When drawing small detail, like the eyes, it helps to zoom in. Click *View*, then *Zoom*, then *Custom*. Then select the zoom level that you want (200%, 400%, or 800%). When you want to zoom back out, repeat these steps and select *100%* as the zoom level.

Step 7: When you are finished drawing the spider, click *File* on the menu bar, then click *Save*. As shown in Figure 5-19, save the image as `Spider2.bmp`, and select *24-bit Bitmap* as the file type.

Figure 5-19 Save the image as a 24-bit bitmap

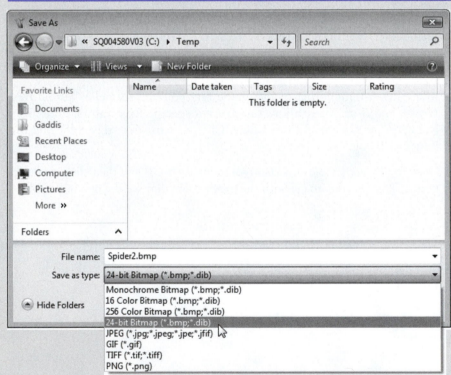

NOTE: When you are saving an image that contains a key color for transparency, it is important that you use the `bmp` file format. The `bmp` file format saves each pixel's RGB values exactly as you created them. Other file formats, such as `jpg`, compress the image to make it smaller on the disk. As a result, some of the pixel colors are slightly changed. This can make some of the transparent pixels appear in the image when it is displayed.

Now that we've created the `Spider2.bmp` image, we can display it along with the `Spider.bmp` and `Web.bmp` images that you saw earlier. Program 5-6 demonstrates this. In line 17 the `Spider2.bmp` file is loaded as image #3. Then, in line 30 it is displayed as the coordinates (50, 50) with transparency. The program's output is shown in Figure 5-20.

Program 5-6   (TwoSpiders.cpp)

```
1   // This program displays two spiders on a web.
2   #include "DarkGDK.h"
3
4   void DarkGDK()
5   {
6       // Set the key color to green.
7       // (Red = 0, Green = 255, Blue = 0)
8       dbSetImageColorKey(0, 255, 0);
9
10      // Open the Web.bmp file as image #1.
11      dbLoadImage("Web.bmp", 1);
12
13      // Open the Spider.bmp file as image #2.
14      dbLoadImage("Spider.bmp", 2);
15
16      // Open the Spider2.bmp file as image #3.
17      dbLoadImage("Spider2.bmp", 3);
18
19      // Display image #1 (the web) at the
20      // coordinates (0,0). This is the background
21      // image, so we won't use transparency.
22      dbPasteImage(1, 0, 0, 0);
23
24      // Display image #2 (the first spider) at the
25      // coordinates (300, 150), with transparency.
26      dbPasteImage(2, 300, 150, 1);
27
28      // Display image #3 (the second spider) at
29      // the coordinates (50, 50), with transparency.
30      dbPasteImage(3, 50, 50, 1);
31
32      // Wait for the user to press a key.
33      dbWaitKey();
34  }
```

Figure 5-20 Output of Program 5-6

In the Spotlight:

Adding a Key Color to Digital
Photos and Other Images

Although you can use a graphics program like Microsoft Paint to create your own images, sometimes you will want to use existing images from other sources. For example, you might want to use a photo that you took with your digital camera, or perhaps a clipart image that you have purchased.

If you want to use transparency with an existing image, you will need to edit the image with a graphics program, and add the key color to all of the parts of the image that you want to make transparent. For example, Figure 5-21 shows a photo of a dog. On the left is the original photo, which shows a brick wall behind the dog. On the right is a modified version of the photo in which we have erased the background and replaced it with a key color. (See the color insert for a color version of Figure 5-21.)

We deleted the background of the photo using Microsoft Paint. We simply zoomed in on the image and use the eraser tool to erase everything but the dog. Then, we used the *Fill with Color* tool to fill the background with the key color (green). This method can be time consuming; however, some graphics programs, such as Adobe Photoshop, provide tools that make it easy to select and erase the background regions of an image.

Figure 5-21 Original photo and modified photo

This figure also appears in this book's full-color insert.

After the photo has been modified, it is important to save it using the bmp file format. As previously mentioned, the bmp file format saves each pixel's RGB values exactly as you created them. Other file formats, such as jpg, compress the image to make it smaller on the disk. As a result, some of the key-colored pixels might be changed slightly, and they will not be transparent.

Program 5-7 demonstrates how we can take the modified photo of the dog (saved to a file named Dog.bmp) and display it over several different background images. First, the dog is displayed with a beach background. After the user presses a key, the dog is displayed with a snow background. After the user presses a key again, the dog is displayed with a mountain background. Figure 5-22 shows the program output. (See the color insert for a color version of Figure 5-22.)

Program 5-7   (TravelingDog.cpp)

```
1   // This program uses transparency to display
2   // a digital photo against several different
3   // background images.
4   #include "DarkGDK.h"
5
6   // Function Prototypes
7   void loadImages();
8   void displayDog(int);
9
10  void DarkGDK()
11  {
12      // Load the images.
13      loadImages();
14
15      // Display the dog against the
16      // 1st background image.
17      displayDog(1);
18
```

```
19          // Display the dog against the
20          // 2nd background image.
21          displayDog(2);
22
23          // Display the dog against the
24          // 3rd background image.
25          displayDog(3);
26      }
27
28      // The loadImages function sets the key color and
29      // loads all of the images into memory.
30      void loadImages()
31      {
32          // Set the key color to green.
33          // (Red = 0, Green = 255, Blue = 0)
34          dbSetImageColorKey(0, 255, 0);
35
36          // Open the Beach.bmp file as image #1.
37          dbLoadImage("Beach.bmp", 1);
38
39          // Open the Snow.bmp file as image #2.
40          dbLoadImage("Snow.bmp", 2);
41
42          // Open the Mountains.bmp file as image #3.
43          dbLoadImage("Mountains.bmp", 3);
44
45          // Open the Dog.bmp file as image #4.
46          dbLoadImage("Dog.bmp", 4);
47      }
48
49      // The displayDog function accepts an argument specifying
50      // a background image number. It displays image #4
51      // against the specified background image.
52      void displayDog(int backgroundImage)
53      {
54          // Display the background image at (0,0)
55          // with no transparency.
56          dbPasteImage(backgroundImage, 0, 0, 0);
57
58          // Display image #4 at 190, 90 with transparency.
59          dbPasteImage(4, 320, 241, 1);
60
61          // Wait for the user to press a key.
62          dbWaitKey();
63      }
```

Figure 5-22 Output of Program 5-7

This figure also appears in this book's full-color insert.

Deleting Images from Memory

After a program is finished using the images it has loaded into memory, it can remove them with the dbDeleteImage function. You pass an image number as an argument to the function and it removes that image from memory. Here is an example:

```
dbDeleteImage(1);
```

This statement removes the first image from memory. In many programs it's a good idea to remove images once the program has finished using them. Some images are very large, so removing them after they are no longer needed frees memory and can improve the program's performance.

NOTE: The dbDeleteImage function removes an image from memory only. It does not delete the image file from your disk.

Checkpoint

5.10. Describe how color key, or chroma key, is used to make a TV weather person appear as if he or she is standing in front of a giant weather map.

5.11. What are the valid image numbers that can be used when an image is loaded with the `dbLoadImage` function?

5.12. How do you display an image that has been loaded with the `dbLoadImage` function?

5.13. When you display an image, how do you make its key color pixels transparent?

5.14. What is the default key color?

5.15. How do you change the key color?

5.16. What file format should you use when saving an image that contains a key color? Why can't you use other formats, such as `jpg`?

Review Questions

Multiple Choice

1. To load a bitmap and display it you call _____.
   a. `dbDisplayBitmap`
   b. `dbLoadBitmap`
   c. `dbLoadGraphic`
   d. `dbBitmap`

2. The Dark GDK allows you to have _____ bitmaps loaded into memory at one time.
   a. 30
   b. 256
   c. 32
   d. an unlimited number of

3. Only this bitmap is displayed on the screen.
   a. bitmap number 1
   b. bitmap number 0
   c. bitmap number 255
   d. the last bitmap loaded

4. You use the _____ function to display a bitmap that is not bitmap 0.
   a. `dbDisplayBitmap`
   b. `dbRenumberBitmap`
   c. `dbMoveBitmap`
   d. `dbCopyBitmap`

5. You use the _____ to get a bitmap's size.

a. `dbBitmapSize` function

b. `dbBitmapWidth` and `dbBitmapHeight` functions

c. `dbBitmapXSize` and `dbBitmapYSize` functions

d. `dbBitmapResolution` function

6. The _____ function returns the maximum number of colors that the bitmap can display.

a. `dbBitmapDepth`

b. `dbBitmapColors`

c. `dbBitmapMaxColors`

d. `dbBitmapResolution`

7. To blend two images into one, _____ is widely used for special effects in movies and television.

a. image morphing

b. color blending

c. color key

d. white screen

8. You use the _____ function to display an image using transparency.

a. `dbPasteImage`

b. `dbDisplayImage`

c. `dbDisplayTransparentImage`

d. `dbTransparent`

9. The default key color with images is _____.

a. green (RGB = 0, 255, 0)

b. blue (RGB = 0, 0, 255)

c. black (RGB = 0, 0, 0)

d. white (RGB = 255, 255, 255)

10. You use the _____ function to change the key color used with images.

a. `dbSetKeyColor`

b. `dbSetImageColorKey`

c. `dbSetImageTransparency`

d. `dbColorKey`

True or False

1. Regardless of the number of bitmaps that are loaded, only bitmap 0 is displayed.

2. Having many large images loaded into memory can slow a program's performance.

3. When calling the `dbFadeBitmap` function, an argument of 100 fades the bitmap completely to black, and an argument of 0 performs no fading.

4. When calling the `dbBlurBitmap` function, an argument of 1 slightly blurs the bitmap, and a value of 9 greatly blurs it.

5. You can use the `dbLoadBitmap` function to load an image and use a key color for transparency.

6. If you are going to change the key color used with images, you must do so before the images are loaded.

7. The jpg file format is not a good choice for saving images that contain a key color for transparency.

Short Answer

1. What are the valid bitmap numbers?

2. How do you display a bitmap that is not bitmap 0?

3. Why is it a good idea for a program to delete a bitmap from memory when it is no longer needed?

4. How does color key technology work to create transparency in an image?

5. When saving an image that contains a key color for transparency, what file format should you use, and why?

Algorithm Workbench

1. Write a statement that loads the file VacationPhoto.jpg and displays it.

2. Write a statement that loads the file VacationPhoto.jpg as bitmap number 5.

3. Write code that prompts the user to enter a bitmap image's file name, then loads and displays that image.

4. Assume you have a bitmap loaded as bitmap number 10. Write a statement that displays the bitmap.

5. Write the code to flip vertically and mirror horizontally bitmap number 2.

6. Write a statement that displays image number 4 at the coordinates (100, 100), using transparency.

7. Write a statement to change the image key color to blue (RGB = 0, 0, 255).

Programming Exercises

1. **Snowman Background**
   Programming Exercise #1 in Chapter 4 asked you to write a modular program that displays a snowman. Modify the program so that it displays an image as a background for the snowman. Use Microsoft Paint (or any graphics program you choose) to create the background, or use a digital photo.

2. **Blurs and Fades**
   Write a program that prompts the user for the name of a bitmap to display. The program should display the image, wait one second, and then display the image with a blur level of 3. The program should wait one more second, and then display the image with a blur level of 6. After one more second, the program should display the image with a blur level of 9.

   Next, the program should wait one second, and then display the image with a fade level of 75. After one more second, the image should be displayed with a fade level of 50. After an additional second, the image should be displayed with a fade level of 25. After one last second the image should be faded completely to black.

3. **Landing Spaceship**
   Use Microsoft Paint, or any other graphics program, to draw an image of a spaceship. Select a key color to use as the background. Then, draw a second image of a planet surface. (If you prefer not to draw your own images, you can use the ones provided as part of the book's online resources, available for download at aw.com/gaddis.)

   After you have created the images, write a program that displays the planet surface with the spaceship above it. Each time the user presses a key, the spaceship should be displayed at a lower position (as if it is landing). After the user has pressed a key five times, the ship should be positioned on the planet's surface and the program should end.

4. **Buried Treasure**
   Use Microsoft Paint, or any other graphics program, to draw a pirate treasure map. (For inspiration, search the Internet for examples. If you prefer not to draw your own map, you can use the one provided as part of the book's online resources, available for download at aw.com/gaddis.)

   Write a program that asks the user for the *XY* coordinates of the buried treasure. It should then display the map with a red X over those coordinates.

5. **Virtual Tourist**
   Have a friend take a digital photo of you, and at least three photos of different locations (school, the mall, the park, and so forth). Transfer the images to your computer. Use a graphics program to replace the background of your picture with the key color of your choice. Then, write a program that displays the image of you over the various background images. (This program will be similar to Program 5-7.) The key color pixels in your picture should be transparent so it looks like you are at each of the locations.

6 Control Structures

TOPICS

6.1 Introduction

6.2 Writing a Decision Structure with the `if` Statement

6.3 The `if-else` Statement

6.4 Nested Decision Structures and the `if-else-if` Statement

6.5 Repetition Structures: The `while` Loop and the `do-while` Loop

6.6 The Increment and Decrement Operators

6.7 Repetition Structures: The `for` Loop

6.8 Using the `for` Loop to Process Pixels in an Image

6.9 Logical Operators

6.10 The `switch` Statement

6.11 Numeric Truth, Flags, and `bool` Variables

6.1 Introduction

CONCEPT: Control structures affect the order in which statements execute. There are three main types of control structures: sequence, decision, and repetition.

A *control structure* determines the order in which a set of statements execute. Back in the 1960s a group of mathematicians proved that only three control structures are needed to write any type of program: the sequence structure, the decision structure, and the repetition structure. The simplest of these structures is the *sequence structure*, which is a set of statements that execute in the order that they appear. Without realizing it, you have already used the sequence structure many times. For example, look at the following `DarkGDK` function:

```
void DarkGDK()
{
    dbSetWindowTitle("A Simple Program");
    dbText(10, 10, "Hello World!");
    dbWaitKey();
}
```

The statements inside the function are a sequence structure because they execute in the order that they are written, from the top of the function to the bottom of the function. When programmers are designing programs, they sometimes draw diagrams known as flowcharts, which show a program's logical flow of execution. Figure 6-1 shows a flowchart for the DarkGDK function previously shown. The elliptical symbols at the top and bottom of the flowchart are known as *terminals* because they mark the algorithm's start and end points. The symbols that appear between the terminals are the steps taken in the algorithm. Notice that the symbols are connected by arrows that represent the flow of execution. To step through the algorithm, you begin at the *Start* terminal, and follow the arrows until you reach the *End* terminal. As you can see, this flowchart depicts a sequence structure because the steps are taken one after another, from the beginning to the end.

 NOTE: Flowcharts are planning tools that programmers sometimes use to design a program's logic. Notice that there is no actual code written in Figure 6-1. The steps are written as informal statements that simply describe the actions that must take place. Once the programmer has determined all of the actions that must take place, and the order in which they must be performed, he or she can refer to the flowchart while writing the code.

Although the sequence structure is heavily used in programming, it cannot handle every type of task. This is because some problems simply cannot be solved by performing a set of ordered steps, one after the other. In some programs, a set of state-

Figure 6-1 Flowchart for a sequence structure

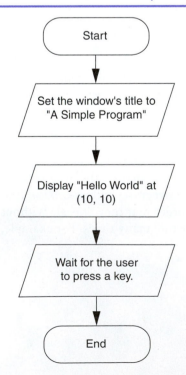

ments must be executed only under certain circumstances. If those circumstances do not exist, the statements should be skipped. Here's an example: Consider a company payroll program that determines whether an employee has worked overtime. If the employee has worked more than 40 hours, he or she gets paid a higher wage for the hours over 40. Otherwise, the overtime calculation should be skipped. This can be accomplished with a *decision structure*.

Suppose the same payroll program calculates pay for all employees. This means that it has to perform the same steps for each employee. This requires a repetition structure. A *repetition structure*, which is also known as a *loop*, is a structure that repeats a set of statements as many times as necessary.

In this chapter, we will discuss the fundamental decision structures and repetition structures provided by C++.

 Checkpoint

> 6.1. What does a control structure determine?
>
> 6.2. Name three types of control structures.
>
> 6.3. What type of control structure have you used so far as you work through this book?

6.2 Writing a Decision Structure with the if Statement

CONCEPT: The **if** statement is used to create a decision structure, which allows a program to have more than one path of execution. The **if** statement causes one or more statements to execute only when a Boolean expression is true.

In a decision structure's simplest form, a specific action is performed only if a certain condition exists. If the condition does not exist, the action is not performed. Figure 6-2 shows part of a flowchart. The figure shows how the logic of an everyday decision can be diagrammed as a decision structure. The diamond symbol represents a true/false condition. If the condition is true, we follow one path, which leads to an action being performed. If the condition is false, we follow another path, which skips the action.

In the flowchart, the diamond symbol indicates some condition that must be tested. In this case, we are determining whether the condition *Cold outside* is true or false. If this condition is true, the action *Wear a coat* is performed. If the condition is false, the action is skipped. The action is *conditionally executed* because it is performed only when a certain condition is true.

Programmers call the type of decision structure shown in Figure 6-2 a *single alternative decision structure*. This is because it provides only one alternative path of execution. If the condition in the diamond symbol is true, we take the alternative path.

Figure 6-2 A simple decision structure

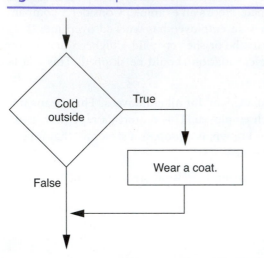

Otherwise, we exit the structure. Figure 6-3 shows a more elaborate example, where three actions are taken only when it is cold outside. It is still a single alternative decision structure, because there is one alternative path of execution.

Figure 6-3 A decision structure that performs three actions if it is cold outside

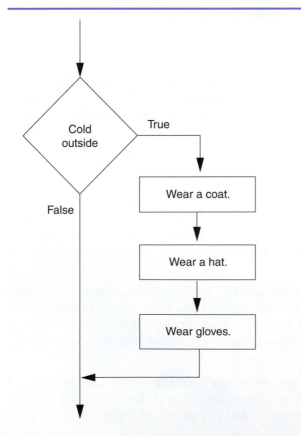

In C++, you use the `if` statement to write a single alternative decision structure. Here is the general format of the `if` statement:

```
if (expression)
{
    statement
    statement
    etc.
}
```

The statement begins with the word `if`, followed by an *expression* that is enclosed in a set of parentheses. Beginning on the next line is a set of statements that are enclosed in curly braces.

The expression that appears inside the parentheses is a Boolean expression. A *Boolean expression* is an expression that can be evaluated as either true or false. When the `if` statement executes, the Boolean expression is tested. If it is true, the statements that appear inside the curly braces are executed. If the Boolean expression is false, however, the statements inside the curly braces are skipped. We say that the statements inside the curly braces are conditionally executed because they are executed only if the Boolean expression is true.

If you are writing an `if` statement that has only one conditionally executed statement, you do not have to enclose the conditionally executed statement inside curly braces. Such an `if` statement can be written in the following general format:

```
if (expression)
    statement
```

When an `if` statement written in this format executes, the Boolean expression is tested. If it is true, the one statement that appears on the next line will be executed. If the Boolean expression is false, however, that one statement is skipped.

Although the curly braces are not required when there is only one conditionally executed statement, it is still a good idea to use them, as shown in the following general format:

```
if (expression)
{
    statement
}
```

This is a good style for writing `if` statements because it minimizes errors. Remember, if you have more than one conditionally executed statement, those statements *must* be enclosed in curly braces. If you get into the habit of always enclosing the conditionally executed statements in a set of curly braces, it's less likely that you will forget them.

Boolean Expressions and Relational Operators

The value of a Boolean expression can be either true or false. Boolean expressions are named in honor of the English mathematician George Boole. In the 1800s, Boole invented a system of mathematics in which the abstract concepts of true and false can be used in computations.

Typically, the Boolean expression that is tested by an `if` statement is formed with a relational operator. A *relational operator* determines whether a specific relationship exists between two values. For example, the greater than operator (>) determines whether one value is greater than another. The equal to operator (==) determines whether two values are equal. Table 6-1 lists the relational operators that are available in C++.

Table 6-1 Relational operators

Operator	Meaning
>	Greater than
<	Less than
>=	Greater than or equal to
<=	Less than or equal to
==	Equal to
!=	Not equal to

The following is an example of an expression that uses the greater than (>) operator to compare two variables, `length` and `width`:

```
length > width
```

This expression determines whether the value of the `length` variable is greater than the value of the `width` variable. If `length` is greater than `width`, the value of the expression is true. Otherwise, the value of the expression is false. The following expression uses the less than operator to determine whether `length` is less than `width`:

```
length < width
```

Table 6-2 shows examples of several Boolean expressions that compare the variables `x` and `y`.

Table 6-2 Boolean expressions using relational operators

Expression	Meaning
x > y	Is x greater than y?
x < y	Is x less than y?
x >= y	Is x greater than or equal to y?
x <= y	Is x less than or equal to y?
x == y	Is x equal to y?
x != y	Is x not equal to y?

The >= and <= Operators

Two of the operators, >= and <=, test for more than one relationship. The >= operator determines whether the operand on its left is greater than *or* equal to the operand on its right. The `<=` operator determines whether the operand on its left is less than *or* equal to the operand on its right.

For example, assume the variable a is assigned 4. All of the following expressions are true:

```
a >= 4
a >= 2
8 >= a
a <= 4
a <= 9
4 <= a
```

The == Operator

The `==` operator determines whether the operand on its left is equal to the operand on its right. If the values of both operands are the same, the expression is true. Assuming that a is 4, the expression a `==` 4 is true and the expression a `==` 2 is false.

> **NOTE:** The equality operator is two = symbols together. Don't confuse this operator with the assignment operator, which is one = symbol.

The != Operator

The `!=` operator is the not-equal-to operator. It determines whether the operand on its left is not equal to the operand on its right, which is the opposite of the `==` operator. As before, assuming a is 4, b is 6, and c is 4, both a `!=` b and b `!=` c are true because a is not equal to b and b is not equal to c. However, a `!=` c is false because a is equal to c.

Putting It All Together

Let's look at the following example of the `if` statement:

```
if (sales > 50000)
{
    bonus = 500;
}
```

This statement uses the `>` operator to determine whether `sales` is greater than 50,000. If the expression `sales > 50000` is true, the variable `bonus` is assigned 500. If the expression is false, however, the assignment statement is skipped. Figure 6-4 shows a flowchart for this section of code.

The following example conditionally executes three statements. Figure 6-5 shows a flowchart for this section of code.

```
if (x > 639)
{
    dbPrint("The x coordinate is off screen.");
    dbPrint("I am resetting it to 0.")
    x = 0;
}
```

Figure 6-4 Example decision structure   **Figure 6-5** Example decision structure

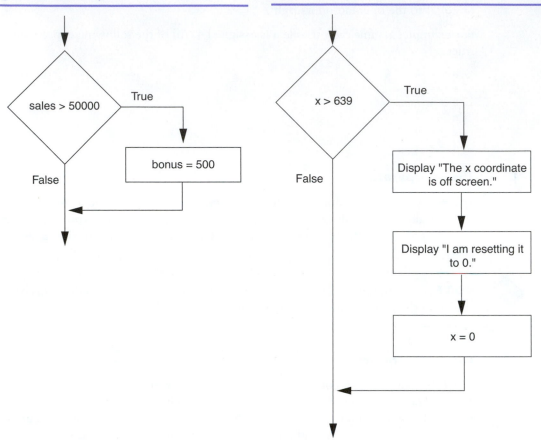

Notice that in both of the previous `if` statement examples, the conditionally executed statements were indented. This indentation is not required, but it makes the code easier to read and debug. By indenting the conditionally executed statements, you visually set them apart from the surrounding code. This allows you to tell at a glance what part of the program is controlled by the `if` statement. Most programmers use this style of indentation when writing `if` statements.

Let's look at a complete program that uses an `if` statement. Suppose you've taken three exams in your computer science class and you want to practice your coding skills by writing a program that calculates the average of the three scores. If the average is greater than 95, it should display the image stored in a file named `Congrats.bmp`. Here is the algorithm in pseudocode:

Get the first test score
Get the second test score
Get the third test score
Calculate the average
Display the average
If the average is greater than 95:
        Display the Congrats.bmp image

Program 6-1 shows the code for the program. Figure 6-6 shows two examples of the program's output. In the top screen the average is not greater than 95, and in the bottom screen the average is greater than 95.

Program 6-1   (`TestAverage.cpp`)

```
1   // This program prompts the user to enter three
2   // tests scores. It then displays the average of
3   // those scores. If the average is greater than
4   // 95 the Congrats.bmp image is displayed.
5   #include "DarkGDK.h"
6
7   void DarkGDK()
8   {
9       // Variables to hold the test scores
10      // and the average.
11      float score1, score2, score3, average;
12
13      // Get the three test scores.
14      dbPrint("Enter the first test score.");
15      score1 = atof( dbInput() );
16
17      dbPrint("Enter the second test score.");
18      score2 = atof( dbInput() );
19
20      dbPrint("Enter the third test score.");
21      score3 = atof( dbInput() );
22
23      // Calculate the average.
24      average = (score1 + score2 + score3) / 3;
25
26      // Display the average.
27      dbPrint();
28      dbPrint("Your average is:");
29      dbPrint( dbStr(average) );
30
31      // If the average is greater than 95
32      // then display the Congrats.bmp image
33      // at the coordinates (200, 120).
34      if (average > 95)
35      {
36          dbLoadImage("Congrats.bmp", 1);
37          dbPasteImage(1, 200, 120);
38      }
39
40      // Wait for the user to press a key.
41      dbWaitKey();
42  }
```

Figure 6-6 Output of Program 6-1

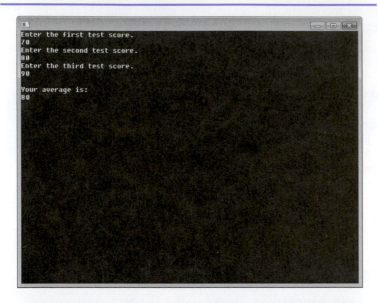

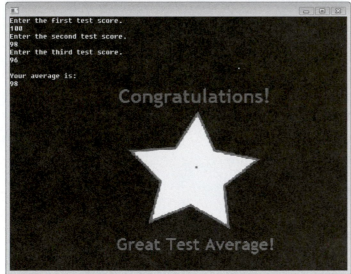

Testing Colors

You can use the relational operators to compare RGB color values. For example, suppose you have two DWORD variables named color1 and color2. The following if statement determines whether they hold the same value.

```
if (color1 == color2)
{
    dbPrint("Those are the same colors.");
}
```

If you need to test the color of a specific point on the screen, you can use the dbPoint function to get that point's color value. You pass two arguments, an X coordinate and a *Y* coordinate, to the dbPoint function, and it returns a DWORD value containing the color of that point. The following code shows an example:

```
DWORD pixelColor;
pixelColor = dbPoint(100, 150);
```

The first statement declares a DWORD variable named pixelColor. The second statement calls the dbPoint function to get the color of the pixel located at (100, 150). The color of that pixel is returned and assigned to the pixelColor variable.

The following code shows another example. This code gets the color of the pixel located at (10, 10). If that pixel's color is blue, it is changed to red.

```
// Declare variables for the colors
// red and blue.
DWORD red = dbRGB(255, 0, 0);
DWORD blue = dbRGB(0, 0, 255);

// Declare a variable to hold a pixel's
// color value.
DWORD pixelColor;

// Get the color of the pixel at (10,10).
pixelColor = dbPoint(10, 10);

// If that pixel is blue, set it to red.
if (pixelColor == blue)
{
    dbDot(10, 10, red);
}
```

 Checkpoint

6.4. What is a single alternative decision structure?

6.5. What is a Boolean expression?

6.6. What types of relationships between values can you test with relational operators?

6.7. Write an if statement that assigns 0 to x if y is equal to 20.

6.8. Write an if statement that displays the message "The line is too long" if the value of the variable length is greater than 640.

6.3 The if-else Statement

CONCEPT: An if-else statement will execute one block of statements if its Boolean expression is true, or another block if its Boolean expression is false.

The previous section introduced the single alternative decision structure (the if statement), which has one alternative path of execution. Now we will look at the *dual alternative decision structure*, which has two possible paths of execution—one path is taken if the Boolean expression is true, and the other path is taken if the Boolean expression is false. Figure 6-7 shows an example flowchart for a dual alternative decision structure.

Figure 6-7 A dual alternative decision structure

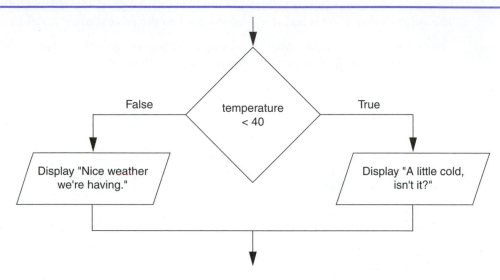

The decision structure in the flowchart tests the expression `temperature < 40`. If this expression is true, the message "A little cold, isn't it?" is displayed. If the expression is false, the message "Nice weather we're having." is displayed.

In code we write a dual alternative decision structure as an `if-else` statement. Here is the general format of the `if-else` statement:

```
if (expression)
{
     statement
     statement
     etc.
}
else
{
     statement
     statement
     etc.
}
```

An `if-else` statement has two parts: an `if` clause and an `else` clause. Just like a regular `if` statement, the `if-else` statement tests a Boolean expression. If the expression is true, the block of statements following the `if` clause is executed, and then control of the program jumps to the statement that follows the `if-else` statement. If the Boolean expression is false, the block of statements following the `else` clause is executed, and then control of the program jumps to the statement that follows the `if-else` statement. This action is described in Figure 6-8.

Figure 6-8 Conditional execution in an `if-else` statement

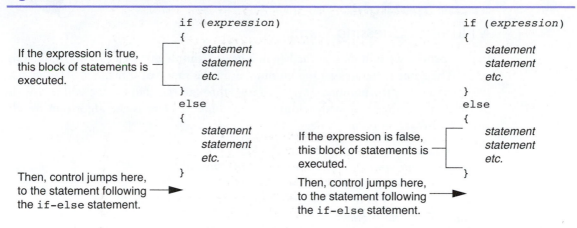

The `if-else` statement has two sets of conditionally executed statements. One set is executed only under the condition that the Boolean expression is true, and the other set is executed only under the condition that the Boolean expression is false. Under no circumstances will both sets of conditionally executed statements be executed.

If either set of conditionally executed statements contains only one statement, the curly braces are not required. For example, the following general format shows only one statement following the `if` clause and only one statement following the `else` clause:

```
if (expression)
     statement
else
     statement
```

Although the curly braces are not required when there is only one conditionally executed statement, it is still a good idea to use them, as shown in the following general format:

```
if (expression)
{
     statement
}
else
{
     statement
}
```

When we were discussing the regular `if` statement we mentioned that this is a good style of programming because it cuts down on errors. If there is more than one conditionally executed statement following either the `if` clause or the `else` clause, those statements *must* be enclosed in curly braces. If you get into the habit of always enclosing the conditionally executed statements in a set of curly braces, it's less likely that you will forget them.

In the Spotlight:

A Number Guessing Game

In this section, we will look at the beginnings of a simple number guessing game program. The game generates a random number in the range of 0 through 10, and asks the user to guess the number. As we progress through the chapter, we will revisit the program and enhance it with additional capabilities. Here is the algorithm for the game, expressed in pseudocode:

Seed the random number generator
Generate a random number in the range of 0 through 10
Display "Can you guess the number I'm thinking of?"
Display "Hint: It's in the range of 0 through 10."
Display "Enter your guess."
Read the user's guess
If the user's guess is equal to the random number
    Display "Congratulations! You guessed it!"
Else
    Display "Sorry, that is not the number."

Program 6-2 shows the code for the program.

Program 6-2   (NumberGuessVersion1.cpp)

```
1   // Version 1 of the number guessing game
2   #include "DarkGDK.h"
3
4   void DarkGDK()
5   {
6      // Variables
7      int myNumber;     // To hold the random number
8      int guess;        // To hold the user's guess
9
10     // Constant for the number's maximum range.
11     const int MAX_NUMBER = 10;
12
13     // Seed the random number generator.
14     dbRandomize( dbTimer() );
15
16     // Get a random number
17     myNumber = dbRND(MAX_NUMBER);
18
19     // Prompt the user for a guess.
20     dbPrint("Can you guess the number I'm thinking of?");
21     dbPrint("Hint: It's in the range of 0 through 10.");
22     dbPrint("Enter your guess.");
23     guess = atoi( dbInput() );
24
25     // Test the user's guess and display
26     // an appropriate message.
```

```
27        if (guess == myNumber)
28        {
29            dbPrint("Congratulations! You guessed it!");
30        }
31        else
32        {
33            dbPrint("Sorry, that is not the number.");
34        }
35
36        // Wait for the user to press a key.
37        dbPrint();
38        dbPrint("Press any key to end the program...");
39        dbWaitKey();
40  }
```

Lines 7 and 8 declare two variables. The myNumber variable will hold the random number and the guess variable will hold the user's guess. Line 11 declares a constant named MAX_NUMBER, initialized with the value 10. This constant will be used as the maximum limit for the random number. Line 14 seeds the random number generator. Line 17 gets a random number from the dbRND function and assigns it to myNumber.

Lines 20 through 22 display messages introducing the game, and prompt the user to enter his or her guess. Line 23 uses dbInput to read the user's input from the keyboard, uses atoi to convert the input to an int, and assigns the resulting value to the guess variable.

The if-else statement that begins in line 27 determines whether the user guessed the number. If the expression guess == myNumber is true, the statement in line 29 is executed, and then the program jumps to the statement in line 37. If the expression is false, the statement in line 33 is executed, and then the program jumps to the statement in line 37. Figure 6-9 shows three example executions of the program.

Figure 6-9 Three example executions of Program 6-2

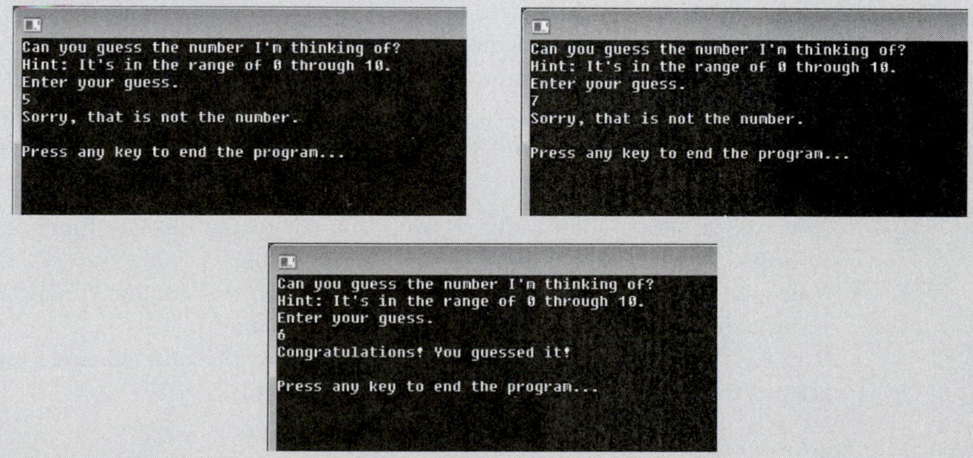

Checkpoint

6.9. Describe how a dual alternative decision structure works.

6.10. In an if-else statement, under what circumstances do the statements that appear after the else clause?

6.11. Write an if-else statement that determines whether y is less than 0. If this is true, set x to 0. Otherwise, set x to 320.

6.4   Nested Decision Structures and the if-else-if Statement

CONCEPT: To test more than one condition, a decision structure can be nested inside another decision structure.

In Section 6.1, we mentioned that a control structure determines the order in which a set of statements execute. Programs are usually designed as combinations of different control structures. For example, Figure 6-10 shows a flowchart that combines a decision structure with two sequence structures.

The flowchart in the figure starts with a sequence structure. Assuming you have an outdoor thermometer in your window, the first step is *Go to the window*, and the next step is *Read thermometer*. A decision structure appears next, testing the condition *Cold outside*. If this is true, the action *Wear a coat* is performed. Another sequence structure appears next. The step *Open the door* is performed, followed by *Go outside*.

Quite often, structures must be nested inside of other structures. For example, look at the partial flowchart in Figure 6-11. It shows a decision structure with a sequence structure nested inside. The decision structure tests the condition *Cold outside*. If that condition is true, the steps in the sequence structure are executed.

You can also nest decision structures inside of other decision structures. This is commonly done in programs that need to test more than one condition. For example, suppose you want to determine whether the pixel located at a specific location has a reddish tint, such that its red component is at least 200, and its green and blue components are each less than 100. You can use the dbRGBR, dbRGBG, and dbRGBB functions to extract the red, green, and blue components of a color. The functions work like this:

- You pass a DWORD color value as an argument to the dbRGBR function and it returns that color's red component as an int value.
- You pass a DWORD color value as an argument to the dbRGBG function and it returns that color's green component as an int value.
- You pass a DWORD color value as an argument to the dbRGBB function and it returns that color's blue component as an int value.

Figure 6-10 Combining sequence structures with a decision structure

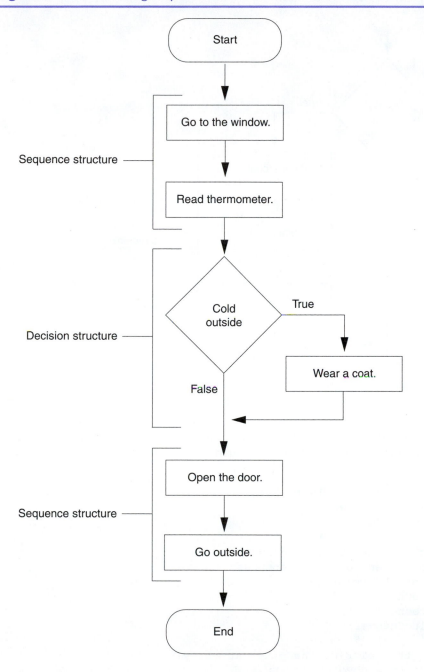

Figure 6-11 A sequence structure nested inside a decision structure

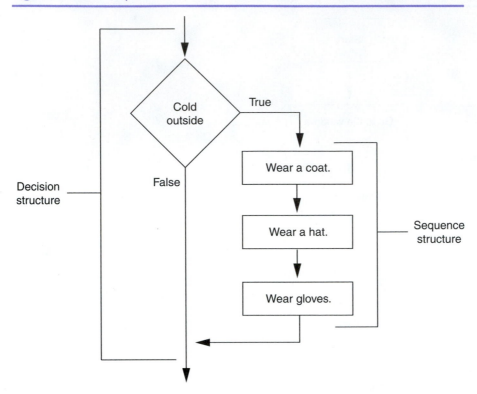

Assume the variables x and y hold a set of *XY* coordinates. The following code shows how you can get the color of the pixel located at (x, y) and determine whether the color is of the reddish tint described earlier.

```
// Declare a variable to hold the
// color of a pixel.
DWORD pixelColor;

// Declare variables to hold the
// red, green, and blue components
// of an RGB color.
int redChannel;
int greenChannel;
int blueChannel;

// Get the color of the pixel at (x, y).
pixelColor = dbPoint(x, y);

// Extract the red, green, and blue
// components of the color.
redChannel = dbRGBR(pixelColor);
greenChannel = dbRGBG(pixelColor);
blueChannel = dbRGBB(pixelColor);
```

```
// Determine whether this is the desired
// reddish shade.
if (redChannel >= 200)
{
    if (greenChannel < 100)
    {
        if (blueChannel < 100)
        {
            dbPrint("That pixel is reddish.");
        }
    }

}
```

Let's take a closer look at the nested `if` statements. The first `if` statement tests the expression `redChannel >= 200`. If this is true, the next `if` statement tests the expression `greenChannel < 100`. If this is true, the next `if` statement tests the expression `blueChannel < 100`. If this is true, the message "That pixel is reddish" is displayed. Figure 6-12 shows a flowchart for nested `if` statements.

Figure 6-12 Flowchart for nested `if` statements

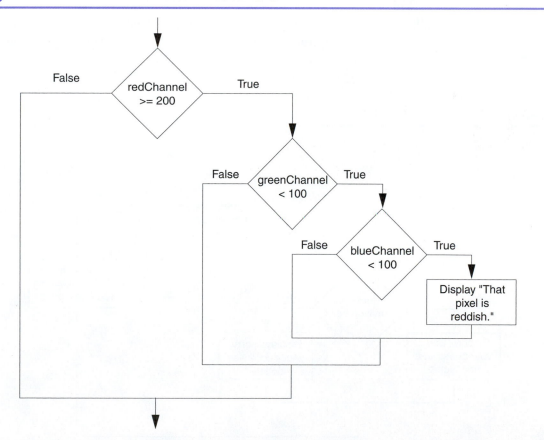

In the Spotlight:

Enhancing the Number Guessing
Game with Feedback

Suppose we want to enhance the number guessing game that we discussed previously so it gives some feedback. If the user guesses the wrong number, the program should indicate whether the guess was too low or too high. We need two decision structures. The first determines whether the user guessed correctly. If the user did not guess correctly, the second determines whether the guess was too low or too high. The following pseudocode shows how we can develop the logic by nesting an `if-else` statement inside another `if-else` statement:

> *If the user's guess is equal to the random number*
>> *Display "Congratulations! You guessed it!"*
> *Else*
>> *If the user's guess is less than the random number*
>>> *Display "Sorry, your guess was too low."*
>> *Else*
>>> *Display "Sorry, your guess was too high.*

Figure 6-13 shows a flowchart for the algorithm.

If we follow the flow of execution, we see that the expression `guess == myNumber` is tested. If this expression is true, there is no need to perform further tests; we know that the user has guessed the number. If the expression is false, however, we use a nested decision structure to test the expression `guess < myNumber`. If this expression is true,

Figure 6-13 A nested decision structure

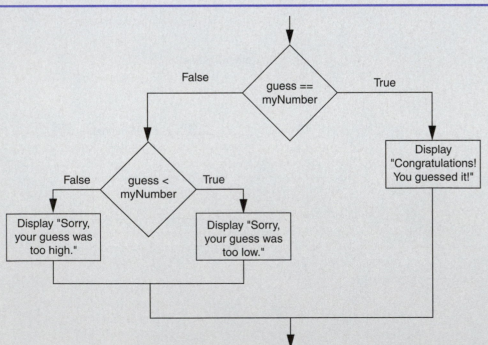

we display a message indicating the guess was too low. If this expression is false, we display a message indicating the guess was too high. Program 6-3 shows the code for the complete program. Figure 6-14 shows the output of two example executions.

Program 6-3   **(NumberGuessVersion2.cpp)**

```
1    // Version 2 of the number guessing game
2    #include "DarkGDK.h"
3
4    void DarkGDK()
5    {
6        // Variables
7        int myNumber;   // To hold the random number
8        int guess;      // To hold the user's guess
9
10       // Constant for the number's maximum range.
11       const int MAX_NUMBER = 10;
12
13       // Seed the random number generator.
14       dbRandomize( dbTimer() );
15
16       // Get a random number
17       myNumber = dbRND(MAX_NUMBER);
18
19       // Prompt the user for a guess.
20       dbPrint("Can you guess the number I'm thinking of?");
21       dbPrint("Hint: It's in the range of 0 through 10.");
22       dbPrint("Enter your guess.");
23       guess = atoi( dbInput() );
24
25       // Test the user's guess and display
26       // an appropriate message.
27       if (guess == myNumber)
28       {
29           dbPrint("Congratulations! You guessed it!");
30       }
31       else
32       {
33           if (guess < myNumber)
34           {
35               dbPrint("Sorry, your guess was too low.");
36           }
37           else
38           {
39               dbPrint("Sorry, your guess was too high.");
40           }
41       }
42
43       // Wait for the user to press a key.
44       dbPrint();
45       dbPrint("Press any key to end the program...");
46       dbWaitKey();
47   }
```

Figure 6-14 Output of two example executions of Program 6-3

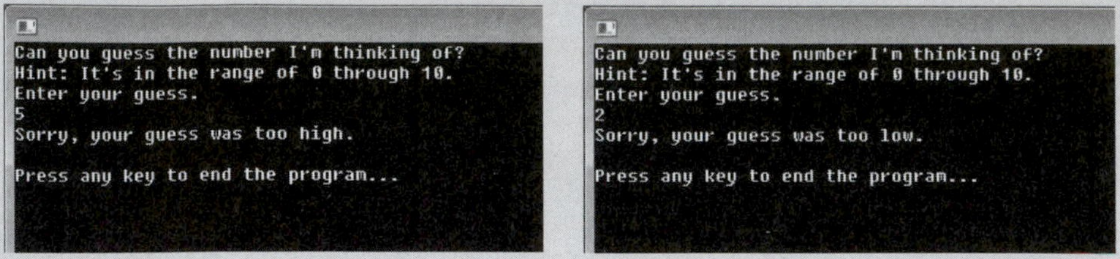

```
Can you guess the number I'm thinking of?
Hint: It's in the range of 0 through 10.
Enter your guess.
5
Sorry, your guess was too high.

Press any key to end the program...
```

```
Can you guess the number I'm thinking of?
Hint: It's in the range of 0 through 10.
Enter your guess.
2
Sorry, your guess was too low.

Press any key to end the program...
```

Programming Style and Nested Decision Structures

For debugging purposes, it is important to use proper alignment and indentation in a nested decision structure. This makes it easier to see which actions are performed by each part of the structure. For example, the following code is functionally equivalent to lines 25 through 39 in Program 6-3. Although this code is logically correct, it would be very difficult to debug because it is not properly indented.

```
if (guess == myNumber)
{
dbPrint("Congratulations! You guessed it!");
}
else
{
if (guess < myNumber)
{
dbPrint("Sorry, your guess was too low.");
}
else
{
dbPrint("Sorry, your guess was too high.");
}
}
```

Proper indentation and alignment also makes it easier to see which `if` and `else` clauses belong together, as shown in Figure 6-15.

Figure 6-15 Alignment of `if` and `else` clauses

```
              ┌──► if (guess == myNumber)
This if       │    {
and else ─────┤        dbPrint("Congratulations! You guessed it!");
go together.  │    }
              └──► else
                   {
                 ┌──► if (guess < myNumber)
This if          │    {
and else ────────┤        dbPrint("Sorry, your guess was too low.");
go together.     │    }
                 └──► else
                      {
                          dbPrint("Sorry, your guess was too high.");
                      }
                   }
```

The `if-else-if` Statement

Even though Program 6-3 is a simple example, the logic of nested decision structures can become complex. C++ provides a special version of the decision structure known as the `if-else-if` statement, which makes this type of logic simpler to write. Here is the general format of the `if-else-if` statement:

```
if (BooleanExpression_1)
{
    statement
    statement
    etc.
}
else if (BooleanExpression_2)
{
    statement
    statement
    etc.
}
Insert as many else if clauses as necessary...
else
{
    statement
    statement
    etc.
}
```

When the statement executes, `BooleanExpression_1` is tested. If `BooleanExpression_1` is true, the block of statements that immediately follows is executed, and the rest of the structure is skipped. If `BooleanExpression_1` is false, however, the program jumps to the very next `else if` clause and tests `BooleanExpression_2`. If it is true, the block of statements that immediately follows is executed, and the rest the structure is then skipped. This process continues until a condition is found to be true, or no more `else if` clauses are left. If none of the conditions is true, the block of statements following the `else` clause is executed.

The code shown in Program 6-4 is another revision of the number guessing game. This version of the program uses an `if-else-if` statement instead of nested `if-else` statements. The output is the same as that of Program 6-3.

Program 6-4   (`NumberGuess3.cpp`)

```
1   // Version 3 of the number guessing game
2   #include "DarkGDK.h"
3
4   void DarkGDK()
5   {
6       // Variables
7       int myNumber;   // To hold the random number
8       int guess;      // To hold the user's guess
9
10      // Constant for the number's maximum range.
11      const int MAX_NUMBER = 10;
```

```
12
13        // Seed the random number generator.
14        dbRandomize( dbTimer() );
15
16        // Get a random number
17        myNumber = dbRND(MAX_NUMBER);
18
19        // Prompt the user for a guess.
20        dbPrint("Can you guess the number I'm thinking of?");
21        dbPrint("Hint: It's in the range of 0 through 10.");
22        dbPrint("Enter your guess.");
23        guess = atoi( dbInput() );
24
25        // Test the user's guess and display the
26        // appropriate message.
27        if (guess == myNumber)
28        {
29            dbPrint("Congratulations! You guessed it!");
30        }
31        else if (guess < myNumber)
32        {
33            dbPrint("Sorry, your guess was too low.");
34        }
35        else
36        {
37            dbPrint("Sorry, your guess was too high.");
38        }
39
40        // Wait for the user to press a key.
41        dbPrint();
42        dbPrint("Press any key to end the program...");
43        dbWaitKey();
44    }
```

Notice the alignment and indentation that is used with the if-else-if statement: The if, else if, and else clauses are all aligned, and the conditionally executed statements are indented.

You never have to use the if-else-if statement because its logic can be coded with nested if-else statements. However, a long series of nested if-else statements has two particular disadvantages when you are debugging code:

- The code can grow complex and become difficult to understand.
- Because indenting is important in nested statements, a long series of nested if-else statements can become too long to be displayed on the computer screen without horizontal scrolling. Also, long statements tend to "wrap around" when printed on paper, making the code even more difficult to read.

The logic of an if-else-if statement is usually easier to follow than a long series of nested if-else statements. And, because all of the clauses are aligned in an if-else-if statement, the lengths of the lines in the statement tend to be shorter.

Checkpoint

6.12. Convert the following set of nested `if-else` statements to an `if-else-if` statement:

```
if (number == 1)
{
    dbPrint("One");
}
else
{
    if (number == 2)
    {
        dbPrint("Two");
    }
    else
    {
        if (number == 3)
        {
            dbPrint("Three");
        }
        else
        {
            dbPrint("Unknown");
        }
    }
}
```

6.5

Repetition Structures: The while Loop and the do-while Loop

CONCEPT: A repetition structure causes a statement or set of statements to execute repeatedly.

Programmers commonly have to write code that performs the same task over and over. For example, suppose you want to write a program that fills the screen with randomly placed dots to create the background of a space-themed game. Although it would not be a good design, one approach would be to write the code to draw a single dot, and then repeat that code for the remaining dots. For example, look at the following:

```
// Generate a random point
dotX = dbRND(MAX_X);
dotY = dbRND(MAX_Y)

// Draw a dot
dbDot(dotX, dotY);

// Generate a random point
dotX = dbRND(MAX_X);
dotY = dbRND(MAX_Y)
```

```
// Draw a dot
dbDot(dotX, dotY);

// Generate a random point
dotX = dbRND(MAX_X);
dotY = dbRND(MAX_Y)

// Draw a dot
dbDot(dotX, dotY);

// Generate a random point
dotX = dbRND(MAX_X);
dotY = dbRND(MAX_Y)

// Draw a dot
dbDot(dotX, dotY);
```

And this code goes on and on . . .

As you can see, this code is one long sequence structure containing a lot of duplicated code. There are several disadvantages to this approach, including the following:

- The duplicated code makes the program large.
- Writing a long sequence of statements can be time consuming.
- If part of the duplicated code has to be corrected or changed then the correction or change has to be done many times.

Instead of writing the same sequence of statements over and over, a better way to perform an operation repeatedly is to write the code for the operation once, and then place that code in a structure that makes the computer repeat it as many times as necessary. This can be done with a *repetition structure*, which is more commonly known as a *loop*.

Condition-Controlled and Count-Controlled Loops

We will look at two broad categories of loops: condition-controlled and count-controlled. A *condition-controlled loop* uses a true/false condition to control the number of times that it repeats. A *count-controlled loop* repeats a specific number of times. In C++, you use the `while` and `do-while` statements to write condition-controlled loops, and you use the `for` statement to write a count-controlled loop. In this chapter, we will demonstrate how to write both types of loops.

The `while` Loop

The `while` loop gets its name from the way it works: *while a Boolean expression is true, do some task*. The loop has two parts: (1) a Boolean expression that is tested for a true or false value, and (2) a statement or set of statements that is repeated as long as the Boolean expression is true. The flowchart in Figure 6-16 shows the logic of a `while` loop.

The diamond symbol represents the Boolean expression that is tested. Notice what happens if the Boolean expression is true: one or more statements are executed and

Figure 6-16 The logic of a while loop

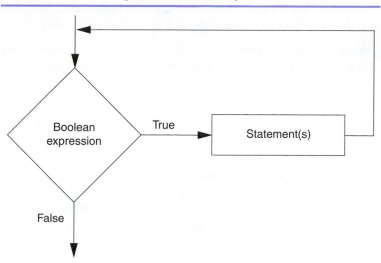

the program's execution flows back to the point just above the diamond symbol. The Boolean expression is tested again, and if it is true, the process repeats. If the Boolean expression is false, the program exits the loop. Each time the loop executes its statement or statements, we say the loop is *iterating*, or performing an *iteration*.

Here is the general format of the while loop:

```
while (BooleanExpression)
{
        statement
        statement
        etc.
}
```

We will refer to the first line as the *while clause*. The while clause begins with the word while, followed by a Boolean expression that is enclosed in parentheses. Beginning on the next line is a block of statements that are enclosed in curly braces. This block of statements is known as the *body* of the loop.

When the while loop executes, the Boolean expression is tested. If the Boolean expression is true, the statements that appear in the body of the loop are executed, and then the loop starts over. If the Boolean expression is false, the loop ends and the program resumes execution at the statement immediately following the loop.

We say that the statements in the body of the loop are conditionally executed because they are executed only under the condition that the Boolean expression is true. If you are writing a while loop that has only one statement in its body, you do not have to enclose the statement inside curly braces. Such a loop can be written in the following general format:

```
while (BooleanExpression)
        statement
```

When a `while` loop written in this format executes, the Boolean expression is tested. If it is true, the one statement that appears on the next line will be executed, and then the loop starts over. If the Boolean expression is false, however, the loop ends.

Although the curly braces are not required when there is only one statement in the loop's body, it is still a good idea to use them, as shown in the following general format:

```
while (BooleanExpression)
{
    statement
}
```

When we discussed the various `if` statements, we mentioned that this is a good style of programming because it cuts down on errors. If you have more than one statement in the body of a loop, those statements *must* be enclosed in curly braces. If you get into the habit of always enclosing the conditionally executed statements in a set of curly braces, it's less likely that you will forget them.

You should also notice that the statements in the body of the loop are indented. As with `if` statements, this indentation makes the code easier to read and debug. By indenting the statements in the body of the loop you visually set them apart from the surrounding code. Most programmers use this style of indentation when writing loops.

In the Spotlight:

Enhancing the Number Guessing Game with a `while` Loop

Now we will revise the number guessing game with a major enhancement. We will add a `while` loop that repeatedly allows the user to enter guesses until he or she gets the right number. Program 6-5 shows the code, and Figure 6-17 shows an example output of the program.

Program 6-5   (`NumberGuess4.cpp`)

```
1    // Version 4 of the number guessing game
2    #include "DarkGDK.h"
3
4    void DarkGDK()
5    {
6        // Variables
7        int myNumber;    // To hold the random number
8        int guess;       // To hold the user's guess
9
10       // Constant for the number's maximum range.
11       const int MAX_NUMBER = 10;
12
```

```
13        // Seed the random number generator.
14        dbRandomize( dbTimer() );
15
16        // Get a random number
17        myNumber = dbRND(MAX_NUMBER);
18
19        // Prompt the user for the first guess.
20        dbPrint("Can you guess the number I'm thinking of?");
21        dbPrint("Hint: It's in the range of 0 through 10.");
22        dbPrint("Enter your guess.");
23        guess = atoi( dbInput() );
24
25        // Let the user continue to guess until
26        // he or she gets the right number.
27        while (guess != myNumber)
28        {
29            // Give the user a hint.
30            if (guess < myNumber)
31            {
32                dbPrint("Sorry, that's too low. Guess again.");
33            }
34            else
35            {
36                dbPrint("Sorry, that's too high. Guess again");
37            }
38
39            // Get the user's next guess.
40            guess = atoi( dbInput() );
41        }
42
43        // Congratulate the user.
44        dbPrint("Congratulations! You guessed it!");
45
46        // Wait for the user to press a key.
47        dbPrint();
48        dbPrint("Press any key to end the program...");
49        dbWaitKey();
50    }
```

Figure 6-17 Output of Program 6-5

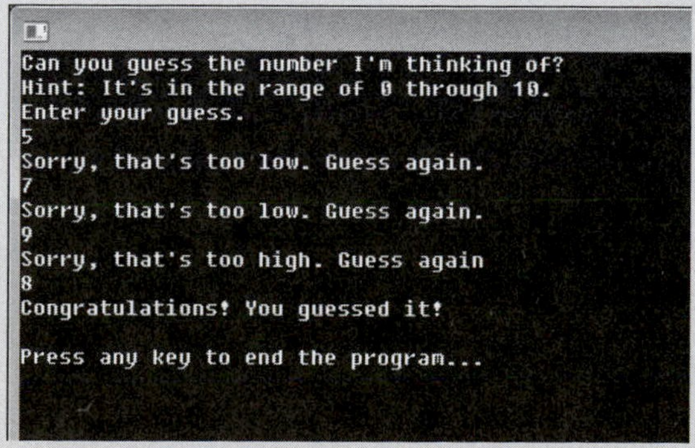

The first part of this program, through line 23, is identical to the previous versions. After the user's guess has been entered, and assigned to the guess variable, the while loop that begins at line 27 executes. The loop begins like this:

```
while (guess != myNumber)
```

When the loop starts executing, it tests the expression guess != myNumber. If the expression is true (guess is not equal to myNumber), the block of statements in lines 28 through 41 is executed. Inside this block of statements, the if-else statement in lines 30 through 37 determines whether the user's guess is too low or too high, and displays a message saying so. Then, the user's next guess is read from the keyboard in line 40 and assigned to the guess variable.

After that, the loop starts over at line 27. Once again, it tests the expression guess != myNumber. If the expression is true, the block of statements in lines 28 through 41 is executed again. This cycle repeats until the expression guess != myNumber is tested in line 27 and found to be false. When that happens the loop ends, as shown in Figure 6-18.

Figure 6-18 The while loop in Program 6-5

The while Loop Is a Pretest Loop

The while loop is known as a *pretest* loop, which means it tests its Boolean expression *before* performing an iteration. For example, in Program 6-5, the following statement in line 23 reads the user's input and assigns it to the guess variable:

```
guess = atoi( dbInput() );
```

Then, the while loop in line 27 begins:

```
while (guess != myNumber)
```

The loop will perform an iteration only if the expression guess != myNumber is true. This means that if the user's first guess is the correct number, the loop will not iterate at all. Figure 6-19 shows an example of the program's output when this happens.

Figure 6-19 Output of Program 6-5 when the user's first guess is correct

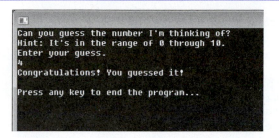

This is an important characteristic of the while loop: it will never execute if its condition is false to start with. In some programs, if you want to make sure the loop executes the first time, you will have to set things up properly. For example, Program 6-6 uses a loop to draw 10 bricks at random locations on the screen. (You saw a program similar to this in Chapter 4.)

Program 6-6   **(RandomBricksLoop.cpp)**

```
 1   // This program uses a loop to draw random bricks.
 2   #include "DarkGDK.h"
 3
 4   // Function prototype
 5   void drawBrick(int, int);
 6
 7   //****************************************************
 8   // DarkGDK function                                 *
 9   //****************************************************
10   void DarkGDK ()
11   {
12       // Variables to hold XY coordinates.
13       int x, y;
14
15       // Variable to hold the number of bricks.
16       // This variable must be initialized.
17       int numBricks = 10;
18
19       // Seed the random number generator.
20       dbRandomize( dbTimer() );
21
22       // Draw the bricks.
23       while (numBricks > 0)
24       {
25           // Draw a brick at a random location.
```

```
26            x = dbRND(600);
27            y = dbRND(460);
28            drawBrick(x, y);
29
30            // Subtract 1 from numBricks.
31            numBricks -= 1;
32        }
33
34        // Pause the program until the user presses a key.
35        dbWaitKey();
36    }
37
38    //*********************************************************
39    // The drawBrick function draws a red brick. The leftX *
40    // and leftY parameters specify the XY coordinates of  *
41    // the brick's lower left corner. The brick will be 40 *
42    // pixels wide and 20 pixels high.                      *
43    //*********************************************************
44    void drawBrick(int leftX, int leftY)
45    {
46        // Constants for the brick's width and height
47        const int WIDTH = 40;
48        const int HEIGHT = 20;
49
50        // Color constants
51        const DWORD RED = dbRGB(255, 0, 0);
52        const DWORD BLACK = dbRGB(0, 0, 0);
53
54        // Set the drawing color to red.
55        dbInk(RED, BLACK);
56
57        // Draw a brick at the specified coordinates.
58        // The brick is 40 pixels wide by 20 pixels high.
59        dbBox(leftX, leftY, leftX+WIDTH, leftY+HEIGHT);
60    }
```

Notice that the while loop, in line 23, starts like this:

```
while (numBricks > 0)
```

The loop will perform an iteration only if the expression numBricks > 0 is true. This means that the numBricks variable must already contain a value that is greater than 0. To make sure this expression is true the first time the loop executes, we initialized the variable with the value 10 in line 17. Figure 6-20 shows an example of the program's output.

Let's take a closer look at what happens inside the loop. The statements in lines 26 and 27 get random numbers for the x and y variables. Line 28 calls the drawBrick function, passing x and y as arguments. The function draws a "brick" (a red rectangle) at the coordinates specified by the arguments x and y. Then the statement in line 31 subtracts 1 from numBricks. This statement is important for the operation of the loop. The numBricks variable starts with the value 10, and each time the loop iterates, line 31 subtracts 1 from numBricks. When numBricks reaches 0, the loop stops.

Figure 6-20 Output of Program 6-6

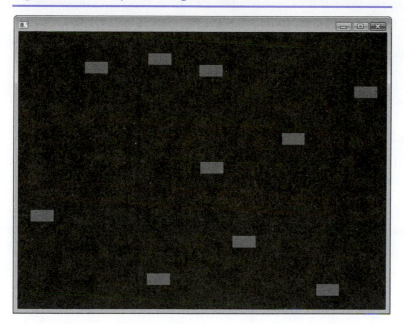

The numBricks variable is an example of a *loop control variable*. Its value is tested by the loop, and controls whether the loop will iterate.

Infinite Loops

In all but rare cases, loops must contain within themselves a way to terminate. This means that something inside the loop must eventually make the loop's Boolean expression false. The loop in Program 6-6 stops when the expression numBricks > 0 is false. The numBricks variable eventually reaches the value 0 because a statement inside the loop (line 31) subtracts 1 from numBricks. The value of numBricks gets smaller with each iteration, and when it reaches 0, the loop stops.

If a loop does not have a way of stopping, it is called an infinite loop. An *infinite loop* continues to repeat until the program is interrupted. Infinite loops usually occur when the programmer forgets to write code inside the loop that makes the test condition false. For example, in Program 6-6, suppose we forgot to write the statement that subtracts 1 from numBricks, as shown here:

```
while (numBricks > 0)
{
    // Draw a brick at a random location.
    x = dbRND(600);
    y = dbRND(460);
    drawBrick(x, y);
}
```

Each time the expression numBricks > 0 is tested at the beginning of the loop, numBricks will contain the value 10. As a consequence, the loop has no way of stopping.

> **NOTE:** If you decide to try this by removing line 31 from Program 6-6, you may not see anything displayed in the program's window. This is because the infinite loop interferes with the way that the Dark GDK refreshes the screen. In Chapter 7 we will discuss the screen refreshing system, and how you can write programs that manage it.

The `do-while` Loop: A Posttest Loop

You have learned that the `while` loop is a pretest loop, which means it tests its Boolean expression before performing an iteration. The `do-while` loop is a *posttest* loop. This means it performs an iteration before testing its Boolean expression. As a result, the `do-while` loop always performs at least one iteration, even if its Boolean expression is false to begin with. The logic of a `do-while` loop is shown in Figure 6-21.

Figure 6-21 The logic of a `do-while` loop

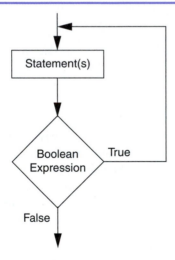

In the flowchart, one or more statements are executed, and then a Boolean expression is tested. If the Boolean expression is true, the program's execution flows back to the point just above the first statement in the body of the loop, and this process repeats. If the Boolean expression is false, the program exits the loop.

In code, the `do-while` loop looks something like an inverted `while` loop. Here is the general format of the `do-while` loop:

```
do
{
    statement
    statement
    etc.
} while (BooleanExpression);
```

As with the while loop, the braces are optional if there is only one statement in the body of the loop. This is the general format of the do-while loop with only one conditionally executed statement:

```
do
    statement
while (BooleanExpression);
```

Notice that a semicolon appears at the very end of the do-while statement. This semicolon is required; leaving it out is a common error.

The do-while loop is a posttest loop. This means it does not test its Boolean expression until it has completed an iteration. As a result, the do-while loop always performs at least one iteration, even if the expression is false to begin with. This differs from the behavior of a while loop. For example, in the following while loop the statement that calls dbPrint will not execute at all:

```
int number = 1;
while (number < 0)
{
    dbPrint( dbStr(number) );
}
```

But, the statement that calls dbPrint in the following do-while loop will execute one time because the do-while loop does not test the expression number < 0 until the end of the iteration.

```
int number = 1;
do
{
    dbPrint( dbStr(number) );
} while (number < 0);
```

Checkpoint

6.13. What is a repetition structure?

6.14. What is a condition-controlled loop? What is a count-controlled loop?

6.15. What is a loop iteration?

6.16. What is the difference between a pretest loop and a posttest loop?

6.17. Does the while loop test its condition before or after it performs an iteration?

6.18. Does the do-while loop test its condition before or after it performs an iteration?

6.19. What is an infinite loop?

6.6   The Increment and Decrement Operators

CONCEPT: To increment a variable means to increase its value, and to decrement a variable means to decrease its value. C++ provides special operators to increment and decrement variables.

To *increment* a variable means to increase its value and to *decrement* a variable means to decrease its value. Both of the following statements increment the variable num by one:

```
num = num + 1;
num += 1;
```

And num is decremented by one in both of the following statements:

```
num = num - 1;
num -= 1;
```

Incrementing and decrementing is so commonly done in programs that C++ provides a set of simple unary operators designed just for incrementing and decrementing variables. The increment operator is ++ and the decrement operator is --. The following statement uses the ++ operator to add 1 to num:

```
num++;
```

After this statement executes, the value of num will be increased by 1. The following statement uses the -- operator to subtract 1 from num:

```
num--;
```

NOTE: The ++ operator is pronounced "plus plus" and the -- operator is pronounced "minus minus." The expression num++ is pronounced "num plus plus" and the expression num-- is pronounced "num minus minus."

In these examples, we have written the ++ and -- operators after their operands (or, on the right side of their operands). This is called *postfix mode*. The operators can also be written before (or, on the left side) of their operands, which is called *prefix mode*. Here are examples:

```
++num;
--num;
```

When you write a simple statement to increment or decrement a variable, such as the ones shown here, it doesn't matter if you use prefix mode or postfix mode. The operators do the same thing in either mode. However, if you write statements that mix these operators with other operators or with other operations, there is a difference in the way the two modes work. Such complex code can be difficult to understand and debug. When we use the increment and decrement operators, we will do so only in ways that are straightforward and easy to understand, such as the statements previously shown.

We introduce these operators at this point because they are commonly used in certain types of loops. In the next section, which discusses the for loop, you will see these operators used often.

6.7 Repetition Structures: The for Loop

CONCEPT: A count-controlled loop iterates a specific number of times. In C++, you use the **for** statement to write a count-controlled loop.

As mentioned earlier, a count-controlled loop iterates a specific number of times. Count-controlled loops are commonly used in programs. For example, suppose a business is open six days per week, and you are going to write a program that calculates the total sales for a week. You will need a loop that iterates exactly six times. Each time the loop iterates, it will prompt the user to enter the sales for one day.

The way that a count-controlled loop works is simple: the loop keeps a count of the number of times it iterates, and when the count reaches a specified amount, the loop stops. A count-controlled loop uses a variable known as a *counter variable*, or simply *counter*, to store the number of iterations that it has performed. Using the counter variable, the loop performs the following three actions, which are known as the *initialization*, *test*, and *increment*:

1. **Initialization:** Before the loop begins, the counter variable is initialized to a starting value. In many situations the starting value will be 1, but it can be other values depending on the nature of the problem.
2. **Test:** The loop tests the counter variable by comparing it to a maximum value. If the counter variable has not reached the maximum value yet, the loop iterates. If the counter has reached the maximum value, the program exits the loop.
3. **Increment:** To *increment* a variable means to increase its value. During each iteration, the loop increments the counter variable by adding 1 to it.

Figure 6-22 shows the general logic of a count-controlled loop. The initialization, test, and increment operations are indicated with the ①, ②, and ③ callouts.

Figure 6-22 Logic of a count-controlled loop

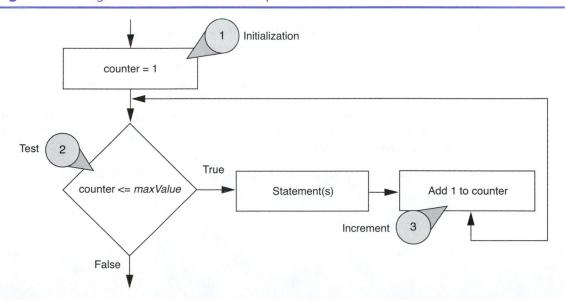

In the flowchart, assume that `counter` is an `int` variable. The first step is to set `counter` to the value 1. Then, we determine whether `counter` is less than or equal to a maximum value. If this is true, we execute the body of the loop. Otherwise, we exit the loop. Notice that in the body of the loop we execute one or more statements, and then we add one to `counter`. Adding one to the counter variable is critical because without this step the loop would iterate an infinite number of times.

Using the logic shown in the flowchart, the *maxValue* that we use in the comparison will be the number of times that we want the loop to iterate. For example, if we want the loop to iterate six times, we will test the expression `counter <= 6`. Likewise, if we want the loop to iterate 100 times, we will test the expression `counter <= 100`.

Count-controlled loops are so common that C++ provides a type of loop just for them. It is known as the *for loop*. The `for` loop is specifically designed to initialize, test, and increment a counter variable. Here is the general format of the `for` loop:

```
for ( InitializationExpression; TestExpression; IncrementExpression)
{
    statement
    statement
    etc.
}
```

The statements that appear inside the curly braces are the body of the loop. These are the statements that are executed each time the loop iterates. As with other control structures, the curly braces are optional if the body of the loop contains only one statement, as shown in the following general format:

```
for ( InitializationExpression; TestExpression; IncrementExpression)
    statement
```

As with other control structures, we always recommend using the curly braces, even if there is only one statement in the body of the loop. Let's look at each part of the loop.

The first line of the `for` loop is the *loop header*. After the key word `for`, there are three expressions inside the parentheses, separated by semicolons. (Notice that there is not a semicolon after the third expression.)

The first expression is the *initialization expression*. It is normally used to initialize a counter variable to its starting value. This is the first action performed by the loop, and it is only done once. The second expression is the *test expression*. This is a Boolean expression that controls the execution of the loop. As long as this expression is true, the body of the `for` loop will repeat. The `for` loop is a pretest loop, so it evaluates the test expression before each iteration. The third expression is the *increment expression*. It executes at the end of each iteration. Typically, this is a statement that increments the loop's counter variable.

Here is an example of a simple `for` loop that prints "Hello" five times:

```
for (count = 1; count <= 5; count++)
{
    dbPrint("Hello");
}
```

In this loop, the initialization expression is count = 1, the test expression is count <= 5, and the increment expression is count++. The body of the loop has one statement, which is the call to dbPrint. This is a summary of what happens when this loop executes:

1. The initialization expression count = 1 is executed. This assigns 1 to the count variable.
2. The expression count <= 5 is tested. If the expression is true, continue with Step 3. Otherwise, the loop is finished.
3. The statement dbPrint("Hello"); is executed.
4. The increment expression count++ is executed. This adds 1 to the count variable.
5. Go back to Step 2.

Okay, we've explained enough! Let's look at an actual program. Program 6-7 uses the for loop to draw 100 dots at random locations on the screen.

Program 6-7   (StarrySky.cpp)

```
1   // This program uses a for loop to
2   // draw 100 dots at random locations.
3   #include "DarkGDK.h"
4
5   void DarkGDK()
6   {
7       // Constants
8       const int MAX_X = 639;   // Maximum X value
9       const int MAX_Y = 479;   // Maximum Y value
10
11      // Variables
12      int count;   // Loop counter
13      int x, y;    // To hold X and Y coordinates
14
15      // Seed the random number generator.
16      dbRandomize( dbTimer() );
17
18      // Draw 100 random dots.
19      for (count = 1; count <= 100; count++)
20      {
21          // Get  set of random coordinates.
22          x = dbRND(MAX_X);
23          y = dbRND(MAX_Y);
24
25          // Draw a dot at that location.
26          dbDot(x, y);
27      }
28
29      // Wait for the user to press a key.
30      dbWaitKey();
31  }
```

In lines 8 and 9 we declare the constants MAX_X and MAX_Y to hold the maximum *X* and *Y* coordinate values. In line 12 we declare count, which we will use as the counter variable in the loop. In line 13 we declare the variables x and y, which will hold *X* and *Y* coordinates. In line 16 we seed the random number generator.

The for loop that draws the dots appears in lines 19 through 27. This is what's happening in the loop header:

- The initialization expression is count = 1. This assigns 1 to the count variable.
- The test expression is count <= 100.
- The increment expression is count++.

As a result of these expressions, the loop will iterate 100 times. As the loop iterates, the count variable will have the values 1 through 100.

NOTE: There are different ways to setup the counter variable in a for loop to achieve the same results. For example, the loop in Program 6-7 could have started like this:

```
for (count = 0; count < 100; count++)
```

In this example count is initialized with the value 0, and the loop iterates as long as count is less than 100. This loop will also iterate 100 times.

Declaring the Counter Variable in the Initialization Expression

Not only may the counter variable be initialized in the initialization expression, but also it may be declared there. The following code shows an example:

```
for (int count = 1; count <= 5; count++)
{
    dbPrint("Hello");
}
```

In this loop, the count variable is both declared and initialized in the initialization expression. If the variable is used only in the loop, it makes sense to declare it in the loop header. This makes the variable's purpose clearer.

When a variable is declared in the initialization expression of a for loop, the scope of the variable is limited to the loop. This means you cannot access the variable in statements outside the loop. For example, the following code would cause a compiler error because the last statement (the dbPrint call) cannot access the count variable.

```
for (int count = 1; count <= 5; count++)
{
    dbPrint("Hello");
}
dbPrint( dbStr(count) );
```

Using the Counter Variable in the Body of the Loop

In a count-controlled loop, the primary purpose of the counter variable is to keep a count of the number of times that the loop has iterated. In some situations, it is also helpful to use the counter variable in a calculation or other task within the body of the loop. For example, look at Program 6-8, which draws five concentric circles around the screen's center point. Figure 6-23 shows the program's output.

Program 6-8   **(LoopCircles.cpp)**

```
1   // This program draws five concentric circles
2   // around the screen's center point.
3   #include "DarkGDK.h"
4
5   void DarkGDK()
6   {
7       // Constants for the screen's center point
8       const int CENTER_X = dbScreenWidth() / 2;
9       const int CENTER_Y = dbScreenHeight() / 2;
10
11      // Constant for the first circle's radius
12      const int STARTING_RADIUS = 50;
13
14      // Variable to hold a circle's radius
15      int radius;
16
17      // Draw five concentric circles.
18      for (int count = 1; count <= 5; count++)
19      {
20          // Calculate this circle's radius.
21          radius = STARTING_RADIUS * count;
22
23          // Draw the circle.
24          dbCircle(CENTER_X, CENTER_Y, radius);
25      }
26
27      // Wait for the user to press a key.
28      dbWaitKey();
29  }
```

Look at line 18, which is the first line of the for loop. Notice that the counter variable is named count, and is initialized with the value 1. The loop iterates five times, and count is incremented after each iteration. Next, look at line 21. Notice that the count variable is used in the calculation of the circle's radius. The first circle's radius will be 50, the second circle's radius will be 100, the third circle's radius will be 150, and so forth.

Figure 6-23 Output of Program 6-8

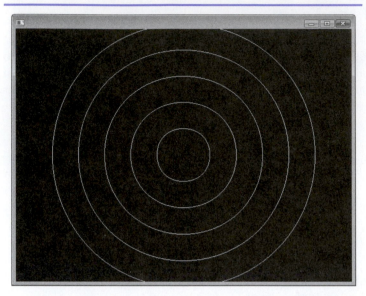

Incrementing by Values Other Than 1

The amount by which the counter variable is incremented in a for loop is typically 1. This makes it convenient to use the ++ operator in the increment expression. This is not a requirement, however. You can write virtually any expression you wish as the increment expression. For example, the following loop increments count by 10.

```
for (int count = 1; count <= 50; count += 10)
{
    // Calculate this circle's radius.
    radius = STARTING_RADIUS * count;

    // Draw the circle.
    dbCircle(CENTER_X, CENTER_Y, radius);
}
```

Notice that in this example the increment expression is count += 10. This means that at the end of each iteration, 10 will be added to count. During the first iteration count will be set to 1, during the second iteration count will be set to 11, during the third iteration count will be set to 21, and so forth.

Counting Backward by Decrementing the Counter Variable

Although the counter variable is usually incremented in a count-controlled loop, you can alternatively decrement the counter variable. For example, look at the following loop:

```
for (int count = 10; count >= 0; count--)
{
    dbPrint( dbStr(count) );
}
dbPrint("Blastoff!");
```

In this loop the `count` variable is initialized with the value 10. The loop iterates as long as `count` is greater than or equal to 0. At the end of each iteration, `count` is decremented by 1.

During the first iteration `counter` is 10, during the second iteration `counter` is 9, and so forth. If this were in an actual program, it would display the numbers 10, 9, 8, and so forth, down to 0, and then display Blastoff!

 Checkpoint

6.20. When you increment or decrement a variable, what are you doing?

6.21. What is a counter variable?

6.22. What three actions do count-controlled loops typically perform using the counter variable?

6.23. After the following code executes, what value will be stored in the `number` variable?

```
int number = 5;
number++;
```

6.24. What would the following code display?

```
for (int counter = 1; count <= 5; count++)
{
    dbPrint( dbStr(counter) );
}
```

6.25. What would the following code display?

```
for (int counter = 0; count <= 500; count += 100)
{
    dbPrint( dbStr(counter) );
}
```

 6.8

Using the `for` Loop to Process Pixels in an Image

CONCEPT: You can use the **for** loop to get the color of each pixel in an image and perform some operation using that color value.

An interesting use of loops is to step through each pixel in an image and perform some operation involving that pixel's color value. For example, suppose we want to load an image and count the number of pure blue pixels (with an RGB value of 0, 0, 255) contained in the image. Well, before we try to tackle the entire image, let's see if we can count just the number of pure blue pixels in the image's top row. First, we load the image like this:

```
dbLoadBitmap("Beach.jpg", 0);
```

Because the image is loaded as bitmap number 0, it will also be displayed on the screen. Next, we use the following statement to get the width of bitmap number 0 and assign that value to the width variable:

```
int width = dbBitmapWidth(0);
```

After this statement executes, the width variable will contain the number of pixels in each row. (For example, if the image has a resolution of 640 by 480, the width variable will be set to 640.)

Now let's think about how we are going to get the color of each pixel in the image's top row. Recall that the dbPoint function accepts a pixel's X and Y screen coordinates as arguments, and returns the color of that pixel. All of the pixels in the top row have a Y coordinate of 0, and their X coordinates range from 0 through 639. We can step through each pixel in the top row by writing a loop such as the one in the following code:

```
DWORD pixelColor;

for (int x = 0; x < width; x++)
{
    pixelColor = dbPoint(x, 0);
}
```

The first time the loop iterates, the x variable will be set to 0, so the statement in the body of the loop will get the color of the pixel at (0, 0). The second time the loop iterates, the x variable will be set to 1, so the statement in the body of the loop will get the color of the pixel at (1, 0). This continues until the last iteration, which will get the color of the pixel at (639, 0).

The code previously shown gets the color of each pixel in the image's top row, but doesn't do anything with those color values. Program 6-9 shows how we can perform the operation we originally set out to do—count the number of pure blue pixels in the top row. The program loads an image named BlueBars.bmp that we have specially designed to test our code. The program's output is shown in Figure 6-24. As you can see from the output, the image's top row has 442 pure blue pixels.

Program 6-9   (TopRowBluePixels.cpp)

```
 1   // This program loads an image and counts the number of
 2   // pure blue (RGB = 0,0,255) pixels in the top row.
 3   #include "DarkGDK.h"
 4
 5   void DarkGDK()
 6   {
 7       // Declare a constant for the color blue.
 8       const DWORD BLUE = dbRGB(0, 0, 255);
 9
10       // Variables
11       DWORD pixelColor;    // To hold a pixel color
12       int width;           // To hold the image's width
13       int totalBlue = 0;   // To hold the number of blue pixels
14
```

```
15        // Load an image as bitmap 0.
16        dbLoadBitmap("BlueBars.bmp", 0);
17
18        // Get the image's width.
19        width = dbBitmapWidth(0);
20
21        // Count the blue pixels in the top row.
22        for (int x = 0; x < width; x++)
23        {
24            // Get a pixel's color.
25            pixelColor = dbPoint(x, 0);
26
27            // If the pixel is blue, increment totalBlue.
28            if (pixelColor == BLUE)
29            {
30                totalBlue++;
31            }
32        }
33
34        // Prompt the user to press a key.
35        dbCenterText(319, 450, "Press any key.");
36        dbWaitKey();
37
38        // Clear the screen and display the number of blue pixels.
39        dbClear(0, 0, 0);
40        dbPrint("Number of pure blue pixels in the top row:");
41        dbPrint( dbStr(totalBlue) );
42
43        // Wait for the user to press a key.
44        dbWaitKey();
45  }
```

Figure 6-24 Output of Program 6-9

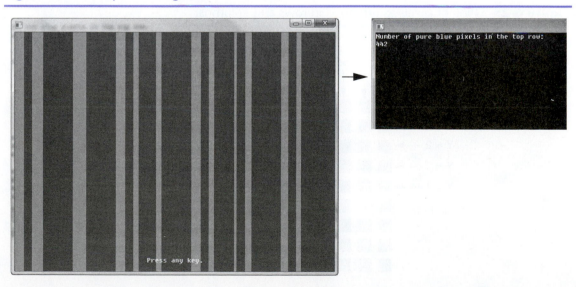

Let's take a closer look at the program. The following declarations are made in lines 8 through 13:

- Line 8 declares a constant named BLUE for the color blue.
- Line 11 declares a DWORD variable named pixelColor. We will use this variable to hold a pixel's color value.
- Line 12 declares an int named width. This variable will hold the width of a bitmap image.
- Line 13 declares an int named totalBlue, and initializes it with the value 0. We will use this variable to keep count of the total number of blue pixels that we find in the image's top row. As you will see in a moment, it is critical that this variable is initialized with 0.

Line 16 loads an image named BlueBars.bmp as bitmap number 0. Then, line 19 gets the bitmap's width and assigns it to the width variable.

The loop in lines 22 through 32 steps through each pixel in the image's top row. When the loop iterates, a pixel's color value is assigned to pixelColor in line 25. The if statement in line 28 determines whether the color is blue, and if so, it increments the totalBlue variable in line 30.

Can you see now why it was critical that the totalBlue variable was initialized with the value 0? Each time the loop gets a blue pixel, it adds one to the totalBlue variable. If the totalBlue variable started with any value other than 0, it will not contain the correct total when the loop finishes.

Now we can expand the program so it scans an entire image for blue pixels. To scan an entire image, we need to think of the pixels as being arranged in rows and columns. The rows correspond to the *Y* coordinates in the image. For example, the pixels in the first row have a *Y* coordinate of 0, the pixels in the second row have a *Y* coordinate of 1, and so forth. The columns correspond to the *X* coordinates in the image. For example, the pixels in the first column have an *X* coordinate of 0, the pixels in the second column have an *X* coordinate of 1, and so forth. This is illustrated in Figure 6-25.

Figure 6-25 Think of pixels as arranged in rows and columns

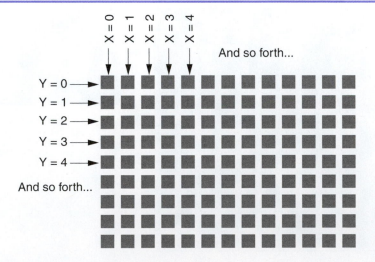

To step through each of the pixels, we need two loops, one nested inside the other. The outer loop will step through the rows (the *Y* coordinates), and the inner loop will step through the columns (the *X* coordinates). The following is an example. Assume that `height` and `width` contain the height and width of the image, and `pixelColor` is a DWORD variable.

```
for (int y = 0; y < height; y++)
{
    for (int x = 0; x < width; x++)
    {
        pixelColor = dbPoint(x, y);
    }
}
```

The outer loop (the one that uses y as its counter variable) will iterate once for each row of pixels in the image. Each time this loop iterates, the inner loop will run through its entire set of iterations. This inner loop iterates once for each column of pixels in the image. As a result, the statement that calls dbPoint will execute once for each pixel in the image. Program 6-10 shows how we can use this technique to count all of the pure blue pixels in an image. The program's output is shown in Figure 6-26. As you can see from the output, the image contains 212,160 pure blue pixels. (There are a total of 307,200 pixels in the image.)

Program 6-10   (CountBluePixels.cpp)

```
 1   // This program loads an image and counts the number of
 2   // pure blue (RGB = 0,0,255) pixels in the entire image.
 3   #include "DarkGDK.h"
 4
 5   void DarkGDK()
 6   {
 7       // Declare a constant for the color blue.
 8       const DWORD BLUE = dbRGB(0, 0, 255);
 9
10       // Variables
11       DWORD pixelColor;      // To hold a pixel color
12       int width;             // To hold the image's width
13       int height;            // To hold the image's height
14       int totalBlue = 0;     // To hold the number of blue pixels
15
16       // Load an image as bitmap 0.
17       dbLoadBitmap("BlueBars.bmp", 0);
18
19       // Get the image's width and height.
20       width = dbBitmapWidth(0);
21       height = dbBitmapHeight(0);
22
23       // Count the blue pixels in the top row.
24       for (int y = 0; y < height; y++)
25       {
26           for (int x = 0; x < width; x++)
27           {
28               // Get the next pixel's color.
29               pixelColor = dbPoint(x, 0);
```

```
30
31                    // If the pixel is blue, increment totalBlue.
32                    if (pixelColor == BLUE)
33                    {
34                        totalBlue++;
35                    }
36          }
37      }
38
39      // Prompt the user to press a key.
40      dbCenterText(319, 450, "Press any key.");
41      dbWaitKey();
42
43      // Clear the screen and display the number of blue pixels.
44      dbClear(0, 0, 0);
45      dbPrint("Number of pure blue pixels in the image:");
46      dbPrint( dbStr(totalBlue) );
47
48      // Wait for the user to press a key.
49      dbWaitKey();
50  }
```

Figure 6-26 Output of Program 6-10

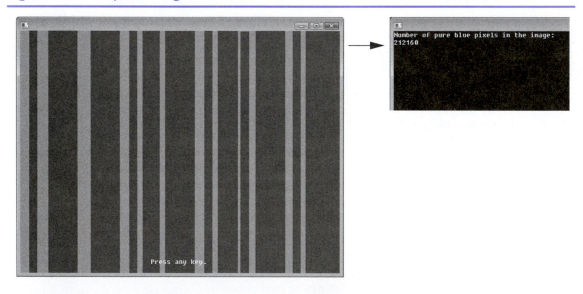

6.9 Logical Operators

CONCEPT: The logical AND operator (`&&`) and the logical OR operator (`||`) allow you to connect multiple Boolean expressions to create a compound expression. The logical NOT operator (`!`) reverses the truth of a Boolean expression.

The C++ language provides a set of operators known as *logical operators*, which you can use to create complex Boolean expressions. Table 6-3 describes these operators.

Table 6-3 Logical operators

Operator	Meaning
&&	This is the logical AND operator. It connects two Boolean expressions into one compound expression. Both subexpressions must be true for the compound expression to be true.
||	This is the logical OR operator. It connects two Boolean expressions into one compound expression. One or both subexpressions must be true for the compound expression to be true. It is only necessary for one of the subexpressions to be true, and it does not matter which.
!	This is the logical NOT operator is a unary operator, meaning it works with only one operand. The operand must be a Boolean expression. The NOT operator reverses the truth of its operand. If it is applied to an expression that is true, the operator returns false. If it is applied to an expression that is false, the operator returns true.

Table 6-4 shows examples of several compound Boolean expressions that use logical operators.

Table 6-4 Compound Boolean expressions using logical operators

Expression	Meaning
x > y && a < b	Is x greater than y AND is a less than b?
x == y || x == z	Is x equal to y OR is x equal to z?
! (x > y)	Is the expression x > y NOT true?

The && Operator

The && operator takes two Boolean expressions as operands and creates a compound Boolean expression that is true only when both subexpressions are true. The following is an example of an if statement that uses the && operator:

```
if ( pixelColor == blue && xCoordinate > 0 )
    dbPrint("The game has started.");
```

In this statement, the two Boolean expressions pixelColor == blue and xCoordinate > 0 are combined into a compound expression. The dbPrint function will be called only if pixelColor is equal to blue and xCoordinate is greater than 0. If either of the Boolean subexpressions is false, the compound expression is false and the message is not displayed. Here is another example:

```
if ( x > 319 && y > 239 )
    dbPrint("That is the lower right screen quadrant.");
```

This statement determines whether x is greater than 319 and y is greater than 239. If both subexpressions are true, the compound expression is true and the statement dbPrint function is called.

Table 6-5 shows a truth table for the && operator. The truth table lists expressions showing all the possible combinations of true and false connected with the && operator. The resulting values of the expressions are also shown.

Table 6-5 Truth table for the and operator

Expression	Value of the Expression
true && false	false
false && true	false
false && false	false
true && true	true

As the table shows, both sides of the && operator must be true for the operator to return a true value.

The || Operator

The || operator takes two Boolean expressions as operands and creates a compound Boolean expression that is true when either of the subexpressions is true. The following is an example of an if statement that uses the || operator:

```
if ( xCoordinate < 319 || yCoordinate > 239 )
    dbPrint("Game Over!");
```

The dbPrint function will be called only if xCoordinate is less than 319 or yCoordinate is greater than 239. If either subexpression is true, the compound expression is true. Here is another example:

```
if ( pixelColor == blue || pixelColor == green )
    blueGreenPixelCount++;
```

This statement determines whether pixelColor is equal to blue or pixelColor is equal to green. If either subexpression is true, the compound expression is true and the statement blueGreenPixelCount++ is executed. Table 6-6 shows a truth table for the || operator.

Table 6-6 Truth table for the || operator

Expression	Value of the Expression
true || false	true
false || true	true
false || false	false
true || true	true

All it takes for an || expression to be true is for one side of the || operator to be true. It doesn't matter if the other side is false or true.

Short-Circuit Evaluation

Both the && and || operators perform *short-circuit evaluation*. Here's how it works with the && operator: If the expression on the left side of the and operator is false, the expression on the right side will not be checked. Because the compound expression will be false if only one of the subexpressions is false, it would waste CPU time to check the remaining expression. So, when the && operator finds that the expression on its left is false, it short circuits and does not evaluate the expression on its right.

Here's how short-circuit evaluation works with the || operator: If the expression on the left side of the || operator is true, the expression on the right side will not be checked. Because it is only necessary for one of the expressions to be true, it would waste CPU time to check the remaining expression.

The ! Operator

The ! operator is a unary operator that takes a Boolean expression as its operand and reverses its logical value. In other words, if the expression is true, the ! operator returns false, and if the expression is false, the ! operator returns true. The following is an if statement using the ! operator:

```
if ( !(points > MINIMUM) )
    dbPrint("Try again.");
```

First, the expression (points > MINIMUM) is tested and a value of either true or false is the result. Then the ! operator is applied to that value. If the expression (points > MINIMUM) is true, the ! operator returns false. If the expression (points > MINIMUM) is false, the ! operator returns true. The code is equivalent to asking: "Is points not greater than MINIMUM?"

Notice that in this example, we have put parentheses around the expression points > MINIMUM. This is necessary because the ! operator has higher precedence than the relational operators. If we did not put the parentheses around the expression points > MINIMUM, the ! operator would have been applied just to the points variable.

Here is another example:

```
if ( !(pixelColor == green) )
    nonGreenPixels++;
```

First, the expression (pixelColor == green) is tested and a value of either true or false is the result. Then the ! operator is applied to that value. If the expression (pixelColor == green) is true, the ! operator returns false. If the expression (pixelColor == green) is false, the ! operator returns true. The code is equivalent to asking: "Is pixelColor not equal to green?"

Table 6-7 shows a truth table for the ! operator.

Table 6-7 Truth table for the ! operator

Expression	Value of the Expression
! true	false
! false	true

Precedence of the Logical Operators

We mentioned earlier that the ! operator has higher precedence than the relational operators. The && and || logical operators have lower precedence than the relational operators. For example, look at the following expression:

```
pixelColor == blue || pixelColor == green
```

When this expression is evaluated, the == operators work first, and then the || operator works. The expression is the same as the following:

```
(pixelColor == blue) || (pixelColor == green)
```

If you prefer, you can enclose the expressions that are to the left and the right of a logical operator in parentheses, as shown here. Even though the parentheses are not required, many programmers prefer to use them, just to make the expression easier to understand.

In many situations you will find the need to write expressions containing more than one logical operator. For example, suppose the variables pointX and pointY contain the *XY* coordinates of a point on the screen, and we want to know whether that point is inside the box shown in Figure 6-27. As shown in the figure, the variables upperX and upperY contain the coordinates of the box's upper-left corner, and the variables lowerX and lowerY contain the coordinates of the box's lower-right corner.

Figure 6-27 A box on the screen

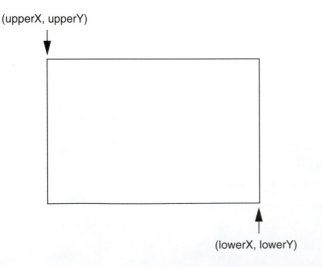

(upperX, upperY)

(lowerX, lowerY)

If the location specified by `pointX` and `pointY` is inside the box, then all of the following will be true:

- `pointX` will be greater than `upperX`
- `pointX` will be less than `lowerX`
- `pointY` will be greater than `upperY`
- `pointY` will be less than `lowerY`

To determine whether the point is inside the box we can write an `if` statement like this:

```
if ( pointX > upperX && pointX < lowerX && pointY > upperY && pointY < lowerY)
{
    Code here executes if the point is inside the box.
}
```

In some situations you might need to enclose parts of a compound Boolean expression inside parentheses because the `&&` operator has slightly higher precedence than the `||` operator. For example, suppose we want to know whether `pixelColor` is equal to either `blue` or `green`, and whether y is less than 300. We might begin an `if` statement like this:

```
if ( pixelColor == blue || pixelColor == green && y < 300 )
```

This expression will not be evaluated the way we want, however, because the `&&` operator has higher precedence than the `||` operator. First, the expression `pixelColor == green && y < 300` will be evaluated, giving a true or false value. That value will then be used on the right side of the `||` operator. Instead, we should use parentheses to make sure the `||` operator works first, as shown here:

```
if ( (pixelColor == blue || pixelColor == green) && y < 300 )
```

 Checkpoint

6.26. What is a compound Boolean expression?

6.27. The following truth table shows various combinations of the values true and false connected by a logical operator. Complete the table by circling T or F to indicate whether the result of such a combination is true or false.

Logical Expression	Result (circle T or F)	
true && false	T	F
true && true	T	F
false && true	T	F
false && false	T	F
true || false	T	F
true || true	T	F
false || true	T	F
false || false	T	F
! true	T	F
! false	T	F

6.28. Assume the variables a = 2, b = 4, and c = 6. Circle T or F for each of the following conditions to indicate if it is true or false.

a == 4 || b > 2	T	F
6 <= c && a > 3	T	F
1 != b && c != 3	T	F
a >= -1 || a <= b	T	F
!(a > 2)	T	F

6.29. Explain how short-circuit evaluation works with the && and || operators.

6.30. Write an if statement that displays the message "The number is valid" if the variable speed is within the range 0 through 200.

6.31. Write an if statement that displays the message "The number is not valid" if the variable speed is outside the range 0 through 200.

6.10 The switch Statement

CONCEPT: The switch statement lets the value of a variable or an expression determine which path of execution the program will take.

The *switch statement* is a *multiple alternative decision structure*. It allows you to test the value of an integer variable or an expression and then use that value to determine which statement or set of statements to execute. Figure 6-28 shows an example of how a switch statement looks in a flowchart.

Figure 6-28 A switch statement

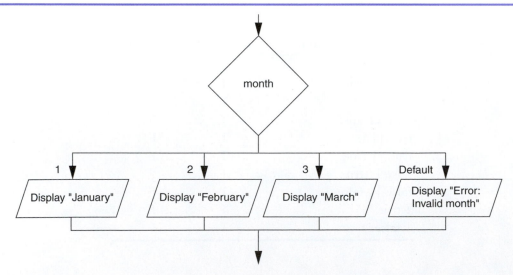

In the flowchart, the diamond symbol contains the name of an integer variable named `month`. If the variable contains the value 1, then `"January"` is displayed. If the variable contains the value 2, then `"February"` is displayed. If the variable contains the value 3, then `"March"` is displayed. If the variable contains none of these values, the box labeled `Default` is executed. In this case, the message `"Error: Invalid month"` is displayed.

Here is the general format of the `switch` statement:

```
switch (testExpression)  ──── This is an integer variable or an expression.
{
    case value_1:
        statement  ┐
        statement  ├ These statements are executed if the
        etc.       │ testExpression is equal to value_1.
        break;     ┘

    case value_2:
        statement  ┐
        statement  ├ These statements are executed if the
        etc.       │ testExpression is equal to value_2.
        break;     ┘
```

Insert as many case sections as necessary

```
    case value_N:
        statement  ┐
        statement  ├ These statements are executed if the
        etc.       │ testExpression is equal to value_N.
        break;     ┘

    default:
        statement  ┐ These statements are executed if the testExpression
        statement  ├ is not equal to any of the values listed after the case
        etc.       ┘ statements.
}  ──────────── This is the end of the switch statement.
```

The first line of the structure starts with the word `switch`, followed by a `testExpression` which is enclosed in parentheses. The `testExpression` is usually an integer variable, but it can also be any expression that gives an integer value. Beginning at the next line is a block of code enclosed in curly braces. Inside this block of code is one or more *case sections*. A `case` section begins with the word `case`, followed by a value, followed by a colon. Each `case` section contains one or more statements, followed by a `break` statement. At the end is an optional *default section*.

When the `switch` statement executes, it compares the value of the `testExpression` with the values that follow each of the `case` statements (from top to bottom). When it finds a `case` value that matches the `testExpression`'s value, the program branches to the `case` statement. The statements that follow the `case` statement are executed, until a `break` statement is encountered. At that point, the program jumps out of the `switch` statement. If the `testExpression` does not match any of the `case` values, the program branches to the `default` statement and executes the statements that immediately follow it.

For example, the following code performs the same operation as the flowchart in Figure 6-28:

```
switch (month)
{
    case 1:
        dbPrint("January");
        break;

    case 2:
        dbPrint("February");
        break;

    case 3:
        dbPrint("March");
        break;

    default:
        dbPrint("Error: Invalid month");
}
```

In this example, the *testExpression* is the month variable. If the value in the month variable is 1, the program will branch to the case 1: section and execute the dbPrint("January") statement that immediately follows it. If the value in the month variable is 2, the program will branch to the case 2: section and execute the dbPrint("February") statement that immediately follows it. If the value in the month variable is 3, the program will branch to the case 3: section and execute the dbPrint("March") statement that immediately follows it. If the value in the month variable is not 1, 2, or 3, the program will branch to the default: section and execute the dbPrint("Error: Invalid month") statement that immediately follows it.

Here are some important points to remember about the switch statement:

- The *testExpression* must be a variable that is of an integer data type (this includes DWORD variables), or an expression that gives an integer value.
- The value that follows the word case must be an integer literal or an integer constant. It cannot be a variable.
- The break statement that appears at the end of a case section is optional, but in most situations you will need it. If the program executes a case section that does not end with a break statement, it will continue executing the code in the very next case section.
- The default section is optional, but in most situations you should have one. The default section is executed when the *testExpression* does not match any of the case values.
- Because the default section appears at the end of the switch statement, it does not need a break statement.

Let's look at another example. Program 6-11 displays a menu, which is a list of choices that the user can select from. The user can enter 1 to see a red background, 2 to see a green background, 3 to see a blue background, or 4 to end the program. A loop repeatedly allows the user to make selections until 4 is entered.

Program 6-11   (SetBackground.cpp)

```cpp
1   // This program demonstrates the switch statement.
2   #include "DarkGDK.h"
3
4   // Function prototype
5   void displayMenu();
6
7   //*********************************************************
8   // DarkGDK function                                       *
9   //*********************************************************
10  void DarkGDK()
11  {
12      // Color constants
13      const DWORD RED   = dbRGB(255, 0, 0);
14      const DWORD GREEN = dbRGB(0, 255, 0);
15      const DWORD BLUE  = dbRGB(0, 0, 255);
16
17      // Constant for a time delay
18      const int TWO_SECONDS = 2000;
19
20      // Variable to hold the user's selection
21      int selection = 0;
22
23      // Let the user make selections from the menu.
24      // A selection of 4 ends the program.
25      while (selection != 4)
26      {
27          // Display the menu.
28          displayMenu();
29
30          // Get the user's selection.
31          selection = atoi( dbInput() );
32
33          // Process the selection.
34          switch (selection)
35          {
36          case 1:
37              dbCLS(RED);
38              break;
39
40          case 2:
41              dbCLS(GREEN);
42              break;
43
44          case 3:
45              dbCLS(BLUE);
46              break;
47
48          case 4:
49              dbPrint("Goodbye!");
50              dbWait(TWO_SECONDS);
51              break;
```

```
52
53              default:
54                  dbPrint("The valid choices are 1 - 4.");
55                  dbPrint("Try again.");
56              }
57          }
58  }
59
60  //*********************************************************
61  // The displayMenu function displays a menu of choices    *
62  // that the user can select from.                         *
63  //*********************************************************
64  void displayMenu()
65  {
66      dbPrint();
67      dbPrint("Make a selection:");
68      dbPrint("1 = Red background");
69      dbPrint("2 = Green background");
70      dbPrint("3 = Blue background");
71      dbPrint("4 = Exit Program");
72  }
```

Inside the loop, the menu is displayed by line 28. The user's selection is read from the keyboard in line 31, converted to an int, and assigned to the selection variable. The switch statement that begins at line 34 processes the user's selection in the following way:

- If the selection variable is equal to 1, the program jumps to the case 1: statement in line 36. The screen is cleared to red, and then the program breaks out of the switch statement.
- If the selection variable is equal to 2, the program jumps to the case 2: statement in line 40. The screen is cleared to green, and then the program breaks out of the switch statement.
- If the selection variable is equal to 3, the program jumps to the case 3: statement in line 44. The screen is cleared to blue, and then the program breaks out of the switch statement.
- If the selection variable is equal to 4, the program jumps to the case 4: statement in line 48. The message "Goodbye!" is displayed, the program waits two seconds, and then breaks out of the switch statement.
- If the selection variable contains any value other than 1, 2, 3, or 4, the program jumps to the default: section in line 53. An error message is displayed and the program jumps out of the switch statement.

Checkpoint

6.32. Convert the following if-else-if code to a switch statement:

```
if (choice == 1)
{
    dbPrint("You chose 1.");
}
```

```
    else if (choice == 2)
    {
        dbPrint("You chose 2.");
    }
    else if (choice == 3)
    {
        dbPrint("You chose 3.");
    }
    else
    {
        dbPrint("Make another choice.");
    }
```

6.11 Numeric Truth, Flags, and `bool` Variables

CONCEPT: In addition to the values of relational expressions, you can use numeric values to represent true or false conditions. You can store the values `true` and `false` in `bool` variables, which are commonly used as flags.

In this chapter, you've seen how relational expressions such as `x > 100` and `color == blue` give true or false values. In addition to relational expressions, C++ also considers the numeric value 0 as false, and any numeric value other than 0 as true.

Let's look at a practical way that we can use this. Recall from Chapter 5 that you can use the `dbLoadBitmap` function to load an image file into memory. If the specified image file does not exist however, the function simply loads nothing without giving an indication that anything went wrong. Ideally, you should check to see if the file exists before you try to load it. You can do that with a function named `dbFileExist`. When you call `dbFileExist` you pass the name of a file as an argument, and the function returns either a 0 or a 1 to indicate whether the file exists. If the file does not exist, the function returns 0. Otherwise it returns 1. Here is an example of how we might use it:

```
if ( dbFileExist("Galaxy.bmp") )
{
    dbLoadBitmap("Galaxy.bmp", 0);
}
else
{
    dbPrint("ERROR: Galaxy.bmp does not exist.");
}
```

The `if` statement calls the `dbFileExist` function, and then treats the value that it returns as either true or false. If the function returns 1, that value is considered true, so the image file is loaded. However, if the function returns 0, that value is considered false, so the error message is displayed.

The previous code can also be written this way:

```
if ( !dbFileExist("Galaxy.bmp") )
{
    dbPrint("ERROR: Galaxy.bmp does not exist.");
}
else
{
    dbLoadBitmap("Galaxy.bmp", 0);
}
```

Notice that we have used the ! operator to reverse the value returned by the dbFileExist function. You can read the code this way: If the file Galaxy.bmp does not exist, display an error message. Otherwise, load the file.

There are other functions in the DarkGDK library that return numeric values to indicate a true or false value. For example, you can call the dbBitmapMirrored function, passing a bitmap number as an argument, and it will return 1 if the specific bitmap is mirrored, or 0 if it is not mirrored. Another example is dbBitmapFlipped. You pass a bitmap number as an argument and the function returns 1 if the bitmap is flipped, or 0 if it is not flipped.

bool Variables

The C++ language provides a special data type named bool that you can use to create variables that hold true or false values. Here is an example of the declaration of a bool variable:

```
bool grandMaster;
```

This declares a bool variable named grandMaster. In the program we can assign the special values true or false to the variable, as shown here:

```
if (points > 5000)
{
    grandMaster = true;
}
else
{
    grandMaster = false;
}
```

Variables of the bool data type are commonly used as flags. A *flag* is a variable that signals when some condition exists in the program. When the flag variable is set to false, it indicates that the condition does not yet exist. When the flag variable is set to true, it means the condition does exist. For example, the previous code might be used in a game to determine whether the user is a "grand master." If he or she has earned more than 5,000 points we set the grandMaster variable to true. Otherwise, we set the variable to false. Later in the program we can test the grandMaster variable, like this:

```
if (grandMaster)
{
    powerLevel += 500;
}
```

This code performs the following: If `grandMaster` is true, add 500 to `powerLevel`. Here is another example:

```
if (!grandMaster)
{
    powerLevel = 100;
}
```

This code performs the following: If `grandMaster` is not true, set `powerLevel` to 100.

Checkpoint

6.33. What numeric value is considered true by C++? What numeric value is considered false?

6.34. What special values can you store in a Boolean variable?

6.35. What is a flag variable?

Review Questions

Multiple Choice

1. A _____ structure executes a set of statements only under certain circumstances.
   a. sequence
   b. circumstantial
   c. decision
   d. Boolean

2. A _____ structure provides one alternative path of execution.
   a. sequence
   b. single alternative decision
   c. one path alternative
   d. single execution decision

3. A(n) _____ expression has a value of either true or false.
   a. binary
   b. decision
   c. unconditional
   d. Boolean

4. The symbols >, <, and == are all _____ operators.
   a. relational
   b. logical
   c. conditional
   d. ternary

5. A(n) _____ structure tests a condition and then takes one path if the condition is true, or another path if the condition is false.
   a. `if` statement
   b. single alternative decision
   c. dual alternative decision
   d. sequence

6. You use a(n) _____ statement to write a single alternative decision structure.
   a. `test-jump`
   b. `if`
   c. `if-else`
   d. `if-call`

7. You use a(n) _____ statement to write a dual alternative decision structure.
   a. `test-jump`
   b. `if`
   c. `if-else`
   d. `if-call`

8. A _____-controlled loop uses a true/false condition to control the number of times that it repeats.
   a. Boolean
   b. condition
   c. decision
   d. count

9. A _____-controlled loop repeats a specific number of times.
   a. Boolean
   b. condition
   c. decision
   d. count

10. Each repetition of a loop is known as a(n) _____.
    a. cycle
    b. revolution
    c. orbit
    d. iteration

11. The `while` loop is a _____ type of loop.
    a. pretest
    b. no-test
    c. prequalified
    d. posttest

12. The `do-while` loop is a _____ type of loop.
    a. pretest
    b. no-test
    c. prequalified
    d. posttest

13. A(n) _____ loop has no way of ending and repeats until the program is interrupted.
    a. indeterminate
    b. interminable
    c. infinite
    d. timeless

14. &&, ||, and ! are _____ operators.
    a. relational
    b. logical
    c. conditional
    d. ternary

15. A compound Boolean expression created with the _____ operator is true only if both of its subexpressions are true.
    a. &&
    b. ||
    c. !
    d. both

16. A compound Boolean expression created with the _____ operator is true if either of its subexpressions is true.
    a. &&
    b. ||
    c. !
    d. either

17. The _____ operator takes a Boolean expression as its operand and reverses its logical value.
    a. &&
    b. ||
    c. !
    d. either

18. The _____ statement allows you to test the value of an integer variable or expression and then use that value to determine which statement or set of statements to execute.
    a. menu
    b. branch
    c. select
    d. switch

19. The _____ section of a switch statement is branched to if none of the case values matches the test expression.
    a. else
    b. default
    c. case
    d. otherwise

20. A _____ is a Boolean variable that signals when some condition exists in the program.
   a. flag
   b. signal
   c. sentinel
   d. siren

True or False

1. You can write any program using only sequence structures.

2. A program can be made of only one type of control structure. You cannot combine structures.

3. A single alternative decision structure tests a condition and then takes one path if the condition is true, or another path if the condition is false.

4. A decision structure can be nested inside another decision structure.

5. A compound Boolean expression that has two subexpressions connected with the `&&` operator is true only when both subexpressions are true.

6. A compound Boolean expression that has two subexpressions connected with the `||` operator is true only when both subexpressions are true.

7. A condition-controlled loop always repeats a specific number of times.

8. The `while` loop is a pretest loop.

9. An infinite loop will automatically stop after 256 seconds.

10. The test expression in a `switch` statement must have an integer value.

Short Answer

1. What is meant by the term "conditionally executed"?

2. You need to test an expression and then execute one set of statements if the expression is true. If the expression is false, you need to execute a different set of statements. What structure will you use?

3. What is a condition-controlled loop?

4. What is a count-controlled loop?

5. What is an infinite loop? Write the code for an infinite loop.

6. Briefly describe how the `&&` operator works.

7. Briefly describe how the `||` operator works.

8. Briefly describe how the `!` operator works.

9. What is a flag and how does it work?

10. If you need to test the value of an integer variable and use that value to determine which statement or set of statements to execute, which statement would be a good choice?

Algorithm Workbench

1. Write an `if` statement that assigns 20 to the variable `y` and assigns 40 to the variable `z` if the variable `x` is greater than 100.

2. Write an `if` statement that assigns 0 to the variable `b` and assigns 1 to the variable `c` if the variable `a` is less than 10.

3. Write an `if-else` statement that assigns 0 to the variable `b` if the variable `a` is less than 10. Otherwise, it should assign 99 to the variable `b`.

4. Write nested decision structures that perform the following: If `amount1` is greater than 10 and `amount2` is less than 100, display the greater of `amount1` and `amount2`.

5. Write an `if-else` statement that displays `"Speed is normal"` if the value of the `speed` variable is at least 24 but no more than 56. If the `speed` variable's value is outside this range, display `"Speed is abnormal"`.

6. Write an `if-else` statement that determines whether the value of the `points` variable is less than 9 or greater than 51. If this is true, display "Invalid points." Otherwise, display "Valid points."

7. Write a `while` loop that lets the user enter a number. The number should be multiplied by 10, and the result assigned to a variable named `product`. The loop should iterate as long as `product` is less than 100.

8. Write a `while` loop that asks the user to enter two numbers. The numbers should be added and the sum displayed. The loop should ask the user if he or she wishes to perform the operation again. If so, the loop should repeat, otherwise it should terminate.

9. Write a `for` loop that displays the following set of numbers:

   ```
   0, 10, 20, 30, 40, 50 . . . 1000
   ```

10. Rewrite the following `if-else-if` statement as a `switch` statement.

    ```
    if (selection == 1)
    {
        dbPrint("You selected A.");
    }
    else if (selection == 2)
    {
        dbPrint("You selected 2.");
    }
    else if (selection == 3)
    {
        dbPrint("You selected 3.");
    }
    else if (selection == 4)
    {
        dbPrint("You selected 4.");
    }
    else
    {
        dbPrint("Not good with numbers, eh?");
    }
    ```

Programming Exercises

1. **Brick Wall**
   Program 6-6 (RandomBricksLoop.cpp) uses a function named drawBrick that draws a brick (a red rectangle) at a specified location. Write a program that uses loops to call this function (or one similar to it) so that the entire Dark GDK window is filled with bricks in a pattern like that shown in Figure 6-29.

Figure 6-29 Brick wall

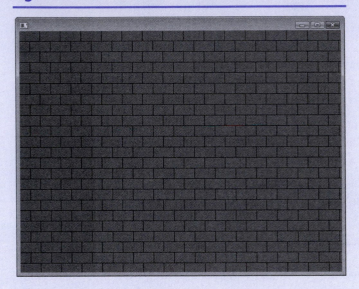

2. **Roman Numerals**
   Use Microsoft Paint, or any other graphics program, to create bitmap images of the Roman numerals I through V. Figure 6-30 shows an example. Then, write a program that asks the user to enter a number in the range of 1 through 5. After the user enters a number, display the bitmap for the Roman numeral version of that number. If the user enters any value outside the range of 1 through 5, display an error message.

Figure 6-30 Roman numerals

3. **Red Shift**
   Write a program that loads and displays an image, and waits for the user to press a key. After a key is pressed, the program should step through each pixel in the image, setting its red color component to 255. (The green and blue components should be left as they are.) After performing this operation, the image should appear to have a red tint.

4. **Red and Blue Swap**
   Write a program that loads and displays an image, and waits for the user to press a key. After a key is pressed, the program should step through each pixel in the image. Each pixel's red component should be swapped with its blue component. For example, if a pixel's RGB value is 127, 10, 200, it should be changed to 200, 10, 127.

5. **Color Manipulator**
   Write a program that loads and displays an image, and waits for the user to press a key. After a key is pressed, the program should step through each pixel in the image. If a pixel's green component and blue component are both less than 100, the pixel should be changed to black.

6. **Color Gradient**
   Write a program that displays a window that is 256 pixels wide by 256 pixels high. Every pixel's blue component should be set to 255. The pixels in the left-most row (row 0) should have their red and green components set to 0. The pixels in the next row (row 1) should have their red and green components set to 1. This pattern should continue until the pixels in the rightmost row (row 255) have their red, green, and blue components set to 255. As a result, the window should show a color gradient that is blue on the left edge, and blends to white on the right edge.

7. **Round Peg in a Square Hole**
   Write a program that displays a 50 by 50 pixel square at a random location. The program should ask the user to guess the X and Y coordinates of the square's center point. A circle with a radius of 25 should be drawn, centered at the XY location entered by the user. If the circle is completely inside the square, congratulate the user and end the program. Otherwise, clear the screen and repeat the steps with a new square.

8. **Shape Menu**
   Write a program that displays the following menu:

   ```
   1 = Square
   2 = Circle
   3 = Ellipse
   4 = End program
   ```

   When the user selects a shape from the menu, the program should ask for any necessary data (such as the length of the square's side, the circle's radius, and so forth) and then it should draw that shape in the center of the screen. Use a loop to repeat this process until the user enters 4.

7

The Game Loop and Animation

TOPICS

7.1 The Game Loop

7.2 Simple Animation

7.3 Controlling Objects with the Keyboard

7.4 Sprites

7.5 Cel Animation and Sprite Sheets

7.6 Sprite Collision Detection

7.1 The Game Loop

CONCEPT: The game loop is a special loop used in games and animation programs. It synchronizes the refreshing of the screen with the program's other operations.

In Chapter 6, you learned about loops, which are control structures that cause one or more statements to repeat. In this chapter, you will use loops to create animations. Before we demonstrate how to write an animation loop, you need to learn a few things about how the Dark GDK updates the screen.

When a Dark GDK program displays output, that output is not actually sent to the screen until the window's contents are refreshed. By default, the Dark GDK refreshes a program's window as fast as it can. However, code that performs an intensive amount of work can interfere with the refresh rate. For example, consider Program 7-1, which uses an infinite loop to display randomly placed dots.

The infinite loop appears in lines 21 through 29. Recall from Chapter 6, that the word `true` is a keyword in C++ that represents the Boolean value true. Any `while` loop that begins `while (true)` will be an infinite loop because the value `true` will always be true!

Program 7-1 (InfiniteLoop.cpp)

```
 1  // This program attempts to fill the screen
 2  // with randomly placed dots. Unfortunately,
 3  // the infinite while loop interferes with
 4  // the Dark GDK's ability to automatically
 5  // update the program's window.
 6  #include "DarkGDK.H"
 7
 8  void DarkGDK()
 9  {
10      // Constants for the screen size
11      const int MAX_X = dbScreenWidth();
12      const int MAX_Y = dbScreenHeight();
13
14      // Variables for XY coordinates
15      int x, y;
16
17      // Seed the random number generator.
18      dbRandomize( dbTimer() );
19
20      // Draw an infinite number of dots.
21      while (true)
22      {
23          // Get a set of random coordinates.
24          x = dbRND(MAX_X);
25          y = dbRND(MAX_Y);
26
27          // Draw a dot at the coordinates.
28          dbDot(x, y);
29      }
30  }
```

The statements inside the loop perform the following operations over and over:

- Random values are generated for the x and y variables (lines 24 and 25).
- A dot is drawn using those variables as coordinates (line 28).

If you run this program, you would expect to see its window being filled with dots, drawn one-by-one at random locations. However, when you run this program you probably won't see any output. The program's window will appear blank, and the program will seem to have malfunctioned. To end the program you will have to click the standard *Close* button in the upper-right corner of the window.

Although the code inside the loop looks very simple, it repeats over and over, never giving the Dark GDK time to update the screen. We could say that the program isn't behaving very nicely. Its code is like a bully that grabs the CPU and refuses to let the Dark GDK perform its automatic screen updates.

Virtually all games and animation programs have a loop of some sort that continuously performs operations such as calculations, gathering input, moving objects on the screen, playing sounds, and so forth. When writing such a program, you have to be sure that the loop tells the Dark GDK to update the screen at the appropriate time.

In other words, you have to *synchronize* the loop with the updating of the screen. The Dark GDK library provides the following functions that you can use for this purpose:

- dbSyncOn—This function tells the Dark GDK that we want our program to handle the updating of the screen. As a result, the Dark GDK will not attempt to update the screen until we tell it to.
- dbSyncRate—This function accepts an argument that specifies the maximum times per second that the screen should be updated. This value is commonly referred to as the *frame rate* or the *refresh rate*.
- LoopGDK—This function is used to control the number of times that a loop executes per second. It also tells us, via its return value, whether the user has attempted to end the program. It returns zero if the user has closed the program's window, or pressed the *Esc* key. Otherwise it returns a nonzero value.
- dbSync—This function forces a screen update.

Let's look at how we can use these functions to modify Program 7-1 so it actually displays the random dots on the screen. Program 7-2 shows the code.

Program 7-2   (**InfiniteDots.cpp**)

```
1    // This program displays randomly placed dots.
2    #include "DarkGDK.H"
3
4    void DarkGDK()
5    {
6        // Constants for the screen size
7        const int MAX_X = dbScreenWidth();
8        const int MAX_Y = dbScreenHeight();
9
10       // Variables for XY coordinates
11       int x, y;
12
13       // Seed the random number generator.
14       dbRandomize( dbTimer() );
15
16       // Specify that the program is now in
17       // control of refreshing the screen.
18       dbSyncOn();
19
20       // Specify that we want a maximum screen
21       // refresh rate of 60 times per second.
22       dbSyncRate(60);
23
24       // Draw dots until the user closes the
25       // window or presses the Esc key.
26       // NOTE: Because we specified a refresh
27       // rate of 60 times per second, this loop
28       // will execute a maximum of 60 times
29       // per second.
30       while ( LoopGDK() )
31       {
32           // Get a set of random coordinates.
33           x = dbRND(MAX_X);
```

```
34              y = dbRND(MAX_Y);
35
36              // Draw a dot at the coordinates.
37              dbDot(x, y);
38
39              // Refresh the screen.
40              dbSync();
41          }
42      }
```

Let's take a closer look. Line 18 calls the dbSyncOn function, which tells the Dark GDK that we will control the updating of the screen from this program. As a result, it will not automatically update the screen. Line 22 specifies a maximum screen refresh rate of 60 times per second. (In this example, we use 60 times per second, which is a typical refresh rate. Depending on the nature of the program, you might want to specify a lower value, to produce a slower animation, or a higher value to speed up the action. You can specify a refresh rate of 0 through 1,000. Specifying 0 tells the Dark GDK to refresh as fast as possible.)

Line 30 is the start of a while loop. Inside the parentheses a call to the LoopGDK function appears. This function's return value indicates whether the user has ended the program. If the user has clicked the standard *Close* button in the window's upper-right corner, or pressed the *Esc* key, the function returns 0 (which is interpreted as false). This action causes the loop to end. If none of this has happened, the function returns a nonzero value (which is interpreted as true), causing the loop to iterate.

The LoopGDK function is also tied to the screen refresh rate that we specified in line 22. Because we specified a screen refresh rate of 60 times per second, the LoopGDK function will make sure that the while loop iterates no more than 60 times per second.

Inside the loop we get random values for the x and y variables (lines 33 and 34) and then we draw a dot using those values as coordinates (line 37). Then, in line 40 we call the dbSync function, which causes the screen to be updated. As a result, the dot that was drawn in line 37 will be displayed in the program's window. When you run this program you will see the window fill with randomly placed dots. Closing the window or pressing the *Esc* key will end the program.

The Game Loop

From this point forward, many of the Dark GDK programs that you will write will require the special type of loop that you saw in Program 7-2. We will refer to this loop as the *game loop*. The game loop, and the code required to set it up properly, will always be written in the general format shown in Figure 7-1. Let's go over each part.

1. Before the loop, call the dbSyncOn function to disable automatic screen refreshing.

Figure 7-1 Game loop code

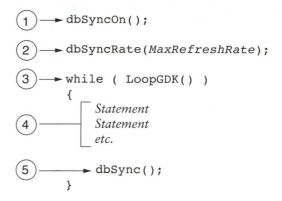

2. Before the loop, call the `dbSyncRate` function to establish a refresh rate. The *MaxRefreshRate* argument is an integer in the range of 0 through 1,000. Passing 0 tells the Dark GDK to refresh the screen as fast as possible.

3. The game loop is a `while` loop that calls the `LoopGDK` function as its Boolean expression. The value that is returned from the `LoopGDK` function will be either true (a nonzero value) or false (zero). The function will return true until the user closes the program's window or presses the *Esc* key. When that happens, it returns false. So, the game loop will continue to iterate until the user chooses to end the program.

   Also, remember that the `LoopGDK` function synchronizes the loop's execution speed with the screen refresh rate that you specified in Step 2. For example, if you specify a refresh rate of 60 times per second, the `LoopGDK` function will let the loop iterate a maximum of 60 times per second.

4. The statements inside the loop perform the operations necessary for displaying graphics on the screen.

5. At the end of the loop, you will call the `dbSync` function to refresh the screen.

 NOTE: Don't forget to call the `dbSync` function at the end of the game loop. If you leave out this function call, the system will not update the screen.

Giving Control Back to the Dark GDK

The Dark GDK library also has a function named `dbSyncOff` that causes automatic screen updating to start again. You can call this function whenever you want the Dark GDK to take over updating the screen. You won't need this function very often, but it can be helpful in some situations. For example, if you have code inside the game loop that prompts the user for some value, and then waits for the user to enter that value, the prompt won't display until the `dbSync` function is called. To remedy this, you can call `dbSyncOff` just before you display the prompt, and then call `dbSyncOn` after the user has entered the value.

Checkpoint

7.1. Briefly describe the following Dark GDK functions:

```
dbSyncOn
dbSyncRate
LoopGDK
dbSync
```

7.2. What is the connection between the LoopGDK function and the screen refresh rate that you specify with the dbSyncRate function?

7.3. Why is it important to call dbSync at the end of the game loop?

7.2 Simple Animation

CONCEPT: A simple way to create an animation is to write a game loop that draws a shape at a different location during each iteration. Be sure to clear the screen of anything displayed during the previous iteration, though!

Now that you know how to set up and write a game loop, let's look at a simple animation program. Program 7-3 displays the ball shown in Figure 7-2. As the program runs, the ball moves from the bottom of the screen to the top of the screen. When it reaches the top of the screen, the animation starts over with the ball at the bottom.

Program 7-3   (MovingBall.cpp)

```cpp
 1   // This program displays an animation of
 2   // a ball moving from the bottom of the screen
 3   // to the top.
 4   #include "DarkGDK.H"
 5
 6   void DarkGDK()
 7   {
 8       // The RADIUS constant holds the ball's radius.
 9       const int RADIUS = 50;
10
11       // The DISTANCE constant holds the distance that
12       // the ball moves during each loop iteration.
13       const int DISTANCE = 10;
14
15       // The CENTER_X constant holds the ball's
16       // X coordinate, which will be in the
17       // center of the screen.
18       const int CENTER_X = dbScreenWidth() / 2;
19
```

```
20        // The BOTTOM_Y constant holds the ball's
21        // bottom Y coordinate. This will position
22        // the bottom of the ball at the bottom of
23        // the screen.
24        const int BOTTOM_Y = dbScreenHeight() - RADIUS;
25
26        // The TOP_Y constant holds the ball's
27        // top Y coordinate. When the ball reaches
28        // this position, it will appear to be at the
29        // top of the screen.
30        const int TOP_Y = RADIUS;
31
32        // The y variable holds the ball's Y coordinate
33        // as it moves up and down. We initialize
34        // it with BOTTOM_Y.
35        int y = BOTTOM_Y;
36
37        // Specify that the program is now in
38        // control of refreshing the screen.
39        dbSyncOn();
40
41        // Specify that we want a maximum screen
42        // refresh rate of 60 times per second.
43        dbSyncRate(60);
44
45        // Display the animation.
46        while ( LoopGDK() )
47        {
48            // Clear the screen.
49            dbCLS();
50
51            // Draw the ball at the current location.
52            dbCircle(CENTER_X, y, RADIUS);
53
54            // Calculate the Y coordinate for
55            // the next iteration.
56            if (y > TOP_Y)
57            {
58                // Decrease the value of y. This
59                // will move the ball up the screen.
60                y -= DISTANCE;
61            }
62            else
63            {
64                // Move the ball back to the bottom
65                // of the screen.
66                y = BOTTOM_Y;
67            }
68
69            // Refresh the screen.
70            dbSync();
71        }
72    }
```

Figure 7-2 Output of Program 7-3

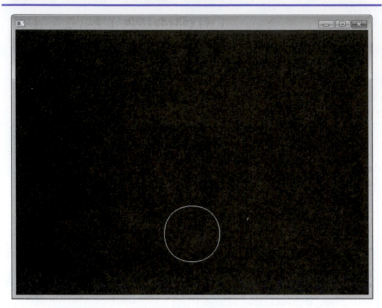

First, let's look at the constants and variables that are declared:

- Line 9: The RADIUS constant specifies the radius of the ball.
- Line 13: The DISTANCE constant specifies the distance that we will move the ball during each loop iteration.
- Line 18: The CENTER_X constant holds the X coordinate of the points in the center of the screen. When we draw the ball, we will use this value as its X coordinate.
- Line 24: The BOTTOM_Y constant holds a value that is calculated as 50 pixels from the bottom of the screen. We will use this constant as the ball's Y coordinate at the beginning of the animation. Because the ball has a radius of 50 pixels, this will make the bottom of the ball appear at the bottom of the screen.
- Line 30: The TOP_Y constant is initialized with the value 50 (the ball's radius). This will be the topmost Y coordinate that the ball will have during the animation. Because the ball has a radius of 50 pixels, the top of the ball will appear at the top of the screen when the ball reaches this Y coordinate.
- Line 35: The y variable will be used to hold the ball's Y coordinate as it moves up the screen. The variable is initialized with the value of BOTTOM_Y. Each time the game loop iterates, it will calculate a new value for the y variable.

Now let's look at the steps taken in this program. Line 39 calls the dbSyncOn function to disable automatic screen refreshing, and line 43 calls the dbSyncRate function to set the refresh rate at 60 times per second. The game loop begins in line 46.

Inside the game loop, in line 49, first we clear the screen with the dbCLS function. (In a moment, we will further discuss the importance of clearing the screen during each iteration.) Then, in line 52 we draw a circle. The circle's X coordinate will always be CENTER_X, which places it vertically at the center of the screen. The Y coordinate is specified by the y variable, and the radius is specified by the RADIUS constant.

Next, in line 56, we have an `if-else` statement that determines the circle's Y coordinate for the next iteration. It works like this: If the `y` variable is greater-than `TOP_Y`, then the ball has not reached the top of the screen yet. (Remember, the Y coordinates at the top of the screen are less than the ones at the bottom.) In this case, we subtract `DISTANCE` from the value in `y` in line 60. Otherwise, we know that the ball has reached the top of the screen, so we reset `y` to `BOTTOM_Y` in line 66.

Then, in line 70, we call `dbSync` to update the screen. This displays the ball that we drew back in line 52. After that, the loop starts over.

Clearing the Screen in the Game Loop

In line 49, we called the `dbCLS` function to clear the screen. This is important because during each iteration of the game loop we are drawing a new circle. If we want the animation to appear as a ball moving on the screen, we have to clear the screen before drawing a new circle. Otherwise, all of the circles drawn by the program will be visible on the screen. Figure 7-3 shows how the program's output would appear if we had forgotten to clear the screen.

Figure 7-3 Drawing the ball without clearing the screen

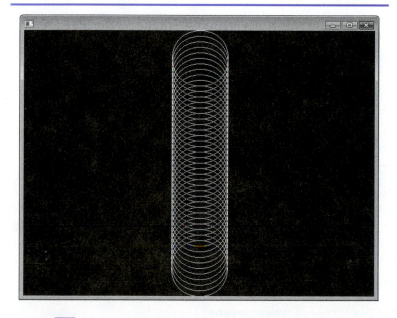

7.3 Controlling Objects with the Keyboard

CONCEPT: The Dark GDK provides functions that let you know whether certain keys, such as the arrow keys, spacebar, *Enter* key, and so forth are being pressed. Many games and animation programs allow the user to control objects on the screen with such keys.

Games commonly allow the player to use keys on the keyboard to control objects on the screen. For example, the *Up*, *Down*, *Left*, and *Right* arrow keys are typically used to move objects. Also, other keys such as the spacebar, the *Ctrl* key, the *Shift* key, the *Esc* key, and the *Enter* key are sometimes used to perform actions. The Dark GDK provides the functions listed in Table 7-1 for the purpose of detecting whether the user has pressed any of these keys.

Table 7-1 Key detection functions

Function	Description
dbUpKey	Returns 1 (true) if the *Up* arrow key is being pressed. Otherwise it returns 0 (false).
dbDownKey	Returns 1 (true) if the *Down* arrow key is being pressed. Otherwise it returns 0 (false).
dbLeftKey	Returns 1 (true) if the *Left* arrow key is being pressed. Otherwise it returns 0 (false).
dbRightKey	Returns 1 (true) if the *Right* arrow key is being pressed. Otherwise it returns 0 (false).
dbControlKey	Returns 1 (true) if the *Ctrl* key is being pressed. Otherwise it returns 0 (false).
dbShiftKey	Returns 1 (true) if the *Shift* key is being pressed. Otherwise it returns 0 (false).
dbReturnKey	Returns 1 (true) if the *Enter* key is being pressed. Otherwise it returns 0 (false).
dbEscapeKey	Returns 1 (true) if the *Esc* key is being pressed. Otherwise it returns 0 (false).
dbSpaceKey	Returns 1 (true) if the spacebar is being pressed. Otherwise it returns 0 (false).

Each of the functions listed in Table 7-1 returns an integer indicating whether a specific key is being pressed. A return value of 1 (true) indicates that the key is being pressed, and a return value of 0 (false) indicates that the key is not being pressed. Typically, you call these functions from an `if` statement. Here is an example that determines whether the user is pressing the spacebar:

```
if ( dbSpaceKey() )
{
    dbPrint("You pressed the spacebar.");
}
```

In this `if` statement, the `dbSpaceKey` function is called and its return value is tested as either true or false. If the user was pressing the spacebar at the moment the function was called, the function returns 1 (true) and the message "You pressed the spacebar." is displayed. If the user is not pressing the spacebar, the `dbSpaceKey` function returns 0 (false), and the message is not displayed.

Program 7-4 shows an example of how you can use these functions in the game loop. The loop uses a series of `if` statements to detect whether the user is pressing any of the arrow keys. If so, a message is displayed indicating which key is being pressed.

Program 7-4   `(KeyDetection.cpp)`

```cpp
1   // This program demonstrates how to perform
2   // continuous key detection in the game loop.
3   #include "DarkGDK.h"
4
5   void DarkGDK()
6   {
7       dbSyncOn();              // Disable auto screen refresh
8       dbSyncRate(60);          // Set the maximum screen refresh rate
9
10      while ( LoopGDK() )
11      {
12          // Is the user pressing any of the arrow keys?
13          if ( dbUpKey() )
14          {
15              dbPrint("You pressed the up arrow key.");
16          }
17
18          if ( dbDownKey() )
19          {
20              dbPrint("You pressed the down arrow key.");
21          }
22
23          if ( dbLeftKey() )
24          {
25              dbPrint("You pressed the left arrow key.");
26          }
27
28          if ( dbRightKey() )
29          {
30              dbPrint("You pressed the right arrow key.");
31          }
32
33          // Update the screen.
34          dbSync();
35      }
36  }
```

Notice that in this program we intentionally do not clear the screen inside the game loop. This way you can see each message that is displayed. Figure 7-4 shows an example of the program's output.

In the example output, the user pressed the *Up* arrow key, then the *Down* arrow key, then the *Right* arrow key, then the *Left* arrow key. Notice that the message for each key press is displayed multiple times. For example, when the program started and the user pressed the *Up* arrow key, the message "You pressed the up arrow key." was displayed four times. This is because the loop iterated four times while the user was holding down the *Up* arrow key. Likewise, when the user pressed the *Down* arrow key, the loop iterated seven times.

> **NOTE:** You might be wondering why we used a series of `if` statements instead of an `if-else-if` statement. The reason is that the user can press multiple keys at the same time. By having separate `if` statements, the loop will test each key during an iteration. As a result, we will see messages appear for all of the arrow keys that are being pressed. If we had used an `if-else-if` statement, we would see only one message appear during an iteration, regardless of the number of arrow keys that the user is pressing.

Figure 7-4 Example output of Program 7-4

Letting the User Move an Object

Now let's look at an example of how we can let the user move an object on the screen by pressing the arrow keys. When Program 7-5 starts, a circle is drawn in the center of the screen, as shown in Figure 7-5. The user can then move the circle up, down, left, or right by pressing the arrow keys.

Line 9 declares RADIUS, a constant for the circle's radius, initialized with the value 50. Lines 14 and 15 declare the variables x and y, which we use to hold the *XY* coordinates for the circle's center point. Notice that we initialize these variables with the coordinates of the center of the screen.

Lines 17 and 18 disable automatic screen refreshing and set the maximum screen refresh rate at 60. The game loop starts at line 21.

Inside the game loop we first clear the screen (line 24) and then we draw the circle at its current location (line 27). The first time the loop iterates this will be at the center of the screen. Then, in line 31 an `if` statement checks to see if the *Up* arrow key is being pressed. If so, the y variable is decremented. This will have the effect of moving the circle up one pixel during the next iteration. Similar `if` statements appear in lines 36, 41, and 46 to determine whether any of the other arrow keys are being pressed. If so, the x and/or y variables are adjusted.

Program 7-5 (MoveTheCircle.cpp)

```
1    // This program draws a circle in the center of the
2    // screen. The user can then move the circle using
3    // the arrow keys.
4    #include "DarkGDK.h"
5
6    void DarkGDK()
7    {
8        // Constant for the circle's radius
9        const int RADIUS = 50;
10
11       // Variables for the circle's XY coordinates.
12       // We initialize these with the coordinates of
13       // the center of the screen.
14       int x = dbScreenWidth() / 2;
15       int y = dbScreenHeight() / 2;
16
17       dbSyncOn();     // Disable auto screen refresh
18       dbSyncRate(60); // Set the maximum screen refresh rate
19
20       // The game loop
21       while ( LoopGDK() )
22       {
23           // Clear the screen.
24           dbCLS();
25
26           // Draw the circle at its current location.
27           dbCircle(x, y, RADIUS);
28
29           // If any arrow key is being pressed, then
30           // move the circle accordingly.
31           if ( dbUpKey() )
32           {
33               y--;
34           }
35
36           if ( dbDownKey() )
37           {
38               y++;
39           }
40
41           if ( dbLeftKey() )
42           {
43               x--;
44           }
45
46           if ( dbRightKey() )
47           {
48               x++;
49           }
50
51           // Update the screen.
52           dbSync();
53       }
54   }
```

Figure 7-5 Program 7-5 at startup

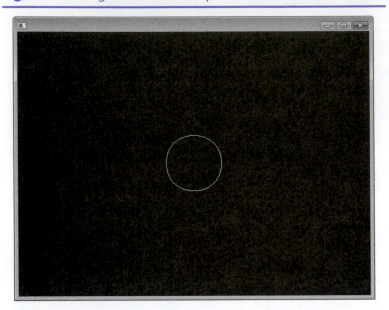

Performing Other Operations with the Keyboard

In addition to moving objects, your programs can let the user perform other operations with the keyboard. For example, when Program 7-6 starts, it also displays a circle with a radius of 50 pixels in the center of the screen. If the user presses the spacebar, then the circle's radius grows. If the user presses the *Ctrl* key and the spacebar at the same time, the circle's radius shrinks.

Program 7-6 **(ResizeCircle.cpp)**

```
 1   // This program draws a circle in the center of the
 2   // screen. The user can then use the spacebar to
 3   // increase the circle's radius, or Ctrl+spacebar
 4   // to decrease the circle's radius.
 5   #include "DarkGDK.h"
 6
 7   void DarkGDK()
 8   {
 9       // Constant for the circle's starting radius
10       const int STARTING_RADIUS = 50;
11
12       // Variables for the circle's XY coordinates.
13       // We initialize these with the coordinates of
14       // the center of the screen.
15       int x = dbScreenWidth() / 2;
16       int y = dbScreenHeight() / 2;
17
18       // Variable for the circle's radius
19       int radius = STARTING_RADIUS;
20
21       dbSyncOn();                 // Disable auto screen refresh
```

```
22          dbSyncRate(60);           // Set the maximum screen refresh rate
23
24          // The game loop
25          while ( LoopGDK() )
26          {
27              // Clear the screen.
28              dbCLS();
29
30              // Draw the circle using the current radius.
31              dbCircle(x, y, radius);
32
33              // If the spacebar is being pressed, AND the
34              // Ctrl key is NOT being pressed, then increase
35              // the circle's radius.
36              if ( dbSpaceKey() && !dbControlKey() )
37              {
38                  radius++;
39              }
40
41              // If the spacebar is being pressed, AND the
42              // Ctrl key is being pressed, then decrease
43              // the circle's radius.
44              if ( dbSpaceKey() && dbControlKey() )
45              {
46                  radius--;
47              }
48
49              // Update the screen.
50              dbSync();
51          }
52 }
```

Notice the use of the logical `&&` and `!` operators in line 36. You should read the logic this way: If the `dbSpaceKey` function returns true *and* the `dbControlKey` function does *not* return true, then increment `radius`. In plain English we would say "If the spacebar is being pressed and the *Ctrl* key is not being pressed, increase the circle's radius."

The `if` statement in line 44 determines whether the spacebar is being pressed and the *Ctrl* key is being pressed. If so, `radius` is decremented.

 Checkpoint

> 7.4. What functions do you call to see if the following keys are being pressed?
> - *Up* arrow
> - *Down* arrow
> - *Right* arrow
> - *Left* arrow
> - *Ctrl*
> - *Shift*
> - *Enter*
> - *Esc*

7.4   Sprites

CONCEPT: A sprite is a graphic image that is used as an element in a game. Sprites can be moved and manipulated in various ways.

In Chapter 5, we discussed loading graphic images from files, displaying them on the screen, and manipulating them in various ways. Graphic images are used extensively in computer games. The graphics for the background scenery, the game characters, and practically everything else are images that are loaded from graphic files. The graphic images that perform actions in a computer game are commonly known as *sprites*. The Dark GDK provides many functions for creating and using sprites.

Creating a Sprite

To create a sprite, you perform two actions: You use the `dbLoadImage` function to load an image into memory that you want to use as the sprite, and you use the `dbSprite` function to designate that image as a sprite and display it. Here is the general format of how you call the `dbSprite` function:

```
dbSprite(SpriteNumber, X, Y, ImageNumber);
```

In the general format, `SpriteNumber` is an integer number that you are assigning to the sprite. This can be any number in the range of 1 through 65,535. Once the sprite is created, you will use this number to identify it in subsequent operations. The `X` and `Y` arguments are integers specifying the screen coordinates where the sprite's upper-left corner will be positioned. `ImageNumber` is the number of the image that you want to use for the sprite.

For example, suppose we have an image file named `LadyBug.bmp` that we want to use as a sprite. The following code shows how we can load that image into memory and then designate it as a sprite:

```
dbLoadImage("LadyBug.bmp", 1);
dbSprite(1, 320, 240, 1);
```

The first statement loads the `LadyBug.bmp` file as image number 1. The second statement designates that image as sprite number 1, and positions it at the screen coordinates (320, 240). When this statement executes, the sprite will be displayed on the screen.

By default, black (RGB = 0, 0, 0) is used as the key color for sprite transparency. You can use the `dbSetImageColorKey` function to designate a different key color. For example, suppose we have two images stored in the files `Space.bmp` and `UFO.bmp`, as shown in Figure 7-6, which also appears in this book's color insert. The `UFO.bmp` image is set on a green background (RGB = 0, 255, 0). Program 7-7 demonstrates how we can set the key color to green, and then display the UFO image on top of the space image.

Figure 7-6 The Space.bmp and UFO.bmp images

UFO.bmp

Space.bmp

This figure also appears in this book's full-color insert.

Program 7-7   (SpriteDemo.cpp)

```
1   // This program displays sprites.
2   #include "DarkGDK.h"
3
4   void DarkGDK()
5   {
6       // Set the key color to green.
7       dbSetImageColorKey(0, 255, 0);
8
9       // Load two images.
10      dbLoadImage("Space.bmp", 1);        // image #1
11      dbLoadImage("UFO.bmp", 2);          // image #2
12
13      // Make sprite #1 and display it
14      // at (0, 0). We will use image #1.
15      dbSprite(1, 0, 0, 1);
16
17      // Make sprite #2 and display it
18      // at (400, 100). We will use image #2.
19      dbSprite(2, 400, 100, 2);
20
21      // Wait for the user to press a key
22      dbWaitKey();
23  }
```

Figure 7-7 shows the program's output.

Figure 7-7 Output of Program 7-7

Moving a Sprite

Once you have created and displayed a sprite with the dbSprite function, you can move it to a new location on the screen by calling the dbSprite function again, using the same sprite number and image number, but passing different values for the *X* and *Y* coordinates. For example, the following statement creates sprite number 1 at the coordinates (100, 200), using image number 5 as the graphic for the sprite:

```
dbSprite(1, 100, 200, 5);
```

Later in the program, suppose we want to move the sprite to the coordinates (300, 20). To do so, we simply call the function again, like this:

```
dbSprite(1, 300, 20, 5);
```

After this function call, the sprite will no longer appear at its previous location. It will now appear at (300, 20).

 NOTE: If you call dbSprite passing a sprite number that has not been used in the program, you are creating a new sprite and assigning that number to it. If you call dbSprite passing an existing sprite number, you are manipulating the existing sprite. As demonstrated here, you can pass new *XY* coordinates for the sprite's location. You can also pass a new image number, to change the image associated with the sprite.

To demonstrate how to move a sprite, look at Program 7-8, which displays the space background and the UFO. This program has a game loop that allows the user to move the UFO by pressing the arrow keys.

Program 7-8   (`MoveSprite.cpp`)

```cpp
1   // This program allows the user to move a sprite
2   // with the arrow keys.
3   #include "DarkGDK.h"
4
5   // Constant for the refresh rate.
6   const int REFRESH_RATE = 60;
7
8   // The following constants are for the image numbers
9   // and sprite numbers used in this program.
10  const int SPACE_IMAGE_NUMBER    = 1;
11  const int SPACE_SPRITE_NUMBER   = 1;
12  const int UFO_IMAGE_NUMBER      = 2;
13  const int UFO_SPRITE_NUMBER     = 2;
14
15  // Constants for the UFO's starting
16  // XY coordinates
17  const int UFO_STARTING_X = 400;
18  const int UFO_STARTING_Y = 100;
19
20  // Function prototypes
21  void createSprites();
22  void getUFOcoordinates(int &, int &);
23
24  //********************************************
25  // The DarkGDK function                      *
26  //********************************************
27  void DarkGDK()
28  {
29      // Variables for the UFO's x and y coordinates.
30      int ufoX = UFO_STARTING_X;
31      int ufoY = UFO_STARTING_Y;
32
33      dbSyncOn();                  // Disable auto refresh
34      dbSyncRate(REFRESH_RATE);    // Set the refresh rate
35
36      // Create the sprites.
37      createSprites();
38
39      // Game loop
40      while ( LoopGDK() )
41      {
42          // Get the coordinates for the UFO.
43          // Note that ufoX and ufoY are passed
44          // by reference. After the function call
45          // they will contain the new coordinates
46          // for the UFO.
47          getUFOcoordinates(ufoX, ufoY);
48
49          // Display the UFO at its new location.
50          dbSprite(UFO_SPRITE_NUMBER, ufoX, ufoY, UFO_IMAGE_NUMBER);
51
52          // Refresh the screen.
53          dbSync();
54      }
```

```
 55      }
 56
 57   //*********************************************
 58   // The createSprites function creates the space *
 59   // and UFO sprites.                             *
 60   //*********************************************
 61   void createSprites()
 62   {
 63       // Set the key color to green.
 64       dbSetImageColorKey(0, 255, 0);
 65
 66       // Load the Space.bmp and UFO.bmp images.
 67       dbLoadImage("Space.bmp", SPACE_IMAGE_NUMBER);
 68       dbLoadImage("UFO.bmp", UFO_IMAGE_NUMBER);
 69
 70       // Create the space sprite. Because this is used
 71       // as the background, we will display it at (0, 0).
 72       dbSprite(SPACE_SPRITE_NUMBER, 0, 0, SPACE_IMAGE_NUMBER);
 73
 74       // Create the UFO sprite and display it at its
 75       // starting coordinates.
 76       dbSprite(UFO_SPRITE_NUMBER, UFO_STARTING_X,
 77                UFO_STARTING_Y, UFO_IMAGE_NUMBER);
 78   }
 79
 80   //*********************************************
 81   // The getUFOcoordinates accepts two arguments  *
 82   // by reference. These arguments are for the    *
 83   // UFO's X and Y coordinates. The function      *
 84   // determines whether the user is pressing an   *
 85   // arrow key and updates these values           *
 86   // accordingly.                                 *
 87   //*********************************************
 88   void getUFOcoordinates(int &x, int &y)
 89   {
 90       if ( dbUpKey() )
 91       {
 92           y--;
 93       }
 94
 95       if ( dbDownKey() )
 96       {
 97           y++;
 98       }
 99
100       if ( dbLeftKey() )
101       {
102           x--;
103       }
104
105       if ( dbRightKey() )
106       {
107           x++;
108       }
109   }
```

Let's take a closer look at the program. The following global constants are declared in lines 6 through 18:

- Line 6 declares REFRESH_RATE, a constant for the screen refresh rate.
- Lines 10 through 13 declare constants for the image numbers and sprite numbers that we will use in this program.
  - SPACE_IMAGE_NUMBER is declared and initialized with 1. We will use this constant whenever we need to refer to the image number for the Space.bmp graphic.
  - SPACE_SPRITE_NUMBER is declared and initialized with 1. We will use this constant whenever we need to refer to the sprite number for the Space.bmp graphic.
  - UFO_IMAGE_NUMBER is declared and initialized with 2. We will use this constant whenever we need to refer to the image number for the UFO.bmp graphic.
  - UFO_SPRITE_NUMBER is declared and initialized with 2. We will use this constant whenever we need to refer to the sprite number for the UFO.bmp graphic.

    The reason that we created constants for the image numbers and sprite numbers is that the constant names are sometimes easier to remember than the numbers.
- Lines 17 and 18 declare the UFO_STARTING_X and UFO_STARTING_Y constants, which are used for the UFO's starting *X* and *Y* coordinates.

Inside the DarkGDK function, we declare the variables ufoX and ufoY in lines 30 and 31. These variables will hold the UFO's *X* and *Y* coordinates, and are initialized with the values of the UFO_STARTING_X and UFO_STARTING_Y constants.

Lines 33 and 34 disable automatic screen refreshing and set the maximum refresh rate at 60 times per second.

Line 37 calls the createSprites function, which loads the Space.bmp and UFO.bmp images, and displays them as sprites. (The createSprites function definition appears in lines 61 through 78.)

The game loop begins in line 40. Inside the loop, the getUFOcoordinates function is called in line 47. The ufoX and ufoY variables are passed by reference to the function. The function (which appears in lines 88 through 109) checks to see whether any of the arrow keys are being pressed. If so, it adjusts the value of the arguments accordingly. After this function finishes, the ufoX and ufoY variables will contain the new coordinates for the UFO.

Line 50 displays the UFO sprite at its new location, and line 53 refreshes the screen.

Getting a Sprite's *X* and *Y* Coordinates

You can get the current screen coordinates of any previously created sprite by calling the dbGetSpriteX and dbGetSpriteY functions, passing the sprite number as an argument. For example, the following statements get the *X* and *Y* coordinates for sprite 1 and assign those values to the int variables spriteX and spriteY:

```
spriteX = dbSpriteX(1);
spriteY = dbSpriteY(1);
```

Getting the Width and Height of a Sprite

You can get the width of an existing sprite by calling the `dbSpriteWidth` function, passing the sprite number as an argument. The function returns the width of the sprite as an integer. The following shows an example. Assume that `spriteWidth` is an `int` variable.

```
spriteWidth = dbSpriteWidth(1);
```

After this statement executes, `spriteWidth` will contain the width of sprite number 1.

You can get the height of an existing sprite by calling the `dbSpriteHeight` function, passing the sprite number as an argument. The function returns the height of the sprite as an integer. The following shows an example. Assume that `spriteHeight` is an `int` variable.

```
spriteHeight = dbSpriteHeight(1);
```

After this statement executes, `spriteHeight` will contain the height of sprite number 1.

Rotating a Sprite

You can use the `dbRotateSprite` function to rotate a sprite around its *insertion point*, which by default is the sprite's upper-left corner. A sprite can be rotated around its insertion point at any angle from 0 degrees through 359 degrees. Here is the general format of how you call the function:

```
dbRotateSprite(SpriteNumber, Angle);
```

SpriteNumber is the number of the sprite that you want to rotate, and *Angle* is a floating-point value indicating the angle of rotation, in degrees.

Program 7-9 shows an example. This program displays the space background and the UFO. It has a game loop that allows the user to rotate the UFO by pressing the *Up* or *Down* arrow keys. Figure 7-8 shows examples of the UFO rotated at different angles.

Program 7-9   **(RotateSprite.cpp)**

```
 1  // This program allows the user to rotate a sprite
 2  // with the up and down arrow keys.
 3  #include "DarkGDK.h"
 4
 5  // Constant for the refresh rate.
 6  const int REFRESH_RATE = 60;
 7
 8  // The following constants are for the image numbers
 9  // and sprite numbers used in this program.
10  const int SPACE_IMAGE_NUMBER  = 1;
11  const int SPACE_SPRITE_NUMBER = 1;
12  const int UFO_IMAGE_NUMBER    = 2;
13  const int UFO_SPRITE_NUMBER   = 2;
```

```
14
15   // Constants for the UFO's XY coordinates
16   const int UFO_X = 400;
17   const int UFO_Y = 100;
18
19   // Constant for the UFO's starting angle.
20   const float STARTING_ANGLE = 0.0;
21
22   // Function prototypes
23   void createSprites();
24   void updateUFO(float &);
25
26   //**********************************************
27   // The DarkGDK function                        *
28   //**********************************************
29   void DarkGDK()
30   {
31       // Variable for the UFO's angle.
32       float ufoAngle = STARTING_ANGLE;
33
34       // Setup for the game loop
35       dbSyncOn();
36       dbSyncRate(REFRESH_RATE);
37
38       // Create the sprites.
39       createSprites();
40
41       // Game loop
42       while ( LoopGDK() )
43       {
44           // Update the UFO's angle.
45           // Note that ufoAngle is passed by
46           // reference. After the function call
47           // it will contain the UFO's new angle.
48           updateUFO(ufoAngle);
49
50           // Display the UFO.
51           dbSprite(UFO_SPRITE_NUMBER, UFO_X, UFO_Y, UFO_IMAGE_NUMBER);
52
53           // Refresh the screen.
54           dbSync();
55       }
56   }
57
58   //****************************************************
59   // The createSprites function creates the space      *
60   // and UFO sprites.                                   *
61   //****************************************************
62   void createSprites()
63   {
64       // Set the key color to green.
65       dbSetImageColorKey(0, 255, 0);
66
67       // Load the Space.bmp and UFO.bmp images.
68       dbLoadImage("Space.bmp", SPACE_IMAGE_NUMBER);
69       dbLoadImage("UFO.bmp", UFO_IMAGE_NUMBER);
```

```
70
71          // Create the space sprite. Because this is used
72          // as the background, we will display it at (0, 0).
73          dbSprite(SPACE_SPRITE_NUMBER, 0, 0, SPACE_IMAGE_NUMBER);
74
75          // Create the UFO sprite and display it.
76          dbSprite(UFO_SPRITE_NUMBER, UFO_X, UFO_Y, UFO_IMAGE_NUMBER);
77     }
78
79     //*****************************************************
80     // The updateUFO function accepts a float argument    *
81     // by reference. This argument holds the UFO's angle  *
82     // of rotation. The function determines whether the   *
83     // user is pressing the up or down arrow key. If so,   *
84     // it increments or decrements the angle and then      *
85     // rotates the UFO sprite.                             *
86     //*****************************************************
87     void updateUFO(float &angle)
88     {
89          // If the up arrow key is being pressed, increment
90          // the UFO's angle.
91          if ( dbUpKey() )
92          {
93               angle++;
94          }
95
96          // If the down arrow key is being pressed, decrement
97          // the UFO's angle.
98          if ( dbDownKey() )
99          {
100              angle--;
101         }
102
103         // Rotate the sprite.
104         dbRotateSprite(UFO_SPRITE_NUMBER, angle);
105    }
```

You can get the angle of a rotated sprite by calling the `dbSpriteAngle` function with the sprite number of the sprite you want to get the angle for. For example, the following statement declares a `float` variable named `angle` and initializes it with sprite number 1's current angle of rotation:

```
float angle = dbSpriteAngle(1);
```

Offsetting a Sprite's Insertion Point

By default, a sprite's insertion point is its upper-left corner. By this, we mean that when the sprite is displayed at a specified location, it is the sprite's upper-left corner that is positioned at that location. You can change the sprite's insertion point by calling the `dbOffsetSprite` function. Here is the general format of how you call the function:

```
dbOffsetSprite(SpriteNumber, XOffset, YOffset);
```

Figure 7-8 UFO sprite rotated at various angles

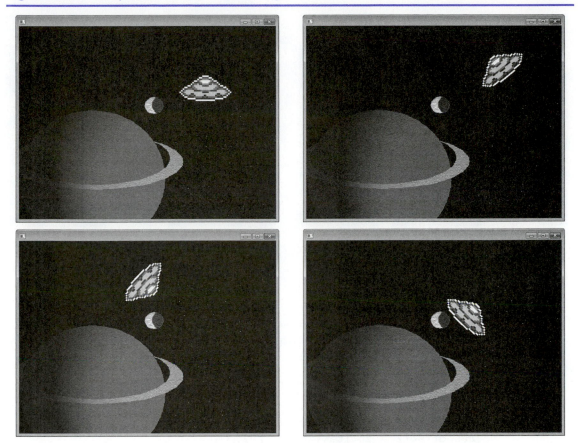

SpriteNumber is the number of the sprite you want to offset. *XOffset* is an integer value for the amount you want to offset from the insertion point along the X axis. *YOffset* is an integer value for the amount you want to offset from the insertion point along the Y axis.

For example, let's say that sprite number 1 has a size of 64 × 64 pixels. Its insertion point is the image's upper-left corner. The following statement moves the sprite's insertion point 32 pixels to the right (along the image's X axis) and 32 pixels down (along the image's Y axis).

```
dbOffsetSprite(1, 32, 32);
```

After this statement executes, the sprite's insertion point will be at its center, not at its upper-left corner. Figure 7-9 shows two examples of a sprite placed at the center of the screen using the screen coordinates (319, 239). Lines have been drawn to help show the center of the screen. The image on the left shows the sprite placed at the center of the screen with no offset, using the upper-left corner as its insertion point. The image on the left shows the sprite placed at the center of the screen, with its insertion point offset to the center of the sprite image. Notice how the offset sprite appears precisely in the center of the screen, while the sprite with no offset appears to be quite a bit off center.

Figure 7-9 A sprite before and after it has been offset

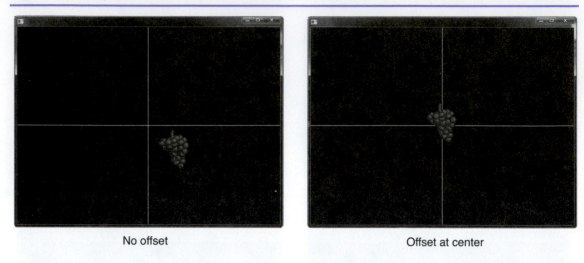

No offset   Offset at center

If you want to offset a sprite's insertion point so it is at the sprite's center, you can get the sprite's width and height to calculate the amount to offset along each axis. The following code shows an example:

```
// Create sprite 1 at (100, 100) using image 1.
dbSprite(1, 100, 100, 1);

// Calculate the X and Y offset amounts.
int offsetX = spriteWidth(1) / 2;
int offsetY = spriteHeight(1) / 2;

// Offset the insertion point.
dbOffsetSprite(1, offsetX, offsetY);

// Display the sprite using the new insertion point.
dbSprite(1, 100, 100, 1);
```

NOTE: Recall from our sprite rotation example that a sprite rotates around its insertion point. In most cases, you will want to rotate a sprite around its center point, not its upper-left corner. By offsetting a sprite's insertion point to its center, all rotations will be done around the sprite's center. If you have downloaded the book's example programs from www.aw.com/gaddis, you will find a project named RotateSpriteWithOffset. This project contains a modified version of Program 7-9 in which the UFO sprite rotates about its center.

You can get the current *X* offset of a sprite by calling the dbSpriteOffsetX function, passing the sprite number as an argument. For example, the following statement stores the *X* offset of sprite 1 in the variable sprite1OffsetX:

```
int sprite1OffsetX = dbSpriteOffsetX(1);
```

You can get the current *Y* offset of a sprite by calling the dbSpriteOffsetY function, passing the sprite number as an argument. For example, the following statement stores the *Y* offset of sprite 1 in the variable sprite1OffsetY:

```
int sprite1OffsetY = dbSpriteOffsetY(1);
```

Showing and Hiding Sprites

You can prevent a sprite from being displayed by calling the dbHideSprite function. Here is the general format of how you call the function:

```
dbHideSprite(SpriteNumber);
```

SpriteNumber is the number of the sprite you want to hide. After a sprite has been hidden, you can display it again with the dbShowSprite function. Here is the general format:

```
dbShowSprite(SpriteNumber);
```

SpriteNumber is the number of the sprite you want to show.

You can hide all sprites by calling the dbHideAllSprites function. Since this function hides all sprites, you simply call the function by its name, without passing any arguments. Here is an example:

```
dbHideAllSprites();
```

You can show all sprites that have been previously hidden by calling the dbShowAllSprites function. Like the dbHideAllSprites function, the dbShowAllSprites function is called without any arguments. Here is an example:

```
dbShowAllSprites();
```

You can determine whether a sprite has been hidden or is being shown by calling the dbSpriteVisible function, passing the sprite number as an argument. If the sprite is visible, the function returns 1 (true). If the sprite is hidden, it returns 0 (false). Here is an example:

```
if ( dbSpriteVisible(1) )
{
    dbHideSprite(1);
}
```

Resizing a Sprite

You can change the size of an existing sprite by calling the dbSizeSprite function. Here is the general format of how you call the function:

```
dbSizeSprite(SpriteNumber, XSize, YSize);
```

The *SpriteNumber* is the number of the sprite you want to size. *XSize* is an integer specifying the size of the sprite (in pixels) along the *X* axis, and *YSize* is an integer specifying the size of the sprite (in pixels) along the *Y* axis. For example, suppose you have a sprite that is 64×64 pixels, if you call the dbSizeSprite function passing 32 as the *XSize* and 32 as the *YSize*, the sprite will shrink to half its size.

The `dbStretchSprite` function can be used to scale a sprite by stretching it or shrinking it. Here is the general format of how you call the function:

```
dbStretchSprite(SpriteNumber, XStretch, YStretch);
```

SpriteNumber is the number of the sprite you want to stretch. *XStretch* is an integer value that represents the percentage the sprite will be expanded or shrunk along the *X* axis. *YStretch* is an integer value that represents the percentage the sprite will be expanded or shrunk along the *Y* axis. For example, passing 50 as both of these arguments will shrink the sprite to half its size, and passing 200 as both of these arguments will expand the sprite to twice its size. If you pass 0 as both arguments, the sprite will vanish.

You can get the amount that a sprite has been scaled along the *X* axis by calling the `dbSpriteScaleX` function, passing the sprite number as an argument. For example, the following statement gets the amount of scale applied to sprite number 1 along the *X* axis and assigns that value to the variable `spriteScaleX`:

```
int spriteScaleX = dbSpriteScaleX(1);
```

You can get the value of how much a sprite has been scaled along the *Y* axis by calling the `dbSpriteScaleY` function, passing the sprite number as an argument. For example, the following statement gets the scale factor of sprite 1 along the *Y* axis and assigns that value to the variable `spriteScaleY`:

```
int spriteScaleY = dbSpriteScaleY(1);
```

Setting a Sprite's Priority

Sprite's have a *priority* that can be used to control the order in which they are drawn on the screen. By default, all sprites have a priority of 0. When all sprites have the same priority, they are drawn on the screen in the order that they are displayed with the `dbSprite` function.

When a sprite is drawn on the screen, it will appear on top of any other sprite that has already been drawn at the same location. For example, the following programming statements will draw three sprites at the location (300, 200). Sprite 1 will be drawn first, then sprite 2, then sprite 3. As a result, sprite 3 will appear on top of sprites 2 and 1, and sprite 2 will appear on top of sprite 1.

```
dbSprite(1, 300, 200, 1);
dbSprite(2, 300, 200, 2);
dbSprite(3, 300, 200, 3);
```

You can change the order in which a sprite is drawn on the screen by changing its priority. The higher a sprite's priority, the later it will be drawn. To change a sprite's priority you call the `dbSetSpritePriority` function. Here is the general format of how you call the function:

```
dbSetSpritePriority(SpriteNumber, Priority);
```

SpriteNumber is the number of the sprite you want to set the priority for. *Priority* is an integer value that sets the priority of the sprite being drawn last to the screen. For example, in the code previously shown, suppose we want to make sure sprite 1 is drawn last (on top of sprites 2 and 3). We can do so without modifying the order in which dbSprite functions are called by changing sprite 1's priority to a higher value. Here is an example:

```
dbSprite(1, 320, 240, 1);
dbSprite(2, 320, 240, 2);
dbSprite(3, 320, 240, 3);
dbSetSpritePriority(1, 1);
```

By changing the priority of sprite 1 to the value 1, it will be drawn last. This is because sprites 2 and 3 have a default priority of 0.

Determining Whether a Sprite Exists

You can determine whether a sprite has been created successfully by calling the dbSpriteExist function. You pass the sprite number as an argument and it returns 1 (true) if the sprite exists, or 0 (false) otherwise. Here is an example:

```
if ( !dbSpriteExist(1) )
{
    dbCLS();
    dbPrint("Error! Sprite expected to exist.");
}
```

Changing the Sprite Image

One way to change the image that is associated with a sprite is to call the dbSprite function, passing a different image number as an argument. For example, assume that the following statement creates sprite number 1 at the coordinates (100, 50) and associates that sprite with image number 10:

```
dbSprite(1, 100, 50, 10);
```

Later in the program we can associate this sprite with image number 20 by calling the dbSprite function again:

```
dbSprite(1, 100, 50, 20);
```

Another way to change a sprite's image is with the dbSetSpriteImage function. Here is the general format of the function:

```
dbSetSpriteImage(SpriteNumber, ImageNumber);
```

SpriteNumber is the number of the sprite that you want to change the image for, and *ImageNumber* is the number of the image you want to the sprite to display. For example the following statement would cause sprite 1 to display image 20:

```
dbSetSpriteImage(1, 20);
```

You can get the image number that a sprite is currently using by calling the dbSpriteImage function. For example, the following statement gets the image number that is associated with sprite 1 and assigns that image number to the spriteImage variable:

```
int spriteImage = dbSpriteImage(1);
```

Flipping and Mirroring a Sprite

You can flip a sprite vertically by calling the dbFlipSprite function. Here is the general format of how you call the function:

```
dbFlipSprite(SpriteNumber);
```

The *SpriteNumber* is the number of the sprite you want to flip. When a sprite is flipped it appears upside down as shown in Figure 7-10.

Figure 7-10 A flipped sprite

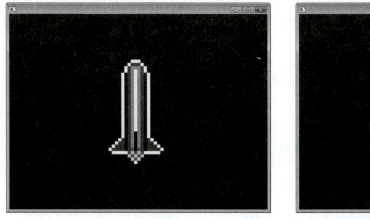

Original sprite   Flipped sprite

You can mirror a sprite horizontally by calling the dbMirrorSprite function. Here is the general format of how you call the function:

```
dbMirrorSprite(SpriteNumber);
```

The *SpriteNumber* is the number of the sprite you want to mirror. When a sprite is mirrored it appears as a horizontal mirror image of the original sprite. Figure 7-11 shows an example.

Figure 7-11 A mirrored sprite

Original sprite   Mirrored sprite

You can determine whether a sprite has been flipped or mirrored by calling the dbSpriteFlipped and dbSpriteMirrored functions, passing a sprite number as an argument. The dbSpriteFlipped function returns 1 if the sprite has been flipped, or 0 otherwise. The dbSpriteMirrored function returns 1 if the sprite has been mirrored, or 0 otherwise.

Setting the Back Save and Transparency Features

By default, a sprite is set to restore its background as it moves, and use transparency. You can change these features by calling the dbSetSprite function. Here is the general format of how you call the function:

```
dbSetSprite(SpriteNumber, BackSave, Transparency);
```

SpriteNumber is the number of the sprite that you want to set. *BackSave* is an integer value. A value of 1 will enable back save, and a value of 0 will disable back save. When back save is disabled, the sprite will not restore the background and leave a trail as it moves. For example, the following statement disables the back save feature for sprite number 2:

```
dbSetSprite(2, 0, 1);
```

Transparency is an integer value. A value of 1 will enable transparency. A value of 0 will disable transparency. If transparency is disabled, then all key color pixels will appear black. For example, the following statement disables the transparency feature for sprite number 2:

```
dbSetSprite(2, 1, 0);
```

NOTE: If the numeric values 0 and 1 are a little confusing, you might consider using the Boolean keywords true or false instead. For example, the following statements accomplish the same thing:

```
dbSetSprite(1, 1, 0);
dbSetSprite(1, true, false);
```

Using a Sprite's Alpha Value to Change Its Opacity

Except for those pixels that are of a key color, a sprite normally appears completely opaque, meaning that you cannot see through it. However, sprites have an *alpha value* that can be used to make them semitransparent. A sprite's alpha value is an integer in the range of 0 through 255. If a sprite's alpha value is set to 255 (which is the default value) then the sprite is completely opaque, and you cannot see through it. An alpha value of 0 makes a sprite completely invisible. Alpha values between 0 and 255 will make the sprite semitransparent.

You use the dbSetSpriteAlpha function to set a sprite's alpha value. Here is the general format for calling the function:

```
dbSetSpriteAlpha(SpriteNumber, AlphaValue);
```

SpriteNumber is the number of the sprite you want to change the alpha value for. *AlphaValue* is an integer value ranging from 0 through 255.

You can get the alpha value of a sprite by calling the dbSpriteAlpha function, passing the sprite number as an argument. For example, the following statement gets the alpha value of sprite 1 and assigns it to the variable spriteAlpha:

```
int spriteAlpha = dbSpriteAlpha(1);
```

If you have downloaded the book's example programs from www.aw.com/gaddis, you will find a project named StealthJet that demonstrates the dbSetSpriteAlpha and dbSpriteAlpha functions. When the program initially runs, it displays the image of the jet shown on the left in Figure 7-12. By pressing the down arrow key you can decrease the jet's alpha value so it becomes less opaque, as shown on the right in the figure. Pressing the *Up* arrow key increases the jet's alpha value.

Figure 7-12 Example output of the StealthJet program

Deleting a Sprite from Memory

After a program is finished using a sprite it has loaded into memory, it can remove it with the dbDeleteSprite function. You pass a sprite number as an argument to the function and it removes that sprite from memory. Here is an example:

```
dbDeleteSprite(10);
```

This statement removes sprite number 10 from memory. Deleting unused sprites frees memory and can improve the program's performance. If a program has several sprites loaded, and continues to run when those sprite are no longer needed, it's a good idea to delete them to increase system performance.

Displaying Sprites, Images, and Primitive Graphics

When you create a sprite in a Dark GDK program, the program goes into a special mode that allows sprites to move around on the screen, passing in front of and behind each other, without interfering with each other's images. Suppose we have two sprites that we will call sprite A and sprite B. If sprite A moves on top of sprite B, the system will make a copy of the part of sprite B that is covered up. Then, when sprite A moves away from sprite B, the system can restore sprite B's image. This process is known as *back saving*. You saw how this works in Program 7-8 and Program 7-9. In those programs we display the UFO sprite on top of the space background sprite. When the UFO sprite moves, the part of the space background sprite that was under it is restored. This gives the appearance that the UFO sprite is on top of the space background sprite.

Sometimes you will need to create programs that display sprites along with regular images and primitive graphics. For example, your program will perform a bit faster if you create sprites only for the game elements that will move around the screen, or be involved in the game action. The back saving process can cause problems, however, when you mix sprites with non-sprite graphics. When the system performs the back save process, it erases everything but sprites from the screen. To demonstrate this, look at Program 7-10. This program loads the `Space.bmp` image and the `UFO.bmp` image in lines 25 and 26. It then pastes the space image to the screen in line 29. In line 32 the UFO image is used to create a sprite. When you run this program, the UFO sprite will be visible, but the space background will not, as shown in Figure 7-13.

Program 7-10   (`MissingBackground.cpp`)

```
1    // This program attempts to display a sprite
2    // on top of a regular image.
3    #include "DarkGDK.h"
4
5    // Constant for the refresh rate.
6    const int REFRESH_RATE = 60;
7
8    // Constants are for the image numbers
9    const int UFO_IMAGE_NUMBER    = 1;
10   const int SPACE_IMAGE_NUMBER  = 2;
11
12   // Constant for the UFO sprite number
13   const int UFO_SPRITE_NUMBER   = 1;
14
15   // Constants for the UFO's XY coordinates
16   const int UFO_X = 400;
17   const int UFO_Y = 100;
18
19   void DarkGDK()
20   {
21       // Set the key color to green.
22       dbSetImageColorKey(0, 255, 0);
23
24       // Load the two images.
25       dbLoadImage("Space.bmp", SPACE_IMAGE_NUMBER);
26       dbLoadImage("UFO.bmp",   UFO_IMAGE_NUMBER);
27
```

```
28      // Paste the space background image.
29      dbPasteImage(SPACE_IMAGE_NUMBER, 0, 0);
30
31      // Make the UFO sprite.
32      dbSprite(UFO_SPRITE_NUMBER, UFO_X, UFO_Y, UFO_IMAGE_NUMBER);
33
34      // Wait for the user to press a key
35      dbWaitKey();
36  }
```

Figure 7-13 Output of Program 7-10

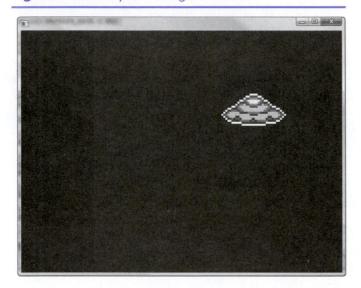

This problem can be easily resolved. Anytime a program needs to display a sprite along with a pasted image, you write a game loop that pastes the image during each iteration. You do the same when you want to display a sprite with primitive graphics or text: in the game loop you draw the primitive graphics and/or display the text during each iteration. Program 7-11 shows an example. It displays the UFO sprite on top of the pasted space image. It also displays text instructing the user to use the arrow keys to move the UFO. The program's output is shown in Figure 7-14. Notice that inside the game loop, in line 45 we paste the space image to the screen, in lines 48 though 49 we display text on the screen, and in line 59 we display the sprite. These actions take place with each iteration of the loop.

Program 7-11   (MoveSprite2.cpp)

```
1   // This program displays a sprite on top of an image.
2   // It allows the user to move the UFO sprite with
3   // the arrow keys.
4   #include "DarkGDK.h"
5
6   // Constant for the refresh rate.
```

```
 7   const int REFRESH_RATE = 60;
 8
 9   // Constants are for the image numbers
10   const int UFO_IMAGE_NUMBER   = 1;
11   const int SPACE_IMAGE_NUMBER = 2;
12
13   // Constant for the UFO sprite number
14   const int UFO_SPRITE_NUMBER  = 1;
15
16   // Constants for the UFO's starting
17   // XY coordinates
18   const int UFO_STARTING_X = 400;
19   const int UFO_STARTING_Y = 100;
20
21   // Constants for the text position
22   const int TEXT_X = 319;
23   const int TEXT_Y = 20;
24
25   // Function prototypes
26   void setUp();
27   void getUFOcoordinates(int &, int &);
28
29   //*********************************************
30   // The DarkGDK function                       *
31   //*********************************************
32   void DarkGDK()
33   {
34       // Variables for the UFO's x and y coordinates.
35       int ufoX = UFO_STARTING_X;
36       int ufoY = UFO_STARTING_Y;
37
38       // Perform setup operations.
39       setUp();
40
41       // Game loop
42       while ( LoopGDK() )
43       {
44           // Paste the background image at (0, 0).
45           dbPasteImage(SPACE_IMAGE_NUMBER, 0, 0);
46
47           // Display instructions.
48           dbCenterText(TEXT_X, TEXT_Y,
49               "Use the arrow keys to move the UFO");
50
51           // Get the coordinates for the UFO.
52           // Note that ufoX and ufoY are passed
53           // by reference. After the function call
54           // they will contain the new coordinates
55           // for the UFO.
56           getUFOcoordinates(ufoX, ufoY);
57
58           // Display the UFO at its new location.
59           dbSprite(UFO_SPRITE_NUMBER, ufoX, ufoY, UFO_IMAGE_NUMBER);
60
61           // Refresh the screen.
62           dbSync();
```

```
 63          }
 64    }
 65
 66    //*********************************************
 67    // The setUp function performs setup operations.*
 68    //*********************************************
 69    void setUp()
 70    {
 71         // Set the key color to green.
 72         dbSetImageColorKey(0, 255, 0);
 73
 74         // Load the two images.
 75         dbLoadImage("Space.bmp", SPACE_IMAGE_NUMBER);
 76         dbLoadImage("UFO.bmp",   UFO_IMAGE_NUMBER);
 77
 78         // Create the UFO sprite and display it at its
 79         // starting coordinates.
 80         dbSprite(UFO_SPRITE_NUMBER, UFO_STARTING_X,
 81                  UFO_STARTING_Y, UFO_IMAGE_NUMBER);
 82
 83         // Disable auto refresh and set the refresh rate.
 84         dbSyncOn();
 85         dbSyncRate(REFRESH_RATE);
 86    }
 87
 88    //*********************************************
 89    // The getUFOcoordinates accepts two arguments  *
 90    // by reference. These arguments are for the    *
 91    // UFO's X and Y coordinates. The function      *
 92    // determines whether the user is pressing an   *
 93    // arrow key and updates these values           *
 94    // accordingly.                                 *
 95    //*********************************************
 96    void getUFOcoordinates(int &x, int &y)
 97    {
 98         if ( dbUpKey() )
 99         {
100             y--;
101         }
102
103         if ( dbDownKey() )
104         {
105              y++;
106         }
107
108         if ( dbLeftKey() )
109         {
110              x--;
111         }
112
113         if ( dbRightKey() )
114         {
115              x++;
116         }
117    }
```

Figure 7-14 Output of Program 7-11

Pasting and Cloning Sprites

There are two ways to make a copy of a sprite: pasting and cloning. When you paste a sprite, you make a copy that is dependent on the original sprite. When you rotate, resize, flip, or mirror the original sprite, the same operation will happen to any pasted copy of the sprite. You use the dbPasteSprite function to paste a copy of a sprite. Here is the general format of how you call the function:

```
dbPasteSprite(SpriteNumber, X, Y);
```

SpriteNumber is the number of the original sprite. *X* and *Y* are integers for the screen coordinates where you want to place the copy. For example, Program 7-12 creates the UFO sprite, and pastes two copies. Each time the game loop iterates, it rotates the original sprite. As a result, the two copies also rotate. Figure 7-15 shows an example of the program's output.

Program 7-12   **(PastedSpriteCopy.cpp)**

```
1   // This program pastes two copies of a sprite.
2   #include "DarkGDK.h"
3
4   // Constant for the refresh rate.
5   const int REFRESH_RATE = 60;
6
7   // Constants are for the image numbers
8   const int UFO_IMAGE_NUMBER      = 1;
9   const int SPACE_IMAGE_NUMBER    = 2;
10
11  // Constant for the UFO sprite number
12  const int UFO_SPRITE_NUMBER     = 1;
13
```

```
14   // Constants for the UFO's coordinates
15   const int UFO_X = 400;
16   const int UFO_Y = 100;
17
18   // Function prototype
19   void setUp();
20
21   //*********************************************
22   // The DarkGDK function                      *
23   //*********************************************
24   void DarkGDK()
25   {
26       // Variable to hold the sprite angle.
27       float angle = 0.0;
28
29       // Perform setup operations.
30       setUp();
31
32       // Game loop
33       while ( LoopGDK() )
34       {
35           // Paste the background image at (0, 0).
36           dbPasteImage(SPACE_IMAGE_NUMBER, 0, 0);
37
38           // Display the UFO.
39           dbSprite(UFO_SPRITE_NUMBER, UFO_X, UFO_Y, UFO_IMAGE_NUMBER);
40
41           // Paste two copies of the UFO sprite.
42           dbPasteSprite(UFO_SPRITE_NUMBER, UFO_X - 100, UFO_Y + 50);
43           dbPasteSprite(UFO_SPRITE_NUMBER, UFO_X + 50, UFO_Y + 100);
44
45           // Rotate the UFO sprite. As a result, the copies
46           // will also rotate.
47           angle++;
48           dbRotateSprite(UFO_SPRITE_NUMBER, angle);
49
50           // Refresh the screen.
51           dbSync();
52       }
53   }
54
55   //*********************************************
56   // The setUp function performs setup operations. *
57   //*********************************************
58   void setUp()
59   {
60       // Set the key color to green.
61       dbSetImageColorKey(0, 255, 0);
62
63       // Load the two images.
64       dbLoadImage("Space.bmp", SPACE_IMAGE_NUMBER);
65       dbLoadImage("UFO.bmp",    UFO_IMAGE_NUMBER);
66
67       // Create the UFO sprite and display it at its
68       // starting coordinates.
```

```
69          dbSprite(UFO_SPRITE_NUMBER, UFO_X,
70                   UFO_Y, UFO_IMAGE_NUMBER);
71
72          // Disable auto refresh and set the refresh rate.
73          dbSyncOn();
74          dbSyncRate(REFRESH_RATE);
75    }
```

Figure 7-15 Screen displayed by Program 7-12

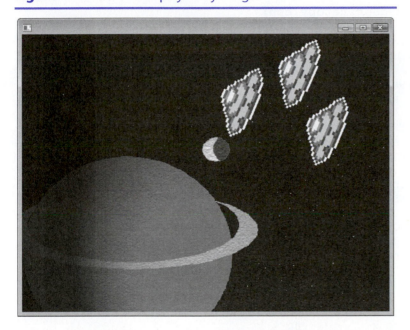

When you clone a sprite, you are making a copy that is independent from the original sprite. When a clone is created, it has all of the characteristics of the original sprite, such as size, rotation angle, etc. If you resize, flip, or mirror the original sprite, it has no effect on the sprite's clones. The opposite is also true: if you resize, flip, or mirror a clone, it has no effect on the original sprite.

You clone a sprite by calling the dbCloneSprite function. Here is the general format for calling the function:

```
dbCloneSprite(SpriteNumber, DestinationSpriteNumber);
```

SpriteNumber is the number of the original sprite, and *DestinationSpriteNumber* is the number you want to assign to the clone. For example the following statement creates sprite number 1, located at (100, 100), using image number 1:

```
dbSprite(1, 100, 100, 1);
```

Then, the following statement creates sprite number 2 as a clone of sprite number 1:

```
dbCloneSprite(1, 2);
```

Next we would use the following statement to display the cloned sprite at (200, 200), using image number 1:

```
dbSprite(2, 200, 200, 1);
```

Program 7-13 demonstrates cloning a sprite. It creates a UFO sprite in lines 84 and 85, then makes two clones of the sprite in lines 88 and 89. The clones are then resized to half of their original size in lines 92 and 93. Inside the game loop, the first UFO sprite is rotated in line 63. This rotation has no effect on the clones. Figure 7-16 shows an example screen from the program.

Program 7-13   (ClonedSpriteCopy.cpp)

```
1   // This program clones a sprite.
2   #include "DarkGDK.h"
3
4   // Constant for the refresh rate.
5   const int REFRESH_RATE = 60;
6
7   // Constants are for the image numbers
8   const int UFO_IMAGE_NUMBER   = 1;
9   const int SPACE_IMAGE_NUMBER = 2;
10
11  // Constants for the UFO sprite numbers
12  const int FIRST_UFO_SPRITE   = 1;
13  const int SECOND_UFO_SPRITE  = 2;
14  const int THIRD_UFO_SPRITE   = 3;
15
16  // Constants for the first UFO's coordinates
17  const int FIRST_UFO_X        = 400;
18  const int FIRST_UFO_Y        = 100;
19
20  // Constants for the second UFO's coordinates
21  const int SECOND_UFO_X       = 200;
22  const int SECOND_UFO_Y       = 150;
23
24  // Constants for the third UFO's coordinates
25  const int THIRD_UFO_X        = 500;
26  const int THIRD_UFO_Y        = 50;
27
28  // Function prototype
29  void setUp();
30
31  //*********************************************
32  // The DarkGDK function                       *
33  //*********************************************
34  void DarkGDK()
35  {
36      // Variable to hold the sprite angle.
37      float angle = 0.0;
38
39      // Perform setup operations.
40      setUp();
41
42      // Game loop
```

Figure 3-21   Red, green, and blue channels

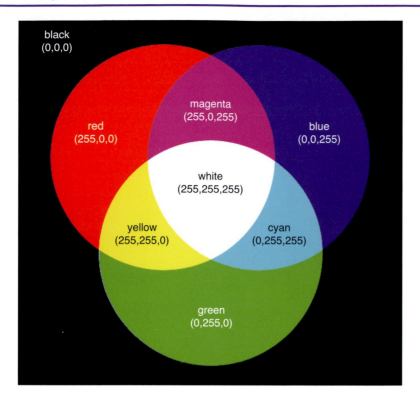

Figure 3-23   Output of Program 3-15

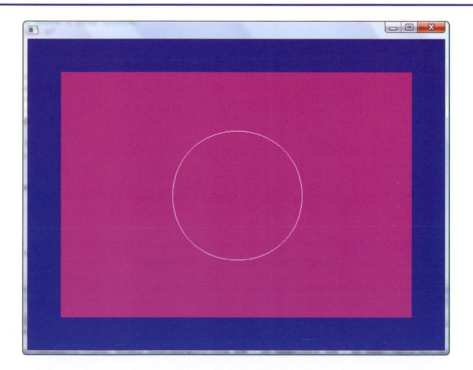

Figure 3-24 Output of Programs 3-16, 3-17, and 4-14

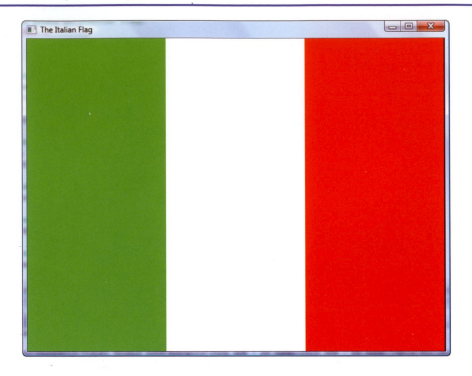

Figure 3-27 Flags

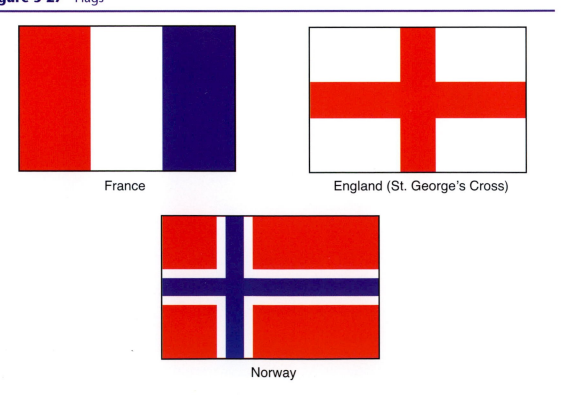

France

England (St. George's Cross)

Norway

Figure 5-3 Final output of Program 5-2

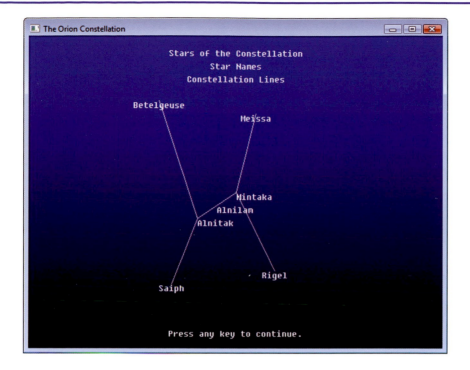

Figure 5-12 Images in Program 5-5

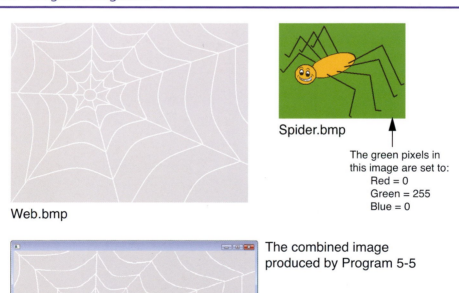

Figure 5-21 ·Original photo and modified photo

Figure 5-22 Output of Program 5-7

Figure 7-6   The `Space.bmp` and `UFO.bmp` images

UFO.bmp

Space.bmp

Figure 8-10   Vulture Trouble title screen and introductory screen

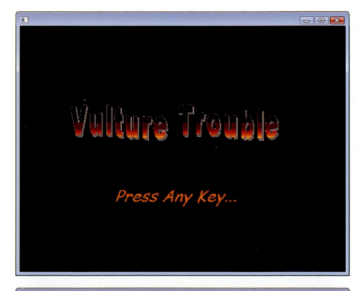

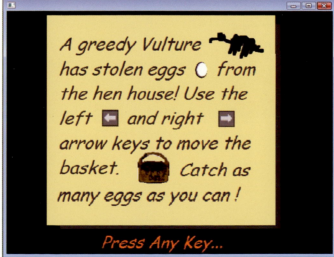

Figure 8-11   Vulture Trouble main screen and summary screen

Figure 8-12   Images used in the Vulture Trouble game

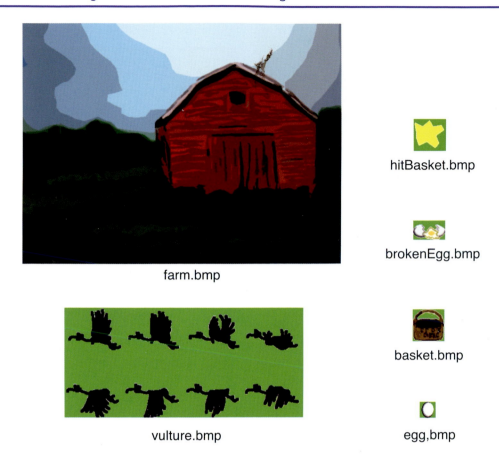

farm.bmp

hitBasket.bmp

brokenEgg.bmp

basket.bmp

vulture.bmp

egg,bmp

Figure 9-5   Output of Program 9-3

Figure 9-6 Output of Program 9-4

Figure 9-18 Screens from the Bug Zapper game

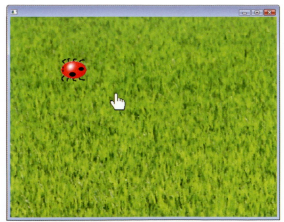

```
43          while ( LoopGDK() )
44          {
45              // Paste the background image at (0, 0).
46              dbPasteImage(SPACE_IMAGE_NUMBER, 0, 0);
47
48              // Display the first UFO.
49              dbSprite(FIRST_UFO_SPRITE, FIRST_UFO_X, FIRST_UFO_Y,
50                  UFO_IMAGE_NUMBER);
51
52              // Display the second UFO.
53              dbSprite(SECOND_UFO_SPRITE, SECOND_UFO_X, SECOND_UFO_Y,
54                  UFO_IMAGE_NUMBER);
55
56              // Display the third UFO.
57              dbSprite(THIRD_UFO_SPRITE, THIRD_UFO_X, THIRD_UFO_Y,
58                  UFO_IMAGE_NUMBER);
59
60              // Rotate the first UFO sprite. This does not affect
61              // the clones.
62              angle++;
63              dbRotateSprite(FIRST_UFO_SPRITE, angle);
64
65              // Refresh the screen.
66              dbSync();
67          }
68  }
69
70  //*********************************************
71  // The setUp function performs setup operations. *
72  //*********************************************
73  void setUp()
74  {
75      // Set the key color to green.
76      dbSetImageColorKey(0, 255, 0);
77
78      // Load the two images.
79      dbLoadImage("Space.bmp", SPACE_IMAGE_NUMBER);
80      dbLoadImage("UFO.bmp",   UFO_IMAGE_NUMBER);
81
82      // Create the first UFO sprite and display it at its
83      // starting coordinates.
84      dbSprite(FIRST_UFO_SPRITE, FIRST_UFO_X,
85          FIRST_UFO_Y, UFO_IMAGE_NUMBER);
86
87      // Make two clones of the first UFO.
88      dbCloneSprite(FIRST_UFO_SPRITE, SECOND_UFO_SPRITE);
89      dbCloneSprite(FIRST_UFO_SPRITE, THIRD_UFO_SPRITE);
90
91      // Scale the two clones to half their current size.
92      dbStretchSprite(SECOND_UFO_SPRITE, 50, 50);
93      dbStretchSprite(THIRD_UFO_SPRITE, 50, 50);
94
95      // Disable auto refresh and set the refresh rate.
96      dbSyncOn();
97      dbSyncRate(REFRESH_RATE);
98  }
```

Figure 7-16 Screen displayed by Program 7-13

 Checkpoint

7.5. What two actions do you perform to create a sprite?

7.6. How do you move an existing sprite?

7.7. What functions do you call to get an existing sprite's current coordinates?

7.8. What functions do you call to get a sprite's width and height?

7.9. Give an example of how you would rotate sprite number 1 at an angle of 47.5 degrees.

7.10. Give an example of how you would offset sprite number 1's insertion point to the center of the sprite.

7.11. Give examples of how you would do the following:
   a. Hide sprite number 1
   b. Show sprite number 1
   c. Hide all of the existing sprites
   d. Show all of the existing sprites
   e. Change the size of sprite number 1 so it is 64 pixels in the X direction and 128 pixels in the Y direction
   f. Scale sprite number 2 so it is 50 percent its current size in both the X and Y directions
   g. Set sprite number 3's priority to 1
   h. Flip sprite number 2
   i. Mirror sprite number 2
   j. Set sprite number 1's alpha level to 10
   k. Make a cloned copy of sprite number 1. The clone should be sprite number 2.

7.5 Cel Animation and Sprite Sheets

CONCEPT: You can create a simple animation by displaying a sequence of images one after the other. This can be done by manually loading and displaying separate images, or via an animated sprite sheet.

Perhaps you've seen simple animations created with flip books. The first page in a flip book shows an image. The next page shows a nearly identical image, but with a slight change. Following this pattern, each page in the book is slightly different from the previous page. When you flip rapidly through the pages, the illusion of movement is created. This type of animation is often called *cel animation*. The term "cel" is an abbreviation of the word "celluloid," which was the material onto which animators once painted the individual images of cartoons.

You can create simple cel animations by displaying a sequence of images, one after the other, in the same location on the screen. If the images are similar except for slight changes, and are displayed in the correct order, the illusion of movement can be created.

For example, look at the sequence of eight images shown in Figure 7-17. Each image shows a cartoon person in a different position. When the images are viewed one after the other, the person appears to be walking.

Figure 7-17 Cel animation images

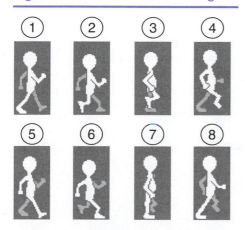

The eight images shown in Figure 7-17 are named `WalkingMan1.bmp`, `WalkingMan2.bmp`, and so forth. Each image is considered a frame in the animation sequence. Program 7-14 loads these images and then displays them one after the other. After the last image is displayed, the program starts over with the first image.

The following global constants are declared in lines 5 through 9:

- The `REFRESH_RATE` constant is declared in line 5 and initialized with the value 10. We will use this constant to set the screen refresh rate. We chose 10, a low

Program 7-14   **(CelAnimation.cpp)**

```
1   // This program demonstrates cel animation.
2   #include "DarkGDK.h"
3
4   // Global constants
5   const int REFRESH_RATE = 10;    // Screen refresh rate
6   const int FIRST_IMAGE = 1;      // First image number
7   const int LAST_IMAGE = 8;       // Last image number
8   const int SPRITE_X = 303;       // Sprite's X coordinate
9   const int SPRITE_Y = 207;       // Sprite's Y coordinate
10
11  // Function prototype
12  void setUp();
13
14  //*****************************************
15  // DarkGDK function                       *
16  //*****************************************
17  void DarkGDK()
18  {
19      // Variable to hold the image number
20      // of the current image to display.
21      int currentImage = FIRST_IMAGE;
22
23      // Load the images and perform set up
24      // for the game loop.
25      setUp();
26
27      // Game loop
28      while ( LoopGDK() )
29      {
30          // Display sprite #1 using the current image.
31          dbSprite(1, SPRITE_X, SPRITE_Y, currentImage);
32
33          // Update the current image number for the
34          // next loop iteration.
35          if (currentImage == LAST_IMAGE)
36          {
37              currentImage = FIRST_IMAGE;
38          }
39          else
40          {
41              currentImage++;
42          }
43
44          // Refresh the screen.
45          dbSync();
46      }
47  }
48
49  //*****************************************
50  // The setUp function loads the images,   *
51  // creates an initial sprite for the      *
52  // animation, and performs the necessary  *
53  // setup for the game loop.               *
```

```
54  //****************************************
55  void setUp()
56  {
57      // Load the walking man images.
58      dbLoadImage("WalkingMan1.bmp", 1);
59      dbLoadImage("WalkingMan2.bmp", 2);
60      dbLoadImage("WalkingMan3.bmp", 3);
61      dbLoadImage("WalkingMan4.bmp", 4);
62      dbLoadImage("WalkingMan5.bmp", 5);
63      dbLoadImage("WalkingMan6.bmp", 6);
64      dbLoadImage("WalkingMan7.bmp", 7);
65      dbLoadImage("WalkingMan8.bmp", 8);
66
67      // Disable auto refresh.
68      dbSyncOn();
69
70      // Set the refresh rate.
71      dbSyncRate(REFRESH_RATE);
72  }
```

value, because we want the animation to run somewhat slowly. (If we use a high refresh rate, the cartoon man will appear to be running instead of walking!)
- Lines 6 and 7 declare the FIRST_IMAGE constant (initialized with 1) and the LAST_IMAGE constant (initialized with 8). These are the image numbers that we will use for the first and last images in the animation sequence.
- Lines 8 and 9 declare the SPRITE_X and SPRITE_Y constants. These are initialized to the screen coordinates we will use to position the sprite.

Inside the DarkGDK function, we first declare an int variable named currentImage (line 21) and initialize it with FIRST_IMAGE. This variable will hold the image number of the current image to display.

In line 25, we call the setup function, which is defined in lines 55 through 72. The setup function loads the eight images, disables auto screen refresh, and sets up the refresh rate.

The game loop starts in line 28. In line 31, we display sprite number 1, using the value of currentImage as the image number. Then the if statement in line 35 determines whether currentImage is equal to LAST_IMAGE. If so, we reset currentImage to FIRST_IMAGE in line 37. Otherwise, we increment currentImage in line 41. In line 45, we refresh the screen.

Simplifying Animation with Sprite Sheets

Although Program 7-14 illustrates the fundamental idea behind cel animation, the Dark GDK supports a simpler way to achieve the same results. Instead of having separate image files for the frames in an animation sequence stored on your disk, you can create one image file that contains all of the images. Such a file is known as a *sprite sheet*. Figure 7-18 shows an example of a sprite sheet containing all of the images for the walking man animation we looked at previously.

Figure 7-18 A sprite sheet

The images in a sprite sheet are organized in rows and columns. The sprite sheet shown in Figure 7-18 has one row and eight columns. When this sprite sheet is used to create an animation, the images are displayed from left to right. This means the image (or frame) in the first column is displayed, then the image (or frame) in the second column is displayed, and so forth.

The Dark GDK can calculate the positions of each image in a sprite sheet because all of the rows must be the same height, and all of the columns must be the same width. For example, the entire sprite sheet shown in Figure 7-18 is 256 pixels wide by 64 pixels high. There are eight columns in the sprite sheet, so each column is 32 pixels wide. The first 32 by 64 pixel block contains the first image, the second 32 by 64 pixel block contains the second image, and so forth.

Figure 7-19 shows another example of a sprite sheet. This one has two rows and four columns. Each image in the sprite sheet occupies an area that is 172 pixels wide by 172 pixels high. The entire sprite sheet is 688 pixels wide by 344 pixels high.

Figure 7-19 A sprite sheet with two rows and four columns

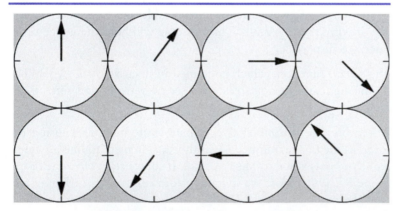

When a sprite sheet containing multiple rows is used to create an animation, the images in the first row are displayed from left to right, then the images in the second row are displayed from left to right, and so forth.

This is consistent with the internal numbering system that the Dark GDK uses to identify the images in a sprite sheet. The images are numbered, starting at 1, from left to right. If the sprite sheet contains multiple rows, the numbering continues from one row to the next. For example, in the sprite sheet shown in Figure 7-19, the images in the first row would be numbered 1, 2, 3, and 4, and the images in the second row would be numbered 5, 6, 7, and 8.

Playing Sprite Animations with the Dark GDK

To play an animation using the images in a sprite sheet, you create an animated sprite. An *animated sprite* is a single sprite that is used to display the images in a sprite sheet, one by one. To create an animated sprite, you call the `dbCreateAnimatedSprite` function, using the following general format:

```
dbCreateAnimatedSprite(SpriteNumber, FileName, Columns,
                       Rows, ImageNumber);
```

SpriteNumber is the sprite number you will use for the animated sprite, *FileName* is the name of the image file that contains the sprite sheet, *Columns* is the number of columns contained horizontally in the sprite sheet. *Rows* is the number of rows contained vertically in the sprite sheet. *ImageNumber* is the image number you are assigning to the image file. Here is an example:

```
dbCreateAnimatedSprite(1, "animation.bmp", 3, 2, 10);
```

This statement creates sprite number 1 as an animated sprite. It loads the file `"animation.bmp"` as image number 10. The file contains a sprite sheet with three rows and two columns.

Once you have created an animated sprite, you use the `dbPlaySprite` function to extract an image from the sprite sheet. Here is the general format of how you call the function:

```
dbPlaySprite(SpriteNumber, StartFrame, EndFrame, Delay);
```

SpriteNumber is the number of the animated sprite. *StartFrame* is the number of the image inside the sprite sheet that you want to display first. *EndFrame* is the number of the image that you want to display last. *Delay* is the number of milliseconds that the program will wait before displaying the next frame in the animation sequence. Here is an example:

```
dbPlaySprite(1, 1, 6, 1000);
```

This statement extracts the next image from animated sprite number 1. The animation sequence begins with frame 1 and ends with frame 6. (After frame 6 is extracted, the sequence starts over with frame 1.) There is a 1,000 millisecond (1 second) delay between frames.

Although the `dbPlaySprite` function extracts an image from an animated sprite, it does not display the image. To do that you need to call the `dbSprite` function, passing the animated sprite number as an argument. To demonstrate, look at Program 7-15. This program loads the clock sprite sheet shown in Figure 7-19 and plays the animation.

In the `setUp` function we create an animated sprite in lines 48 and 49. Notice that we are using constants for the sprite number, the number of columns, the number of rows, and the image number. After the statement executes, sprite number 1 will be an animated sprite. It will contain the images found in the file `ClockSpriteSheet.bmp`. There are four rows and two columns of images.

Program 7-15 **(SpriteSheetClock.cpp)**

```
 1   // This program uses a sprite sheet to
 2   // diaplay an animated clock.
 3   #include "DarkGDK.h"
 4
 5   // Global constants
 6   const int REFRESH_RATE = 10;      // Screen refresh rate
 7   const int CLOCK_IMAGE_NUM = 1;    // Clock image number
 8   const int CLOCK_SPRITE_NUM = 1;   // Clock sprite number
 9   const int NUM_ROWS = 2;           // Number of sprite rows
10   const int NUM_COLS = 4;           // Number of sprite columns
11   const int DELAY = 200;            // Animation delay
12   const int SPRITE_X = 233;         // Sprite X coordinate
13   const int SPRITE_Y = 153;         // Sprite Y coordinate
14
15   // Function prototype
16   void setUp();
17
18   //*******************************************
19   // DarkGDK function                         *
20   //*******************************************
21   void DarkGDK()
22   {
23       // Perform program setup.
24       setUp();
25
26       // Game loop
27       while ( LoopGDK() )
28       {
29           // Retrieve an image from the sprite sheet.
30           dbPlaySprite(CLOCK_SPRITE_NUM, 1, 8, DELAY);
31
32           // Display the sprite image.
33           dbSprite(CLOCK_SPRITE_NUM, SPRITE_X, SPRITE_Y,
34                   CLOCK_IMAGE_NUM);
35
36           // Refresh the screen.
37           dbSync();
38       }
39   }
40
41   //*******************************************
42   // The setUp function loads the sprite sheet *
43   // and performs setup for the game loop.     *
44   //*******************************************
45   void setUp()
46   {
47       // Create an animated sprite from the sprite sheet.
48       dbCreateAnimatedSprite(CLOCK_SPRITE_NUM, "ClockSpriteSheet.bmp",
49                             NUM_COLS, NUM_ROWS, CLOCK_IMAGE_NUM);
50
51       // Disable auto refresh and set the
52       // refresh rate.
53       dbSyncOn();
54       dbSyncRate(REFRESH_RATE);
55   }
```

Inside the game loop, in line 30, we call the `dbPlaySprite` function to extract an image from the animated sprite. Notice that the animation sequence begins with frame 1 (the first image in the sprite sheet) and ends with frame 8 (the last image in the sprite sheet). The program will pause 200 milliseconds between each frame. In lines 33 and 34 we call the `dbSprite` function to display the extracted image, and then in line 37 we refresh the screen.

 Checkpoint

7.12. What is a sprite sheet?

7.13. What Dark GDK function do you call to create an animated sprite?

7.14. What Dark GDK function do you call to extract an image from an animated sprite?

 7.6 **Sprite Collision Detection**

CONCEPT: A collision between sprites occurs when one sprite's bounding rectangle comes in contact with another sprite's bounding rectangle. Collisions between sprites can be detected.

When a sprite is displayed on the screen, it is displayed within a rectangle that is known as the sprite's *bounding rectangle*. The bounding rectangle is normally invisible, but if transparency is turned off, or if the sprite's background color is not used as the key color, you may be able to see the bounding rectangle on the screen. This is illustrated in Figure 7-20.

 NOTE: A sprite's bounding rectangle will be the size, in pixels, of the sprite's image file. For example, suppose you use Microsoft Paint to create an image file that is 64 pixels wide by 96 pixels high. If you use this image as a sprite, the sprite's bounding rectangle will be 64 pixels wide by 96 pixels high.

Figure 7-20 A sprite displayed inside its bounding rectangle

Bounding rectangle

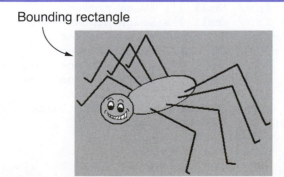

When one sprite's bounding rectangle comes in contact with another sprite's bounding rectangle, it is said that the two sprites have *collided*. In games, sprite collisions are usually an important part of the game play. For this reason, it is important that you can detect collisions between sprites in your programs.

The Dark GDK provides a function named `dbSpriteCollision` that determines whether two sprites have collided. You pass two sprite numbers as arguments, and the function returns 1 (true) if the bounding rectangles of the two sprites are overlapping, or 0 (false) otherwise. The following code shows an example; it determines whether sprites 1 and 2 have collided, and if so, hides both sprites:

```
if ( dbSpriteCollision(1, 2) )
{
    dbHideSprite(1);
    dbHideSprite(2);
}
```

Sometimes you just want to know whether a particular sprite has collided with any other sprite. You make this determination by passing a sprite number as the first argument and 0 as the second argument. If the sprite specified by the first argument has collided with any other sprite the function returns 1 (true). Otherwise it returns true. The following code shows an example. It determines whether sprite 1 has collided with any other sprite. If so, it hides sprite 1.

```
if ( dbSpriteCollision(1, 0) )
{
    dbHideSprite(1);
}
```

Program 7-16 shows a complete example that detects sprite collisions. When the program runs, it displays the two bowling ball sprites shown in Figure 7-21. The sprites move toward each other until a collision is detected. When that happens, they are reset back to their original positions.

Program 7-16   **(SpriteCollision.cpp)**

```
 1   // This program demonstrates how sprite collisions
 2   // can be detected.
 3   #include "DarkGDK.h"
 4
 5   // Global constants
 6   const int BALL1_IMAGE_NUM = 1;   // Ball 1's image number
 7   const int BALL2_IMAGE_NUM = 2;   // Ball 2's image number
 8   const int BALL1_SPRITE_NUM = 1;  // Ball 1's sprite number
 9   const int BALL2_SPRITE_NUM = 2;  // Ball 2's sprite number
10   const int BALL1_X = 0;           // Ball 1's initial X position
11   const int BALL2_X = 511;         // Ball 2's initial X position
12   const int BALL_Y = 175;          // Both ball's Y position
13   const int DISTANCE = 10;         // Distance to move the balls
14   const int REFRESH_RATE = 10;     // Refresh rate
15
16   // Function prototypes
17   void setUp();
```

```
18   void moveBowlingBalls();
19   void detectCollision();
20
21   //***************************************************
22   // The DarkGDK function                             *
23   //***************************************************
24   void DarkGDK()
25   {
26       // Perform setup.
27       setUp();
28
29       // Game loop
30       while ( LoopGDK() )
31       {
32           // Move the bowling balls toward each other.
33           moveBowlingBalls();
34
35           // Check for a collision.
36           detectCollision();
37
38           // Refresh the screen.
39           dbSync();
40       }
41   }
42
43   //***************************************************
44   // The setUp function loads the images, creates the*
45   // sprites, and sets things up for the game loop.  *
46   //***************************************************
47   void setUp()
48   {
49       // Set the key color to green.
50       dbSetImageColorKey(0, 255, 0);
51
52       // Load the bowling ball images.
53       dbLoadImage("BowlingBall1.bmp", BALL1_IMAGE_NUM);
54       dbLoadImage("BowlingBall2.bmp", BALL2_IMAGE_NUM);
55
56       // Make the sprites.
57       dbSprite(BALL1_SPRITE_NUM, BALL1_X, BALL_Y,
58                BALL1_IMAGE_NUM);
59       dbSprite(BALL2_SPRITE_NUM, BALL2_X, BALL_Y,
60                BALL2_IMAGE_NUM);
61
62       // Disable auto refresh.
63       dbSyncOn();
64
65       // Set the refresh rate.
66       dbSyncRate(REFRESH_RATE);
67   }
68
69   //***************************************************
70   // The moveBowlingBalls function moves the bowling  *
71   // balls toward each other.                         *
72   //***************************************************
73   void moveBowlingBalls()
```

```
 74   {
 75       // Variable to hold X coordinates
 76       int x;
 77
 78       // Get bowling ball #1's X coordinate.
 79       x = dbSpriteX(BALL1_SPRITE_NUM);
 80
 81       // Increment the coordinate.
 82       x += DISTANCE;
 83
 84       // Move bowling ball #1.
 85       dbSprite(BALL1_SPRITE_NUM, x, BALL_Y,
 86               BALL1_IMAGE_NUM);
 87
 88       // Get bowling ball #2's X coordinate.
 89       x = dbSpriteX(BALL2_SPRITE_NUM);
 90
 91       // Decrement the coordinate.
 92       x -= DISTANCE;
 93
 94       // Move bowling ball #2.
 95       dbSprite(BALL2_SPRITE_NUM, x, BALL_Y,
 96               BALL2_IMAGE_NUM);
 97
 98   }
 99
100   //***************************************************
101   // The detectCollision function determines whether  *
102   // the two bowling ball sprites have collided. If    *
103   // so, they are reset to their original positions.   *
104   //***************************************************
105   void detectCollision()
106   {
107       if ( dbSpriteCollision(BALL1_SPRITE_NUM, BALL2_SPRITE_NUM) )
108       {
109           // Reset the sprites back at their initial positions.
110           dbSprite(BALL1_SPRITE_NUM, BALL1_X, BALL_Y,
111               BALL1_IMAGE_NUM);
112           dbSprite(BALL2_SPRITE_NUM, BALL2_X, BALL_Y,
113               BALL2_IMAGE_NUM);
114       }
115   }
```

Let's look at the program. Here is a summary of the global constants:

- Lines 6 through 9 declare constants for the bowling ball image numbers and sprite numbers.
- Lines 10 and 11 declare constants for ball 1's initial X coordinate and ball 2's initial X coordinate. Line 12 declares a constant that will be used for both balls' Y coordinate.
- Line 13 declares a constant for the distance, in pixels, that each ball will move during an iteration of the game loop.
- Line 14 declares a constant for the screen refresh rate.

Figure 7-21 Sprites displayed by Program 7-16

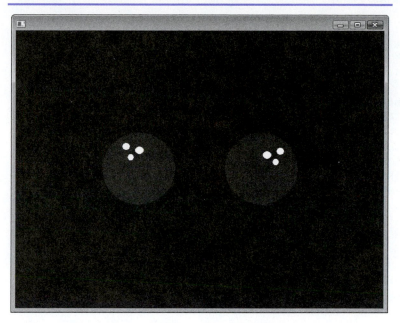

The `DarkGDK` function appears in lines 24 through 41. Line 27 calls the `setUp` function, which loads the images, makes the sprites, and sets things up for the game loop (see lines 47 through 67 for the function definition).

The game loop begins in line 30. Inside the loop, in line 33, we call the `moveBowlingBalls` function, which moves the two bowling ball sprites toward each other (see lines 73 through 98 for the function definition).

In line 36, we call the `detectCollision` function, which checks for a collision between the two sprites. If a collision has happened, it resets the sprites to their original positions (see lines 105 through 115 for the function definition). In line 39, we call `dbSync` to refresh the screen.

In the Spotlight:
The PizzaBot Game

Program 7-17 is called `PizzaBot` because the main character is a pizza eating robot! Figure 7-22 shows the sprite sheet that we will use to create an animated sprite for the robot. The image is saved in a file named `Robot.bmp`. Notice that the sprite sheet has one row and three columns.

When the program runs, the robot will appear in the lower-right corner of the screen. The slice of pizza shown on the left in Figure 7-23 will also appear, in a random location. This image is saved in a file named `Pizza.bmp`. The object of the game is to use the arrow keys to move the robot to the slice of pizza. When the robot collides with the slice of pizza, the Yum! image shown on the right in Figure 7-23 will appear in place of the pizza. It is saved in a file named `Yum.bmp`.

Program 7-17 (`PizzaBot.cpp`)

```cpp
1   // This program lets the user chase randomly generated
2   // pizza slices with a robot. It demonstrates collision
3   // detection with sprites.
4   #include "DarkGDK.h"
5
6   // Global constants
7   const int ROBOT_IMAGE_NUM = 1;   // Robot image number
8   const int ROBOT_SPRITE_NUM = 1;  // Robot sprite number
9   const int ROBOT_COLS = 3;        // Number of robot columns
10  const int ROBOT_ROWS = 1;        // Number of robot rows
11  const int START_FRAME = 1;       // Robot animation starting frame
12  const int END_FRAME = 3;         // Robot animation ending frame
13  const int ROBOT_X = 500;         // Robot's starting X coordinate
14  const int ROBOT_Y = 350;         // Robot's starting Y coordinate
15  const int ROBOT_MOVE = 10;       // Amount to move the robot
16  const int DELAY = 200;           // Sprite delay
17  const int PIZZA_IMAGE_NUM = 2;   // Pizza image number
18  const int PIZZA_SPRITE_NUM = 2;  // Pizza sprite number
19  const int YUM_IMAGE_NUM = 3;     // Yum! image number
20  const int REFRESH_RATE = 30;     // Screen refresh rate
21
22  // Function prototypes
23  void setUp();
24  void updateRobot();
25  void detectCollision();
26  void showYum();
27  void generatePizza();
28
29  //*********************************************************
30  // DarkGDK function                                       *
31  //*********************************************************
32  void DarkGDK()
33  {
34      // Perform setup.
35      setUp();
36
37      // Game loop
38      while ( LoopGDK() )
39      {
40          // Update the robot's position.
41          updateRobot();
42
43          // Check for a collision between the robot
44          // and the pizza.
45          detectCollision();
46
47          // Refresh the screen.
48          dbSync();
49      }
50  }
51
52  //*********************************************************
53  // The setUp function performs various setup operations.  *
```

```
54   //**********************************************************
55   void setUp()
56   {
57       // Seed the random number generator.
58       dbRandomize( dbTimer() );
59
60       // Set the key color to green.
61       dbSetImageColorKey(0, 255, 0);
62
63       // Create an animated sprite for the robot.
64       dbCreateAnimatedSprite(ROBOT_SPRITE_NUM, "Robot.bmp",
65                              ROBOT_COLS, ROBOT_ROWS,
66                              ROBOT_IMAGE_NUM);
67
68       // Extract an image for the robot sprite.
69       dbPlaySprite(ROBOT_SPRITE_NUM, START_FRAME, END_FRAME,
70                    DELAY);
71
72       // Display the robot image sprite.
73       dbSprite(ROBOT_SPRITE_NUM, ROBOT_X, ROBOT_Y,
74                ROBOT_IMAGE_NUM);
75
76       // Load the pizza image.
77       dbLoadImage("Pizza.bmp", PIZZA_IMAGE_NUM);
78
79       // Display the pizza at a random location.
80       generatePizza();
81
82       // Load the Yum! image.
83       dbLoadImage("Yum.bmp", YUM_IMAGE_NUM);
84
85       // Disable auto refresh and set the frame rate.
86       dbSyncOn();
87       dbSyncRate(REFRESH_RATE);
88   }
89
90   //**********************************************************
91   // The updateRobot function moves the robot if the user *
92   // is pressing an arrow key.                            *
93   //**********************************************************
94   void updateRobot()
95   {
96       // Get the robot's XY coordinates.
97       int x = dbSpriteX(ROBOT_SPRITE_NUM);
98       int y = dbSpriteY(ROBOT_SPRITE_NUM);
99
100      // Check for arrow keys.
101      if ( dbUpKey() )
102      {
103          y -= ROBOT_MOVE;
104      }
105
106      if ( dbDownKey() )
107      {
108          y += ROBOT_MOVE;
```

```
109            }
110
111            if ( dbRightKey() )
112            {
113                x += ROBOT_MOVE;
114            }
115
116            if ( dbLeftKey() )
117            {
118               x -= ROBOT_MOVE;
119            }
120
121            // Extract the next image from the animated sprite.
122            dbPlaySprite(ROBOT_SPRITE_NUM, START_FRAME, END_FRAME,
123                        DELAY);
124
125            // Display the sprite.
126            dbSprite(ROBOT_SPRITE_NUM, x, y, ROBOT_IMAGE_NUM);
127        }
128
129        //**********************************************************
130        // The detectCollision function determines whether the    *
131        // robot has collided with the pizza. If so, a new slice  *
132        // of pizza is generated.                                 *
133        //**********************************************************
134        void detectCollision()
135        {
136            if ( dbSpriteCollision(ROBOT_SPRITE_NUM, PIZZA_SPRITE_NUM) )
137            {
138                // Show the Yum! image in place of the pizza.
139                showYum();
140
141                // Generate a new slice of pizza.
142                generatePizza();
143            }
144        }
145
146        //**********************************************************
147        // The showYum function momentarily displays the Yum!     *
148        // image in place of the pizza image.                     *
149        //**********************************************************
150        void showYum()
151        {
152            // Get the pizza's coordinates.
153            int x = dbSpriteX(PIZZA_SPRITE_NUM);
154            int y = dbSpriteY(PIZZA_SPRITE_NUM);
155
156            // Enable auto refresh.
157            dbSyncOff();
158
159            // Display the Yum! image in place of the pizza.
160            dbSprite(PIZZA_SPRITE_NUM, x, y, YUM_IMAGE_NUM);
161
162            // Wait...
163            dbWait(DELAY);
```

```
164
165        // Disable auto refresh.
166        dbSyncOn();
167    }
168
169    //*********************************************************
170    // The generatePizza function generates a new slice of   *
171    // pizza at a random location.                           *
172    //*********************************************************
173    void generatePizza()
174    {
175        // Get the screen sizes.
176        int screenWidth = dbScreenWidth();
177        int screenHeight = dbScreenHeight();
178
179        // Calculate the maximum X and Y coordinates.
180        int maxX = screenWidth - dbSpriteWidth(PIZZA_SPRITE_NUM);
181        int maxY = screenHeight - dbSpriteHeight(PIZZA_SPRITE_NUM);
182
183        // Get random XY coordinates.
184        int x = dbRND(maxX);
185        int y = dbRND(maxY);
186
187        // Display a new slice of pizza.
188        dbSprite(PIZZA_SPRITE_NUM, x, y, PIZZA_IMAGE_NUM);
189    }
```

Figure 7-22 Robot sprite sheet

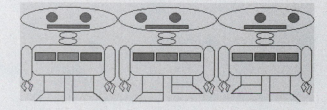

Figure 7-23 The pizza and Yum! images

The Yum! image will appear only briefly, and then disappear. After that, another slice of pizza will be randomly placed on the screen.

In addition to collision detection, this program incorporates many of the new topics that we have covered in this chapter. Let's review each part of the program.

Global Constants

Several global constants are declared in lines 7 through 20, summarized here:

- Lines 7 and 8 declare `ROBOT_IMAGE_NUM` and `ROBOT_SPRITE_NUM` to represent the robot's image number and sprite number.
- Lines 9 and 10 declare `ROBOT_COLS` and `ROBOT_ROWS` to represent the number of columns and rows in the robot sprite sheet.
- Line 11 and 12 declare `START_FRAME` and `END_FRAME` to represent the robot sprite sheet's starting frame number and ending frame number.
- Lines 13 and 14 declare `ROBOT_X` and `ROBOT_Y` to represent the robot's starting *X* and *Y* screen coordinates.
- Line 15 declares `ROBOT_MOVE`, which holds the amount by which the robot will move (10 pixels) when the user presses an arrow key.
- Line 16 declares `DELAY`, which represents the number milliseconds to wait between frames in the robot animation sequence.
- Lines 17 and 18 declare `PIZZA_IMAGE_NUM` and `PIZZA_SPRITE_NUM` to represent the pizza's image number and sprite number.
- Line 19 declares `YUM_IMAGE_NUM` to represent the image number for the Yum! image.
- Line 20 declares `REFRESH_RATE` to represent the screen refresh rate.

The `DarkGDK` Function

The `DarkGDK` function is defined in lines 32 through 50. It calls the `setUp` function in line 35 to perform setup operations. The game loop appears in lines 38 through 49. Inside the game loop, first we call the `updateRobot` function in line 41. This function determines whether an arrow key has been pressed, and if so, updates the robot's position accordingly. Then, we call the `detectCollision` function in line 45. This function determines whether the robot has collided with the pizza. If so, it displays the Yum! image for a brief instant, and then generates a new slice of pizza at a random location. Line 48 calls the `dbSync` function to refresh the screen.

The `setUp` Function

The `setUp` function is defined in lines 55 through 88. First, it seeds the random number generator (line 58), and then it sets the key color to green (line 61). The statement in lines 64 through 66 calls `dbCreateAnimatedSprite` to create an animated sprite for the robot. The sprite sheet is loaded from the file `Robot.bmp`, with three columns and one row.

The statement in lines 69 through 70 calls the `dbPlaySprite` function to extract an image of the robot from the animated sprite. The statement in lines 73 through 74 calls `dbSprite` to display the sprite's image.

Line 77 loads the `Pizza.bmp` image, and then line 80 calls the `generatePizza` function. The `generatePizza` function (which is defined in lines 173 through 189) draws the pizza sprite at a random location on the screen.

Line 83 loads the Yum! image into memory. Line 86 disables auto screen refresh, and line 87 sets the refresh rate.

The `updateRobot` Function

The `updateRobot` function is defined in lines 94 through 127. Its purpose is to determine whether the user is pressing an arrow key, and update the robot's position accordingly. The statements in lines 97 and 98 get the robot sprite's current *X* and *Y* screen coordinates, and assigns those values to the local `x` and `y` variables.

The `if` statements that appear in lines 101 through 119 check each of the arrow keys. If any of them are being pressed, the `x` and `y` variables are adjusted accordingly.

The `dbPlaySprite` function is called in lines 122 through 123 to extract the next image in the robot animation sequence, and the `dbSprite` function is called in line 126 to display the robot sprite image.

The `detectCollision` Function

The `detectCollision` function is defined in lines 134 through 144. Its purpose is to determine whether the robot sprite has collided with the pizza sprite. The `if` statement in line 136 calls the `dbSpriteCollision` function to make this determination. If the sprites have collided, the `showYum` function is called (line 139) to display the Yum! image, and then the `generatePizza` function is called in line 142 to show the pizza sprite at a new location.

The `showYum` Function

The `showYum` function is defined in lines 150 through 167. Its purpose is to display the Yum! image in place of the pizza image. (This occurs when the robot collides with the pizza.) Lines 153 and 154 get the pizza sprite's *X* and *Y* screen coordinates and assigns those values to the local `x` and `y` variables.

Line 157 calls `dbSyncOff` to temporarily enable auto screen refresh. We display the Yum! image in place of the pizza image in line 160, we wait for a short delay in line 163, and then we disable auto screen refresh in line 166.

The `generatePizza` Function

The `generatePizza` function is defined in lines 173 through 189. Its purpose is to display the pizza sprite at a random screen location. Lines 176 and 177 get the screen width and height, and assign those values to the local `screenWidth` and `screenHeight` variables. Lines 180 and 181 calculate the maximum *X* and *Y* coordinates that we can use, to make sure the pizza image doesn't get placed somewhere off-screen. Then, lines 184 and 185 generate random values for the local variables `x` and `y`. These values are used to display the pizza sprite in line 188.

 Checkpoint

7.15. What is a sprite's bounding rectangle?

7.16. What constitutes a sprite collision?

7.17. How do you detect a collision between two sprites?

7.18. How would you determine whether sprite number 1 has collided with any other sprite?

Review Questions

Multiple Choice

1. _____ disables automatic screen refreshing.
   a. dbSyncOn
   b. dbSyncOff
   c. dbAutoRefreshOff
   d. dbDisableRefresh

2. The LoopGDK function returns false (zero) when _____.
   a. the user has not provided input to the program
   b. the user has pressed the *Esc* key
   c. the user has closed the program's window
   d. the user has pressed the *Esc* key and has closed the program's window

3. _____ causes the screen to be refreshed.
   a. dbScreenUpdate
   b. dbRefresh
   c. dbSync
   d. dbDisplay

4. _____ causes automatic screen refreshing to resume.
   a. dbSyncOn
   b. dbSyncOff
   c. dbAutoRefreshOff
   d. dbDisableRefresh

5. _____ returns true or false indicating whether or not the spacebar is being pressed.
   a. dbTestSpaceBar
   b. dbSpaceKey
   c. dbSpaceBarDown
   d. dbSpaceBar

6. _____ returns true or false indicating whether or not the *Enter* key is being pressed.
   a. dbTestEnter
   b. dbEnterKey
   c. dbEnterKeyDown
   d. dbReturnKey

7. By default, a sprite's insertion point is _____.
   a. its upper-left corner
   b. its upper-right corner
   c. its center point
   d. its lower-right corner

8. A sprite's opacity is determined by _____.
   a. its omega value
   b. its alpha value
   c. its priority
   d. the order in which it is drawn

9. A _____ is an image file that contains all of the frames of an animation sequence.
   a. sprite sheet
   b. cel sheet
   c. flipbook file
   d. CGI file

10. When _____ overlap, a sprite collision occurs.
    a. two sprite images
    b. two pure green pixels
    c. two sprite bounding rectangles
    d. two copies of the same sprite

True or False

1. The LoopGDK function controls the maximum speed at which the game loop executes.

2. You can only call the dbSprite function once for a particular sprite, and that is when you create the sprite.

3. The dbPlaySprite function displays an image from a sprite sheet on the screen.

4. A sprite with the priority 1 is drawn after a sprite with the priority 0.

5. All of the rows in a sprite sheet must be the same height, and all of the columns must be the same width.

Short Answer

1. How do you turn automatic screen refreshing off? How do you turn it back on again?

2. What happens if you call dbSyncRate and pass 0 as the argument?

3. Why should you always remember to call dbSync at the end of the game loop?

4. If the dbUpKey function returns true, does it mean that the *Up* arrow key has been previously pressed, or is being pressed now?

5. In this chapter, we discussed two ways that you can change the image associated with a sprite. What are they?

6. What does a sprite's priority determine?

7. What is a sprite's bounding rectangle?

Algorithm Workbench

1. Write code that uses a game loop that displays a row of dots, one next to the other, from (0, 100) to (639, 100).

2. Write code that displays the message OK if the spacebar is not being pressed.

3. Assume that sprite number 1 is an animated sprite that has already been created with the dbCreateAnimatedSprite function. Complete the following game loop so it displays frames 1 through 4 of the animated sprite, with a delay of 1

second between frames. The sprite frames should be displayed at the coordinates (10, 20). Assume that the sprite sheet has been loaded as image number 1.

```
dbSyncOn();
dbSyncRate(REFRESH_RATE);

while ( LoopGDK() )
{
    // Write your code here.
    dbSync();
}
```

4. Write code that determines whether sprites 1 and 2 have collided. If so, mirror both sprites.

Programming Exercises

1. **Random Circles**
   Write a program that draws circles at random locations. Each circle's radius should also be randomly generated. The program should execute until the user closes its window or presses the *Esc* key.

2. **Bouncing Ball**
   Program 7-3 shows an animated ball that moves from the bottom of the screen to the top of the screen. When the ball reaches the top of the screen, the animation starts over with the ball at the bottom. Modify the program so that when the ball reaches the top, it reverses direction and moves back to the bottom. When it reaches the bottom, it reverses again and moves back to the top.

3. **Two Bouncing Balls**
   Modify the program that you wrote for Exercise 2 so it displays an animation of two bouncing balls. The two balls should not bounce together, however. One ball should start at the bottom of the screen, and the other should start at the top.

4. **Moving and Resizing an Ellipse**
   Write a program that draws an ellipse in the center of the screen. When the program starts, the ellipse's X radius should be 100 and its Y radius should be 50. Allow the user to perform the following actions:

   - Move the ellipse on the screen by pressing the arrow keys.
   - Increase the ellipse's X radius by pressing the spacebar.
   - Decrease the ellipse's X radius by pressing the *Ctrl* key and the spacebar.
   - Increase the ellipse's Y radius by pressing the *Enter* key.
   - Decrease the ellipse's Y radius by pressing the *Ctrl* key and the *Enter* key.

5. **Make Your Head Spin**
   Have a friend use a digital camera to take photos of your head from different angles. (For example, your left profile, your face, your right profile, the back of your head, and so forth.) Copy the photos to your computer, and put them together as a sprite sheet. Then, write a program that creates an animated sprite that shows your head spinning.

6. **Randomly Moving Bowling Balls**

   The SpriteCollision program shown in this chapter (see Program 7-16) shows two bowling balls that initially appear on opposite sides of the screen. The balls move toward each other, and when they collide, they are repositioned back at their original locations and the animation repeats. Modify the program so the bowling balls move in random directions. If a ball reaches the edge of the screen, it should change directions. If the bowling balls collide, they should be repositioned back at their original locations.

7. **Invisible Pizza Modification**

   Modify the PizzaBot game (see Program 7-17) so the slice of pizza is shown on the screen for half a second, and then becomes invisible. The user must then guide the robot to the invisible slice of pizza.

8. **Lunar Lander, Part 1**

   Use Microsoft Paint, or any graphics program of your choice, to create a drawing of a spacecraft and a background drawing of the moon's surface. Write a program that initially displays the spacecraft on the moon's surface. When the user presses the spacebar, the spacecraft should slowly lift off the surface, and continue to lift as long as the spacebar is held down. When the user releases the spacebar, the spacecraft should slowly descend toward the surface, and stop when it gets there.

9. **Lunar Lander, Part 2**

   Enhance the lunar lander program (see Programming Exercise 8) so the user can press the left or right arrow keys, along with the spacebar, to guide the spacecraft slowly to the left or right. If the spacebar is not pressed, however, the left and right arrow keys should have no effect.

10. **Lunar Lander, Part 3**

    Enhance the lunar lander program (see Programming Exercises 8 and 9) so the spacecraft initially appears on one side of the screen and a landing pad appears on the opposite side. The user should try to fly the spacecraft and guide it so that it lands on the landing pad. If the spacecraft successfully lands on the landing pad, display a message congratulating the user.

8

The Vulture Trouble Game: Introducing Audio, Physics, and Text Effects

TOPICS

8.1 Introduction

8.2 Playing Sound Effects and Music

8.3 Simulating Falling Objects

8.4 Text Effects

8.5 The Vulture Trouble Game

8.1 Introduction

We've covered a lot of programming topics in the previous chapters, and now it's time to put all of them into practice. At the end of this chapter, we will demonstrate a game called Vulture Trouble. In the game, a greedy vulture has stolen eggs from a farmer's hen house. The vulture realizes he's been caught, and is dropping the eggs one by one. The player's objective is to use a basket to catch as many of the eggs as possible. If the player does not catch an egg, it hits the ground and breaks.

To make the game more interesting, we will incorporate music, sound effects, and a bit of physics. We will also manipulate the appearance and size of the game's text. Before we present the code for the game, we will explore those areas of programming.

8.2 Playing Sound Effects and Music

CONCEPT: The Dark GDK lets you play audio files that have been saved in the WAV, MIDI, or MP3 formats, as well as music tracks on an audio CD. The library provides numerous functions for working with these audio files.

Sound effects are important in games, as they are often used to signal events like colliding objects, selecting items, completing part of a game, and gaining extra power.

Background music also plays an important role in games. It can create a particular mood, for example, by making the game seem silly and whimsical or dark and mysterious.

The Dark GDK allows you to play sound from audio files that are stored in the WAV, MIDI, and MP3 formats. In the Dark GDK, audio that is saved in the WAV format is classified as *sound*, and audio that is saved in the MIDI or MP3 format is classified as *music*. There are two sets of functions for loading and playing audio: one for sound files and one for music files.

> **NOTE:** When you installed the Dark GDK, a collection of sample sound and music files was also installed in the folder `C:\Program Files\The Game Creators\ Dark GDK\Media`. This book's online resources, downloadable from www.aw.com/ gaddis, also contain sample audio files.

Sound Files

Audio files that are saved in the WAV format are considered sound files by the Dark GDK. To use a sound file first you must load it into memory. Then you can play the sound file and perform other operations with it.

Loading a Sound File

You load a sound file into memory by calling the `dbLoadSound` function. Here is the general format of how you call the function:

```
dbLoadSound(FileName, SoundNumber);
```

FileName is the name of the sound you would like to load into the program's memory. *SoundNumber* is an integer number that you are assigning to the sound. You will use the sound number to identify the sound when you want to play it, or perform other operations with it. For example, the following statement loads the sound file `MySound.wav` as sound number 1:

```
dbLoadSound("MySound.wav", 1);
```

In this example, we have specified only the file name, without a path. In order for the program to find the `MySound.wav` file, the file must be located in the program's project folder.

Another technique is to specify the file's path, as well as its name, when you call the `dbLoadSound` function. This eliminates the need to copy the sound file to the program's project folder. For example, suppose the `MySound.wav` file is stored in the folder `C:\Audio`. The file's name, including path, would be as follows:

```
C:\Audio\MySound.wav
```

Remember that when you write a Windows path as a string literal in a C++ program, each backslash character must be written as *two* backslashes. Here is an example:

```
dbLoadSound("C:\\Audio\\MySound.wav");
```

When this statement executes, the program will load the sound file `C:\Audio\MySound.wav`.

Playing a Sound

Once you have loaded a sound file into memory you can play it with the `dbPlaySound` function. Here is the general format of how you call the function:

```
dbPlaySound(SoundNumber);
```

SoundNumber is the number of the sound that you want to play. For example, the following statement plays sound number 1:

```
dbPlaySound(1);
```

When you call the `dbPlaySound` function, the specified sound will be played. Program 8-1 shows an example.

Program 8-1   **(PlaySound.cpp)**

```cpp
1   // This program loads a sound file and plays it.
2   #include "DarkGDK.h"
3
4   void DarkGDK()
5   {
6       // Load the sound file radio.wav as
7       // sound number 1.
8       dbLoadSound("radio.wav", 1);
9
10      // Play sound number 1.
11      dbPlaySound(1);
12
13      // Wait for the user to press a key.
14      dbWaitKey();
15  }
```

The statement in line 8 loads the sound file `radio.wav` as sound number 1, and the statement in line 11 plays the sound. Line 14 waits for the user to press a key.

Program 8-2 shows another example. We originally used this program in Chapter 7 to demonstrate sprite collisions. Two bowling balls move toward each other and collide. In this example, we have modified the program to play a sound when the collision is detected. Figure 8-1 shows the program's output.

Program 8-2   **(CollisionWithSound.cpp)**

```cpp
1   // This program demonstrates two colliding sprites
2   // with sound.
3   #include "DarkGDK.h"
4
5   // Global constants
6   const int COLLISION_SOUND = 1;  // Collision sound number
7   const int BALL1_IMAGE_NUM = 1;  // Ball 1's image number
```

```
 8   const int BALL2_IMAGE_NUM = 2;   // Ball 2's image number
 9   const int BALL1_SPRITE_NUM = 1; // Ball 1's sprite number
10   const int BALL2_SPRITE_NUM = 2; // Ball 2's sprite number
11   const int BALL1_X = 0;           // Ball 1's initial X position
12   const int BALL2_X = 511;         // Ball 2's initial X position
13   const int BALL_Y = 175;          // Both ball's Y position
14   const int DISTANCE = 10;         // Distance to move the balls
15   const int REFRESH_RATE = 10;     // Refresh rate
16
17   // Function prototypes
18   void setUp();
19   void moveBowlingBalls();
20   void detectCollision();
21
22   //*****************************************************
23   // The DarkGDK function                              *
24   //*****************************************************
25   void DarkGDK()
26   {
27       // Perform setup.
28       setUp();
29
30       // Game loop
31       while ( LoopGDK() )
32       {
33           // Move the bowling balls toward each other.
34           moveBowlingBalls();
35
36           // Check for a collision.
37           detectCollision();
38
39           // Refresh the screen.
40           dbSync();
41       }
42   }
43
44   //*****************************************************
45   // The setUp function loads the images, creates the *
46   // sprites, and sets things up for the game loop.    *
47   //*****************************************************
48   void setUp()
49   {
50       // Set the key color to green.
51       dbSetImageColorKey(0, 255, 0);
52
53       // Load the bowling ball images.
54       dbLoadImage("BowlingBall1.bmp", BALL1_IMAGE_NUM);
55       dbLoadImage("BowlingBall2.bmp", BALL2_IMAGE_NUM);
56
57       // Make the sprites.
58       dbSprite(BALL1_SPRITE_NUM, BALL1_X, BALL_Y,
59               BALL1_IMAGE_NUM);
60       dbSprite(BALL2_SPRITE_NUM, BALL2_X, BALL_Y,
61               BALL2_IMAGE_NUM);
62
63       // Load the collision sound.
64       dbLoadSound("Hit metal.wav", COLLISION_SOUND);
65
```

```
66          // Disable auto refresh.
67          dbSyncOn();
68
69          // Set the refresh rate.
70          dbSyncRate(REFRESH_RATE);
71     }
72
73     //****************************************************
74     // The moveBowlingBalls function moves the bowling  *
75     // balls toward each other.                         *
76     //****************************************************
77     void moveBowlingBalls()
78     {
79          // Variable to hold X coordinates
80          int x;
81
82          // Get bowling ball #1's X coordinate.
83          x = dbSpriteX(BALL1_SPRITE_NUM);
84
85          // Increment the coordinate.
86          x += DISTANCE;
87
88          // Move bowling ball #1.
89          dbSprite(BALL1_SPRITE_NUM, x, BALL_Y,
90                  BALL1_IMAGE_NUM);
91
92          // Get bowling ball #2's X coordinate.
93          x = dbSpriteX(BALL2_SPRITE_NUM);
94
95          // Decrement the coordinate.
96          x -= DISTANCE;
97
98          // Move bowling ball #2.
99          dbSprite(BALL2_SPRITE_NUM, x, BALL_Y,
100                 BALL2_IMAGE_NUM);
101    }
102
103    //****************************************************
104    // The detectCollision function determines whether  *
105    // the two bowling ball sprites have collided. If    *
106    // so, a sound is played and they are reset to       *
107    // their original positions.                         *
108    //****************************************************
109    void detectCollision()
110    {
111         if ( dbSpriteCollision(BALL1_SPRITE_NUM, BALL2_SPRITE_NUM) )
112         {
113              // Play the collision sound.
114              dbPlaySound(COLLISION_SOUND);
115
116              // Reset the sprites back at their initial positions.
117              dbSprite(BALL1_SPRITE_NUM, BALL1_X, BALL_Y,
118                      BALL1_IMAGE_NUM);
119              dbSprite(BALL2_SPRITE_NUM, BALL2_X, BALL_Y,
120                      BALL2_IMAGE_NUM);
121         }
122    }
```

Let's look at how sound is incorporated into this version of the program. Notice that in line 6 we declare an `int` constant named `COLLISION_SOUND`, initialized with the value 1. We will use this constant whenever we need to refer to the sound number for the audio that we will play when the bowling balls collide.

In the `setUp` function, line 64 loads a sound file named `Hit metal.wav`. This is one of the sample media files that is installed with the Dark GDK. As the file name indicates, it is the sound of metal objects hitting. When we were developing this program, we copied the file into the program's project folder. Inside the `detectCollision` function, line 114 plays the sound file when a sprite collision occurs.

> **NOTE:** In Program 8-2, the `Hit metal.wav` sound file plays for three seconds. When you run this program, you might notice that as the sound plays, the action on the screen continues. Once the `dbPlaySound` function starts a sound playing, the program continues executing while the sound plays.

Figure 8-1 Colliding bowling ball sprites displayed by Program 8-2

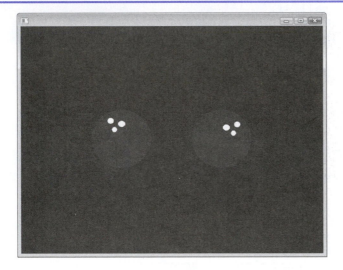

Looping a Sound File

To loop a sound means to play it repeatedly. You can loop a sound by calling the `dbLoopSound` function. Here is the general format of how you call the function:

```
dbLoopSound(SoundNumber);
```

SoundNumber is the number of the sound that you want to loop. Program 8-3 demonstrates sound looping. It loops a sound while drawing random dots on the screen.

Line 46, inside the `setUp` function, loads a sound file named `Magic tree.wav`. This is also one of the sample media files that is installed with the Dark GDK. Line 54 calls the `dbLoopSound` function to start the sound looping. Once the sound starts, it will play repeatedly while the rest of the statements in the program execute.

Program 8-3   **(LoopSound.cpp)**

```cpp
1   // This program loops a sound.
2   #include "DarkGDK.h"
3
4   // Constants
5   const int SOUND_NUM    = 1;       // Sound number
6   const int REFRESH_RATE = 60;      // Refresh rate
7
8   // Function prototype
9   void setUp();
10
11  //***********************************************
12  // DarkGDK function                            *
13  //***********************************************
14  void DarkGDK()
15  {
16      // Variables to hold XY coordinates
17      int x, y;
18
19      // Perform setup operations.
20      setUp();
21
22      // Game loop
23      while ( LoopGDK() )
24      {
25          // Get a random set of coordinates.
26          x = dbRND( dbScreenWidth() - 1 );
27          y = dbRND( dbScreenHeight() - 1 );
28
29          // Draw a random dot.
30          dbDot(x, y);
31
32          // Refresh the screen.
33          dbSync();
34      }
35  }
36
37  //***********************************************
38  // The setUp function performs setup operations. *
39  //***********************************************
40  void setUp()
41  {
42      // Seed the random number generator.
43      dbRandomize( dbTimer() );
44
45      // Load the Magic tree.wav sound file.
46      dbLoadSound("Magic tree.wav", SOUND_NUM);
47
48      // Disable auto refresh and set the
49      // maximum refresh rate.
50      dbSyncOn();
51      dbSyncRate(REFRESH_RATE);
52
53      // Start the sound loop.
54      dbLoopSound(SOUND_NUM);
55  }
```

Stopping a Sound

You can stop a sound that is currently playing by calling the dbStopSound function. Here is the general format of how you call the function:

```
dbStopSound(SoundNumber);
```

SoundNumber is the number of the sound that you want to stop.

Determining Whether a Sound Is Playing or Looping

You can determine whether a sound is playing by calling the dbSoundPlaying function, passing a sound number as an argument. The dbSoundPlaying function returns 1 (true) if the sound is playing, or 0 (false) if the sound is not playing. For example, the following code determines whether sound number 1 is playing, and if it is, it stops the sound:

```
if ( dbSoundPlaying(1) )
{
    dbStopSound(1);
}
```

You can determine whether a sound is looping by calling the dbSoundLooping function, passing the sound number as an argument. The dbSoundLooping function returns 1 (true) if the sound is looping, or 0 (false) if the sound is not looping. For example, the following code determines whether sound number 1 is looping. If sound number 1 is looping, the sound is stopped.

```
if ( dbSoundLooping(1) )
{
    dbStopSound(1);
}
```

Playing or Looping Part of a Sound File

When you call the dbPlaySound function, you can pass an optional second argument that specifies the starting byte number in the sound file. This allows you to skip part of the sound file. Here is the general format:

```
dbPlaySound(SoundNumber, StartingByte);
```

For example, the following statement plays sound number 1, beginning at byte 500:

```
dbPlaySound(1, 500);
```

When this statement executes, bytes 0 through 499 in the sound file will be skipped.

The dbLoopSound function also allows you to loop a portion of a sound file. Here are various optional formats in which the function may be called:

```
dbLoopSound(SoundNumber, StartingByte);
dbLoopSound(SoundNumber, StartingByte, EndingByte);
dbLoopSound(SoundNumber, StartingByte, EndingByte, Initial);
```

- In the first format *SoundNumber* is the number of the sound that you want to loop, and *StartingByte* is the starting byte number. The sound will play, beginning at the starting byte number, and then repeat.

- In the second format *SoundNumber* is the number of the sound that you want to loop, *StartingByte* is the starting byte number, and *EndingByte* is the ending byte number. The sound will play, from the starting byte number to the ending byte number, and then repeat.
- In the third format *SoundNumber* is the number of the sound that you want to loop, *StartingByte* is the starting byte number, *EndingByte* is the ending byte number, and *Initial* is the initial byte number for the first loop. When the sound is played, the first loop will begin at the initial byte number and end at the ending byte number. Subsequent loops will repeat from the starting byte number to the ending byte number, and then repeat.

Deleting a Sound from Memory

When a sound is no longer needed by the program, it can be removed from memory by calling the dbDeleteSound function, passing the sound number as an argument. For example, the following statement deletes sound number 1 from memory:

```
dbDeleteSound(1);
```

Determining Whether a Sound Exists

You can determine whether a sound is loaded in the program's memory by calling the dbSoundExist passing the sound number as an argument. The function returns 1 (true) if the sound has been loaded, or 0 (false) if the sound has not been loaded. For example, the following code segment checks for the existence of sound number 1 before deleting it from memory:

```
if ( dbSoundExist(1) )
{
    dbDeleteSound(1);
}
```

The following code segment determines whether sound number 1 does not exist before loading the file sample.wav and assigning it the sound number 1:

```
if ( !dbSoundExist(1) )
{
    dbLoadSound("sample.wav", 1);
}
```

Pausing and Resuming a Sound

A sound that is currently playing can be paused by calling the dbPauseSound function, passing the sound number as an argument. For example, the following statement will cause sound number 1 to pause:

```
dbPauseSound(1);
```

You can resume a sound that is paused by calling the dbResumeSound function passing the sound number as an argument. For example, the following statement causes sound number 1 to resume play:

```
dbResumeSound(1);
```

You can determine whether a sound is paused by calling the dbSoundPaused function, passing the sound number as an argument. The dbSoundPaused function returns 1 (true) if the specified sound is currently paused, or 0 (false) if the specified sound is not paused. For example, look at the following code segment:

```
if ( dbSoundPaused(1) )
{
    dbResumeSound(1);
}
```

This code segment determines whether sound 1 is paused. If so, it resumes the playing of the sound.

Cloning a Sound

Sometimes you might want to have multiple copies of the same sound, each referenced with a different sound number. Because making identical copies of a sound is not memory efficient, the Dark GDK allows you to clone a sound. Cloning a sound merely creates a new sound number and assigns it to an existing sound. This allows for multiple sound numbers to reference the same sound in memory. You clone a sound by calling the dbCloneSound function. Here is the general format of how you call the function:

```
dbCloneSound(ExistingSoundNumber, NewSoundNumber);
```

ExistingSoundNumber is the number of the existing sound that you want to clone. *NewSoundNumber* is the new sound number that you want to create to reference the existing sound. Here is an example:

```
dbCloneSound(1, 2);
```

This statement creates sound number 2, which references the same sound as sound number 1.

Sound Volume

Windows provides a volume control that allows users to adjust the volume of sounds being played. The Dark GDK also allows you to adjust the volume of specific sounds in your program with the dbSetSoundVolume function. Here is the general format of how you call the function:

```
dbSetSoundVolume(SoundNumber, Volume);
```

SoundNumber is the number of the sound for which you want to change the volume. *Volume* is an integer value that specifies a volume percentage. You can pass a value in the range of 0 through 100 for the *Volume*. For example, the following statement sets the volume of sound 1 to 75 percent. This means that sound 1's volume will be 75 percent of the current Windows volume setting.

```
dbSetSoundVolume(1, 75);
```

You can get the volume of a sound by calling the dbSoundVolume function, passing the sound number as an argument. For example, the following statement stores the volume of sound number 1 in the integer variable currentVolume:

```
currentVolume = dbSoundVolume(1);
```

Sound Speed

You can get the playing speed of a sound by calling the dbSoundSpeed function, passing the sound number as an argument. For example, the following statement stores the playing speed of sound number 1 in the integer variable currentSpeed:

```
currentSpeed = dbSoundSpeed(1);
```

WAV files typically have a playing speed of 44,100 Hz. This means that when the sound was recorded, 44,100 sound samples were recorded each second. (This is commonly known as the frequency.) You can change the playing speed of a sound by calling the dbSetSoundSpeed function. Here is the general format of how you call the function:

```
dbSetSoundSpeed(SoundNumber, Speed);
```

SoundNumber is the number of the sound for which you want to change the speed. *Speed* is an integer value that sets the speed of the sound. The speed can range from a value of 100 to 100,000. Lower values will produce slower, low-pitched sounds, while higher values will produce very fast, high-pitched sounds. For example, when you increase the speed of a voice recording, it produces a "chipmunk" sound. Here is an example of code that loads a sound and sets its playing speed to twice its original value:

```
// Load a sound.
dbLoadSound("MySound.wav", 1);

// Get the sounds current playing speed.
int speed = dbSoundSpeed(1);

// Double the playing speed.
speed = speed * 2;
dbSetSoundspeed(1, speed);

// Play the sound at its new speed.
dbPlaySound(1);
```

Panning Sounds

Sounds can also pan from the left speaker to the right, or vice-versa. This effect is particularly noticeable when the user is wearing headphones. You can use sound panning to simulate the sound of a person walking across the room, the sound of a car driving by, the sound of a plane flying over, and many other interesting effects. You set the sound pan by calling the dbSetSoundPan function. Here is the general format of how you call the function:

```
dbSetSoundPan(SoundNumber, Pan);
```

SoundNumber is the number of the sound for which you want to set the pan. *Pan* is an integer value ranging from −10,000 to 10,000. A value of 0 equally distributes the sound output between the left and right speakers. A negative value shifts the sound output to the left speaker. A positive value shifts the sound output to the right speaker. For example, Program 8-4 loads two of the sample Dark GDK sound files:

Program 8-4   **(SoundsLeftRight.cpp)**

```
 1   // This program plays a guitar sound in the
 2   // left speaker and a cowbell sound in the
 3   // right speaker.
 4   #include "DarkGDK.h"
 5
 6   void DarkGDK()
 7   {
 8       // Load two sounds.
 9       dbLoadSound("guitar.wav", 1);
10       dbLoadSound("cowbell.wav", 2);
11
12       // Set sound 1 (guitar) to the left speaker.
13       dbSetSoundPan(1, -10000);
14
15       // Set sound 2 (cowbell) to the right speaker.
16       dbSetSoundPan(2, 10000);
17
18       // Start both sounds looping.
19       dbLoopSound(1);
20       dbLoopSound(2);
21
22       // Wait for the user to press a key.
23       dbWaitKey();
24   }
```

guitar.wav and cowbell.wav. In line 13, the guitar sound is positioned completely in the left speaker (with a pan value of –10,000) and in line 16, the cowbell sound is positioned completely in the right speaker (with a pan value of 10,000). Lines 19 and 20 start both sounds looping. The program will run until you press a key.

Program 8-5 shows another example of sound panning. This program loops a sample Dark GDK sound file named Wood 1 slow.wav. This file has the sound of footsteps, slowly walking on a wooden floor. The sound starts playing in the left speaker. The for loop in lines 28 through 38 iterates eight times. Each time, it waits for half a second and then pans the sound toward the right speaker. This creates the effect of someone walking across the room, from the left to the right. When the loop finishes, the program ends.

Program 8-5   **(WalkingPan.cpp)**

```
 1   // This program pans a walking sound from
 2   // the left speaker to the right speaker.
 3   #include "DarkGDK.h"
 4
 5   void DarkGDK()
 6   {
 7       // Constants
 8       const int SOUND_NUM    = 1;    // Sound number
```

```
 9      const int NUM_PANS     = 8;         // Number of pans
10      const int DELAY        = 500;       // Delay between pans
11      const int PAN_INCREASE = 2500;      // Pan increase
12
13      // Variable to hold the pan value, initialized
14      // with -10,000 for the left speaker.
15      int pan = -10000;
16
17      // Load the sound file.
18      dbLoadSound("Wood 1 slow.wav", SOUND_NUM);
19
20      // Position the sound in the left speaker.
21      dbSetSoundPan(SOUND_NUM, pan);
22
23      // Start the sound looping.
24      dbLoopSound(SOUND_NUM);
25
26      // This loop pans the sound eight times
27      // toward right speaker.
28      for (int count = 0; count < NUM_PANS; count++)
29      {
30          // Wait for half a second.
31          dbWait(DELAY);
32
33          // Increase the pan amount.
34          pan += PAN_INCREASE;
35
36          // Pan the sound.
37          dbSetSoundPan(SOUND_NUM, pan);
38      }
39  }
```

You can get a sound's pan value by calling the dbSoundPan function, passing the sound number as an argument. For example, the following statement stores the pan value of sound number 1 in the integer variable currentPan:

```
currentPan = dbSoundPan(1);
```

Music Files

Music files are files that are saved in the MIDI or MP3 format. The Dark GDK provides many of the same operations for music files as sound files; however, there are some limitations. For example, you can have a maximum of 32 music files loaded into memory at one time, you cannot clone a music file, and you cannot pan a music file. The Dark GDK does allow you to load music files from audio CDs. Let's take a closer look at some of the things you can do with music files.

Loading a Music File

Before you can use a music file you have to load it into memory. You load a music file into memory by calling the dbLoadMusic function. Here is the general format of how you call the function:

```
dbLoadMusic(FileName, MusicNumber);
```

FileName is the name of the music file that you would like to load into the program's memory. *MusicNumber* is an integer number that you are assigning to the music. This can be an integer in the range of 1 through 32. You will use the music number to identify the music when you want to play it, or perform other operations with it. For example, the following statement loads the file `MyMusic.mp3` as music number 1.

```
dbLoadMusic("MySound.mp3", 1);
```

Playing Music

Once you have loaded a music file into memory you can play it with the `dbPlayMusic` function. Here is the general format of how you call the function:

```
dbPlayMusic(MusicNumber);
```

MusicNumber is the number of the music that you want to play. For example, the following statement plays music number 1:

```
dbPlayMusic(1);
```

Looping Music

To loop music means to play it repeatedly. You can loop music by calling the `dbLoopMusic` function. Here is the general format of how you call the function:

```
dbLoopMusic(MusicNumber);
```

MusicNumber is the number of the music that you want to loop.

Stopping Music

You can stop music that is currently playing by calling the `dbStopMusic` function. Here is the general format of how you call the function:

```
dbStopMusic(MusicNumber);
```

MusicNumber is the number of the sound that you want to stop.

Determining Whether Music Is Playing or Looping

You can determine whether music is playing by calling the `dbMusicPlaying` function, passing a music number as an argument. The `dbMusicPlaying` function returns 1 (true) if the music is playing, or 0 (false) if the sound is not playing. For example, the following code determines whether music number 1 is playing, and if it is, it stops it:

```
if ( dbMusicPlaying(1) )
{
    dbStopMusic(1);
}
```

You can determine whether music is looping by calling the `dbMusicLooping` function, passing the music number as an argument. The `dbMusicLooping` function returns 1 (true) if the music is looping, or 0 (false) if the music is not looping. For example, the following code segment checks to see whether music number 1 is looping. If it is, then the music is stopped.

```
if ( dbMusicLooping(1) )
{
    dbStopMusic(1);
}
```

Deleting Music from Memory

When music is no longer needed by the program, it can be removed from memory by calling the dbDeleteMusic function, passing the music number as an argument. For example, the following statement deletes music number 1 from memory:

```
dbDeleteMusic(1);
```

Determining Whether or Not Music Exists

You can determine whether or not music is loaded in the program's memory by calling the dbMusicExist function, passing the sound number as an argument. The function returns 1 (true) if the music has been loaded, or 0 (false) if the music has not been loaded. For example, the following code segment checks for the existence of music number 1 before deleting it from memory:

```
if ( dbMusicExist(1) )
{
    dbDeleteMusic(1);
}
```

Pausing and Resuming Music

Music that is currently playing can be paused by calling the dbPauseMusic function, passing the music number as an argument. For example, the following statement will cause music number 1 to pause:

```
dbPauseMusic(1);
```

You can resume music that is paused by calling the dbResumeMusic function, passing the music number as an argument. For example, the following statement causes music number 1 to resume play:

```
dbResumeMusic(1);
```

You can determine whether or not music is paused by calling the dbMusicPaused function, passing the music number as an argument. The dbMusicPaused function returns 1 (true) if the specified music is currently paused, or 0 (false) if the specified music is not paused. For example, the following code segment determines whether or not music number 1 is paused, and if so, resumes its playing:

```
if ( dbMusicPaused(1) )
{
    dbResumeMusic(1);
}
```

Music Volume

Windows allows users to adjust the volume of sounds being played. The Dark GDK also allows you to adjust the volume of music in your program with the `dbSetMusicVolume` function. Here is the general format of how you call the function:

```
dbSetMusicVolume(MusicNumber, Volume);
```

MusicNumber is the number of the music for which you want to change the volume. *Volume* is an integer value that specifies a volume percentage. You can pass a value in the range of 0 through 100 for the *Volume*. For example, the following statement sets the volume of music 1 to 50 percent. This means that music 1's volume will be 50 percent of the current Windows volume setting.

```
dbSetMusicVolume(1, 50);
```

You can get the volume of music by calling the `dbMusicVolume` function, passing the music number as an argument. For example, the following statement stores the volume of music number 1 in the integer variable `currentVolume`:

```
currentVolume = dbMusicVolume(1);
```

Music Speed

A music file's normal playing speed is considered 100 percent. However, you can change the playing speed to make the music slower or faster. To change a particular music's playing speed you call the `dbSetMusicSpeed`, with the following general format:

```
dbSetMusicSpeed(MusicNumber, Speed);
```

MusicNumber is the number of the music for which you want to change the speed. *Speed* is an integer value that specifies the speed as a percentage. For example, the value 50 will cause the music to play at half its normal speed, and the value 200 will cause the music to play at twice its normal speed.

You can get the playing speed of music by calling the `dbMusicSpeed` function, passing the music number as an argument. For example, the following statement gets the playing speed of music number 1 and assigns it to the integer variable `currentSpeed`:

```
currentSpeed = dbMusicSpeed(1);
```

Loading Music from a CD

You can load music from a CD by calling the `dbLoadCDMusic` function. Here is the general format of how you call the function:

```
dbLoadCDMusic(TrackNumber, MusicNumber);
```

TrackNumber is the number of the track you wish to play from the CD. *MusicNumber* is the number you want to assign to the music. For example, the following statement loads track 1 into the program's memory and assigns it to music number 1:

```
dbLoadCDMusic(1, 1);
```

Once the track is loaded, you can call `dbPlayMusic` to play it. Only one CD track at a time can be loaded into the program's memory, however. If you want to load another track from the CD, first you must delete the previous track. Program 8-6 demonstrates this. When you run the program, make sure you have already inserted a music CD into the computer's CD drive. The program will play 10 seconds from track 1, 10 seconds from track 2, and 10 seconds from track 3.

Program 8-6   (CDSampler.cpp)

```
1   // This program plays 10 seconds from tracks
2   // 1, 2, and 3 of the loaded CD.
3   #include "DarkGDK.h"
4
5   void DarkGDK()
6   {
7       const int MUSIC_NUM = 1;        // Music number
8       const int DELAY     = 10000;    // Time delay
9
10      // Play 10 seconds from track #1.
11      dbLoadCDMusic(1, MUSIC_NUM);
12      dbPrint("Now playing from track #1.");
13      dbPlayMusic(MUSIC_NUM);
14      dbWait(DELAY);
15
16      // Play 10 seconds from track #2.
17      dbDeleteMusic(MUSIC_NUM);
18      dbLoadCDMusic(2, MUSIC_NUM);
19      dbPrint("Now playing from track #2.");
20      dbPlayMusic(MUSIC_NUM);
21      dbWait(DELAY);
22
23      // Play 10 seconds from track #3.
24      dbDeleteMusic(MUSIC_NUM);
25      dbLoadCDMusic(3, MUSIC_NUM);
26      dbPrint("Now playing from track #3.");
27      dbPlayMusic(MUSIC_NUM);
28      dbWait(DELAY);
29
30      // Stop track #3 and wait for the user
31      // to press a key.
32      dbStopMusic(MUSIC_NUM);
33      dbPrint("Press any key to end.");
34      dbWaitKey();
35  }
```

You can get the number of tracks that are on a CD by calling the dbGetNumberOfCDTracks function. The function returns the number of tracks on the currently loaded CD, or a value of zero if no CD media is present. This function is important because it can tell you whether a CD is available, as well as the total number of tracks present on the CD. Program 8-7 demonstrates this function. The program determines whether a CD is loaded in the computer's CD drive, and if so, it prompts the user for a track number. That track is loaded from the CD and played.

Program 8-7 (MusicCD.cpp)

```cpp
1  // This program lets the user specify a track to
2  // load from a CD and play.
3  #include "DarkGDK.h"
4
5  // Function prototype
6  void playTrack();
7
8  //*********************************************
9  // DarkGDK function                          *
10 //*********************************************
11 void DarkGDK()
12 {
13     // If a CD is loaded, play a track.
14     if ( dbGetNumberOfCDTracks() > 0 )
15     {
16         playTrack();
17     }
18     else
19     {
20         dbPrint("No CD loaded.");
21     }
22
23     // Wait for the user to press a key.
24     dbPrint("Press any key to end.");
25     dbWaitKey();
26 }
27
28 //*********************************************
29 // The playTrack function gets a CD track    *
30 // number from the user and plays that track. *
31 //*********************************************
32 void playTrack()
33 {
34     const int MUSIC_NUM = 1;     // Music number
35     int tracks;                  // Number of tracks
36     int trackToPlay;             // The track to play
37
38     // Get the number of tracks on the CD.
39     tracks = dbGetNumberOfCDTracks();
40
41     // Display the number of tracks.
42     dbPrint("Number of tracks on the CD:");
43     dbPrint( dbStr(tracks) );
44
45     // Get the track number to play.
46     dbPrint("Which track do you want to hear?");
47     trackToPlay = atoi( dbInput() );
48
49     // If the user entered a valid track number,
50     // load and play that track.
51     if ( trackToPlay > 0 && trackToPlay <= tracks )
```

```
52        {
53              dbLoadCDMusic(trackToPlay, MUSIC_NUM);
54              dbPlayMusic(MUSIC_NUM);
55        }
56        else
57        {
58              // Display an error message.
59              dbPrint("Invalid track number.");
60        }
61 }
```

Checkpoint

8.1. In the Dark GDK, what is the difference between a sound file and a music file?

8.2. The Dark GDK provides functions to perform many operations with sound and music files. Complete the following table, listing the names of the Dark GDK functions that perform the specified operation. If the Dark GDK does not perform one of the listed operations, write "None."

Operation	Sound Function	Music Function
Load sound or music into memory		
Play		
Loop		
Delete sound or music from memory		
Pause		
Resume		
Pan		
Set the volume		
Set the playing speed		
Clone		
Load a track from a CD		
Determine whether a sound or music exists in memory		
Determine whether a sound or music is playing		
Determine whether a sound or music is looping		
Determine whether a sound or music is paused		
Determine the pan value		
Determine the playing speed		
Determine the volume setting		

8.3 Simulating Falling Objects

CONCEPT: When an object in the real world falls to Earth, its speed increases as it falls. If you want to write a program that realistically simulates falling objects, you will need to incorporate this acceleration into your program.

Game programmers often need to simulate moving objects, and in many cases the objects must move realistically. For example, suppose you are writing a program that shows an object falling toward the ground. You could design a loop that merely moves the object down the screen's *Y* axis the same amount each time the loop iterates. The resulting animation would not be realistic, however, because in the world, objects do not fall at a steady speed.

Designing programs that simulate realistic motion requires some knowledge of simple physics. In this section, we will discuss the motion of an object that is falling toward Earth because of gravity. Then we will look at how that motion can be reasonably simulated in a computer program.

NOTE: If you're thinking "Wait a minute, I didn't sign up to learn physics. I want to learn programming!"—then relax. You don't need to master physics in order to program realistic motion. Understanding a little about the physics of gravity and free fall, however, will go a long way in helping you to understand the code that we will write later.

Gravity is a force that attracts objects to one another. The more massive the objects are, the greater the gravitational attraction between them. For example, the Earth is so massive that its gravitational pull keeps us from floating off into space. When an apple falls from a tree, it falls because it is attracted to the Earth by gravity.

If you watch an object fall from a considerable height, such as the top of a building, you will notice that the object's speed increases as it falls. The object's increase in speed is known as *acceleration*. When an object falls in a vacuum (where there are no air molecules to slow it down), its speed increases at a rate of 9.8 meters per second, *each second*. Did you get that? For each second that an object falls, its speed increases by an additional 9.8 meters per second.

For example, suppose a construction worker is building a skyscraper, and he accidentally drops a brick from the top of the building. If we forget about the fact that the air will slow the brick down a small amount, we can calculate how fast the brick will be traveling each second as it plummets to the ground:

- At one second the brick is falling at a speed of 9.8 meters per second.
- At two seconds the brick is falling at a speed of 19.6 meters per second.
- At three seconds the brick is falling at a speed of 29.4 meters per second.
- At four seconds the brick is falling at a speed of 39.2 meters per second.
- And so forth.

This is illustrated in Figure 8-2.

Figure 8-2 Speed of a falling brick at various time intervals (not drawn to scale)

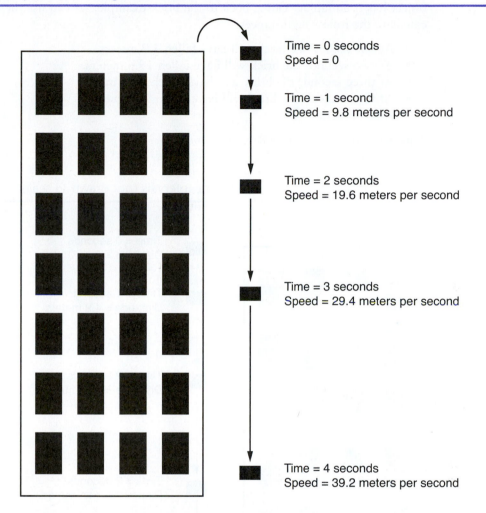

Time = 0 seconds
Speed = 0

Time = 1 second
Speed = 9.8 meters per second

Time = 2 seconds
Speed = 19.6 meters per second

Time = 3 seconds
Speed = 29.4 meters per second

Time = 4 seconds
Speed = 39.2 meters per second

If this is interesting enough to make you want to read a physics book, you will see the acceleration rate of a falling object written as 9.8 m/s² (which is pronounced "9.8 meters per second squared"). The letter *g* is commonly used to represent the acceleration rate of a falling object in formulas.

Now let's talk about the distance that an object falls over time. When an object is moving, two factors determine the distance that the object moves: the object's speed and the amount of time that the object is moving. For example, a ball that is moving at a constant speed of 12 meters per second will travel a distance of 24 meters in two seconds. By constant speed, we mean that the ball is not speeding up or slowing down; it is moving steadily at 12 meters per second. However, a falling object does not move at a constant speed. A falling object speeds up as it falls. As a result, a falling object travels downward an increasingly greater distance each second that it falls. We can use the following formula to calculate the distance that a falling object falls:

$$d = \frac{1}{2}\,gt^2$$

In this formula, *d* is the distance, *g* is 9.8, and *t* is the number of seconds that the object has been falling. Going back to the brick example, we can use the formula to calculate the following distances:

- At one second the brick will have fallen 4.9 meters.
- At two seconds the brick will have fallen 19.6 meters.
- At three seconds the brick will have fallen 44.1 meters.
- At four seconds the brick will have fallen 78.4 meters.
- And so forth.

This is illustrated in Figure 8-3.

Figure 8-3 A falling brick's distance at various time intervals (not drawn to scale)

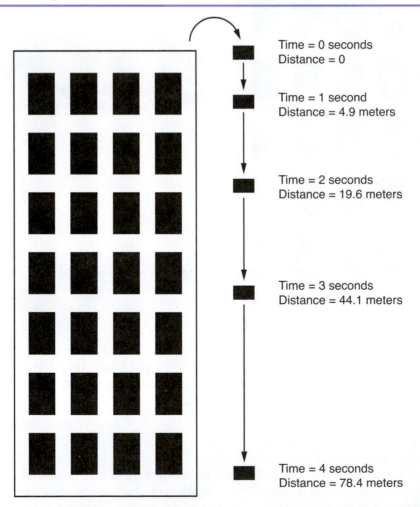

So how do you simulate the behavior of falling objects in a program? After all, a computer screen is measured in pixels, not meters. Because of this, the formula for calculating the distance that a falling object moves on the screen will have to be "tweaked."

First, you have to decide how accurate the simulation must be. If your program will be used for scientific research, it will need to be accurate. If you are creating a game, however, accuracy is probably not essential. That's the case with the Vulture Trouble game that is presented later in this chapter. We want to display eggs that are falling realistically, but also we want the falling motion to work for the game and the game player. If the eggs fall too fast, then the player might get frustrated because the game is too difficult to play. Likewise, if the eggs fall too slowly, then the game will not be challenging enough.

Program 8-8 shows how we can approximate the motion of a falling object, at a speed that is slow enough to easily observe, yet fast enough to seem realistic. When the program runs, it displays the ball sprite shown in Figure 8-4 falling from the top of the screen to the bottom. To achieve the falling motion we have used the value 0.98 as the gravitational acceleration, and a screen refresh rate of 60 times per second.

Program 8-8   **(FreeFall.cpp)**

```
1   // This program simulates a falling ball.
2   #include "DarkGDK.h"
3
4   // Constants
5   const int    BALL_IMAGE    = 1;
6   const int    BALL_SPRITE   = 1;
7   const int    REFRESH_RATE  = 60;
8   const float ACCELERATION   = 0.98;
9
10  // Function prototype
11  void setUp();
12
13  //****************************************************
14  // DarkGDK function                                 *
15  //****************************************************
16  void DarkGDK()
17  {
18      // Variables for the ball's XY coordinates
19      int ballX, ballY;
20
21      // Variable to hold the simulated time that
22      // the ball has been falling
23      int time = 0;
24
25      // Variable to hold the falling distance
26      float distance;
27
28      // Perform setup operations.
29      setUp();
30
31      // Calculate the maximum Y coordinate for
32      // the ball sprite.
33      int maxY = dbScreenHeight() -
34                  dbSpriteHeight(BALL_SPRITE);
35
```

```
36        // Game loop
37        while ( LoopGDK() )
38        {
39            // Get the ball's X and Y coordinates.
40            ballX = dbSpriteX(BALL_SPRITE);
41            ballY = dbSpriteY(BALL_SPRITE);
42
43            // If the ball is above the bottom of the
44            // screen, then update its position.
45            if ( ballY < maxY )
46            {
47                // Calculate the object's distance using
48                // the distance formula.
49                distance = 0.5 * ACCELERATION * time * time;
50
51                // Set the ball's Y coordinate to the
52                // distance.
53                ballY = distance;
54
55                // Increment time.
56                time++;
57            }
58            // Else, set the ball's Y coordinate at the
59            // bottom of the screen.
60            else
61            {
62                ballY = maxY;
63            }
64
65            // Draw the ball sprite.
66            dbSprite(BALL_SPRITE, ballX, ballY, BALL_IMAGE);
67
68            // Refresh the screen.
69            dbSync();
70        }
71 }
72
73 //*****************************************************
74 // The setUp function performs setup operations.      *
75 //*****************************************************
76 void setUp()
77 {
78    // Set the key color.
79    dbSetImageColorKey(0, 255, 0);
80
81    // Load the ball image.
82    dbLoadImage("Ball.bmp", BALL_IMAGE);
83
84    // Calculate the ball's X coordinate.
85    int ballX = dbScreenWidth() / 2;
86
87    // The ball's Y coordinate is 0.
88    int ballY = 0;
89
90    // Create the ball sprite.
```

```
91        dbSprite(BALL_SPRITE, ballX, ballY, BALL_IMAGE);
92
93        // Disable auto refresh and set the maximum
94        // refresh rate.
95        dbSyncOn();
96        dbSyncRate(REFRESH_RATE);
97 }
```

Figure 8-4 Ball sprite from Program 8-8

In lines 5 through 7, we declare global constants for the ball's image number, sprite number, and the screen refresh rate. In line 8, we declare a `float` constant named `ACCELERATION`, initialized with the value 0.98. We will use this value for gravitational acceleration. If you're wondering how we decided to use the value 0.98, we used the trial-and-error method. When we tried the value 9.8, it produced motion that was so fast the ball could barely be seen. So, we knew that we needed to scale down the acceleration value. Next, we tried the value 0.98 and we were happy with the results.

The `setUp` function, in lines 76 through 97, does the following:

- It sets the key color to green (line 79).
- It loads the ball image (line 82).
- It calculates the ball's *X* coordinate (line 85) and sets the ball's *Y* coordinate to 0 (line 88).
- It creates the ball sprite (line 91).
- It disables auto-refresh and sets the maximum refresh rate (lines 95 and 96).

The `DarkGDK` function starts with the following actions:

- It declares the local `int` variables `ballX` and `ballY` (line 19). These variables will hold the ball sprite's *X* and *Y* coordinates.
- It declares the local `int` variable `time` (line 23), initialized with the value 0. This variable will keep a count of the game loop's iterations. We will use it as the time value in the distance calculation.
- It declares the local `float` variable `distance` (line 26). This variable will hold the distance that the ball sprite falls during each iteration of the game loop.
- It calls the `setUp` function (line 29).
- It calculates the maximum *Y* coordinate for the sprite and assigns that value to the `maxY` variable (lines 33 and 34). As long as the sprite's insertion point is above this position, the ball hasn't hit the bottom edge of the screen.

Then, the game loop starts in line 37. Inside the game loop the following is done:

- The ball sprite's *X* and *Y* coordinates are retrieved and assigned to the `ballX` and `ballY` variables (lines 40 and 41).
- The `if` statement in line 45 determines whether the ball sprite's *Y* coordinate is less than `maxY`. If so, the ball can continue to fall. In that case, line 49 uses the distance formula you saw earlier to calculate the distance that the ball has fallen down the screen. Then, line 53 sets the `ballY` variable to this distance. Line 56 increments the `time` variable.
- The `else` clause in line 60 handles things if the ball has reached the bottom of the screen. If that is the case, the `ballY` variable is set to `maxY`.
- The `dbSprite` statement in line 66 draws the ball sprite at the coordinates specified by the `ballX` and `ballY` variables, and line 69 refreshes the screen.

NOTE: Line 53 assigns `distance`, a `float` variable, to `ballY`, an `int` variable. Recall that when a floating-point value is assigned to an integer variable, the floating-point value is truncated. This means that the portion of the number after the decimal point is dropped. This does not adversely affect the motion of the ball because we only need a reasonable amount of accuracy in our simulation.

Simulating Motion in Two Directions

In the previous example, we simulated a ball that was moving in one direction: straight down. But what about situations in which an object is moving in two directions simultaneously? For example, when a baseball pitcher throws the ball toward the catcher, the baseball is moving in two directions simultaneously:

- It is moving horizontally, toward the catcher, because the pitcher threw it in that direction.
- It is moving vertically, toward the ground, because gravity is pulling it down.

To simulate this type of motion, we need to update the falling object's position along both the *X* and *Y* axes. Program 8-9 shows an example. In this program, a ball is initially positioned in the upper-right corner of the window. As the ball accelerates toward the bottom of the screen, it also moves to the left along the *X* axis at a constant speed. The resulting animation looks like the ball was not merely dropped, but

Program 8-9   **(DualMotion.cpp)**

```
1   // This program simulates a ball that is falling
2   // and moving horizontally.
3   #include "DarkGDK.h"
4
5   // Constants
6   const int   BALL_IMAGE    = 1;
7   const int   BALL_SPRITE   = 1;
8   const int   REFRESH_RATE  = 60;
9   const int   X_MOVEMENT    = 10;
10  const float ACCELERATION  = 0.98;
11
12  // Function prototype
13  void setUp();
14
15  //****************************************************
16  // DarkGDK function                                  *
17  //****************************************************
18  void DarkGDK()
19  {
20      // Variables for the ball's XY coordinates
21      int ballX, ballY;
22
23      // Variable to hold the simulated time that
24      // the ball has been falling
25      int time = 0;
26
27      // Variable to hold the falling distance
28      float distance;
29
30      // Perform setup operations.
31      setUp();
32
33      // Calculate the maximum Y coordinate for
34      // the ball sprite.
35      int maxY = dbScreenHeight() -
36                 dbSpriteHeight(BALL_SPRITE);
37
38      // Game loop
39      while ( LoopGDK() )
40      {
41          // Get the ball's X and Y coordinates.
42          ballX = dbSpriteX(BALL_SPRITE);
43          ballY = dbSpriteY(BALL_SPRITE);
44
45          // If the ball is above the bottom of the screen,
46          // then update its position.
47          if ( ballY < maxY )
48          {
49              // Move the ball to the left.
50              ballX -= X_MOVEMENT;
51
52              // Calculate the object's distance using
53              // the distance formula.
```

```
54                     distance = 0.5 * ACCELERATION * time * time;
55
56                     // Set the ball's Y coordinate to the
57                     // distance.
58                     ballY = distance;
59
60                     // Increment time.
61                     time++;
62             }
63             // Else, set the ball's Y coordinate at the
64             // bottom of the screen.
65             else
66             {
67                 ballY = maxY;
68             }
69
70             // Draw the ball sprite.
71             dbSprite(BALL_SPRITE, ballX, ballY, BALL_IMAGE);
72
73             // Refresh the screen.
74             dbSync();
75
76             dbWaitKey();
77         }
78 }
79
80 //*******************************************************
81 // The setUp function performs setup operations.        *
82 //*******************************************************
83 void setUp()
84 {
85     // Set the key color.
86     dbSetImageColorKey(0, 255, 0);
87
88     // Load the ball image.
89     dbLoadImage("Ball.bmp", BALL_IMAGE);
90
91     // Calculate the ball's X coordinate so we can
92     // place the ball at the right edge of the screen.
93     int ballX = dbScreenWidth() -
94                 dbGetImageWidth(BALL_IMAGE);
95
96     // The ball's Y coordinate is 0.
97     int ballY = 0;
98
99     // Create the ball sprite.
100     dbSprite(BALL_SPRITE, ballX, ballY, BALL_IMAGE);
101     dbWaitKey();
102
103     // Disable auto refresh and set the maximum
104     // refresh rate.
105     dbSyncOn();
106     dbSyncRate(REFRESH_RATE);
107 }
```

also given a slight kick toward the left side of the screen. In Figure 8-5 we have captured four different frames from the program's output and superimposed them so you can see the ball's path as it falls.

Figure 8-5 Four frames captured from Program 8-9's output

This program's code is very similar to Program 8-8. In line 9, we have declared a constant named X_MOVEMENT, initialized with the value 10. This is the distance that the ball will move along the *X* axis each time the game loop iterates.

Inside the game loop we subtract X_MOVEMENT from ballX in line 50, and we assign distance to ballY in line 58. As a result, the ball moves to the left 10 pixels, and accelerates down toward the bottom of the screen each time the game loop iterates.

NOTE: If you have downloaded the book's sample programs from www.aw.com/gaddis, you will find an additional program named DropTheBall that provides a more in-depth example of horizontal and vertical motion.

 **Checkpoint**

> 8.3. When gravity causes an object to fall in a vacuum toward Earth, does the object fall at a steady speed, or does its speed increase as it falls?
>
> 8.4. If gravity is causing an object to fall in a vacuum toward Earth, how far will the object have fallen at 10 seconds?

8.4 Text Effects

CONCEPT: You can change the font, size, and style of text that is displayed by the **dbPrint**, **dbText**, and **dbCenterText** functions.

Until now, when your programs have displayed text using the dbPrint, dbText, and dbCenterText functions, the text appears on the screen using the default font and size. The *font* is the name of the typeface that defines the way characters appear. For example, if you have used word processing software, you have probably seen different fonts such as Times Roman, Arial, and Courier. Each of these fonts has a unique appearance. The default font that is used by the Dark GDK is called Fixedsys. The size of text is measured in *points*. One point is 1/72 of an inch. The default text size in the Dark GDK is 12 points.

The Dark GDK provides functions for changing the font and text size, which gives you the ability to customize the appearance of messages displayed by your programs. You can also change the style of text to make it appear bold and/or italic.

Changing the Text Size

The dbSetTextSize function can be used to set the point size of the current font. As previously mentioned, one point is 1/72 of an inch. For example, the following statement sets the text size to be displayed at 24 point:

```
dbSetTextSize(24);
```

After the statement executes, any text that is subsequently displayed will be 24 points in size. This size setting will remain in effect until you change it by calling the dbSetTextSize again. Text can be set to any size supported by the font type that is currently being used. If you specify a size that is not supported, the text size will not change. An unsupported point size will not result in an error.

You can get the current text size by calling the dbFontSize function. The dbFontSize function returns an integer value for the current text size. The following shows an example. Assume that currentSize is an int variable.

```
currentSize = dbFontSize();
```

After this statement executes, the currentSize variable will hold the current text size.

Changing the Text Font

You can change the current text font by calling the dbSetTextFont function and passing the font name as a string argument. For example, the following statement sets the font to Arial:

```
dbSetTextFont("Arial");
```

After this statement executes, all subsequent text displayed by the program will appear in the Arial font. This font setting will remain in effect until you change it by calling the `dbSetTextFont` again. If the font name is misspelled or the font is not supported, the font will not change, but unsupported or misspelled fonts will not result in an error.

You can get the name of the current font by calling the `dbTextFont` function. This is a value-returning function that returns the current font name as a string. For example, the following statement will print the name of the current font:

```
dbPrint( dbTextFont() );
```

NOTE: You can see a list of all the fonts installed on your system by clicking the *Start* button, clicking *Control Panel*, and then opening *Fonts*. The Dark GDK can use any TrueType font that is installed on your system.

Using Bold and Italic Styles

In addition to changing the text size and font, you can also change the text style to bold, italic, or both. Here is a summary of the functions that you call to change the text style:

- The `dbSetTextToBold` function sets the current text style to bold.
- The `dbSetTextToItalic` function sets the current text style to italic.
- The `dbSetTextToBoldItalic` function sets the current text style to both bold and italic.
- The `dbSetTextToNormal` function sets the current text style to normal, which is non-bold and non-italic.

NOTE: You have to call the `dbSetTextToBoldItalic` function if you want your text to be both bold and italic. Calling the `dbSetTextToBold` function causes text to be bold and non-italic, and calling the `dbSetTextToItalic` function causes text to be italic and non-bold.

If you want to know the current text style setting, you can call the `dbTextStyle` function. This is a value-returning function that returns the following integer values:

- 0 if the current text style is normal (non-bold and non-italic)
- 1 if the current text style is italic
- 2 if the current text style is bold
- 3 if the current text style is bold and italic

Here is an example:

```
if ( dbTextStyle() == 1 )
{
    dbPrint("The current style is italic.");
}
else if ( dbTextStyle() == 2 )
{
    dbPrint("The current style is bold.");
}
```

```
        else if ( dbTextStyle() == 3 )
        {
            dbPrint("The current style is bold and italic.");
        }
        else
        {
            dbPrint("The current style is normal.");
        }
```

Program 8-10 demonstrates how to change the font and text size, and how to display text in bold and/or italic. The program's output is shown in Figure 8-6.

Program 8-10   (TextEffects.cpp)

```
 1   // This program demonstrates how to set the text
 2   // font, size, and style.
 3   #include "DarkGDK.h"
 4
 5   void DarkGDK()
 6   {
 7       // Demonstrate Arial font, 36 points.
 8       dbSetTextFont("Arial");
 9       dbSetTextSize(36);
10       dbPrint("This is 36 point Arial.");
11
12       // Demonstrate Freestyle Script font,
13       // 42 points.
14       dbSetTextFont("Freestyle Script");
15       dbSetTextSize(42);
16       dbPrint("This is 42 point Freestyle Script.");
17
18       // Demonstrate Rockwell font, 24 points.
19       dbSetTextFont("Rockwell");
20       dbSetTextSize(24);
21       dbPrint("This is 24 point Rockwell.");
22
23       // Set the current font to italic.
24       dbSetTextToItalic();
25       dbPrint("This is italic Rockwell.");
26
27       // Set the current font to bold.
28       dbSetTextToBold();
29       dbPrint("This is bold Rockwell.");
30
31       // Set the current font to bold and italic.
32       dbSetTextToBoldItalic();
33       dbPrint("This is bold italic Rockwell.");
34
35       // Wait for the user to press a key.
36       dbWaitKey();
37   }
```

Figure 8-6 Output of Program 8-10

Text Background Transparency

When text is displayed, it is displayed in a rectangular area that we call the text's background. By default, the background is transparent. Any graphics or imagery on which you display text will be visible through the text's background. For example, the image on the left in Figure 8-7 shows text with a transparent background displayed on top of a bitmap image. If you want the text background to be opaque (not transparent), you can call the `dbSetTextOpaque` function, as shown here:

```
dbSetTextOpaque();
```

Figure 8-7 Text displayed on transparent and opaque backgrounds

Text displayed on a transparent background

Text displayed on an opaque background

After calling this function, subsequent text will be displayed on an opaque background, as shown in the image on the right in Figure 8-7. The default background color is black, however you can change that with the `dbInk` function. Recall from Chapter 3 that the `dbInk` function takes two DWORD arguments: the first specifies the foreground color and the second specifies the background color. When you display text on an opaque background, the color of the background will be the background color that is currently set by the `dbInk` function. For example, the following code sets the background color to red and then displays the string "Warning!" in white letters on a red opaque background.

```
DWORD white = dbRGB(255, 255, 255);
DWORD red = dbRGB(255, 0, 0);
dbInk(white, red);
dbSetTextOpaque();
dbPrint("Warning!");
```

You can call the dbSetTextTransparent function to set the text background back to transparent, as shown here:

```
dbSetTextTransparent();
```

After calling this function, subsequent text will be displayed on a transparent background.

If you want to know what the current background setting is, you can call the dbTextBackgroundType function. This is a value-returning function that returns the integer 1 if the current background setting is transparent, or 0 if the current background setting is opaque. Here is an example:

```
if ( dbTextBackgroundType() == 1 )
{
    dbPrint("The background setting is transparent.");
}
else
{
    dbPrint("The background setting is opaque.");
}
```

Getting Text Width and Height

In some situations you might want to know the size that a string will be, in pixels, when it is displayed. You can use the dbTextWidth and dbTextHeight functions to get the width and the height of a string, in pixels, using the current font and text size. Program 8-11 demonstrates these functions. It displays the string "Bonjour!" using the Arial font, set to 36 points. It then draws lines around the text to form a box. The program's output is shown in Figure 8-8.

Program 8-11   (TextInTheBox.cpp)

```
 1   // This program displays text and then draws
 2   // a box around the text.
 3   #include "DarkGDK.h"
 4
 5   void DarkGDK()
 6   {
 7       // Variables
 8       int upperX = 50;      // Text X coordinate
 9       int upperY = 50;      // Text Y coordinate
10       int width;            // Text width
11       int height;           // Text height
12
```

```
13      // Set the font to Arial and the size
14      // to 36 points.
15      dbSetTextFont("Arial");
16      dbSetTextSize(36);
17
18      // Display some text.
19      dbText(upperX, upperY, "Bonjour!");
20
21      // Get the width of the text we just displayed.
22      width = dbTextWidth("Bonjour!");
23      height = dbTextHeight("Bonjour!");
24
25      // Draw a horizontal line above the text.
26      dbLine(upperX, upperY, upperX+width, upperY);
27
28      // Draw a horizontal line below the text.
29      dbLine(upperX, upperY+height, upperX+width, upperY+height);
30
31      // Draw a vertical line to the left of the text.
32      dbLine(upperX, upperY, upperX, upperY+height);
33
34      // Draw a vertical line to the right of the text.
35      dbLine(upperX+width, upperY, upperX+width, upperY+height);
36
37      // Wait for the user to press a key.
38      dbWaitKey();
39  }
```

Figure 8-8 Output of Program 8-11

Setting the Cursor Position

You've already learned that the dbPrint function prints a line of output to the program window. The first time you call dbPrint, its output is printed at the top of the window, justified along the left side. (This is the same as calling the dbText function, passing 0, 0 as the text position.) Each subsequent time that you call dbPrint, it prints a line of output below the previous line of output.

You can change the location of the dbPrint function's output by calling the dbSetCursor function before calling dbPrint. When you call the dbSetCursor function you pass a set of *XY* coordinates as arguments. The *cursor*, which marks the position at which text is displayed, will be moved to that location. Here is an example:

```
dbSetCursor(10, 20);
dbPrint("Hello world!");
```

In the example, the cursor will be positioned at the coordinates (10, 20). When the `dbPrint` function executes, the string "Hello world!" will be printed from that location. The result will be the same as the following statement:

```
dbText(10, 20, "Hello world!");
```

You can use the `dbSetCursor` function along with the `dbTextWidth` and/or `dbTextHeight` functions to get better control over the way text output is displayed. For example, look at the following code segment:

```
int points = 5000;

dbPrint("You have earned");
dbPrint( dbStr(points) );
dbPrint(" points.");
```

When this code executes it will display output similar to the following:

```
You have earned
5000
points.
```

The output of each `dbPrint` function call is displayed on a separate line. The output would look better, however, if it all appeared on the same line, as follows:

```
You have earned 5000 points.
```

This output can be achieved with the `dbSetCursor` function, as demonstrated in Program 8-12. The program's output is shown in Figure 8-9.

Program 8-12   **(DisplayPoints.cpp)**

```
 1  // This program demonstrates how to set the
 2  // cursor position and control the output of
 3  // the dbPrint function.
 4  #include "DarkGDK.h"
 5
 6  void DarkGDK()
 7  {
 8      int points = 5000;    // Points earned
 9      int x = 20, y = 50;   // Text coordinates
10
11      // Set the font to Arial and the text
12      // size to 24 points.
13      dbSetTextFont("Arial");
14      dbSetTextSize(24);
15
16      // Set the cursor position.
17      dbSetCursor(x, y);
18
```

```
19          // Print the first part of the message.
20          dbPrint("You have earned ");
21
22          // Calculate the X position of the next
23          // part of the message.
24          x += dbTextWidth("You have earned ");
25
26          // Set the cursor position.
27          dbSetCursor(x, y);
28
29          // Print the value of the points variable.
30          dbPrint( dbStr(points) );
31
32          // Calculate the X position of the next
33          // part of the message.
34          x += dbTextWidth( dbStr(points) );
35
36          // Set the cursor position.
37          dbSetCursor(x, y);
38
39          // Print the last part of the message.
40          dbPrint(" points.");
41
42          // Wait for the user to press a key.
43          dbWaitKey();
44   }
```

Figure 8-9 Output of Program 8-12

 Checkpoint

8.5. What function do you call to change the current font?

8.6. What function do you call to change the current text size?

8.7. What function do you call to set the current text style to bold?

8.8. What function do you call to set the current text style to italic?

8.9. What function do you call if you want text to be non-bold and non-italic?

8.10. What function do you call if you want text to be transparent?

8.11. What function do you call if you do not want text to be transparent?

8.12. What function do you call to set the text cursor position?

8.13. What value-returning functions do you call to get the following data:
- The current text size
- The current font
- The current text width
- The current text height
- The current text style
- The current text background transparency setting

8.5 The Vulture Trouble Game

In this section, we will demonstrate the Vulture Trouble game. In the game, a greedy vulture has stolen eggs from a farmer's hen house. The vulture realizes he's been caught, and is dropping the eggs one by one. The player's objective is to use a basket to catch as many of the eggs as possible. If the player does not catch an egg, it hits the ground and breaks.

The top screen shown in Figure 8-10 (located in this book's color insert) shows the game's title screen, which is displayed when the program starts. The bottom screen is the introductory screen that is displayed after the user presses a key. The introductory screen gives the user instructions for playing the game. The top screen shown in Figure 8-11 (located in this book's color insert) shows the game's main screen, which appears next. The vulture is an animated sprite that moves back and forth across the screen. The egg that is dropped from the vulture, as well as the basket that appears at the bottom of the screen, are also sprites. The player uses the left and right arrow keys to move the basket sprite, and hopefully catch the eggs as they fall. The vulture has stolen a total of 40 eggs.

When the game begins, a row of 40 mini eggs appears across the top of the screen. This serves as an indicator of the number of eggs left. Each time the vulture drops an egg, one of the mini eggs is removed from the top of the screen. The program keeps count of the number of eggs that the player catches, as well as the number of broken eggs. After the last egg has been dropped, a summary screen like the one shown at the bottom of Figure 8-11 appears.

Figure 8-12 (located in this book's color insert) shows all of the images that we will use in the game. Here is a summary of each:

- The `farm.bmp` image will serve as the background for the game.
- The `vulture.bmp` image contains the frames we will use to create an animated sprite for the flying vulture.
- The `egg.bmp` image shows an egg.
- The `basket.bmp` image shows the basket that the player will use to catch eggs.
- The `hitBasket.bmp` image will be displayed briefly when an egg hits the basket.
- The `brokenEgg.bmp` image will be displayed briefly when an egg hits the ground.

Now let's look at the game's code in Program 8-13. Rather than presenting all of the code at once, we will show a section at a time, discussing each part. The first part of the program shows the global constant declarations.

Program 8-13   (`VultureTrouble.cpp` *partial listing*)

```
 1   //*******************************************
 2   // Vulture Trouble Game                     *
 3   //*******************************************
 4   #include "DarkGDK.h"
 5
 6   // Constants for the image numbers
 7   const int TITLE_SCREEN_IMAGE  = 1;
 8   const int INTRO_SCREEN_IMAGE  = 2;
 9   const int EGG_IMAGE           = 3;
10   const int BROKEN_EGG_IMAGE    = 4;
11   const int FARM_IMAGE          = 5;
12   const int BASKET_IMAGE        = 6;
13   const int HIT_BASKET_IMAGE    = 7;
14   const int VULTURE_IMAGE       = 8;
15
16   // Constants for the sprite numbers
17   const int FARM_SPRITE         = 1;
18   const int BASKET_SPRITE       = 2;
19   const int EGG_SPRITE          = 3;
20   const int HIT_BASKET_SPRITE   = 4;
21   const int BROKEN_EGG_SPRITE   = 5;
22   const int VULTURE_SPRITE      = 6;
23
24   // Constants for the vulture animated sprite
25   const int VULTURE_COLS        = 4;
26   const int VULTURE_ROWS        = 2;
27   const int START_FRAME         = 1;
28   const int END_FRAME           = 8;
29
30   // Constants for the sound numbers
31   const int POP_SOUND           = 1;
32   const int CLAP_SOUND          = 2;
33   const int TYPE_SOUND          = 3;
34   const int COMPLETE_SOUND      = 4;
35   const int PERFECT_SCORE_SOUND = 5;
36
37   // Constants for the music numbers
38   const int INTRO_MUSIC         = 1;
39   const int MAIN_MUSIC          = 2;
40
41   // Time delay constants
42   const int TENTH_SECOND        = 100;
43   const int ONE_SECOND          = 1000;
44   const int FOUR_SECONDS        = 4000;
45
46   // Other constants
47   const int MAX_EGGS            = 40;   // Total number of eggs
48   const int BASKET_MOVE         = 4;    // Amount to move the basket
49   const int VULTURE_MOVE        = 2;    // Amount to move the vulture
50   const float ACCELERATION      = 0.5;  // Gravity acceleration
51   const int REFRESH_RATE        = 60;   // Refresh rate
52
```

Here is a summary of the constant declarations:

- Lines 7 through 14 declare constants for the image numbers that we will use.
- Lines 17 through 22 declare constants for the sprite numbers that we will use.
- Lines 25 through 28 declare constants that we will use to work with the vulture animated sprite.
- Lines 31 through 35 declare constants for the sound numbers that we will use.
- Lines 38 and 39 declare constants for the music numbers that we will use.
- Lines 42 through 44 declare constants for various time delays that we will use.
- Lines 47 through 51 declare these other constants:
  - MAX_EGGS is the total number of eggs that the vulture has stolen.
  - BASKET_MOVE specifies the number of pixels that the basket moves horizontally when the left or right arrow key is pressed.
  - VULTURE_MOVE specifies the number of pixels that the vulture moves horizontally during each iteration of the game loop.
  - ACCELERATION is the value that we will use for gravitational acceleration.
  - REFRESH_RATE specifies the maximum screen refresh rate.

Lines 53 through 68 hold the function prototypes, and then the DarkGDK function is shown:

Program 8-13   (**VultureTrouble.cpp** *continued*)

```
69   //*****************************************
70   // DarkGDK function                       *
71   //*****************************************
72   void DarkGDK()
73   {
74       // Local variables
75       int eggs = MAX_EGGS;        // Number of eggs in play
76       int caught = 0;             // Number of eggs caught
77       int broken = 0;             // Number of eggs broken
78       int basketX, basketY;       // Basket's XY coordinates
79       int vultureX, vultureY;     // Vulture's XY coordinates
80       int eggX, eggY;             // Egg's XY coordinates
81       int time = 0;               // Time, for distance formula
82
83       // Load the game resources.
84       loadResources();
85
86       // Display the title and intro screens.
87       intro();
88
89       // Create the sprites.
90       createSprites(basketX, basketY, eggX, eggY,
91                   vultureX, vultureY);
92
93       // Execute the game loop.
94       while ( LoopGDK() && eggs > 0 )
95       {
96           // Move the basket.
97           moveBasket(basketX);
98
```

```
 99              // Move the vulture.
100              moveVulture(vultureX);
101
102              // Move the egg.
103              moveEgg(vultureX, vultureY,
104                      eggX, eggY, time);
105
106              // Check for collisions.
107              checkCollisions(vultureY, eggY, caught,
108                              broken, eggs, time);
109
110              // Render the scene.
111              render(basketX, basketY, eggX, eggY,
112                     vultureX, vultureY);
113          }
114
115      // Display the summary screen.
116      summaryScreen(caught, broken);
117  }
118
```

Here is a summary of the DarkGDK function's local variables, declared in lines 75 through 81:

- The eggs variable, declared in line 75, will hold the number of eggs currently in play. This variable is initialized with MAX_EGGS and is decremented each time that an egg is caught or broken.
- The caught variable, declared and initialized to 0 in line 76, keeps count of the number of eggs caught. The broken variable, declared and initialized to 0 in line 77, keeps count of the number of eggs broken.
- The basketX and basketY variables, declared in line 78, will hold the basket's *X* and *Y* coordinates.
- The vultureX and vultureY variables, declared in line 79, will hold the vulture's *X* and *Y* coordinates.
- The eggX and eggY variables, declared in line 80, will hold the egg's *X* and *Y* coordinates.
- The time variable, declared and initialized to 0 in line 81, will keep a count of the game loop's iterations. We will use it as the time value in the distance formula to calculate the egg's falling distance.

In line 84, the loadResources function, which loads the image and audio files is called. Then, line 87 calls the intro function. The intro function displays the game's title screen, followed by the intro screen. Then, lines 90 and 91 call the createSprites function, which creates all of the game's sprites. The createSprites function requires the basketX, basketY, eggX, eggY, vultureX, and vultureY variables as arguments. These variables are passed by reference, and after the function executes, they will hold the coordinates for the basket, the first falling egg, and the vulture.

The game loop begins in line 94. Notice that the loop iterates as long as the LoopGDK function returns true *and* the eggs variable is greater than 0. When there are no more eggs, the loop will stop and the game will be over.

Inside the game loop, in line 97, the moveBasket function is called, passing basketX by reference as an argument. The moveBasket function will detect whether the user has pressed the right or left arrow key, and move the basket accordingly. After the function executes, the basketX variable will hold the basket's updated X coordinate. (The function does not require the basketY variable as an argument because the basket moves only horizontally.)

In line 100, the moveVulture function is called, passing vultureX by reference as an argument. The moveVulture function moves the vulture across the screen. After the function executes, the vultureX variable will hold the vulture's updated X coordinate. (The function does not require the vultureY variable as an argument because the vulture moves only horizontally.)

In lines 103 and 104, the moveEgg function is called, passing vultureX, vultureY, eggX, eggY, and time as arguments. The vultureX and vultureY variables are passed by value, and the eggX, eggY, and time variables are passed by reference. The moveEgg function updates the egg's position as it falls. After the function executes, the eggX and eggY variables will hold the egg's updated coordinates and the time variable will be incremented.

In lines 107 and 108, the checkCollisions function is called, passing vultureY, eggY, caught, broken, eggs, and time as arguments. The vultureY variable is passed by value, and the eggY, caught, broken, eggs, and time variables are passed by reference. The checkCollisions function determines whether the egg has hit the basket or has hit the ground. If either of these conditions exists, it displays the appropriate animation and updates the caught and broken variables.

In lines 111 and 112, the render function is called with basketX, basketY, eggX, eggY, vultureX, and vultureY variables passed as arguments. The render function draws the current scene on the screen.

Outside the game loop, line 116 calls the summaryScreen function passing caught and broken as arguments. The summaryScreen function displays the summary screen that reports the number of eggs caught, the number of eggs broken, and the number of points earned.

Next, is the loadResources function:

Program 8-13   (**VultureTrouble.cpp** *continued*)

```
119    // *****************************************************
120    // The loadResources function loads all the images    *
121    // and audio files.                                    *
122    // *****************************************************
123    void loadResources()
124    {
125        // Set the color key to green.
126        dbSetImageColorKey(0, 255, 0);
127
128        // Load the images.
129        dbLoadImage("titleScreen.bmp", TITLE_SCREEN_IMAGE);
130        dbLoadImage("intro.bmp", INTRO_SCREEN_IMAGE);
```

```
131        dbLoadImage("farm.bmp", FARM_IMAGE);
132        dbLoadImage("egg.bmp", EGG_IMAGE);
133        dbLoadImage("brokenEgg.bmp", BROKEN_EGG_IMAGE);
134        dbLoadImage("basket.bmp", BASKET_IMAGE);
135        dbLoadImage("hitBasket.bmp", HIT_BASKET_IMAGE);
136
137        // Load the intro music
138        dbLoadMusic("vultureTrouble.mp3", INTRO_MUSIC);
139        dbLoadMusic("vultureLevel.mp3", MAIN_MUSIC);
140
141        // Load the sound effcts.
142        dbLoadSound("pop.wav", POP_SOUND);
143        dbLoadSound("clap.wav", CLAP_SOUND);
144        dbLoadSound("type.wav", TYPE_SOUND);
145        dbLoadSound("complete.wav", COMPLETE_SOUND);
146        dbLoadSound("vulturePerfect.wav", PERFECT_SCORE_SOUND);
147    }
148
```

This function is straightforward. Line 126 sets the key color to green. Lines 129 through 135 load the images. Lines 138 and 139 load the music files. Lines 142 through 146 load the sound files.

Next, is the intro function:

Program 8-13   (**VultureTrouble.cpp** *continued*)

```
149    // ****************************************************
150    // The intro function displays a title screen, followed *
151    // by an intro screen while playing music.             *
152    // ****************************************************
153    void intro()
154    {
155        // Set the window title.
156        dbSetWindowTitle("Vulture Trouble");
157
158        // Loop the intro music.
159        dbLoopMusic(INTRO_MUSIC);
160
161        // Paste the title screen image and wait for
162        // the user to press a key.
163        dbPasteImage(TITLE_SCREEN_IMAGE, 0, 0);
164        dbWaitKey();
165
166        // Clear the screen.
167        dbCLS();
168
169        // Paste the intro image and wait for the
170        // user to press a key.
171        dbPasteImage(INTRO_SCREEN_IMAGE, 0, 0);
172        dbWaitKey();
```

```
173
174        // Stop the music.
175        dbStopMusic(INTRO_MUSIC);
176
177        // Disable auto refresh and set the
178        // refresh rate.
179        dbSyncOn();
180        dbSyncRate(REFRESH_RATE);
181    }
182
```

Line 156 sets the window's title text. Line 159 starts the intro music looping. Lines 163 and 164 display the game's title screen and wait for the user to press a key. (Figure 8-10 in the color insert shows the title screen on the top.) After the user presses a key, line 167 clears the screen, then lines 171 and 172 display the intro screen and wait for the user to press a key. (Figure 8-10 in the color insert shows the intro screen on the bottom.) After the user presses a key line 175 stops the intro music. Lines 179 and 180 disable auto refresh and set the screen refresh rate.

Next, is the createSprites function:

Program 8-13   (`VultureTrouble.cpp` continued)

```
183    // ***********************************************************
184    // The createSprites function creates the sprites.          *
185    // Parameter summary:                                        *
186    //   basketX: The basket's X coordinate (by reference)       *
187    //   basketY: The basket's X coordinate (by reference)       *
188    //      eggX: The egg's X coordinate (by reference)          *
189    //      eggY: The egg's X coordinate (by reference)          *
190    // vultureX: The vulture's X coordinate (by reference)       *
191    // vultureY: The vulture's X coordinate (by reference)       *
192    // ***********************************************************
193    void createSprites(int &basketX, int &basketY, int &eggX,
194                       int &eggY, int &vultureX, int &vultureY)
195    {
196        // Variable to hold calculated sprite numbers.
197        int spriteNum;
198
199        // Create the sprites, initially positioned at (0, 0).
200        dbSprite(FARM_SPRITE, 0, 0, FARM_IMAGE);
201        dbSprite(BASKET_SPRITE, 0, 0, BASKET_IMAGE);
202        dbSprite(EGG_SPRITE, 0, 0, EGG_IMAGE);
203        dbSprite(HIT_BASKET_SPRITE, 0, 0, HIT_BASKET_IMAGE);
204        dbSprite(BROKEN_EGG_SPRITE, 0, 0, BROKEN_EGG_IMAGE);
205
206        // Hide the hit basket and broken egg sprites.
```

```
207            dbHideSprite(HIT_BASKET_SPRITE);
208            dbHideSprite(BROKEN_EGG_SPRITE);
209
210            // Create the animated vulture sprite.
211            dbCreateAnimatedSprite(VULTURE_SPRITE, "vulture.bmp",
212                                   VULTURE_COLS, VULTURE_ROWS,
213                                   VULTURE_IMAGE);
214
215            // Set the starting position of the vulture to
216            // the center of the top of the screen.
217            vultureX = dbScreenWidth() / 2 -
218                       dbSpriteWidth(VULTURE_SPRITE) / 2;
219            vultureY = 0;
220
221            // Set the starting position of the egg so it
222            // is at the vulture's beak.
223            eggX = vultureX + dbSpriteWidth(VULTURE_SPRITE) -
224                   dbSpriteWidth(EGG_SPRITE);
225            eggY = vultureY +
226                   dbSpriteHeight(VULTURE_SPRITE) / 2;
227
228            // Set the basket's starting X position to a
229            // random location on the screen.
230            dbRandomize( dbTimer() );
231            basketX = dbRND( dbScreenWidth() -
232                             dbSpriteWidth(BASKET_SPRITE) );
233
234            // Set the basket's starting Y position to the bottom
235            // of the screen.
236            basketY = dbScreenHeight() -
237                      dbSpriteHeight(BASKET_SPRITE);
238
239            // Clone the egg sprite to display mini eggs at the
240            // top of the screen. The cloned mini eggs sprite
241            // numbers will begin at 101.
242            for(int count = 0; count < MAX_EGGS; count++)
243            {
244                // Calculate a new sprite number.
245                spriteNum = 100 + count;
246
247                // Clone the egg sprite.
248                dbCloneSprite(EGG_SPRITE, spriteNum);
249
250                // Scale the sprite to 50%.
251                dbScaleSprite(spriteNum, 50);
252
253                // Place the sprite in the status bar.
254                dbSprite(spriteNum,
255                         dbSpriteWidth(EGG_SPRITE) / 2 * count ,
256                         0,
257                         EGG_IMAGE);
258            }
259    }
260
```

The `createSprites` function creates the sprites that will be used in the game. Notice in lines 193 and 194 that `basketX`, `basketY`, `eggX`, `eggY`, `vultureX`, and `vultureY` are all reference parameters. When the function finishes, the `basketX` and `basketY` parameters will be set to the basket's *XY* coordinates, the `eggX` and `eggY` parameters will be set to the egg's *XY* coordinates, and the `vultureX` and `vultureY` parameters will be set to the vulture's *XY* coordinates. Let's take a closer look at the function.

In line 197, we declare a local variable named `spriteNum`. Recall that a row of mini eggs will be displayed at the top of the screen, representing the number of eggs remaining. Each of the mini eggs will be an individual sprite. We will use the `spriteNum` variable to hold the sprite number of the mini eggs as we create them.

In lines 200 through 204, we create the following sprites, initially located at (0, 0):

- The `FARM_SPRITE` will serve as the background scene.
- The `BASKET_SPRITE` is the basket that the user moves back and forth with the arrow keys.
- The `EGG_SPRITE` is the egg that will be falling from the vulture.
- The `HIT_BASKET_SPRITE` will be displayed briefly when the egg hits the basket.
- The `BROKEN_EGG_SPRITE` will be displayed briefly when the egg hits the ground.

In lines 207 and 208, we hide the hit basket sprite and the broken egg sprite. We want these two sprites to remain invisible until we need them.

In lines 211 through 213, we call the `dbCreateAnimatedSprite` function to create the vulture sprite. This is an animated sprite created from the file `vulture.bmp`. (Figure 8-12 in the color insert shows the image contained in the file.) In lines 217 through 219, we set the vulture's *XY* coordinates. The vulture's *X* coordinate is calculated at the center of the screen, and the *Y* coordinate is set to 0. As a result, the vulture will initially appear at the top-center of the screen.

In lines 223 through 226, we set the egg's *XY* coordinates. The calculations that are performed in these lines will place the egg just below the vulture's beak, as shown in Figure 8-13. When the vulture drops the egg, this will give the appearance that it is dropping it from its beak.

Figure 8-13 Egg positioned below the vulture's beak

Line 230 seeds the random number generator and lines 231 and 232 get a random number for the basket's *X* coordinate. Lines 236 and 237 calculate the basket's *Y* coordinate so the basket will be at the bottom of the screen. As a result of these statements, the basket will be randomly positioned somewhere at the bottom of the screen.

The loop in lines 242 through 258 creates the row of mini eggs at the top of the screen. Notice in line 242 that we are using a variable named count to control the loop. The count variable starts at 0 and is incremented after each loop iteration. The loop iterates as long as count is less than MAX_EGGS. Since MAX_EGGS is set to 40, this loop will iterate 40 times. As it iterates, the count variable will be set to the values 0 through 39. Each time the loop iterates, it will create one of the mini eggs at the top of the screen. Let's look at the code inside the loop.

Line 245 assigns the value of 100 + count to the spriteNum variable. This will be the sprite number of the mini egg that we are creating. Line 248 clones the EGG_SPRITE and assigns spriteNum as the clone's sprite number. Line 251 scales the size of the new sprite by 50 percent. Then lines 254 through 257 place the sprite in its position at the top of the screen. When the loop finishes all of its iterations, a row of 40 egg sprites will appear at the top of the screen, as shown in Figure 8-14. Their sprite numbers will be 100 through 139. Each will be half the size of the original egg sprite that they were cloned from.

Figure 8-14 Row of mini egg sprites at the top of the screen

Next is the moveBasket function:

Program 8-13	(**VultureTrouble.cpp** *continued*)

```
261   // ****************************************************
262   // The moveBasket function detects keyboard input and  *
263   // moves the basket accordingly.                       *
264   // Parameter summary:                                  *
265   // basketX: The basket's X coordinate (by reference)   *
266   // ****************************************************
267   void moveBasket(int &basketX)
268   {
269       // Check if the left key is pressed.
270       if( dbLeftKey() )
271       {
272           // Stop the basket at the left edge of the screen.
273           if (basketX <= 0)
274           {
275               basketX = 0;
276           }
277           // Move the basket left.
278           else
279           {
280               basketX -= BASKET_MOVE;
```

```
281                    }
282            }
283
284            // Check if the right key is pressed.
285            if( dbRightKey() )
286            {
287                    // Stop the basket at the right edge of the screen.
288                    if (basketX + dbSpriteWidth(BASKET_SPRITE) >= dbScreenWidth())
289                    {
290                            basketX = dbScreenWidth() - dbSpriteWidth(BASKET_SPRITE);
291                    }
292                    // Move the basket right.
293                    else
294                    {
295                            basketX += BASKET_MOVE;
296                    }
297            }
298    }
299
```

The moveBasket function detects whether the left or right arrow key is being pressed, and if so, moves the basket accordingly. The function's parameter, basketX , is a reference variable. When the function finishes executing, the parameter will hold the basket's updated *X* coordinate.

The if statement that begins in line 270 determines whether the left arrow key is being pressed. If so, the if statement that begins in line 273 determines whether the basket is at the left edge of the screen. If this is the case, line 275 sets the basketX parameter to 0, which keeps the basket from moving off the screen. Otherwise, the value of the basketX parameter is decreased in line 280.

The if statement that begins in line 285 determines whether the right arrow key is being pressed. If so, the if statement that begins in line 288 determines whether the basket is at the right edge of the screen. If this is the case, line 290 calculates a value for the basketX parameter to keep the basket at the right edge of the screen. Otherwise, the value of the basketX parameter is increased in line 295.

Next is the moveVulture function:

Program 8-13 (**VultureTrouble.cpp** *continued*)

```
300    // ****************************************************
301    // The moveVulture function moves the vulture back and *
302    // forth across the top of the screen.                 *
303    // Parameter summary:                                  *
304    // vultureX: The vulture's X coordinate (by reference) *
305    // ****************************************************
306    void moveVulture(int &vultureX)
307    {
308            // Play the vulture animation sequence.
309            dbPlaySprite(VULTURE_SPRITE, START_FRAME,
310                        END_FRAME, TENTH_SECOND);
```

```
311
312          // Check the vulture X position. If it is less
313          // than or equal to 0, mirror the vulture sprite.
314          if (vultureX <= 0)
315          {
316              dbMirrorSprite(VULTURE_SPRITE);
317          }
318
319          // If the vulture is at the right edge of the
320          // screen, mirror the vulture sprite.
321          if (vultureX + dbSpriteWidth(VULTURE_SPRITE) >= dbScreenWidth())
322          {
323              dbMirrorSprite(VULTURE_SPRITE);
324          }
325
326          // If the vulture is currently mirrored, move right.
327          if ( dbSpriteMirrored(VULTURE_SPRITE) )
328          {
329              vultureX += VULTURE_MOVE;
330          }
331          // If the vulture is not mirrored, move left.
332          else
333          {
334              vultureX -= VULTURE_MOVE;
335          }
336  }
337
```

The moveVulture function moves the animated vulture sprite. When the game begins, the vulture is facing left, and flies horizontally across the top of the screen. When it reaches the left edge of the screen, it turns around and flies in the other direction. This continues as the game plays. Each time the vulture reaches the edge of the screen, it turns around and flies in the opposite direction. The function's parameter, vultureX, is a reference variable. When the function finishes executing, the parameter will hold the vulture's updated X coordinate.

Lines 309 and 310 get the next frame of the vulture animation. Notice that there is a delay of a tenth of a second between each animation frame. The if statement in line 314 determines whether the vulture is at the left edge of the screen. If so, line 316 mirrors the sprite so the vulture is facing in the opposite direction.

The if statement in line 321 performs a similar operation to determine whether the vulture is at the right edge of the screen. If this is the case, line 323 mirrors the sprite so the vulture is facing in the opposite direction.

The if statement in line 327 determines whether the sprite is mirrored. (If the vulture is facing its original direction of left, then it is not mirrored and the dbSpriteMirrored function will return false. If the vulture is facing right, then it is mirrored and the dbSpriteMirrored function will return true.) If the sprite is mirrored, then we know the vulture is flying toward the right, so line 329 increases the value of the vultureX parameter. Otherwise, we know that the vulture is flying toward the left and line 334 decreases the value of the vultureX parameter.

Next is the `moveEgg` function:

Program 8-13   (**VultureTrouble.cpp** *continued*)

```
338  // ******************************************************
339  // The moveEgg function moves the egg sprite both      *
340  // down the screen and across the screen.              *
341  // Parameter summary:                                  *
342  // vultureX: The vulture's X coordinate                *
343  // vultureY: The vulture's Y coordinate                *
344  //     eggX: The egg's X coordinate (by reference)     *
345  //     eggY: The egg's Y coordinate (by reference)     *
346  //     time: The falling time (by reference)           *
347  // ******************************************************
348  void moveEgg(int vultureX, int vultureY,
349              int &eggX, int &eggY, int &time)
350  {
351      // Local varible to hold the falling distance
352      float distance;
353
354      // Set the egg's X position so it is below the
355      // vulture's beak. This will depend on whether
356      // the vulture is mirrored.
357      if( dbSpriteMirrored(VULTURE_SPRITE) )
358      {
359          eggX = vultureX +
360                  dbSpriteWidth(VULTURE_SPRITE) -
361                  dbSpriteWidth(EGG_SPRITE);
362      }
363      else
364      {
365          eggX = vultureX;
366      }
367
368      // Calculate the falling distance.
369      distance = 0.5 * ACCELERATION * time * time;
370
371      // update the egg Y position.
372      eggY = distance + vultureY +
373              dbSpriteHeight(VULTURE_SPRITE) / 2;
374
375      // Increment the falling time.
376      time++;
377  }
378
```

The `moveEgg` function updates the egg's position as it falls to the ground. To simulate realistic motion, the egg must move both horizontally and vertically. The vulture flies horizontally across the screen as it carries the stolen eggs. This means that the eggs are also moving horizontally. When the vulture drops an egg, the falling egg will continue its horizontal motion as it falls to the ground. This is illustrated in Figure 8-15. The figure shows four frames, from right to left. In the first frame, the vulture has just dropped the egg. In the second frame you can see that the egg has fallen toward the ground, but it has also continued moving horizontally, at a constant speed. (In fact, the egg is moving horizontally at the same speed as the vulture.) In the third and fourth frames you can see that this motion continues until the egg hits the ground.

Figure 8-15 An egg moving horizontally and vertically

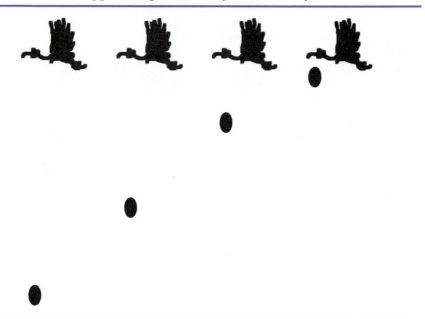

The `moveEgg` function has five parameters: `vultureX`, `vultureY`, `eggX`, `eggY`, and `time`. The first two, `vulture` and `vultureY`, are passed by value because the function does not need to update the vulture's position. The `eggX` and `eggY` parameters are reference variables because the egg's position is updated by this function. The `time` parameter is also a reference variable because it will be updated by the function.

In line 352, we declare a local variable named `distance` that will hold the egg's falling distance. Next, we update the egg's X coordinate. The `if` statement in line 357 determines whether the vulture is mirrored. If so, then the vulture is flying toward the right and lines 359 through 361 calculate the egg's new X position. (This calculation keeps the egg positioned horizontally with the vulture.) If the vulture is not mirrored, then it is flying toward the left and line 365 sets the egg's X coordinate to the same value as the vulture's X coordinate.

Next, we update the egg's Y coordinate. Line 369 uses the distance formula you saw earlier in this chapter to calculate the distance that the egg will fall down the screen. Lines 372 and 373 add this distance to the egg's starting Y coordinate, and assign the result to `eggY`. Line 376 increments the `time` parameter.

Next, is the checkCollisions function:

Program 8-13   (**VultureTrouble.cpp** *continued*)

```
379   // *****************************************************
380   // The checkCollisions function checks for a collision *
381   // between the egg and basket or the ground.           *
382   // Parameter summary:                                  *
383   // vultureY: The vulture's Y coordinate                *
384   //     eggY: The egg's Y coordinate (by reference)     *
385   //   caught: The number of caught eggs (by reference) *
386   //   broken: The number of broken eggs (by reference) *
387   //     eggs: The number of eggs in play (by reference)*
388   //     time: The falling time (by reference)           *
389   // *****************************************************
390   void checkCollisions(int vultureY, int &eggY, int &caught,
391                       int &broken, int &eggs, int &time)
392   {
393       // The egg has hit the basket.
394       if ( dbSpriteCollision(EGG_SPRITE, BASKET_SPRITE) )
395       {
396           // Increment number of caught eggs.
397           caught++;
398
399           // Decrement number of eggs in play.
400           eggs--;
401
402           // Show the hit basket effect.
403           showHitBasket();
404
405           // Reset the egg.
406           resetEgg(eggs, vultureY, eggY);
407
408           // Reset the falling time.
409           time = 0;
410       }
411       // The egg has missed the basket.
412       else if ( eggY > dbScreenHeight() )
413       {
414           // Increment the number of broken eggs.
415           broken++;
416
417           // Decrement the number of eggs in play.
418           eggs--;
419
420           // Show the broken egg effect.
421           showBrokenEgg();
422
423           // Reset the egg.
424           resetEgg(eggs, vultureY, eggY);
425
426           // Reset the falling time.
427           time = 0;
428       }
429   }
430
```

The `checkCollisions` function determines whether the egg has hit the basket or has hit the ground. The function has six parameters: `vultureY`, `eggY`, `caught`, `broken`, `eggs`, and `time`. All of these except `vultureY` are reference variables.

The `if` statement in line 394 determines whether a collision has occurred between the egg sprite and the basket sprite. If so, then the user has caught the egg in the basket. The `caught` variable, which keeps count of the number of caught eggs, is incremented in line 397, and the `eggs` variable, which keeps count of the number of eggs in play, is decremented in line 400. Line 403 calls the `showHitBasket` function, which displays the hit basket sprite, and the `resetEgg` function is called in line 406, which resets the egg sprite. The `time` variable is set to 0 in line 409.

The `else if` clause in line 412 takes over if there is not a collision between the egg sprite and the basket sprite. It determines whether the egg's *Y* coordinate is greater than the height of the screen. If so, the egg has reached the bottom of the screen (without hitting the basket). When this is the case, the `broken` variable, which keeps count of the number of broken eggs, is incremented in line 415, and the `eggs` variable, which keeps count of the number of eggs in play, is decremented in line 418. Line 421 calls the `showBrokenEgg` function, which displays the broken egg sprite, and the `resetEgg` function is called in line 424, which resets the egg sprite. The `time` variable is set to 0 in line 427.

It's worth noting that when this function executes, if the egg has not come into contact with the basket and has not hit the ground, it is still falling and the function performs no operation.

Next, is the `showHitBasket` function:

Program 8-13   (**VultureTrouble.cpp** *continued*)

```
431   //************************************************
432   // The showHitBasket function displays the hit    *
433   // basket effect and plays the pop sound.         *
434   //************************************************
435   void showHitBasket()
436   {
437       // Temporarily enable auto refresh.
438       dbSyncOff();
439
440       // Show the hit basket sprite.
441       dbShowSprite(HIT_BASKET_SPRITE);
442
443       // Play the pop sound.
444       dbPlaySound(POP_SOUND);
445
446       // Wait for a tenth of a second.
447       dbWait(TENTH_SECOND);
448
449       // Hide the hit basket sprite.
450       dbHideSprite(HIT_BASKET_SPRITE);
451
452       // Disable auto refresh.
```

```
453        dbSyncOn();
454    }
455
```

The showHitBasket function is called when an egg hits the basket. Line 438 calls dbSyncOff to enable auto screen refresh temporarily. Line 441 makes the hit basket sprite visible on the screen, as shown in Figure 8-16. (Because we've enabled auto refresh, the sprite will immediately be displayed.) Line 444 plays the pop sound effect. Line 447 causes the program to wait for a tenth of a second so the user will be able to see the hit basket sprite. Then, line 450 makes the hit basket sprite invisible again. Line 453 disables auto refresh once again.

Figure 8-16 The hit basket sprite displayed

Next, is the showBrokenEgg function:

Program 8-13 (**VultureTrouble.cpp** *continued*)

```
456    //*************************************************
457    // The showBrokenEgg function displays the broken *
458    // egg effect and plays the clap sound.           *
459    //*************************************************
460    void showBrokenEgg()
461    {
462        // Temporarily enable auto refresh.
463        dbSyncOff();
464
465        // Show the broken egg sprite.
466        dbShowSprite(BROKEN_EGG_SPRITE);
467
468        // Play the clap sound.
469        dbPlaySound(CLAP_SOUND);
470
471        // Wait for a tenth of a second.
472        dbWait(TENTH_SECOND);
473
474        // Hide the broken egg sprite.
475        dbHideSprite(BROKEN_EGG_SPRITE);
476
477        // Disable auto refresh.
478        dbSyncOn();
```

```
479   }
480
```

The `showBrokenEgg` function is called when an egg hits the ground. Line 463 calls `dbSyncOff` to enable auto screen refresh temporarily. Line 466 makes the broken egg sprite visible on the screen, as shown in Figure 8-17. (Because we've enabled auto refresh, the sprite will immediately be displayed.) Line 469 plays the clap sound effect. Line 472 causes the program to wait for a tenth of a second so the user will be able to see the broken egg sprite. Then, line 475 makes the broken egg sprite invisible again. Line 478 disables auto refresh once again.

Figure 8-17 The broken egg sprite displayed

Next, is the `resetEgg` function:

Program 8-13   (**VultureTrouble.cpp** *continued*)

```
481   //*******************************************************
482   // The resetEgg function resets the egg after it has    *
483   // either been caught in the basket, or hit the ground.*
484   // Parameter summary:                                   *
485   //      eggs: The number of eggs in play                *
486   // vultureY: The vulture's Y coordinate                 *
487   //      eggY: The egg's Y coordinate (by reference)     *
488   //*******************************************************
489   void resetEgg(int eggs, int vultureY, int &eggY)
490   {
491       // If a clone of this egg sprite exists in the
492       // status bar, delete it.
493       if ( dbSpriteExist(eggs + 100) )
494       {
495           dbDeleteSprite(eggs + 100);
496       }
497
498       // Wait for a tenth of a second.
499       dbWait(TENTH_SECOND);
500
501       // Reset the egg Y position.
502       eggY = vultureY +
503               dbSpriteHeight(VULTURE_SPRITE) / 2;
504   }
505
```

When an egg is either caught in the basket, or hits the ground, the following actions must take place:

- One of the mini eggs at the top of the screen must be deleted.
- The egg sprite must be repositioned so it once again appears just below the vulture's beak.

The resetEgg function performs both of these. The function accepts as arguments the number of eggs currently in play, the vulture's *Y* coordinate (by value), and the egg's *Y* coordinate (by reference).

First, we delete one of the mini egg sprites at the top of the screen. As we delete the mini eggs, we will do so from right to left, so the sprite that we want to delete is the rightmost egg. We can calculate its sprite number with the expression eggs + 100. (Recall that eggs holds the number of eggs in play.) The if statement in line 493 makes sure that particular sprite exists, and if so, line 495 deletes it. Line 499 pauses the program for a tenth of a second. Lines 502 and 503 calculate the egg's *Y* position so it appears under the vulture's beak, and assigns that value to the eggY parameter.

Next, is the render function:

Program 8-13   (**VultureTrouble.cpp** *continued*)

```
506  // *******************************************************
507  // The render function draws the screen.              *
508  // Parameter summary:                                 *
509  //   basketX: The basket's X coordinate               *
510  //   basketY: The basket's Y coordinate               *
511  //      eggX: The egg's X coordinate                  *
512  //      eggX: The egg's Y coordinate                  *
513  // vultureX: The vulture's X coordinate               *
514  // vultureY: The vulture's Y coordinate               *
515  // *******************************************************
516  void render(int basketX, int basketY, int eggX, int eggY,
517              int vultureX, int vultureY)
518  {
519      // Draw the sprites.
520      dbSprite(BASKET_SPRITE, basketX, basketY, BASKET_IMAGE);
521      dbSprite(EGG_SPRITE, eggX, eggY, EGG_IMAGE);
522      dbSprite(HIT_BASKET_SPRITE, basketX, basketY, HIT_BASKET_IMAGE);
523      dbSprite(BROKEN_EGG_SPRITE, eggX,
524              dbScreenHeight() - dbSpriteHeight(BROKEN_EGG_SPRITE),
525              BROKEN_EGG_IMAGE);
526      dbSprite(VULTURE_SPRITE, vultureX, vultureY, VULTURE_IMAGE);
527
528      // Refresh the screen.
529      dbSync();
530  }
531
```

The render function displays all of the sprites in their updated positions and refreshes the screen. It accepts as arguments the basket's *XY* coordinates, the egg's *XY* coordinates, and the vulture's *XY* coordinates. Notice that even though the hit basket sprite and the broken egg sprite may be invisible at the time this function is called, their positions are still updated in lines 522 through 525.

Next, is the summaryScreen function:

Program 8-13　　　(**VultureTrouble.cpp** *continued*)

```
532   // ********************************************************
533   // The summaryScreen function displays a summary of      *
534   // player's performance, including points earned.         *
535   // Each caught egg earns 1000 points.                     *
536   // Parameter summary:                                     *
537   // caught: The number of eggs caught in the basket        *
538   // broken: The number of broken eggs                      *
539   // ********************************************************
540   void summaryScreen(int caught, int broken)
541   {
542       // Delete the sprites and get them off the screen.
543       deleteSprites();
544
545       // Enable auto refresh and clear the screen.
546       dbSyncOff();
547       dbCLS();
548
549       // Set the text size.
550       dbSetTextSize(36);
551
552       // Display the text.
553       dbCenterText(dbScreenWidth() / 2, 100, "GAME OVER!");
554
555       // Play the game complete sound.
556       dbPlaySound(COMPLETE_SOUND);
557
558       // Wait four seconds for sound to finish.
559       dbWait(FOUR_SECONDS);
560
561       // Count the eggs caught and tally the
562       // score.
563       for(int caughtCount = 0; caughtCount <= caught; caughtCount++)
564       {
565           // Clear the screen.
566           dbCLS();
567
568           // Paste the images.
569           dbPasteImage(EGG_IMAGE, 200, 240);
570           dbPasteImage(BROKEN_EGG_IMAGE, 300, 240);
571
572           // Display the text.
573           dbCenterText(dbScreenWidth() / 2,
```

```
574                              100, "GAME RESULTS");
575              dbText(240,240,"x");
576              dbText(380,240,"x");
577              dbText(260,240,dbStr(caughtCount));
578              dbText(400,240, dbStr(broken) );
579
580              // Play the type sound.
581              dbPlaySound(TYPE_SOUND);
582
583              // Wait for a tenth of a second.
584              dbWait(TENTH_SECOND);
585
586              // Display the score, which is 1000 points
587              // for each caught egg.
588              dbCenterText(dbScreenWidth() / 2,
589                          400, dbStr(caughtCount * 1000));
590          }
591
592          // If no eggs were broken, display a special message.
593          if (caught == MAX_EGGS)
594          {
595              // Display the perfect score message.
596              dbCenterText(dbScreenWidth() / 2,
597                          200, "PERFECT SCORE!");
598
599              // Play the sound.
600              dbPlaySound(PERFECT_SCORE_SOUND);
601
602              // Wait for one second.
603              dbWait(ONE_SECOND);
604          }
605
606          // Wait for the player to press a key.
607          dbWaitKey();
608      }
609
```

The summaryScreen function displays the summary screen, as shown on the bottom of Figure 8-11 in the color insert. This screen displays a summary of the eggs caught, eggs broken, and points earned. It accepts as arguments the number of eggs caught and the number of eggs broken.

Line 543 calls the deleteSprites function, which deletes the sprites and takes them off the screen. Line 546 enables auto refresh, and line 547 clears the screen. Line 550 sets the text size to 36 points.

Line 553 displays the message "GAME OVER" to let the user know that the game has ended. The message is centered horizontally, just under pixel 100 on the screen's Y axis. Line 556 plays an accompanying sound. Line 559 causes the program to wait four seconds, which is enough time for the sound to complete.

The loop that starts in line 563 displays the summary information along with some special effects. Admittedly, we could have skipped the special effects and simply displayed the number of caught eggs, the number of broken eggs, and the number of points earned. We thought we could make the game appear more professional, how-ever, if we made this screen more interesting. If you've played the game already, then you've noticed that the summary screen goes through an animated tally of the num-ber of eggs caught and the number of points earned. Let's take a closer look at the loop.

In the loop's header, the `caughtCount` variable is initialized with 0, and is incre-mented at the end of each iteration. The loop executes as long as `caughtCount` is less than or equal to `caught` (which is the total number of caught eggs). As a result, this loop will iterate once for each egg that was caught. Let's look at what happens dur-ing each iteration:

- Line 566 clears the screen.
- Line 569 pastes the egg image at (200, 400) and line 570 pastes the broken egg image at (300, 240).
- Lines 573 and 574 display the message "GAME RESULTS" centered horizon-tally, just under pixel 100 on the screen's Y axis.
- Lines 575 and 576 display the two x characters.
- Line 577 displays the current value of the `caughtCount` variable at (260, 240). As the loop iterates, this statement will cause the values 0 up through the total number of eggs caught to appear at this location on the screen. This creates the tallying animation for the number of eggs caught.
- Line 578 displays the total number of broken eggs at (400, 240).
- Line 581 plays the "type" sound.
- Line 584 causes the program to wait a tenth of a second.
- Lines 588 and 589 displays the value of `caughtCount * 1000` on the screen. The user earns 1000 points for each caught egg, and this statement creates the tallying animation for the number of points earned.

After the loop finishes, the `if` statement that begins in line 593 determines whether the user caught every egg. If so, lines 596 and 597 display the message "PERFECT SCORE," line 600 plays the perfect score sound effect and line 603 causes the pro-gram to wait for one second while the sound plays. Line 607 waits for the user to press a key.

The `deleteSprites` function is shown next. This function deletes all of the sprites.

Program 8-13   (`VultureTrouble.cpp` *continued*)

```
610    //***************************************************
611    // The deleteSprites function deletes the sprites.   *
612    //***************************************************
613    void deleteSprites()
614    {
615        dbDeleteSprite(FARM_SPRITE);
616        dbDeleteSprite(BASKET_SPRITE);
617        dbDeleteSprite(EGG_SPRITE);
618        dbDeleteSprite(HIT_BASKET_SPRITE);
619        dbDeleteSprite(BROKEN_EGG_SPRITE);
620        dbDeleteSprite(VULTURE_SPRITE);
621    }
```

Review Questions

Multiple Choice

1. You use the _____ function to load a WAV file into memory.
   a. dbLoadWAV
   b. dbLoadSound
   c. dbLoadMusic
   d. dbLoadAudio

2. You use the _____ function to load a MIDI file into memory.
   a. dbLoadWAV
   b. dbLoadSound
   c. dbLoadMusic
   d. dbLoadAudio

3. You use the _____ function to make a sound come from the left or right speaker.
   a. dbSetSoundPan
   b. dbSoundLeftRight
   c. dbShiftSound
   d. dbMoveSound

4. You can have a maximum of _____ music files loaded into memory.
   a. 1
   b. 100
   c. 256
   d. 32

5. A pan value of _____ equally distributes a sound between the left and right speakers.
   a. 10,000
   b. 0
   c. −10,000
   d. 1

6. Without considering the effects of air resistance, suppose a boy drops a marble off the top of a building. The marble's speed will _____.
   a. increase as it falls
   b. be the same all the way down
   c. decreases as it falls
   d. alternatively decrease and increase

7. The name of the typeface that defines the way characters appear is _____.
   a. style
   b. typograph
   c. font
   d. points

8. In text sizes, one point equals _____.
   a. one pixel
   b. 1/72 of an inch
   c. one inch on the screen
   d. ten pixels

9. The _____ function returns the current text size.
   a. `dbSize`
   b. `dbTextSize`
   c. `dbCharSize`
   d. `dbFontSize`

10. You use the _____ function to set the text style to italic, but not bold.
    a. `dbSetTextToItalic`
    b. `dbItalicNoBold`
    c. `dbNormalItalic`
    d. None of the above. This requires multiple function calls.

True or False

1. You use the `dbLoadMusic` function to load a WAV file into memory.

2. To loop a sound, you have to write a `while` loop that repeatedly calls the `dbPlaySound` function.

3. When you play a WAV file, you can start at a byte other than the beginning.

4. Cloning a sound is not memory efficient because it makes a copy of a sound in memory.

5. Panning a sound means to alter it so it sounds like it is in a pan.

6. You cannot pan an MP3 file.

7. You cannot clone a MIDI file.

8. You can load all of the tracks from a CD into memory at one time.

9. When gravity causes an object to fall toward Earth, the object's speed increases as it falls.

10. If the text size is set to 24 points, then characters will be 24 pixels high on the screen.

Short Answer

1. What audio file formats can you load and play with the Dark GDK?

2. What does a pan value of −10,000 specify?

3. Suppose gravity is causing an object to fall in a vacuum, toward Earth. At 3 seconds, what is the object's speed?

4. If gravity is causing an object to fall in a vacuum, toward Earth, how far will the object have fallen at three seconds?

5. If you call the `dbSetTextToBold` function, and then call the `dbSetTextToItalic` function, will subsequent text be displayed in bold, italic, or both?

Algorithm Workbench

1. Write code that loads an audio file named `gong.wav`, sets the volume to 50 percent, and plays the file.

2. Write code that plays sound number 1, beginning at byte number 256.

3. Write code that loops the section of sound number 1 beginning at byte 256 and ending at byte 1024.

4. Write code that loads the two audio files `Steve.wav` and `Sally.wav`. The code should play `Steve.wav` in the left speaker and `Sally.wav` in the right speaker.

5. Assume an MP3 file has been loaded as music number 5. Write code that sets the playing speed of the music to 50 percent of its normal playing speed.

6. Write an `if-else` statement that determines whether a CD is available, and if so, plays track number 1. If no CD is available, display a message telling the user to insert a CD.

7. Write code that sets the text font to Arial, the text size to 28 points, and the text style to bold and italic.

8. Write code that sets the font size to twice its current value.

Programming Exercises

1. **Random CD Music Sampler**
   Write a program that plays the first 15 seconds of randomly selected tracks from a music CD. When each track begins to play, the volume should start at 25 percent, and increase to 100 percent. When each track ends, rather than abruptly stopping, the volume should fade from 100 percent down to 0 percent.

2. **Moon Gravity**
   In this chapter, you learned that on Earth, falling objects accelerate at a rate of 9.8 meters per second, per second. On the moon falling objects accelerate at only 1.6 meters per second, per second. (This is about one-sixth the acceleration.) Write a program that shows two dropping balls, side by side. One of the balls should simulate Earth's gravity and the other should simulate moon gravity. Your simulation does not have to be exact, just close enough to give a reasonable demonstration.

3. **Stormy Weather**
   Assuming you have installed the Dark GDK, you will find sample sound files named `wind.wav`, `rain.wav`, and `thunder.wav` in the folder `C:\Program Files\The Game Creators\Dark GDK\Media\Sounds\weather`. Write a program that loops the `wind.wav` file and the `rain.wav` file. When the user presses the spacebar, the program should play the `thunder.wav` file and display lightning on the screen.

4. **Vulture Trouble Modification**
   Modify the Vulture Trouble game so the gravitational acceleration increases a slight amount for each egg that drops. This will make the game more challenging because the eggs will fall faster and faster as play continues.

5. **Catch the Boulder Game**
   Design and create a game named Catch the Boulder. The object of the game is to catch falling boulders in a cart that can be moved back and forth on a railroad

track. In many ways the game can be patterned after the Vulture Trouble game presented in this chapter. The book's online resources (downloadable from `www .aw.com/gaddis`) provide several images that you can use to create the game. Figure 8-18 shows an example of a screen from the game.

Figure 8-18 Sample screen from Catch the Boulder

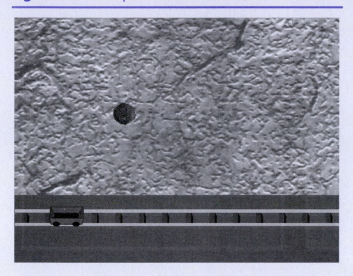

6. **Balloon Ace Game**

   Design and create a game named Balloon Ace. When the game runs, the user will control the movement of an airplane. Yellow and green balloons will randomly appear from the right edge of the screen and move toward the left edge of the screen. This will give the appearance that the plane is flying toward the balloons. The object of the game is to pop the green balloons by colliding into them with the plane, and to avoid the yellow balloons. At the end of the game the program should award points to the user for the number of green balloons popped and the number of yellow balloons avoided. The book's online resources (downloadable from `www.aw.com/gaddis`) provide several images that you can use to create the game. Figure 8-19 shows an example of a screen from the game.

Figure 8-19 Sample screen from Balloon Ace

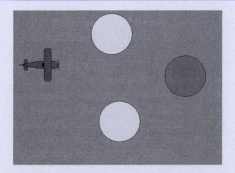

Value-Returning Functions and Mouse Input

TOPICS

9.1 Writing a Value-Returning Function

9.3 The Bug Zapper Game

9.2 Working with the Mouse

9.1 Writing a Value-Returning Function

CONCEPT: A value-returning function is a function that returns a value to the part of the program that called it. The Dark GDK provides numerous value-returning functions that you have already used. You can also write your own value-returning functions.

In Chapter 3, you learned about `void` functions. A `void` function is a group of statements that exist within a program for the purpose of performing a specific task. When you need the function to perform its task, you call the function. This causes the statements inside the function to execute. When the function is finished, control of the program returns to the statement appearing immediately after the function call.

A *value-returning function* is a special type of function. It is like a `void` function in the following ways:

- It is a group of statements that perform a specific task.
- When you want to execute the function, you call it.

When a value-returning function finishes, however, it returns a value to the statement that called it. The value that is returned from a function can be used like any other value: it can be assigned to a variable, displayed on the screen, used in a mathematical expression (if it is a number), and so on.

You have already used many of the value-returning functions that are in the Dark GDK library. For example, the dbRND function returns a random number. Let's review how that function works. Here is an example:

```
number = dbRND(100);
```

The part of the statement that reads dbRND(100) is a call to the dbRND function. The argument 100 specifies the maximum value of the random number. As a result, the function will return a random number in the range of 0 through 100. Figure 9-1 illustrates this part of the statement.

Figure 9-1 A statement that calls the dbRND function

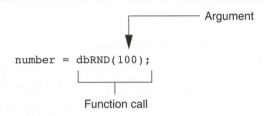

Notice that the call to the dbRND function appears on the right side of an = operator. When the function is called, it will generate a random number in the range of 0 through 100 and then *return* that number. The number that is returned will be assigned to the number variable, as shown in Figure 9-2.

Figure 9-2 The random function returns a value

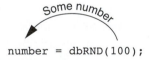

A random number in the range of
0 through 100 will be assigned to
the number variable.

Writing Your Own Value-Returning Functions

You write a value-returning function in the same way that you write a void function, with two exceptions:

- You must specify a data type for a value-returning function. The value that is returned from the function must be of the specified data type.
- A value-returning function must have a return statement. The return statement causes a value to be returned from the function.

Here is the general format of a value-returning function definition in C++:

```
DataType FunctionName(ParameterList)
{
    statement
    statement
    etc.
    return expression;
}
```

- `DataType` is the data type of the value that the function returns. We commonly call this the function's *return type*. For example, if the function returns an integer, the word `int` will appear here. If the function returns a floating-point value, then `float` or `double` will appear here. Likewise, if the function returns a color value, the word `DWORD` will appear here.
- `FunctionName` is the name of the function.
- `ParameterList` is an optional parameter list. If the function does not accept arguments, then an empty set of parentheses will appear.

One of the statements inside the function must be a `return` statement, which takes the following form:

```
return expression;
```

The value of the `expression` that follows the key word `return` will be sent back to the statement that called the function. This can be any value, variable, or expression that has a value (such as a math expression).

The following is an example of a value-returning function. The name of this function is `getCenterX`, and its purpose is to return the *X* coordinate of the screen's center point. Notice that the function's return type is `int`. This means that when the function executes, it will return an `int` value.

```
int getCenterX()
{
    // Calculate the center X coordinate.
    int centerX = dbScreenWidth() / 2;

    // Return the coordinate.
    return centerX;
}
```

Let's look at the body of the function to see how it works. Here is the first statement:

```
int centerX = dbScreenWidth() / 2;
```

This statement declares a local `int` variable named `centerX`, and initializes it with the result of a calculation. The calculation divides the screen's width by 2, which gives us the *X* coordinate of the center point. Next, we have the following `return` statement:

```
return centerX;
```

When the `return` statement executes, it causes the function to end execution, and it sends the value of the variable `centerX` back to the statement that called the function.

If we are going to write a function that returns the *X* coordinate of the screen's center point, we should also write a function that returns the *Y* coordinate of the screen's center point. Here it is:

```
int getCenterY()
{
    // Calculate the center Y coordinate.
    int centerY = dbScreenHeight() / 2;

    // Return the coordinate.
    return centerY;
}
```

The first statement declares a local `int` variable named `centerY`, and initializes it with the result of a calculation. The calculation divides the screen's height by 2, which gives us the *Y* coordinate of the center point. After that, a `return` statement returns the value of the `centerY` variable.

Program 9-1 demonstrates how we can define and call these two functions. The `getCenterX` function is defined in lines 39 through 46, and the `getCenterY` function is defined in lines 52 through 59. Notice that we have written prototypes for the functions in lines 6 and 7.

Program 9-1   **(ValueReturningFunctions.cpp)**

```
1   // This program demonstrates how you can define
2   // and call your own value-returning functions.
3   #include "DarkGDK.h"
4
5   // Function prototypes
6   int getCenterX();
7   int getCenterY();
8
9   //*******************************************
10  // The DarkGDK function                     *
11  //*******************************************
12  void DarkGDK()
13  {
14      // Constant for the circle's radius
15      const int RADIUS = 200;
16
17      // Declare variables to hold a
18      // set of XY coordinates.
19      int x, y;
20
21      // Get the center X coordinate.
22      x = getCenterX();
23
24      // Get the center Y coordinate.
25      y = getCenterY();
26
27      // Display a circle around the
28      // center point.
29      dbCircle(x, y, RADIUS);
```

```
30
31       // Wait for the user to press a key.
32       dbWaitKey();
33  }
34
35  //*******************************************
36  // The getCenterX function returns the X    *
37  // coordinate of the screen's center point. *
38  //*******************************************
39  int getCenterX()
40  {
41       // Calculate the center X coordinate.
42       int centerX = dbScreenWidth() / 2;
43
44       // Return the coordinate.
45       return centerX;
46  }
47
48  //*******************************************
49  // The getCenterY function returns the Y    *
50  // coordinate of the screen's center point. *
51  //*******************************************
52  int getCenterY()
53  {
54       // Calculate the center Y coordinate.
55       int centerY = dbScreenHeight() / 2;
56
57       // Return the coordinate.
58       return centerY;
59  }
```

The program calls the getCenterX function in line 22 and assigns its return value to the x variable. Then it calls the getCenterY function in line 25 and assigns its return value to the y variable. These variables are used to draw a circle around the screen's center point in line 29. The program's output is shown in Figure 9-3.

Making the Most of the return Statement

Look again at the getCenterX function presented in Program 9-1:

```
int getCenterX()
{
     // Calculate the center X coordinate.
     int centerX = dbScreenWidth() / 2;

     // Return the coordinate.
     return centerX;
}
```

Notice that two things happen inside this function: (1) the value of the expression dbScreenWidth() / 2 is assigned to the centerX variable, and (2) the value of the centerX variable is returned. Although this function does what it sets out to do, it

Figure 9-3 Output of Program 9-1

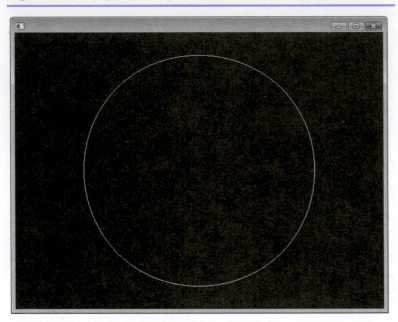

can be simplified. Because the return statement can return the value of an expression, we can eliminate the centerX variable and rewrite the function as follows:

```
int getCenterX()
{
    return dbScreenWidth() / 2;
}
```

This version of the function does not store the value of dbScreenWidth() / 2 in a variable. Instead, it takes advantage of the fact that the return statement can return the value of an expression. This version of the function does the same thing as the previous version, but in only one step. We can revise the getCenterY function in a similar manner, as shown here:

```
int getCenterY()
{
    return dbScreenHeight() / 2;
}
```

Let's look at another example. Program 9-2 uses a game loop to get random *X* and *Y* coordinates, and then display a dot at that location. The program has the following value-returning functions:

- getMaximumX—This function returns the maximum *X* coordinate in the visible area of the screen. The function definition appears in lines 59 through 62.
- getMaximumY—This function returns the maximum *Y* coordinate in the visible area of the screen. The function definition appears in lines 68 through 71.

The program uses these functions to make sure the coordinates generated by the dbRND function are in the visible area of the screen. Figure 9-4 shows an example of the program's output after it has executed for about one minute.

Program 9-2   (`RandomDots.cpp`)

```cpp
 1   // This program uses functions to get the maximum
 2   // X and Y coordinates within the visible screen area.
 3   #include "DarkGDK.h"
 4
 5   // Function prototypes
 6   void setUp();
 7   int getMaximumX();
 8   int getMaximumY();
 9
10   //************************************************
11   // DarkGDK function                             *
12   //************************************************
13   void DarkGDK()
14   {
15       // Variables to hold coordinates.
16       int x, y;
17
18       // Perform setup operations.
19       setUp();
20
21       // Game loop
22       while ( LoopGDK() )
23       {
24           // Get a set of random XY coordinates
25           // within the bounds of the screen.
26           x = dbRND( getMaximumX() );
27           y = dbRND( getMaximumY() );
28
29           // Draw a dot at that location.
30           dbDot(x, y);
31
32           // Refresh the screen.
33           dbSync();
34       }
35   }
36
37   //************************************************
38   // The setUp function performs various setup     *
39   // operations.                                   *
40   //************************************************
41   void setUp()
42   {
43       // Constant for the refresh rate.
44       const int REFRESH_RATE = 60;
45
46       // Seed the random number generator.
47       dbRandomize( dbTimer() );
48
49       // Disable auto refresh and set the
50       // refresh rate.
51       dbSyncOn();
52       dbSyncRate(REFRESH_RATE);
53   }
```

```
54
55  //***********************************************
56  // The getMaximumX function returns the maximum   *
57  // X coordinate within the visible screen area.   *
58  //***********************************************
59  int getMaximumX()
60  {
61      return dbScreenWidth() - 1;
62  }
63
64  //***********************************************
65  // The getMaximumY function returns the maximum   *
66  // Y coordinate within the visible screen area.   *
67  //***********************************************
68  int getMaximumY()
69  {
70      return dbScreenHeight() - 1;
71  }
```

Figure 9-4 Example output of Program 9-2

Take a closer look at line 26, where we generate the random *X* coordinate:

```
x = dbRND( getMaximumX() );
```

Notice that we have written nested function calls. When this statement executes, the getMaximumX function is called, and the value it returns is passed as an argument to the dbRND function. Line 27 has a similar statement that generates a random *Y* coordinate:

```
y = dbRND( getMaximumY() );
```

When this statement executes, the value that is returned from the `getMaximumY` function is passed as an argument to the `dbRND` function.

In the Spotlight:
Returning a Color from a Function

You can write value-returning functions that return values of any data type. For example, if you want to write a function that returns a color, that function would return a `DWORD` value. Program 9-3 demonstrates this. It has a function named `randomColor` (defined in lines 75 through 92) that returns a randomly generated color. The program uses a game loop to draw squares of random colors at random locations. Figure 9-5 (in the book's color insert) shows an example of the program's output after running for a short time.

Program 9-3   **(RandomColors.cpp)**

```
1   // This program displays squares of random colors at
2   // random locations on the screen.
3   #include "DarkGDK.h"
4
5   // Function prototypes
6   void setUp();
7   DWORD randomColor();
8   int getMaximumX();
9   int getMaximumY();
10
11  //***********************************************
12  // DarkGDK function                             *
13  //***********************************************
14  void DarkGDK()
15  {
16      // Constants
17      const int SIZE = 50;                    // Square size
18      const DWORD BLACK = dbRGB(0, 0, 0);     // Background color
19
20      // Variables to hold coordinates.
21      int upperX, upperY, lowerX, lowerY;
22
23      // Variable to hold a color value.
24      DWORD color;
25
26      // Perform setup operations.
27      setUp();
28
29      // Game loop
30      while ( LoopGDK() )
31      {
32          // Get a random color.
33          color = randomColor();
34
```

```
35                 // Get a set of coordinates for the box's
36                 // upper-left and lower-right corners.
37                 upperX = dbRND( getMaximumX() - SIZE );
38                 upperY = dbRND( getMaximumY()  - SIZE);
39                 lowerX = upperX + SIZE;
40                 lowerY = upperY + SIZE;
41
42                 // Change the drawing color.
43                 dbInk(color, BLACK);
44
45                 // Draw a box.
46                 dbBox(upperX, upperY, lowerX, lowerY);
47
48                 // Refresh the screen.
49                 dbSync();
50         }
51   }
52
53   //*************************************************
54   // The setUp function performs various setup      *
55   // operations.                                    *
56   //*************************************************
57   void setUp()
58   {
59        // Constant for the refresh rate.
60        const int REFRESH_RATE = 60;
61
62        // Seed the random number generator.
63        dbRandomize( dbTimer() );
64
65        // Disable auto refresh and set the
66        // refresh rate.
67        dbSyncOn();
68        dbSyncRate(REFRESH_RATE);
69   }
70
71   //*************************************************
72   // The randomColor function returns a DWORD value *
73   // containing a randomly generated color.         *
74   //*************************************************
75   DWORD randomColor()
76   {
77        // Constant for the max color value
78        const int MAX_COLOR = 255;
79
80        // Declare variables for the RGB components
81        // and initialize them with random values.
82        int red = dbRND(MAX_COLOR);
83        int green = dbRND(MAX_COLOR);
84        int blue = dbRND(MAX_COLOR);
85
86        // Declare a DWORD variable and initialize
87        // it with a color value.
88        DWORD color = dbRGB(red, green, blue);
89
```

```
 90        // Return the color.
 91        return color;
 92   }
 93
 94   //*********************************************
 95   // The getMaximumX function returns the maximum   *
 96   // X coordinate within the visible screen area.   *
 97   //*********************************************
 98   int getMaximumX()
 99   {
100        return dbScreenWidth() - 1;
101   }
102
103   //*********************************************
104   // The getMaximumY function returns the maximum   *
105   // Y coordinate within the visible screen area.   *
106   //*********************************************
107   int getMaximumY()
108   {
109        return dbScreenHeight() - 1;
110   }
```

Before we look at the `randomColor` function, let's examine the overall logic of the `DarkGDK` function. Line 17 declares a constant named `SIZE` that is initialized with 50. This is for the size of the boxes that we will draw. Line 18 declares a constant named `BLACK` to represent the color black. This will be used as the background color when we call the `dbInk` function.

Line 21 declares four `int` variables: `upperX`, `upperY`, `lowerX`, and `lowerY`. When we draw a box, these variables will hold the coordinates of the box's upper-left and lower-right corners. Line 24 declares a `DWORD` variable named `color`, which will be used to hold the color that is returned from the `randomColor` function.

Line 27 calls the `setUp` function, and the game loop begins in line 30. Inside the loop, the `randomColor` function is called in line 33 and its return value is assigned to the `color` variable. Lines 37 and 38 call the `dbRND` function to get random values for the `upperX` and `upperY` variables. Notice that we use the expression `getMaximumX() - SIZE` to specify the maximum value for the *X* coordinate, and `getMaximumY() - SIZE` to specify the maximum value for the *Y* coordinate. This ensures that the entire box will be drawn in the visible part of the screen. Lines 39 and 40 calculate the coordinates for the lower-right corner. Line 43 sets the foreground drawing color to the random color that was previously generated, and line 46 draws a box. Line 49 refreshes the screen.

Now let's look at the `randomColor` function. First, notice that its return type is `DWORD`. This is shown in the function prototype (line 7) and the function header (line 75). The function works like this: In lines 82 through 84 it generates three random integers, which are assigned to the local variables `red`, `green`, and `blue`. Those variables are used to generate a color in line 88, which is assigned to the local variable `color`. The `color` variable is then returned in line 91.

Returning Boolean Values

You can write *Boolean functions* in C++, which return the `bool` values `true` or `false`. You can use a Boolean function to test a condition, and then return either `true` or `false` to indicate whether or not the condition exists.

Boolean functions are useful for simplifying complex logic. For example, suppose you want to know whether a color is a shade of gray. When a color's red, green, and blue components are set to the same value, that color is a shade of gray. The following Boolean function accepts a `DWORD` argument containing a color and returns `true` if that argument is a shade of gray, or `false` otherwise.

```cpp
bool isGray(DWORD color)
{
    // Declare a bool variable to indicate whether
    // the color is a shade of gray.
    bool setToGray;

    // Get the color's RGB components.
    int red = dbRGBR(color);
    int green = dbRGBG(color);
    int blue = dbRGBG(color);

    // Determine whether the components are
    // set to the same value.
    if (red == green && red == blue)
    {

        setToGray = true;
    }
    else
    {
        setToGray = false;
    }

    // Return the result.
    return setToGray;
}
```

In this function, we extract the `color` parameter's red, green, and blue components. Then, in the `if` statement, we determine whether the red component is equal to both the green component and the blue component. If so, we set the `bool` variable `setToGray` to `true`. If not, we set `setToGray` to `false`. At the end of the function, we return the value of the `setToGray` variable. Program 9-4 shows an example of how we might use the function. The program loads a bitmap image and then counts the number of gray pixels in the image. The program's output is shown in Figure 9-6. (A color version of Figure 9-6 appears in the color insert.)

Program 9-4   (CountGray.cpp)

```cpp
1   // This program counts the number of gray pixels
2   // in an image.
3   #include "DarkGDK.h"
4
```

```
 5    // Function prototype
 6    bool isGray(DWORD);
 7
 8    //***************************************************
 9    // Dark GDK function                                *
10    //***************************************************
11    void DarkGDK()
12    {
13        // Variable to hold the number of gray pixels
14        int grayCount = 0;
15
16        // Variable to hold a color.
17        DWORD pixelColor;
18
19        // Load a bitmap image.
20        dbLoadBitmap("Statue.jpg", 0);
21
22        // Scan the entire image, counting gray pixels.
23        for (int x = 0; x < 640; x++)
24        {
25            for (int y = 0; y < 480; y++)
26            {
27                // Get a pixel color.
28                pixelColor = dbPoint(x, y);
29
30                // If the pixel is gray, count it.
31                if ( isGray(pixelColor) )
32                {
33                    grayCount++;
34                }
35            }
36        }
37
38        // Let the user press a key to continue.
39        dbText(500, 450, "Press any key...");
40        dbWaitKey();
41
42        // Clear the screen and report the number of
43        // gray pixels.
44        dbCLS();
45        dbPrint("Number of gray pixels in the image:");
46        dbPrint( dbStr(grayCount) );
47
48        // Wait for the user to press a key.
49        dbWaitKey();
50    }
51
52    //***************************************************
53    // The isGray function accepts a DWORD color as     *
54    // an argument. It returns true if the color is     *
55    // a shade of gray, or false otherwise.             *
56    //***************************************************
57    bool isGray(DWORD color)
58    {
59        // Declare a bool variable to indicate whether
```

```
60        // the color is a shade of gray.
61        bool setToGray;
62
63        // Get the color's RGB components.
64        int red = dbRGBR(color);
65        int green = dbRGBG(color);
66        int blue = dbRGBG(color);
67
68        // Determine whether the components are
69        // set to the same value.
70        if (red == green && red == blue)
71        {
72            setToGray = true;
73        }
74        else
75        {
76            setToGray = false;
77        }
78
79        // Return the result.
80        return setToGray;
81  }
```

Figure 9-6 Output of Program 9-4

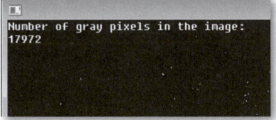

Number of gray pixels in the image:
17972

This figure also appears in this book's full-color insert.

In the Spotlight:
Constraining a Sprite to the Screen's Visible Area

Suppose you are writing a program that lets the user move a sprite around on the screen and you want to prevent the sprite from moving out of the visible area. There are many different ways to make sure that a sprite does not move off the screen. In this section, we will look at one approach.

When an arrow key is pressed, you determine whether or not moving the sprite a particular distance in the specified direction will move it off the screen. If such a move will not position the sprite off the screen, you move it. Otherwise, you do not move it. Let's look at the specific steps you take when each of the four arrow keys are pressed.

Moving a Sprite Up

Here is an example of what we need to do when the user presses the *Up* arrow key:

- Get the *Y* coordinate of the sprite's top edge.
- Subtract the distance that the sprite will move from the sprite's top *Y* coordinate.
- If the result is less than 0 (which is the screen's top *Y* coordinate), then the sprite can move up that distance without going off the screen.

Figure 9-7 shows the relationship between the sprite's top *Y* coordinate and the top of the screen.

Figure 9-7 Relationship between the sprite's top *Y* coordinate and the screen's top *Y* coordinate

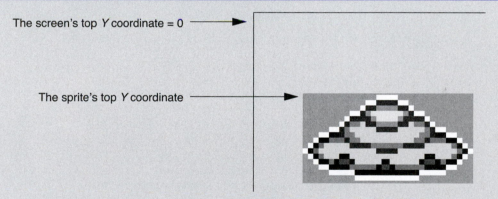

The screen's top *Y* coordinate = 0

The sprite's top *Y* coordinate

First, we will define the following function, `spriteTopY`, which accepts a sprite number as an argument, and returns the sprite's topmost *Y* coordinate. Here is the function definition:

```
int spriteTopY(int spriteNum)
{
    // Get the sprite's Y coordinate.
    int y = dbSpriteY(spriteNum);

    // Get the sprite's Y offset.
    int offsetY = dbSpriteOffsetY(spriteNum);

    // Calculate the Y coordinate of the
    // sprite's topmost edge.
    int topY = y - offsetY;
```

```
    // Return the Y coordinate.
    return topY;
}
```

In the function, we call `dbSpriteY` to get the Y coordinate of the sprite's insertion point. This value is assigned to the y variable. Recall that by default, the sprite's insertion point is the sprite's upper-left corner. However, the insertion point can be offset, so in the next statement, we call the `dbSpriteoffsetY` function to get the amount of Y offset. (If there is no offset, this function returns 0.) This value is assigned to the `offsetY` variable. Then, we subtract `offsetY` from y, which gives us the Y coordinate of the top of the sprite. This value is assigned to the `topY` variable. Last, we return the value of the `topY` variable.

 NOTE: In a nutshell, the function calculates the sprite's top Y coordinate by subtracting the sprite's Y offset from the Y coordinate of the sprite's insertion point. The resulting value is returned from the function.

Next, we define a Boolean function named `canMoveUp`, which accepts a sprite number and a distance as arguments. If the specified sprite can move up the screen the specified distance without going off the screen, the function returns `true`. Otherwise, it returns `false`. Here is the code for the function:

```
bool canMoveUp(int spriteNum, int distance)
{
    // Declare a bool variable to indicate whether
    // the sprite can move up.
    bool canMove;

    // If the sprite's top Y coordinate minus the
    // specified distance to move the sprite is greater
    // than 0, then the sprite can move up.
    // Otherwise, sprite cannot move up.
    if ( (spriteTopY(spriteNum) - distance) > 0 )
    {
        canMove = true;
    }

    else
    {
        canMove = false;
    }

    // Return the value of canMove.
    return canMove;
}
```

Here is a summary of how the function works: First, we declare a local `bool` variable named `canMove`. We will use this variable to hold the value that we will return from the function, which will be either `true` or `false`. Then, we have an `if` statement that subtracts the distance from the sprite's top edge. If that value is greater than 0, then the sprite can make the move without going off the screen. In that case, we assign true to canMove. Else, we assign false to canMove. At the end of the function we return the value of canMove.

The following shows an example of how we might use the canMoveUp function. Assume that spriteNumber is the sprite number and distance is the distance that we want to move the sprite.

```
if ( dbUpKey() )
{
    if ( canMoveUp(spriteNumber, distance) )
    {
        // Code goes here to move the sprite up
        // the specified distance.
    }
}
```

Moving a Sprite Down

Here is an example of what we need to do when the user presses the *Down* arrow key:

- Get the *Y* coordinate of the sprite's bottom edge.
- Get the screen's maximum *Y* coordinate. (This is the *Y* coordinate of the screen's bottom edge.)
- Add the distance that the sprite will move to the sprite's bottom *Y* coordinate.
- If the result is less than the screen's maximum *Y* coordinate, then the sprite can move down that distance without going off the screen.

Figure 9-8 shows the relationship between the sprite's bottom *Y* coordinate and the screen's maximum *Y* coordinate.

Figure 9-8 Relationship between the sprite's bottom *Y* coordinate and the screen's maximum *Y* coordinate

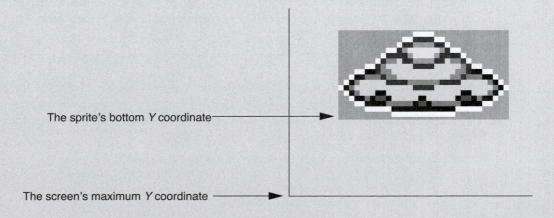

The sprite's bottom *Y* coordinate

The screen's maximum *Y* coordinate

First, we will define the following function, `spriteBottomY`, which accepts a sprite number as an argument, and returns the sprite's bottom *Y* coordinate. Here is the function definition:

```
int spriteBottomY(int spriteNum)
{
    // Get the sprite's Y coordinate.
    int y = dbSpriteY(spriteNum);

    // Get the sprite's Y offset.
    int offsetY = dbSpriteOffsetY(spriteNum);

    // Get the height of the sprite.
    int height = dbSpriteHeight(spriteNum);

    // Calculate the Y coordinate of the
    // sprite's bottom edge.
    int bottomY = y - offsetY + height;

    // Return the Y coordinate.
    return bottomY;
}
```

Here is a summary of how the function works: First, we call `dbSpriteY` to get the *Y* coordinate of the sprite's insertion point. This value is assigned to the `y` variable. Because the insertion point can be offset, in the next statement we call the `dbSpriteoffsetY` function to get the amount of *Y* offset. (If there is no offset, this function returns 0.) This value is assigned to the `offsetY` variable. Next, we call the `dbSpriteHeight` function to get the height of the sprite and assign that value to the `height` variable.

Then, we subtract `offsetY` from `y` (which gives us the *Y* coordinate of the top of the sprite) and add the sprite's height. This final result, which is the sprite's bottom *Y* coordinate, is assigned to the `bottomY` variable. Last, we return the value of the `bottomY` variable.

NOTE: In a nutshell, the function calculates the sprite's bottom *Y* coordinate by subtracting the sprite's *Y* offset from the *Y* coordinate of the sprite's insertion point, and adding the height of the sprite. The resulting value is returned from the function.

Next, we define a Boolean function named `canMoveDown`, which accepts a sprite number and a distance as arguments. If the specified sprite can move down the screen the specified distance without going off the screen, the function returns `true`. Otherwise, it returns `false`. Here is the code for the function:

```
bool canMoveDown(int spriteNum, int distance)
{
    // Declare a bool variable to indicate whether
    // the sprite can move down.
    bool canMove;
```

```
    // If the sprite's bottom Y coordinate plus the
    // specified distance to move the sprite is less
    // than the screen's maximum Y coordinate, then the
    // sprite can move down. Otherwise, the sprite cannot
    // move down.
    if ( (spriteBottomY(spriteNum) + distance) < getMaximumY() )
    {
        canMove = true;
    }
    else
    {
        canMove = false;
    }

    // Return the value of canMove.
    return canMove;
}
```

Here is a summary of how the function works:

- First, we declare a local `bool` variable named `canMove`. We will use this variable to hold the value that we will return from the function, which will be either `true` or `false`.
- Then, we have an `if` statement that adds the distance to the sprite's bottom edge. If that value is greater than the screen's maximum *Y* coordinate, then the sprite can make the move without going off the screen. In that case, we assign `true` to `canMove`. Else, we assign `false` to `canMove`. (Notice that we are using the `getMaximumY` function that we developed earlier in this chapter.)
- At the end of the function we return the value of `canMove`.

The following shows an example of how we might use the `canMoveDown` function. Assume that `spriteNumber` is the sprite number and `distance` is the distance that we want to move the sprite.

```
if ( dbDownKey() )
{
    if ( canMoveDown(spriteNumber, distance) )
    {
        // Code goes here to move the sprite down
        // the specified distance.
    }
}
```

Moving a Sprite to the Left

Here is an example of what we need to do when the user presses the *Left* arrow key:

- Get the *X* coordinate of the sprite's left edge.
- Subtract the distance that the sprite will move from the sprite's left *X* coordinate.
- If the result is greater than 0 (the screen's leftmost *X* coordinate), then the sprite can move left that distance without going off the screen.

Figure 9-9 shows the relationship between the sprite's left *X* coordinate and the left side of the screen.

Figure 9-9 Relationship between the sprite's left *X*
coordinate and the screen's left *X* coordinate

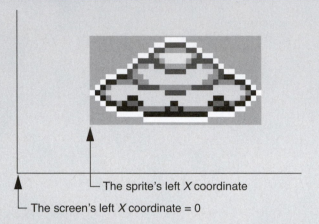

The sprite's left *X* coordinate

The screen's left *X* coordinate = 0

First, we will define the following function, `spriteLeftX`, which accepts a sprite number as an argument, and returns the sprite's left *X* coordinate. Here is the function definition:

```
int spriteLeftX(int spriteNum)
{
    // Get the sprite's X coordinate.
    int x = dbSpriteX(spriteNum);

    // Get the sprite's X offset.
    int offsetX = dbSpriteOffsetX(spriteNum);

    // Calculate the X coordinate of the
    // sprite's left edge.
    int leftX = x - offsetX;

    // Return the X coordinate.
    return leftX;
}
```

Here is a summary of how the function works:

- First, we call `dbSpriteX` to get the *X* coordinate of the sprite's insertion point. This value is assigned to the `x` variable.
- Because the insertion point can be offset, in the next statement we call the `dbSpriteoffsetX` function to get the amount of *X* offset. (If there is no offset, this function returns 0.) This value is assigned to the `offsetX` variable.
- Then, we subtract `offsetX` from `x`, which gives us the *X* coordinate of the sprite's left edge. This value is assigned to the `leftX` variable.
- Last, we return the value of the `leftX` variable.

NOTE: In a nutshell, the function calculates the sprite's left *X* coordinate by subtracting the sprite's *X* offset from the *X* coordinate of the sprite's insertion point. The resulting value is returned from the function.

Next, we define a Boolean function named `canMoveLeft`, which accepts a sprite number and a distance as arguments. If the specified sprite can move left the specified distance without going off the screen, the function returns `true`. Otherwise, it returns `false`. Here is the code for the function:

```
bool canMoveLeft(int spriteNum, int distance)
{
    // Declare a bool variable to indicate whether
    // the sprite can move left.
    bool canMove;

    // If the sprite's left X coordinate minus the specified
    // distance is greater than 0, then the sprite can move
    // left. Otherwise, it cannot move left.
    if ( (spriteLeftX(spriteNum) - distance) > 0 )
    {
        canMove = true;
    }
    else
    {
        canMove = false;
    }

    // Return the value of canMove.
    return canMove;
}
```

Here is a summary of how the function works:

- First, we declare a local `bool` variable named `canMove`. We will use this variable to hold the value that we will return from the function, which will be either `true` or `false`.
- Then, we have an `if` statement that subtracts the distance from the X coordinate of the sprite's left edge. If that value is greater than 0 (which is the screen's leftmost X coordinate), then the sprite can make the move without going off the screen. In that case, we assign `true` to `canMove`. Else, we assign `false` to `canMove`.
- At the end of the function we return the value of `canMove`.

The following shows an example of how we might use the `canMoveLeft` function. Assume that `spriteNumber` is the sprite number and `distance` is the distance that we want to move the sprite.

```
if ( dbLeftKey() )
{
    if ( canMoveLeft(spriteNumber, distance) )
    {
        // Code goes here to move the sprite left
        // the specified distance.
    }
}
```

Moving a Sprite to the Right

Here is an example of what we need to do when the user presses the *Right* arrow key:

- Get the *X* coordinate of the sprite's right edge.
- Get the screen's maximum *X* coordinate.
- Add the distance that the sprite will move to the sprite's right *X* coordinate.
- If the result is less than the screen's maximum *X* coordinate, then the sprite can move right that distance without going off the screen.

Figure 9-10 shows the relationship between the sprite's right *X* coordinate and the screen's maximum *X* coordinate.

Figure 9-10 Relationship between the sprite's right *X* coordinate and the screen's maximum *X* coordinate

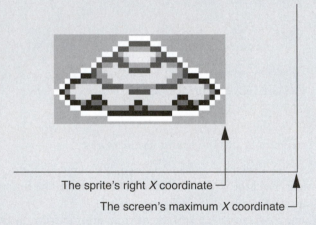

The sprite's right *X* coordinate ⏋

The screen's maximum *X* coordinate ⏋

First, we will define the following function, `spriteRightX`, which accepts a sprite number as an argument, and returns the *X* coordinate of the sprite's right edge. Here is the function definition:

```
int spriteRightX(int spriteNum)
{
    // Get the sprite's X coordinate.
    int x = dbSpriteX(spriteNum);

    // Get the sprite's X offset.
    int offsetX = dbSpriteOffsetX(spriteNum);

    // Get the sprite's width.
    int width = dbSpriteWidth(spriteNum);

    // Calculate the X coordinate of the
    // sprite's right edge.
    int rightX = x - offsetX + width;

    // Return the X coordinate.
    return rightX;
}
```

Here is a summary of how the function works:

- First, we call `dbSpriteX` to get the *X* coordinate of the sprite's insertion point. This value is assigned to the `x` variable.
- Because the insertion point can be offset, in the next statement we call the `dbSpriteoffsetX` function to get the amount of *X* offset. (If there is no offset, this function returns 0.) This value is assigned to the `offsetX` variable.
- Next, we call the `dbSpriteWidth` function to get the width of the sprite and assign that value to the `width` variable.
- Then, we subtract `offsetX` from `x` (which gives us the *X* coordinate of the sprite's left edge) and add the sprite's width. This final result, which is the *X* coordinate of the sprite's right edge, is assigned to the `rightX` variable. Last, we return the value of the `rightX` variable.

> **NOTE:** In a nutshell, the function calculates the sprite's right *X* coordinate by subtracting the sprite's *X* offset from the *X* coordinate of the sprite's insertion point, and adding the width of the sprite. The resulting value is returned from the function.

Next, we define a Boolean function named `canMoveRight`, which accepts a sprite number and a distance as arguments. If the specified sprite can move right the specified distance without going off the screen, the function returns `true`. Otherwise, it returns `false`. Here is the code for the function:

```
bool canMoveRight(int spriteNum, int distance)
{
    // Declare a bool variable to indicate whether
    // the sprite can move right.
    bool canMove;

    // If the sprite's right X coordinate plus the specified
    // distance is less than the screen's maximum X coordinate,
    // then the sprite can move right. Otherwise, the sprite
    // cannot move right.
    if ( (spriteRightX(spriteNum) + distance) < getMaximumX() )
    {
        canMove = true;
    }
    else
    {
        canMove = false;
    }

    // Return the value of canMove.
    return canMove;
}
```

Here is a summary of how the function works:

- First, we declare a local `bool` variable named `canMove`. We will use this variable to hold the value that we will return from the function, which will be either `true` or `false`.

- Then, we have an `if` statement that adds the distance to the *X* coordinate of the sprite's right edge. If that value is less than the screen's maximum *X* coordinate, then the sprite can make the move without going off the screen. In that case, we assign `true` to `canMove`. Else, we assign `false` to `canMove`. (Notice that we are using the `getMaximumX` function that we developed earlier in this chapter.)
- At the end of the function we return the value of `canMove`.

The following shows an example of how we might use the `canMoveRight` function. Assume that `spriteNumber` is the sprite number and `distance` is the distance that we want to move the sprite.

```
if ( dbRightKey() )
{
    if ( canMoveRight(spriteNumber, distance) )
    {

        // Code goes here to move the sprite right
        // the specified distance.
    }
}
```

Program 9-5 demonstrates these functions. It displays the UFO sprite and allows the user to move it around the screen with the arrow keys. The sprite will not move out of the screen's visible area. Figure 9-11 shows an example of the program's output.

Program 9-5   (`ConstrainSprite.cpp`)

```
 1  // This program allows the user to move a sprite
 2  // with the arrow keys, and constrains the sprite
 3  // to the visible area of the screen.
 4  #include "DarkGDK.h"
 5
 6  // Constants
 7  const int REFRESH_RATE = 60;
 8  const int UFO_SPRITE_NUM = 1;
 9  const int UFO_IMAGE_NUM = 1;
10  const int DISTANCE = 10;
11
12  // Function prototypes
13  void setUp();
14  void updateUFO();
15  bool canMoveUp(int, int);
16  bool canMoveDown(int, int);
17  bool canMoveRight(int, int);
18  bool canMoveLeft(int, int);
19  int spriteTopY(int);
20  int spriteBottomY(int);
21  int spriteLeftX(int);
22  int spriteRightX(int);
23  int getMaximumX();
24  int getMaximumY();
25
26  //*********************************************************
27  // The DarkGDK function                                  *
```

```
28    //********************************************************
29    void DarkGDK()
30    {
31        // Perform setup.
32        setUp();
33
34        // Game loop
35        while ( LoopGDK() )
36        {
37            // Update the UFO's position.
38            updateUFO();
39
40            // Refresh the screen.
41            dbSync();
42        }
43    }
44
45    //********************************************************
46    // The setUp function performs setup operations.        *
47    //********************************************************
48    void setUp()
49    {
50        // Set the key color to green.
51        dbSetImageColorKey(0, 255, 0);
52
53        // Load the UFO image and make a sprite.
54        dbLoadImage("UFO.bmp", UFO_IMAGE_NUM);
55        dbSprite(UFO_SPRITE_NUM, 10, 10, UFO_IMAGE_NUM);
56
57        // Disable auto-refresh and set the refresh rate.
58        dbSyncOn();
59        dbSyncRate(REFRESH_RATE);
60    }
61
62    //********************************************************
63    // The updateUFO function checks the arrow keys and     *
64    // updates the UFO's position accordingly.              *
65    //********************************************************
66    void updateUFO()
67    {
68        // Get the UFO sprite's XY coordinates.
69        int x = dbSpriteX(UFO_SPRITE_NUM);
70        int y = dbSpriteY(UFO_SPRITE_NUM);
71
72        // Check the down arrow key.
73        if ( dbDownKey() )
74        {
75            // If the sprite can move down, then move it down.
76            if ( canMoveDown(UFO_SPRITE_NUM, DISTANCE) )
77            {
78                y += DISTANCE;
79            }
80        }
81
82        // Check the up arrow key.
```

```
83            if ( dbUpKey() )
84            {
85                // If the sprite can move up, then move it up.
86                if ( canMoveUp(UFO_SPRITE_NUM, DISTANCE) )
87                {
88                    y -= DISTANCE;
89                }
90            }
91
92            // Check the left arrow key.
93            if ( dbLeftKey() )
94            {
95                // If the sprite can move left, then move it left.
96                if ( canMoveLeft(UFO_SPRITE_NUM, DISTANCE) )
97                {
98                    x -= DISTANCE;
99                }
100           }
101
102           // Check the right arrow key.
103           if ( dbRightKey() )
104           {
105               // If the sprite can move right, then move it right.
106               if ( canMoveRight(UFO_SPRITE_NUM, DISTANCE) )
107               {
108                   x += DISTANCE;
109               }
110           }
111
112           // Display the sprite.
113           dbSprite(UFO_SPRITE_NUM, x, y, UFO_IMAGE_NUM);
114    }
115
116    //********************************************************
117    // The canMoveUp function returns true if the sprite     *
118    // can move up the specified distance without going off*
119    // the screen. Otherwise it returns false.               *
120    //********************************************************
121    bool canMoveUp(int spriteNum, int distance)
122    {
123        // Declare a bool variable to indicate whether
124        // the sprite can move up.
125        bool canMove;
126
127        // If the sprite's top Y coordinate minus the
128        // specified distance to move the sprite is greater
129        // than 0, then the sprite can move up.
130        // Otherwise, sprite cannot move up.
131        if ( (spriteTopY(spriteNum) - distance) > 0 )
132        {
133            canMove = true;
134        }
135        else
136        {
137            canMove = false;
```

```
138         }
139
140         // Return the value of canMove.
141         return canMove;
142    }
143
144    //********************************************************
145    // The canMoveDown function returns true if the sprite  *
146    // can move down the specified distance without going   *
147    // off the screen. Otherwise it returns false.          *
148    //********************************************************
149    bool canMoveDown(int spriteNum, int distance)
150    {
151         // Declare a bool variable to indicate whether
152         // the sprite can move down.
153         bool canMove;
154
155         // If the sprite's bottom Y coordinate plus the
156         // specified distance to move the sprite is less
157         // than the screen's maximum Y coordinate, then the
158         // sprite can move down. Otherwise, the sprite cannot
159         // move down.
160         if ( (spriteBottomY(spriteNum) + distance) < getMaximumY() )
161         {
162             canMove = true;
163         }
164         else
165         {
166             canMove = false;
167         }
168
169         // Return the value of canMove.
170         return canMove;
171    }
172
173    //********************************************************
174    // The canMoveLeft function returns true if the sprite  *
175    // can move left the specified distance without going   *
176    // off the screen. Otherwise it returns false.          *
177    //********************************************************
178    bool canMoveLeft(int spriteNum, int distance)
179    {
180         // Declare a bool variable to indicate whether
181         // the sprite can move left.
182         bool canMove;
183
184         // If the sprite's left X coordinate minus the specified
185         // distance is greater than 0, then the sprite can move
186         // left. Otherwise, it cannot move left.
187         if ( (spriteLeftX(spriteNum) - distance) > 0 )
188         {
189             canMove = true;
190         }
191         else
192         {
```

```
193                canMove = false;
194            }
195
196            // Return the value of canMove.
197            return canMove;
198        }
199
200        //**********************************************************
201        // The canMoveRight function returns true if the sprite  *
202        // can move right the specified distance without going   *
203        // off the screen. Otherwise it returns false.           *
204        //**********************************************************
205        bool canMoveRight(int spriteNum, int distance)
206        {
207            // Declare a bool variable to indicate whether
208            // the sprite can move right.
209            bool canMove;
210
211            // If the sprite's right X coordinate plus the specified
212            // distance is less than the screen's maximum X coordinate,
213            // then the sprite can move right. Otherwise, the sprite
214            // cannot move right.
215            if ( (spriteRightX(spriteNum) + distance) < getMaximumX() )
216            {
217                canMove = true;
218            }
219            else
220            {
221                canMove = false;
222            }
223
224            // Return the value of canMove.
225            return canMove;
226        }
227
228        //**********************************************************
229        // The spriteTopY function returns the specified sprite's *
230        // top Y coordinate.                                      *
231        //**********************************************************
232        int spriteTopY(int spriteNum)
233        {
234            // Get the sprite's Y coordinate.
235            int y = dbSpriteY(spriteNum);
236
237            // Get the sprite's Y offset.
238            int offsetY = dbSpriteOffsetY(spriteNum);
239
240            // Calculate the Y coordinate of the
241            // sprite's topmost edge.
242            int topY = y - offsetY;
243
244            // Return the Y coordinate.
245            return topY;
246        }
247
```

```
248    //**********************************************************
249    // The spriteBottomY function returns the specified        *
250    // sprite's bottom Y coordinate.                           *
251    //**********************************************************
252    int spriteBottomY(int spriteNum)
253    {
254        // Get the sprite's Y coordinate.
255        int y = dbSpriteY(spriteNum);
256
257        // Get the sprite's Y offset.
258        int offsetY = dbSpriteOffsetY(spriteNum);
259
260        // Get the height of the sprite.
261        int height = dbSpriteHeight(spriteNum);
262
263        // Calculate the Y coordinate of the
264        // sprite's bottom edge.
265        int bottomY = y - offsetY + height;
266
267        // Return the Y coordinate.
268        return bottomY;
269    }
270
271    //**********************************************************
272    // The spriteRightX function returns the specified         *
273    // sprite's rightmost X coordinate.                        *
274    //**********************************************************
275    int spriteRightX(int spriteNum)
276    {
277        // Get the sprite's X coordinate.
278        int x = dbSpriteX(spriteNum);
279
280        // Get the sprite's X offset.
281        int offsetX = dbSpriteOffsetX(spriteNum);
282
283        // Get the sprite's width.
284        int width = dbSpriteWidth(spriteNum);
285
286        // Calculate the X coordinate of the
287        // sprite's right edge.
288        int rightX = x - offsetX + width;
289
290        // Return the X coordinate.
291        return rightX;
292    }
293
294    //**********************************************************
295    // The spriteLeftX function returns the specified          *
296    // sprite's leftmost X coordinate.                         *
297    //**********************************************************
298    int spriteLeftX(int spriteNum)
299    {
300        // Get the sprite's X coordinate.
301        int x = dbSpriteX(spriteNum);
302
```

```
303         // Get the sprite's X offset.
304         int offsetX = dbSpriteOffsetX(spriteNum);
305
306         // Calculate the X coordinate of the
307         // sprite's left edge.
308         int leftX = x - offsetX;
309
310         // Return the X coordinate.
311         return leftX;
312     }
313
314     //****************************************************
315     // The getMaximumX function returns the maximum    *
316     // X coordinate within the visible screen area.    *
317     //****************************************************
318     int getMaximumX()
319     {
320         return dbScreenWidth() - 1;
321     }
322
323     //****************************************************
324     // The getMaximumY function returns the maximum    *
325     // Y coordinate within the visible screen area.    *
326     //****************************************************
327     int getMaximumY()
328     {
329         return dbScreenHeight() - 1;
330     }
```

Figure 9-11 Example output of Program 9-5

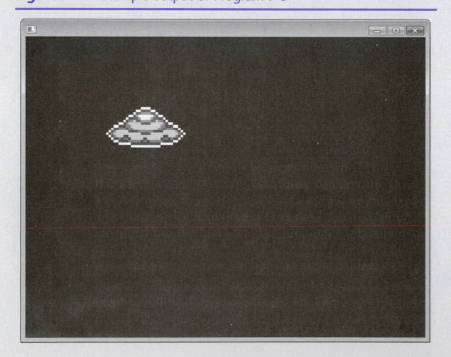

Checkpoint

9.1. How does a value-returning function differ from a `void` function?

9.2. What is the purpose of the `return` statement in a function?

9.3. Look at the following function definition:

```
int doSomething(int number)
{
    return number * 2;
}
```

a.   What is the name of the function?
b.   What type of data does the function return?
c.   Given the function definition, what will the following statement display?
`dbPrint( dbStr( doSomething(10) ) );`

9.4. What is a Boolean function?

9.2 Working with the Mouse

CONCEPT: The Dark GDK provides functions that your program can use to interact with the mouse.

The mouse is an important input device that most computer users are accustomed to using. The Dark GDK provides functions that you can use to work with the mouse. These functions allow you to track the mouse pointer's location on the screen, and determine when the user is pressing one of the mouse buttons.

Getting the Mouse Coordinates

You can call the `dbMouseX` and `dbMouseY` functions to get the current coordinates of the mouse pointer. The following code shows an example. Assume that `x` and `y` are `int` variables.

```
x = dbMouseX();
y = dbMouseY();
```

After this code executes, `x` will contain the mouse pointer's X coordinate and `y` will contain the mouse pointer's Y coordinate. Program 9-6 demonstrates how these functions work. The program uses a game loop that continuously gets the mouse pointer's coordinates (lines 27 and 28), and draws a circle that is centered around that location (line 32). This is shown in Figure 9-12. As the user moves the mouse pointer, the circle moves with it.

Program 9-6   (`CircleMouse.cpp`)

```cpp
1   // This program demonstrates how to get
2   // the mouse pointer's location.
3   #include "DarkGDK.h"
4
5   void DarkGDK()
6   {
7       // Constants
8       const int REFRESH_RATE = 60;
9       const int RADIUS = 50;
10
11      // Variables to hold the mouse pointer's
12      // X and Y coordinates.
13      int mouseX, mouseY;
14
15      // Disable auto refresh and set the
16      // refresh rate.
17      dbSyncOn();
18      dbSyncRate(REFRESH_RATE);
19
20      // Game loop
21      while ( LoopGDK() )
22      {
23          // Clear the screen.
24          dbCLS();
25
26          // Get the mouse pointer's location.
27          mouseX = dbMouseX();
28          mouseY = dbMouseY();
29
30          // Draw a circle centered around the
31          // mouse pointer's location.
32          dbCircle(mouseX, mouseY, RADIUS);
33
34          // Refresh the screen.
35          dbSync();
36      }
37  }
```

Figure 9-12 Example output of Program 9-6

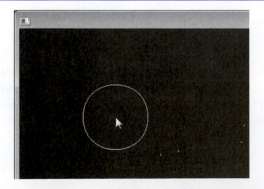

Showing, Hiding, and Positioning the Mouse

By default, the mouse pointer is visible when a Dark GDK program is running. You can control the mouse pointer's visibility, however, with the `dbHideMouse` and `dbShowMouse` functions. Here is the general format of how you call these functions:

```
dbHideMouse();
ShowMouse();
```

When you call the `dbHideMouse` function, the mouse pointer becomes invisible within the program's window. (When the user moves the mouse pointer outside the program's window, it becomes visible again.) When the mouse is hidden, it is still active within the program's window. For example, you can still call `dbMouseX` and `dbMouseY` to get its position. To make the mouse pointer visible again, you call the `dbShowMouse` function.

You can position the mouse pointer anywhere in the program's window, at any time, by calling the `dbPositionMouse` function. Here is the general format of how you call the function:

```
dbPositionMouse(X, Y);
```

The mouse pointer will be positioned at the coordinates specified by the arguments that you pass for *X* and *Y*. For example, the following statement will position the mouse pointer at the coordinates (620, 440).

```
dbPositionMouse(620, 440);
```

The following code shows an example that positions the mouse pointer at the center of the screen. In this code, we pass the expression `dbScreenWidth() / 2` for the *X* coordinate, and the expression `dbScreenHeight() / 2` for the *Y* coordinate.

```
dbPositionMouse( dbScreenWidth() / 2, dbScreenHeight() / 2);
```

Detecting Button Clicks

You can use the `dbMouseClick` function to determine whether the user is pressing a mouse button. On the typical PC, the mouse has at least two buttons—one on the left and one on the right. Some mice have more than two buttons, and the `dbMouseClick` function can detect up to four buttons.

The `dbMouseClick` function returns an integer that indicates which, if any, of the mouse buttons is being pressed. Here is a summary of the values that the function returns:

- 0 if no mouse button is being pressed
- 1 if the left mouse button is being pressed
- 2 if the right mouse button is being pressed
- 4 if the third mouse button is being pressed
- 8 if the fourth mouse button is being pressed

Program 9-7 demonstrates how you can detect mouse clicks. When the user clicks the left mouse button on a point in the window, the program draws a circle around that point. Notice that inside the game loop we do not clear the screen. As a result, the circles that are drawn by the user remain on the screen. Figure 9-13 shows an example of the program's output after the user has clicked the left mouse button several times at different locations.

Program 9-7   (MouseClick.cpp)

```
1   // This program demonstrates how to detect
2   // mouse clicks.
3   #include "DarkGDK.h"
4
5   void DarkGDK()
6   {
7       // Constants
8       const int REFRESH_RATE = 60;
9       const int RADIUS = 50;
10
11      // Variables to hold the mouse pointer's
12      // X and Y coordinates.
13      int mouseX, mouseY;
14
15      // Disable auto refresh and set the
16      // refresh rate.
17      dbSyncOn();
18      dbSyncRate(REFRESH_RATE);
19
20      // Game loop
21      while ( LoopGDK() )
22      {
23          // Get the mouse pointer's location.
24          mouseX = dbMouseX();
25          mouseY = dbMouseY();
26
27          // If the user is pressing the left mouse
28          // button, draw a circle at the mouse
29          // pointer's location.
30          if ( dbMouseClick() == 1 )
31          {
32              dbCircle(mouseX, mouseY, RADIUS);
33          }
34
35          // Refresh the screen.
36          dbSync();
37      }
38  }
```

 NOTE: If the user presses more than one mouse button at the same time, the dbMouseClick function returns the sum of those buttons' individual return values. For example, if the user is pressing both the left and right buttons, the dbMouseClick function returns the value 3. On a four-button mouse, if the user is pressing both the third and fourth buttons, the dbMouseClick function returns the value 12.

Figure 9-13 Example output of Program 9-7

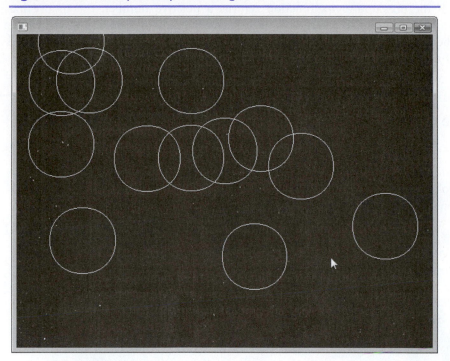

Displaying the System's Hourglass Pointer

Programs commonly change the mouse pointer to another image known as an *hourglass* when the program is busy performing a lengthy operation. Although the hourglass pointer doesn't look like an hourglass on all systems, the pointer's purpose is to give the user a visual cue that the program is busy. In a Dark GDK program, you can change the mouse to the system's hourglass pointer with the dbChangeMouse function. When you call the function, you pass the integer 1 to change the pointer to the hourglass, as shown here:

```
dbChangeMouse(1);
```

To change the pointer back to the system pointer, you call the dbChangeMouse function passing 0 as the argument, as shown here:

```
dbChangeMouse(0);
```

Getting Mouse Movement Distances

The Dark GDK provides two functions named dbMouseMoveX and dbMouseMoveY that return mouse movement distances. When you call the dbMouseMoveX function, it returns the distance, in pixels that the mouse has moved along the screen's *X* axis since the last time the function was called. The dbMouseMoveY function works similarly. It returns the distance, in pixels, that the mouse has moved along the screen's *Y* axis since the last time the function was called. Here is an example:

```
distanceX = dbMouseMoveX();
distanceY = dbMouseMoveY();
```

These functions can also be used to determine the direction that the mouse has moved. If the dbMouseMoveX function returns a positive number, the mouse has moved toward the right. If it returns a negative number, the mouse has moved to the left. If the dbMouseMoveY function returns a positive number, the mouse has moved down. If it returns a negative number, the mouse has moved up.

In the Spotlight:
Processing Full Mouse Clicks

Take a moment to run Program 9-7 (MouseClick.cpp) again, and see what happens if you hold down the mouse button while moving the pointer around on the screen. You should see a trail of circles being drawn, as shown in Figure 9-14.

Figure 9-14 Holding down the mouse button while running Program 9-7

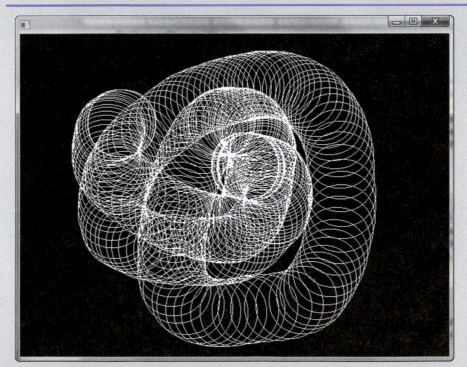

The program has this effect because the game loop simply determines whether the left mouse button is being pressed, and if so, draws a circle at the mouse pointer's location. As long as the user is holding down the left mouse button, the program draws circles.

In some situations, you might not want this behavior. When the user presses a mouse button, you might prefer to wait until the user releases the mouse button before performing an action. That would ensure that the action is performed only once per mouse click. (This is the way that most commercial applications work.)

For the purpose of discussion, let's use the term *full mouse click* to describe the action of pressing and releasing the mouse button. The Dark GDK does not provide a function to detect a full mouse click, so we will have to write our own function. The logic of detecting a full mouse click is as follows:

> *If the mouse button is pressed*
> > *Get the mouse pointer's XY coordinates*
> > *While the mouse button is being pressed*
> > > *Do nothing*

In the logic, we determine whether or not the mouse button is being pressed. If so, we get the mouse pointer coordinates, and then perform a loop that does nothing as long as the mouse button is being pressed. The purpose of the loop is to make the program wait until the mouse button is released before continuing.

The following code segment shows a function named `mouseFullClick`. The function returns `true` indicating that a full mouse click has been performed, or `false` otherwise. The function has two reference parameters, `x` and `y`. If the mouse button is pressed, the mouse pointer's coordinates will be stored in these parameters. (Just as we do with complete program listings, we've numbered the lines so we can discuss specific parts of the code.)

```
 1   bool mouseFullClick(int &x, int &y)
 2   {
 3       // Variable to hold the return value.
 4       bool buttonClick = false;
 5
 6       // If the mouse button is pressed, process
 7       // a full clicking action.
 8       if ( dbMouseClick() == 1 )
 9       {
10           // Get the mouse pointer coordinates.
11           x = dbMouseX();
12           y = dbMouseY();
13
14           // Wait for the user to release the
15           // mouse button.
16           while ( dbMouseClick() == 1)
17           {
18               // Do nothing in this loop.
19           }
20
21           // Set buttonClick to true.
22           buttonClick = true;
23       }
24
25       // Return true or false to indicate whether the
26       // mouse was clicked.
27       return buttonClick;
28   }
```

Let's take a closer look at the function. In line 4, we declare a local `bool` variable named `buttonClick`, and initialize it with `false`. This function will return `true` or `false` to indicate whether the mouse button was clicked, and we will use the `buttonClick` variable to hold that return value.

In line 8, we call `dbMouseClick` to determine whether the left mouse button is being pressed. If so, we do the following:

- In lines 11 and 12, we get the mouse pointer's coordinates and store those values in the x and y parameter variables. Recall that x and y are reference parameters, so these values will actually be stored in the variables that are passed as arguments to the function.
- In lines 16 through 19, we have a `while` loop that executes as long as the left mouse button is being pressed. There are no statements inside the loop, so it simply does nothing as long as the user is pressing the left mouse button.
- In line 22, we set the `buttonClick` variable to `true`, to indicate that the user clicked the mouse button.

The last statement, in line 27, returns the value of the `buttonClick` variable.

Program 9-8 demonstrates the function. This program draws a circle each time the user performs a full mouse click.

Program 9-8   **(FullMouseClick.cpp)**

```
 1   // This program demonstrates how to detect a full
 2   // mouse click, which is the action of pressing the
 3   // mouse button and then releasing it.
 4   #include "DarkGDK.h"
 5
 6   // Function prototype
 7   bool mouseFullClick(int &, int &);
 8
 9   void DarkGDK()
10   {
11       // Constants
12       const int REFRESH_RATE = 60;
13       const int RADIUS = 50;
14
15       // Variables to hold the mouse pointer's
16       // X and Y coordinates.
17       int mouseX, mouseY;
18
19       // Disable auto refresh and set the
20       // refresh rate.
21       dbSyncOn();
22       dbSyncRate(REFRESH_RATE);
23
24       // Game loop
25       while ( LoopGDK() )
26       {
```

```
27              // If the user has clicked the mouse
28              // button, draw a circle at the mouse
29              // pointer's location.
30              if ( mouseFullClick(mouseX, mouseY) )
31              {
32                  dbCircle(mouseX, mouseY, RADIUS);
33              }
34
35              // Refresh the screen.
36              dbSync();
37      }
38  }
39
40  //*********************************************************
41  // The mouseFullClick function processes a full mouse    *
42  // click. If the user is pressing the left mouse button  *
43  // it gets the mouse pointer's coordinates and then      *
44  // waits for the user to release the button. It returns  *
45  // true to indicate that the mouse was clicked, and the  *
46  // reference parameters are set to the mouse pointer's   *
47  // coordinates. If the user is not pressing the mouse    *
48  // button, the function returns false.                   *
49  //*********************************************************
50  bool mouseFullClick(int &x, int &y)
51  {
52      // Variable to hold the return value.
53      bool buttonClick = false;
54
55      // If the mouse button is pressed, process
56      // a full clicking action.
57      if ( dbMouseClick() == 1 )
58      {
59          // Get the mouse pointer coordinates.
60          x = dbMouseX();
61          y = dbMouseY();
62
63          // Wait for the user to release the
64          // mouse button.
65          while ( dbMouseClick() == 1)
66          {
67              // Do nothing in this loop.
68          }
69
70          // Set buttonClick to true.
71          buttonClick = true;
72      }
73
74      // Return true or false to indicate whether the
75      // mouse was clicked.
76      return buttonClick;
77  }
```

In the Spotlight:

Clicking Sprites

A common technique in games and graphics programs is to display an image that the user can click with the mouse. When the user clicks the image, an action takes place. One way to accomplish this is to create a sprite using the image, and then each time the user clicks the mouse button, determine whether the mouse pointer's coordinates are inside the sprite's bounding rectangle. We can make this determination if we know the *XY* coordinates of the sprite's upper-left corner and lower-right corner, as shown in Figure 9-15.

Figure 9-15 A sprite's upper-left and lower-right corner coordinates

Sprite's upper-left
XY coordinates

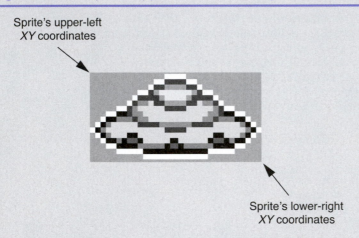

Sprite's lower-right
XY coordinates

Here is the logic that we use to determine whether the mouse pointer is within the sprite's bounding rectangle:

> *If the mouse's X coordinate is greater than or equal to the sprite's upper-left*
> *X coordinate, AND*
> *the mouse's Y coordinate is greater than or equal to the sprite's upper-left*
> *Y coordinate, AND*
> *the mouse's X coordinate is less than or equal to the sprite's lower-right*
> *X coordinate, AND*
> *the mouse's Y coordinate is less than or equal to the sprite's lower-right*
> *Y coordinate,*
> *Then*
> *the mouse pointer is inside the sprite's bounding rectangle.*
> *Else*
> *the mouse pointer is not inside the sprite's bounding rectangle.*

Program 9-9 demonstrates how we can do this. When the program starts, it displays an image of a penny. When the user clicks the penny with the mouse, it changes to a quarter. Figure 9-16 shows an example of the program's output.

Program 9-9   (`ClickCoin.cpp`)

```cpp
1    // This program demonstrates how to determine whether or not
2    // the user has clicked a sprite.
3    #include "DarkGDK.h"
4
5    // Constants
6    const int PENNY_IMAGE = 1;        // The penny's image number
7    const int QUARTER_IMAGE = 2;      // The quarter's image number
8    const int COIN_SPRITE = 1;        // The coin sprite number
9    const int COIN_X = 50;            // The coin sprite's X coordinate
10   const int COIN_Y = 50;            // The coin sprite's Y coordinate
11   const int REFRESH_RATE = 60;      // The refresh rate
12
13   // Function prototypes
14   void setUp();
15   bool onSprite(int, int, int);
16   bool mouseFullClick(int &, int &);
17
18   //*************************************************************
19   // DarkGDK function                                          *
20   //*************************************************************
21   void DarkGDK()
22   {
23       // Variables to hold the mouse pointer's
24       // X and Y coordinates.
25       int mouseX, mouseY;
26
27       // Perform setup operations.
28       setUp();
29
30       // Game loop
31       while ( LoopGDK() )
32       {
33           // Determine whether the user has clicked the
34           // left mouse button.
35           if ( mouseFullClick(mouseX, mouseY) )
36           {
37               // Determine whether the user clicked on the coin.
38               if ( onSprite(COIN_SPRITE, mouseX, mouseY) )
39               {
40                   // Replace the coin with the quarter image.
41                   dbSprite(COIN_SPRITE, COIN_X, COIN_Y, QUARTER_IMAGE);
42               }
43           }
44
45           // Refresh the screen.
46           dbSync();
47       }
48   }
49   //*************************************************************
50   // The setUp function performs setup operations.             *
51   //*************************************************************
52   void setUp()
53   {
```

```
54          // Set the key color to green.
55          dbSetImageColorKey(0, 255, 0);
56
57          // Load the coin images.
58          dbLoadImage("Penny.bmp", PENNY_IMAGE);
59          dbLoadImage("Quarter.bmp", QUARTER_IMAGE);
60
61          // Make the sprite, using the penny image.
62          dbSprite(COIN_SPRITE, COIN_X, COIN_Y, PENNY_IMAGE);
63
64          // Disable auto refresh and set the refresh rate.
65          dbSyncOn();
66          dbSyncRate(REFRESH_RATE);
67      }
68
69      //*************************************************************
70      // The onSprite function takes a sprite number and a set of  *
71      // XY coordinates as arguments. The function returns true     *
72      // if the coordinates are located on the sprite's bounding    *
73      // rectangle, or false otherwise.                             *
74      //*************************************************************
75      bool onSprite(int spriteNum, int pointX, int pointY)
76      {
77          // Variable to hold the value to return.
78          bool insideSprite;
79
80          // Get the X coordinate of the sprite's upper-left corner.
81          int upperX = dbSpriteX(spriteNum) - dbSpriteOffsetX(spriteNum);
82
83          // Get the Y coordinate of the sprite's upper-left corner.
84          int upperY = dbSpriteY(spriteNum) - dbSpriteOffsetY(spriteNum);
85
86          // Get the X coordinate of the sprite's lower-right corner.
87          int lowerX = upperX + dbSpriteWidth(spriteNum);
88
89          // Get the Y coordinate of the sprite's lower-right corner.
90          int lowerY = upperY + dbSpriteHeight(spriteNum);
91
92          // Determine whether (pointX, pointY) is inside the
93          // sprite's bounding rectangle.
94          if (pointX >= upperX && pointY >= upperY &&
95              pointX <= lowerX && pointY <= lowerY)
96          {
97              insideSprite = true;
98          }
99          else
100         {
101             insideSprite = false;
102         }
103
104         // Return the value of insideSprite.
105         return insideSprite;
106     }
107
```

```
108   //*********************************************************
109   // The mouseFullClick function processes a full mouse      *
110   // click. If the user is pressing the left mouse button    *
111   // it gets the mouse pointer's coordinates and then        *
112   // waits for the user to release the button. It returns    *
113   // true to indicate that the mouse was clicked, and the    *
114   // reference parameters are set to the mouse pointer's     *
115   // coordinates. If the user is not pressing the mouse      *
116   // button, the function returns false.                     *
117   //*********************************************************
118   bool mouseFullClick(int &x, int &y)
119   {
120       // Variable to hold the return value.
121       bool buttonClick = false;
122
123       // If the mouse button is pressed, process
124       // a full clicking action.
125       if ( dbMouseClick() == 1 )
126       {
127           // Get the mouse pointer coordinates.
128           x = dbMouseX();
129           y = dbMouseY();
130
131           // Wait for the user to release the
132           // mouse button.
133           while ( dbMouseClick() == 1)
134           {
135               // Do nothing in this loop.
136           }
137
138           // Set buttonClick to true.
139           buttonClick = true;
140       }
141
142       // Return true or false to indicate whether the
143       // mouse was clicked.
144       return buttonClick;
145   }
```

Figure 9-16 Output of Program 9-9

Before clicking   After clicking

Look at the Boolean function named onSprite, which is defined in lines 75 through 106. The function takes three arguments: a sprite number, an X coordinate, and a Y coordinate. If the XY coordinates are within the sprite's bounding rectangle, the function returns true. Otherwise, it returns false. It works like this: Line 81 gets the sprite's upper-left X coordinate, and line 84 gets the sprite's upper-left Y coordinate. Line 87 gets the sprite's lower-right X coordinate, and line 90 gets the sprite's lower-right Y coordinate. The if statement that starts in line 94 determines whether the coordinates that were passed as arguments are within the sprite's bounding rectangle. If so, the insideSprite variable is assigned true in line 97. Otherwise insideSprite is assigned false in line 101. The value of insideSprite is returned in line 105.

Inside the game loop, line 35 determines whether the user has clicked the left mouse button. (Notice that we are using the mouseFullClick function that was introduced in *In the Spotlight: Clicking Sprites*.) If so, the if statement in line 38 calls the onSprite function, passing the coin sprite's number and the mouse pointer's coordinates as arguments. If the mouse pointer is inside the sprite's bounding rectangle, the function returns true and the statement in line 41 changes the penny to a quarter.

In the Spotlight:
Creating a Custom Mouse Pointer

Creating a custom mouse pointer is a simple procedure:

1. Create a sprite with the image that you want to use for the mouse pointer.
2. Hide the regular mouse pointer.
3. In the game loop, get the mouse pointer's coordinates and move the sprite to that location.

Program 9-10 demonstrates how this is done. The program uses the image file HandPointer.bmp to create a sprite, which is then displayed at the mouse coordinates. Figure 9-17 shows the image.

Program 9-10   (CustomPointer.cpp)

```
1   // This program demonstrates how to use a sprite as
2   // a custom mouse pointer.
3   #include "DarkGDK.H"
4
5   // Constants
6   const int HAND_IMAGE = 1;        // Hand image number
7   const int HAND_SPRITE = 1;       // Hand sprite number
8   const int OFFSET_X = 13;         // Sprite X offset
9   const int OFFSET_Y = 0;          // Sprite Y offset
10  const int REFRESH_RATE = 60;     // Refresh rate
11
12  // Function prototype
13  void setUp();
14
```

```
15  //***************************************************************
16  // DarkGDK function                                             *
17  //***************************************************************
18  void DarkGDK()
19  {
20      // Variables to hold mouse coordinates
21      int mouseX, mouseY;
22
23      // Perform setup operations.
24      setUp();
25
26      // Game loop
27      while ( LoopGDK() )
28      {
29          // Get the mouse location.
30          mouseX = dbMouseX();
31          mouseY = dbMouseY();
32
33          // Update the sprite's location.
34          dbSprite(HAND_SPRITE, mouseX, mouseY, HAND_IMAGE);
35
36          // Refresh the screen.
37          dbSync();
38      }
39  }
40
41  //***************************************************************
42  // The setUp function performs setup operations.               *
43  //***************************************************************
44  void setUp()
45  {
46      // Set the key color to green.
47      dbSetImageColorKey(0, 255, 0);
48
49      // Load the hand image.
50      dbLoadImage("HandPointer.bmp", HAND_IMAGE);
51
52      // Get the mouse pointer location.
53      int mouseX = dbMouseX();
54      int mouseY = dbMouseY();
55
56      // Hide the mouse.
57      dbHideMouse();
58
59      // Display the sprite at the mouse pointer location.
60      dbSprite(HAND_SPRITE, mouseX, mouseY, HAND_IMAGE);
61
62      // Offset the sprite so its insertion point is at
63      // the finger's tip.
64      dbOffsetSprite(HAND_SPRITE, OFFSET_X, OFFSET_Y);
65
66      // Disable auto refresh and set the refresh rate.
67      dbSyncOn();
68      dbSyncRate(REFRESH_RATE);
69  }
```

Figure 9-17 Custom mouse pointer displayed by Program 9-10

 NOTE: In the bitmap file `HandPointer.bmp`, the tip of the index finger is located at (13, 0). In lines 62 through 64 of Program 9-10 we call the `dbOffsetSprite` function to offset the sprite's insertion point to these coordinates. That causes the tip of the index finger to be positioned at the mouse pointer's location.

 Checkpoint

9.5. How do you get the mouse pointer's current location on the screen?

9.6. How do you move the mouse pointer to a specific location on the screen?

9.7. How do you make the mouse invisible? Once you've made it invisible, how do you make it visible again?

9.8. How do you tell if the user is pressing a particular mouse button, such as the left button?

9.9. How do you tell if the user is pressing more than one mouse button simultaneously?

9.10. How do you change the mouse pointer to the hourglass pointer? How do you change it back to the regular system pointer?

 9.3 **The Bug Zapper Game**

In this section, we will look at a simple game that incorporates many of the topics that we have discussed in this chapter. The Bug Zapper game displays an animated sprite of a bug. The user zaps the bug by clicking it with the mouse. When this happens, a new bug appears at a random location on the screen. The game will run for 10 seconds before ending. The object of the game is to zap as many bugs as possible within the allotted time. When the game ends, a screen displays the number of bugs that were zapped.

Figure 9-18 shows some screens from the game. The intro screen shown in the top-left is displayed when the game begins. The user presses a key on the keyboard and a screen similar to the one in the top-right is displayed. The user zaps as many bugs as possible until time runs out. Then the bottom screen is displayed, showing the number of bugs that were zapped.

Figure 9-18 Screens from the Bug Zapper game

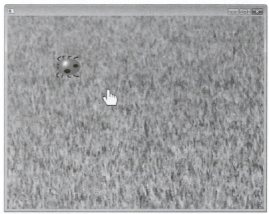

This figure also appears in this book's full-color insert.

Program 9-11 shows the code for the game, but rather than showing all of the code at once, we will show sections of it, with a description following each section. Lines 1 through 31 are shown first.

Program 9-11   (`BugZapper.cpp` *Partial Listing*)

```
1   // Bug Zapper Game
2   #include "DarkGDK.h"
3
4   // Constants
5   const int POINTER_IMAGE   = 1;   // Mouse pointer image number
6   const int BUG_IMAGE       = 2;   // Bug image number
7   const int INTRO_IMAGE     = 3;   // Intro screen image number
8   const int GRASS_IMAGE     = 4;   // Grass image number
9   const int POINTER_SPRITE  = 1;   // Pointer sprite number
10  const int BUG_SPRITE      = 2;   // Bug sprite number
```

```
11   const int OFFSET_X      = 13;         // Pointer sprite X offset
12   const int OFFSET_Y      = 0;          // Pointer sprite Y offset
13   const int ROWS          = 1;          // Animated sprite rows
14   const int COLS          = 2;          // Animated sprite columns
15   const int DELAY         = 500;        // Animation delay
16   const int MAX_TIME      = 10000;      // Max game time (10 seconds)
17   const int REFRESH_RATE  = 60;         // Refresh rate
18
19   // Function Prototypes
20   void setUp();
21   void displayIntro();
22   void initMouse();
23   void initBug();
24   void updateMouse();
25   void updateBug();
26   void generateNewBug();
27   int  elapsedTime(int);
28   void displayBugsZapped(int);
29   bool mouseFullClick(int &, int &);
30   bool onSprite(int, int, int);
31
```

These lines have the required #include directive, declare global constant declarations, and function prototypes. Here is a summary of the global constant declarations:

- The POINTER_IMAGE, BUG_IMAGE, INTRO_IMAGE, and GRASS_IMAGE constants will be used as image numbers for the mouse pointer image, the bug image, the intro screen image, and the grass background image.
- The POINTER_SPRITE and BUG_SPRITE constants will be used as sprite numbers for the mouse pointer sprite and the bug sprite.
- The OFFSET_X and OFFSET_Y constants will be used as the X and Y offset amounts for the mouse pointer sprite.
- The ROWS and COLS constants specify the number of rows and columns in the sprite sheet file that will be used for the bug.
- The DELAY constant specifies the amount of delay, in milliseconds, between each frame in the bug animation. The constant is initialized with the value 500, which specifies a half-second delay.
- The MAX_TIME constant specifies the number of milliseconds that the game will run. The constant is initialized with the value 10,000, which specifies 10 seconds.
- The REFRESH_RATE constant specifies the screen refresh rate.

Next, as Program 9-11 continues, the DarkGDK function, is shown:

Program 9-11   (Bugzapper.cpp *continued*)

```
32   //***************************************************
33   // The DarkGDK function                            *
34   //***************************************************
```

```
35   void DarkGDK()
36   {
37       // Variables to hold the mouse pointer coordinates
38       int mouseX, mouseY;
39
40       // Variable to keep count of the number
41       // of bugs zapped.
42       int bugsZapped = 0;
43
44       // Boolean flag to indicate whether the game is
45       // still playing. This is set to false when time
46       // runs out.
47       bool stillPlaying = true;
48
49       // Perform setup.
50       setUp();
51
52       // Get the current system time, in milliseconds.
53       int startTime = dbTimer();
54
55       // Game loop
56       while ( LoopGDK() && stillPlaying )
57       {
58           // Paste the grass background image.
59           dbPasteImage(GRASS_IMAGE, 0, 0);
60
61           // Update the mouse pointer.
62           updateMouse();
63
64           // Update the bug animation.
65           updateBug();
66
67           // Did the user click the mouse?
68           if ( mouseFullClick(mouseX, mouseY) )
69           {
70               // Was the mouse on the bug?
71               if ( onSprite(BUG_SPRITE, mouseX, mouseY) )
72               {
73                   // Update the count.
74                   bugsZapped++;
75
76                   // Generate a new bug.
77                   generateNewBug();
78               }
79           }
80
81           // See how many seconds we've been playing. If more
82           // than MAX_TIME, then time's up.
83           if ( elapsedTime(startTime) > MAX_TIME )
84           {
85               // Set the stillPlaying flag to false.
86               // This indicates that we are out of time.
87               stillPlaying = false;
88
89               // Display the number of bugs zapped.
```

```
90                     displayBugsZapped(bugsZapped);
91              }
92
93              // Refresh the screen.
94              dbSync();
95        }
96  }
97
```

In line 38 we declare the int variables mouseX and mouseY. These will be used to hold the mouse pointer's *XY* coordinates. In line 42 we declare the int variable bugZapped, which will hold the number of bugs that the user zaps. The bugZapped variable is initialized with 0. In line 47 we declare the bool variable stillPlaying, which will be used to indicate whether the game is still playing. When we run out of time, we will set the stillPlaying variable to false, as a signal that the game is over.

In line 50 we call the setUp function, which handles all of the image and sprite setup. It also seeds the random number generator, sets up the mouse, and displays the intro screen.

In line 53 we call the dbTimer function to get the internal system time and assign that value to the startTime variable. This is the time that the game officially begins. As the game plays we can continually get the system time and compare that value with the startTime variable. This will allow us to determine when the user's time is up.

The game loop begins in line 56. Notice that the loop tests a compound expression:

```
while ( LoopGDK() && stillPlaying )
```

The loop will execute as long as the LoopGDK function returns true and the stillPlaying variable contains true. In a moment you will see that the stillPlaying variable is set to false when the game's time is up. That will cause the game loop to stop.

Inside the game loop we perform the following actions:

- In line 59 we paste the grass background image to the screen.
- In line 62 we call the updateMouse function, which updates the position of the mouse's custom pointer.
- In line 65 we call the updateBug function, which displays the next frame of the bug animation.
- Line 68 is the beginning of an if statement that determines whether the user has clicked the mouse button. (We call the mouseFullClick function, which was introduced earlier in this chapter.) If the user did click the mouse, we have another if statement in line 71 that determines whether the mouse pointer is located on the bug sprite. If that is true, we add one to bugsZapped in line 74, and we call the generateNewBug function in line 77. The generateNewBug function causes the bug animation to appear at a new location on the screen.
- In line 83 we call the elapsedTime function, passing the startTime variable as an argument. The elapsedTime function gets the system time and returns the number of milliseconds that have elapsed since startTime. If this amount

of time is greater than MAX_TIME, then the game's time is up. If that is the case, we set stillPlaying to false in line 87, and then we call the displayBugsZapped function in line 90. The displayBugsZapped function takes an argument, which is the number of bugs zapped. It displays that value on the game's ending screen.

- In line 94 we call dbSync to refresh the screen.

The setUp function is shown next:

Program 9-11   (**Bugzapper.cpp** *continued*)

```
98   //*****************************************************
99   // The setUp function performs setup operations.      *
100  //*****************************************************
101  void setUp()
102  {
103      // Display the intro screen.
104      displayIntro();
105
106      // Seed the random number generator.
107      dbRandomize( dbTimer() );
108
109      // Set the key color.
110      dbSetImageColorKey(0, 255, 0);
111
112      // Initialize the mouse.
113      initMouse();
114
115      // Initialize the bug.
116      initBug();
117
118      // Load the grass background image.
119      dbLoadImage("Grass.bmp", GRASS_IMAGE);
120
121      // Disable auto refresh and set the refresh rate.
122      dbSyncOn();
123      dbSyncRate(REFRESH_RATE);
124  }
125
```

In line 104 we call the displayIntro function to display the intro screen, in line 107 we seed the random number generator, and in line 110 we set the key color for image transparency to green. In line 113 we call the initMouse function to initialize the mouse, and in line 116 we call the initBug function to create the animated sprite for the bug. In line 119 we load the grass image that is used as a background for the game, and in lines 122 through 123 we disable auto screen refresh and set the refresh rate.

The displayIntro function is shown next, which simply loads the intro screen image, pastes it to the screen, and waits for the user to press a key.

Program 9-11 (`Bugzapper.cpp` *continued*)

```
126   //****************************************************
127   // The displayIntro function displays the intro screen *
128   // and waits for the user to press a key.              *
129   //****************************************************
130   void displayIntro()
131   {
132       // Load the intro screen image.
133       dbLoadImage("Intro.bmp", INTRO_IMAGE);
134       dbPasteImage(INTRO_IMAGE, 0, 0);
135
136       // Wait for the user to press a key.
137       dbWaitKey();
138   }
139
```

The `initMouse` function is shown next:

Program 9-11 (`Bugzapper.cpp` *continued*)

```
140   //****************************************************
141   // The initMouse function initializes the mouse.      *
142   //****************************************************
143   void initMouse()
144   {
145       // Hide the mouse pointer.
146       dbHideMouse();
147
148       // Get the screen center point.
149       int centerX = dbScreenWidth() / 2;
150       int centerY = dbScreenHeight() / 2;
151
152       // Position the mouse at the center.
153       dbPositionMouse(centerX, centerY);
154
155       // Load the hand pointer image.
156       dbLoadImage("HandPointer.bmp", POINTER_IMAGE);
157
158       // Create the hand pointer sprite.
159       dbSprite(POINTER_SPRITE, centerX, centerY, POINTER_IMAGE);
160
161       // Offset the mouse pointer.
162       dbOffsetSprite(POINTER_SPRITE, OFFSET_X, OFFSET_Y);
163
164       // Set the pointer sprite's priority to 1 so it will
165       // always be drawn on top of the bug. (The bug will
166       // have a priority of 0.)
167       dbSetSpritePriority(POINTER_SPRITE, 1);
168   }
169
```

First, we hide the system mouse pointer in line 146. Then, we get the screen's center coordinates in lines 149 through 150. Next, we position the mouse to these coordinates in line 153.

Next, in line 156 we load the image that we will use as the mouse pointer, and in line 159 we create a sprite using that image. The sprite is positioned at the center of the screen, the same location as the mouse pointer.

In line 162 we offset the mouse pointer sprite's insertion point. The image that we are using for the mouse pointer is a hand with its index finger extended. This offset places the insertion point at the tip of the index finger.

In line 167 we set the mouse pointer sprite's priority to 1. This ensures that the mouse pointer sprite will be drawn on top of the bug sprite, which will have a priority of 0.

The `initBug` function is shown next:

Program 9-11   (`Bugzapper.cpp` *continued*)

```
170    //****************************************************
171    // The initBug function creates the animated sprite   *
172    // for the bug and places the first bug on the screen.*
173    //****************************************************
174    void initBug()
175    {
176        // Create the bug animated sprite.
177        dbCreateAnimatedSprite(BUG_SPRITE, "ShinyBug.bmp",
178                               COLS, ROWS, BUG_IMAGE);
179
180        // Make sure the sprite has a priority of 0
181        // so it will not be drawn on top of the
182        // mouse pointer.
183        dbSetSpritePriority(BUG_SPRITE, 0);
184
185        // Generate a bug at a random location.
186        generateNewBug();
187    }
188
```

The statement in lines 176 and 177 create the animated sprite for the bug. Line 183 sets the sprite's priority to 0. (A sprite's priority is 0 by default, but we explicitly set it to 0 here so anyone reading the code knows that this is happening.) Line 186 calls the `generateNewBug` function, which positions the bug at a random location on the screen.

The `updateMouse` function is shown next. This function simply gets the mouse pointer's current coordinates, and then displays the custom mouse pointer sprite at that location.

Program 9-11   (`Bugzapper.cpp` *continued*)

```
189    //********************************************************
190    // The updateMouse function moves the custom mouse    *
191    // to the mouse's current location.                   *
192    //********************************************************
193    void updateMouse()
194    {
195        // Get the mouse pointer's location.
196        int mouseX = dbMouseX();
197        int mouseY = dbMouseY();
198
199        // Move the hand pointer to the mouse location.
200        dbSprite(POINTER_SPRITE, mouseX, mouseY, POINTER_IMAGE);
201    }
202
```

The `updateBug` function is shown next. This function gets the bug sprite's current coordinates (lines 210 and 211), gets the next animation frame for the bug (line 214), and then displays the animation frame (line 215).

Program 9-11   (`Bugzapper.cpp` *continued*)

```
203    //********************************************************
204    // The updateBug function displays the next animation *
205    // frame for the bug.                                 *
206    //********************************************************
207    void updateBug()
208    {
209        // Get the bug's location.
210        int bugX = dbSpriteX(BUG_SPRITE);
211        int bugY = dbSpriteY(BUG_SPRITE);
212
213        // Play the bug animation.
214        dbPlaySprite(BUG_SPRITE, ROWS, COLS, DELAY);
215        dbSprite(BUG_SPRITE, bugX, bugY, BUG_IMAGE);
216    }
217
```

The `generateNewBug` function is shown next:

Program 9-11   (`Bugzapper.cpp` *continued*)

```
218    //********************************************************
219    // The generateNewBug function generates a new bug at *
220    // a random location.                                 *
221    //********************************************************
```

```
222   void generateNewBug()
223   {
224       // Get the screen dimensions.
225       int screenWidth = dbScreenWidth();
226       int screenHeight = dbScreenHeight();
227
228       // Get the bug's width and height.
229       int bugWidth = dbSpriteWidth(BUG_SPRITE);
230       int bugHeight = dbSpriteHeight(BUG_SPRITE);
231
232       // Generate a new location.
233       int x = dbRND(screenWidth - bugWidth);
234       int y = dbRND(screenHeight - bugHeight);
235
236       // Put the bug at that location.
237       dbSprite(BUG_SPRITE, x, y, BUG_IMAGE);
238   }
239
```

In lines 225 and 226 we get the width and height of the screen. In lines 229 and 230 we get the width and height of the bug sprite. Then, in line 233 we generate a random number for the bug's *X* coordinate. We do not want the bug to be positioned offscreen, so we specify the maximum value for the random number with the expression `screenWidth - bugWidth`. In line 234 we perform a similar operation to generate a random number for the bug's *Y* coordinate. To prevent the bug from being positioned offscreen, we specify the maximum value for the random number with the expression `screenHeight - bugHeight`. In line 237 we display the bug sprite at the random coordinates.

The `elapsedTime` function is shown next:

Program 9-11   (`Bugzapper.cpp` *continued*)

```
240   //****************************************************
241   // The elapsedTime function accepts a previously taken *
242   // time reading as an argument and returns the number *
243   // of milliseconds that have elapsed since that time. *
244   //****************************************************
245   int elapsedTime(int startTime)
246   {
247       return dbTimer() - startTime;
248   }
249
```

The purpose of the `elapsedTime` function is to accept an argument specifying a time in milliseconds, and return the number of milliseconds that have elapsed since that time. The function does this by subtracting the argument from the current system time (gotten via the `dbTimer` function). The result is returned.

The `displayBugsZapped` function is shown next:

Program 9-11   (`Bugzapper.cpp` *continued*)

```
250  //*********************************************************
251  // The displayBugsZapped function displays the closing   *
252  // screen showing the number of bugs zapped. The number  *
253  // of bugs is passed as an argument.                      *
254  //*********************************************************
255  void displayBugsZapped(int bugs)
256  {
257      // Get the center coordinates.
258      int centerX = dbScreenWidth() / 2;
259      int centerY = dbScreenHeight() / 2;
260
261      // Enable auto refresh.
262      dbSyncOff();
263
264      // Delete all sprites.
265      dbDeleteSprite(BUG_SPRITE);
266      dbDeleteSprite(POINTER_SPRITE);
267
268      // Clear the screen.
269      dbCLS();
270
271      // Display the number of bugs zapped.
272      dbCenterText(centerX, centerY, "Number of bugs zapped:");
273      dbCenterText(centerX, centerY + 20, dbStr(bugs));
274      dbCenterText(centerX, centerY + 40, "Press any key...");
275
276      // Wait for the user to press a key.
277      dbWaitKey();
278
279      // Disable auto refresh.
280      dbSyncOn();
281  }
282
```

The purpose of the `displayBugsZapped` function is to display the game's ending screen that shows the number of bugs the user zapped. The number of bugs zapped is passed to the function as an argument.

Lines 258 and 259 calculate the coordinates of the screen's center. Line 262 enables auto screen refresh. Lines 265 and 266 delete the bug and mouse pointer sprites. Line 269 clears the screen, and then lines 272 through 274 display the message showing the number of bugs zapped. Line 277 waits for the user to press a key, and line 280 disables auto screen refresh.

The `mouseFullClick` function is shown next. This function, which we discussed earlier in the chapter, detects a full mouse click (button down and then released) and stores the mouse's coordinates in the function's reference parameters. (See *In the Spotlight: Processing Full Mouse Clicks* for more details about this function.)

Program 9-11   (`Bugzapper.cpp` *continued*)

```
283   //**********************************************************
284   // The mouseFullClick function processes a full mouse    *
285   // click. If the user is pressing the left mouse button  *
286   // it gets the mouse pointer's coordinates and then      *
287   // waits for the user to release the button. It returns  *
288   // true to indicate that the mouse was clicked, and the  *
289   // reference parameters are set to the mouse pointer's   *
290   // coordinates. If the user is not pressing the mouse    *
291   // button, the function returns false.                   *
292   //**********************************************************
293   bool mouseFullClick(int &x, int &y)
294   {
295       // Variable to hold the return value.
296       bool buttonClick = false;
297
298       // If the mouse button is pressed, process
299       // a full clicking action.
300       if ( dbMouseClick() == 1 )
301       {
302           // Get the mouse pointer coordinates.
303           x = dbMouseX();
304           y = dbMouseY();
305
306           // Wait for the user to release the
307           // mouse button.
308           while ( dbMouseClick() == 1)
309           {
310               // Do nothing in this loop.
311           }
312
313           // Set buttonClick to true.
314           buttonClick = true;
315       }
316
317       // Return true or false to indicate whether the
318       // mouse was clicked.
319       return buttonClick;
320   }
321
```

The onSprite function is shown next. This function, which we also discussed earlier in the chapter, returns true or false to indicate whether a set of coordinates are located within a sprite's bounding rectangle. (See *In the Spotlight: Clicking Sprites* for more details about this function.)

Program 9-11   (`Bugzapper.cpp` continued)

```
322    //*************************************************************
323    // The onSprite function takes a sprite number and a set of   *
324    // XY coordinates as arguments. The function returns true      *
325    // if the coordinates are located on the sprite's bounding     *
326    // rectangle, or false otherwise.                              *
327    //*************************************************************
328    bool onSprite(int spriteNum, int pointX, int pointY)
329    {
330        // Variable to hold the value to return.
331        bool insideSprite;
332
333        // Get the X coordinate of the sprite's upper-left corner.
334        int upperX = dbSpriteX(spriteNum) - dbSpriteOffsetX(spriteNum);
335
336        // Get the Y coordinate of the sprite's upper-left corner.
337        int upperY = dbSpriteY(spriteNum) - dbSpriteOffsetY(spriteNum);
338
339        // Get the X coordinate of the sprite's lower-right corner.
340        int lowerX = upperX + dbSpriteWidth(spriteNum);
341
342        // Get the Y coordinate of the sprite's lower-right corner.
343        int lowerY = upperY + dbSpriteHeight(spriteNum);
344
345        // Determine whether (pointX, pointY) is inside the
346        // sprite's bounding rectangle.
347        if (pointX >= upperX && pointY >= upperY &&
348            pointX <= lowerX && pointY <= lowerY)
349        {
350            insideSprite = true;
351        }
352        else
353        {
354            insideSprite = false;
355        }
356
357        // Return the value of insideSprite.
358        return insideSprite;
359    }
```

Review Questions

Multiple Choice

1. The _____ is the part of a function definition that specifies a function's return type.
   a. header
   b. footer
   c. body
   d. return statement

2. _____ causes a function to end and sends a value back to the part of the program that called the function.
   a. `end`
   b. `send`
   c. `exit`
   d. `return`

3. A function type that returns either true or false is _____.
   a. `binary`
   b. `TrueFalse`
   c. `bool`
   d. `logical`

4. _____ return the mouse pointer's *X* and *Y* coordinates.
   a. `dbMousePositionX` and `dbMousePositionY`
   b. `dbMouseX` and `dbMouseY`
   c. `dbMX` and `dbMY`
   d. `dbMouseAcross` and `dbMouseDown`

5. _____ make the mouse pointer visible or invisible.
   a. `dbAddMouse` and `dbRemoveMouse`
   b. `dbMouseVisible` and `dbMouseInvisible`
   c. `dbShowMouse` and `dbHideMouse`
   d. `dbMouseReveal` and `dbMouseCloak`

6. The `dbMouseClick` function returns _____ if the left mouse button is being pressed.
   a. `0`
   b. `1`
   c. `2`
   d. `-1`

7. The `dbMouseClick` function returns _____ if both the left and right mouse buttons are being pressed.
   a. `12`
   b. `10`
   c. `20`
   d. `3`

8. You would use _____ to move the mouse pointer to (100, 50).
   a. `dbMouseX(100); dbMouseY(50);`
   b. `dbPositionMouse(100, 50);`
   c. `dbMoveMouse(100, 50);`
   d. `dbMouseXY(100, 50);`

9. You use _____ to change the mouse pointer to an hourglass.
   a. `dbChangeMouse`
   b. `dbHourglassMouse`
   c. `dbHourglass`
   d. `dbSetMouseHourglass`

10. _____ gets the distance that the mouse pointer has moved along the screen's *X* axis since the last time the function was called.
    a. `dbMouseDistanceX`
    b. `dbMouseX`
    c. `dbMouseMoveX`
    d. `dbLastDistanceX`

True or False

1. A value-returning function must have a `return` statement.

2. The `dbMouseClick` function returns a non-zero value if the user has pressed and then released the mouse button.

3. When you make the mouse pointer invisible in your Dark GDK program, it will become visible again when the user moves it outside the program's window.

4. You use the `dbMouseX` function to set the mouse's *X* coordinate to a specific location.

5. The `dbMouseMoveY` function moves the mouse a specific distance along the screen's *Y* axis.

Short Answer

1. What is the difference between a `void` function and a value-returning function?

2. How do you get the current location of the mouse pointer on the screen?

3. If the user is pressing one of the mouse buttons, how do you tell which one is being pressed?

4. How do you tell if the user is pressing more than one mouse button simultaneously?

Algorithm Workbench

1. The following statement calls a function named `half`. The `half` function returns a value that is half that of the argument. (Assume both the `result` and `number` variables are `float`.) Write the function definition for the `half` function.

   ```
   result = half(number);
   ```

2. A program contains the following function definition:

   ```
   int cube(int num)
   {
       return num * num * num;
   }
   ```
   Write a statement that passes the value 4 to this function and assigns its return value to the variable `result`.

3. Write the code for a function named `timesTen` that accepts an `int` argument. When the function is called, it should return the value of its argument multiplied times 10.

4. Write code that changes the mouse pointer to the hourglass pointer, waits two seconds, and then changes it back to the system pointer.

5. Write code that detects when the left mouse button is pressed, and then displays the message "Can I help you?" when the button is released.

Programming Exercises

1. **Color Addition**
   Write a function named addColors that adds two colors together to produce a third color. The function should work like this:

   - It should accept two DWORD color values as arguments.
   - Extract each argument's red, green, and blue components.
   - Add the two red components. The sum is the third color's red component.
   - Add the two green components. The sum is the third color's green component.
   - Add the two blue components. The sum is the third color's blue component.
   - Use the third color's red, green, and blue components to produce a DWORD value.
   - Return the third color's DWORD value.

   Demonstrate the function in a program that displays three boxes. The colors of the first two boxes should be randomly generated. (See the randomColor function that was demonstrated in this chapter.) Pass the colors of these two boxes as arguments to the addColors function. The value that is returned from the function should be used as the third box's color.

2. **Coin Toss**
   Write a function named coinToss that returns a random number in the range of 0 through 1. Demonstrate the function in a program that simulates the tossing of a coin. The program should wait for the user to press a key, and then call the coinToss function. If the function returns 0, the program should display the image of a coin with heads facing up. If the function returns 1, the program should display the image of a coin with tails facing up. (You can create your own coin images, or use the ones provided in the book's online resources, downloadable from www.aw.com/gaddis.)

3. **PizzaBot Modification**
   Modify the PizzaBot game that is presented in Chapter 7 so the robot will not move outside of the visible area of the screen.

4. **Mouse Crosshairs**
   Write a program that tracks the movement of the mouse cursor with a set of crosshairs. Figure 9-19 shows an example. As the user moves the mouse pointer, the crosshairs should move with it.

Figure 9-19 Mouse crosshairs example

5. **Custom Mouse Pointers**
   Design a set of two custom mouse pointers: one that is to be displayed when no buttons are being pressed, and another that is to be displayed when the left button is pressed. Demonstrate the pointers in a program.

6. **Mouse Rollover**
   Write a program that displays an image. When the user moves the mouse pointer over the image, it should change to a second image. The second image should remain displayed as long as the mouse pointer is over it. When the user moves the mouse pointer away from the image, it should change back to the first image.

7. **Change for a Dollar Game**
   The book's online resources (downloadable from www.aw.com/gaddis) provide images of a penny, nickel, dime, and quarter. Create a game that displays each of these images, plus another image showing the text Count Change. The game should let the user click any of the coins, in any order. To win the game, the user must click the coins that, when added together, equal $1. When the user clicks the Count Change image the program should show the amount of money that the user clicked. If the amount equals $1 the program should indicate that the user won the game.

Programming Exercises **471**

8. **Rock, Paper, Scissors Game**

   Write a program that lets the user play the game of Rock, Paper, Scissors against the computer. The program should work as follows:

   1. When the program begins, a random number in the range of 0 through 2 is generated. If the number is 0, then the computer has chosen rock. If the number is 1, then the computer has chosen paper. If the number is 2, then the computer has chosen scissors. (Don't display the computer's choice yet.)

   2. To make his or her selection, the user clicks an image on the screen. (You can find images for this game included in the book's online resources at www.aw.com/gaddis.)

   3. The computer's choice is displayed.

   4. A winner is selected according to the following rules:

      • If one player chooses rock and the other player chooses scissors, then rock wins. (Rock smashes scissors.)

      • If one player chooses scissors and the other player chooses paper, then scissors wins. (Scissors cuts paper.)

      • If one player chooses paper and the other player chooses rock, then paper wins. (Paper wraps rock.)

      • If both players make the same choice, the game ends in a tie.

10 Arrays and Tile Mapping

TOPICS

10.1 Array Basics

10.2 Sorting Arrays

10.3 Two-Dimensional Arrays

10.4 Tile Maps

10.1 Array Basics

CONCEPT: In the programs you have designed so far, you have used variables to store data in memory. The simplest way to store a value in memory is to store it in a variable. Variables work well in many situations, but they have limitations.

For example, they can hold only one value at a time. Consider the following variable declaration:

```
int number = 99;
```

This statement declares an `int` variable named `number`, initialized with the value 99. Consider what happens if the following statement appears later in the program:

```
number = 5;
```

This statement assigns the value 5 to the variable `number`, replacing the value 99 that was previously stored there. Because `number` is an ordinary variable, it can hold only one value at a time.

Because variables hold only a single value, they can be cumbersome in programs that process sets of data. For example, suppose you are writing a program that will draw a bar chart comparing 20 different values. Imagine declaring 20 variables to hold each of those values:

```
int value1;
int value2;
int value3;
```

and so on...

```
int value20;
```

473

Then, imagine writing the code that allows the user to input all 20 values:

```
// Get the first value.
dbPrint "Enter value #1."
value1 = atoi( dbInput() );

// Get the second value.
dbPrint "Enter value #2."
value2 = atoi( dbInput() );

// Get the third value.
dbPrint "Enter value #3."
value3 = atoi( dbInput() );
```

and so on...

```
// Get the twentieth value.
dbPrint "Enter value #20."
value20 = atoi( dbInput() );
```

As you can see, variables are not well suited for storing and processing sets of data. Each variable is a separate item that must be declared and individually processed. Fortunately, you can create *arrays*, which are specifically designed for storing and processing sets of data. Like a variable, an array is a named storage location in memory. Unlike a variable, an array can hold a group of values. All of the values in an array must be the same data type. You can have an array of `int` values, an array of `float` values, an array of `DWORD` values, and so forth, but you cannot store a mixture of data types in an array. Here is an example of how you can declare an `int` array:

```
int values[20];
```

Notice that this statement looks like a regular `int` variable declaration except for the number inside the brackets. The number inside the brackets is known as a *size declarator*. The size declarator specifies the number of values that the array can hold. This statement declares an array named `values` that can hold 20 integer values. The array size declarator must be a nonnegative integer. Here is another example:

```
float salesAmounts[7];
```

This statement declares an array named `salesAmounts` that can hold 7 `float` values. The following statement shows one more example. This statement declares an array that can hold 50 `DWORD` values. The name of the array is `colors`.

```
DWORD colors[50];
```

An array's size cannot be changed while the program is running. If you have written a program that uses an array, and then find that you must change the array's size, you have to change the array's size declarator in the source code. Then you must recompile the program with the new size declarator. To make array sizes easier to maintain, many programmers prefer to use named constants as array size declarators. Here is an example:

```
const int SIZE = 20;
int values[SIZE];
```

As you will see later in this chapter, many array processing techniques require you to refer to the array's size. When you use a named constant as an array's size declarator, you can use the constant to refer to the size of the array in your algorithms. If you ever need to modify the program so that the array is a different size, you only need to change the value of the named constant.

Array Elements and Subscripts

The storage locations in an array are known as *elements*. In memory, an array's elements are located in consecutive memory locations. Each element in an array is assigned a unique number known as a *subscript*. Subscripts are used to identify specific elements in an array. In C++, the first element is assigned the subscript 0, the second element is assigned the subscript 1, and so forth. For example, suppose we have the following declarations in a program:

```
const int SIZE = 5;
int numbers[SIZE];
```

As shown in Figure 10-1, the `numbers` array has five elements. The elements are assigned the subscripts 0 through 4. (Because subscript numbering starts at zero, the subscript of the last element in an array is one less than the total number of elements in the array.)

Figure 10-1 Array subscripts

```
const int SIZE = 5;
int numbers[SIZE];
```

| Element 0 | Element 1 | Element 2 | Element 3 | Element 4 |

Assigning Values to Array Elements

You access the individual elements in an array by using their subscripts. For example, assuming `numbers` is the `int` array previously described, the following code assigns values to each of its five elements:

```
numbers[0] = 20;
numbers[1] = 30;
numbers[2] = 40;
numbers[3] = 50;
numbers[4] = 60;
```

This code assigns the value 20 to element 0, the value 30 to element 1, and so forth. Figure 10-2 shows the contents of the array after these statements execute.

NOTE: The expression `numbers[0]` is pronounced "numbers sub zero."

Figure 10-2 Values assigned to each element

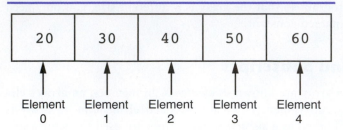

You can read values from the keyboard and store them in an array element as you can with a regular variable. Program 10-1 demonstrates this. The program asks the user to enter a radius for three different circles. The values entered for each are stored in an array, and then the array elements are used to draw the circles. Figure 10-3 shows an example of the program's output, where the user entered the values 50, 100, and 150 as the three radii.

Program 10-1   (`ArrayDemo.cpp`)

```
1   // This program provides a simple array demonstration.
2   #include "DarkGDK.h"
3
4   void DarkGDK()
5   {
6       // Declare a constant for the number of circles.
7       const int NUM_CIRCLES = 3;
8
9       // Declare an array to hold the circle radii.
10      int radius[NUM_CIRCLES];
11
12      // Declare variables for the XY coordinates.
13      int x, y;
14
15      // Get the radius for the first circle.
16      dbPrint("Enter the radius for the first circle:");
17      radius[0] = atoi( dbInput() );
18
19      // Get the radius for the second circle.
20      dbPrint("Enter the radius for the second circle:");
21      radius[1] = atoi( dbInput() );
22
23      // Get the radius for the third circle.
24      dbPrint("Enter the radius for the third circle:");
25      radius[2] = atoi( dbInput() );
26
27      // Get the screen's center.
28      x = dbScreenWidth() / 2;
29      y = dbScreenHeight() / 2;
30
31      // Draw the three circles around the center point.
```

```
32        dbCircle(x, y, radius[0]);
33        dbCircle(x, y, radius[1]);
34        dbCircle(x, y, radius[2]);
35
36        // Wait for the user to press a key.
37        dbWaitKey();
38   }
```

Figure 10-3 Output of Program 10-1

Let's take a closer look at the program. A named constant, NUM_CIRCLES is declared in line 7 and initialized with the value 3. Then, an int array named radius is declared in line 10. The NUM_CIRCLES constant is used as the array size declarator, so the radius array will have three elements. Line 13 declares two int variables, x and y, to hold XY coordinate values.

The statements in lines 17, 21, and 25 read values from the keyboard and store those values in the elements of the radius array. The statements in lines 28 and 29 calculate the coordinates for the screen's center point. Then, the dbCircle statements in lines 32 through 34 draw the three circles using the values stored in the array as the circle radii. The first circle is drawn in line 32 with the value of radius[0] as the radius. The second circle is drawn in line 33 with the value of radius[1] as the radius. The third circle is drawn in line 34 with the value of radius[2] as the radius.

In the example, the user entered the values 50, 100, and 150, which were stored in the radius array. Figure 10-4 shows the contents of the array after these values are stored in it.

Figure 10-4 Contents of the `radius` array

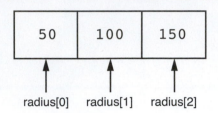

No Array Bounds Checking in C++

The C++ language does not perform *array bounds checking*, which means the C++ compiler does not check the values that you use as array subscripts to make sure they are valid. For example, look at the following code:

```
// Create an array
const int SIZE = 5;
int numbers[SIZE];

// ERROR! This statement uses an invalid subscript!
numbers[5] = 99;
```

This code declares an array with five elements. The subscripts for the array's elements are 0 through 4. The last statement, however, attempts to assign a value to `numbers[5]`, a nonexistent element. If this code were part of a complete program, it would compile and execute. When the assignment statement executes, however, it will attempt to write the value 99 to an invalid location in memory. This is an error and will most likely cause the program to crash.

Using a Loop to Step through an Array

In C++ you can store a number in a variable, and then use that variable as an array subscript. This makes it possible to use a loop to step through an entire array, performing the same operation on each element. For example, look at the following code:

```
// Declare a constant for the array size.
const int SIZE = 10;

// Declare an array.
int numbers[SIZE];

// Set each array element to 100.
for (int index = 0; index < SIZE; index++)
{
    numbers[index] = 100;
}
```

This code declares an `int` array named `numbers`, with 10 elements. In the `for` loop, the `index` variable is initialized with the value 0, and is incremented at the end of each iteration. The loop iterates as long as `index` is less than `SIZE`. As a result, the loop will iterate 10 times. As it iterates, the index variable will be assigned the values 0 through 9.

The first time the loop iterates, index is set to 0, so the statement inside the loop assigns 100 to the array element numbers[0]. The second time the loop iterates, index is set to 1, so the statement inside the loop assigns 100 to the array element numbers[1]. This continues until the last loop iteration, in which 100 is assigned to numbers[9].

> **NOTE:** We should emphasize the fact that the loop shown in the previous code iterates as long as index *is less than* SIZE. Remember, the subscript of the last element in an array is one less than the size of the array. In this case, the subscript of the last element of the numbers array is 9, which is one less than SIZE. It would be an error to write the loop as shown in the following:
>
> ```cpp
> // Declare a constant for the array size.
> const int SIZE = 10;
>
> // Declare an array.
> int numbers[SIZE];
>
> // ERROR! This loop writes outside the array!
> for (int index = 0; index <= SIZE; index++)
> {
>     numbers[index] = 100;
> }
> ```
>
> Can you spot the error in this code? The for loop iterates as long as index is less than or equal to SIZE. The last time the loop iterates, the index variable will be set to 10 and the statement inside the loop will try to assign the value 100 to numbers[10], which is a nonexistent element.

Let's look at another example. Program 10-2 shows how we can redesign Program 10-1 to use two for loops: one for inputting the values into the array and the other for drawing the circles. Figure 10-5 shows an example of the program's output.

Program 10-2   (ArrayLoopDemo.cpp)

```cpp
1  // This program provides a simple array demonstration.
2  #include "DarkGDK.h"
3
4  void DarkGDK()
5  {
6      // Declare a constant for the number of circles.
7      const int NUM_CIRCLES = 3;
8
9      // Declare an array to hold the circle radii.
10     int radius[NUM_CIRCLES];
11
```

```
12          // Declare variables for the XY coordinates.
13          int x, y;
14
15          // Tell the user what we are doing.
16          dbPrint("Enter three radii and I will draw three circles.");
17
18          // Get the radius for each circle.
19          for (int index = 0; index < NUM_CIRCLES; index++)
20          {
21              dbPrint("Enter a radius:");
22              radius[index] = atoi( dbInput() );
23          }
24
25          // Get the screen's center.
26          x = dbScreenWidth() / 2;
27          y = dbScreenHeight() / 2;
28
29          // Draw the three circles around the center point.
30          for (int index = 0; index < NUM_CIRCLES; index++)
31          {
32              dbCircle(x, y, radius[index]);
33          }
34
35          // Wait for the user to press a key.
36          dbWaitKey();
37      }
```

Figure 10-5 Output of Program 10-2

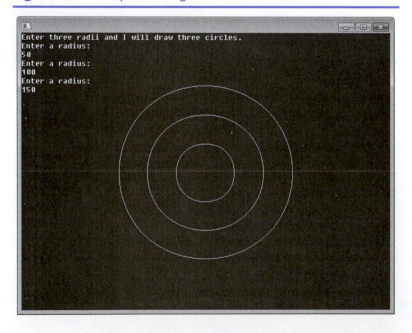

Let's take a closer look at the first `for` loop, which appears in lines 19 through 23. Here is the first line of the loop:

```
for (int index = 0; index < NUM_CIRCLES; index++)
```

This specifies that the `index` variable will be initialized with the value 0, and will be incremented at the end of each iteration. The loop will iterate as long as `index` is less than `NUM_CIRCLES`. As a result, the `index` variable will be assigned the values 0 through 2 as the loop executes. Inside the loop, in line 22, the `index` variable is used as a subscript:

```
radius[index] = atoi( dbInput() );
```

During the loop's first iteration, the `index` variable will be set to 0, so the user's input is stored in `radius[0]`. During the next iteration, the user's input is stored in `radius[1]`. Then, during the last iteration the user's input is stored in `radius[2]`. Notice that the loop correctly starts and ends the `index` variable with valid subscript values (0 through 2).

The second `for` loop appears in lines 30 through 33. This loop also uses a variable named `index`, which takes on the values 0 through 2 as the loop iterates. The first time the loop iterates, the statement in line 32 draws a circle using `radius[0]` as the radius. The second time the loop iterates, the statement draws a circle using `radius[1]` as the radius. The third time the loop iterates, the statement draws a circle using `radius[2]` as the radius.

Array Initialization

You can optionally initialize an array with values when you declare it. Here is an example:

```
const int SIZE = 5;
int numbers[SIZE] = { 10, 20, 30, 40, 50 };
```

The series of values separated with commas and enclosed inside curly braces is called an *initialization list*. These values are stored in the array elements in the order they appear in the list. (The first value, 10, is stored in `numbers[0]`; the second value, 20, is stored in `numbers[1]`, and so forth). Program 10-3 shows another example. The program draws 10 lines, and the coordinates for each line's endpoints are stored in four arrays:

- The `startX` array is initialized in lines 12 and 13 with each line's starting *X* coordinate.
- The `startY` array is initialized in lines 17 and 18 with each line's starting *Y* coordinate.
- The `endX` array is initialized in lines 22 and 23 with each line's ending *X* coordinate.
- The `endY` array is initialized in lines 27 and 28 with each line's ending *Y* coordinate.

The program's output is shown in Figure 10-6.

Program 10-3   **(LineArrays.cpp)**

```
1   // This program draws 10 lines. The line's coordinates are
2   // stored in arrays.
3   #include "DarkGDK.h"
4
5   void DarkGDK()
6   {
7       // Declare a constant for the array sizes.
8       const int SIZE = 10;
9
10      // Declare and initialize an array containing
11      // the starting X coordinate for each line.
12      int startX[SIZE] = { 100, 150, 200, 250, 300,
13                           350, 400, 450, 500, 550 };
14
15      // Declare and initialize an array containing
16      // the starting Y coordinate for each line.
17      int startY[SIZE] = {   0,  10,  20,  40,  60,
18                            80, 100, 120, 140, 160 };
19
20      // Declare and initialize an array containing
21      // the ending X coordinate for each line.
22      int endX[SIZE]   = { 550, 500, 450, 400, 350,
23                           300, 250, 200, 150, 100 };
24
25      // Declare and initialize an array containing
26      // the ending Y coordinate for each line.
27      int endY[SIZE]   = { 390, 400, 410, 420, 430,
28                           440, 450, 460, 470, 480 };
29
30      // Use the arrays to draw lines.
31      for (int index = 0; index < SIZE; index++)
32      {
33          dbLine(startX[index], startY[index],
34                 endX[index], endY[index]);
35      }
36
37      // Wait for the user to press a key.
38      dbWaitKey();
39  }
```

Let's take a closer look at the for loop that appears in lines 31 through 35. Here is the first line of the loop:

```
for (int index = 0; index < SIZE; index++)
```

The first time through the loop, index will be set to 0. The second time through the loop, index will be set to 1. This continues until the last iteration, in which index is set to 9. Inside the loop, lines 33 and 34 call the dbLine function to draw a line:

```
dbLine(startX[index], startY[index],
       endX[index], endY[index]);
```

Figure 10-6 Output of Program 10-3

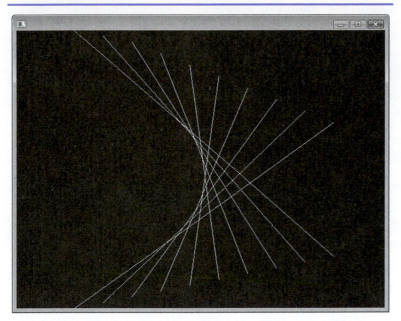

During the first loop iteration, `index` will equal 0, so this statement draws a line from (100, 0) to (550, 390). During the second loop iteration, index will equal 1, so this statement draws a line from (150, 10) to (500, 400). This continues until all of the values stored in the arrays have been used as line coordinates.

DWORD Color Arrays

Program 10-4 demonstrates how you can create a DWORD array to hold color values. Lines 7 through 10 declare constants for the colors red, green, blue, and magenta. Then, line 19 creates a DWORD array named colors. The colors array has four elements, initialized with the color constants. Inside the game loop, line 31 gets a random number in the range of 0 through 3 and assigns it to the index variable. In line 34, the index variable is used as a subscript to get an element of the colors array, and that value is passed as an argument to the dbCLS function. As a result, the screen is cleared to a color that is randomly selected from the colors array. The program clears the screen to a randomly selected color every half a second.

Program 10-4   **(ColorArray.cpp)**

```
1    // This program demonstrates an array of colors.
2    #include "DarkGDK.h"
3
4    void DarkGDK()
5    {
6        // Color constants
7        const DWORD RED        = dbRGB(255, 0, 0);
```

```
 8      const DWORD GREEN       = dbRGB(0, 255, 0);
 9      const DWORD BLUE        = dbRGB(0, 0, 255);
10      const DWORD MAGENTA     = dbRGB(255, 0, 255);
11
12      // Constant for time delay (half a second)
13      const int DELAY = 500;
14
15      // Constant for the array size
16      const int SIZE = 4;
17
18      // Array of colors
19      DWORD colors[SIZE] = { RED, GREEN, BLUE, MAGENTA };
20
21      // Variable to use as an array index
22      int index;
23
24      // Seed the random number generator.
25      dbRandomize( dbTimer() );
26
27      // Repeatedly clear the screen with random colors.
28      while ( LoopGDK() )
29      {
30          // Get a random number
31          index = dbRND( SIZE - 1 );
32
33          // Clear the screen to a random color.
34          dbCLS( colors[index] );
35
36          // Wait.
37          dbWait(DELAY);
38      }
39  }
```

Implicit Array Sizing

In C++, you can declare an array without specifying its size, as long as you provide an initialization list. C++ automatically makes the array large enough to hold all the initialization values. For example, the following statement declares an array with five elements:

```
int numbers[] = { 2, 4, 6, 8, 10 };
```

Because the size declarator is omitted, C++ will make the array just large enough to hold the values in the initialization list.

NOTE: If you leave the size declarator out of an array declaration, you *must* provide an initialization list. Otherwise, C++ doesn't know how large to make the array.

Copying an Array

If you need to copy the contents of one array to another, you have to assign the individual elements of the array that you are copying to the elements of the other array. Usually this is best done with a loop. For example, look at the following code:

```
const int SIZE = 5;
int firstArray[SIZE] = { 100, 200, 300, 400, 500 };
int secondArray[SIZE];
```

Suppose you wish to copy the values in firstArray to secondArray. The following code assigns each element of firstArray to the corresponding element in secondArray.

```
for (int index = 0; index < SIZE; index++)
{
      secondArray[index] = firstArray[index];
}
```

Passing an Array as an Argument to a Function

You can pass an entire array as an argument to a function, which gives you the ability to modularize many of the operations that you perform on the array. Passing an array as an argument typically requires that you pass two arguments: (1) the array itself, and (2) an integer that specifies the number of elements in the array.

Program 10-5 shows an example. This program has two functions that accept an array of DWORD color values: clearToBlack and drawDots. The clearToBlack function sets each element of the array to the color black, and the drawDots function uses the elements of the array to draw a row of dots across the screen. When you run the program you will see a red screen with a black line drawn across the center of the screen. The black line is actually a row of black dots that were drawn by the drawDots function.

Program 10-5   (PassArray.cpp)

```
1    // This program demonstrates how an array can be
2    // passed as an argument to a function.
3    #include "DarkGDK.h"
4
5    // Function prototype
6    void clearToBlack(DWORD [], int);
7    void drawDots(DWORD [], int);
8
9    //***************************************************
10   // The DarkGDK function                            *
11   //***************************************************
12
13   void DarkGDK()
14   {
```

```
15      // Constant for the color red
16      const DWORD RED = dbRGB(255, 0, 0);
17
18      // Constant for the array size
19      const int SIZE = 640;
20
21      // Array to hold color values
22      DWORD colors[SIZE];
23
24      // Clear the screen to red.
25      dbCLS(RED);
26
27      // Set each element of the array to black.
28      clearToBlack(colors, SIZE);
29
30      // Draw a row of dots across the screen,
31      // using the colors array to specify the
32      // color of the dots.
33      drawDots(colors, SIZE);
34
35      // Wait for the user to press a key.
36      dbWaitKey();
37  }
38
39  //*****************************************************
40  // The clearToBlack function accepts two arguments:  *
41  // (1) A DWORD array, and (2) an int specifying the  *
42  // size of the array. The function sets each element *
43  // of the array to the color black.                  *
44  //*****************************************************
45  void clearToBlack(DWORD colorArray[], int size)
46  {
47      for (int index = 0; index < size; index++)
48      {
49          colorArray[index] = dbRGB(0, 0, 0);
50      }
51  }
52
53  //*****************************************************
54  // The drawDots function accepts two arguments:      *
55  // (1) A DWORD array, and (2) an int specifying the  *
56  // size of the array. The function draws a row of    *
57  // dots across the center of the screen, using the   *
58  // elements of the array to specify the color of     *
59  // each dot.                                         *
60  //*****************************************************
61  void drawDots(DWORD dots[], int size)
62  {
63      // Get the Y coordinate of the center of the
64      // screen.
65      int y = dbScreenHeight() / 2;
66
67      // Draw the row of dots across the center of
68      // the screen.
69      for (int x = 0; x < size; x++)
```

```
70        {
71            dbDot(x, y, dots[x]);
72        }
73  }
```

Take a closer look at the `clearToBlack` function. First, look at the function header in line 45:

```
void clearToBlack(DWORD colorArray[], int size)
```

The function has two parameters: a `DWORD` array named `colorArray`, and an `int` named `size`. When this function is called, a `DWORD` array should be passed into the `colorArray` parameter, and an `int` specifying the array's size should be passed into the `size` parameter. Notice that the `colorArray` parameter name is followed by a set of empty brackets. This indicates that `colorArray` will accept an array argument.

In C++, arrays are always passed by reference. This means that when the `clearToBlack` function is called, the `colorArray` parameter will reference the actual array that is passed as an argument, not a copy of the array. As a result, any changes that are made to the array parameter are made to the actual array that was passed as an argument. In this function, the `for` loop that starts in line 47 iterates once for each element in the `colorArray` parameter. Each time the loop iterates, it sets an element of the array to the color black.

Now let's look at the `drawDots` function. Notice that the function header in line 61 has a `DWORD` array parameter named `dots` and an `int` named `size`. When this function is called, a `DWORD` array should be passed into the `dots` parameter, and an `int` specifying the array's size should be passed into the `size` parameter.

Line 65 declares a local `int` variable named `y`, and initializes it with the *Y* coordinate of the center of the screen. This variable will be used as the *Y* coordinate for each dot that the function draws.

As the `for` loop in lines 69 through 72 iterates, the `x` variable will be assigned the values 0 through `size` −1. Each time the loop iterates, the statement in line 71 draws a dot on the screen, using `x` and `y` as the coordinates. Notice that the `x` variable is also used as a subscript to get a value from the `dots` array. The first element in the array specifies the color of the first dot; the second element in the array specifies the color of the second dot, and so forth.

In the Spotlight:

Drawing Polylines

A *polyline* is a line that is made up of one or more connected line segments. Figure 10-7 shows an example of a polyline that is a series of five connected line segments. Each line segment has its own endpoints, which are shown by the small circles in the figure.

Figure 10-7 A polyline with five line segments and six endpoints

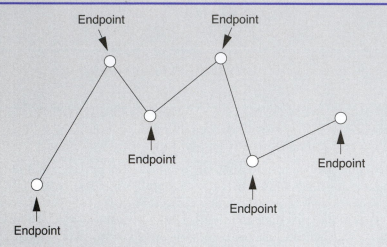

The `DarkGDK` provides a function to draw simple lines, but it does not provide a function to draw polylines. Program 10-6 shows an example of how we can write our own polyline function. The function, which is defined in lines 39 through 45, accepts the following three arguments:

- An int array that contains the X coordinates of each endpoint in the polyline
- An int array that contains the Y coordinates of each endpoint in the polyline
- An int that specifies the number of endpoints in the polyline

Program 10-6   **(Polyline.cpp)**

```
 1   // This program demonstrates the polyline function.
 2   #include "DarkGDK.h"
 3
 4   // Function prototype
 5   void polyline(int [], int [], int);
 6
 7   //*****************************************************
 8   // DarkGDK function                                   *
 9   //*****************************************************
10   void DarkGDK()
11   {
12       // Declare a constant for the number of endpoints
13       // in the polyline.
14       const int POINTS = 5;
15
16       // The xPoints array is initialized with the X
17       // coordinate of each endpoint in the polyline.
18       int xPoints[POINTS] = { 0,  160, 320, 480, 640 };
19
20       // The yPoints array is initialized with the Y
21       // coordinate of each endpoint in the polyline.
```

```
22          int yPoints[POINTS] = { 320,   160, 320, 160, 320 };
23
24          // Draw the polyline.
25          polyline(xPoints, yPoints, POINTS);
26
27          // Wait for the user to press a key.
28          dbWaitKey();
29  }
30
31  //*********************************************************
32  // The polyline function draws a polyline, which is a  *
33  // series of connected line segments. The x parameter  *
34  // is an array that contains the X coordinates of each *
35  // endpoint. The y parameter is an array that contains *
36  // the Y coordinates of each endpoint. The numPoints   *
37  // parameter specifies the number of endpoints.        *
38  //*********************************************************
39  void polyline(int x[], int y[], int numPoints)
40  {
41      for (int index = 0; index < numPoints - 1; index++)
42      {
43              dbLine(x[index], y[index], x[index+1], y[index+1]);
44      }
45  }
```

In the function, the parameters x and y are the arrays that contain the coordinates for each endpoint. For example, the first endpoint will be located at x[0], y[0]; the second endpoint will be located at x[1], y[1], and so forth.

Inside the DarkGDK function, the xPoints array is declared and initialized in line 18, and the yPoints array is declared and initialized in line 22. These arrays, along with the number of points, are passed as arguments to the polyline function. The program's output is shown in Figure 10-8. The figure is annotated to show the values of the xPoints and yPoints arrays, as well as the coordinates of each endpoint in the polyline.

Figure 10-8 Annotated output of Program 10-6

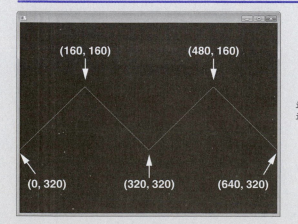

```
int xPoints[POINTS] = {    0, 160, 320, 480, 640 };
int yPoints[POINTS] = {  320, 160, 320, 160, 320 };
```

Comparing Two Arrays

If you need to compare two arrays to determine whether they contain the same values, you have to write a loop that steps through both arrays, comparing their corresponding elements. The following code shows an example:

```
const int SIZE = 5;
int arrayA[SIZE] = { 1, 2, 3, 4, 5 };
int arrayB[SIZE] = { 1, 2, 3, 4, 5 };

bool arraysEqual = true;
int index = 0;

while ( index < SIZE && arraysEqual )
{
    if ( arrayA[index] != arrayB[index] )
    {
        arraysEqual = false;
    }
}

if ( arraysEqual )
{
    dbPrint("Both arrays contain the same values.");
}
else
{
    dbPrint("The arrays do not contain the same values.");
}
```

This code determines if `arrayA` and `arrayB` contain the same values. `arraysEqual`, a `bool` variable that is initialized to `true`, is used to signal whether the arrays are equal. Another variable, `index`, which is initialized to 0, is used in the loop as a subscript.

Then a `while` loop begins. The loop executes as long as `arraysEqual` is true and the `index` variable is less than `SIZE`. During each iteration, it compares a set of corresponding elements in the arrays. When it finds two corresponding elements that have different values, the `arraysEqual` variable is set to `false`. After the loop finishes, an `if` statement examines the `arraysEqual` variable. If the variable is `true`, then the arrays are equal and a message indicating so is displayed. Otherwise they are not equal, and a different message is displayed.

In the Spotlight:

The Memory Match Game

Program 10-7 shows the code for a simple game called Memory Match. The user's objective is to remember a sequence of five random numbers that are briefly displayed on the screen, and enter them in the same order in which they were displayed. When the game runs, the screen shown on the left in Figure 10-9 appears. When the user presses a key, the screen is cleared and five random numbers are displayed in the

Figure 10-9 Memory match opening screens

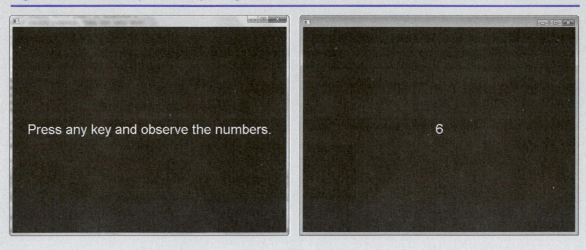

Press any key and observe the numbers.

6

range of 0 through 20. The numbers appear one at a time, as shown in the screen on the right in Figure 10-9. Next, the screen on the left in Figure 10-10 appears. After pressing a key, the user is prompted to enter the five numbers, pressing *Enter* after each number. After the fifth number is entered, the program displays the screen shown on the right in Figure 10-10. This screen displays the random numbers selected by the computer, the numbers entered by the user, and the number of matches. If the user enters all five numbers correctly, he or she is congratulated on having a perfect match.

Figure 10-10 Memory match screens

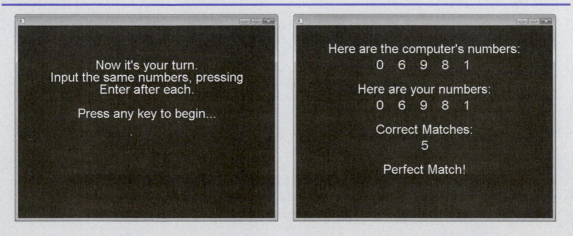

Now it's your turn.
Input the same numbers, pressing
Enter after each.

Press any key to begin...

Here are the computer's numbers:
0 6 9 8 1

Here are your numbers:
0 6 9 8 1

Correct Matches:
5

Perfect Match!

Now let's look at the game's code. Rather than presenting all the code at once, we will examine it a section at a time. The first section of code, which follows, shows the DarkGDK function.

Program 10-7   (`MemoryMatch.cpp` *partial listing*)

```
1   // This is the memory match game. It displays a
2   // sequence of random numbers, then the user must
3   // try to remember the numbers and enter them in
4   // the correct order.
5   #include "DarkGDK.h"
6
7   // Function prototypes
8   void generateRandom(int [], int);
9   void setText();
10  void displayRandom(int [], int);
11  void getUserNumbers(int [], int);
12  void displayResults(int [], int [], int);
13  int  matchingNumbers(int [], int [], int);
14  void displayArray(int, int, int [], int);
15
16  //*****************************************************
17  // The DarkGDK function                              *
18  //*****************************************************
19  void DarkGDK()
20  {
21      // Constant for array sizes
22      const int SIZE = 5;
23
24      // Array declarations
25      int random[SIZE];        // Random numbers
26      int user[SIZE];          // User's numbers
27
28      // Generate the random numbers.
29      generateRandom(random, SIZE);
30
31      // Set the font and text size.
32      setText();
33
34      // Display the random numbers.
35      displayRandom(random, SIZE);
36
37      // Get the user's numbers.
38      getUserNumbers(user, SIZE);
39
40      // Display the results.
41      displayResults(random, user, SIZE);
42
43      // Wait for the user to press a key.
44      dbWaitKey();
45  }
46
```

Line 22 declares SIZE as a constant. This will be used as an array size declarator. Line 25 declares an int array named random. This array will hold the computer's random numbers. Line 26 declares an int array named user. This array will hold the numbers that the user enters.

Line 29 calls the generateRandom function, passing the random array and SIZE as arguments. This function fills the random array with random numbers. Line 32 calls the setText function, which sets the font to Arial and the text size to 36 points.

Line 35 calls the displayRandom function, passing the random array and SIZE as arguments. This function displays the numbers in the random array on the screen, one at a time, with a brief pause between each one.

Line 38 calls the getUserNumbers function, passing the user array and SIZE as arguments. This function prompts the user to enter the five numbers, and stores them in the user array.

Line 41 calls the displayResults function, passing the random array, the user array, and SIZE as arguments. This function displays the game results. Line 44 waits for the user to press a key.

The code for the generateRandom function is shown next. The function steps through the array that is passed to it as an argument, storing random numbers (in the range of 0 through 20) in each element.

Program 10-7   (MemoryMatch.cpp *continued*)

```
47  //*******************************************************
48  // The generateRandom function accepts two arguments:  *
49  // (1) an array of ints, and (2) an int specifying     *
50  // the array size. The function fills the array with   *
51  // random numbers.                                     *
52  //*******************************************************
53  void generateRandom(int numbers[], int size)
54  {
55      // Seed the random number generator.
56      dbRandomize( dbTimer() );
57
58      // Fill the array with random numbers in
59      // the range of 0 through 20.
60      for (int index = 0; index < size; index++)
61      {
62          numbers[index] = dbRND(20);
63      }
64  }
65
```

The code for the setText function appears next. It sets the font to Arial, and the text size to 36 points:

Program 10-7 (`MemoryMatch.cpp` *continued*)

```
66   //****************************************************
67   // The setText function sets the font and text size. *
68   //****************************************************
69   void setText()
70   {
71       dbSetTextFont("Arial");
72       dbSetTextSize(36);
73   }
74
```

The `displayRandom` function is shown next. When this function is called, the random array is passed as an argument. The function displays the array's elements one at a time in the center of the screen, with a short time delay separating each one.

Program 10-7 (`MemoryMatch.cpp` *continued*)

```
75   //*********************************************************
76   // The displayRandom function accepts two arguments:  *
77   // (1) an array of ints, and (2) int specifying the   *
78   // array size. The function displays the numbers in   *
79   // the array one at a time, with a short delay         *
80   // between each number.                                *
81   //*********************************************************
82   void displayRandom(int numbers[], int size)
83   {
84       // Constant for the time delay
85       const int DELAY = 300;
86
87       // Get the height of a character.
88       int textHeight = dbTextHeight("0");
89
90       // Calculate the XY coordinates for the text.
91       int x = dbScreenWidth() / 2;
92       int y = (dbScreenHeight() / 2) - (textHeight / 2);
93
94       // Prompt the user for a key press.
95       dbCLS();
96       dbCenterText(x, y, "Press any key and observe the numbers.");
97       dbWaitKey();
98       dbCLS();
99
100      // Display the random numbers.
101      for (int index = 0; index < size; index++)
102      {
103          dbCenterText( x, y, dbStr(numbers[index]) );
104          dbWait(DELAY);
105          dbCLS();
106          dbWait(DELAY);
107      }
108  }
109
```

The `getUserNumbers` function is shown next. When this function is called, the user array is passed as an argument. The function prompts the user to enter the numbers that were previously displayed. The numbers are stored in the array.

Program 10-7   (`MemoryMatch.cpp` *continued*)

```
110    //*******************************************************
111    // The getUserNumbers function accepts two arguments: *
112    // (1) an array of ints, and (2) int specifying the   *
113    // array size. The function prompts the user to enter *
114    // the numbers and stores them in the array.          *
115    //*******************************************************
116    void getUserNumbers(int numbers[], int size)
117    {
118        // Get the height of a character.
119        int textHeight = dbTextHeight("0");
120
121        // The coordinates for the text.
122        int x = dbScreenWidth() / 2;
123        int y = 80;
124
125        // Prompt the user for a key press.
126        dbCLS();
127        dbCenterText(x, y, "Now it's your turn.");
128        dbCenterText(x, y+30, "Input the same numbers, pressing");
129        dbCenterText(x, y+60, "Enter after each.");
130        dbCenterText(x, y+120, "Press any key to begin...");
131        dbWaitKey();
132        dbCLS();
133
134        // Get the width of two characters.
135        int textWidth = dbTextWidth("00");
136
137        // Calculate the XY coordinates for the input.
138        x = (dbScreenWidth() / 2) - (textWidth / 2);
139        y = (dbScreenHeight() / 2) - (textHeight / 2);
140
141        // Get the user's numbers.
142        for (int index = 0; index < size; index++)
143        {
144            dbSetCursor(x, y);
145            numbers[index] = atoi( dbInput() );
146            dbCLS();
147        }
148    }
149
```

The `displayResults` function is shown next. When this function is called, the random array, the user array, and the `SIZE` constant are passed as arguments. The function displays the random numbers selected by the computer, the numbers entered by the user, and the number of matching numbers. If the user entered all five numbers correctly, a message is displayed indicating a perfect match.

Program 10-7   (`MemoryMatch.cpp` *continued*)

```
150    //*******************************************************
151    // The displayResults function accepts three arguments: *
152    // (1) an array holding the random numbers,              *
153    // (2) an array holding the user's numbers, and          *
154    // (3) an int specifying the size of both arrays.        *
155    // The function displays the game results.               *
156    //*******************************************************
157    void displayResults(int random[], int user[], int size)
158    {
159        // Constants for each line of text output
160        const int LINE_1_X = dbScreenWidth() / 2;
161        const int LINE_1_Y = 40;
162
163        const int LINE_2_X = 200;
164        const int LINE_2_Y = 80;
165
166        const int LINE_3_X = dbScreenWidth() / 2;
167        const int LINE_3_Y = 140;
168
169        const int LINE_4_X = 200;
170        const int LINE_4_Y = 180;
171
172        const int LINE_5_X = dbScreenWidth() / 2;
173        const int LINE_5_Y = 240;
174
175        const int LINE_6_X = dbScreenWidth() / 2;
176        const int LINE_6_Y = 280;
177
178        const int LINE_7_X = dbScreenWidth() / 2;
179        const int LINE_7_Y = 340;
180
181        // Variable to hold the number of matches
182        int matches = matchingNumbers(random, user, size);
183
184        // Display the computer's random numbers.
185        dbCLS();
186        dbCenterText( LINE_1_X,    LINE_1_Y,
187            "Here are the computer's numbers:");
188        displayArray(LINE_2_X, LINE_2_Y, random, size);
189
190        // Display the user's numbers.
191        dbCenterText( LINE_3_X,    LINE_3_Y,
192            "Here are your numbers:");
193        displayArray(LINE_4_X, LINE_4_Y, user, size);
194
195        // Display the number of matches.
196        dbCenterText( LINE_5_X, LINE_5_Y,
197            "Correct Matches:");
198        dbCenterText( LINE_6_X, LINE_6_Y, dbStr(matches) );
199
200        // Display a special message if the
201        // user remembered all the numbers.
202        if ( matches == size )
```

```
203          {
204              dbCenterText( LINE_7_X, LINE_7_Y, "Perfect Match!" );
205          }
206    }
207
```

Take a closer look at line 182. This statement declares an `int` variable named `matches`. It calls a function named `matchingNumbers`, which determines the number of matching numbers entered by the user and returns that value. The value is assigned to the `matches` variable. The code for the `matchingNumbers` function is shown next.

Program 10-7   (`MemoryMatch.cpp` *continued*)

```
208    //***********************************************************
209    // The matchingNumbers function accepts three arguments:  *
210    // (1) an array holding the random numbers,               *
211    // (2) an array holding the user's numbers, and           *
212    // (3) an int specifying the size of both arrays.         *
213    // The function returns the number of matching numbers    *
214    // in both arrays.                                        *
215    //***********************************************************
216    int matchingNumbers(int random[], int user[], int size)
217    {
218        // Variable to hold the number of matches
219        int matches = 0;
220
221        // Compare the computer's numbers with the
222        // user's numbers and count the matches.
223        for (int index = 0; index < size; index++)
224        {
225            if ( random[index] == user[index] )
226            {
227                matches++;
228            }
229        }
230
231        // Return the number of matches.
232        return matches;
233    }
234
```

When the `matchingNumbers` function is called, the `random` array, the `user` array, and the size of the arrays are passed as arguments. In line 219, a local variable named `matches` is declared and initialized with the value 0. This variable will be used to keep count of the number of matching elements in both arrays. The `for` loop that starts in line 223 steps through the arrays, using the `index` variable as a subscript. The `if` statement in line 225 compares `random[index]` with `users[index]`, and if they are equal, the `matches` variable is incremented in line 227. The function returns the number of matching elements in line 232.

The code for the `displayArray` function is shown next. This function accepts as arguments *X* and *Y* coordinates, an `int` array, and the size of the array. It displays the values stored in the array's elements, beginning at the specified coordinates.

Program 10-7   (**MemoryMatch.cpp** *continued*)

```
235   //*********************************************************
236   // The displayArray function displays the contents of an  *
237   // array on the screen. It accepts the following four     *
238   // arguments:                                             *
239   // (1) an X coordinate for the output                     *
240   // (2) a Y coordinate for the output                      *
241   // (3) an int array to display                            *
242   // (4) the size of the array                              *
243   //*********************************************************
244   void displayArray(int x, int y, int numbers[], int size)
245   {
246       // Get the width of a single character. This is
247       // used to calculate the output position of each
248       // array element.
249       int charWidth = dbTextWidth("0");
250
251       // Display the contents of the array.
252       for (int index = 0; index < size; index++)
253       {
254           // Display an element.
255           dbText( x, y, dbStr(numbers[index]) );
256
257           // Increase x by the width of three characters.
258           x = x + (charWidth * 3);
259       }
260   }
```

In the Spotlight:
Shuffling an Array

To *shuffle* an array means to randomly rearrange its contents. Quite often, game programs need to shuffle the contents of an array to simulate the shuffling of a deck of cards, the rearranging of a set of puzzle pieces, and so forth.

Program 10-8 demonstrates an example of a shuffling algorithm. The program loads a set of images, and then stores their image numbers in an array. The images are displayed on the screen, from left to right, in the order that their image numbers appear in the array. When the user presses the spacebar, the array is shuffled and the images are redisplayed in their new order. Figure 10-11 shows an example of the program's output. The screen on the left shows the images displayed in their original order, and the screen on the right shows the images after they have been shuffled.

Program 10-8   **(Shuffle.cpp)**

```cpp
1   // This program shuffles an array of image numbers.
2   #include "DarkGDK.h"
3
4   // Constants to use for image numbers
5   const int APPLE        = 1;
6   const int BANANA       = 2;
7   const int CHERRIES     = 3;
8   const int GRAPES       = 4;
9   const int ORANGE       = 5;
10
11  // Other constants
12  const int REFRESH_RATE = 60;
13  const int TEXT_X       = 319;
14  const int TEXT_Y       = 120;
15
16  // Function prototypes
17  void setUp();
18  void displayImages(int [], int);
19  void shuffle(int [], int);
20  void swap(int &, int &);
21
22  //****************************************************
23  // DarkGDK function                                  *
24  //****************************************************
25  void DarkGDK()
26  {
27      // Create an array to hold the image numbers.
28      const int SIZE = 5;
29      int images[SIZE] = { APPLE, BANANA, CHERRIES,
30                           GRAPES, ORANGE };
31
32      // Perform setup operations.
33      setUp();
34
35      // Game loop
36      while ( LoopGDK() )
37      {
38          // Check to see if the spacebar is being pressed.
39          if ( dbSpaceKey() )
40          {
41              // Wait until the user releases the spacebar.
42              while ( dbSpaceKey() )
43              {   // Do nothing.
44              }
45
46              // Shuffle the images in the array.
47              shuffle(images, SIZE);
48          }
49
50          // Display the images in the order that their
51          // numbers appear in the images array.
52          displayImages(images, SIZE);
53
```

```
54                   // Prompt the user to press the spacebar.
55                   dbCenterText( TEXT_X, TEXT_Y,
56                      "Press and release the spacebar to shuffle the images.");
57
58                   // Refresh the screen.
59                   dbSync();
60          }
61   }
62
63   //*******************************************************
64   // The setUp function performs setup operations.       *
65   //*******************************************************
66   void setUp()
67   {
68       // Load the images.
69       dbLoadImage("Apple.bmp",    APPLE);
70       dbLoadImage("Banana.bmp",   BANANA);
71       dbLoadImage("Cherries.bmp", CHERRIES);
72       dbLoadImage("Grapes.bmp",   GRAPES);
73       dbLoadImage("Orange.bmp",   ORANGE);
74
75       // Set the text to 24 point Arial font.
76       dbSetTextFont("Arial");
77       dbSetTextSize(24);
78
79       // Disable auto-refresh and set the
80       // refresh rate.
81       dbSyncOn();
82       dbSyncRate(REFRESH_RATE);
83   }
84
85   //*******************************************************
86   // The displayImages function accepts two arguments: *
87   // (1) an array of image numbers, and                 *
88   // (2) an int that specifies the array size.          *
89   // After the function executes, the images will be    *
90   // displayed in a row across the screen, in the       *
91   // order that their numbers appear in the array.      *
92   //*******************************************************
93   void displayImages(int images[], int size)
94   {
95       // Variables for the image XY coordinates
96       int x = 0;
97       int y = (dbScreenHeight() / 2) -
98               (dbGetImageHeight(images[0]) / 2);
99
100      // Display the images.
101      for (int index = 0; index < size; index++)
102      {
103          // Display an image.
104          dbPasteImage( images[index], x, y );
105
106          // Increase x for the next image.
107          x += dbGetImageWidth( images[index] );
108      }
```

```
109   }
110
111   //*****************************************************
112   // The shuffle function accepts two arguments:      *
113   // (1) an array of ints, and                        *
114   // (2) an int that specifies the array size.        *
115   // After the function executes, the array's elements *
116   // will be randomly shuffled.                        *
117   //*****************************************************
118   void shuffle(int numbers[], int size)
119   {
120       // Variable to hold a random subscript
121       int randomSub;
122
123       // Seed the random number generator.
124       dbRandomize( dbTimer() );
125
126       // Step through the array, swapping each element
127       // with a random element.
128       for (int index = 0; index < size; index++)
129       {
130           // Get a random subscript.
131           randomSub = dbRND(size - 1);
132
133           // Swap two elements.
134           swap( numbers[index], numbers[randomSub] );
135       }
136   }
137
138   //*****************************************************
139   // The swap function accepts two int arguments       *
140   // passed by reference. The function swaps the        *
141   // contents of the two arguments.                     *
142   //*****************************************************
143   void swap(int &a, int &b)
144   {
145       // Assign a to temp.
146       int temp = a;
147
148       // Assign b to a.
149       a = b;
150
151       // Assign temp to b.
152       b = temp;
153   }
```

The game loop begins in line 36. Inside the loop, the if statement in line 39 determines whether the spacebar is being pressed. If it is, the while loop that appears in lines 42 through 44 causes the program to wait until the user releases the spacebar. Then, once the user has released the spacebar, the shuffle function is called in line 47. The images array and the SIZE constant are passed as arguments.

Figure 10-11 Images before and after being shuffled

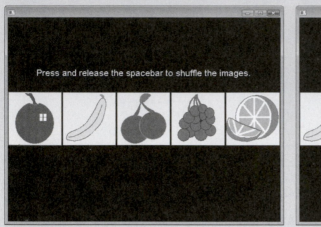 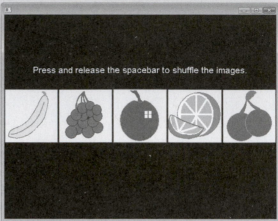

 NOTE: You might be wondering why we use the `while` loop in lines 42 through 44 to wait until the user releases the spacebar. If we don't do this, when the user presses the spacebar, the game loop iterates several times before the spacebar is released. As a result, the `shuffle` function is called several times. By inserting the `while` loop, we make sure the `shuffle` function is called only once each time the spacebar is pressed.

The `shuffle` function, which appears in lines 118 through 136, performs the shuffle. Before we look at the code, let's take a look at the general logic used to shuffle the array's contents. The algorithm works like this:

For each element in the array:
  Randomly select another element
  Swap the contents of this element with the randomly selected element

Now let's look at the code. Line 121 declares a local `int` variable named `randomSub`, which will hold a randomly generated subscript. Line 124 seeds the random number generator. The loop that begins in line 128 iterates once for each element in the array. As the loop iterates, the `index` variable is assigned the values 0 through `size - 1`. Line 131 generates a random number in the range of 0 through `size - 1` and assigns the number to `randomNum`. Then line 134 calls the `swap` function, passing `numbers[index]` and `numbers[randomNum]` as arguments. These arguments are passed by reference, and after the function call is complete, the contents of the two array elements will be swapped.

Swapping Array Elements

Before we look at the code for the `swap` function, let's briefly discuss the process of swapping two items in computer memory. Assume we have the following variable declarations:

```
int a = 1;
int b = 9;
```

Suppose we want to swap the values in these variables so the variable a contains 9 and the variable b contains 1. At first, you might think that we only need to assign the variables to each other, like this:

```
// ERROR! This does NOT swap the variables.
a = b;
b = a;
```

To understand why this doesn't work, let's step through the code. The first statement is a = b;. This causes the value 9 to be assigned to a. But, what happens to the value 1 that was previously stored in a? Remember, when you assign a new value to a variable, the new value replaces any value that was previously stored in the variable. So the old value, 1, will be thrown away. Then the next statement is b = a;. Since the variable a contains 9, this assigns 9 to b. After these statements execute, both variables a and b will contain the value 9.

To successfully swap the contents of two variables, we need a third variable to serve as a temporary storage location:

```
int temp;
```

Then we can perform the following steps to swap the values in the variables a and b:

- Assign the value of a to temp.
- Assign the value of b to a.
- Assign the value of temp to b.

Now let's look at the code for the swap function, which appears in lines 143 through 153. The function has two reference parameters, a and b. It is critical that these parameters be reference variables because the function will need to change the values of the arguments that are passed into them. Line 146 assigns the value of a to the local variable temp, line 149 assigns the value of b to a, and line 152 assigns the value of temp to b. After these steps have been performed, the arguments that were passed into a and b will be swapped.

Partially Filled Arrays

Sometimes you need to store a series of items in an array, but you do not know the total number of items. As a result, you do not know the exact number of elements needed for the array. One solution is to make the array large enough to hold the largest possible number of items. This can lead to another problem, however. If the actual number of items stored in the array is less than the number of elements, the array will only be partially filled. When you process a partially filled array, you must process only the elements that contain valid data items.

A partially filled array is normally used with an accompanying integer variable that holds the number of items stored in the array. For example, suppose a program uses the following code to create an array named myNumbers with 100 elements., and an int variable named count that will hold the number of items stored in the array:

```
const int SIZE = 100;
int myNumbers[SIZE];
int count = 0;
```

Each time we add an item to the array, we must increment count. The following code demonstrates:

```
int number;

// Get a number from the user.
dbPrint( "Enter a number or -1 to quit:");
number = atoi( dbInput() );

// Add numbers to the myNumbers array until the user
// enters -1.
while (number != -1 && count < SIZE)
{
    // Increment count.
    count++;

    // Add the number to the array.
    myNumbers[count - 1] = number;

    // Get the next number
    dbPrint("Enter a number or -1 to quit:");
    number = atoi( dbInput() );
}
```

Each iteration of this loop allows the user to enter a number to be stored in the array, or −1 to quit. The count variable is incremented, and then used to calculate the subscript of the next available element in the array. When the user enters −1, or count exceeds 99, the loop stops. The following code displays all of the valid items in the array:

```
for (int index = 0; index < count; index++)
{
    dbPrint( myNumbers[index] );
}
```

Notice that this code uses count instead of the array size to determine where the array subscripts end.

In the Spotlight:
Dealing Cards with Partially Filled Arrays

In this section, we will discuss how partially filled arrays can be used to simulate card dealing. Program 10-9 loads 10 images, which are used as cards in a deck. The deck is shuffled and the screen shown in the top left of Figure 10-12 is displayed. This screen instructs the user to press the spacebar to deal a card. Each time the user presses the spacebar, a card is dealt and displayed on the screen. The top right image in Figure 10-12 shows an example of the screen after one card has been dealt. The bottom left image shows an example after two cards are dealt. The bottom right image shows an example after five cards are dealt. After the fifth card is dealt, the program informs the user that a full hand has been dealt, and it will deal no more cards.

Program 10-9   (`CardDealer.cpp`)

```
1    // This program demonstrates how partially filled arrays
2    // can be used to simulate card dealing.
3    #include "DarkGDK.h"
4
5    // Constants to use for image numbers
6    const int APPLE        = 1;
7    const int BANANA       = 2;
8    const int CHERRIES     = 3;
9    const int GRAPES       = 4;
10   const int LEMON        = 5;
11   const int LIME         = 6;
12   const int ORANGE       = 7;
13   const int PEAR         = 8;
14   const int STRAWBERRY   = 9;
15   const int WATERMELON   = 10;
16
17   // Constant for the sound file.
18   const int DEAL_SOUND   = 1;
19
20   // Other constants
21   const int REFRESH_RATE = 60;
22   const int TEXT_X       = 319;
23   const int TEXT_Y       = 120;
24
25   // Function prototypes
26   void setUp();
27   void shuffle(int [], int);
28   void swap(int &, int &);
29   void displayImages(int [], int);
30
31   //*****************************************************
32   // DarkGDK function                                   *
33   //*****************************************************
34   void DarkGDK()
35   {
36       // Create an array to represent the deck of cards.
37       const int DECK_SIZE = 10;
38       int deck[DECK_SIZE] = { APPLE, BANANA, CHERRIES, GRAPES, LEMON,
39                               LIME, ORANGE, PEAR, STRAWBERRY, WATERMELON };
40
41       // Create an array to represent the dealt hand.
42       const int HAND_SIZE = 5;
43       int hand[HAND_SIZE];
44
45       // Variable to hold the number of cards in the deck.
46       int deckCount = DECK_SIZE;
47
48       // Variable to hold the number of cards in the hand.
49       int handCount = 0;
50
51       // Perform setup operations.
52       setUp();
53
```

```
54        // Shuffle the deck.
55        shuffle(deck, DECK_SIZE);
56
57        // Game loop
58        while ( LoopGDK() )
59        {
60            // Clear the screen.
61            dbCLS();
62
63            if ( handCount < HAND_SIZE )
64            {
65                // Prompt the user to deal a card.
66                dbCenterText(TEXT_X, TEXT_Y,
67                    "Press the spacebar to deal a card.");
68
69                // If a full hand has not been dealt, deal a card.
70                if ( dbSpaceKey() )
71                {
72                    // Wait for the user to release the spacebar
73                    // before continuing. This ensures that we deal
74                    // only one card at a time.
75                    while ( dbSpaceKey() )
76                    { // Do nothing...
77                    }
78
79                    // Deal a card from the deck into the hand.
80                    hand[handCount] = deck[deckCount - 1];
81
82                    // We just increased the size of the hand by one
83                    // card, so increment handCount.
84                    handCount++;
85
86                    // We just decreased the size of the deck by one
87                    // card, so decrement deckCount.
88                    deckCount--;
89
90                    // Wait.
91                    dbPlaySound(DEAL_SOUND);
92                }
93            }
94            else
95            {
96                // Let the user know the full hand has been dealt.
97                dbCenterText(TEXT_X, TEXT_Y,
98                    "A full hand has been dealt.");
99            }
100
101            // Display the cards currently in the hand.
102            displayImages(hand, handCount);
103
104            // Refresh the screen.
105            dbSync();
106        }
107    }
108
```

```
109    //********************************************************
110    // The setUp function performs setup operations.      *
111    //********************************************************
112    void setUp()
113    {
114        // Load the images.
115        dbLoadImage("Apple.bmp",        APPLE);
116        dbLoadImage("Banana.bmp",       BANANA);
117        dbLoadImage("Cherries.bmp",     CHERRIES);
118        dbLoadImage("Grapes.bmp",       GRAPES);
119        dbLoadImage("Lemon.bmp",        LEMON);
120        dbLoadImage("Lime.bmp",         LIME);
121        dbLoadImage("Orange.bmp",       ORANGE);
122        dbLoadImage("Pear.bmp",         PEAR);
123        dbLoadImage("Strawberry.bmp",   STRAWBERRY);
124        dbLoadImage("Watermelon.bmp",   WATERMELON);
125
126        // Load the sound for dealing a card.
127        dbLoadSound("select.wav", DEAL_SOUND);
128
129        // Set the font to 24 point Arial.
130        dbSetTextFont("Arial");
131        dbSetTextSize(24);
132
133        // Disable auto-refresh and set the
134        // refresh rate.
135        dbSyncOn();
136        dbSyncRate(REFRESH_RATE);
137    }
138
139    //********************************************************
140    // The shuffle function accepts two arguments:         *
141    // (1) an array of ints, and                           *
142    // (2) an int that specifies the array size.           *
143    // After the function executes, the array's elements   *
144    // will be randomly shuffled.                          *
145    //********************************************************
146    void shuffle(int numbers[], int size)
147    {
148        // Variable to hold a random subscript
149        int randomSub;
150
151        // Seed the random number generator.
152        dbRandomize( dbTimer() );
153
154        // Step through the array, swapping each element
155        // with a random element.
156        for (int index = 0; index < size; index++)
157        {
158            // Get a random subscript.
159            randomSub = dbRND(size - 1);
160
161            // Swap two elements.
162            swap( numbers[index], numbers[randomSub] );
163        }
```

```
164    }
165
166    //******************************************************
167    // The swap function accepts two int arguments         *
168    // passed by reference. The function swaps the         *
169    // contents of the two arguments.                      *
170    //******************************************************
171    void swap(int &a, int &b)
172    {
173        // Assign a to temp.
174        int temp = a;
175
176        // Assign b to a.
177        a = b;
178
179        // Assign temp to b.
180        b = temp;
181    }
182
183    //******************************************************
184    // The displayImages function accepts two arguments:   *
185    // (1) an array of image numbers, and                  *
186    // (2) an int that specifies the array size.           *
187    // After the function executes, the images will be     *
188    // displayed in a row across the screen, in the order  *
189    // that their numbers appear in the array.             *
190    //******************************************************
191    void displayImages(int images[], int size)
192    {
193        // Variables for the image XY coordinates
194        int x = 0;
195        int y = (dbScreenHeight() / 2) -
196               (dbGetImageHeight(images[0]) / 2);
197
198        // Display the images.
199        for (int index = 0; index < size; index++)
200        {
201            // Display an image.
202            dbPasteImage( images[index], x, y );
203
204            // Increase x for the next sprite.
205            x += dbGetImageWidth( images[index] );
206        }
207    }
```

As you will see when we analyze the code, this program uses two arrays: one to hold the deck of cards, and another to hold the hand of cards that are dealt. Each time a card is dealt, it is removed from the array that represents the deck, and added to the array that represents the hand.

Lines 6 through 23 declare constants that we will use for image numbers (lines 6 through 15), a sound number (line 18), the refresh rate (line 21), and coordinates for

Figure 10-12 Example output of Program 10-9

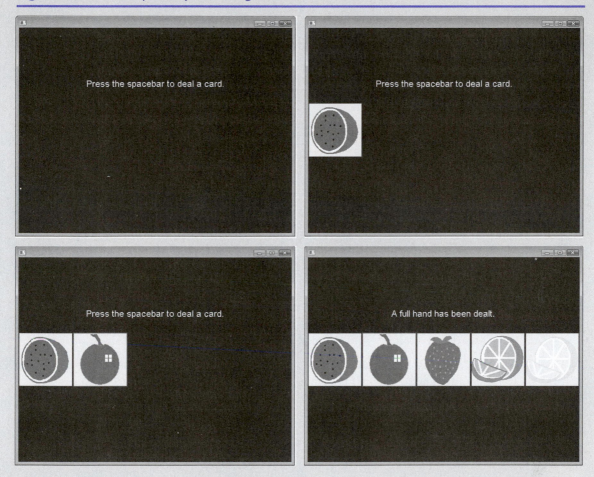

displaying text output (lines 22 and 23). The function prototypes appear in lines 26 through 29.

Inside the DarkGDK function, in lines 38 and 39, we create an array named deck that represents the deck of cards. We have a total of 10 cards, so deck will be an array of 10 integers. We initialize the array with the image numbers for all of the cards.

In line 43, we create another array. This one is named hand, and it will represent the hand of cards that will be dealt. Each time we deal a card, we will add that card's image number to the hand array. We will deal a maximum of five cards, so hand will be an array of five integers.

As the program runs, we will need to treat the deck array as a partially filled array, even though it starts with values in all of its elements. Each time we deal a card from the deck, we want to remove the card so it won't be dealt again. That means we have to remove the card's image number from the deck array. Line 46 declares a variable named deckCount that will hold the number of cards currently in the deck array. Because we start with 10 cards in the deck array, the deckCount variable is initialized with the value 10 (the value of the DECK_SIZE constant).

In line 49, we declare another `int` variable named `handCount`. The `handCount` variable will hold the number of cards that are dealt. This will also be the number of image numbers currently stored in the `hand` array. The `handCount` variable is initialized with 0 because no cards have been dealt when the program begins.

Line 52 calls the `setUp` function, which loads the images, loads a sound file that is played when a card is dealt, sets the text font and size, and disables auto screen refresh.

We need the deck to be shuffled before any cards are dealt, so line 55 calls the `shuffle` function (discussed earlier), passing the `deck` array and the `DECK_SIZE` constant as arguments.

The game loop begins in line 58. First, the screen is cleared in line 61. Then, the `if` statement in line 63 determines whether another card can be dealt. The `HAND_SIZE` constant is the maximum number of cards that we can deal, so, if `handCount` is less than `HAND_SIZE`, we can still deal another card. If we can still deal a card, the `if` statement in line 70 determines whether the user is pressing the spacebar. If so, the `while` loop in lines 75 through 77 causes the program to wait until the user releases the spacebar. (That is to make sure that we deal only one card when the user presses the spacebar.) Then the statement in line 80 deals a card by copying a value from the `deck` array into the `hand` array:

```
hand[handCount] = deck[deckCount - 1];
```

This statement assigns the image number that is stored in `deck[deckCount - 1]` to the `hand[handCount]` array element.

Line 84 increments the `handCount` variable. This is necessary because we've just added a new value to the `hand` array. Then line 88 decrements the `deckCount` variable, which is necessary because we have removed a card from the `deck` array. (We haven't actually removed it from the array. By decrementing the `deckCount` variable, however, we have made the element unavailable.) Then line 91 plays the "card deal" sound.

The `else` clause that appears in line 94 executes if five cards have already been dealt. It simply displays the message "A full hand has been dealt."

Line 102 calls the `displayImages` function, passing the `hand` array and the `handCount` variable as arguments. As a result, all of the cards that have been dealt will be displayed. Then line 105 refreshes the screen.

 Checkpoint

10.1. Can you store a mixture of data types in an array?

10.2. What is an array size declarator?

10.3. Can the size of an array be changed while the program is running?

10.4. What is an array element?

10.5. What is a subscript?

10.6. What is the first subscript in an array?

10.7. Look at the following code and answer questions a through d:

```
const int SIZE = 7;
float numbers[SIZE];
```

a. What is the name of the array that is being declared?
b. How many elements will the array have?
c. What data type are the array elements?
d. What is the subscript of the last element in the array?

10.8. Look at the following code and answer questions a through c:

```
int numbers[] = { 10, 20, 30 };
```

a. Is this a legal declaration of an array?
b. How many elements will the array have?
c. What is the subscript of the last element in the array?

10.9. Does C++ perform array bounds checking? What does this mean?

10.10. How do you copy the contents of one array to another array?

10.2 Sorting Arrays

CONCEPT: A sorting algorithm rearranges the contents of an array so they appear in a specific order. The selection sort is a specific example of a sorting algorithm.

Many programming tasks require that the data in an array be sorted in some order. If an array is sorted in *ascending order*, it means the values in the array are stored from lowest to highest. If the values are sorted in *descending order*, they are stored from highest to lowest. To sort the data in an array, the programmer must use an appropriate sorting algorithm. A *sorting algorithm* is a technique for stepping through an array and rearranging its contents in some order. In this chapter, we will examine the *selection sort algorithm*.

The selection sort algorithm works like this: The smallest value in the array is located and moved to element 0. Then, the next smallest value is located and moved to element 1. This process continues until all of the elements have been placed in their proper order. Let's see how the selection sort works when arranging the elements of the array in Figure 10-13.

The selection sort scans the array, starting at element 0, and locates the element with the smallest value. Then the contents of this element are swapped with the contents of element 0. In this example, the 1 stored in element 5 is swapped with the 5 stored in element 0. After the swap, the array appears as shown in Figure 10-14.

Then, the algorithm repeats the process, but because element 0 already contains the smallest value in the array, it can be left out of the procedure. This time, the algorithm begins the scan at element 1. In this example, the value in element 2 is swapped with the value in element 1. Then the array appears as shown in Figure 10-15.

Figure 10-13 Values in an array

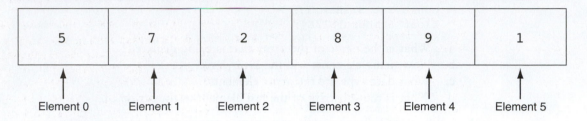

Figure 10-14 Values in the array after the first swap

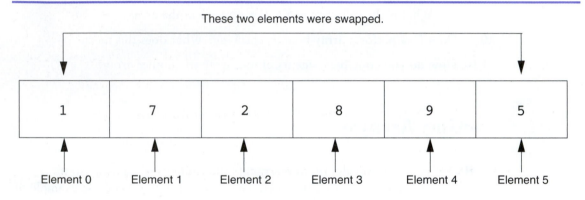

Figure 10-15 Values in the array after the second swap

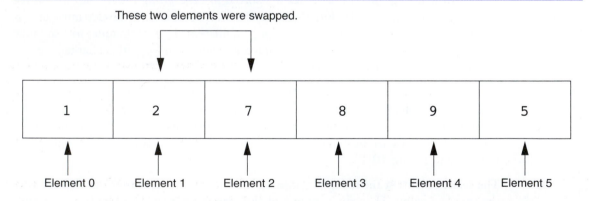

Once again the process is repeated, but this time the scan begins at element 2. The algorithm will find that element 5 contains the next smallest value. This element's value is swapped with that of element 2, causing the array to appear as shown in Figure 10-16.

Next, the scanning begins at element 3. Its value is swapped with that of element 5, causing the array to appear as shown in Figure 10-17.

Figure 10-16 Values in the array after the third swap

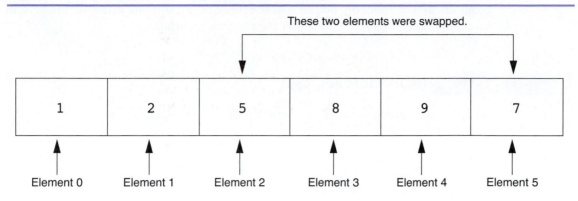

Figure 10-17 Values in the array after the fourth swap

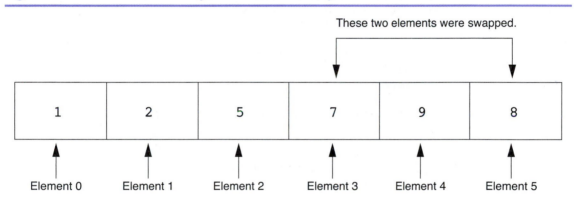

At this point there are only two elements left to sort. The algorithm finds that the value in element 5 is smaller than that of element 4, so the two are swapped. This puts the array in its final arrangement, as shown in Figure 10-18.

Figure 10-18 Values in the array after the fifth swap

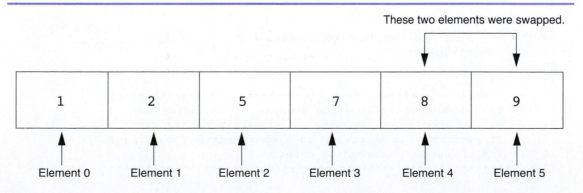

Program 10-10 shows a simple demonstration of the selection sort algorithm. This program uses a function named `selectionSort` to sort an array of integers in ascending order. Figure 10-19 shows the program's output.

Program 10-10   **(SelectionSort.cpp)**

```cpp
1   // This program demonstrates the selection sort algorithm.
2   #include "DarkGDK.h"
3
4   // Function prototype
5   void selectionSort(int [], int);
6   void swap(int &a, int &b);
7
8   void DarkGDK()
9   {
10      // Create an int array with test values.
11      const int SIZE = 6;
12      int numbers[SIZE] = { 4, 6, 1, 3, 5, 2 };
13
14      // Set the text to 28 point Arial.
15      dbSetTextFont("Arial");
16      dbSetTextSize(28);
17
18      // Display the array in its original order.
19      dbPrint("Original order: ");
20      for (int index = 0; index < SIZE; index++)
21      {
22          dbPrint( dbStr(numbers[index]) );
23      }
24
25      // Sort the array.
26      selectionSort(numbers, SIZE);
27
28      // Display a blank line.
29      dbPrint();
30
31      // Display the sorted array.
32      dbPrint("Sorted order: ");
33      for (int index = 0; index < SIZE; index++)
34      {
35          dbPrint( dbStr(numbers[index]) );
36      }
37
38      // Wait for the user to press a key.
39      dbWaitKey();
40  }
41
42  //*********************************************************
43  // The selectionSort function accepts an int array and   *
44  // an int specifying the size of the array as arguments  *
45  // It performs the selection sort on the array, sorting  *
46  // its contents in ascending order.                      *
47  //*********************************************************
```

```
48   void selectionSort(int numbers[], int size)
49   {
50       int startScan;        // Starting position of the scan
51       int index;            // To hold a subscript value
52       int minIndex;         // Element with smallest value in the scan
53       int minValue;         // The smallest value found in the scan
54
55       // The outer loop iterates once for each element in the
56       // numbers array. The startScan variable marks the position
57       // where the scan should begin.
58       for (startScan = 0; startScan < (size - 1); startScan++)
59       {
60           // Assume the first element in the scannable area
61           // is the smallest value.
62           minIndex = startScan;
63           minValue = numbers[startScan];
64
65           // Scan the array starting at the 2nd element in the
66           // scannable area. We are looking for the smallest
67           // value in the scannable area.
68           for(index = startScan + 1; index < size; index++)
69           {
70               if (numbers[index] < minValue)
71               {
72                   minValue = numbers[index];
73                   minIndex = index;
74               }
75           }
76
77           // Swap the element with the smallest value
78           // with the first element in the scannable area.
79           swap( numbers[minIndex], numbers[startScan] );
80       }
81   }
82
83   //****************************************************
84   // The swap function accepts two int arguments        *
85   // passed by reference. The function swaps the        *
86   // contents of the two arguments.                     *
87   //****************************************************
88   void swap(int &a, int &b)
89   {
90       // Assign a to temp.
91       int temp = a;
92
93       // Assign b to a.
94       a = b;
95
96       // Assign temp to b.
97       b = temp;
98   }
```

> **NOTE:** You can modify the `selectionSort` function so it sorts the array in descending order by changing the less-than operator in line 70 to a greater-than operator, as shown here:
>
> ```
> if ( numbers[index] > maxValue )
> ```
>
> Notice that we have also changed the name of the `minValue` variable to `maxValue`, which is more appropriate for a descending order sort. You would need to make this change throughout the function.

Figure 10.19 Output of Program 10-10

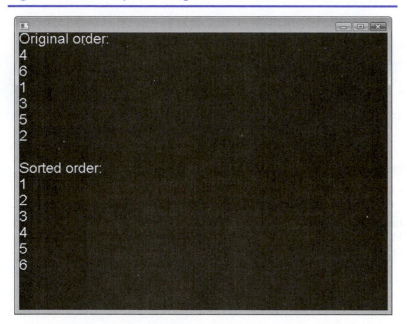

Program 10-11 shows an example that uses both the `selectionSort` and the `shuffle` functions. The program loads a set of images, and then stores their image numbers in an array. The images are displayed on the screen, from left to right, in the order that their image numbers appear in the array. When the user presses the *Shift* key, the array is shuffled. When the user presses the *Ctrl* key, the array is sorted. Figure 10-20 shows an example of the program's output. The screen on the left shows the images displayed in their sorted order (after the user has pressed the *Ctrl* key), and the screen on the right shows the images after the user has pressed the *Shift* key to shuffle them.

Program 10-11   **(SortAndShuffle.cpp)**

```
1    // This program sorts and shuffles an array.
2    #include "DarkGDK.h"
3
4    // Constants to use for image numbers
5    const int APPLE        = 1;
6    const int BANANA       = 2;
7    const int CHERRIES     = 3;
8    const int GRAPES       = 4;
9    const int ORANGE       = 5;
10
11   // Other constants
12   const int REFRESH_RATE  = 60;
13   const int TEXT_X        = 319;
14   const int TEXT_Y        = 120;
15
16   // Function prototypes
17   void setUp();
18   void displayImages(int [], int);
19   void shuffle(int [], int);
20   void selectionSort(int [], int);
21   void swap(int &, int &);
22
23   //*****************************************************
24   // DarkGDK function                                   *
25   //*****************************************************
26   void DarkGDK()
27   {
28       // Create an array to hold the image numbers.
29       const int SIZE = 5;
30       int images[SIZE] = { APPLE, BANANA, CHERRIES,
31                            GRAPES, ORANGE };
32
33       // Perform setup operations.
34       setUp();
35
36       // Game loop
37       while ( LoopGDK() )
38       {
39           // Check to see if the shift key is being pressed.
40           if ( dbShiftKey() )
41           {
42               // Wait until the user releases the shift key.
43               while ( dbShiftKey() )
44               {   // Do nothing.
45               }
46
47               // Shuffle the images in the array.
48               shuffle(images, SIZE);
49           }
50
51           // Check to see if the Ctrl key is being pressed.
52           if ( dbControlKey() )
53           {
```

```
54                   // Wait until the user releases the Ctrl key.
55                   while ( dbControlKey() )
56                   {   // Do nothing.
57                   }
58
59                   // Sort the images in the array.
60                   selectionSort(images, SIZE);
61           }
62
63
64           // Display the images in the order that their
65           // numbers appear in the images array.
66           displayImages(images, SIZE);
67
68           // Prompt the user to press the spacebar.
69           dbCenterText( TEXT_X, TEXT_Y,
70              "Press SHIFT to shuffle or CTRL to sort the images.");
71
72           // Refresh the screen.
73           dbSync();
74       }
75   }
76
77   //*****************************************************
78   // The setUp function performs setup operations.      *
79   //*****************************************************
80   void setUp()
81   {
82       // Load the images.
83       dbLoadImage("Apple.bmp",     APPLE);
84       dbLoadImage("Banana.bmp",    BANANA);
85       dbLoadImage("Cherries.bmp",  CHERRIES);
86       dbLoadImage("Grapes.bmp",    GRAPES);
87       dbLoadImage("Orange.bmp",    ORANGE);
88
89       // Set the text to 24 point Arial font.
90       dbSetTextFont("Arial");
91       dbSetTextSize(24);
92
93       // Disable auto-refresh and set the
94       // refresh rate.
95       dbSyncOn();
96       dbSyncRate(REFRESH_RATE);
97   }
98
99   //*******************************************************
100  // The displayImages function accepts two arguments:    *
101  // (1) an array of image numbers, and                   *
102  // (2) an int that specifies the array size.            *
103  // After the function executes, the images will be      *
104  // displayed in a row across the screen, in the order   *
105  // that their numbers appear in the array.              *
106  //*******************************************************
107  void displayImages(int images[], int size)
108  {
```

```
109         // Variables for the image XY coordinates
110         int x = 0;
111         int y = (dbScreenHeight() / 2) -
112                 (dbGetImageHeight(images[0]) / 2);
113
114         // Display the images.
115         for (int index = 0; index < size; index++)
116         {
117             // Display an image.
118             dbPasteImage( images[index], x, y );
119
120             // Increase x for the next image.
121             x += dbGetImageWidth( images[index] );
122         }
123     }
124
125     //********************************************************
126     // The shuffle function accepts two arguments:          *
127     // (1) an array of ints, and                            *
128     // (2) an int that specifies the array size.            *
129     // After the function executes, the array's elements    *
130     // will be randomly shuffled.                           *
131     //********************************************************
132     void shuffle(int numbers[], int size)
133     {
134         // Variable to hold a random subscript
135         int randomSub;
136
137         // Seed the random number generator.
138         dbRandomize( dbTimer() );
139
140         // Step through the array, swapping each element
141         // with a random element.
142         for (int index = 0; index < size; index++)
143         {
144             // Get a random subscript.
145             randomSub = dbRND(size - 1);
146
147             // Swap two elements.
148             swap( numbers[index], numbers[randomSub] );
149         }
150     }
151
152     //************************************************************
153     // The selectionSort function accepts an int array and      *
154     // an int specifying the size of the array as arguments.    *
155     // It performs the selection sort on the array, sorting     *
156     // its contents in ascending order.                         *
157     //************************************************************
158     void selectionSort(int numbers[], int size)
159     {
160         int startScan;      // Starting position of the scan
161         int index;          // To hold a subscript value
162         int minIndex;       // Element with smallest value in the scan
163         int minValue;       // The smallest value found in the scan
```

```
164
165        // The outer loop iterates once for each element in the
166        // numbers array. The startScan variable marks the position
167        // where the scan should begin.
168        for (startScan = 0; startScan < (size - 1); startScan++)
169        {
170            // Assume the first element in the scannable area
171            // is the smallest value.
172            minIndex = startScan;
173            minValue = numbers[startScan];
174
175            // Scan the array starting at the 2nd element in the
176            // scannable area. We are looking for the smallest
177            // value in the scannable area.
178            for(index = startScan + 1; index < size; index++)
179            {
180                if (numbers[index] < minValue)
181                {
182                    minValue = numbers[index];
183                    minIndex = index;
184                }
185            }
186
187            // Swap the element with the smallest value
188            // with the first element in the scannable area.
189            swap( numbers[minIndex], numbers[startScan] );
190        }
191 }
192
193 //****************************************************
194 // The swap function accepts two int arguments      *
195 // passed by reference. The function swaps the      *
196 // contents of the two arguments.                   *
197 //****************************************************
198 void swap(int &a, int &b)
199 {
200     // Assign a to temp.
201     int temp = a;
202
203     // Assign b to a.
204     a = b;
205
206     // Assign temp to b.
207     b = temp;
208 }
```

Figure 10-20 Example output of Program 10-11

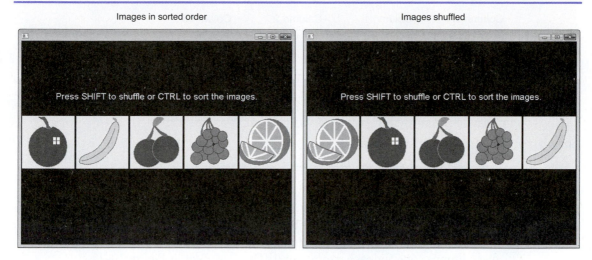

Images in sorted order   Images shuffled

 Checkpoint

10.11. What is a sorting algorithm?

10.12. What is the difference between an ascending order sort and a descending order sort?

10.13. Briefly describe the process used by the selection sort algorithm to sort the contents of an array.

 10.3 **Two-Dimensional Arrays**

CONCEPT: A two-dimensional array is like several identical arrays put together. It is useful for storing multiple sets of data.

The arrays that you have studied so far are known as one-dimensional arrays. They are called *one dimensional* because they can only hold one set of data. Two-dimensional arrays, which are also called *2D arrays*, can hold multiple sets of data. It's best to think of a two-dimensional array as having rows and columns of elements, as shown in Figure 10-21. This figure shows a two-dimensional array having three rows and four columns. Notice that the rows are numbered 0, 1, and 2, and the columns are numbered 0, 1, 2, and 3. There are 12 elements in the array.

Two-dimensional arrays are useful for working with multiple sets of data. For example, suppose you are designing a grade-averaging program for a teacher. The teacher has six students and each student takes five exams during the semester. One approach is to create six one-dimensional arrays, one for each student. Each of these arrays

Figure 10-21 A two-dimensional array

	Column 0	Column 1	Column 2	Column 3
Row 0				
Row 1				
Row 2				

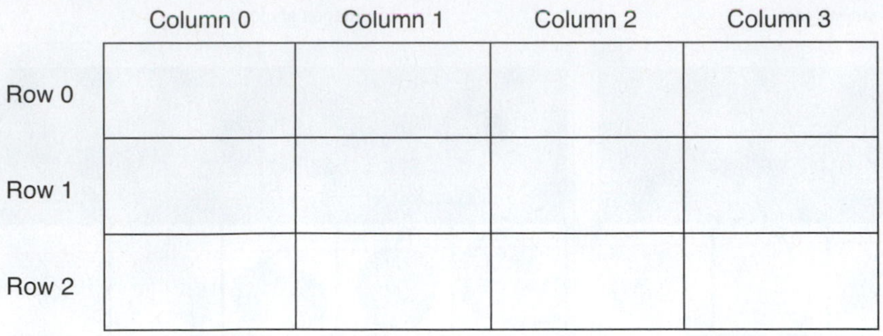

would have five elements, one for each exam score. This approach is cumbersome, however, because you would have to separately process each of the arrays. A better approach is to use a two-dimensional array with six rows (one for each student) and five columns (one for each exam score). This is shown in Figure 10-22.

Figure 10-22 Two-dimensional array with six rows and five columns

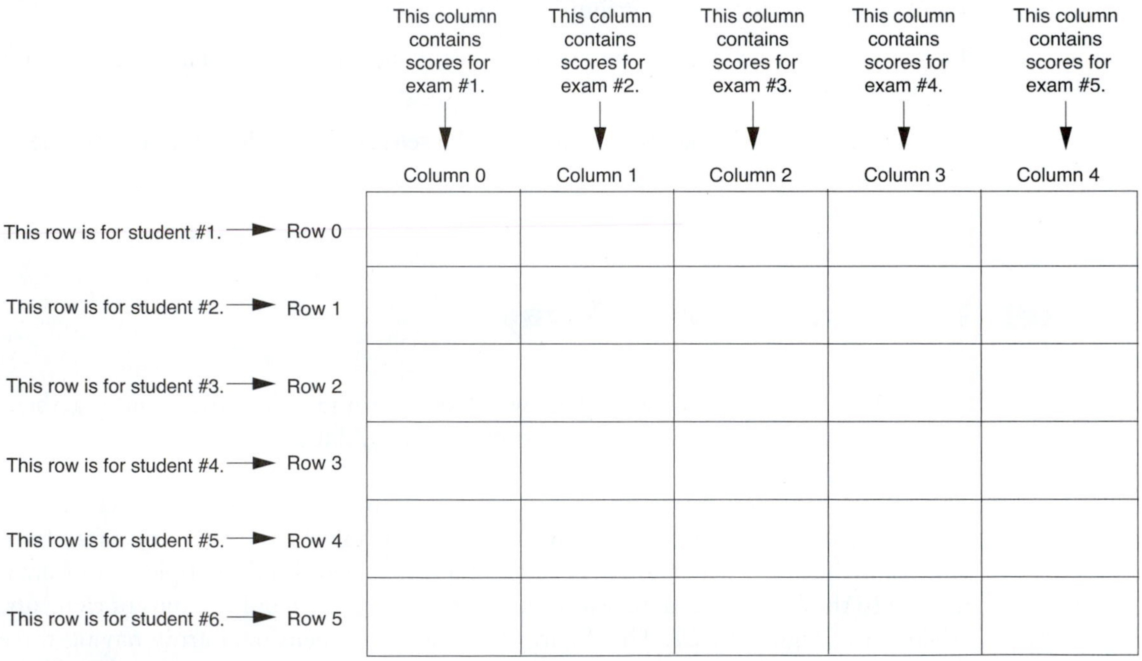

	This column contains scores for exam #1.	This column contains scores for exam #2.	This column contains scores for exam #3.	This column contains scores for exam #4.	This column contains scores for exam #5.
	↓	↓	↓	↓	↓
	Column 0	Column 1	Column 2	Column 3	Column 4
This row is for student #1. → Row 0					
This row is for student #2. → Row 1					
This row is for student #3. → Row 2					
This row is for student #4. → Row 3					
This row is for student #5. → Row 4					
This row is for student #6. → Row 5					

Declaring a Two-Dimensional Array

To declare a two-dimensional array, two size declarators are required: The first one is for the number of rows and the second one is for the number of columns. The following shows an example of how to declare a two-dimensional array of integers:

```
int values[3][4];
```

This statement declares a two-dimensional `int` array with three rows and four columns. The name of the array is `values`. There are 12 elements in the array. As with one-dimensional arrays, it is best to use named constants as the size declarators. Here is an example:

```
const int ROWS = 3;
const int COLS = 4;
int values[ROWS][COLS];
```

When processing the data in a two-dimensional array, each element has two subscripts: one for its row and another for its column. In the `values` array, the elements in row 0 are referenced as follows:

```
values[0][0]
values[0][1]
values[0][2]
values[0][3]
```

The elements in row 1 are referenced as follows:

```
values[1][0]
values[1][1]
values[1][2]
values[1][3]
```

And the elements in row 2 are referenced as follows:

```
values[2][0]
values[2][1]
values[2][2]
values[2][3]
```

Figure 10-23 illustrates the array with the subscripts shown for each element.

Figure 10-23 Subscripts for each element of the `values` array

	Column 0	Column 1	Column 2	Column 3
Row 0	values[0][0]	values[0][1]	values[0][2]	values[0][3]
Row 1	values[1][0]	values[1][1]	values[1][2]	values[1][3]
Row 2	values[2][0]	values[2][1]	values[2][2]	values[2][3]

Accessing the Elements in a Two-Dimensional Array

To access one of the elements in a two-dimensional array, you must use both subscripts. For example, the following statement assigns the number 95 to `values[2][1]`:

```
values[2][1] = 95;
```

Programs that process two-dimensional arrays commonly do so with nested loops. Program 10-12 shows an example. It declares an array with two rows and three columns, prompts the user for values to store in each element, and then displays the values in each element. An example of the program's output is shown in Figure 10-24. In the example output, the user entered the numbers 1, 2, 3, 4, 5, and 6. Figure 10-25 shows how these numbers are stored in the values array.

Program 10-12   (TwoDimArray.cpp)

```
1   // This program demonstrates a two-dimensional array.
2   #include "DarkGDK.h"
3
4   void DarkGDK()
5   {
6       // Create a two-dimensional array.
7       const int ROWS = 2;
8       const int COLS = 3;
9       int values[ROWS][COLS];
10
11      // Get values to store in the array.
12      for (int row = 0; row < ROWS; row++)
13      {
14          for (int col = 0; col < COLS; col++)
15          {
16              dbPrint("Enter a number:");
17              values[row][col] = atoi( dbInput() );
18          }
19      }
20
21      // Display the values in the array.
22      dbPrint();
23      dbPrint("Here are the values you entered:");
24
25      for (int row = 0; row < ROWS; row++)
26      {
27          for (int col = 0; col < COLS; col++)
28          {
29              dbPrint( dbStr(values[row][col]) );
30          }
31      }
32
33      // Wait for the user to press a key.
34      dbWaitKey();
35  }
```

Initializing a Two-Dimensional Array

As with regular, one-dimensional arrays, you can initialize a two-dimensional array with an initialization list when you declare it. Here is an example:

```
const int ROWS = 3;
const int COLS = 2;
int numbers[ROWS][COLS] = { 10, 20, 30, 40, 50, 60 };
```

Figure 10-24 Output of Program 10-12

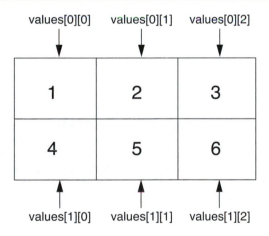

```
Enter a number:
1
Enter a number:
2
Enter a number:
3
Enter a number:
4
Enter a number:
5
Enter a number:
6

Here are the values you entered:
1
2
3
4
5
6
```

Figure 10-25 Numbers stored in the `values` array
in example output of Program 10-12

```
values[0][0]    values[0][1]    values[0][2]

    1               2               3

    4               5               6

values[1][0]    values[1][1]    values[1][2]
```

The values in the initialization list are stored in the array elements, starting at the first element, and proceeding to the last element. In this example, the values are assigned to the `numbers` array in the following manner:

```
numbers[0][0] is set to 10.
numbers[0][1] is set to 20.
numbers[1][0] is set to 30.
numbers[1][1] is set to 40.
numbers[2][0] is set to 50.
numbers[2][1] is set to 60.
```

This is shown in Figure 10-26.

Figure 10-26 Initialization of the numbers array

	Column 0	Column 1
Row 0	10	20
Row 1	30	40
Row 2	50	60

When initializing a two-dimensional array, it helps visually to enclose each row's values in a set of braces. Here is an example:

```
const int ROWS = 3;
const int COLS = 2;
int numbers[ROWS][COLS] = { {10, 20}, {30, 40}, {50, 60} };
```

The same declaration could also be written as follows:

```
const int ROWS = 3;
const int COLS = 2;
int numbers[ROWS][COLS] = { {10, 20},
                            {30, 40},
                            {50, 60}
                          };
```

Passing a Two-Dimensional Array to a Function

Program 10-13 demonstrates passing a two-dimensional array to a function. The program has a function named `showArray` that accepts a two-dimensional `int` array as an argument. The function displays the contents of the array on the screen. Figure 10-27 shows the program's output.

Program 10-13 (Pass2DArray.cpp)

```
1   // This program demonstrates how to pass
2   // a two-dimensional array to a function.
3   #include "DarkGDK.h"
4
5   // Global constants
6   const int ROWS = 3;
7   const int COLS = 2;
8
9   // Function prototype
10  void showArray(int[][COLS], int);
11
```

```
12   //*************************************************
13   // DarkGDK function                               *
14   //*************************************************
15   void DarkGDK()
16   {
17       // Declare a two-dimensional array.
18       int data[ROWS][COLS] = {   {10, 20},
19                                  {30, 40},
20                                  {50, 60}
21                              };
22
23       // Call showArray to display the array.
24       showArray(data, ROWS);
25
26       // Wait for the user to press a key.
27       dbWaitKey();
28   }
29
30   //*************************************************
31   // The showArray function accepts a two-dimensional   *
32   // array of ints with COLS columns, and an int        *
33   // specifying the number of rows as arguments. The    *
34   // function displays the array elements.              *
35   //*************************************************
36   void showArray(int numbers[][COLS], int rows)
37   {
38       for (int r = 0; r < rows; r++)
39       {
40           for (int c = 0; c < COLS; c++)
41           {
42               dbPrint( dbStr(numbers[r][c]) );
43           }
44       }
45   }
```

Figure 10-27 Output of Program 10-13

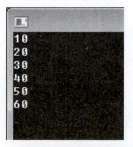

When a two-dimensional array is passed to a function, the parameter must contain a size declarator for the number of columns. Here is the header for the showArray function, from line 36 of Program 10-13:

```
void showArray(int array[][COLS], int rows)
```

COLS is a global constant that is set to 4. The function can accept any two-dimensional integer array, as long as it has four columns. Notice that the number of columns is also specified in the function prototype, in line 10:

```
void showArray( int[][COLS], int);
```

NOTE: When writing a function that accepts a two-dimensional array as an argument, C++ requires the columns to be specified in the function header and prototype because of the way two-dimensional arrays are stored in memory. Although we think of two-dimensional arrays as being organized like tables, with rows and columns, they are actually stored in memory as one long sequence of elements. For example, the data array that is declared in Program 10-13 has three rows and two columns per row. In memory, one row follows the next as shown in Figure 10-28.

When the compiler generates code for accessing the elements of a two-dimensional array, it needs to know the number of columns in each row so it can calculate the location of a given element. For example, suppose we write a statement that accesses the element at row 2, column 0. Since each row has two columns, the compiler knows that it has to skip two rows × two columns = four elements. The next element will be the one we need to access.

Figure 10-28 Storage of a two-dimensional array in memory

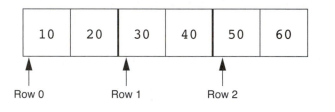

 Checkpoint

10.14. How many rows and how many columns are in the following array?

```
int points[88][100];
```

10.15. Write a statement that assigns the value 100 to the very last element in the points array declared in Checkpoint 10.14.

10.16. Write a declaration for a two-dimensional array initialized with the following table of data:

12	24	32	21	42
14	67	87	65	90
19	1	24	12	8

10.17. Assume a program has the following declarations:

```
const int ROWS = 100;
const int COLS = 50;
int info[ROWS][COLS];
```

Write a set of nested loops that store the value 99 in each element of the info array.

10.18. Assume a program has the following global constants:

```
const int ROWS = 10;
const int COLS = 5;
```

Assume the same program has the following array declaration:

```
int data[ROWS][COLS];
```

Write the function header for a void function named processArray. We should be able to pass the data array as an argument to the processArray function.

10.4 Tile Maps

CONCEPT: Tiles are small rectangular images that are commonly used to construct the background imagery in a game. A tile map is a two-dimensional array that specifies tiles and their locations on the screen.

Tiles are small rectangular images that can be put together to form a larger image. In the early days of video games, computers had much less memory and much lower processing speeds than computers have today. Game developers commonly used tiles to construct the background imagery in games. Breaking a large image down into many smaller ones was more memory efficient, and processing the smaller images was faster. Many game programmers today still prefer to use tiles. In this section, we will discuss how two-dimensional arrays are used to map the locations of tiles on the screen.

For example, the image on the left in Figure 10-29 shows a screen from a game. We are looking down on the scene, which is a grass field with a stone path that leads

Figure 10-29 A tile-based image

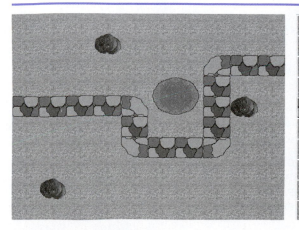 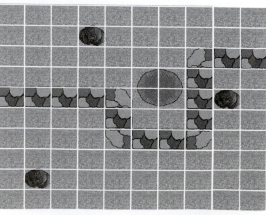

around a tree and some rocks. The image on the right shows how the image is actually constructed of small tiles. In this particular scene there are 10 rows and 10 columns of tiles, for a total of 100 tiles. In this example, the entire screen is 640 pixels wide by 480 pixels high. So each tile is 64 pixels wide by 48 pixels high.

Although there are a total of 100 tiles in the image, many of them are duplicates. The entire image is actually constructed of only 11 tiles, which are shown in Figure 10-30. There is one tile for the grass, five tiles for different sections of the path, one tile for the rocks, and four tiles for the different sections of the tree.

Figure 10-30 Tiles

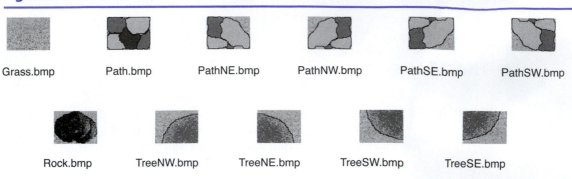

Grass.bmp   Path.bmp   PathNE.bmp   PathNW.bmp   PathSE.bmp   PathSW.bmp

Rock.bmp   TreeNW.bmp   TreeNE.bmp   TreeSW.bmp   TreeSE.bmp

NOTE: The letters NE, NW, SE, and SW in the tile names stand for northeast, northwest, southeast, and southwest.

Let's look at the steps we would take to construct the image shown in Figure 10-29 from the tiles shown in Figure 10-30. As usual we declare constants for the image numbers, as shown here:

```
// Constants for the image numbers
const int GRASS  = 1;
const int PATH   = 2;
const int PATHNE = 3;
const int PATHNW = 4;
const int PATHSE = 5;
const int PATHSW = 6;
const int TREENW = 7;
const int TREENE = 8;
const int TREESW = 9;
const int TREESE = 10;
const int ROCK   = 11;
```

We use these image numbers when we load the tile images, as shown here:

```
dbLoadImage("Grass.bmp",  GRASS);
dbLoadImage("Path.bmp",   PATH);
dbLoadImage("PathNE.bmp", PATHNE);
dbLoadImage("PathNW.bmp", PATHNW);
```

```
dbLoadImage("PathSE.bmp",  PATHSE);
dbLoadImage("PathSW.bmp",  PATHSW);
dbLoadImage("TreeNE.bmp",  TREENE);
dbLoadImage("TreeNW.bmp",  TREENW);
dbLoadImage("TreeSE.bmp",  TREESE);
dbLoadImage("TreeSW.bmp",  TREESW);
dbLoadImage("Rock.bmp",    ROCK);
```

We will also declare constants for the tile image sizes, as shown here:

```
// Constants for the tile image sizes
const int TILE_WIDTH  = 64;
const int TILE_HEIGHT = 48;
```

Then we create a two-dimensional int array to serve as the tile map. A *tile map* is an array that maps the location of each tile on the screen. In this example, the image is constructed using 10 rows of tiles, with each row containing 10 tiles. As a result, our tile map will be an array with 10 rows and 10 columns. Here are the constants that we will use as the array size declarators:

```
// Constants for the tile map size declarators
const int TILE_ROWS = 10;
const int TILE_COLS = 10;
```

Each element of the tile map array will hold the image number for a tile. For example, the element at subscript [0][0] will hold the image number for the first tile in the first row. (This is the tile in the upper-left corner of the screen.) The element at subscript [0][1] will hold the image number for the second tile in the first row. This continues until the last element in the array, at subscript [9][9], which will hold the image number for the tenth tile in the 10th row (the tile in the lower-right corner). The following code shows how we would declare and initialize the array:

```
int tileMap[TILE_ROWS][TILE_COLS] =
{ {GRASS, GRASS, GRASS, GRASS, GRASS, GRASS, GRASS, GRASS,  GRASS, GRASS},
  {GRASS, GRASS, GRASS, ROCK,  GRASS, GRASS, GRASS, GRASS,  GRASS, GRASS},
  {GRASS, GRASS, GRASS, GRASS, GRASS, GRASS, GRASS, PATHNW, PATH,  PATH },
  {GRASS, GRASS, GRASS, GRASS, GRASS, TREENW, TREENE, PATH,  GRASS, GRASS},
  {PATH,  PATH,  PATH,  PATH,  PATHNE, TREESW, TREESE, PATH,  ROCK,  GRASS},
  {GRASS, GRASS, GRASS, GRASS, PATH,  GRASS, GRASS, PATH,   GRASS, GRASS},
  {GRASS, GRASS, GRASS, GRASS, PATHSW, PATH,  PATH,  PATHSE, GRASS, GRASS},
  {GRASS, GRASS, GRASS, GRASS, GRASS, GRASS, GRASS, GRASS,  GRASS, GRASS},
  {GRASS, ROCK,  GRASS, GRASS, GRASS, GRASS, GRASS, GRASS,  GRASS, GRASS},
  {GRASS, GRASS, GRASS, GRASS, GRASS, GRASS, GRASS, GRASS,  GRASS, GRASS}
};
```

To display the tiles we will write a function that accepts the tile map as an argument. The code below shows such a function. This is obviously not a complete program, but we have provided line numbers so we can discuss each part of the code.

```
1   //*************************************************************
2   // The displayTiles function displays tiles. It accepts a    *
3   // two-dimensional int array as the tile map, and an int      *
4   // that specifies the number of rows in the array.           *
5   //*************************************************************
6   void displayTiles(int map[][TILE_COLS], int rows)
```

```
7    {
8        // Variables for the tile coordinates
9        int x = 0, y = 0;
10
11       // Display all the tiles specified in the map.
12       for (int r = 0; r < rows; r++)
13       {
14           // Set x to 0.
15           x = 0;
16
17           // Display all the tiles in this row.
18           for (int c = 0; c < TILE_COLS; c++)
19           {
20               dbPasteImage( map[r][c], x, y );
21               x += TILE_WIDTH;
22           }
23
24           // Increase y for the next row.
25           y += TILE_HEIGHT;
26       }
27   }
```

As you can see from the function header in line 6, this function has the following parameters:

- A two-dimensional `int` array named `map`. The tile map array will be passed into this parameter.
- An `int` named `rows`. This parameter specifies the number of rows in the `map` array.

Inside the function, in line 9, we declare two local `int` variables named `x` and `y`. These variables will hold the coordinates for each tile that we display. The `for` loop in lines 12 through 26 displays each row of tiles. Inside the loop, in line 15, we set `x` to 0 because the *X* coordinate of the first tile in each row is 0. Then the nested `for` loop that appears in lines 18 through 22 displays each of the tiles in the row. When this loop iterates, line 20 pastes a tile image to the screen, and line 21 increases the value of `x` for the next tile. After this loop finishes all of its iterations, a complete row of tiles will have been displayed. Then line 25 increases the `y` variable for the next row.

The code in Program 10-14 demonstrates how this works in a complete program. When you execute this program, it will display the image previously shown on the left of Figure 10-29.

Program 10-14   (`TileDemo.cpp`)

```
1    // This program demonstrates a tile map.
2    #include "DarkGDK.h"
3
4    // Constants for the image numbers
5    const int GRASS        = 1;
6    const int PATH         = 2;
7    const int PATHNE       = 3;
8    const int PATHNW       = 4;
```

```
 9   const int PATHSE          = 5;
10   const int PATHSW          = 6;
11   const int TREENW          = 7;
12   const int TREENE          = 8;
13   const int TREESW          = 9;
14   const int TREESE          = 10;
15   const int ROCK            = 11;
16
17   // Constants for the tile image sizes
18   const int TILE_WIDTH       = 64;
19   const int TILE_HEIGHT      = 48;
20
21   // Constants for the tile map sizes
22   const int TILE_ROWS        = 10;
23   const int TILE_COLS        = 10;
24
25   // Function prototypes
26   void setUp();
27   void displayTiles(int [][TILE_COLS], int);
28
29   //**********************************************************
30   // The DarkGDK function                                    *
31   //**********************************************************
32   void DarkGDK()
33   {
34      // Tile map
35      int tileMap[TILE_ROWS][TILE_COLS] =
36      { {GRASS, GRASS, GRASS, GRASS, GRASS,  GRASS,  GRASS,  GRASS,  GRASS, GRASS},
37        {GRASS, GRASS, GRASS, ROCK,  GRASS,  GRASS,  GRASS,  GRASS,  GRASS, GRASS},
38        {GRASS, GRASS, GRASS, GRASS, GRASS,  GRASS,  GRASS,  PATHNW, PATH,  PATH },
39        {GRASS, GRASS, GRASS, GRASS, GRASS,  TREENW, TREENE, PATH,   GRASS, GRASS},
40        {PATH,  PATH,  PATH,  PATH,  PATHNE, TREESW, TREESE, PATH,   ROCK,  GRASS},
41        {GRASS, GRASS, GRASS, GRASS, PATH,   GRASS,  GRASS,  PATH,   GRASS, GRASS},
42        {GRASS, GRASS, GRASS, GRASS, PATHSW, PATH,   PATH,   PATHSE, GRASS, GRASS},
43        {GRASS, GRASS, GRASS, GRASS, GRASS,  GRASS,  GRASS,  GRASS,  GRASS, GRASS},
44        {GRASS, ROCK,  GRASS, GRASS, GRASS,  GRASS,  GRASS,  GRASS,  GRASS, GRASS},
45        {GRASS, GRASS, GRASS, GRASS, GRASS,  GRASS,  GRASS,  GRASS,  GRASS, GRASS}
46      };
47
48      // Perform setup operations.
49      setUp();
50
51      // Display the tiles.
52      displayTiles(tileMap, TILE_ROWS);
53
54      // Wait for the user to press a key.
55      dbWaitKey();
56   }
57
58   //**********************************************************
59   // The setUp function loads the tile images.               *
60   //**********************************************************
61   void setUp()
62   {
63      dbLoadImage("Grass.bmp",  GRASS);
```

```
64     dbLoadImage("Path.bmp",    PATH);
65     dbLoadImage("PathNE.bmp", PATHNE);
66     dbLoadImage("PathNW.bmp", PATHNW);
67     dbLoadImage("PathSE.bmp", PATHSE);
68     dbLoadImage("PathSW.bmp", PATHSW);
69     dbLoadImage("TreeNE.bmp", TREENE);
70     dbLoadImage("TreeNW.bmp", TREENW);
71     dbLoadImage("TreeSE.bmp", TREESE);
72     dbLoadImage("TreeSW.bmp", TREESW);
73     dbLoadImage("Rock.bmp",    ROCK);
74  }
75
76  //*************************************************************
77  // The displayTiles function displays tiles. It accepts a *
78  // two-dimensional int array as the tile map, and an int  *
79  // that specifies the number of rows in the array.        *
80  //*************************************************************
81  void displayTiles(int map[][TILE_COLS], int rows)
82  {
83      // Variables for the tile coordinates
84      int x = 0, y = 0;
85
86      // Display all the tiles specified in the map.
87      for (int r = 0; r < rows; r++)
88      {
89          // Set x to 0.
90          x = 0;
91
92          // Display all the tiles in this row.
93          for (int c = 0; c < TILE_COLS; c++)
94          {
95              dbPasteImage( map[r][c], x, y );
96              x += TILE_WIDTH;
97          }
98
99          // Increase y for the next row.
100         y += TILE_HEIGHT;
101     }
102 }
```

Now that we've demonstrated the basic technique for displaying a set of tiles using a tile map, let's add some action. Program 10-15 displays the same set of tiles as Program 10-14, and also displays a sprite of a character that we've named Alec. When you run the program, you can use the arrow keys to make Alec walk around the screen.

Program 10-15 (WalkingAlec.cpp)

```
1  // This program allows the user to move an animated sprite
2  // around a tile-based screen.
3  #include "DarkGDK.h"
4
```

```
 5   // Constants for the tile image numbers
 6   const int GRASS       = 1;
 7   const int PATH        = 2;
 8   const int PATHNE      = 3;
 9   const int PATHNW      = 4;
10   const int PATHSE      = 5;
11   const int PATHSW      = 6;
12   const int TREENW      = 7;
13   const int TREENE      = 8;
14   const int TREESW      = 9;
15   const int TREESE      = 10;
16   const int ROCK        = 11;
17
18   // Constants for the tile image sizes
19   const int TILE_WIDTH  = 64;
20   const int TILE_HEIGHT = 48;
21
22   // Constants for the tile map sizes
23   const int TILE_ROWS   = 10;
24   const int TILE_COLS   = 10;
25
26   // Constants for the Alec sprite sheet
27   const int ALEC        = 12;     // Alec's sprite and image number
28   const int ALEC_ROWS   = 4;      // Number of sprite sheet rows
29   const int ALEC_COLS   = 4;      // Number of sprite sheet columns
30   const int EAST_START  = 1;      // First frame for going east
31   const int EAST_END    = 4;      // Last frame for going east
32   const int NORTH_START = 5;      // First frame for going north
33   const int NORTH_END   = 8;      // Last frame for going north
34   const int SOUTH_START = 9;      // First frame for going south
35   const int SOUTH_END   = 12;     // Last frame for going south
36   const int WEST_START  = 13;     // First frame for going west
37   const int WEST_END    = 16;     // Last frame for going west
38   const int DELAY       = 200;    // Animation delay
39
40   // Constants for Alec's direction
41   const int NORTH       = 1;
42   const int SOUTH       = 2;
43   const int EAST        = 3;
44   const int WEST        = 4;
45
46   // Refresh rate
47   const int REFRESH_RATE = 60;
48
49   // Function prototypes
50   void setUp();
51   void displayTiles(int [][TILE_COLS], int);
52   bool arrowKeyPressed();
53   void updateDirection(int &);
54   void moveAlec(int);
55
56   //*************************************************************
57   // The DarkGDK function.                                      *
58   //*************************************************************
59   void DarkGDK()
```

```
60   {
61       // Tile map
62       int tileMap[TILE_ROWS][TILE_COLS] =
63       { {GRASS, GRASS, GRASS, GRASS, GRASS,  GRASS,  GRASS,   GRASS,   GRASS,  GRASS},
64         {GRASS, GRASS, GRASS, ROCK,  GRASS,  GRASS,  GRASS,   GRASS,   GRASS,  GRASS},
65         {GRASS, GRASS, GRASS, GRASS, GRASS,  GRASS,  GRASS,   PATHNW,  PATH,   PATH },
66         {GRASS, GRASS, GRASS, GRASS, GRASS,  TREENW, TREENE,  PATH,    GRASS,  GRASS},
67         {PATH,  PATH,  PATH,  PATH,  PATHNE, TREESW, TREESE,  PATH,    ROCK,   GRASS},
68         {GRASS, GRASS, GRASS, GRASS, PATH,   GRASS,  GRASS,   PATH,    GRASS,  GRASS},
69         {GRASS, GRASS, GRASS, GRASS, PATHSW, PATH,   PATH,    PATHSE,  GRASS,  GRASS},
70         {GRASS, GRASS, GRASS, GRASS, GRASS,  GRASS,  GRASS,   GRASS,   GRASS,  GRASS},
71         {GRASS, ROCK,  GRASS, GRASS, GRASS,  GRASS,  GRASS,   GRASS,   GRASS,  GRASS},
72         {GRASS, GRASS, GRASS, GRASS, GRASS,  GRASS,  GRASS,   GRASS,   GRASS,  GRASS}
73       };
74
75       // Variable for Alec's direction. We start Alec facing east.
76       int direction = EAST;
77
78       // Perform setup operations.
79       setUp();
80
81       // Game loop
82       while ( LoopGDK() )
83       {
84           // Display the tiles.
85           displayTiles(tileMap, TILE_ROWS);
86
87           // If an arrow key is being pressed...
88           if ( arrowKeyPressed() )
89           {
90               // Update the direction.
91               updateDirection(direction);
92
93               // Move Alec.
94               moveAlec(direction);
95           }
96
97           // Refresh the screen.
98           dbSync();
99       }
100  }
101
102  //*************************************************************
103  // The setUp function loads the tile images.                *
104  //*************************************************************
105  void setUp()
106  {
107      // Load the tile images.
108      dbLoadImage("Grass.bmp",   GRASS);
109      dbLoadImage("Path.bmp",    PATH);
110      dbLoadImage("PathNE.bmp",  PATHNE);
111      dbLoadImage("PathNW.bmp",  PATHNW);
112      dbLoadImage("PathSE.bmp",  PATHSE);
113      dbLoadImage("PathSW.bmp",  PATHSW);
114      dbLoadImage("TreeNE.bmp",  TREENE);
```

```
115         dbLoadImage("TreeNW.bmp",    TREENW);
116         dbLoadImage("TreeSE.bmp",    TREESE);
117         dbLoadImage("TreeSW.bmp",    TREESW);
118         dbLoadImage("Rock.bmp",      ROCK);
119
120         // Set the image color key to magenta.
121         dbSetImageColorKey(255, 0, 255);
122
123         // Create the Alec animated sprite.
124         dbCreateAnimatedSprite(ALEC, "Alec.bmp",
125                           ALEC_COLS, ALEC_ROWS, ALEC);
126
127         // Start the sprite with Alec facing east.
128         dbPlaySprite(ALEC, EAST_START, EAST_END, DELAY);
129
130         // Display Alec in the upper-left corner.
131         dbSprite(ALEC, 0, 0, ALEC);
132
133         // Disable auto-refresh and set the refresh rate.
134         dbSyncOn();
135         dbSyncRate(REFRESH_RATE);
136     }
137
138     //*************************************************************
139     // The displayTiles function displays tiles. It accepts a     *
140     // two-dimensional int array as the tile map, and an int that  *
141     // specifies the number of rows in the array.                  *
142     //*************************************************************
143     void displayTiles(int map[][TILE_COLS], int rows)
144     {
145         // Variables for the tile coordinates
146         int x = 0, y = 0;
147
148         // Display all the tiles specified in the map.
149         for (int r = 0; r < rows; r++)
150         {
151             // Set x to 0.
152             x = 0;
153
154             // Display all the tiles in this row.
155             for (int c = 0; c < TILE_COLS; c++)
156             {
157                 dbPasteImage( map[r][c], x, y );
158                 x += TILE_WIDTH;
159             }
160
161             // Increase y for the next row.
162             y += TILE_HEIGHT;
163         }
164     }
165
166     //*********************************************************
167     // The arrowKeyPressed function returns true if any of the *
168     // arrow keys are being pressed.                           *
169     //*********************************************************
```

```
170   bool arrowKeyPressed()
171   {
172       // Variable to indicate whether an arrow key is
173       // being pressed.
174       bool status = false;
175
176       // If any of the arrow keys are being pressed,
177       // set status to true.
178       if ( dbRightKey() || dbLeftKey() ||
179            dbUpKey() || dbDownKey() )
180       {
181           status = true;
182       }
183
184       // Return the value of the status variable.
185       return status;
186   }
187
188   //*****************************************************************
189   // The updateDirection function accepts the direction variable   *
190   // by reference. If any of the arrow keys are being pressed it    *
191   // updates the variable.                                          *
192   //*****************************************************************
193   void updateDirection(int &direction)
194   {
195       if ( dbRightKey() )
196       {
197           direction = EAST;
198       }
199       else if ( dbLeftKey() )
200       {
201           direction = WEST;
202       }
203       else if ( dbUpKey() )
204       {
205           direction = NORTH;
206       }
207       else if ( dbDownKey() )
208       {
209           direction = SOUTH;
210       }
211   }
212
213   //*********************************************************
214   // The moveAlec function accepts Alec's direction as an   *
215   // argument and updates the sprite's position and frame.  *
216   //*********************************************************
217   void moveAlec(int direction)
218   {
219       // Get Alec's coordinates.
220       int x = dbSpriteX(ALEC);
221       int y = dbSpriteY(ALEC);
222
223       // Variables to indicate the starting and
224       // ending frame numbers for Alec.
```

```
225        int startFrame, endFrame;
226
227        // Update Alec's position and frame numbers
228        // based on his direction.
229        switch (direction)
230        {
231            case NORTH:
232                y--;
233                startFrame = NORTH_START;
234                endFrame = NORTH_END;
235                break;
236
237            case SOUTH:
238                y++;
239                startFrame = SOUTH_START;
240                endFrame = SOUTH_END;
241                break;
242
243            case EAST:
244                x++;
245                startFrame = EAST_START;
246                endFrame = EAST_END;
247                break;
248
249            case WEST:
250                x--;
251                startFrame = WEST_START;
252                endFrame = WEST_END;
253                break;
254        }
255
256        // Get a frame from the sprite sheet.
257        dbPlaySprite(ALEC, startFrame, endFrame, DELAY);
258
259        // Display the sprite.
260        dbSprite(ALEC, x, y, ALEC);
261 }
```

The Alec character is an animated sprite, created from the Alec.bmp sprite sheet shown in Figure 10-31. When you press the *Right* arrow key, the program uses the four frames in the top row (frames 1 through 4) to make Alec face east as he walks. When you press the *Up* arrow key, the program uses the four frames in the second row (frames 5 through 8) to make Alec face north as he walks. When you press the *Down* arrow key, the program uses the four frames in the third row (frames 9 through 12) to make Alec face south as he walks. When you press the *Left* arrow key, the program uses the four frames in the fourth row (frames 13 through 16) to make Alec face west as he walks.

Figure 10-32 shows the screen that is displayed when you start the program, with Alec positioned in the upper-left corner.

Figure 10-31 Animated sprite frames for the
Alec character (stored in `Alec.bmp`)

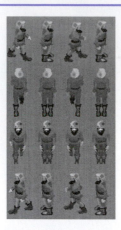

Figure 10-32 Starting screen from Program 10-15

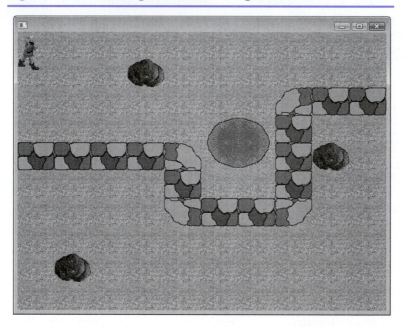

Let's analyze the program. Lines 6 through 16 declare the constants that we will use as image numbers for the tiles. Lines 19 and 20 declare constants for the tile image width and height. Lines 23 and 24 declare constants for the numbers of tile rows and columns that we will display. (These constants will be used as size declarators for the two-dimensional tile map array.)

Lines 27 through 38 declare the following constants that are used for the Alec character's animated sprite:

- Line 27: ALEC is the number that we will use for both the image number and sprite number for the Alec character.

- Lines 28 and 29: `ALEC_ROWS` and `ALEC_COLS` are the number of rows and columns in the `Alec.bmp` sprite sheet.
- Lines 30 and 31: `EAST_START` is the frame number for Alec's first east-facing frame, and `EAST_END` is the frame number for Alec's last east-facing frame.
- Lines 32 and 33: `NORTH_START` is the frame number for Alec's first north-facing frame, and `NORTH_END` is the frame number for Alec's last north-facing frame.
- Lines 34 and 35: `SOUTH_START` is the frame number for Alec's first south-facing frame, and `SOUTH_END` is the frame number for Alec's last south-facing frame.
- Lines 36 and 37: `WEST_START` is the frame number for Alec's first west-facing frame, and `WEST_END` is the frame number for Alec's last west-facing frame.
- Line 38: `DELAY` specifies the time delay between frames for the animation.

Lines 41 through 44 declare the constants `NORTH`, `SOUTH`, `EAST`, and `WEST`, initialized with the values 1, 2, 3, and 4 respectively. We will use these constants to indicate the direction that Alec is facing.

Line 47 declares the `REFRESH_RATE` constant that specifies the maximum screen refresh rate. The function prototypes are shown in lines 50 through 54.

Inside the `DarkGDK` function, we declare the `tileMap` array in lines 62 through 73, and initialize it with image number constants. In line 76, we declare an `int` variable named `direction`. This variable will be used to indicate the direction that the Alec character is facing. Notice that we have initialized it with the value of the `EAST` constant. As a result, Alec will be facing east when the program starts. In line 79, we call the `setUp` function, which performs such things as loading all of the images and creating the Alec sprite.

The game loop begins in line 82. Inside the loop, in line 85, we call the `displayTiles` function to display the tile map. In line 88, an `if` statement calls the `arrowKeyPressed` function. The `arrowKeyPressed` function returns `true` if one of the arrow keys is being pressed, or `false` otherwise. If the function returns `true`, the following actions take place:

- In line 91, we call the `updateDirection` function, passing the `direction` variable as an argument. Note that the `direction` variable is passed by reference. The function determines which arrow key is being pressed, and when it finishes, the `direction` variable will be updated to reflect Alec's direction.
- In line 94, we call the `moveAlec` function, passing the `direction` variable as an argument. This function moves Alec in the direction that the character is facing.
- In line 98, we call `dbSync` to refresh the screen.

The `setUp` function appears in lines 105 through 136. It loads all of the tile images in lines 108 through 118. Line 121 sets the key color to magenta. (This is the key color used in the `Alec.bmp` sprite sheet.) Lines 124 and 125 create the animated sprite for the Alec character. Line 128 starts the animation, specifying the east-facing row of frames. Line 131 displays the Alec sprite at (0, 0). Lines 134 and 135 disable auto-refresh and set the maximum screen refresh rate.

The `displayTiles` function appears in lines 143 through 164. This code is identical to the `displayTiles` function that you saw in Program 10-14.

The `arrowKeyPressed` function appears in lines 170 through 186. This function returns `true` if any of the arrow keys are being pressed, or `false` otherwise.

The `updateDirection` function appears in lines 193 through 211. When we call this function, we pass the `direction` variable by reference as an argument. This function determines which arrow key is being pressed and then updates the `direction` variable with the value of the appropriate directional constant. For example, if the *Right Arrow* key is being pressed, the value of the `EAST` constant will be assigned to the `direction` variable. If the *Left* arrow key is being pressed, the value of the `WEST` constant is assigned to the `direction` variable, and so forth.

The `moveAlec` function appears in lines 217 through 261. When we call this function, we pass the `direction` variable as an argument. In lines 220 and 221, we declare two `int` variables named x and y, and initialize them with the X and Y coordinates of the `ALEC` sprite. In line 225, we declare two `int` variables named `startFrame` and `endFrame`. We will use these variables to indicate the starting and ending frame numbers for the `ALEC` sprite's animation. If you look back at Figure 10-31, you will see that we want to use frames 1 through 4 when Alec is facing east, frames 5 through 8 when Alec is facing north, frames 9 through 12 when Alec is facing south, and frames 13 through 16 when Alec is facing west. The `startFrame` and `endFrame` variables will be used to indicate these values.

In line 229, a `switch` statement begins. The purpose of this switch statement is to update the Alec character's position, and set the appropriate starting and ending frame numbers. The `switch` statement tests the value of the `direction` parameter, which indicates the direction that the Alec character is currently facing. If the `direction` parameter is equal to `NORTH`, the program jumps to the `case` statement in line 231. If the `direction` parameter is equal to `SOUTH`, the program jumps to the `case` statement in line 237. If the `direction` parameter is equal to `EAST`, the program jumps to the `case` statement in line 243. If the `direction` parameter is equal to `WEST`, the program jumps to the `case` statement in line 249. In each of these case sections, either the x or y variable is updated to indicate the character's new position, and the `startFrame` and `endFrame` variables are assigned the appropriate frame numbers.

After the `switch` statement, we get the next frame in the animation sequence in line 257, and in line 260 we display the `ALEC` sprite.

Displaying Layered Sets of Tiles

In Program 10-15, the user can make the Alec character walk anywhere on the screen on top of the background tiles. This includes the rock tiles and the tiles that make up the tree. To make the program more realistic, we should treat the rocks and the tree as obstacles, and prevent Alec from walking on those tiles.

To achieve this, we will first use layered tiles. This means that we will display a set of tiles on the screen, and then display a partial set of tiles on top of the first set. The second set of tiles will contain the images of the obstacles, which in this case are the rocks and the tree. When we display the second set of tiles (the obstacles), we will turn them into sprites. Then when we move Alec around on the screen, we will check for collisions. If Alec collides with any other sprite, we will prevent him from moving on top of that sprite. Program 10-16 demonstrates how this is done.

Program 10-16   (`LayeredMaps.cpp`)

```
 1   // This program allows the user to move an animated sprite
 2   // around a screen layered with two sets of tiles: one for
 3   // the background and one for obstacles.
 4   #include "DarkGDK.h"
 5
 6   // Constants for the background tile image numbers
 7   const int GRASS       = 1;
 8   const int PATH        = 2;
 9   const int PATHNE      = 3;
10   const int PATHNW      = 4;
11   const int PATHSE      = 5;
12   const int PATHSW      = 6;
13
14   // Constants for the obstacle image numbers
15   const int NONE        = 0;
16   const int TREENW      = 7;
17   const int TREENE      = 8;
18   const int TREESW      = 9;
19   const int TREESE      = 10;
20   const int ROCK        = 11;
21
22   // Constants for the tile sizes
23   const int TILE_WIDTH  = 64;
24   const int TILE_HEIGHT = 48;
25
26   // Constants for the tile map sizes
27   const int TILE_ROWS   = 10;
28   const int TILE_COLS   = 10;
29
30   // Constant for the first obstacle sprite number
31   const int FIRST_OBSTACLE_SPRITE = 100;
32
33   // Constants for the Alec sprite sheet
34   const int ALEC        = 12;   // Alec's sprite and image number
35   const int ALEC_ROWS   = 4;    // Number of sprite sheet rows
36   const int ALEC_COLS   = 4;    // Number of sprite sheet columns
37   const int EAST_START  = 1;    // First frame for going east
38   const int EAST_END    = 4;    // Last frame for going east
39   const int NORTH_START = 5;    // First frame for going north
40   const int NORTH_END   = 8;    // Last frame for going north
41   const int SOUTH_START = 9;    // First frame for going south
42   const int SOUTH_END   = 12;   // Last frame for going south
43   const int WEST_START  = 13;   // First frame for going west
44   const int WEST_END    = 16;   // Last frame for going west
45   const int DELAY       = 200;  // Animation delay
46
47   // Constants for Alec's direction
48   const int NORTH       = 1;
49   const int SOUTH       = 2;
50   const int EAST        = 3;
51   const int WEST        = 4;
52
53   // Sound number for the "thump" sound
```

```
54   const int THUMP_SOUND = 1;
55
56   // Refresh rate
57   const int REFRESH_RATE = 60;
58
59   // Function prototypes
60   void setUp();
61   void displayTiles(int [][TILE_COLS], int);
62   void displayObstacles(int [][TILE_COLS], int);
63   bool arrowKeyPressed();
64   void updateDirection(int &);
65   void moveAlec(int);
66   void checkCollisions(int);
67
68   //**************************************************************
69   // The DarkGDK function.                                       *
70   //**************************************************************
71   void DarkGDK()
72   {
73      // Tile map for the background
74      int tileMap[TILE_ROWS][TILE_COLS] =
75      { {GRASS, GRASS, GRASS, GRASS, GRASS,  GRASS, GRASS, GRASS,  GRASS, GRASS},
76        {GRASS, GRASS, GRASS, GRASS, GRASS,  GRASS, GRASS, GRASS,  GRASS, GRASS},
77        {GRASS, GRASS, GRASS, GRASS, GRASS,  GRASS, GRASS, PATHNW, PATH,  PATH },
78        {GRASS, GRASS, GRASS, GRASS, GRASS,  GRASS, GRASS, PATH,   GRASS, GRASS},
79        {PATH,  PATH,  PATH,  PATH,  PATHNE, GRASS, GRASS, PATH,   GRASS, GRASS},
80        {GRASS, GRASS, GRASS, GRASS, PATH,   GRASS, GRASS, PATH,   GRASS, GRASS},
81        {GRASS, GRASS, GRASS, GRASS, PATHSW, PATH,  PATH,  PATHSE, GRASS, GRASS},
82        {GRASS, GRASS, GRASS, GRASS, GRASS,  GRASS, GRASS, GRASS,  GRASS, GRASS},
83        {GRASS, GRASS, GRASS, GRASS, GRASS,  GRASS, GRASS, GRASS,  GRASS, GRASS},
84        {GRASS, GRASS, GRASS, GRASS, GRASS,  GRASS, GRASS, GRASS,  GRASS, GRASS}
85      };
86
87      // Tile map for the rock and tree obstacles
88      int obstacleMap[TILE_ROWS][TILE_COLS] =
89      { {NONE, NONE, NONE, NONE, NONE, NONE,   NONE,   NONE, NONE, NONE},
90        {NONE, NONE, NONE, ROCK, NONE, NONE,   NONE,   NONE, NONE, NONE},
91        {NONE, NONE, NONE, NONE, NONE, NONE,   NONE,   NONE, NONE, NONE},
92        {NONE, NONE, NONE, NONE, NONE, TREENW, TREENE, NONE, NONE, NONE},
93        {NONE, NONE, NONE, NONE, NONE, TREESW, TREESE, NONE, ROCK, NONE},
94        {NONE, NONE, NONE, NONE, NONE, NONE,   NONE,   NONE, NONE, NONE},
95        {NONE, NONE, NONE, NONE, NONE, NONE,   NONE,   NONE, NONE, NONE},
96        {NONE, NONE, NONE, NONE, NONE, NONE,   NONE,   NONE, NONE, NONE},
97        {NONE, ROCK, NONE, NONE, NONE, NONE,   NONE,   NONE, NONE, NONE},
98        {NONE, NONE, NONE, NONE, NONE, NONE,   NONE,   NONE, NONE, NONE}
99      };
100
101     // Variable for Alec's direction. We start Alec facing east.
102     int direction = EAST;
103
104     // Perform setup operations.
105     setUp();
106
107     // Game loop
108     while ( LoopGDK() )
```

```
109            {
110                // Display the background tiles.
111                displayTiles(tileMap, TILE_ROWS);
112
113                // Display the obstacle sprites
114                displayObstacles(obstacleMap, TILE_ROWS);
115
116                // If an arrow key is being pressed...
117                if ( arrowKeyPressed() )
118                {
119                    // Update the direction.
120                    updateDirection(direction);
121
122                    // Move Alec.
123                    moveAlec(direction);
124
125                    // Check for collisions.
126                    checkCollisions(direction);
127                }
128
129                // Refresh the screen.
130                dbSync();
131            }
132  }
133
134  //***********************************************************
135  // The setUp function loads the tile images.                *
136  //***********************************************************
137  void setUp()
138  {
139      // Load the tile images.
140      dbLoadImage("Grass.bmp",  GRASS);
141      dbLoadImage("Path.bmp",   PATH);
142      dbLoadImage("PathNE.bmp", PATHNE);
143      dbLoadImage("PathNW.bmp", PATHNW);
144      dbLoadImage("PathSE.bmp", PATHSE);
145      dbLoadImage("PathSW.bmp", PATHSW);
146      dbLoadImage("TreeNE.bmp", TREENE);
147      dbLoadImage("TreeNW.bmp", TREENW);
148      dbLoadImage("TreeSE.bmp", TREESE);
149      dbLoadImage("TreeSW.bmp", TREESW);
150      dbLoadImage("Rock.bmp",   ROCK);
151
152      // Load the thump sound.
153      dbLoadSound("thump.wav", THUMP_SOUND);
154
155      // Set the image color key to magenta.
156      dbSetImageColorKey(255, 0, 255);
157
158      // Create the Alec animated sprite.
159      dbCreateAnimatedSprite(ALEC, "Alec.bmp",
160                             ALEC_COLS, ALEC_ROWS, ALEC);
161
162      // Start the sprite with Alec facing east.
163      dbPlaySprite(ALEC, EAST_START, EAST_END, DELAY);
```

```
164
165        // Display Alec in the upper-left corner.
166        dbSprite(ALEC, 0, 0, ALEC);
167
168        // Disable auto-refresh and set the refresh rate.
169        dbSyncOn();
170        dbSyncRate(REFRESH_RATE);
171    }
172
173    //*****************************************************************
174    // The displayTiles function displays tiles. It accepts a         *
175    // two-dimensional int array as the tile map, and an int that      *
176    // specifies the number of rows in the array.                      *
177    //*****************************************************************
178    void displayTiles(int map[][TILE_COLS], int rows)
179    {
180        // Variables for the tile coordinates
181        int x = 0, y = 0;
182
183        // Display all the tiles specified in the map.
184        for (int r = 0; r < rows; r++)
185        {
186            // Set x to 0.
187            x = 0;
188
189            // Display all the tiles in this row.
190            for (int c = 0; c < TILE_COLS; c++)
191            {
192                dbPasteImage( map[r][c], x, y );
193                x += TILE_WIDTH;
194            }
195
196            // Increase y for the next row.
197            y += TILE_HEIGHT;
198        }
199    }
200
201    //*****************************************************************
202    // The displayObstacles function displays obstacle tiles. It       *
203    // accepts two-dimensional int array as the tile map, and an       *
204    // int that specifies the number of rows in the array.             *
205    //*****************************************************************
206    void displayObstacles(int map[][TILE_COLS], int rows)
207    {
208        // Variable to hold the calculated sprite numbers
209        int spriteNumber = FIRST_OBSTACLE_SPRITE;
210
211        // Variables for the tile coordinates
212        int x = 0, y = 0;
213
214        // Display all the tiles specified in the map.
215        for (int r = 0; r < rows; r++)
216        {
217            // Set x to 0.
218            x = 0;
```

```
219
220                 // Display all the tiles in this row.
221                 for (int c = 0; c < TILE_COLS; c++)
222                 {
223                     // If an obstacle tile is specified, then
224                     // display it.
225                     if ( map[r][c] != NONE )
226                     {
227                         // Display the obstacle tile as a sprite.
228                         dbSprite(spriteNumber, x, y, map[r][c]);
229
230                         // Calculate the next sprite number.
231                         spriteNumber++;
232                     }
233
234                     // Update the x coordinate for the next tile.
235                     x += TILE_WIDTH;
236                 }
237
238             // Increase y for the next row.
239             y += TILE_HEIGHT;
240         }
241 }
242
243 //****************************************************************
244 // The arrowKeyPressed function returns true if any of the      *
245 // arrow keys are being pressed.                                *
246 //****************************************************************
247 bool arrowKeyPressed()
248 {
249     // Variable to indicate whether an arrow key is
250     // being pressed.
251     bool status = false;
252
253     // If any of the arrow keys are being pressed,
254     // set status to true.
255     if ( dbRightKey() || dbLeftKey() ||
256          dbUpKey() || dbDownKey() )
257     {
258         status = true;
259     }
260
261     // Return the value of the status variable.
262     return status;
263 }
264
265 //****************************************************************
266 // The updateDirection function accepts the direction variable  *
267 // by reference. If any of the arrow keys are being pressed it   *
268 // updates the variable.                                         *
269 //****************************************************************
270 void updateDirection(int &direction)
271 {
272     if ( dbRightKey() )
273     {
```

```
274                direction = EAST;
275            }
276        else if ( dbLeftKey() )
277            {
278                direction = WEST;
279            }
280        else if ( dbUpKey() )
281            {
282                direction = NORTH;
283            }
284        else if ( dbDownKey() )
285            {
286                direction = SOUTH;
287            }
288    }
289
290    //************************************************************
291    // The moveAlec function accepts Alec's direction as an       *
292    // argument and updates the sprite's position and frame.      *
293    //************************************************************
294    void moveAlec(int direction)
295    {
296        // Get Alec's coordinates.
297        int x = dbSpriteX(ALEC);
298        int y = dbSpriteY(ALEC);
299
300        // Variables to indicate the starting and
301        // ending frame numbers for Alec.
302        int startFrame, endFrame;
303
304        // Update Alec's position and frame numbers
305        // based on his direction.
306        switch (direction)
307        {
308            case NORTH:
309                y--;
310                startFrame = NORTH_START;
311                endFrame = NORTH_END;
312                break;
313
314            case SOUTH:
315                y++;
316                startFrame = SOUTH_START;
317                endFrame = SOUTH_END;
318                break;
319
320            case EAST:
321                x++;
322                startFrame = EAST_START;
323                endFrame = EAST_END;
324                break;
325
326            case WEST:
327                x--;
328                startFrame = WEST_START;
```

```
329                     endFrame = WEST_END;
330                     break;
331         }
332
333         // Get a frame from the sprite sheet.
334         dbPlaySprite(ALEC, startFrame, endFrame, DELAY);
335
336         // Display the sprite.
337         dbSprite(ALEC, x, y, ALEC);
338    }
339
340    //**********************************************************
341    // The checkCollisions function accepts Alec's direction   *
342    // as an argument. If Alec has collided with a sprite it    *
343    // moves his position in the opposite direction one pixel.*
344    //**********************************************************
345    void checkCollisions(int direction)
346    {
347        // Get Alec's coordinates.
348        int x = dbSpriteX(ALEC);
349        int y = dbSpriteY(ALEC);
350
351        // Determine whether Alec has collided with any
352        // other sprite.
353        if ( dbSpriteCollision(ALEC, 0) )
354        {
355            // Move Alec one pixel in the direction opposite
356            // that which he is facing.
357            switch (direction)
358            {
359                case NORTH:
360                    y++;
361                    break;
362
363                case SOUTH:
364                    y--;
365                    break;
366
367                case EAST:
368                    x--;
369                    break;
370
371                case WEST:
372                    x++;
373                    break;
374            }
375
376            // Display the sprite.
377            dbSprite(ALEC, x, y, ALEC);
378
379            // Play the thump sound.
380            dbPlaySound(THUMP_SOUND);
381        }
382    }
```

This program works in many ways like Program 10-15, but we need to look at the differences. First let's look at the new constants we have declared:

- In line 15, we have declared a constant named NONE, initialized with the value 0. As you will see in a moment, we will use this constant in the obstacle tile map to indicate locations where no tile should be displayed.
- In line 31, we have also declared a constant named FIRST_OBSTACLE_SPRITE, initialized with the value 100. When we create the obstacle sprites, we will start their sprite numbers at this value.
- In line 54, we have declared a constant named THUMP_SOUND. We will use this as the sound number for a sound effect that will play when Alec bumps into an obstacle.

Inside the DarkGDK function, notice that we have two tile map arrays. First we have the tileMap array that is used to display the background, declared in lines 74 through 85:

```
73   // Tile map for the background
74   int tileMap[TILE_ROWS][TILE_COLS] =
75   { {GRASS, GRASS, GRASS, GRASS, GRASS,  GRASS, GRASS, GRASS,  GRASS, GRASS},
76     {GRASS, GRASS, GRASS, GRASS, GRASS,  GRASS, GRASS, GRASS,  GRASS, GRASS},
77     {GRASS, GRASS, GRASS, GRASS, GRASS,  GRASS, GRASS, PATHNW, PATH,  PATH },
78     {GRASS, GRASS, GRASS, GRASS, GRASS,  GRASS, GRASS, PATH,   GRASS, GRASS},
79     {PATH,  PATH,  PATH,  PATH,  PATHNE, GRASS, GRASS, PATH,   GRASS, GRASS},
80     {GRASS, GRASS, GRASS, GRASS, PATH,   GRASS, GRASS, PATH,   GRASS, GRASS},
81     {GRASS, GRASS, GRASS, GRASS, PATHSW, PATH,  PATH,  PATHSE, GRASS, GRASS},
82     {GRASS, GRASS, GRASS, GRASS, GRASS,  GRASS, GRASS, GRASS,  GRASS, GRASS},
83     {GRASS, GRASS, GRASS, GRASS, GRASS,  GRASS, GRASS, GRASS,  GRASS, GRASS},
84     {GRASS, GRASS, GRASS, GRASS, GRASS,  GRASS, GRASS, GRASS,  GRASS, GRASS}
85   };
```

Look carefully at the image number constants in this array and notice that they only specify the tiles for the grass and the stone path. The constants for the rock and tree tiles are not present in this array. Next we have the obstacleMap array in lines 88 through 99, which specifies the locations for the obstacles:

```
87   // Tile map for the rock and tree obstacles
88   int obstacleMap[TILE_ROWS][TILE_COLS] =
89   { {NONE, NONE, NONE, NONE, NONE, NONE,   NONE,   NONE, NONE, NONE},
90     {NONE, NONE, NONE, ROCK, NONE, NONE,   NONE,   NONE, NONE, NONE},
91     {NONE, NONE, NONE, NONE, NONE, NONE,   NONE,   NONE, NONE, NONE},
92     {NONE, NONE, NONE, NONE, NONE, TREENW, TREENE, NONE, NONE, NONE},
93     {NONE, NONE, NONE, NONE, NONE, TREESW, TREESE, NONE, ROCK, NONE},
94     {NONE, NONE, NONE, NONE, NONE, NONE,   NONE,   NONE, NONE, NONE},
95     {NONE, NONE, NONE, NONE, NONE, NONE,   NONE,   NONE, NONE, NONE},
96     {NONE, NONE, NONE, NONE, NONE, NONE,   NONE,   NONE, NONE, NONE},
97     {NONE, ROCK, NONE, NONE, NONE, NONE,   NONE,   NONE, NONE, NONE},
98     {NONE, NONE, NONE, NONE, NONE, NONE,   NONE,   NONE, NONE, NONE}
99   };
```

The obstacle tiles will be displayed on top of the background tiles. Notice that many of the elements in the obstacleMap array are initialized with NONE. In each location that specifies NONE, no obstacle will be displayed. The background tiles in those locations will be visible.

Inside the game loop in line 111 we call the `displayTiles` function, passing the `tileMap` array as an argument to display the background tiles. Then in line 114, we call a function named `displayObstacles`, passing the `obstacleMap` array as an argument. The `displayObstacles` function displays the obstacle tiles specified by the `obstacleMap` array, and makes sprites of each one.

The `if` statement in line 117 determines whether the user is pressing an arrow key. If so, we perform the following:

- Call the `updateDirection` function in line 120 to update the `direction` variable.
- Call the `moveAlec` function in line 123 to move Alec in the specified direction.
- Call the `checkCollisions` function in line 126 to determine whether Alec has collided with any of the obstacle sprites. If so, Alec is moved back one pixel in the opposite direction.

Now let's look at the `displayObstacles` function, which appears in lines 206 through 241. You will notice that in many ways this function is like the `displayTiles` function. This function has the following parameters:

- A two-dimensional `int` array named `map`. A tile map array will be passed into this parameter.
- An `int` named `rows`. This parameter specifies the number of rows in the `map` array.

Inside the function in line 209, we declare a variable named `spriteNumber` and initialize it with the value of `FIRST_OBSTACLE_SPRITE`. When we create sprites for the obstacles, we will calculate their sprite numbers and this variable will be used to hold those sprite numbers.

In line 212, we declare two local `int` variables named `x` and `y`. These variables will hold the coordinates for each tile that we display. The `for` loop in lines 215 through 240 displays each row of tiles. Then the nested `for` loop that appears in lines 221 through 236 displays each of the tiles in the row. When this loop iterates, the `if` statement in line 225 determines whether the array element that we are currently processing contains the value `NONE`. If so, we do not want to display anything in this location. Otherwise, we want to display an obstacle. In line 228, we create a sprite using the value of the `spriteNumber` variable as the sprite number, and using the image specified by the array element `map[r][c]` as the image. In line 231, we increment `spriteNumber` to get the next sprite number.

Now let's look at the `checkCollisions` function in lines 345 through 382. When we call this function we pass the `direction` variable as an argument to specify Alec's current direction. In lines 348 and 349 we declare two `int` variables named `x` and `y` and we initialize them with the `ALEC` sprite's *XY* coordinates. Then the `if` statement in line 353 determines whether the `ALEC` sprite has collided with any other sprite. When you call the `dbSpriteCollision` function, you pass two sprite numbers as arguments, and the function returns `true` (1) if those sprites have collided, or `false` (0) it they have not collided. When you pass 0 as the second argument to `dbSpriteCollision`, as we did in this statement, the function returns `true` if the sprite specified by the first argument has collided with any sprite.

If the ALEC sprite has collided with any other sprite, the switch statement in line 357 executes. The switch statement tests the value of the direction parameter, and then branches to the appropriate case statement to move the ALEC sprite backward by one pixel.

In line 377, we display the ALEC sprite, and in line 380, we play the thump sound effect. (The sound file was loaded in the setUp function.)

 Checkpoint

10.19. What are tiles?

10.20. What is a tile map?

10.21. Suppose you are writing a tile-based game that uses a screen that is 500 pixels wide by 400 pixels high. The tiles that you want to use for the background are 25 pixels wide by 20 pixels high. How many rows and columns will the tile map have?

Review Questions

Multiple Choice

1. A(n) _____ appears in an array declaration and specifies the number of elements in the array.
   a. subscript
   b. size declarator
   c. array name
   d. initialization value

2. To make programs easier to maintain, many programmers use _____ to specify the size of an array.
   a. real numbers
   b. string expressions
   c. math expressions
   d. named constants

3. A(n) _____ is an individual storage location in an array.
   a. element
   b. bin
   c. cubby hole
   d. size declarator

4. A(n) _____ is a number that identifies a storage location in an array.
   a. element
   b. subscript
   c. size declarator
   d. identifier

5. The first subscript in an array is _____.
   a. −1
   b. 1
   c. 0
   d. the size of the array minus one

6. The last subscript in an array is _____.
   a. −1
   b. 99
   c. 0
   d. the size of the array minus one

7. C++ does not perform _____, which means it will allow a program to use an invalid array subscript.
   a. memory checking
   b. bounds checking
   c. type compatibility checking
   d. syntax checking

8. You think of a two-dimensional array as containing _____.
   a. lines and statements
   b. chapters and pages
   c. rows and columns
   d. horizontal and vertical elements

9. Small rectangular images that can be put together to form a larger image are called _____.
   a. tiles
   b. maps
   c. components
   d. elements

10. A _____ is a two-dimensional array that specifies the locations of tiles on the screen.
    a. tile locator
    b. tile specifier
    c. tile bank
    d. tile map

True or False

1. You can store a mixture of different data types in an array.

2. An array's size cannot be changed while the program is running.

3. You can do many things with arrays, but you cannot pass one as an argument to a function.

4. A declaration for a two-dimensional array requires only one size declarator.

Short Answer

1. Look at the following code:

```
const int SIZE = 10;
int values[SIZE];
```

   a. How many elements does the array have?
   b. What is the subscript of the first element in the array?
   c. What is the subscript of the last element in the array?

2. Look at the following code:

```
int values[] = { 1, 2, 3 };
```

   a. How many elements does the array have?
   b. What value is stored in numbers[2]?
   c. What value is stored in numbers[0]?

3. Look at the following array declaration:

```
int data[8][10]
```

   a. How many rows does the array have?
   b. How many columns does the array have?
   c. How many elements does the array have?
   d. Write a statement that assigns the number 0 to the last column of the last row in the array.

4. Suppose you are writing a tile-based game that uses a screen that is 1024 pixels wide by 768 pixels high. The tiles that you want to use for the background are 32 pixels wide by 32 pixels high. How many rows and columns will the tile map have?

Algorithm Workbench

1. Assume data is an int array with 20 elements. Write a for loop that displays each element of the array.

2. Assume the arrays numberArray1 and numberArray2 each have 100 elements. Write code that copies the values in numberArray1 to numberArray2.

3. Write the code for a void function named setToZero. The function should accept an int array as an argument. It should assign 0 to each of the array's elements.

4. Write the code for a void function named set2DToZero. The function should accept a two-dimensional int array as an argument. (The array that is accepted as an argument should have 10 columns.) The function should assign 0 to each of the array's elements.

5. Suppose you have the images shown in Figure 10-33 to use as tiles in a program. In the program you declare the following constants for image numbers:

```
const int GRASS  = 1;
const int PATH   = 2;
const int PATHNE = 3;
```

```
const int PATHNW = 4;
const int PATHSE = 5;
const int PATHSW = 6;
```

Figure 10-33 Tile images

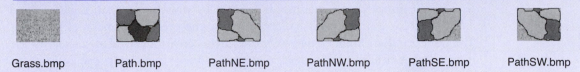

Grass.bmp   Path.bmp   PathNE.bmp   PathNW.bmp   PathSE.bmp   PathSW.bmp

In the same program you load the images using the following statements:

```
dbLoadImage("Grass.bmp",   GRASS);
dbLoadImage("Path.bmp",    PATH);
dbLoadImage("PathNE.bmp", PATHNE);
dbLoadImage("PathNW.bmp", PATHNW);
dbLoadImage("PathSE.bmp", PATHSE);
dbLoadImage("PathSW.bmp", PATHSW);
```

Write the declaration for a tile map that you would use to display the image shown in Figure 10-34. Assume that the screen resolution is 640 by 480, and each of the tiles is 64 pixels wide by 48 pixels high.

Figure 10-34 Tile-based screen

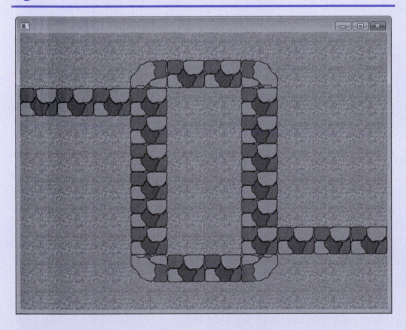

Programming Exercises

1. **ColorArray Program Modification**
   Program 10-4 (ColorArray.cpp) demonstrates how to use a DWORD array of color values. The program randomly clears the screen every half a second to one of these four colors: red, green, blue, or magenta. When you run the program, you might notice that sometimes it appears to wait longer than half a second between color changes. This happens because the program sometimes generates the same random number two or more times consecutively. This results in the screen being cleared to the same color two or more times in a row. Modify the program so it never clears the screen to the same color two times consecutively.

2. **Closed Polyline Function**
   In this chapter, you saw an example of a function that draws a polyline. Write a program that uses a similar function to draw a closed polygon. When a closed polyline is drawn, the last endpoint is connected to the first endpoint.

3. **ESP Game**
   Create a game that can test your ESP abilities. In the book's online resources (located at www.aw.com/gaddis), you will find images for cards with a triangle, a square, and a circle, as well as a face-down card image. The game should work this way:

   Three cards are shown face down. Internally, the program should randomly select values for each card (one triangle, one square, and one circle). The user should be instructed to use the mouse to select which card is the triangle. The selected card should then be revealed.

   Repeat this 10 times and then display the number of times the user correctly identifies the triangle card.

4. **Matching Card Game**
   For this game you will use six of the fruit symbols shown in this chapter to create a deck of 12 cards. There should two of each symbol in the deck. For example, there might be two apple cards, two banana cards, two grape cards, and so forth. (The images are available in the book's online resources at www.aw.com/gaddis.)

   This game is designed for two players. When the game begins the cards should be shuffled and then all of the cards should be shown face down. Each player takes turns picking two cards, with the objective of finding two cards that match. If the two cards match, the player gets points and those two cards are removed from the game. If the two cards don't match, the computer turns them back over and the next player takes a turn. The game ends when all of the matching cards have been selected, and the player with the highest score wins.

5. **Domination Card Game**
   This is a card game where the user plays against the computer. Create a deck of at least 20 cards in which the cards are numbered 1 through 20. When the game begins, the deck is shuffled. Then half of the deck is given to the user and the other half is given to the computer, with no card values showing. At this point in the game, you might want to display the two players' cards as two separate face-down decks, one on the left side of the screen and the other on the right side.

During each turn, one card from the user and one card from the computer are turned over. The player with the highest value gets to keep both cards, which are placed back at the bottom of that player's deck. The game is won when one player has all of the cards. (As an alternative, you can design the game to end after a specified number of turns. The player with the highest value set of cards wins.)

6. **Tic-Tac-Toe**

   Create a game that allows two players to play a game of tic-tac-toe. The program should display a screen similar to the one shown in Figure 10-35. The program should repeat the following steps until one of the players wins, or a tie occurs:

   - Player 1 uses the mouse to select a location for an X.
   - Player 2 uses the mouse to select a location for an O.
   - After each player makes a selection, the program should determine whether a player has won, or a tie has occurred. A player wins by placing three Xs or Os in a row, horizontally, vertically, or diagonally. If all of the spaces have an X or an O placed in them, and there are no three Xs or Os in a row, then a tie has occurred.

Figure 10-35 Tic-Tac-Toe screen

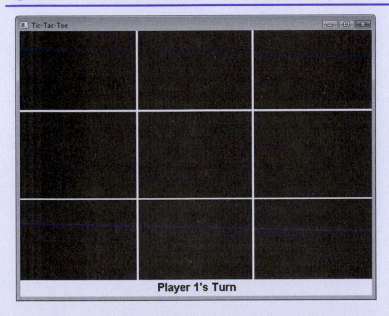

7. **Coins and Snakes**

   In this chapter, you saw Program 10-15, which lets the user move the Alec character around a tile-based screen. Use the same tile images to create a similar game that has at least 10 rocks placed around the screen. Some of the rocks should turn into a coin when Alec comes in contact with them, and some of the rocks should turn into a snake. When a rock turns into a coin, the player earns one point, and when a rock turns into a snake, the player loses one point. When all of the coins or all of the snakes have been uncovered, the game ends. The object of the game is to have at least one point when the game ends. (You will find coin and snake images in the book's online resources at www.aw.com/gaddis.)

11 Strings and Files

TOPICS

11.1 Working with Strings

11.2 Introduction to File Input and Output

11.3 Saving a Game's High Score

11.1 Working with Strings

So far, you have learned how to store numeric data, such as integers and floating point values, in variables. In this chapter, we will show you how to store strings in memory, and perform various operations on those strings.

If you want to store a numeric value in memory, you declare a variable of the appropriate data type. Then you can assign a numeric value to the variable. Storing a string in memory, however, is not as straightforward as storing a numeric value because numeric values occupy established amounts of memory. For example, an int occupies four bytes, regardless of its value. A float occupies eight bytes, regardless of its value. Strings, on the other hand, can vary in length. Suppose you are writing a program that asks the user to enter his or her name. One user might enter "Jim", and someone else using the program might enter "Daphne".

In C++, strings are commonly stored in char arrays. *char* is a C++ data type for storing single characters in memory. Before we can fully explore the way that strings are stored, we need to discuss the basics of the char data type.

The char Data Type

A char variable occupies one byte of memory, and is typically used to hold a single character. Here is an example of how you might declare a char variable named letter:

```
char letter;
```

Now we can assign a character to the variable as follows:

```
letter = 'A';
```

After this statement executes, the character A will be stored in the `letter` variable. Notice that the character literal on the right side of the assignment operator is enclosed in single quotation marks, not the double quotation marks that we use to enclose strings. In C++, a character literal is always enclosed in single quotation marks. An error will occur if you try to assign a string literal to a `char` variable, as shown in the following example:

```
// Declare a char variable.
char letter;

// ERROR! The following statement won't work!
letter = "A";
```

This code attempts to assign the string literal `"A"` to the `char` variable `letter`. Even though the string `"A"` has only one character, it cannot be assigned to a `char` variable because of the way that string literals are stored in memory.

The Way Strings Are Stored in Memory

As previously mentioned, strings can vary in length. When a string is stored in memory, some technique must be used to indicate the string's length. In C++, an extra byte containing the number 0 is appended to the end of a string. This extra byte is called the *null character*, and its purpose is to mark the end of the string. For example, Figure 11-1 illustrates how the strings "Desmond", "Kate", and "Bonnie" would be stored. In the figure, we use the Ø symbol to represent the null character.

Figure 11-1 The strings "Desmond", "Kate", and "Bonnie"

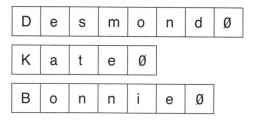

Although the name Desmond is seven characters long, the string "Desmond" uses eight bytes of memory. This is because an extra byte of storage is required for the null character. Likewise, the string "Kate" uses five bytes of memory, and the string "Bonnie" uses seven bytes.

 NOTE: Remember that the null character is not the character `'0'` but the numeric value 0. Its purpose is simply to mark the end of the string. When you print a string on the screen, you do not see the null character.

This explains why you cannot assign strings to `char` variables. Previously, you saw that you can assign a character literal such as `'A'` to a `char` variable, but an error will occur if you assign a string literal such as `"A"` to a `char` variable. This is because a null character is appended, in memory, to the end of all string literals. As shown in Figure 11-2, the character literal `'A'` takes only one byte of memory, but the string literal `"A"` takes two bytes of memory. Because a `char` variable is only one byte in size, it cannot hold a string.

Figure 11-2 Character and string storage

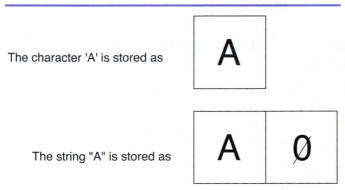

The character 'A' is stored as

The string "A" is stored as

Using `char` Arrays for String Storage

Strings are commonly stored in `char` arrays. You declare a `char` array the same way that you declare arrays of other types. Here is an example:

```
const int SIZE = 12;
char name[SIZE];
```

This code declares `name` as an array of 12 characters. Because strings end with a null character, the `name` array is large enough to hold a string up to 11 characters long. Optionally, we can initialize the array with a string when we declare it, as shown here:

```
const int SIZE = 12;
char name[SIZE] = "Desmond";
```

This code declares `name` as an array of 12 characters, and initializes it with the string "Desmond". The string "Desmond", including the null character, uses only eight bytes, so the array will be only partially filled. This is shown in Figure 11-3.

Figure 11-3 A `char` array partially filled with a string

D	e	s	m	o	n	d	Ø				

Displaying a String Stored in a `char` Array

You can easily display a string that is stored in a `char` array with `dbPrint`, `dbText`, and `dbCenterText`. For example, suppose we have the following declarations:

```
const int SIZE = 6;
char greeting[SIZE] = "Hello";
```

This code declares `greeting` as an array of six characters, and initializes it with the string "Hello". We can then use statements such as the following to display the string:

```
dbPrint( greeting );
dbText( 100, 100, greeting );
dbCenterText( 319, 239, greeting );
```

Using Standard C++ Library Functions to Work with Strings

The standard C++ library provides numerous functions for working with strings. We will discuss several of these functions in this chapter. To use these functions you need to write the following `#include` directive at the top of your program:

```
#include <string.h>
```

This directive includes the contents of the standard C++ header file `string.h` in your program. Notice that the name of the file is enclosed in angled brackets < > instead of quotation marks. This is because `string.h` is part of the standard C++ library.

You are already accustomed to writing an `#include` directive for the `DarkGDK.h` header file. You still need that directive in your programs as well. You can write the `#include` directive for `string.h` either before or after the directive for `DarkGDK.h`.

Using `strcpy` to Copy a String to an Existing Array

Although you can use the = operator to initialize a `char` array with a string, you cannot use the = operator to assign a string to an existing `char` array. For example, the following code will cause an error:

```
// Declare a char array.
const int SIZE = 12;
char name[SIZE];

// ERROR! The following statement will not work!
name = "Desmond";
```

This code declares `name` as a 12 element `char` array. Notice that the array is not initialized with any data. The last statement attempts to use the = operator to assign a string to the array. This will cause an error. In C++, when you assign a group of values to an array, you must assign the values on an element-by-element basis. In this example, the character `'D'` must be assigned to `name[0]`, the character `'e'` must be assigned to `name[1]`, and so forth.

Fortunately, the standard C++ library provides a function named `strcpy` that simplifies the process of assigning a string to a `char` array. Here is the general format of how you call the function:

```
strcpy( Destination, Source );
```

In the general format, `Destination` is the name of the array that you are assigning to, and `Source` is the string that you are assigning. After the function executes, the `Source` string will be copied to the `Destination` array, with a null character placed at the end. Here is an example:

```
// Declare a char array.
const int SIZE = 12;
char name[SIZE];

// Assign "Desmond" to the name array.
strcpy( name, "Desmond" );
```

After this code executes, the `name` array will contain the string "Desmond". You can also use the `strcpy` function to copy a string from one `char` array to another `char` array. Here is an example:

```
// Declare and initialize the name1 char array.
const int SIZE = 12;
char name1[SIZE] = "Desmond";

// Declare name2 as an empty char array.
char name2[SIZE];

// Copy the contents of name1 to name2.
strcpy( name2, name1 );
```

This code declares two `char` arrays named `name1` and `name2`. The `name1` array is initialized with the string "Desmond", and the `name2` array is uninitialized. The last statement uses `strcpy` to copy the contents of `name1` to `name2`. After this code executes, both the `name1` and `name2` arrays will contain the string "Desmond".

> **WARNING!** The `strcpy` function does not determine whether the destination array is large enough to hold the string that is being copied to it. If the string is too large to fit in the destination array, the function will overwrite the bounds of the array, causing an error condition known as a *buffer overflow*.

Using `strcat` to Append a String to an Existing Array

The `strcat` function *concatenates*, or appends, one string to the end of another. Here is the general format of how you call the function:

```
strcat( Destination, Source );
```

In the general format, `Destination` is the name of the array that you are assigning to, and `Source` is the string that you are assigning. Here is an example:

```
// Declare a char array, initialized with "Desmond".
const int SIZE = 50;
char name[SIZE] = "Desmond";
```

```
// Append " was here!" to the end of the string
// stored in the name array.
strcat( name, " was here!" );
```

This code declares `name` as an array of 50 characters, and initializes it with the string "Desmond". The last statement calls `strcat` to append the string "was here!" to the end of the string that is stored in the `name` array. After this code executes, the `name` array will contain the string "Desmond was here!".

> **WARNING!** The `strcat` function does not determine whether the destination array is large enough to hold both strings. If the destination array is not large enough to hold both strings, `strcat` will overwrite the bounds of the array, causing a buffer overflow.

Using `strlen` to Get the Length of a String

The `strlen` function accepts the name of a `char` array as its argument, and it returns the length of the string that is stored in the array. The length of a string is the number of characters in the string, not including the null character. Here is an example:

```
// Declare and initialize the name char array.
const int SIZE = 12;
char name[SIZE] = "Desmond";

// Declare an int named length.
int length;

// Assign the length of the string to the length
// variable.
length = strlen( name );
```

This code declares `name` as an array of 12 characters, and initializes it with the string "Desmond". Then an `int` variable named `length` is declared. The last statement calls the `strlen` function, passing the `name` array as an argument. The function returns the length of the string stored in the array, and that value is assigned to the `length` variable. After this code executes, the `length` variable will be assigned the value 7 because the string "Desmond" has seven characters.

Reading a String as Input

Recall that the Dark GDK function `dbInput` returns input that has been typed at the keyboard as a string. If you need to save that input as a string, you can use `dbInput` along with `strcpy`. You do so in the following general format:

```
strcpy( Destination, dbInput() );
```

Destination is the name of the array that will contain the input. The following code shows an example:

```
// Declare a char array.
const int SIZE = 50;
char name[SIZE];
```

```
// Prompt the user to enter his or her name.
dbPrint( "Enter your name:" );

// Read the input and store it in the name array.
strcpy( name, dbInput() );
```

This code declares `name` as an array of 50 characters, and then prompts the user to enter his or her name. The last statement gets the user's input from the keyboard and stores that input as a string in the `name` array.

Comparing Strings

Suppose a program has two `char` arrays that each contains strings, and you need to determine whether the two strings are the same. To compare the contents of the two `char` arrays, you must use the `strcmp` function. When you call the `strcmp` function, you pass the names of the two arrays as arguments, as shown in the following general format:

```
strcmp( Array1, Array2 )
```

The function returns a value according to the following rules:

- If the strings stored in both arrays are identical, `strcmp` returns 0.
- If the string in `Array1` is less than the string in `Array2`, `strcmp` returns a negative number.
- If the string in `Array1` is greater than the string in `Array2`, `strcmp` returns a positive number.

The following code shows an example. Assume `str1` and `str2` are both `char` arrays that contain strings.

```
if ( strcmp( str1, str2 ) == 0 )
{
    dbPrint("Both strings are the same.");
}
```

You can pass `char` arrays or string literals as arguments to `strcmp`. The following code shows an example that compares a `char` array (`name`) to a string literal.

```
if ( strcmp( name, "Greg" ) == 0 )
{
    dbPrint("Welcome back Greg!");
}
```

The `strcmp` function performs a case sensitive comparison, meaning that uppercase characters are not equivalent to their lowercase counterparts. For example, the string "Manchester" is not the same as the string "manchester".

Program 11-1 shows a simple demonstration. It prompts the user to enter two strings, and it then determines whether the strings are the same. Figure 11-4 shows sample output from the program.

In Program 11-1, the `if` statement in line 22 determines whether `strcmp` returns the value 0 to indicate that `string1` and `string2` are the same. The `strcmp` function can also determine whether one string is greater than or less than another string. If string1 were less than string2, the strcmp function would return a negative number, and if string1 were greater than string2, the strcmp function would return a positive number.

Program 11-1   **(StringsEqual.cpp)**

```
1   // This program demonstrates how to determine
2   // whether two strings are equal.
3   #include "DarkGDK.h"
4   #include <string.h>
5
6   void DarkGDK()
7   {
8       // Declare two char arrays for input.
9       const int SIZE = 50;
10      char string1[SIZE];
11      char string2[SIZE];
12
13      // Prompt the user for the first string.
14      dbPrint("Enter a string:");
15      strcpy( string1, dbInput() );
16
17      // Prompt the user for the second string.
18      dbPrint("Enter another string:");
19      strcpy( string2, dbInput() );
20
21      // Determine whether the strings are the same.
22      if ( strcmp(string1, string2) == 0 )
23      {
24          dbPrint("Those strings are the same.");
25      }
26      else
27      {
28          dbPrint("Those strings are NOT the same.");
29      }
30
31      // Wait for the user to press a key.
32      dbWaitKey();
33  }
```

Figure 11-4 Sample output of Program 11-1

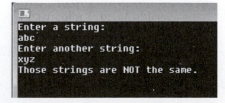

Recall from Chapter 1 that computers do not actually store characters, such as A, B, C, and so forth, in memory. Instead, they store numeric codes that represent the characters. In Chapter 1, we mentioned that ASCII (the American Standard Code for Information Interchange) is the most commonly used character coding system. You can see the set of ASCII codes in Appendix B, but here are some facts:

- The uppercase characters "A" through "Z" are represented by the numbers 65 through 90.
- The lowercase characters "a" through "z" are represented by the numbers 97 through 122.
- When the digits "0" through "9" are stored in memory as characters, they are represented by the numbers 48 through 57. (For example, the string "abc123" would be stored in memory as the codes 97, 98, 99, 49, 50, and 51.)
- A blank space is represented by the number 32.
- The null character is represented by the number 0.

In addition to establishing a set of numeric codes to represent characters in memory, ASCII also establishes an order for characters. The character "A" comes before the character "B", which comes before the character "C", and so forth.

When `strcmp` compares the characters in two strings, it actually compares the codes for the characters. For example, look at how the following code compares the strings "a" and "b":

```
if ( strcmp("a", "b") < 0 )
{
    dbPrint("The letter a is less than the letter b.");
}
```

This code is easy to understand because the strings "a" and "b" each contain only one character. Because the ASCII code for the character a is less than the ASCII code for the character b, the `strcmp` function will return a negative value. If this were part of an actual program it would display the message "The letter a is less than the letter b."

Let's look at how strings containing more than one character are compared. Suppose we have the strings "Mary" and "Mark" stored in memory, as follows:

```
const int SIZE = 5;
char name1[SIZE] = "Mary";
char name2[SIZE] = "Mark";
```

Figure 11-5 shows how the strings "Mary" and "Mark" would actually be stored in memory, using ASCII codes.

Figure 11-5 ASCII codes for the strings "Mary" and "Mark"

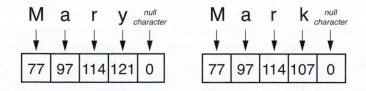

When you use strcmp to compare these strings, they are compared character-by-character. For example, look at the following code:

```
const int SIZE = 5;
char name1[SIZE] = "Mary";
char name2[SIZE] = "Mark";

if ( strcmp(name1, name2) > 0 )
{
    dbPrint("Mary is greater than Mark.");
}
else
{
    dbPrint("Mary is not greater than Mark.");
}
```

The strcmp function compares each character in the strings "Mary" and "Mark," beginning with the first, or leftmost, characters. This is illustrated in Figure 11-6.

Figure 11-6 Comparing each character in a string

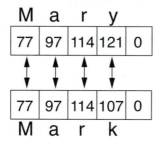

Here is how the comparison takes place:

1. The "M" in "Mary" is compared with the "M" in "Mark." Since these are the same, the next characters are compared.
2. The "a" in "Mary" is compared with the "a" in "Mark." Since these are the same, the next characters are compared.
3. The "r" in "Mary" is compared with the "r" in "Mark." Since these are the same, the next characters are compared.
4. The "y" in "Mary" is compared with the "k" in "Mark." Since these are not the same, the two strings are not equal. The character "y" has a higher ASCII code (121) than "k" (107), so the function returns a positive number to indicate that name1 ("Mary") is greater than name2 ("Mark").

If one of the strings in a comparison is shorter than the other, only the corresponding characters are compared. If the corresponding characters are identical, then the shorter string is considered less than the longer string. For example, suppose the strings "High" and "Hi" were being compared. The string "Hi" would be considered less than "High" because it is shorter.

The `strstr` Function

The `strstr` function searches for a string inside of a string. For instance, it could be used to search for the string "seven" inside the larger string "Four score and seven years ago." The function's first argument is the string to be searched, and the second argument is the string to look for. If the function finds the second string inside the first, it returns a non-zero value to indicate true. Otherwise it returns 0 to indicate false. Here is an example:

```
const int SIZE = 35;
char quote[SIZE] = "Four score and seven years ago";

if ( strstr(quote, "seven") )
{
    dbPrint("seven was found in the string.");
}
```

If this code were run as part of a program, it would display "seven was found in the string".

In the Spotlight:

Getting a File Name and Testing for the File's Existence

When a program prompts the user for the name of a file to load, such as an image file, the program should determine whether the file exists before it tries to load it. The Dark GDK provides a function named `dbFileExist` that can make this determination. You pass the name of a file as an argument, and the function returns 1 (true) if the file exists, or 0 (false) if the file does not exist.

Program 11-2 shows an example. The program prompts the user to enter the name of an image file. The file name that is entered by the user is saved to a `char` array. The program then passes the array as an argument to the `dbFileExist` function to determine whether the file exists before it tries to load it. Figure 11-7 shows an example of the program's output when it cannot locate the file specified by the user's input.

Program 11-2   (FileTest.cpp)

```
 1  // This program gets the name of an image file from the user.
 2  // If the file exists, the file is loaded and displayed.
 3  // Otherwise an error message is displayed.
 4  #include "DarkGDK.h"
 5  #include <string.h>
 6
 7  void DarkGDK()
 8  {
 9      // Declare a const for the image number.
10      const int IMAGE_NUM = 1;
```

```
11
12          // Declare an array to hold the file name.
13          const int SIZE = 50;
14          char filename[SIZE];
15
16          // Prompt the user to enter a file name.
17          dbPrint("Enter the name of an image file:");
18
19          // Get the user's input and copy it to the
20          // filename array.
21          strcpy( filename, dbInput() );
22
23          // If the file exists, load it and display it.
24          // Otherwise, display an error message.
25          if ( dbFileExist(filename) )
26          {
27              // Load the file.
28              dbLoadImage( filename, IMAGE_NUM);
29
30              // Display the image at (0, 0).
31              dbPasteImage(IMAGE_NUM, 0, 0);
32          }
33          else
34          {
35              dbPrint("Sorry, that file is not found.");
36          }
37
38          // Wait for the user to press a key.
39          dbWaitKey();
40      }
```

Figure 11-7 Output of Program 11-2 when
              the specified file cannot be found

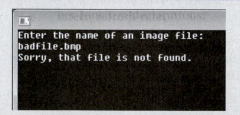

Let's take a closer look at the program. Line 14 declares a `char` array named `filename` that will be used to hold the name of a file. Line 17 prompts the user to enter a file name. Line 21 gets the user's input and stores it in the `filename` array. The `if` statement in line 25 calls the `dbFileExist` function passing the `filename` array as an argument. If the file exists, the program loads and displays the file in lines 28 and 31. If the file does not exist, the program displays an error message in line 35.

In the Spotlight:
Mad Libs Word Games

Mad Libs is a word game that usually involves two people. One person asks the other to provide a list of words, which are written into blanks in a short story. After all of the blanks are filled in, the story is read aloud. The words that were provided usually result in a funny or outlandish story.

In this example, we will demonstrate a program that plays a word game similar to Mad Libs. The program will ask the user to enter the following:

- A year (example: 2001)
- The name of a college
- The name of a food
- The name of an emotion

The program will then insert the user's input into the following story:

In *(year)* I graduated from *(name of a college)*. I quickly went to work in a *(name of a food)* factory. This made my parents very *(name of an emotion)*!

Program 11-3 shows the code for the program, and Figure 11-8 shows an example of the program's output.

Program 11-3   (`WordGame.cpp`)

```
 1   // This program plays a word game similar
 2   // to Mad Libs.
 3   #include "DarkGDK.h"
 4   #include <string.h>
 5
 6   // Function prototypes
 7   void getInput(char[], char[], char[], char[]);
 8   void displayStory(char[], char[], char[], char[]);
 9
10   //*********************************************************
11   // DarkGDK function                                       *
12   //*********************************************************
13   void DarkGDK()
14   {
15       // Constants for array sizes
16       const int WORD_SIZE = 30;
17
18       // Arrays for the user's input
19       char year[WORD_SIZE];
20       char college[WORD_SIZE];
21       char food[WORD_SIZE];
22       char emotion[WORD_SIZE];
23
24       // Get the user's words.
25       getInput(year, college, food, emotion);
26
```

```
27          // Display the story.
28          displayStory(year, college, food, emotion);
29
30          // Wait for the user to press a key.
31          dbPrint("Press any key to exit.");
32          dbWaitKey();
33    }
34
35    //*********************************************************
36    // The getInput function accepts arrays for each of the *
37    // words that the user must provide. It gets input for   *
38    // those words and stores that input in the arrays.      *
39    //*********************************************************
40    void getInput(char year[], char college[], char food[],
41                  char emotion[])
42    {
43          // Get a year.
44          dbPrint("Enter a year (for example, 2001):");
45          strcpy( year, dbInput() );
46
47          // Get the name of a college.
48          dbPrint("Enter the name of a college:");
49          strcpy( college, dbInput() );
50
51          // Get the name of a food.
52          dbPrint("Enter the name of a food:");
53          strcpy( food, dbInput() );
54
55          // Get the name of an emotion.
56          dbPrint("Enter the name of an emotion:");
57          strcpy( emotion, dbInput() );
58    }
59
60    //*********************************************************
61    // The displayStory function accepts arrays containing   *
62    // the user's words. It displays the story with these    *
63    // words filled into the blanks.                         *
64    //*********************************************************
65    void displayStory(char year[], char college[], char food[],
66                  char emotion[])
67    {
68          // Constants for array sizes
69          const int LINE_SIZE = 80;
70
71          // Arrays for the lines of output
72          char line1[LINE_SIZE];
73          char line2[LINE_SIZE];
74          char line3[LINE_SIZE];
75
76          // Build line 1.
77          strcpy( line1, "In " );
78          strcat( line1, year );
79          strcat( line1, " I graduated from " );
80          strcat( line1, college );
81          strcat( line1, "." );
```

```
 82
 83        // Build line 2.
 84        strcpy( line2, "I quickly went to work in a ");
 85        strcat( line2, food );
 86        strcat( line2, " factory.");
 87
 88        // Build line 3.
 89        strcpy( line3, "This made my parents very ");
 90        strcat( line3, emotion );
 91        strcat( line3, "!");
 92
 93        // Display the story.
 94        dbPrint();
 95        dbPrint("Here is your story:");
 96        dbPrint("-------------------");
 97        dbPrint(line1);
 98        dbPrint(line2);
 99        dbPrint(line3);
100        dbPrint();
101    }
```

Figure 11-8 An example of Program 11-3's output

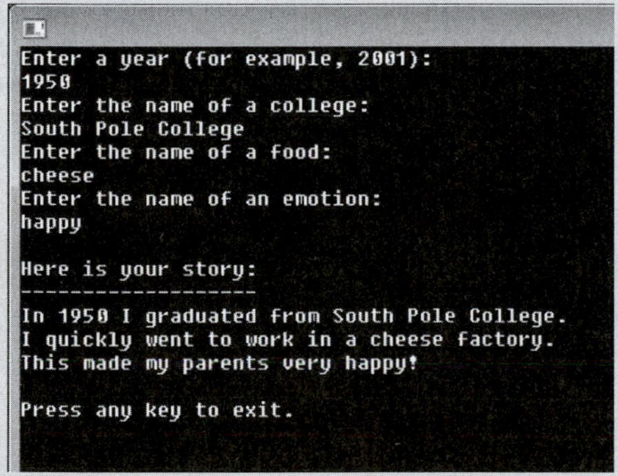

```
Enter a year (for example, 2001):
1950
Enter the name of a college:
South Pole College
Enter the name of a food:
cheese
Enter the name of an emotion:
happy

Here is your story:
-------------------
In 1950 I graduated from South Pole College.
I quickly went to work in a cheese factory.
This made my parents very happy!

Press any key to exit.
```

Inside the `DarkGDK` function, in lines 19 through 22, we declare the `year`, `college`, `food`, and `emotion` arrays to hold the words that the user must enter. We've used 30 as the size for each array, which should be sufficient. In line 25, we call the `getInput` function, passing these arrays as arguments. The function gets input from the user and stores it in the arrays. In line 28, we call the `displayStory` function passing the arrays as arguments. The function uses the contents of the arrays to create the story, which is then displayed on the screen.

The `getInput` function appears in lines 40 through 58. It accepts the `year`, `college`, `food`, and `emotion` arrays as arguments. In line 44, the user is prompted to enter a year. Then in line 45, `strcpy` is used to copy the value returned from `dbInput` into the `year` array. Similar actions take place in lines 48 and 49 to get the name of a college, lines 52 and 53 to get the name of a food, and lines 56 and 57 to get the name of an emotion.

The `displayStory` function appears in lines 65 through 101. It accepts the `year`, `college`, `food`, and `emotion` arrays as arguments. Lines 72 through 74 declare three `char` arrays named `line1`, `line2`, and `line3`. The function will display three lines of output, and these arrays will be used to hold them. We've used 80 as the size of each array, which should be sufficient.

In line 77, we begin building the first line of output, which will be in the form "In _(year)_ I graduated from _(name of a college)_." We use `strcpy` to copy the string "In" to `line1`. Then in line 78, we use `strcat` to append the contents of the `year` array to `line1`. In line 79, we append the string "I graduated from" to `line1`. In line 80, we append the contents of the `college` array to `line1`. Then in line 81, we append a period to `line1`.

In line 84, we begin building the second line of output, which will be in the form "I quickly went to work in a _(name of a food)_ factory." We use `strcpy` to copy the string "I quickly went to work in a" to `line2`. In line 85, we `strcat` to append the contents of the `food` array to `line2`. In line 86, we append the string "factory". to `line2`.

In line 89, we begin building the third line of output, which will be in the form "This made my parents very _(name of an emotion)_!" We use `strcpy` to copy the string "This made my parents very" to `line3`. In line 90, we `strcat` to append the contents of the `emotion` array to `line3`. In line 91, we append the string "!" to `line3`. Lines 94 through 100 then display the story on the screen.

Arrays of Strings

Strings are stored in one-dimensional `char` arrays. If you need to create an array of several strings, you create a two-dimensional `char` array. Figure 11-9 depicts such an array.

Figure 11-9 A two-dimensional `char` array as an array of strings

```
const int ROWS = 4;
const int COLS = 9;
char names[ROWS][COLS] = { "Galileo",
                           "Kepler",
                           "Newton",
                           "Einstein" };
```

G	a	l	i	l	e	o	Ø	
K	e	p	l	e	r	Ø		
N	e	w	t	o	n	Ø		
E	i	n	s	t	e	i	n	Ø

There are four strings in the array, so it must have four rows. The longest string in the array is nine characters long (including the null terminator), so the array must have at least nine columns. The rows that contain strings with less than nine characters will have unused elements.

In the array, the string "Galileo" is stored in row 0, the string "Kepler" is stored in row 1, the string "Newton" is stored in row 2, and the string "Einstein" is stored in row 3. To process the array of strings, we only need to use the row subscript numbers. For example, the following statement will display "Galileo", which is the string in row 0:

```
dbPrint( names[0] );
```

Likewise, the following statement will display "Kepler", which is the string in row 1:

```
dbPrint( names[1] );
```

Program 11-4 demonstrates how a loop can be used to display all of the strings in the array. Figure 11-10 shows the program's output.

Program 11-4   (`ArrayOfStrings.cpp`)

```
1   // This program uses a two-dimensional char array
2   // as an array of strings.
3   #include "DarkGDK.h"
4   #include <string.h>
5
6   void DarkGDK()
7   {
8       // Constants for the array size declarators
9       const int ROWS = 4;
10      const int COLS = 9;
11
12      // Declare a 2D char array and initialize it
13      // with strings.
14      char names[ROWS][COLS] = {  "Galileo",
15                                  "Kepler",
16                                  "Newton",
17                                  "Einstein" };
18
19      // Display each string in the array.
20      for (int index = 0; index < ROWS; index++)
21      {
22          dbPrint( names[index] );
23      }
24
25      // Wait for the user to press a key.
26      dbPrint();
27      dbPrint("Press any key to exit.");
28      dbWaitKey();
29  }
```

Figure 11-10 Output of Program 11-4

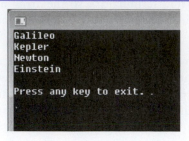

Program 11-5 shows another example. In this program, the user is prompted to enter four names, which are stored in a two-dimensional char array. A loop is then used to display the names. Figure 11-11 shows an example of the program's output.

Program 11-5   (ArrayOfStrings2.cpp)

```
1   // This program gets strings from the user and stores
2   // them in a 2D array.
3   #include "DarkGDK.h"
4   #include <string.h>
5
6   void DarkGDK()
7   {
8       // Constants for the array size declarators
9       const int ROWS = 4;
10      const int COLS = 50;
11
12      // Declare a 2D char array.
13      char names[ROWS][COLS];
14
15      dbPrint("I'm going to ask you to enter 4 names.");
16
17      // Get four strings from the user and store them
18      // in the array.
19      for (int index = 0; index < ROWS; index++)
20      {
21          dbPrint("Enter a name:");
22          strcpy( names[index], dbInput() );
23      }
24
25      dbPrint();
26      dbPrint("Here are the names you entered");
27      dbPrint("-------------------------------");
28
29      // Display each string in the array.
30      for (int index = 0; index < ROWS; index++)
31      {
32          dbPrint( names[index] );
```

```
33       }
34
35       // Wait for the user to press a key.
36       dbPrint();
37       dbPrint("Press any key to exit.");
38       dbWaitKey();
39   }
```

Figure 11-11 Output of Program 11-5

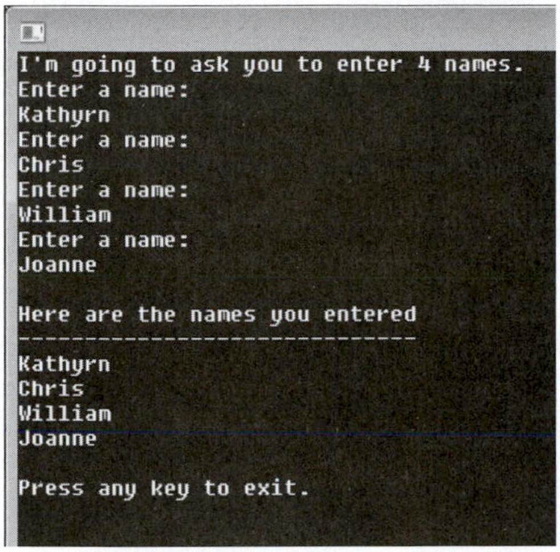

✔ Checkpoint

11.1. What is a char variable? Can char variables hold strings?

11.2. In what are character literals enclosed?

11.3. How many bytes of memory would the string "Maxwell" occupy?

11.4. To use the standard C++ functions discussed in this section, what #include directive do you use?

11.5. What standard C++ function can you use to copy a string to a char array?

11.6. What standard C++ function can you use to append one string to another string?

11.7. What standard C++ function can you use to get the length of a string?

11.8. Describe the meaning of the values that are returned from the strcmp function.

11.9. What is the purpose of the strstr function, and how do you use it?

11.10. Since strings are stored in one-dimensional char arrays, how would you create an array of strings?

11.2 Introduction to File Input and Output

CONCEPT: When a program needs to save data for later use, it writes the data in a file. The data can be read from the file later.

The data that is stored in variables in RAM disappears once the program stops running. If a program is to retain data between the times it runs, it must have a way of saving it. Data is saved in a file, which is usually stored on a computer's disk. Once the data is saved in a file, it will remain there after the program stops running. Data that is stored in a file can be retrieved and used later.

Most of the commercial software packages that you use store data in files. Here are a few examples:

- **Games:** Many computer games keep data stored in files. For example, some games keep a list of player names with their scores stored in a file. Some games also allow you to save your current game status in a file so you can quit the game and then resume playing it without having to start from the beginning.
- **Word Processors:** Word processing programs are used to write letters, memos, reports, and other documents. The documents are then saved in files so they can be edited and printed.
- **Image Editors:** Image editing programs are used to draw graphics and edit images such as the ones that you take with a digital camera. The images that you create or edit with an image editor are saved in files.
- **Spreadsheets:** Spreadsheet programs are used to work with numerical data. Numbers and mathematical formulas can be inserted into the rows and columns of the spreadsheet. The spreadsheet can then be saved in a file for later use.
- **Web Browsers:** Sometimes when you visit a Web page, the browser stores a small file known as a cookie on your computer. Typically, cookies contain information about the browsing session, such the contents of a shopping cart.

Programs that are used in daily business operations rely extensively on files. Payroll programs keep employee data in files, inventory programs keep data about a company's products in files, accounting systems keep data about a company's financial operations in files, and so forth.

Programmers usually refer to the process of saving data in a file as "writing data" to the file. When a piece of data is written to a file, it is copied from a variable in RAM to the file. This is illustrated in Figure 11-12. The term *output file* is used to describe a file that data is written to. It is called an output file because the program stores output in it.

The process of retrieving data from a file is known as "reading data" from the file. When a piece of data is read from a file, it is copied from the file into a variable in RAM, as shown in Figure 11-13. The term *input file* is used to describe a file that data is read from. It is called an input file because the program gets input from the file.

Figure 11-12 Writing data to a file

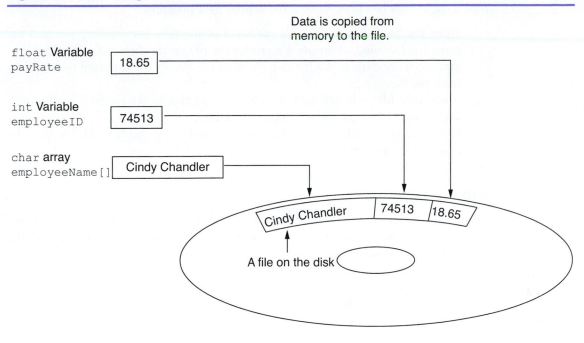

Figure 11-13 Reading data from a file

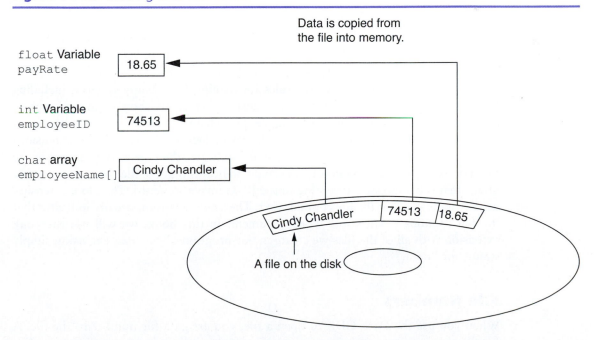

In this section, we will discuss writing data to files and reading data from files. Three steps must always be taken when a file is used by a program:

1. **Open the file** —Opening a file creates a connection between the file and the program. Opening an output file creates the file on the disk and allows the program to write data to it. Opening an input file allows the program to read data from the file.
2. **Process the file** —In this step, data is either written to the file (if it is an output file) or read from the file (if it is an input file).
3. **Close the file** —When the program is finished using the file, the file must be closed. Closing a file disconnects the file from the program.

File Names

Most computer users are accustomed to the fact that a file is identified by a file name. For example, when you create a document with a word processor and then save the document in a file, you have to specify a file name. When you use a utility such as Windows Explorer to examine the contents of your disk, you see a list of file names. Figure 11-14 shows how three files named `cat.jpg`, `notes.txt`, and `resume.doc` might be represented in Windows Explorer.

Figure 11-14 Three files

cat.jpg   notes.txt   resume.doc

Each operating system has its own rules for naming files. Many systems, including Windows, support the use of file name extensions, which are short sequences of characters that appear at the end of a file name, preceded by a period (which is known as a "dot"). For example, the file names shown in Figure 11-14 have the extensions `.jpg`, `.txt`, and `.doc`. The extension usually indicates the type of data stored in the file. For example, the `.jpg` extension usually indicates that the file contains a graphic image that is compressed according to the JPEG image standard. The `.txt` extension usually indicates that the file contains text. The `.doc` extension usually indicates that the file contains a Microsoft Word document. In this book, we will use the `.dat` extension with all of the files we create in our programs. The `.dat` extension simply stands for "data."

File Numbers

When you use the Dark GDK to open a file, you assign a file number to the file. A *file number* is an integer that you use to identify the file in subsequent operations. File numbers must be in the range of 1 through 32. With the Dark GDK, you can have up to 32 different files opened simultaneously.

Opening an Output File

To open an output file with the Dark GDK, you use the `dbOpenToWrite` function. Here is the general format for calling the function:

```
dbOpenToWrite( FileNumber, FileName );
```

FileNumber is the integer file number that you are assigning to the file. *FileName* is a string specifying the name of the file. Here is an example:

```
dbOpenToWrite( 1, "GameData.dat" );
```

After this statement executes, a file named `GameData.dat` will be opened as an output file, which means that we will be able to write data to the file. The file number 1 will be assigned to the file. Most of the time you will want to declare a constant for the file number, as follows:

```
const int OUTPUT_FILE = 1;
dbOpenToWrite( OUTPUT_FILE, "GameData.dat" );
```

Declaring a constant for the file number will make the code easier to read and maintain.

Opening an output file actually creates the file on the disk. When using `dbOpenToWrite` to open an output file, the file must not already exist or the function will fail to open it. For this reason, you should use `dbFileExist` to determine whether the file exists first. If the file exists and you do not want to erase it, you can display an error message as shown in the following example:

```
// If the file exists display an error message. Otherwise,
// open the file.
if ( dbFileExist("GameData.dat") )
{
    dbPrint("Error! GameData.dat already exists.");
}
else
{
    dbOpenToWrite( OUTPUT_FILE, "GameData.dat" );
}
```

If the file exists, and you want to proceed, you can then use the `dbDeleteFile` function to delete the existing file. You pass a file name as an argument to the `dbDeleteFile` function, and the function deletes that file. Here is an example:

```
// If the file exists, delete it.
if ( dbFileExist("GameData.dat") )
{
    dbDeleteFile("GameData.dat");
}

// Open the file for writing.
dbOpenToWrite( OUTPUT_FILE, "GameData.dat" );
```

NOTE: If you do not specify a path when opening a file, the file will be opened in the program's project directory.

Writing Data to an Output File

Once a file has been opened with the dbOpenToWrite function, you can write data to it. The Dark GDK provides several functions for writing data to files. We will discuss three of the most useful functions: dbWriteFile, dbWriteString, and dbWriteFloat.

The dbWriteFile function writes the contents of an int variable to a file. This is the general format:

```
dbWriteFile( FileNumber, Variable );
```

FileNumber is the file number of a file that is open for writing, and Variable is an int variable. The function will write the contents of Variable to the specified file. The following code shows an example. Assume that OUTPUT_FILE is the file number for an open output file and myData is an int variable.

```
dbWriteFile( OUTPUT_FILE, myData );
```

The dbWriteFile function can also be used to write a DWORD value to a file. Here is an example:

```
DWORD color = dbRGB( 255, 0, 0 );
dbWriteFile( OUTPUT_FILE, color );
```

The dbWriteString function writes a string to a file. This is the general format:

```
dbWriteString( FileNumber, String );
```

FileNumber is the file number of a file that is open for writing, and String is a string literal or the name of a char array. The function will write the string to the specified file. The following code shows an example. Assume that OUTPUT_FILE is the file number for an open output file, and name is a char array containing a string.

```
dbWriteString( OUTPUT_FILE, name );
```

Here is an example that writes a string literal to a file:

```
dbWriteString( OUTPUT_FILE, "Activity Log" );
```

The dbWriteFloat function writes the contents of a float variable to a file. This is the general format:

```
dbWriteFloat( FileNumber, Variable );
```

FileNumber is the file number of a file that is open for writing, and Variable is a float variable. The function will write the contents of Variable to the specified file. The following code shows an example. Assume that OUTPUT_FILE is the file number for an open output file and myData is a float variable.

```
dbWriteFloat( OUTPUT_FILE, myData );
```

Closing an Output File

Once a program is finished writing data to a file, it should use the dbCloseFile function to close the file. Closing a file disconnects the program from the file, and frees the file number so it can be used with another file. Here is the general format of the dbCloseFile function:

```
dbCloseFile(FileNumber);
```

FileNumber is the file number of a file that is currently open. After the dbCloseFile function executes, the file associated with that file number will be closed. The following statement shows an example. Assume that OUTPUT_FILE is a constant that specifies the file number of an open file.

```
dbCloseFile(OUTPUT_FILE);
```

Opening an Input File

To open an input file with the Dark GDK you use the dbOpenToRead function. Here is the general format for calling the function:

```
dbOpenToRead( FileNumber, FileName );
```

FileNumber is the integer file number that you are assigning to the file. *FileName* is a string specifying the name of the file. The following code shows an example. Assume that INPUT_FILE is a constant that has been declared to specify the file number.

```
dbOpenToRead( INPUT_FILE, "GameData.dat" );
```

After this statement executes, a file named GameData.dat will be opened as an input file. This means that we will be able to read data from the file. The file number specified by the INPUT_FILE constant will be assigned to the file.

When opening an input file, the file must exist or the dbOpenToRead function will fail. You can use the dbFileExist function to make sure the file exists before attempting to open it, as shown here:

```
// Constant for the file number
const INPUT_FILE = 1;

// If the GameData.dat file exists, open it.
if ( dbFileExist("GameData.dat") )
{
    dbOpenToRead( INPUT_FILE, "GameData.dat" );
}
else
{
    // Display an error message.
    dbPrint("Error! GameData.dat does not exist." );
}
```

 NOTE: If you do not specify a path when opening an input file, the program will assume the file is located in the program's project directory.

Reading Data from an Input File

Once a file has been opened with the dbOpenToRead function, you can read data from it. The Dark GDK provides several functions for reading data from files. We will discuss three of the most useful functions: dbReadFile, dbReadString, and dbReadFloat.

The dbReadFile function is a value-returning function. You pass the file number of a file that is open for reading as an argument. The function reads a value from the file and returns that value as an int. The following code shows an example. Assume that INPUT_FILE is the file number for an open input file and myData is an int variable.

```
myData = dbReadFile( INPUT_FILE );
```

The value that is returned from dbReadFile can also be assigned to a DWORD variable. The following code shows an example. Assume that color is a DWORD variable.

```
color = dbReadFile( INPUT_FILE );
```

The dbReadString function is also a value-returning function. You pass the file number of a file that is open for reading as an argument. The function reads a string from the file and returns that string. The following code shows an example. Assume that INPUT_FILE is the file number for an open input file, and str is a char array.

```
strcpy( str, dbReadString(INPUT_FILE) );
```

After this statement executes, a string will be read from the file specified by INPUT_FILE. The string will be stored in the str array.

The dbReadFloat function is also a value-returning function. You pass the file number of a file that is open for reading as an argument. The function reads a value from the file and returns that value as a float. The following code shows an example. Assume that INPUT_FILE is the file number for an open input file and myData is a float variable.

```
myData = dbReadFormat( INPUT_FILE );
```

Closing an Output File

Once a program is finished reading data from a file, it should use the dbCloseFile function to close the file. As previously mentioned, closing a file disconnects the program from the file, and frees the file number so it can be used with another file. The following statement shows an example. Assume that INPUT_FILE is a constant that specifies the file number of an open file.

```
dbCloseFile(INPUT_FILE);
```

Determining if a File Is Open

In some circumstances you might need to determine if a file is opened before performing operations with the file. This can be done with the dbFileOpen function. You pass a file number as an argument to dbFileOpen and it returns 1 (true) if the file is open, or 0 (false) if the file is not open. Here is an example:

```
if ( dbFileOpen(INPUT_FILE) )
{
        // Code here reads from the file.
}
else
{
        dbPrint("Error: The file is not open.");
}
```

You can use the dbFileOpen function to test both input and output files.

Let's look at an example program that writes data to a file. Program 11-6 prompts the user to enter his or her name, age, and annual salary. The user is also asked to enter a file name. The file is opened and the data is written to the file. Figure 11-15 shows an example of the program running.

Program 11-6   **(FileWrite.cpp)**

```
 1   // This program gets data from the user and writes it
 2   // to a file.
 3   #include "DarkGDK.h"
 4   #include <string.h>
 5
 6   // Constants
 7   const int OUTPUT_FILE = 1;
 8   const int STRING_SIZE = 100;
 9
10   // Function prototypes
11   void getData(char [], int &, float &);
12   void openFile();
13   void writeData(char [], int, float);
14
15   //*********************************************************
16   // The DarkGDK function                                  *
17   //*********************************************************
18   void DarkGDK()
19   {
20       // Arrays and variables for user data
21       char  name[STRING_SIZE];
22       int   age;
23       float salary;
24
25       // Get data from the user.
26       getData(name, age, salary);
27
28       // Open an output file.
29       openFile();
30
31       // If the file is open, write the data to it.
32       if ( dbFileOpen( OUTPUT_FILE ) )
```

```
33         {
34             // Write the data.
35             writeData( name, age, salary );
36
37             // Close the file.
38             dbCloseFile(OUTPUT_FILE);
39
40             // Let the user know we're done.
41             dbPrint("The data is written to the file.");
42         }
43
44         // Wait for the user to press a key.
45         dbPrint("Press any key to exit the program.");
46         dbWaitKey();
47     }
48
49     //**********************************************************
50     // The getData function gets personal data from the user.   *
51     //**********************************************************
52     void getData(char name[], int &age, float &salary)
53     {
54         // Get the user's name.
55         dbPrint("Enter your name:");
56         strcpy( name, dbInput() );
57
58         // Get the user's age.
59         dbPrint("Enter your age:");
60         age = atoi( dbInput() );
61
62         // Get the user's salary.
63         dbPrint("Enter your annual salary:");
64         salary = atof( dbInput() );
65     }
66
67     //**********************************************************
68     // The openFile function gets a file name from the user and *
69     // opens that file for output. The file is not opened if it *
70     // already exists.                                          *
71     //**********************************************************
72     void openFile()
73     {
74         // Char array to hold the file name
75         char filename[STRING_SIZE];
76
77         // Get a file name from the user.
78         dbPrint("Enter the name of the file to save this data:");
79         strcpy( filename, dbInput() );
80
81         // If the file already exists, display an error message.
82         // Otherwise, open the file.
83         if ( dbFileExist(filename) )
84         {
85             dbPrint("Error: That file already exists.");
86         }
87         else
```

```
 88        {
 89            dbOpenToWrite( OUTPUT_FILE, filename );
 90        }
 91  }
 92
 93  //********************************************************
 94  // The writeData function accepts the user's name, age, and *
 95  // salary, and writes that data to the output file.         *
 96  //********************************************************
 97  void writeData(char name[], int age, float salary)
 98  {
 99        // Write the user's name.
100        dbWriteString( OUTPUT_FILE, name );
101
102        // Write the user's age.
103        dbWriteFile( OUTPUT_FILE, age );
104
105        // Write the user's salary.
106        dbWriteFloat( OUTPUT_FILE, salary );
107  }
```

Figure 11-15 Example output of Program 11-6

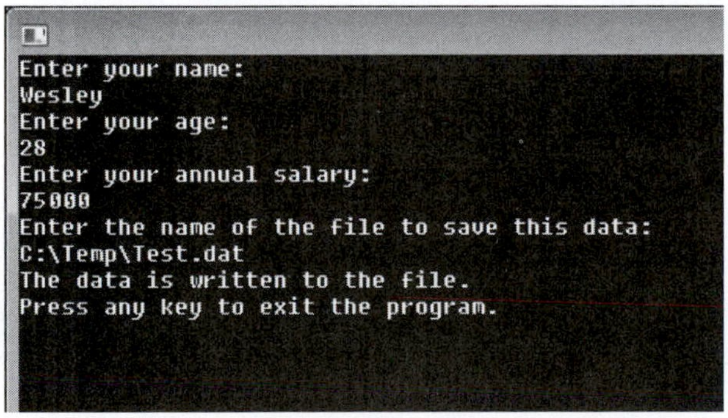

```
Enter your name:
Wesley
Enter your age:
28
Enter your annual salary:
75000
Enter the name of the file to save this data:
C:\Temp\Test.dat
The data is written to the file.
Press any key to exit the program.
```

Let's take a closer look at the program. In the DarkGDK function, in lines 21 through 23, we declare a char array to hold the user's name and variables for the user's age and salary. In line 26, we call the getData function, passing as arguments the name array, the age variable (by reference), and the salary variable (by reference). The getData function gets input from the user and stores it in these arguments. In line 29, we call the openFile function. The openFile function, which is defined in lines 72 through 91, gets a file name from the user. If the file does not exist, it is opened for writing. If the file exists, an error message is displayed.

The if statement in line 32 calls the dbFileOpen function to determine if the output file is opened. If so, the writeData function is called in line 35, passing name, age, and salary as arguments. The writeData function writes these to the output file. Then in line 38, the output file is closed and in line 41 a message is displayed indicating that the data was written to the file.

In the example execution of the program in Figure 11-15, the user entered the name Wesley, the age 28, and the salary 75,000. The user entered `C:\Temp\Test.dat` as the name of the file to which this data will be saved. Figure 11-16 illustrates the contents of the file after this data has been written to it.

Figure 11-16 Contents of `C:\Temp\Test.dat`

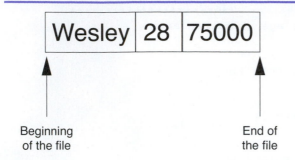

Wesley | 28 | 75000

Beginning of the file

End of the file

Now let's look at a program that reads data from a file. Program 11-7 opens the file that was created by Program 11-6 and reads its contents. Figure 11-17 shows an example of the program's output.

Program 11-7 (FileRead.cpp)

```
1   // This program reads data from a file and displays it.
2   #include "DarkGDK.h"
3   #include <string.h>
4
5   // Constants
6   const int INPUT_FILE  = 1;
7   const int STRING_SIZE = 100;
8
9   // Function prototypes
10  void openFile();
11  void readData(char [], int &, float &);
12  void displayData(char [], int, float);
13
14  //************************************************************
15  // The DarkGDK function                                     *
16  //************************************************************
17  void DarkGDK()
18  {
19      // Arrays and variables for file data
20      char  name[STRING_SIZE];
21      int   age;
22      float salary;
23
24      // Open the input file.
25      openFile();
```

```
26
27          // If the file is open, read data from it.
28          if ( dbFileOpen(INPUT_FILE) )
29          {
30              // Read the data.
31              readData( name, age, salary );
32
33              // Close the file.
34              dbCloseFile(INPUT_FILE);
35
36              // Display the data.
37              displayData(name, age, salary);
38          }
39
40          // Wait for the user to press a key.
41          dbPrint("Press any key to exit the program.");
42          dbWaitKey();
43      }
44
45      //***********************************************************
46      // The openFile function gets a file name from the user and  *
47      // opens that file for input. The file is not opened if it    *
48      // does not exist.                                            *
49      //***********************************************************
50      void openFile()
51      {
52          // Char array to hold the file name
53          char filename[STRING_SIZE];
54
55          // Get a file name from the user.
56          dbPrint("Enter the name of the file:");
57          strcpy( filename, dbInput() );
58
59          // If the file exists, open it for reading.
60          // Otherwise display an error message.
61          if ( dbFileExist(filename) )
62          {
63              dbOpenToRead( INPUT_FILE, filename );
64          }
65          else
66          {
67              dbPrint("Error: That file does not exist.");
68          }
69      }
70
71      //***********************************************************
72      // The readData function reads data from the file.          *
73      //***********************************************************
74      void readData(char name[], int &age, float &salary)
75      {
76          // Read the user's name.
77          strcpy( name, dbReadString( INPUT_FILE ) );
78
79          // Read the user's age.
80          age = dbReadFile(INPUT_FILE);
```

```
81
82          // Read the user's salary.
83          salary = dbReadFloat(INPUT_FILE);
84   }
85
86   //**********************************************************
87   // The displayData function accepts the user's name, age,  *
88   // salary, and displays that data on the screen.           *
89   //**********************************************************
90   void displayData(char name[], int age, float salary)
91   {
92          dbPrint();
93          dbPrint("Here is the data from the file:");
94          dbPrint("-------------------------------");
95          dbPrint(name);
96          dbPrint( dbStr(age) );
97          dbPrint( dbStr(salary) );
98          dbPrint();
99   }
```

Figure 11-17 Output of Program 11-7

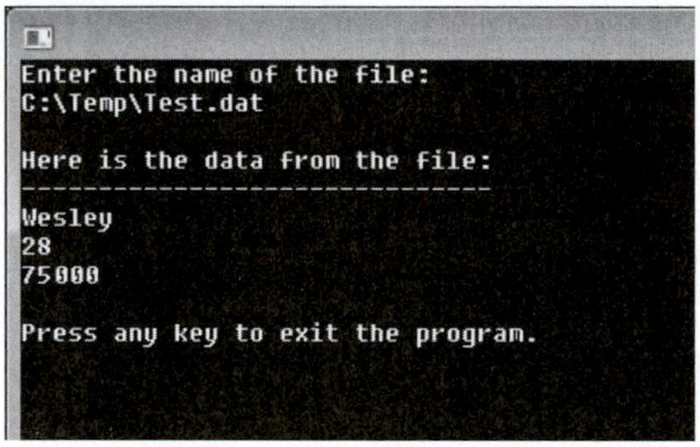

In the DarkGDK function, in lines 20 through 22, we declare a char array to hold the user's name and variables for the user's age and salary. In line 25, we call the openFile function. The openFile function, which is defined in lines 50 through 69, gets a file name from the user. If the file exists, it is opened for reading. If the file does not exist, an error message is displayed.

The if statement in line 28 calls the dbFileOpen function to determine if the input file is opened. If so, the readData function is called in line 31, passing the name array, the age variable (by reference), and the salary variable (by reference) as arguments. The readData function reads values from the input file and stores those values in the arguments. Then in line 34, the input file is closed. In line 37, the displayData function is called with name, age, and salary passed as arguments. The function displays the values of these arguments on the screen.

When a program works with an input file, a special value known as a *read position* is internally maintained for that file. A file's read position marks the location of the next item that will be read from the file. When an input file is opened, its read position is initially set to the first item in the file. In Program 11-7, the input file is opened by the statement in line 63. Once this statement executes, the read position for the `Test.dat` file will be positioned as shown in Figure 11-18.

Figure 11-18 Initial read position

The statement in line 77 reads the first item of data from the file by calling the `dbReadString` function. Once this statement executes, the `name` array will contain the string "Wesley". In addition, the file's read position will be advanced to the next item in the file, as shown in Figure 11-19.

Figure 11-19 Read position after the first item
has been read from the file

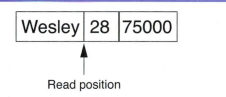

The statement in line 80 executes next. This statement calls the `dbReadFile` function, which reads an item from the file's current read position. The value returned from the function is stored in the `age` variable. Once this statement executes, the `age` variable will contain the value 28. The file's read position will be advanced to the next item, as shown in Figure 11-20.

Figure 11-20 Read position after the second
item has been read from the file

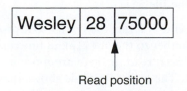

The statement in line 83 executes next. This statement calls the `dbReadFloat` function, which reads an item from the file's current read position. The value returned from the function is stored in the `salary` variable. Once this statement executes, the age variable will contain the value 75,000. The file's read position will be advanced to the end of the file, as shown in Figure 11-21.

Figure 11-21 Read position after the third item has been read from the file

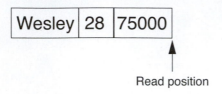

Using Loops to Process Files

Although some programs use files to store only small amounts of data, files are often used to hold large collections of data. When a program uses a file to write or read a large amount of data, a loop is typically involved. For example, suppose the following array declaration appears in a program:

```
const int ARRAY_SIZE = 100;
int values[ARRAY_SIZE];
```

Assuming that the array contains values, the following code could be used to write those values to a file. Assume OUTPUT_FILE is the file number for an output file that has already been opened.

```
for (int index = 0; index < ARRAY_SIZE; index++)
{
    dbWriteFile( OUTPUT_FILE, values[index] );
}
```

Detecting the End of a File

Quite often, a program must read the contents of a file without knowing the number of items that are stored in the file. This presents a problem if you want to write a program that processes all of the items in the file, regardless of how many there are. You can write a loop that reads all of the items in a file, but an error will occur if the program attempts to read beyond the last item in the file.

To prevent a program from reading beyond the end of a file, the Dark GDK provides a function named dbFileEnd. You pass a file number to the dbFileEnd function and it returns 1 (true) if the last item in the file has been read. If there are more items to read from the file, the function returns 0 (false). The following code shows how you typically use the dbFileEnd function to process all the items in a file. Assume INPUT_FILE a file number.

```
// Open a file.
dbOpenToRead( INPUT_FILE, "TestFile.dat");
```

```
        // Process all items in the file.
        while ( !dbFileEnd(INPUT_FILE) )
        {
                // Read an item from the file and process it.
        }

        // Close the file.
        dbCloseFile(INPUT_FILE);
```

Notice the use of the ! operator in the while loop. The loop executes as long as the
end of the file has *not* been reached. This technique is used in Program 11-8. The program generates a set of random colors and saves them to a file. It then reads the values from the file and displays them on the screen.

Program 11-8   (SaveColors.cpp)

```
 1  // This program saves a set of color values to a file. The
 2  // file is then read and those color values displayed.
 3  #include "DarkGDK.h"
 4
 5  // Constants
 6  const int IMAGE_NUM = 1;
 7  const int FILE_NUM  = 1;
 8
 9  // Function prototypes
10  void writeColors();
11  void displayColors();
12
13  //************************************************
14  // The DarkGDK function                         *
15  //************************************************
16  void DarkGDK()
17  {
18      // Generate a set of random color values and
19      // save them to a file.
20      writeColors();
21
22      // Read the color values from the file and
23      // draw them on the screen.
24      displayColors();
25
26      // Wait for the user to press a key.
27      dbPrint("Press any key to exit.");
28      dbWaitKey();
29  }
30
31  //************************************************
32  // The writeColors function writes a set of random *
33  // color values to a file named Colors.dat.        *
34  //************************************************
35  void writeColors()
36  {
37      // Variables to hold RGB color components
38      int r, g, b;
```

```
39
40      // Variable to hold a color
41      DWORD color;
42
43      // If the output file exists, delete it.
44      if ( dbFileExist("Colors.dat") )
45      {
46          dbDeleteFile("Colors.dat");
47      }
48
49      // Open the output file.
50      dbOpenToWrite(FILE_NUM, "Colors.dat");
51
52      // Write a set of random colors to the file.
53      for (int count = 0; count < dbScreenWidth(); count++)
54      {
55          // Generate a random color.
56          r = dbRND(255);
57          g = dbRND(255);
58          b = dbRND(255);
59          color = dbRGB( r, g, b );
60
61          // Write the color to the file.
62          dbWriteFile( FILE_NUM, color );
63      }
64
65      // Close the file.
66      dbCloseFile(FILE_NUM);
67  }
68
69  //****************************************************
70  // The displayColors function reads the color values *
71  // from the Colors.dat file and displays them.       *
72  //****************************************************
73  void displayColors()
74  {
75      // Variables
76      int   x, y;     // To hold coordinates
77      DWORD color;    // To hold a color
78
79      // Set the coordinate values.
80      x = 0;
81      y = dbScreenHeight() / 2;
82
83      // Open the input file.
84      dbOpenToRead( FILE_NUM, "Colors.dat" );
85
86      // Read the color values from the file and
87      // display them in middle line of the screen.
88      while ( !dbFileEnd(FILE_NUM) )
89      {
90          // Read a value from the file.
91          color = dbReadFile(FILE_NUM);
92
93          // Use that color value to draw a pixel.
```

```
94          dbDot( x, y, color );
95
96          // Increment the X coordinate.
97          x++;
98      }
99
100     // Close the file.
101     dbCloseFile(FILE_NUM);
102 }
```

Checkpoint

11.11. What is an output file?

11.12. What is an input file?

11.13. What three steps must be taken by a program when it uses a file?

11.14. What is the purpose of opening a file?

11.15. What is the purpose of closing a file?

11.16. What is a file's read position? Initially, where is the read position when an input file is opened?

11.17. What is the purpose of the `dbFileEnd` function?

11.18. What would it mean if the expression `dbFileEnd(FILE_NUM)` returns `true`?

11.3 Saving a Game's High Score

Many games keep track of the highest score that has been earned in the game. When a player beats the current high score, he or she is usually congratulated, and their score replaces the old high score. This provides motivation for the player to continue playing the game in order to beat the current high score.

A game that keeps track of the high score usually works something like this: A file is kept on the disk that contains the highest score achieved so far. When the player has finished the game, the program reads the file to get the high score. If the player's score is greater than the high score, the player is congratulated and then the player's score is written to the file. The first time the game is played, the file will not exist. In that case, the file is created and the player's score is written to it.

To demonstrate this, Program 11-9 shows a modified version of the Bug Zapper game that was presented in Chapter 9. Recall that the Bug Zapper game displays an animated sprite of a bug. The user zaps the bug by clicking it with the mouse. When this happens, a new bug appears at a random location on the screen. The game will run for 10 seconds before ending. The object of the game is to zap as many bugs as possible within the allotted time. When the game ends, a screen displays the user's score, which is the number of bugs that were zapped. This modified version of the game keeps the high score in a file named `HighScore.dat`. Each time the user beats the

Program 11-9   (BugZapperVersion2.cpp)

```cpp
1   // Bug Zapper Game, version 2.
2   // This version saves the high score.
3   #include "DarkGDK.h"
4
5   // Constants
6   const int HIGH_SCORE_FILE = 1;        // High score file number
7   const int POINTER_IMAGE   = 1;        // Mouse pointer image number
8   const int BUG_IMAGE       = 2;        // Bug image number
9   const int INTRO_IMAGE     = 3;        // Intro screen image number
10  const int GRASS_IMAGE     = 4;        // Grass image number
11  const int POINTER_SPRITE  = 1;        // Pointer sprite number
12  const int BUG_SPRITE      = 2;        // Bug sprite number
13  const int OFFSET_X        = 13;       // Pointer sprite X offset
14  const int OFFSET_Y        = 0;        // Pointer sprite Y offset
15  const int ROWS            = 1;        // Animated sprite rows
16  const int COLS            = 2;        // Animated sprite columns
17  const int DELAY           = 500;      // Animation delay
18  const int MAX_TIME        = 10000;    // Max game time (10 seconds)
19  const int REFRESH_RATE    = 60;       // Refresh rate
20
21  // Function Prototypes
22  void setUp();
23  void displayIntro();
24  void initMouse();
25  void initBug();
26  void updateMouse();
27  void updateBug();
28  void generateNewBug();
29  int  elapsedTime(int);
30  void displayBugsZapped(int);
31  void checkForHighScore(int);
32  void newHighScore(int);
33  bool mouseFullClick(int &, int &);
34  bool onSprite(int, int, int);
35
36  //******************************************************
37  // The DarkGDK function                               *
38  //******************************************************
39  void DarkGDK()
40  {
41      // Variables to hold the mouse pointer coordinates
42      int mouseX, mouseY;
43
44      // Variable to keep count of the number
45      // of bugs zapped.
46      int bugsZapped = 0;
47
48      // Boolean flag to indicate whether the game is
49      // still playing. This is set to false when time
50      // runs out.
51      bool stillPlaying = true;
52
53      // Perform setup.
```

```
54          setUp();
55
56          // Get the current system time, in milliseconds.
57          int startTime = dbTimer();
58
59          // Game loop
60          while ( LoopGDK() && stillPlaying )
61          {
62              // Paste the grass background image.
63              dbPasteImage(GRASS_IMAGE, 0, 0);
64
65              // Update the mouse pointer.
66              updateMouse();
67
68              // Update the bug animation.
69              updateBug();
70
71              // Did the user click the mouse?
72              if ( mouseFullClick(mouseX, mouseY) )
73              {
74                  // Was the mouse on the bug?
75                  if ( onSprite(BUG_SPRITE, mouseX, mouseY) )
76                  {
77                      // Update the count.
78                      bugsZapped++;
79
80                      // Generate a new bug.
81                      generateNewBug();
82                  }
83              }
84
85              // See how many seconds we've been playing. If more
86              // than MAX_TIME, then time's up.
87              if ( elapsedTime(startTime) > MAX_TIME )
88              {
89                  // Set the stillPlaying flag to false.
90                  // This indicates that we are out of time.
91                  stillPlaying = false;
92
93                  // Display the number of bugs zapped.
94                  displayBugsZapped(bugsZapped);
95              }
96
97              // Refresh the screen.
98              dbSync();
99          }
100  }
101
102  //*****************************************************
103  // The setUp function performs setup operations.      *
104  //*****************************************************
105  void setUp()
106  {
107      // Display the intro screen.
108      displayIntro();
```

```
109
110       // Seed the random number generator.
111       dbRandomize( dbTimer() );
112
113       // Set the key color.
114       dbSetImageColorKey(0, 255, 0);
115
116       // Initialize the mouse.
117       initMouse();
118
119       // Initialize the bug.
120       initBug();
121
122       // Load the grass background image.
123       dbLoadImage("Grass.bmp", GRASS_IMAGE);
124
125       // Disable auto refresh and set the refresh rate.
126       dbSyncOn();
127       dbSyncRate(REFRESH_RATE);
128   }
129
130   //*****************************************************
131   // The displayIntro function displays the intro screen*
132   // and waits for the user to press a key.             *
133   //*****************************************************
134   void displayIntro()
135   {
136       // Load the intro screen image.
137       dbLoadImage("Intro.bmp", INTRO_IMAGE);
138       dbPasteImage(INTRO_IMAGE, 0, 0);
139
140       // Wait for the user to press a key.
141       dbWaitKey();
142   }
143
144   //*****************************************************
145   // The initMouse function initializes the mouse.      *
146   //*****************************************************
147   void initMouse()
148   {
149       // Hide the mouse pointer.
150       dbHideMouse();
151
152       // Get the screen center point.
153       int centerX = dbScreenWidth() / 2;
154       int centerY = dbScreenHeight() / 2;
155
156       // Position the mouse at the center.
157       dbPositionMouse(centerX, centerY);
158
159       // Load the hand pointer image.
160       dbLoadImage("HandPointer.bmp", POINTER_IMAGE);
161
162       // Create the hand pointer sprite.
163       dbSprite(POINTER_SPRITE, centerX, centerY, POINTER_IMAGE);
```

```
164
165        // Offset the mouse pointer.
166        dbOffsetSprite(POINTER_SPRITE, OFFSET_X, OFFSET_Y);
167
168        // Set the pointer sprite's priority to 1 so it will
169        // always be drawn on top of the bug. (The bug will
170        // have a priority of 0.)
171        dbSetSpritePriority(POINTER_SPRITE, 1);
172  }
173
174  //*********************************************************
175  // The initBug function creates the animated sprite      *
176  // for the bug and places the first bug on the screen.   *
177  //*********************************************************
178  void initBug()
179  {
180        // Create the bug animated sprite.
181        dbCreateAnimatedSprite(BUG_SPRITE, "ShinyBug.bmp",
182                               COLS, ROWS, BUG_IMAGE);
183
184        // Make sure the sprite has a priority of 0
185        // so it will not be drawn on top of the
186        // mouse pointer.
187        dbSetSpritePriority(BUG_SPRITE, 0);
188
189        // Generate a bug at a random location.
190        generateNewBug();
191  }
192
193  //*********************************************************
194  // The updateMouse function moves the custom mouse        *
195  // to the mouse's current location.                       *
196  //*********************************************************
197  void updateMouse()
198  {
199        // Get the mouse pointer's location.
200        int mouseX = dbMouseX();
201        int mouseY = dbMouseY();
202
203        // Move the hand pointer to the mouse location.
204        dbSprite(POINTER_SPRITE, mouseX, mouseY, POINTER_IMAGE);
205  }
206
207  //*********************************************************
208  // The updateBug function displays the next animation *
209  // frame for the bug.                                  *
210  //*********************************************************
211  void updateBug()
212  {
213        // Get the bug's location.
214        int bugX = dbSpriteX(BUG_SPRITE);
215        int bugY = dbSpriteY(BUG_SPRITE);
216
217        // Play the bug animation.
218        dbPlaySprite(BUG_SPRITE, ROWS, COLS, DELAY);
```

```
219            dbSprite(BUG_SPRITE, bugX, bugY, BUG_IMAGE);
220    }
221
222    //*****************************************************
223    // The generateNewBug function generates a new bug at *
224    // random location.                                   *
225    //*****************************************************
226    void generateNewBug()
227    {
228        // Get the screen dimensions.
229        int screenWidth = dbScreenWidth();
230        int screenHeight = dbScreenHeight();
231
232        // Get the bug's width and height.
233        int bugWidth = dbSpriteWidth(BUG_SPRITE);
234        int bugHeight = dbSpriteHeight(BUG_SPRITE);
235
236        // Generate a new location.
237        int x = dbRND(screenWidth - bugWidth);
238        int y = dbRND(screenHeight - bugHeight);
239
240        // Put the bug at that location.
241        dbSprite(BUG_SPRITE, x, y, BUG_IMAGE);
242    }
243
244    //*****************************************************
245    // The elapsedTime function accepts a previously taken *
246    // time reading as an argument and returns the number  *
247    // of milliseconds that have elapsed since that time.  *
248    //*****************************************************
249    int elapsedTime(int startTime)
250    {
251        return dbTimer() - startTime;
252    }
253
254    //*****************************************************
255    // The displayBugsZapped function displays the closing *
256    // screen showing the number of bugs zapped. The number*
257    // of bugs is passed as an argument.                   *
258    //*****************************************************
259    void displayBugsZapped(int bugs)
260    {
261        // Get the center coordinates.
262        int centerX = dbScreenWidth() / 2;
263        int centerY = dbScreenHeight() / 2;
264
265        // Enable auto refresh.
266        dbSyncOff();
267
268        // Delete all sprites.
269        dbDeleteSprite(BUG_SPRITE);
270        dbDeleteSprite(POINTER_SPRITE);
271
272        // Clear the screen.
273        dbCLS();
```

```
274
275          // Display the number of bugs zapped.
276          dbCenterText(centerX, centerY, "Number of bugs zapped:");
277          dbCenterText(centerX, centerY + 20, dbStr(bugs));
278          dbCenterText(centerX, centerY + 40, "Press any key...");
279
280          // Wait for the user to press a key.
281          dbWaitKey();
282
283          // Determine whether this is the new high score.
284          checkForHighScore(bugs);
285
286          // Disable auto refresh.
287          dbSyncOn();
288      }
289
290      //*******************************************************
291      // The checkForHighScore function reads the high score  *
292      // from the HighScore.dat file and determines whether   *
293      // the user's score is the new high score.              *
294      //*******************************************************
295      void checkForHighScore(int bugs)
296      {
297          // Variable to hold the high score so far.
298          int highScore;
299
300          // If the HighScore.dat file exists, open it and read
301          // its value. Otherwise, set highScore to 0.
302          if ( dbFileExist("HighScore.dat") )
303          {
304              // Open the HighScore.dat file.
305              dbOpenToRead( HIGH_SCORE_FILE, "HighScore.dat" );
306
307              // Read the current high score.
308              highScore = dbReadFile(HIGH_SCORE_FILE);
309
310              // Close the file.
311              dbCloseFile(HIGH_SCORE_FILE);
312          }
313          else
314          {
315              highScore = 0;
316          }
317
318          // Determine whether the user's score is the
319          // new high score.
320          if ( bugs > highScore )
321          {
322              newHighScore(bugs);
323          }
324      }
325
326      //*******************************************************
327      // The newHighScore file congratulates the user for     *
328      // attaining the new high score and updates the         *
```

```
329    // HighScore.dat file.                              *
330    //*****************************************************
331    void newHighScore(int bugs)
332    {
333        // Get the center coordinates.
334        int centerX = dbScreenWidth() / 2;
335        int centerY = dbScreenHeight() / 2;
336
337        // Clear the screen.
338        dbCLS();
339
340        // Congratulate the user.
341        dbCenterText(centerX, centerY, "Congratulations!");
342        dbCenterText(centerX, centerY + 20, "That's the new high score!");
343
344        // If the HighScore.dat file exists, delete it.
345        if ( dbFileExist("HighScore.dat") )
346        {
347            dbDeleteFile("HighScore.dat");
348        }
349
350        // Open the HighScore.dat file for writing.
351        dbOpenToWrite( HIGH_SCORE_FILE, "HighScore.dat" );
352
353        // Write the user's score to the file.
354        dbWriteFile( HIGH_SCORE_FILE, bugs );
355
356        // Close the file.
357        dbCloseFile(HIGH_SCORE_FILE);
358
359        // Wait for the user to press a key.
360        dbCenterText(centerX, centerY + 40, "Press any key...");
361        dbWaitKey();
362    }
363
364    //*****************************************************
365    // The mouseFullClick function processes a full mouse   *
366    // click. If the user is pressing the left mouse button *
367    // it gets the mouse pointer's coordinates and then     *
368    // waits for the user to release the button. It returns *
369    // true to indicate that the mouse was clicked, and the *
370    // reference parameters are set to the mouse pointer's  *
371    // coordinates. If the user is not pressing the mouse   *
372    // button, the function returns false.                  *
373    //*****************************************************
374    bool mouseFullClick(int &x, int &y)
375    {
376        // Variable to hold the return value.
377        bool buttonClick = false;
378
379        // If the mouse button is pressed, process
380        // a full clicking action.
381        if ( dbMouseClick() == 1 )
382        {
383            // Get the mouse pointer coordinates.
384            x = dbMouseX();
385            y = dbMouseY();
```

```
386
387            // Wait for the user to release the
388            // mouse button.
389            while ( dbMouseClick() == 1)
390            {
391                // Do nothing in this loop.
392            }
393
394            // Set buttonClick to true.
395            buttonClick = true;
396        }
397
398        // Return true or false to indicate whether the
399        // mouse was clicked.
400        return buttonClick;
401    }
402
403    //*************************************************************
404    // The onSprite function takes a sprite number and a set of  *
405    // XY coordinates as arguments. The function returns true    *
406    // if the coordinates are located on the sprite's bounding   *
407    // rectangle, or false otherwise.                            *
408    //*************************************************************
409    bool onSprite(int spriteNum, int pointX, int pointY)
410    {
411        // Variable to hold the value to return.
412        bool insideSprite;
413
414        // Get the X coordinate of the sprite's upper-left corner.
415        int upperX = dbSpriteX(spriteNum) - dbSpriteOffsetX(spriteNum);
416
417        // Get the Y coordinate of the sprite's upper-left corner.
418        int upperY = dbSpriteY(spriteNum) - dbSpriteOffsetY(spriteNum);
419
420        // Get the X coordinate of the sprite's lower-right corner.
421        int lowerX = upperX + dbSpriteWidth(spriteNum);
422
423        // Get the Y coordinate of the sprite's lower-right corner.
424        int lowerY = upperY + dbSpriteHeight(spriteNum);
425
426        // Determine whether (pointX, pointY) is inside the
427        // sprite's bounding rectangle.
428        if (pointX >= upperX && pointY >= upperY &&
429            pointX <= lowerX && pointY <= lowerY)
430        {
431            insideSprite = true;
432        }
433        else
434        {
435            insideSprite = false;
436        }
437
438        // Return the value of insideSprite.
439        return insideSprite;
440    }
```

high score, he or she is congratulated with the screen shown in Figure 11-22, and then the user's score is written to the HighScore.dat file, replacing the value previously stored there.

Figure 11-22 High score message

Since we discussed the original Bug Zapper game in detail in Chapter 9, we will discuss only the modifications that were made in this version. When the player's time runs out, the displayBugsZapped function is called to display the number of bugs that were zapped. In this function, in line 284, a function named checkForHighScore is called, with bugs passed as an argument. Recall that the bugs variable holds the number of bugs that the user zapped.

The checkForHighScore function appears in lines 295 through 324. In line 302, the dbFileExist function is called to determine whether the HighScore.dat file exists. If the file exists, it is opened for reading in line 305. In line 308, a value is read from the file and stored in the highScore variable, and then the file is closed in line 311. If the HighScore.dat file does not exist, the highScore variable is assigned 0 in line 315.

The if statement in line 320 determines whether bugs is greater than highScore. If that is true, then the user has beaten the high score, and the newHighScore function is called in line 322, with bugs passed as an argument.

The newHighScore function appears in lines 331 through 362. The first part of the function (lines 333 through 342) displays a congratulatory message. Then the if statement in line 345 determines whether the HighScore.dat file exists. If so, the file is deleted in line 347. This happens because we need to open the file for writing so we can write the user's current score.

In line 351, the file is opened for writing, and in line 354 the value of the bugs variable is written to the file. The file is closed in line 357.

Review Questions

Multiple Choice

1. A _____ variable is used to hold a single character.
   a. character
   b. char
   c. byte
   d. dbSingleChar

2. A(n) _____ is appended to the end of strings in memory.
   a. integer indicating the number of characters in the string
   b. byte containing the number −1
   c. null character
   d. double quotation mark

3. To use the standard C++ string functions discussed in this chapter, you use the _____ directive.
   a. #include <string.h>
   b. #include "string.h"
   c. #include <string_functions.h>
   d. #include "standard_string.h"

4. You use _____ to copy a string to a char array.
   a. stringCopy
   b. arraycpy
   c. strcpy
   d. cpystr

5. You use _____ to append one string to another string.
   a. append
   b. strappend
   c. appendString
   d. strcat

6. String concatenation means _____.
   a. removing all the characters from the string
   b. appending a string to another string
   c. reversing the characters in a string
   d. protecting a string from accidental corruption

7. You use _____ to get the length of a string.
   a. strlen
   b. stringLength
   c. length
   d. str_len

8. You use _____ to compare two strings.
   a. compare
   b. stringCompare
   c. strcmp
   d. str_cmp

9. _____ searches for a string inside a string.
   a. strstr
   b. insideString
   c. string_string
   d. substring

10. A file that data is written to is known as a(n) _____.
    a. input file
    b. output file
    c. sequential access file
    d. binary file

11. A file that data is read from is known as a(n) _____.
    a. input file
    b. output file
    c. sequential access file
    d. binary file

12. Before a file can be used by a program, it must be _____.
    a. formatted
    b. encrypted
    c. closed
    d. opened

13. When a program is finished using a file, it should _____.
    a. erase the file
    b. open the file
    c. close the file
    d. encrypt the file

14. The _____ marks the location of the next item that will be read from a file.
    a. input position
    b. delimiter
    c. pointer
    d. read position

15. You use _____ to open an output file.
    a. dbOpenToWrite
    b. dbOpenToRead
    c. dbOpenOutput
    d. dbOpen

16. You use _____ to open an input file.
    a. dbOpenToWrite
    b. dbOpenToRead
    c. dbOpenInput
    d. dbOpen

17. You use _____ to write an integer value to a file.
    a. dbWriteInteger
    b. dbWriteInt
    c. dbIntegerOut
    d. dbWriteFile

18. _____ returns 1 (true) if the end of the specified file has been reached.
    a. `dbEOF`
    b. `dbFileEnd`
    c. `dbEndOfFile`
    d. `dbEndReached`

19. You use _____ to determine if a file is currently open.
    a. `dbOpen`
    b. `dbIsOpen`
    c. `dbFileOpen`
    d. `dbTestForOpen`

20. You use _____ to determine if a file exists.
    a. `dbFileExist`
    b. `dbFileExists`
    c. `dbExists`
    d. `dbFindFile`

21. You use _____ to delete a file.
    a. `dbEraseFile`
    b. `dbDelete`
    c. `dbDeleteFile`
    d. `dbRemoveFile`

True or False

1. In C++, character literals can be enclosed in either single quotation marks or double quotation marks.

2. A null character is a byte that contains the number 0.

3. The following statement copies the string "Rodney" to a char array named `name`.
   `name = "Rodney";`

4. The `strlen` function returns the amount of memory occupied by a string, including the null character.

5. The `strcmp` function returns 1 if its two arguments are equal, or 0 if they are not equal.

6. When an input file is opened, its read position is initially set to the first item in the file.

7. The `dbOpenToWrite` function will fail if the specified file already exists.

8. When an input file is opened, the read position is set to the last item in the file.

9. The largest file number that you can use with the Dark GDK is 100.

10. You use the same Dark GDK function to close input files and output files.

Short Answer

1. How many bytes of memory would the string `"Agent 99"` occupy?

2. What is string concatenation?

3. Describe the meaning of the values that are returned from the `strcmp` function.

4. What standard C++ function can you use to search for a string inside another string?

5. How would you create an array of strings?

6. Describe the three steps that must be taken when a file is used by a program.

7. What is a file's read position? Where is the read position when a file is first opened for reading?

8. What is the purpose of the `dbFileEnd` function?

9. With the Dark GDK, how many files can you have opened simultaneously?

10. What Dark GDK function do you use to write a floating-point value to a file?

Algorithm Workbench

1. Write the code that declares a `char` array named `dog`, initialized with the string "Fido".

2. Assume that a `char` array named `name` has been declared in a program. Write a statement that copies the string "Rodney" to the `name` array.

3. Assume that a `char` array named `greeting` has been declared and initialized with the string "Good". Write a statement that appends the string "afternoon" to the string that is stored in the `greeting` array.

4. Assume that a `char` array named `playerName` and an `int` variable named `length` have been declared in a program. Write a statement that gets the length of the string stored in the `playerName` array and assigns the length to the `length` variable.

5. Assume that a `char` array named `phoneNumber` has been declared in a program. Write code that prompts the user to enter his or her phone number, and then stores the user's input in the `phoneNumber` array.

6. Assume that two `char` arrays named `playerName` and `selectedPlayer` have been declared in a program. Write code that determines whether the strings in these two arrays are the same. If so, the code should display the message "You have been selected."

7. You need to store the strings "Marley", "Addison", "Rex", and "Henry" in an array. Write code that would create and initialize the appropriate type of array to hold these strings.

8. Write a program that opens an output file with the name `MyName.dat`, writes your name to the file, and then closes the file.

9. Write a program that opens the `MyName.dat` file that was created by the program in question 8, reads your name from the file, displays the name on the screen, and then closes the file.

10. Write a program that does the following: Opens an output file with the name `NumberList.dat`, uses a loop to write the numbers 1 through 100 to the file, and then closes the file.

11. Write a program that does the following: Opens the `NumberList.dat` file that was created by the program created in question 10, reads all of the numbers from the file and displays them, and then closes the file.

12. Modify the program that you created in question 11 so it adds all of the numbers read from the file and displays their total.

Programming Exercises

1. **Mad Lib Game**
   In this chapter, you saw an example of a program that plays the Mad Lib word game. Make up your own Mad Lib story and write a program that plays the game.

2. **Connect the Dots**
   Write a program that lets the user click points on the screen until the spacebar is pressed. The program should save the coordinates to an output file as the user clicks the mouse. When the user presses the spacebar, close the file and then reopen it as an input file, Read the coordinates from the file and draw lines connecting those coordinates.

3. **Bug Zapper High Score**
   In this chapter, you saw a version of the Bug Zapper game that keeps track of the game's highest score. Modify the program so that each time the game ends, the high score and the name of the player who achieved the score are displayed.

4. **Bug Zapper Bonus Time**
   Modify the Bug Zapper game so it reads the high score file when the program begins. If the user beats the high score while the game is playing, the user should immediately get an extra three seconds of play time.

5. **Slide Show List**
   Write a program that first asks the user for the number of image files that he or she wants to display in a slideshow. It should then let the user enter the names of the all the image files. Then write another program that reads the file names from the file created by the first program. It should load and display each specified image with a short delay between each one.

CHAPTER 12 Object-Oriented Programming

TOPICS

12.1 Procedural and Object-Oriented Programming

12.2 Classes and Objects

12.3 Inheritance

12.4 An Object-Oriented Game: Balloon Target

12.1 Procedural and Object-Oriented Programming

CONCEPT: Procedural programming is a method of writing software. It is a programming practice centered on the procedures or actions that take place in a program. Object-oriented programming is centered on objects. Objects are created from abstract data types that encapsulate data and functions together.

There are primarily two methods of programming used today: procedural and object oriented. The earliest programming languages were procedural, meaning a program comprised one or more procedures. A *procedure* is simply a function that performs a specific task such as gathering input from the user, performing calculations, reading or writing files, displaying output, and so forth. So far, the programs you have written have been procedural.

Procedures typically operate on data items that are separate from the procedures. In a procedural program, the data items are commonly passed from one procedure to another. As you might imagine, the focus of procedural programming is on the creation of procedures that operate on the program's data. The separation of data and the code that operates on the data can lead to problems, however, as the program becomes larger and more complex.

611

For example, suppose you are part of a programming team that has developed a game. When the program was initially designed, it kept several image numbers in `int` variables. Your job was to design several functions that accept those variables as arguments and perform operations with them. The software has been operating successfully for some time, but your team has been asked to update it by adding several new features. During the revision process, the senior programmer informs you that the image numbers will no longer be stored in variables. Instead, they will be stored in an `int` array. This means that you will have modify all of the functions that you have designed so they accept and work with an `int` array instead of the variables. Making these extensive modifications is not only a great deal of work, but opens the opportunity for errors to appear in your code.

Whereas procedural programming is centered on creating functions, *object-oriented programming* (*OOP*) is centered on creating objects. An *object* is a software entity that contains fields and methods. An object's *fields* are simply variables, arrays, or other data structures that are stored in the object. An object's *methods* are functions that perform operations on the object's data. The object is, conceptually, a self-contained unit consisting of data (fields) and functions (methods). This is illustrated in Figure 12-1.

Figure 12-1 An object contains data and functions

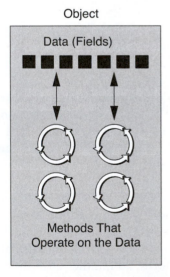

OOP addresses the problem of code/data separation through encapsulation and data hiding. *Encapsulation* refers to the combining of data and code into a single object. *Data hiding* refers to an object's ability to hide its fields from code that is outside the object. Only the object's methods may then directly access and make changes to the object's fields. An object typically hides its fields, but allows outside code to access its methods. As shown in Figure 12-2, the object's methods provide programming statements outside the object with indirect access to the object's fields.

Figure 12-2 Code outside the object interacts with the object's methods

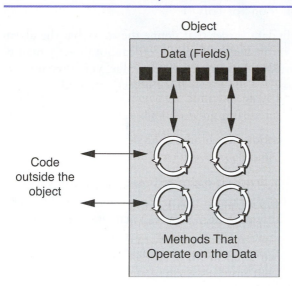

When an object's fields are hidden from outside code and access to those fields is restricted to the object's methods, the fields are protected from accidental corruption. In addition, the programming code outside the object does not need to know about the format or internal structure of the object's fields. The code only needs to interact with the object's methods. When a programmer changes the structure of an object's internal data, he or she also modifies the object's methods so they may properly operate on the data. The way in which outside code interacts with the methods, however, does not change.

Object Reusability

In addition to solving the problems of code/data separation, the use of OOP has also been encouraged by the trend of *object reusability*. An object is not a standalone program, but is used by programs that need its service. For example, Sharon is a programmer who has developed an object for rendering 3D images. She is a math whiz and knows a lot about computer graphics, so her object is coded to perform all the necessary 3D mathematical operations and handle the computer's video hardware. Tom, who is writing a program for an architectural firm, needs his application to display 3D images of buildings. Because he is working under a tight deadline and does not possess a great deal of knowledge about computer graphics, he can use Sharon's object to perform the 3D rendering (for a small fee, of course!).

An Everyday Example of an Object

Think of your alarm clock as an object. It has the following fields:

- The current second (a value in the range of 0–59)
- The current minute (a value in the range of 0–59)

- The current hour (a value in the range of 1–12)
- The time the alarm is set for (a valid hour and minute)
- Whether the alarm is on or off ("on" or "off ")

As you can see, the fields are merely data values that define the *state* that the alarm clock is currently in. You, the user of the alarm clock object, cannot directly manipulate these fields because they are *private*. To change a field's value, you must use one of the object's methods. Here are some of the alarm clock object's methods:

- Set time
- Set alarm time
- Turn alarm on
- Turn alarm off

Each method manipulates one or more of the fields. For example, the "Set time" method allows you to set the alarm clock's time. You activate the method by pressing a button on the clock. By using another button, you can activate the "Set alarm time" method. In addition, another button allows you to execute the "Turn alarm on" and "Turn alarm off" methods. Note that all of these methods can be activated by you, who are outside of the alarm clock. Methods that can be accessed by entities outside the object are known as *public methods*.

OOP Terminology

OOP programmers commonly use the term "fields" to describe the items of data that are stored in an object, and the term "methods" to describe the procedures that operate on an object's data. C++ programmers often refer to fields as *member variables* and refer to methods as *member functions*. These are the terms that we will use, since they are commonly used in C++.

 Checkpoint

12.1. What is an object?

12.2. What is encapsulation?

12.3. Why is an object's internal data usually hidden from outside code?

12.4. What are public methods?

 12.2 Classes and Objects

CONCEPT: A class is code that specifies the member variables and member functions for a particular type of object.

Let's discuss how objects are created in software. Before an object can be created, it must be designed by a programmer. The programmer determines the member variables and member functions that are necessary, and then creates a *class*. A class is code that specifies the member variables and member functions of a particular type of object. Think of a class as a "blueprint" that objects may be created from. It serves a similar purpose as the blueprint for a house. The blueprint itself is not a house, but rather a detailed description of a house. When we use the blueprint to build an actual house, we could say we are building an instance of the house described by the blueprint. If we desire, we can build several identical houses from the same blueprint. Each house is a separate instance of the house described by the blueprint. This idea is illustrated in Figure 12-3.

Figure 12-3 A blueprint and houses built from the blueprint

Blueprint that describes a house.

Instances of the house described by the blueprint.

Another way of thinking about the difference between a class and an object is to think of the difference between a cookie cutter and a cookie. While a cookie cutter itself is not a cookie, it describes a cookie. The cookie cutter can be used to make several cookies, as shown in Figure 12-4. Think of a class as a cookie cutter and the objects created from the class as cookies.

Figure 12-4 The cookie cutter metaphor

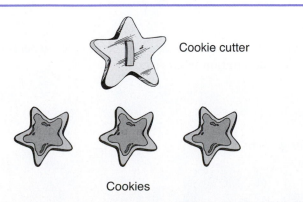

Cookie cutter

Cookies

Think of a class as a cookie cutter and objects as the cookies.

So, a class is not an object, but rather a description of an object. When the program is running, it can use the class to create, in memory, as many objects of a specific type as needed. Each object that is created from a class is called an *instance* of the class.

For example, Jessica is a game programmer. She is developing a game in which the user moves a hero sprite around the screen. During game play, the program automatically moves an enemy sprite around the screen. The user must make sure that the hero sprite does not come in contact with the enemy sprite.

Although the hero and enemy sprites are separate elements in the game, all sprites have the same characteristics. For example, all sprites have a sprite number, an image number, an X coordinate, and a Y coordinate. Jessica decides that she can write a Sprite class that specifies member variables to hold a sprite's data, and member functions that perform operations on a sprite. The Sprite class is not an object, but rather a blueprint that objects may be created from.

Jessica's program will then use the Sprite class to create a hero object in memory. The hero object is an instance of the Sprite class, and it stores data specific to the hero sprite. When the program needs to manipulate the hero sprite, it calls the hero object's member functions. The program will also use the Sprite class to create an enemy object in memory. The enemy object is also an instance of the Sprite class, and it stores data specific to the enemy sprite. When the program needs to manipulate the enemy sprite, it calls the enemy object's member functions. Figure 12-5 illustrates the idea that the hero object and the enemy object are both instances of the Sprite class.

Figure 12-5 The hero and enemy objects are instances of the Sprite class

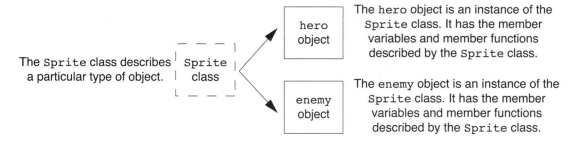

Class Declarations

To create a class, first you write the *class declaration*. This is the general format that we will use to write a class declaration in C++:

```
class ClassName
{
private:

    Member variables go here...

public:

    Member function declarations go here...
};
```

The first line is known as the *class header*. It starts with the key word `class`, followed by the class name. The same rules for naming variables apply to naming classes. Many programmers follow the convention of beginning class names with an uppercase letter. This serves as a visual reminder that the name is that of a class, not a variable.

Following the class header is an opening curly brace. On the line after the opening curly brace we write the key word `private` followed by a colon. This marks the beginning of the class's *private section*. Typically, we declare all of the class's member variables (fields) in the private section. As a result, those member variables can be accessed only by the class's member functions.

After the private section we write the key word `public`, followed by a colon. This marks the beginning of the class's *public section*. Any class members that are declared in the public section can be accessed by code that is outside the class. This is where we typically declare the class's member functions. Declaring member functions in the public section makes them available to code outside the class.

At the end of the class definition is a closing curly brace, followed by a semicolon. Don't forget to write the semicolon, or an error will occur when you compile the code.

NOTE: Normally, you don't write a semicolon after a closing brace, but C++ requires that you write a semicolon after a class's closing brace. Forgetting to do so is a common mistake, and will prevent your code from compiling.

Let's look at an example. Suppose we want to create a `Circle` class. Once the class is complete, we can create objects that represent circles in a Dark GDK program. The class will have private member variables for the following data:

- The *X* coordinate of the circle's center point
- The *Y* coordinate of the circle's center point
- The circle's radius

We will have public member functions to perform the following operations:

- Set the *XY* coordinates for the circle's center point
- Set the circle's radius
- Get the circle's center *X* coordinate
- Get the circle's center *Y* coordinate
- Get the circle's radius
- Draw the circle on the screen

Program 12-1 shows a partial listing for the `CircleClass1.cpp` program. This part of the program shows the definition of the `Circle` class.

Program 12-1 (`CircleClass1.cpp` *partial listing*)

```
1   // This program demonstrates the Circle class.
2   #include "DarkGDK.h"
3
4   //****************************************************
```

```
 5   // Circle class                                              *
 6   //*****************************************************
 7   class Circle
 8   {
 9   private:
10       int centerX;    // Center point X coordinate
11       int centerY;    // Center point Y coordinate
12       int radius;     // Radius
13
14   public:
15       void setCenter(int, int);
16       void setRadius(int);
17       int getCenterX() const;
18       int getCenterY() const;
19       int getRadius() const;
20       void draw() const;
21   };
22
```

The `Circle` class definition appears in lines 7 through 21. Notice that the name of the class begins with an uppercase letter. As previously mentioned, this serves as a visual reminder that `Circle` is a class.

The class's private section begins in line 9. We declare the following member variables in lines 10 through 12:

- `centerX`—holds the *X* coordinate of a circle's center point
- `centerY`—holds the *Y* coordinate of a circle's center point
- `radius`—holds a circle's radius

Because these member variables are declared in the `Circle` class's private section, they can be accessed only by functions that are members of the `Circle` class. We declare the member functions in the class's public section, which begins in line 14. Notice that the member function declarations look just like function prototypes, except that they appear inside the class declaration. Here is a summary of the member function declarations:

- In line 15, we declare a `void` member function named `setCenter`. The function accepts two `int` arguments. These arguments will be assigned to the `centerX` and `centerY` member variables, thus setting *XY* coordinates of a circle's center point.
- In line 16, we declare a `void` member function named `setRadius`. The function accepts an `int` argument, which will be assigned to the `radius` member variable, thus setting a circle's radius.
- In line 17, we declare an `int` member function named `getCenterX`. This function returns the *X* coordinate of the circle's center.
- In line 18, we declare an `int` member function named `getCenterY`. This function returns the *Y* coordinate of the circle's center.
- In line 19, we declare an `int` member function named `getRadius`. This function returns the circle's radius.

- In line 20, we declare a `void` member function named `draw`, which accepts no arguments. The purpose of the function will be to draw a circle on the screen, using the values of the `centerX`, `centerY`, and `radius` member variables to establish the circle's size and position.

Mutators and Accessors

It is common practice to make all of a class's member variables private and to provide public member functions for changing or accessing those member variables. This ensures that the object owning those member variables is in control of all changes being made to them. A member function that stores a value in a member variable or changes the value of a member variable in some other way is known as a *mutator function*. A member function that gets a value from a class's member variable but does not change it is known as an *accessor function*. In the `Circle` class, the `setCenter` and `setRadius` functions are mutators because they assign values to member variables. The `draw` member function is an accessor because it accesses the values of the member variables, but does not change those values.

Notice that in lines 17 through 20 the word `const` appears at the end of the declarations for the `getCenterX`, `getCenterY`, `getRadius`, and `draw` member functions. This specifies that these functions do not change any data stored in the calling object. In any of these functions, if you inadvertently write code that changes the calling object's data, the compiler will generate an error. It is a good programming practice to mark all accessor functions as `const`.

Defining Member Functions

In lines 15 through 20 of the `Circle` class, we declared six member functions. Those declarations alone do nothing. They simply inform the compiler that those functions are members of the class. Now we must write the definitions of those member functions. The definition of the `setCenter` member function is shown in lines 27 through 31, as follows:

Program 12-1   (`CircleClass1.cpp` *continued*)

```
23  //*****************************************************
24  // The Circle::setCenter member function accepts      *
25  // arguments for the circle's X and Y coordinates.    *
26  //*****************************************************
27  void Circle::setCenter(int x, int y)
28  {
29      centerX = x;
30      centerY = y;
31  }
32
```

The function header appears in line 27. Notice that the function name is prefixed with `Circle::`. This indicates that the function is not a regular function, but rather a member of the `Circle` class. The function has two `int` parameter variables, `x` and `y`. These parameters are assigned to the `centerX` and `centerY` member variables in lines 29 and 30.

The definition of the `setRadius` member function is shown in lines 37 through 40, as follows:

Program 12-1   (`CircleClass1.cpp` *continued*)

```
33   //*****************************************************
34   // The Circle::setRadius member function accepts an   *
35   // argument for the circle's radius.                  *
36   //*****************************************************
37   void Circle::setRadius(int rad)
38   {
39       radius = rad;
40   }
41
```

Because `setRadius` is a member of the `Circle` class, we have prefixed the function name with `Circle::`. The function has an `int` parameter named `rad`, which is assigned to the member variable `radius` in line 39.

The definition of the `getCenterX` member function is shown in lines 46 through 49, as follows:

Program 12-1   (`CircleClass1.cpp` *continued*)

```
42   //*****************************************************
43   // The Circle::getCenterX member function returns the *
44   // X coordinate of the circle's center point.         *
45   //*****************************************************
46   int Circle::getCenterX() const
47   {
48       return centerX;
49   }
50
```

Quite often, programs need to query objects to determine the values of their member variables. The `getCenterX` function is an accessor function that returns the *X* coordinate of the circle's center point. Notice that the key word const appears at the end of the function header in line 46. As previously mentioned, this specifies that the function does not modify any of the class's member variables.

The definition of the `getCenterY` member function is shown in lines 55 through 58, as follows. The purpose of this function is to return the *Y* coordinate of the circle's center point.

Program 12-1   (`CircleClass1.cpp` *continued*)

```
51   //******************************************************
52   // The Circle::getCenterY member function returns the *
53   // Y coordinate of the circle's center point.          *
54   //******************************************************
55   int Circle::getCenterY() const
56   {
57       return centerY;
58   }
59
```

The definition of the `getRadius` member function is shown in lines 64 through 67, as follows. The purpose of this function is to return the circle's radius.

Program 12-1   (`CircleClass1.cpp` *continued*)

```
60   //******************************************************
61   // The Circle::getRadius member function returns the   *
62   // circle's radius.                                    *
63   //******************************************************
64   int Circle::getRadius() const
65   {
66       return radius;
67   }
68
```

The definition of the `draw` member function is shown in lines 72 through 75, as follows:

Program 12-1   (`CircleClass1.cpp` *continued*)

```
69   //******************************************************
70   // The Circle::draw member function draws the circle. *
71   //******************************************************
72   void Circle::draw() const
73   {
74       dbCircle( centerX, centerY, radius );
75   }
76
```

The purpose of the `draw` member function is to draw a circle on the screen, using the values of the `centerX`, `centerY`, and `radius` member variables to define the circle's position and size. This is done in line 74, where the `dbCircle` function is called with `centerX`, `centerY`, and `radius` passed as arguments.

Creating an Object

The code that we looked at in lines 7 through 75 of Program 12-1 declares the `Circle` class and defines its member functions. The code does not create any objects, however. Remember that a class is merely the blueprint for one or more objects.

To create an object you write a statement similar to a variable declaration. Here is an example that creates an object from the `Circle` class:

```
Circle myCircle;
```

After this statement executes, an object named `myCircle` will be created in memory. The object will be an instance of the `Circle` class. Because the object is an instance of the `Circle` class, it will contain the `centerX`, `centerY`, and `radius` member variables that are specified in the `Circle` class. This is illustrated in Figure 12-6. Because we haven't yet assigned values to the member variables, their values are undefined.

Figure 12-6 An instance of the `Circle` class

`myCircle` **is a** `Circle` **object.**

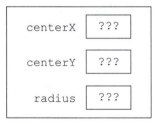

To perform operations on the `myCircle` object's data, you will call the `Circle` class's member functions. For example, the following statement calls the `setCenter` member function:

```
myCircle.setCenter( 100, 75 );
```

The statement is written in *dot notation*. It's called dot notation because programmers refer to the period as a "dot." On the left side of the dot is the name of an object. On the right side of the dot is the name of the member function we are calling. When this statement executes, the `setCenter` member function will be called to operate on the `myCircle` object. We are passing 100 and 75 as arguments. As a result, the value 100 will be assigned to the `myCircle` object's `centerX` member variable and 75 will be assigned to the `myCircle` object's `centerY` member variable. This is illustrated in Figure 12-7.

To set the circle's radius we call the `setRadius` member function, as shown here:

```
myCircle.setRadius(50);
```

This statement calls the `setRadius` member function to operate on the `myCircle` object. The argument, 50, will be assigned to the object's `radius` member variable, as shown in Figure 12-8.

Figure 12-7 Values assigned to `centerX` and `centerY`

The `myCircle` object

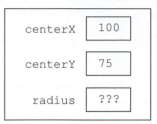

Figure 12-8 Values assigned to `centerX`, `centerY`, and `radius`

The `myCircle` object

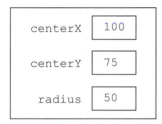

To draw a circle on the screen using the `myCircle` object's data, we call the `draw` member function as shown here:

```
myCircle.draw();
```

Let's see how this works in a program. The complete listing of Program 12-1 is shown, as follows:

Program 12-1   (`CircleClass1.cpp` *complete listing*)

```
1   // This program demonstrates the Circle class.
2   #include "DarkGDK.h"
3
4   //*****************************************************
5   // Circle class                                      *
6   //*****************************************************
7   class Circle
8   {
9   private:
10      int centerX;   // Center point X coordinate
11      int centerY;   // Center point Y coordinate
12      int radius;    // Radius
13
```

```
14   public:
15       void setCenter(int, int);
16       void setRadius(int);
17       int getCenterX() const;
18       int getCenterY() const;
19       int getRadius() const;
20       void draw() const;
21   };
22
23   //********************************************************
24   // The Circle::setCenter member function accepts      *
25   // arguments for the circle's X and Y coordinates.    *
26   //********************************************************
27   void Circle::setCenter(int x, int y)
28   {
29       centerX = x;
30       centerY = y;
31   }
32
33   //********************************************************
34   // The Circle::setRadius member function accepts an   *
35   // argument for the circle's radius.                  *
36   //********************************************************
37   void Circle::setRadius(int rad)
38   {
39       radius = rad;
40   }
41
42   //********************************************************
43   // The Circle::getCenterX member function returns the *
44   // X coordinate of the circle's center point.         *
45   //********************************************************
46   int Circle::getCenterX() const
47   {
48       return centerX;
49   }
50
51   //********************************************************
52   // The Circle::getCenterY member function returns the *
53   // Y coordinate of the circle's center point.         *
54   //********************************************************
55   int Circle::getCenterY() const
56   {
57       return centerY;
58   }
59
60   //********************************************************
61   // The Circle::getRadius member function returns the  *
62   // circle's radius.                                   *
63   //********************************************************
64   int Circle::getRadius() const
65   {
```

```
66          return radius;
67    }
68
69    //*****************************************************
70    // The Circle::draw member function draws the circle. *
71    //*****************************************************
72    void Circle::draw() const
73    {
74          dbCircle( centerX, centerY, radius );
75    }
76
77    //*****************************************************
78    // The DarkGDK function                               *
79    //*****************************************************
80    void DarkGDK()
81    {
82          // Create a Circle object.
83          Circle myCircle;
84
85          // Set the myCircle object's center at (100, 150).
86          myCircle.setCenter(100, 150);
87
88          // Set the myCircle object's radius at 50.
89          myCircle.setRadius(50);
90
91          // Draw the circle.
92          myCircle.draw();
93
94          // Display the circle's data.
95          dbPrint("The circle's center X, center Y, and radius are:");
96          dbPrint( dbStr( myCircle.getCenterX() ) );
97          dbPrint( dbStr( myCircle.getCenterY() ) );
98          dbPrint( dbStr( myCircle.getRadius()  ) );
99
100         // Wait for the user to press a key.
101         dbWaitKey();
102   }
```

Let's take a closer look at the DarkGDK function. The statement in line 83 creates myCircle as an object of the Circle class. Line 86 calls the setCenter member function to set the myCircle object's center point at (100, 150). Line 89 calls the setRadius member function to set the myCircle object's radius to 50. Line 92 calls the draw member function to draw a circle on the screen using the myCircle object's data. The statements in lines 96, 97, and 98 get the circle's center X coordinate, center Y coordinate, and radius, and display those on the screen. Figure 12-9 shows the program's output.

Figure 12-9 Output of Program 12-1

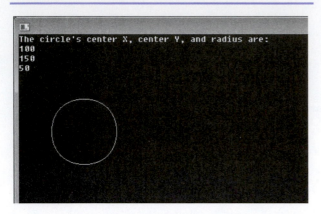

Constructors

A class's member variables cannot be initialized when they are declared, like regular variables. For example, the following class declaration would cause a compiler error:

```
class Circle
{
    private:
        int centerX = 0;   // ERROR! Cannot initialize member
                           // variables
        int centerY = 0;   // ERROR!
        int radius  = 0;   // ERROR!

    public:
        void setCenter(int, int);
        void setRadius(int);
        int getCenterX() const;
        int getCenterY() const;
        int getRadius() const;
        void draw() const;
};
```

To initialize member variables you must write a constructor for the class. A *constructor* is a special member function that is automatically executed when an object is created. It is called a constructor because it helps construct the object. To demonstrate, look at the partial code listing shown in Program 12-2.

Program 12-2   (**CircleClass2.cpp** *partial listing*)

```
1   // This program demonstrates the Circle class constructor.
2   #include "DarkGDK.h"
3
4   //*****************************************************
5   // Circle class                                      *
6   //*****************************************************
7   class Circle
```

```
 8  {
 9  private:
10      int centerX;  // Center point X coordinate
11      int centerY;  // Center point Y coordinate
12      int radius;   // Radius
13
14  public:
15      Circle(int, int, int);
16      void setCenter(int, int);
17      void setRadius(int);
18      int getCenterX() const;
19      int getCenterY() const;
20      int getRadius() const;
21      void draw() const;
22  };
23
24  //*****************************************************
25  // The constructor accepts arguments for the circle's *
26  // X and Y coordinates, and the radius.               *
27  //*****************************************************
28  Circle::Circle(int x, int y, int rad)
29  {
30      centerX = x;
31      centerY = y;
32      radius = rad;
33  }
34
35  //*****************************************************
36  // The Circle::setCenter member function accepts      *
37  // arguments for the circle's X and Y coordinates.    *
38  //*****************************************************
39  void Circle::setCenter(int x, int y)
40  {
41      centerX = x;
42      centerY = y;
43  }
44
45  //*****************************************************
46  // The Circle::setRadius member function accepts an   *
47  // argument for the circle's radius.                  *
48  //*****************************************************
49  void Circle::setRadius(int rad)
50  {
51      radius = rad;
52  }
53
54  //*****************************************************
55  // The Circle::getCenterX member function returns the *
56  // X coordinate of the circle's center point.         *
57  //*****************************************************
58  int Circle::getCenterX() const
59  {
60      return centerX;
61  }
62
```

```
63   //*********************************************************
64   // The Circle::getCenterY member function returns the *
65   // Y coordinate of the circle's center point.            *
66   //*********************************************************
67   int Circle::getCenterY() const
68   {
69        return centerY;
70   }
71
72   //*********************************************************
73   // The Circle::getRadius member function returns the      *
74   // circle's radius.                                       *
75   //*********************************************************
76   int Circle::getRadius() const
77   {
78        return radius;
79   }
80
81   //*********************************************************
82   // The Circle::draw member function draws the circle. *
83   //*********************************************************
84   void Circle::draw() const
85   {
86        dbCircle( centerX, centerY, radius );
87   }
88
```

A constructor has the same name as the class it is a member of. When writing a constructor, you do not specify a return type, not even void. Because you do not explicitly call a constructor (it is automatically called when an object is created), it cannot return a value.

In Program 12-2, the constructor is declared in line 15, and defined in lines 28 through 33. The constructor accepts three int arguments, which are assigned to the centerX, centerY, and radius member variables. A constructor that accepts arguments is sometimes referred to as a *parameterized constructor*.

You pass arguments to the constructor when you create the object. Here is an example:

```
Circle myCircle( 100, 75, 50 );
```

This statement creates an object named myCircle from the Circle class. It passes the arguments 100, 75, and 50 as arguments to the constructor. The constructor then assigns these arguments to the object's centerX, centerY, and radius member variables. To demonstrate, look at the rest of Program 12-2, as follows:

Program 12-2   (**CircleClass2.cpp** *continued*)

```
89   //*********************************************************
90   // The DarkGDK function                                   *
91   //*********************************************************
```

```
 92   void DarkGDK()
 93   {
 94        // Create a Circle object.
 95        Circle myCircle(100, 150, 50);
 96
 97        // Draw the circle.
 98        myCircle.draw();
 99
100        // Display the circle's data.
101        dbPrint("The circle's center X, center Y, and radius are:");
102        dbPrint( dbStr( myCircle.getCenterX() ) );
103        dbPrint( dbStr( myCircle.getCenterY() ) );
104        dbPrint( dbStr( myCircle.getRadius()  ) );
105
106        // Wait for the user to press a key.
107        dbWaitKey();
108   }
```

Line 95 creates a `Circle` object named `myCircle`. The arguments 100, 150, and 50 are passed as arguments to the constructor. Because the constructor assigns these values to the object's member variables, there is no need to call the `setCenter` and `setRadius` member functions. Line 98 calls the `draw` member function to draw a circle on the screen using the `myCircle` object's data. The program's output is the same as shown in Figure 12-9.

Creating Multiple Objects from the Same Class

You can create several objects from the same class in a program. Each object has its own set of member variables. For example, look at Program 12-3. (To save space, we have left out lines 24 through 87, which contain the definitions of the `Circle` class's member functions. The function definitions are the same as those shown in Program 12-2.)

Program 12-3   (`MultipleObjects.cpp`)

```
 1   // This program creates three Circle objects.
 2   #include "DarkGDK.h"
 3
 4   //*****************************************************
 5   // Circle class                                      *
 6   //*****************************************************
 7   class Circle
 8   {
 9   private:
10        int centerX;   // Center point X coordinate
11        int centerY;   // Center point Y coordinate
12        int radius;    // Radius
13
14   public:
15        Circle(int, int, int);
```

```
16          void setCenter(int, int);
17          void setRadius(int);
18          int getCenterX() const;
19          int getCenterY() const;
20          int getRadius() const;
21          void draw() const;
22      };
23
```

Lines 24 through 87 are not shown. See Program 12-2 for reference.

```
88      //****************************************************
89      // The DarkGDK function                             *
90      //****************************************************
91      void DarkGDK()
92      {
93          // Create three Circle objects.
94          Circle c1( 50,  50,  20 );
95          Circle c2( 100, 120, 20 );
96          Circle c3( 40,  100, 20 );
97
98          // Draw the three circles.
99          c1.draw();
100         c2.draw();
101         c3.draw();
102
103         // Wait for the user to press a key.
104         dbPrint("Press any key to exit.");
105         dbWaitKey();
106     }
```

Line 94 creates a `Circle` object named `c1`, passing the arguments 50, 50, and 20 to the constructor. Line 95 creates a `Circle` object named `c2`, passing the arguments 100, 120, and 20 to the constructor. Line 96 creates a `Circle` object named `c3`, passing the arguments 40, 100, and 20 to the constructor. Figure 12-10 shows the state of these three objects.

Line 99 uses the `c1` object to call the `draw` member function. This causes a circle to be drawn on the screen using the data stored in the `c1` object. Line 100 uses the `c2` object to call the `draw` member function, and line 101 uses the `c3` object to call the `draw` member function. The program's output is shown in Figure 12-11.

Figure 12-10 The c1, c2, and c3 objects

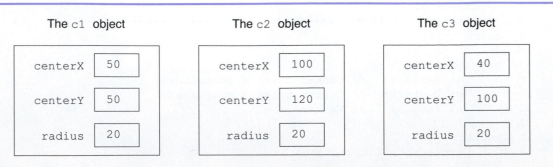

Figure 12-11 Output of Program 12-3

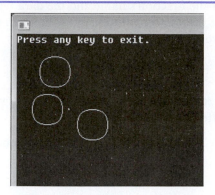

Overloaded Member Functions

Sometimes you need different ways to perform the same operation. For example, the `Circle` class has a `draw` member function that draws a circle on the screen. When the `draw` member function executes, it uses the current drawing color. Suppose you also need a way to draw a circle using a specific color. You could write another member function, with a name such as `drawColor`, which accepts a `DWORD` argument specifying a color. When this function executes, it draws the circle using the specified color.

Although that approach works, a better approach is to *overload* the `draw` member function. When a member function is overloaded, it means that two or more functions in the same class have the same name, but use different parameter lists. Here is an example of two overloaded `draw` member functions:

```
void Circle::draw() const
{
    dbCircle( centerX, centerY, radius );
}

void Circle::draw(DWORD color) const
{
    dbInk( color, color );
    dbCircle( centerX, centerY, radius );
}
```

The first `draw` member function accepts no arguments and draws the circle using the current drawing color. The second `draw` member function accepts a `DWORD` argument. It uses that argument to set the drawing color before drawing the circle.

When we write a call to the `draw` function, the compiler must determine which one of the overloaded functions we intended to call. The process of matching a function call with the correct function is known as *binding*. When an overloaded function is being called, the compiler uses the function's name and parameter list to determine which function to bind the call to. If no arguments are passed to the `draw` function, the version of the function with no parameters is called. Likewise, when a `DWORD` argument is passed to the `draw` function, the version with a `DWORD` parameter is called.

The compiler uses a function's signature to distinguish it from other functions of the same name. A function's *signature* consists of the function's name and the data types of the function's parameters, in the order that they appear. For example, here are the signatures of the draw functions that were previously shown:

```
Circle::draw()
Circle::draw(DWORD)
```

Note that the function's return type is *not* part of the signature. For this reason, you cannot overload functions by giving them different return types.

Program 12-4 demonstrates the Circle class with the overloaded draw member functions.

Program 12-4   (CircleClass3.cpp)

```
 1  // This program demonstrates overloaded draw functions.
 2  #include "DarkGDK.h"
 3
 4  //*****************************************************
 5  // Circle class                                      *
 6  //*****************************************************
 7  class Circle
 8  {
 9  private:
10      int centerX;   // Center point X coordinate
11      int centerY;   // Center point Y coordinate
12      int radius;    // Radius
13
14  public:
15      Circle(int, int, int);
16      void setCenter(int, int);
17      void setRadius(int);
18      int getCenterX() const;
19      int getCenterY() const;
20      int getRadius() const;
21      void draw() const;
22      void draw(DWORD) const;
23  };
24
25  //*****************************************************
26  // The constructor accepts arguments for the circle's *
27  // X and Y coordinates, and the radius.               *
28  //*****************************************************
29  Circle::Circle(int x, int y, int rad)
30  {
31      centerX = x;
32      centerY = y;
33      radius = rad;
34  }
35
36  //*****************************************************
37  // The Circle::setCenter member function accepts      *
38  // arguments for the circle's X and Y coordinates.    *
```

```
39   //********************************************************
40   void Circle::setCenter(int x, int y)
41   {
42       centerX = x;
43       centerY = y;
44   }
45
46   //********************************************************
47   // The Circle::setRadius member function accepts an    *
48   // argument for the circle's radius.                   *
49   //********************************************************
50   void Circle::setRadius(int rad)
51   {
52       radius = rad;
53   }
54
55   //********************************************************
56   // The Circle::getCenterX member function returns the *
57   // X coordinate of the circle's center point.          *
58   //********************************************************
59   int Circle::getCenterX() const
60   {
61       return centerX;
62   }
63
64   //********************************************************
65   // The Circle::getCenterY member function returns the *
66   // Y coordinate of the circle's center point.          *
67   //********************************************************
68   int Circle::getCenterY() const
69   {
70       return centerY;
71   }
72
73   //********************************************************
74   // The Circle::getRadius member function returns the   *
75   // circle's radius.                                    *
76   //********************************************************
77   int Circle::getRadius() const
78   {
79       return radius;
80   }
81
82   //********************************************************
83   // The Circle::draw member function draws the circle. *
84   // This version uses the current drawing color.        *
85   //********************************************************
86   void Circle::draw() const
87   {
88       dbCircle( centerX, centerY, radius );
89   }
90
91   //********************************************************
92   // The Circle::draw member function draws the circle. *
93   // This version uses the color that is passed as an    *
```

```
 94      // argument.                                          *
 95      //****************************************************
 96      void Circle::draw(DWORD color) const
 97      {
 98          dbInk( color, color );
 99          dbCircle( centerX, centerY, radius );
100      }
101
102      //****************************************************
103      // The DarkGDK function                              *
104      //****************************************************
105      void DarkGDK()
106      {
107          // Create some color variables.
108          DWORD red   = dbRGB( 255, 0,   0  );
109          DWORD green = dbRGB( 0,   255, 0  );
110          DWORD blue  = dbRGB( 0,   0,   255);
111
112          // Create four Circle objects.
113          Circle c1( 50,  50,  20 );
114          Circle c2( 100, 120, 20 );
115          Circle c3( 40,  100, 20 );
116          Circle c4( 130, 75,  20 );
117
118          // Draw four circles of different colors.
119          c1.draw();          // Use the default color
120          c2.draw(red);       // Draw a red circle
121          c3.draw(green);     // Draw a green circle
122          c4.draw(blue);      // Draw a blue circle
123
124          // Wait for the user to press a key.
125          dbPrint("Press any key to exit.");
126          dbWaitKey();
127      }
```

Inside the `Circle` class, the two overloaded `draw` member functions are declared in lines 21 and 22. The functions are defined in lines 86 through 89 and 96 through 100. In the `DarkGDK` function, in lines 108 through 110, we declare and initialize the three `DWORD` variables `red`, `green`, and `blue`. In lines 113 through 116, we create four `Circle` objects named `c1`, `c2`, `c3`, and `c4`.

In line 119, we use the `c1` object to call the `draw` member function with no arguments. This causes the `draw` member function that is defined in lines 86 through 89 to execute. As a result, the circle will be drawn using the current drawing color. In line 120, we use the `c2` object to call the `draw` member function, passing the `DWORD` variable `red` as an argument. This causes the `draw` member function that is defined in lines 96 through 100 to execute. As a result, a red circle will be drawn. Line 121 uses the `c3` object to draw a green circle, and line 122 uses the `c4` object to draw a blue circle.

Overloaded Constructors

Constructors can also be overloaded, which means that a class can have more than one constructor. The rules for overloading constructors are the same for overloading other functions: Each version of the constructor must have a different parameter list. As long as each constructor has a unique signature, the compiler can tell them apart. For example, Program 12-5 shows yet another version of the `Circle` class. This one has two overloaded constructors.

Program 12-5   **(CircleClass4.cpp)**

```cpp
1   // This program demonstrates overloaded constructors.
2   #include "DarkGDK.h"
3
4   //****************************************************
5   // Circle class                                     *
6   //****************************************************
7   class Circle
8   {
9   private:
10      int centerX;   // Center point X coordinate
11      int centerY;   // Center point Y coordinate
12      int radius;    // Radius
13
14   public:
15      Circle();
16      Circle(int, int, int);
17      void setCenter(int, int);
18      void setRadius(int);
19      int getCenterX() const;
20      int getCenterY() const;
21      int getRadius() const;
22      void draw() const;
23      void draw(DWORD) const;
24   };
25
26   //****************************************************
27   // The default constructor sets centerX, centerY, and *
28   // radius to 0.                                      *
29   //****************************************************
30   Circle::Circle()
31   {
32      centerX = 0;
33      centerY = 0;
34      radius  = 0;
35   }
36
37   //****************************************************
38   // The constructor accepts arguments for the circle's *
39   // X and Y coordinates, and the radius.              *
40   //****************************************************
41   Circle::Circle(int x, int y, int rad)
```

```
42   {
43       centerX = x;
44       centerY = y;
45       radius = rad;
46   }
47
48   //*******************************************************
49   // The Circle::setCenter member function accepts        *
50   // arguments for the circle's X and Y coordinates.      *
51   //*******************************************************
52   void Circle::setCenter(int x, int y)
53   {
54       centerX = x;
55       centerY = y;
56   }
57
58   //*******************************************************
59   // The Circle::setRadius member function accepts an     *
60   // argument for the circle's radius.                    *
61   //*******************************************************
62   void Circle::setRadius(int rad)
63   {
64       radius = rad;
65   }
66
67   //*******************************************************
68   // The Circle::getCenterX member function returns the   *
69   // X coordinate of the circle's center point.          *
70   //*******************************************************
71   int Circle::getCenterX() const
72   {
73       return centerX;
74   }
75
76   //*******************************************************
77   // The Circle::getCenterY member function returns the   *
78   // Y coordinate of the circle's center point.          *
79   //*******************************************************
80   int Circle::getCenterY() const
81   {
82       return centerY;
83   }
84
85   //*******************************************************
86   // The Circle::getRadius member function returns the    *
87   // circle's radius.                                     *
88   //*******************************************************
89   int Circle::getRadius() const
90   {
91       return radius;
92   }
93
94   //*******************************************************
95   // The Circle::draw member function draws the circle.   *
96   // This version uses the current drawing color.         *
```

```
97   //*****************************************************
98   void Circle::draw() const
99   {
100      dbCircle( centerX, centerY, radius );
101  }
102
103  //*****************************************************
104  // The Circle::draw member function draws the circle. *
105  // This version uses the color that is passed as an   *
106  // argument.                                          *
107  //*****************************************************
108  void Circle::draw(DWORD color) const
109  {
110      dbInk( color, color );
111      dbCircle( centerX, centerY, radius );
112  }
113
114  //*****************************************************
115  // The DarkGDK function                               *
116  //*****************************************************
117  void DarkGDK()
118  {
119      // Create two Circle objects.
120      Circle c1;
121      Circle c2( 100, 120, 20 );
122
123      // Set the c1 object's radius.
124      c1.setRadius(100);
125
126      // Draw the two circles.
127      c1.draw();
128      c2.draw();
129
130      // Wait for the user to press a key.
131      dbText(150, 10, "Press any key to exit.");
132      dbWaitKey();
133  }
```

Inside the Circle class, the two overloaded constructors are declared in lines 15 and 16. The first constructor, which is defined in lines 30 through 35, accepts no arguments. When it executes, it sets the centerX, centerY, and radius member variables to 0. The second constructor is defined in lines 41 through 46. This is the same one that we have seen before, accepting arguments that are assigned to the centerX, centerY, and radius member variables.

When a constructor accepts no arguments, it is called the *default constructor*. This means that the constructor that is defined in lines 30 through 35 is the Circle class's default constructor. Notice that line 120 creates the c1 object, passing no arguments to the constructor. This causes the default constructor to execute. As a result, the c1 object's centerX, centerY, and radius member variables will be set to 0. In line 121, the c2 object is created with three int arguments passed. This causes the constructor that is defined in lines 41 through 46 to execute.

In line 124, we use the c1 object to call the setRadius member function, passing 100 as an argument. This sets the c1 object's radius member variable to 100. Lines 127 and 128 draw the two circles on the screen. Figure 12-12 shows the program's output.

Figure 12-12 Output of Program 12-5

 NOTE: If you write a class with no constructor whatsoever, when the class is compiled C++ will automatically write a default constructor that does nothing. For example, the first version of the Circle class had no constructor; so, when the class was compiled C++ generated the following constructor:

```
Circle::Circle()
{
}
```

 NOTE: If you are creating an object and calling the default constructor, do not write parentheses after the object name. For example, the following statement will cause a compiler error:

```
Circle myCircle();
```

Instead, the statement should be written like this:

```
Circle myCircle;
```

Creating Arrays of Objects

As with any other data type in C++, you can define arrays of class objects. For example, the following creates an array of Circle objects:

```
const int SIZE = 5;
Circle circles[SIZE];
```

This code creates an array of five Circle objects. The name of the array is circles, and the default constructor is called for each object in the array. Program 12-6 declares such an array and demonstrates how to process its elements. (To save space, we have left out lines 25 through 113, which contain the definitions of the Circle class's member functions. The function definitions are the same as those shown in Program 12-5.)

Program 12-6   (`ObjectArray1.cpp` *partial listing*)

```
1    // This program demonstrates an array of objects.
2    #include "DarkGDK.h"
3
4    //******************************************************
5    // Circle class                                        *
6    //******************************************************
7    class Circle
8    {
9    private:
10       int centerX;   // Center point X coordinate
11       int centerY;   // Center point Y coordinate
12       int radius;    // Radius
13
14   public:
15       Circle();
16       Circle(int, int, int);
17       void setCenter(int, int);
18       void setRadius(int);
19       int getCenterX() const;
20       int getCenterY() const;
21       int getRadius() const;
22       void draw() const;
23       void draw(DWORD) const;
24   };
```
         Lines 25 through 113 are not shown. See Program 12-5 for reference.
```
114  //******************************************************
115  // The DarkGDK function                                *
116  //******************************************************
117  void DarkGDK()
118  {
119      // Create an array of Circle objects.
120      const int SIZE = 5;
121      Circle circles[SIZE];
122
123      // Get the coordinates of the center of the screen.
124      int x = dbScreenWidth() / 2;
125      int y = dbScreenHeight() / 2;
126
127      // Variable to hold a circle's radius.
128      int radius = 10;
129
130      // Set each object's position and radius.
131      for ( int index = 0; index < SIZE; index++ )
132      {
133          // Set the center point.
134          circles[index].setCenter( x, y );
135
136          // Set the radius.
```

```
137            circles[index].setRadius( radius );
138
139            // Draw the circle.
140            circles[index].draw();
141
142            // Double the value of radius.
143            radius *= 2;
144        }
145
146    // Wait for the user to press a key.
147    dbPrint("Press any key to exit.");
148    dbWaitKey();
149 }
```

Line 121 creates an array of five `Circle` objects. The name of the array is `circles`, and the default constructor is called for each object. In lines 124 and 125, we declare the `int` variables `x` and `y` and initialize those variables with the coordinates of the center of the screen. In line 128, we declare an `int` variable named `radius` and initialize it with the value 10.

The `for` loop in lines 131 through 144 steps through each element of the `circles` array. In line 134, the element's `setCenter` member function is called. In line 137, the element's `setRadius` member function is called with the `radius` variable passed as an argument. Line 140 calls the element's `draw` member function to draw the circle on the screen. Then, line 143 doubles the value of the `radius` variable so the next circle will be twice as large. Figure 12-13 shows the program's output.

Figure 12-13 Output of Program 12-6

In the previous example, an array of objects was created and the default constructor was called for each object in the array. If you need to call a constructor that requires arguments for the elements, you can do so with an initialization list. Here is an example:

```
const int SIZE = 5;
Circle circles[SIZE] = { Circle(  30, 50, 20 ),
                         Circle(  90, 50, 20 ),
                         Circle( 150, 50, 20 ),
                         Circle( 210, 50, 20 ),
                         Circle( 270, 50, 20 )
                       };
```

Recall that the `Circle` class has a constructor that accepts three `int` arguments. When this code executes, it calls that constructor for each element of the circles array. Program 12-7 demonstrates the code. (As with the previous program, we have left out lines 22 through 83, which contain the definitions of the `Circle` class's member functions. The function definitions are the same as those shown in Program 12-5.) Figure 12-14 shows the program's output.

Program 12-7   (`ObjectArray2.cpp` *partial listing*)

```
1   // This program demonstrates an array of objects.
2   #include "DarkGDK.h"
3
4   //*****************************************************
5   // Circle class                                       *
6   //*****************************************************
7   class Circle
8   {
9   private:
10      int centerX;   // Center point X coordinate
11      int centerY;   // Center point Y coordinate
12      int radius;    // Radius
13
14  public:
15      Circle();
16      Circle(int, int, int);
17      void setCenter(int, int);
18      void setRadius(int);
19      int getCenterX() const;
20      int getCenterY() const;
21      int getRadius() const;
22      void draw() const;
23      void draw(DWORD) const;
24  };
```
Lines 25 through 113 are not shown. See Program 12-5 for reference.
```
114  //*****************************************************
115  // The DarkGDK function                               *
116  //*****************************************************
117  void DarkGDK()
118  {
119      // Create an array of Circle objects.
120      const int SIZE = 5;
```

```
121         Circle circles[SIZE] = { Circle(  30, 50, 20 ),
122                                  Circle(  90, 50, 20 ),
123                                  Circle( 150, 50, 20 ),
124                                  Circle( 210, 50, 20 ),
125                                  Circle( 270, 50, 20 )
126                                };
127
128         // Step through the array drawing each circle.
129         for ( int index = 0; index < SIZE; index++ )
130         {
131             circles[index].draw();
132         }
133
134         // Wait for the user to press a key.
135         dbPrint("Press any key to exit.");
136         dbWaitKey();
137  }
```

Figure 12-14 Output of Program 12-7

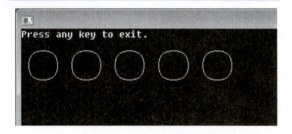

Passing Objects as Arguments to Functions

Objects can be passed as arguments to functions just like regular variables. When you pass an object by value, only a copy of the object is passed into the function. If you want the function to be able to modify the object, you must pass it by reference. Program 12-8 shows an example. In this program we have written a void function named setCircle. The setCircle function accepts a Circle object by reference. It then sets the object's member variables to random values. (As with previous programs, we have left out lines 25 through 113, which contain the definitions of the Circle class's member functions. The function definitions are the same as those shown in Program 12-5.)

Program 12-8   (**PassObject.cpp** *partial listing*)

```
1   // This program passes an object to a function.
2   #include "DarkGDK.h"
3
4   //******************************************************
5   // Circle class                                       *
6   //******************************************************
```

```
 7   class Circle
 8   {
 9   private:
10       int centerX;   // Center point X coordinate
11       int centerY;   // Center point Y coordinate
12       int radius;    // Radius
13
14   public:
15       Circle();
16       Circle(int, int, int);
17       void setCenter(int, int);
18       void setRadius(int);
19       int getCenterX() const;
20       int getCenterY() const;
21       int getRadius() const;
22       void draw() const;
23       void draw(DWORD) const;
24   };
```
      Lines 25 through 113 are not shown. See Program 12-5 for reference.
```
114  // Function prototype
115  void setCircle(Circle &);
116
117  //*****************************************************
118  // The DarkGDK function                              *
119  //*****************************************************
120  void DarkGDK()
121  {
122      // Create a Circle object.
123      Circle myCircle;
124
125      // Set the object's member variables to
126      // random values.
127      setCircle(myCircle);
128
129      // Display the circle.
130      myCircle.draw();
131
132      // Wait for the user to press a key.
133      dbPrint("Press any key to exit.");
134      dbWaitKey();
135  }
136
137  //*****************************************************
138  // The setCircle function accepts a Circle object by *
139  // reference. It sets the object's center point      *
140  // coordinates and radius to random values.          *
141  //*****************************************************
142  void setCircle(Circle &c)
143  {
144      // Seed the random number generator.
145      dbRandomize( dbTimer() );
146
147      // Generate random values for the circle's
148      // center point coordinates and radius.
149      int x = dbRND( dbScreenWidth() );
```

```
150        int y = dbRND( dbScreenHeight() );
151        int radius = dbRND( dbScreenHeight() / 2);
152
153        // Store those values in the Circle object.
154        c.setCenter(x, y);
155        c.setRadius(radius);
156  }
```

Destructors

A destructor is a special member function that is automatically executed when an object is destroyed from memory. A common case in which an object is destroyed is when the function in which it was declared finishes executing. For example, if you declare a `Circle` object in the `DarkGDK` function, that object will be destroyed when the `DarkGDK` function finishes executing. In the same way that constructors set things up when an object is created, destructors perform shutdown procedures when the object goes out of existence.

A destructor's name starts with the tilde character (~), followed by the name of the class. For example, if we were to write a destructor for the `Circle` class, its name would be `~Circle`. The class declaration would then appear as follows:

```
class Circle
{
private:
    int centerX;   // Center point X coordinate
    int centerY;   // Center point Y coordinate
    int radius;    // Radius

public:
    Circle();
    Circle(int, int, int);
    ~Circle();
    void setCenter(int, int);
    void setRadius(int);
    int getCenterX() const;
    int getCenterY() const;
    int getRadius() const;
    void draw() const;
    void draw(DWORD) const;
};
```

The destructor's definition would appear as follows:

```
Circle::~Circle()
{
    // Any code written here will execute when
    // the object is destroyed.
}
```

You don't always need a destructor in a class, but in some situations they are necessary. In the Spotlight presents a class that uses a destructor to delete sprites from memory when they are no longer needed.

In the Spotlight:

A Sprite Class

When designing a game as an object-oriented program, you will want to make objects for all of the major elements in the game. Sprites are excellent candidates to become objects. Earlier in this chapter, we mentioned that all sprites have the same characteristics. For example, all sprites have a sprite number, an image number, an *X* coordinate, and a *Y* coordinate. In addition, all sprites support the same set of operations, such as setting the position, hiding, showing, stretching, flipping, mirroring, and so forth. Because all sprites have so much in common, we can create a `Sprite` class, and then each time we need a sprite in our program, use the class to create an object.

In this section, we will examine a simple `Sprite` class that provides the basic operations needed to create and work with a sprite. The class has the following private member variables:

- `imageNumber`—holds the sprite's image number
- `spriteNumber`—holds the sprite's sprite number

The class also has the following public member functions:

- Constructor—creates the sprite
- `display`—displays the sprite at a specified location
- `display`—displays the sprite at its current location
- `show`—shows the sprite
- `hide`—hides the sprite
- `getImageNumber`—returns the image number for the sprite
- `getSpriteNumber`—returns the sprite number for the sprite
- `getX`—returns the sprite's current *X* coordinate
- `getY`—returns the sprite's current *Y* coordinate
- `destructor`—deletes the sprite from memory

Program 12-9 shows a partial listing for the program that demonstrates the class. The `Sprite` class declaration is shown in lines 7 through 24.

Program 12-9   (`SpriteClass.cpp` *partial listing*)

```
 1   // This program demonstrates the Sprite class.
 2   #include "DarkGDK.h"
 3
 4   //*************************************************
 5   // The Sprite class                              *
 6   //*************************************************
 7   class Sprite
 8   {
 9   private:
10       int imageNumber;
11       int spriteNumber;
12
13   public:
14       Sprite(int, int, char []);
```

```
15          ~Sprite();
16          void display(int, int) const;
17          void display() const;
18          void show() const;
19          void hide() const;
20          int getImageNumber() const;
21          int getSpriteNumber() const;
22          int getX() const;
23          int getY() const;
24      };
25
```

The constructor is shown next, in lines 31 through 39. It accepts arguments for the image number, the sprite number, and the image file name. In lines 34 and 35, the imageNumber and spriteNumber member variables are assigned, and in line 38 the image file is loaded.

Program 12-9 (**SpriteClass.cpp** *continued*)

```
26   //***************************************************
27   // The constructor sets up the sprite. It accepts   *
28   // arguments for the image number, sprite number,   *
29   // and image file name.                             *
30   //***************************************************
31   Sprite::Sprite(int image, int sprite, char filename[])
32   {
33       // Set the image number and sprite number.
34       imageNumber = image;
35       spriteNumber = sprite;
36
37       // Load the image for the sprite.
38       dbLoadImage(filename, imageNumber);
39   }
40
```

The destructor is shown next, in lines 44 through 50. When an instance of this class is destroyed, the destructor deletes the sprite from memory.

Program 12-9 (**SpriteClass.cpp** *continued*)

```
41   //***************************************************
42   // The destructor deletes the sprite.               *
43   //***************************************************
44   Sprite::~Sprite()
45   {
46       if ( dbSpriteExist(spriteNumber) )
47       {
```

```
48              dbDeleteSprite(spriteNumber);
49          }
50  }
51
```

The `display` member function is overloaded. The first version of the function is shown next, in lines 56 through 59. This function accepts arguments specifying an *XY* coordinate, and then displays the sprite at that location.

Program 12-9   (**SpriteClass.cpp** *continued*)

```
52  //****************************************************
53  // This display member function displays the sprite *
54  // at the specified XY coordinates.                  *
55  //****************************************************
56  void Sprite::display(int x, int y) const
57  {
58      dbSprite( spriteNumber, x, y, imageNumber );
59  }
60
```

The second version of the `display` member function is shown next, in lines 65 through 73. This function accepts no arguments, and displays the sprite at its current location.

Program 12-9   (**SpriteClass.cpp** *continued*)

```
61  //****************************************************
62  // This display member function displays the sprite *
63  // at its current XY coordinates.                    *
64  //****************************************************
65  void Sprite::display() const
66  {
67      // Get the sprite's current coordinates.
68      int x = dbSpriteX(spriteNumber);
69      int y = dbSpriteY(spriteNumber);
70
71      // Display the sprite.
72      dbSprite( spriteNumber, x, y, imageNumber );
73  }
74
```

The `show` member function is shown next, in lines 78 through 81. This function can be called to show a sprite that was previously hidden.

Program 12-9   (`SpriteClass.cpp` *continued*)

```
75   //**************************************************
76   // The show member function shows the sprite.      *
77   //**************************************************
78   void Sprite::show() const
79   {
80       dbShowSprite(spriteNumber);
81   }
82
```

The `hide` member function is shown next, in lines 86 through 89. This function can be called to hide the sprite.

Program 12-9   (`SpriteClass.cpp` *continued*)

```
83   //**************************************************
84   // The hide member function hides the sprite.      *
85   //**************************************************
86   void Sprite::hide() const
87   {
88       dbHideSprite(spriteNumber);
89   }
90
```

The `getImageNumber` member function is shown next, in lines 95 through 98. This function returns the image number that is associated with the sprite.

Program 12-9   (`SpriteClass.cpp` *continued*)

```
91   //**************************************************
92   // The getImageNumber member function returns the  *
93   // image number for this sprite.                   *
94   //**************************************************
95   int Sprite::getImageNumber() const
96   {
97       return imageNumber;
98   }
99
```

The `getSpriteNumber` member function is shown next, in lines 104 through 107. This function returns the sprite number that is associated with the sprite.

Program 12-9   (`SpriteClass.cpp` *continued*)

```
100   //*****************************************************
101   // The getSpriteNumber member function returns the  *
102   // sprite number for this sprite.                   *
103   //*****************************************************
104   int Sprite::getSpriteNumber() const
105   {
106        return spriteNumber;
107   }
108
```

The `getX` member function is shown next, in lines 113 through 116. This function returns the sprite's current *X* coordinate.

Program 12-9   (`SpriteClass.cpp` *continued*)

```
109   //*****************************************************
110   // The getX member function returns the sprite's   *
111   // X coordinate.                                   *
112   //*****************************************************
113   int Sprite::getX() const
114   {
115        return dbSpriteX(spriteNumber);
116   }
117
```

The `getY` member function is shown next, in lines 122 through 125. This function returns the sprite's current *Y* coordinate.

Program 12-9   (`SpriteClass.cpp` *continued*)

```
118   //*****************************************************
119   // The getY member function returns the sprite's   *
120   // Y coordinate.                                   *
121   //*****************************************************
122   int Sprite::getY() const
123   {
124        return dbSpriteY(spriteNumber);
125   }
126
```

The `DarkGDK` function is shown next, in lines 130 through 160. The function provides a simple demonstration of many of the `Sprite` class's member functions. It uses the class to create a space background sprite and a UFO sprite.

Program 12-9   (`SpriteClass.cpp` *continued*)

```
127   //****************************************************
128   // The DarkGDK function                             *
129   //****************************************************
130   void DarkGDK()
131   {
132       // Constants for image and sprite numbers
133       const int SPACE = 1;
134       const int UFO   = 2;
135
136       // Set the image key color for transparency.
137       dbSetImageColorKey( 0, 255, 0 );
138
139       // Create a Sprite object for the background.
140       Sprite background(SPACE, SPACE, "Space.bmp");
141
142       // Create a Sprite object for the UFO.
143       Sprite ufo(UFO, UFO, "UFO.bmp");
144
145       // Display the background sprite at (0, 0).
146       background.display(0, 0);
147
148       // Display the UFO sprite in the center of the screen.
149       ufo.display( dbScreenWidth() / 2,
150                    dbScreenHeight() / 2 );
151
152       // Wait for a key press.
153       dbWaitKey();
154
155       // Hide the UFO sprite.
156       ufo.hide();
157
158       // Wait for a key press.
159       dbWaitKey();
160   }
```

In lines 133 and 134, the SPACE and UFO constants are declared. These will be used as image numbers and sprite numbers. In line 137, the transparency key color is set to green. Then in line 140, a Sprite object named background is created. The SPACE constant is passed as both the image number and the sprite number. The file name "Space.bmp" is passed as the image file name.

In line 143, a Sprite object named ufo is created. The UFO constant is passed as both the image number and the sprite number. The file name "UFO.bmp" is passed as the image file name.

In line 146, the background object is used to call the display member function, passing 0, 0 as arguments. This causes the background sprite to be displayed at (0, 0). Then, in lines 149 and 150, the ufo object is used to call the display member function. The arguments that are passed are the calculated coordinates of the screen's center. As a result, the UFO sprite is displayed at the center of the screen. At this point, the screen appears as shown in the left image in Figure 12-15.

Line 153 waits for the user to press a key, and then line 156 uses the ufo object to call the hide member function this hides the UFO sprite, as shown in the right image in Figure 12-15.

Figure 12-15 Output of Program 12-9

 Checkpoint

12.5. You hear someone make the following comment: "A blueprint is a design for a house. A carpenter can use the blueprint to build the house. If the carpenter wishes, he or she can build several identical houses from the same blueprint." Think of this as a metaphor for classes and objects. Does the blueprint represent a class or an object?

12.6. In this chapter, we use the metaphor of a cookie cutter and cookies that are made from the cookie cutter to describe classes and objects. In this metaphor, are objects the cookie cutter or the cookies?

12.7. An object's private members are accessible by what code?

12.8. Are a class's member variables typically declared in the class's public section or private section?

12.9. Are a class's member functions typically declared in the class's public section or private section?

12.10. What is an accessor? What is a mutator?

12.11. What is a constructor?

12.12. What is a parameterized constructor? What is a default constructor?

12.13. What are overloaded member functions?

12.14. What is a destructor?

12.3 Inheritance

CONCEPT: Inheritance allows a new class to extend an existing class. The new class inherits the members of the class it extends.

Generalization and Specialization

In the real world you can find many objects that are specialized versions of other more general objects. For example, the term "insect" describes a very general type of creature with numerous characteristics. Because grasshoppers and bumblebees are insects, they have all the general characteristics of an insect. In addition, they have special characteristics of their own. For example, the bumblebee has its stinger and the grasshopper has its jumping ability. Bumblebees and grasshoppers are specialized versions of an insect, as illustrated in Figure 12-16.

Figure 12-16 Bumblebees and grasshoppers are specialized versions of an insect

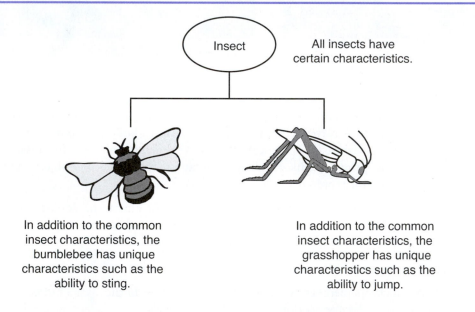

Inheritance and the "Is a" Relationship

When one object is a specialized version of another object, there is an "is a" relationship between them. For example, a grasshopper is an insect. Here are a few other examples of the "is a" relationship:

- A poodle is a dog.
- A car is a vehicle.
- A flower is a plant.
- A rectangle is a shape.
- A football player is an athlete.

When an "is a" relationship exists between objects, it means that the specialized object has all of the characteristics of the general object, plus additional characteristics that make it special. In object-oriented programming, inheritance is used to create an "is a" relationship among classes. This allows you to extend the capabilities of a class by creating another class that is a specialized version of it.

Inheritance involves a base class and a derived class. The *base class* is the general class and the *derived class* is the specialized class. You can think of the derived class as an extended version of the base class. The derived class inherits members from the base class without any of them having to be rewritten. Furthermore, new members may be added to the derived class, and that is what makes it a specialized version of the base class.

Let's look at an example of how inheritance can be used. The `dbCircle` function draws a circle with a line thickness of one pixel. Suppose you need to draw circles that are thicker than one pixel. This can be done with a loop, as shown in the following code:

```
int centerX    = 100;   // Center point X coordinate
int centerY    = 100;   // Center point Y coordinate
int radius     = 20;    // Radius
int thickness = 10;     // Line thickness

// Draw the circle to the specified thickness.
for ( int count = 0; count < thickness; count++ )
{
    // Draw a circle 1 pixel thick.
    dbCircle( centerX, centerY, radius - count );
}
```

This code draws a circle with its center point located at (100, 100), with a radius of 20 pixels, and with a line thickness of 10 pixels. The line thickness is achieved by the loop, which draws 10 concentric circles that are very close together. The first circle is drawn with a radius of 20, the second is drawn with a radius of 19, the third is drawn with a radius of 18, and so forth.

In an object-oriented program, we could create a class named `ThickCircle` that represents a circle with a specified thickness. We have already developed a `Circle` class (in the previous section), that represents a basic circle. Because a thick circle is a specialized version of a regular circle, we can derive the `ThickCircle` class from the `Circle` class.

When we derive the `ThickCircle` class from the `Circle` class, the `ThickCircle` class will inherit all of the members of the `Circle` class. So, when we declare the `ThickCircle` class, we only specify the members that are new to the `ThickCircle` class. We will add the following member variable to the `ThickCircle` class:

- `thickness`—an `int` variable that specifies the circle's line thickness

We will also add the following member functions to the `ThickCircle` class:

- A default constructor that sets `thickness` to 2
- An overloaded constructor that accepts an argument for `thickness`
- A `setThickness` member function that accepts an argument for `thickness`
- A specialized version of the `draw()` member function that draws the thick circle using the current drawing color

- A specialized version of the draw(DWORD) member function that draws the thick circle using a specified color

Program 12-10 demonstrates the ThickCircle class. To save space, we will not show the code in lines 1 through 114. Those lines contain the initial comments, #include directive, and the code for the Circle class. The declaration for the ThickCircle class begins in line 119.

Program 12-10   (**ThickCircleClass.cpp** *partial listing*)

```
115   //*****************************************************
116   // The ThickCircle class is derived from the Circle  *
117   // class.                                            *
118   //*****************************************************
119   class ThickCircle : public Circle
120   {
121   private:
122       int thickness;
123
124   public:
125       ThickCircle();
126       ThickCircle(int);
127       void setThickness(int);
128       void draw() const;
129       void draw(DWORD) const;
130   };
```

The only new notation in this class declaration appears in line 119. After the name of the class, ThickCircle, a colon appears, followed by public Circle. This indicates that the ThickCircle class is derived from the Circle class. (The Thick-Circle class is the derived class and the Circle class is the base class.) Figure 12-17 illustrates this notation.

Figure 12-17 Inheritance notation in the class header

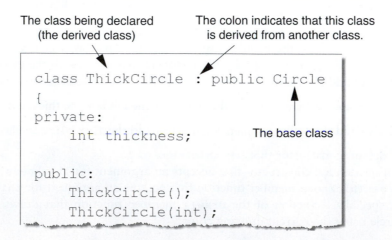

WARNING! When writing the class header for a derived class, don't forget the word `public` that appears after the colon. If you leave out the word `public`, the class will compile, but it will not be able to access any of the base class members.

The `ThickCircle` class has two overloaded constructors, shown here:

Program 12-10   (**ThickCircleClass.cpp** *continued*)

```
132   //****************************************************
133   // The default constructor sets the thickness to 2.  *
134   //****************************************************
135   ThickCircle::ThickCircle()
136   {
137       thickness = 2;
138   }
139
140   //****************************************************
141   // This constructor accepts an argument for thickness. *
142   //****************************************************
143   ThickCircle::ThickCircle(int thick)
144   {
145       thickness = thick;
146   }
147
```

The default constructor, defined in lines 135 through 138, sets the `thickness` member variable to 2. The second constructor, which appears in lines 144 through 146, accepts an argument for the circle's thickness.

When a `ThickCircle` object is created, one of these constructors will be called, depending on whether an argument is passed. But before the code in either of these constructors executes, the `Circle` class's default constructor will be called. Recall that the `Circle` class's default constructor sets the `centerX`, `centerY`, and `radius` member variables to 0.

The `setThickness` member function accepts an argument that is assigned to the `thickness` member variable. The function is defined in lines 152 through 155, as shown here:

Program 12-10   (**ThickCircleClass.cpp** *continued*)

```
148   //****************************************************
149   // The ThickCircle::setThickness member function sets *
150   // the circle's thickness.                            *
151   //****************************************************
152   void ThickCircle::setThickness(int thick)
153   {
154       thickness = thick;
155   }
156
```

Lines 161 through 169 define a member function named draw that accepts no arguments. Recall that the Circle class also has a member function named draw that accepts no arguments. The function that appears here, in the ThickCircle class, is a *redefinition* of the draw() function in the Circle class. When we use a Thick-Circle object to call the draw() member function, it will call the one defined in the ThickCircle class, not the one defined in the Circle class. We use the term *overriding* to describe this behavior. The draw() function in the derived class overrides the draw() function in the base class.

In the ThickCircle class, we redefined the draw() function because the draw() function in the Circle class is not adequate for the needs of the ThickCircle class. The draw() function in the Circle class draws circles with a line thickness of one pixel. In the ThickCircle class, we need to use the algorithm that was previously shown to achieve greater line thicknesses. The redefined draw() function is shown here:

Program 12-10   (**ThickCircleClass.cpp** *continued*)

```
157  //*****************************************************
158  // The ThickCircle::draw member function draws the    *
159  // thick circle using the current drawing color.      *
160  //*****************************************************
161  void ThickCircle::draw() const
162  {
163      // Get the circle's center point coordinates
164      // and radius from the base class.
165      int x = getCenterX();
166      int y = getCenterY();
167      int rad = getRadius();
168
169      // Draw the circle to the specified thickness.
170      for ( int count = 0; count < thickness; count++ )
171      {
172          // Draw a circle 1 pixel thick.
173          dbCircle( x, y, rad - count );
174      }
175  }
176
```

In lines 165 through 167, we get the circle's center X coordinate, center Y coordinate, and radius. Notice that instead of getting these values directly from the centerX, centerY, and radius member variables, we call the base class functions getCenterX, getCenterY, and getRadius to access these values. This is because the centerX, centerY, and radius member variables are declared as private in the base class. A derived class cannot directly access the private members of its base class. Instead, it must use the base class's public accessor functions to get those variables' values.

Lines 182 through 192 define the draw member function that accepts a DWORD argument specifying the circle's color. This is also a redefinition of a base class function.

Program 12-10   (**ThickCircleClass.cpp** *continued*)

```
177   //*******************************************************
178   // This version of the ThickColor::draw member         *
179   // function draws the thick circle using the color      *
180   // passed as an argument.                                *
181   //*******************************************************
182   void ThickCircle::draw(DWORD color) const
183   {
184       // Set the drawing color.
185       dbInk( color, color );
186
187       // Draw the circle.
188       draw();
189   }
190
```

Line 185 sets the drawing color to the value specified by the color argument. Then, line 188 calls the `ThickCircle` class's other `draw` function (the one defined in lines 161 through 175).

> **NOTE:** Sometimes it is necessary to call a base class function that has been redefined in the derived class. For example, suppose that in one of the `ThickCircle` class's member functions we need to call the `draw()` function that was defined in the base class. We could do so with the following statement:
>
> ```
> Circle::draw();
> ```

The program's `DarkGDK` function is shown in lines 194 through 224:

Program 12-10   (**ThickCircleClass.cpp** *continued*)

```
191   //*******************************************************
192   // The DarkGDK function                                 *
193   //*******************************************************
194   void DarkGDK()
195   {
196       // Create a regular Circle object.
197       Circle c1( 100, 100, 50 );
198
199       // Create two ThickCircle objects.
200       ThickCircle c2( 10 );
201       ThickCircle c3( 20 );
202
203       // Set the c2 (ThickCircle) object's center point
204       // and radius.
205       c2.setCenter( 250, 100 );
206       c2.setRadius( 50 );
207
208       // Set the c3 (ThickCircle) object's center point
```

```
209         // and radius.
210         c3.setCenter( 400, 100 );
211         c3.setRadius( 50 );
212
213         // Create a DWORD variable for the color red.
214         DWORD red = dbRGB( 255, 0, 0 );
215
216         // Draw the three circles.
217         c1.draw();
218         c2.draw();
219         c3.draw(red);
220
221         // Wait for the user to press a key.
222         dbPrint("Press any key to exit.");
223         dbWaitKey();
224   }
```

Line 197 creates a regular `Circle` object named `c1`. Then, lines 200 and 201 create two `ThickCircle` objects named `c2` and `c3`. A value of 10 is passed as an argument to `c2`'s constructor and a value of 20 is passed as an argument to `c3`'s constructor. Lines 205 and 206 set `c2`'s center point and radius, and lines 210 and 211 set `c3`'s center point and radius.

Line 214 creates a `DWORD` variable named `red`, initialized with the RGB values for the color red. Then, line 217 calls the `c1` object's `draw` member function. The `c1` object is an instance of the `Circle` class, so this will draw a regular circle with a line thickness of one pixel. Line 218 calls the `c2` object's `draw` member function. This will draw a circle with a thickness of 10 pixels, using the current drawing color. Then, line 219 calls the `c3` object's `draw` member function, passing the `red` variable as an argument. This will draw a red circle with a thickness of 20 pixels. The program's output is shown in Figure 12-18.

Figure 12-18 Output of Program 12-10

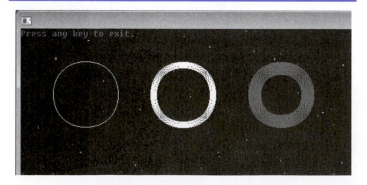

Passing Arguments to the Base Class Constructor

When either of the `ThickCircle` class's constructors execute, the `Circle` class's default constructor is executed first. Recall that the `Circle` class also has a parameterized constructor that accepts arguments for the center X coordinate, the center Y

coordinate, and the radius. What if we want to call that constructor instead of the `Circle` class's default constructor when we create a `ThickCircle` object? We can do so by letting the `ThickCircle` class's constructor explicitly call the `Circle` class's constructor, passing any necessary arguments to it.

Program 12-11 demonstrates how this is done. In the program we have created another version of the `ThickCircle` class, which is declared in lines 119 through 130.

Program 12-11   (**ThickCircleClass2.cpp** *partial listing*)

```
115  //****************************************************
116  // The ThickCircle class is derived from the Circle  *
117  // class.                                            *
118  //****************************************************
119  class ThickCircle : public Circle
120  {
121  private:
122      int thickness;
123
124  public:
125      ThickCircle();
126      ThickCircle(int, int, int, int);
127      void setThickness(int);
128      void draw() const;
129      void draw(DWORD) const;
130  };
```

In this version of the class, we have declared a default constructor in line 125, and an overloaded constructor inline 126 that accepts four `int` arguments. That constructor is defined in lines 145 through 149, as shown here:

Program 12-11   (**ThickCircleClass.cpp** *continued*)

```
140  //****************************************************
141  // This constructor accepts arguments for the center *
142  // X coordinate, the center Y coordinate, the radius,*
143  // and the thickness.                                *
144  //****************************************************
145  ThickCircle::ThickCircle(int x, int y, int rad, int thick)
146              : Circle(x, y, rad)
147  {
148      thickness = thick;
149  }
```

Here is a summary of the constructor's parameters:

- The `x` parameter will receive the *X* coordinate of the circle's center point.
- The `y` parameter will receive the *Y* coordinate of the circle's center point.
- The `rad` parameter will receive the circle's radius.
- The `thick` parameter will receive the line thickness.

Notice the new notation that appears in line 146:

```
: Circle(x, y, rad)
```

This is an explicit call to the `Circle` class constructor, passing x, y, and rad as arguments. To understand how this works, consider the following statement:

```
ThickCircle myCircle( 100, 200, 50, 20 );
```

This statement creates a `ThickCircle` object named `myCircle`. The constructor is called and 100 is passed into the x parameter, 200 is passed into the y parameter, 50 is passed into the rad parameter, and 20 is passed into the `thick` parameter. The code that appears in line 146 then calls the `Circle` class constructor passing x, y, and rad as arguments.

The program's `DarkGDK` function, in lines 197 through 208, demonstrates. The declaration in line 200 creates a `ThickCircle` object specifying 100 as the center *X* coordinate, 100 as the center *Y* coordinate, 50 as the radius, and 20 as the line thickness. The program's output is shown in Figure 12-19.

Program 12-11 (`ThickCircleClass.cpp` *continued*)

```
194   //****************************************************
195   // The DarkGDK function                             *
196   //****************************************************
197   void DarkGDK()
198   {
199       // Create a ThickCircle object.
200       ThickCircle myCircle( 100, 100, 50, 20 );
201
202       // Draw the thick circle.
203       myCircle.draw();
204
205       // Wait for the user to press a key.
206       dbPrint("Press any key to exit.");
207       dbWaitKey();
208   }
```

Figure 12-19 Output of Program 12-11

In the Spotlight:

The `MoveableSprite` Class

The previous In the Spotlight section showed a simple `Sprite` class that provides the basic operations needed to create and work with a sprite. Here, we will examine a `MoveableSprite` class that is derived from the `Sprite` class. The `MoveableSprite` class will give the ability to move the sprite on the screen. The `MoveableSprite` class will have the following private member variables:

- `distance`—holds the sprite's moving distance (the number of pixels that the sprite is to move, each time it is moved)

The `MoveableSprite` class will also have the following public member functions:

- Constructor—accepts as arguments the image number for the sprite, the sprite number, the image file name, and the sprite's moving distance
- `setDistance`—accepts an argument for the sprite's moving distance and assigns it to the distance member variable
- `getDistance`—returns the sprite's moving distance
- `moveUp`—moves the sprite up
- `moveDown`—moves the sprite down
- `moveLeft`—moves the sprite to the left
- `moveRight`—moves the sprite to the right

Program 12-12 demonstrates the `MoveableSprite` class. To save space, we will not show the code in lines 1 through 126. Those lines contain the initial comments, `#include` directive, and the code for the `Sprite` class. The declaration for the `MoveableSprite` class begins in line 131.

Program 12-12   (`MoveableSpriteClass.cpp` *partial listing*)

```
127  //************************************************
128  // The MoveableSprite class is derived from the    *
129  // Sprite class.                                   *
130  //************************************************
131  class MoveableSprite : public Sprite
132  {
133  private:
134      int distance;
135  public:
136      MoveableSprite(int, int, char [], int);
137      void setDistance(int);
138      int getDistance() const;
139      void moveUp() const;
140      void moveDown() const;
141      void moveLeft() const;
142      void moveRight() const;
143  };
144
```

The constructor is defined in lines 149 through 154, as follows:

Program 12-12 (`MoveableSpriteClass.cpp` *continued*)

```
145  //**************************************************
146  // The MoveableSprite constructor calls the Sprite *
147  // constructor.                                     *
148  //**************************************************
149  MoveableSprite::MoveableSprite(int image, int sprite,
150                                 char filename[], int dist)
151               : Sprite(image, sprite, filename)
152  {
153      distance = dist;
154  }
155
```

The constructor accepts arguments for the sprite's image number, sprite number, image file name, and moving distance. In line 151, the `Sprite` class constructor is explicitly called, passing the image number, sprite number, and image file name as arguments. In line 153, the argument passed as the moving distance is assigned to the `distance` member variable.

The `setDistance` member function is defined in lines 160 through 163, as follows:

Program 12-12 (`MoveableSpriteClass.cpp` *continued*)

```
156  //**************************************************
157  // The setDistance member function sets the moving *
158  // distance for the sprite.                         *
159  //**************************************************
160  void MoveableSprite::setDistance(int dist)
161  {
162      distance = dist;
163  }
164
```

The `getDistance` member function is defined in lines 169 through 172, as follows:

Program 12-12 (`MoveableSpriteClass.cpp` *continued*)

```
165  //**************************************************
166  // The getDistance member function returns the     *
167  // sprite's moving distance.                        *
168  //**************************************************
169  int MoveableSprite::getDistance() const
170  {
171      return distance;
172  }
173
```

The `moveUp` member function is defined in lines 177 through 188, as follows:

Program 12-12   (`MoveableSpriteClass.cpp` *continued*)

```
174   //****************************************************
175   // The moveUp member function moves the sprite up. *
176   //****************************************************
177   void MoveableSprite::moveUp() const
178   {
179       // Get the sprite's current coordinates.
180       int x = getX();
181       int y = getY();
182
183       // Decrease y.
184       y -= distance;
185
186       // Display the sprite at its new location.
187       display( x, y );
188   }
189
```

Lines 180 and 181 call the `Sprite` class's `getX` and `getY` member functions to get the sprite's current *XY* coordinates. Those values are assigned to the local variables x and y. Line 184 decreases the value of y by the value of the `distance` member variable. Line 187 calls the `Sprite` class's `display` function to display the sprite at its new location.

The `moveDown` member function is defined in lines 194 through 205, as follows:

Program 12-12   (`MoveableSpriteClass.cpp` *continued*)

```
190   //****************************************************
191   // The moveDown member function moves the sprite    *
192   // down.                                            *
193   //****************************************************
194   void MoveableSprite::moveDown() const
195   {
196       // Get the sprite's current coordinates.
197       int x = getX();
198       int y = getY();
199
200       // Increase y.
201       y += distance;
202
203       // Display the sprite at its new location.
204       display( x, y );
205   }
206
```

Lines 197 and 198 call the Sprite class's getX and getY member functions to get the sprite's current *XY* coordinates. Those values are assigned to the local variables x and y. Line 201 increases the value of y by the value of the distance member variable. Line 204 calls the Sprite class's display function to display the sprite at its new location.

The moveLeft member function is defined in lines 211 through 222, as follows:

Program 12-12   (**MoveableSpriteClass.cpp** *continued*)

```
207  //****************************************************
208  // The moveLeft member function moves the sprite   *
209  // left.                                           *
210  //****************************************************
211  void MoveableSprite::moveLeft() const
212  {
213      // Get the sprite's current coordinates.
214      int x = getX();
215      int y = getY();
216
217      // Decrease x.
218      x -= distance;
219
220      // Display the sprite at its new location.
221      display( x, y );
222  }
223
```

Lines 214 and 215 call the Sprite class's getX and getY member functions to get the sprite's current *XY* coordinates. Those values are assigned to the local variables x and y. Line 218 decreases the value of x by the value of the distance member variable. Line 221 calls the Sprite class's display function to display the sprite at its new location.

The moveRight member function is defined in lines 228 through 239, as follows:

Program 12-12   (**MoveableSpriteClass.cpp** *continued*)

```
224  //****************************************************
225  // The moveRight member function moves the sprite  *
226  // right.                                          *
227  //****************************************************
228  void MoveableSprite::moveRight() const
229  {
230      // Get the sprite's current coordinates.
231      int x = getX();
232      int y = getY();
233
234      // Increase x.
235      x += distance;
236
```

```
237        // Display the sprite at its new location.
238        display( x, y );
239   }
240
```

Lines 231 and 232 call the `Sprite` class's `getX` and `getY` member functions to get the sprite's current *XY* coordinates. Those values are assigned to the local variables `x` and `y`. Line 235 increases the value of `x` by the value of the `distance` member variable. Line 238 calls the `Sprite` class's `display` function to display the sprite at its new location.

The program's `DarkGDK` function, which is shown in lines 244 through 299, demonstrates an object of the class.

Program 12-12   (`MoveableSpriteClass.cpp` *continued*)

```
241   //***************************************************
242   // The DarkGDK function                            *
243   //***************************************************
244   void DarkGDK()
245   {
246        // Constants
247        const int SPACE   = 1;
248        const int UFO     = 2;
249        const int REFRESH = 60;
250
251        // Set the image key color for transparency.
252        dbSetImageColorKey( 0, 255, 0 );
253
254        // Create a Sprite object for the background.
255        Sprite background(SPACE, SPACE, "Space.bmp");
256
257        // Create a MoveableSprite object for the UFO.
258        MoveableSprite ufo(UFO, UFO, "UFO.bmp", 10);
259
260        // Display the background sprite at (0, 0).
261        background.display(0, 0);
262
263        // Display the UFO sprite in the center of the screen.
264        ufo.display( dbScreenWidth() / 2,
265                     dbScreenHeight() / 2 );
266
267        // Disable auto-refresh and set the refresh rate.
268        dbSyncOn();
269        dbSyncRate(REFRESH);
270
271        // Game loop
272        while ( LoopGDK() )
273        {
274            // If any of the arrow keys are pressed, move
275            // the UFO sprite.
276            if ( dbUpKey() )
```

```
277                 {
278                       ufo.moveUp();
279                 }
280
281                 if ( dbDownKey() )
282                 {
283                       ufo.moveDown();
284                 }
285
286                 if ( dbLeftKey() )
287                 {
288                       ufo.moveLeft();
289                 }
290
291                 if ( dbRightKey() )
292                 {
293                       ufo.moveRight();
294                 }
295
296                 // Refresh the screen.
297                 dbSync();
298           }
299    }
```

Lines 247 through 249 declare constants for the image and sprite numbers, and the screen refresh rate. Line 252 sets the key color for transparency to green. Line 255 creates a `Sprite` object named `background`. The `SPACE` constant is passed as the image number and the sprite number, and the image file name is `Space.bmp`. This sprite will be displayed as the background.

Line 258 creates a `MoveableSprite` object named `ufo`. The `UFO` constant is passed as the image number and the sprite number, the image file name is `UFO.bmp`, and 10 is passed as the sprite's moving distance.

Line 261 displays the background sprite at (0, 0). Lines 264 and 265 display the UFO sprite at the center of the screen. Lines 268 and 269 disable auto-refresh and set the screen refresh rate.

The game loop begins in line 272. A series of `if` statements appear in lines 276 through 294. These `if` statements determine whether one of the arrow keys is being pressed, and if so, call the `ufo` object's appropriate member function. Line 297 refreshes the screen.

When the program runs, the screen shown in Figure 12-20 appears. When the user presses any of the arrow keys, the UFO sprite moves accordingly.

Figure 12-20 Output of Program 2-12

 Checkpoint

12.15. In this section we discussed base classes and derived classes. Which is the general class and which is the specialized class?

12.16. What does it mean to say there is an "is a" relationship between two objects?

12.17. What does a derived class inherit from its base class?

12.18. Look at the following code which is the first line of a class declaration. What is the name of the base class? What is the name of the derived class?

```
class Canary : public Bird
```

12.19. Can a derived class have a member function with the same name as base class member function?

12.4   **An Object-Oriented Game: Balloon Target**

In this section, we will examine an object-oriented game program named Balloon Target. Figure 12-21 shows a screen from the game. In the game, a balloon moves repeatedly across the screen, from left to right. Each time the balloon starts at the left side of the screen, its speed randomly changes. A dart is positioned at the bottom of the screen. When the user presses the spacebar, the dart is launched. The object of the game is to hit the balloon with the dart as many times as possible.

Figure 12-21 The Balloon Target game

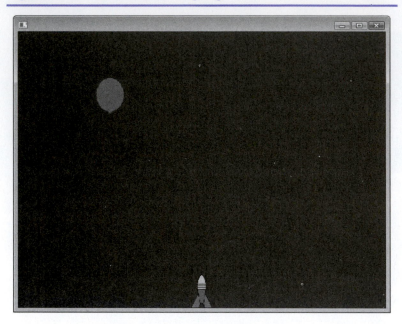

Program 12-13 shows the code. In the program, we create instances of the `MoveableSprite` class (discussed in the previous section) to represent the balloon and the dart. To save space, we will not show the code in lines 1 through 240. Those lines contain the initial comments, `#include` directive, the code for the `Sprite` class, and the code for the `MoveableSprite` class.

Lines 242 through 247 declare global constants, as shown here:

Program 12-13   (**BalloonTarget.cpp** *partial listing*)

```
241  // Constants
242  const int BALLOON          = 1;      // Image and sprite number
243  const int DART             = 2;      // Image and sprite number
244  const int DART_DIST        = 10;     // Dart moving distance
245  const int REFRESH          = 60;     // Refresh rate
246  const int POP_SOUND        = 1;      // Sound number
247  const int MAX_BALLOON_DIST = 14;     // Maximum balloon distance
248
```

Here is a summary of the constants:

- `BALLOON` and `DART` will be used as image numbers and sprite numbers.
- `DART_DIST` is the dart sprite's moving distance.
- `REFRESH` is the screen refresh rate.
- `POP_SOUND` will be used as a sound number.
- `MAX_BALLOON_DIST` is used to calculate the maximum moving distance for the balloon sprite. The greater the balloon's moving distance, the faster it moves

across the screen.

The function prototypes are listed in lines 250 through 255, as shown here:

Program 12-13   (**BalloonTarget.cpp** *continued*)

```
249   // Function prototypes
250   void restartBalloon(MoveableSprite &);
251   void restartDart(MoveableSprite &);
252   void moveBalloon(MoveableSprite &);
253   bool spacebarPressed();
254   void moveDart(MoveableSprite &, bool &);
255   void checkForCollision(MoveableSprite &, MoveableSprite &, bool &);
256
```

The `DarkGDK` function is shown next:

Program 12-13   (**BalloonTarget.cpp** *continued*)

```
257   //**************************************************
258   // The DarkGDK function                            *
259   //**************************************************
260   void DarkGDK()
261   {
262       // Variable to indicate whether the dart has
263       // been launched.
264       bool dartLaunched = false;
265
266       // Set the image key color for transparency.
267       dbSetImageColorKey( 0, 255, 0 );
268
269       // Seed the random number generator.
270       dbRandomize( dbTimer() );
271
272       // Create MoveableSprite objects for the
273       // balloon and the dart.
274       MoveableSprite balloon(BALLOON, BALLOON, "Balloon.bmp", 0);
275       MoveableSprite dart(DART, DART, "Dart.bmp", DART_DIST);
276
277       // Position the balloon and dart.
278       restartBalloon(balloon);
279       restartDart(dart);
280
281       // Disable auto-refresh and set the refresh rate.
282       dbSyncOn();
283       dbSyncRate(REFRESH);
284
285       // Game loop
286       while ( LoopGDK() )
287       {
288           // Move the balloon.
```

```
289            moveBalloon(balloon);
290
291            // See if the spacebar has been pressed.
292            if ( spacebarPressed() )
293            {
294                dartLaunched = true;
295            }
296
297            // If the dart has been launched, move it.
298            if (dartLaunched)
299            {
300                moveDart( dart, dartLaunched );
301            }
302
303            // Check for collisions.
304            checkForCollision( dart, balloon, dartLaunched );
305
306            // Refresh the screen.
307            dbSync();
308        }
309    }
310
```

In line 264, we declare a bool variable named `dartLaunched`, initialized with the value `false`. This variable will be used as a flag to indicate whether the dart has been launched. In line 267, we set the transparency key color to green. In line 270, we seed the random number generator.

In line 274, we create a `MoveableSprite` object named `balloon`. This object will represent the balloon. We pass the `BALLOON` constant as arguments for both the image number and the sprite number, the string `"Balloon.bmp"` as the argument for the image file name, and 0 as the argument for the moving distance. At this point, the value that we pass for the balloon's moving distance is unimportant because it will soon be set to a random value.

In line 275, we create a `MoveableSprite` object named `dart`. This object will represent the dart. We pass the `DART` constant as arguments for both the image number and the sprite number, the string `"Dart.bmp"` as the argument for the image file name, and `DART_DIST` as the argument for the moving distance.

In line 278, we call the `restartBalloon` function, passing the `balloon` object as an argument. Note that the `balloon` object is passed by reference to the function. The `restartBalloon` function positions the balloon at a random location along the screen's left edge, and sets the balloon's moving distance to a random value.

In line 279, we call the `restartDart` function, passing the `dart` object as an argument. The `dart` object is passed by reference to the function. The `restartDart` function horizontally centers the dart at the bottom of the screen.

Lines 282 and 283 disable auto-refresh and set the screen refresh rate. The game loop begins in line 286.

Inside the game loop, line 289 calls the `moveBalloon` function, passing the `balloon` object by reference. The `moveBalloon` function moves the balloon toward the screen's right edge. If the balloon is at the edge of the screen, it is restarted.

The `if` statement in line 292 determines whether the user is pressing the spacebar. If so, the `dartLaunched` variable is set to `true` to indicate that the dart has been launched.

The `if` statement in line 298 determines whether the `dartLaunched` variable is set to `true`. If so, the `moveDart` function is called in line 300 with the `dart` object and the `dartLaunched` variable passed by reference as arguments. The `moveDart` function moves the dart up the screen. If the dart is at the top of the screen, it is reset and `dartLaunched` is set to `false`.

Line 304 calls the `checkForCollision` function, passing the `dart` object, the `balloon` object, and the `dartLaunched` variable as arguments. All three arguments are passed by reference. The `checkForCollision` function determines whether the dart and the balloon have collided. If so, a pop sound is played, both the balloon and the dart are reset, and the `dartLaunched` variable is set to `false`.

Line 307 refreshes the screen.

The definition of the `restartBalloon` function is shown in lines 317 through 337, as follows:

Program 12-13   (`BalloonTarget.cpp` *continued*)

```
311   //**************************************************
312   // The restartBalloon function accepts by reference *
313   // the balloon's MoveableSprite object. It restarts *
314   // the balloon along the left edge of the screen,   *
315   // with a random moving distance.                   *
316   //**************************************************
317   void restartBalloon(MoveableSprite &balloon)
318   {
319       // We want to keep the balloon in the top
320       // two-thirds of the screen. Calculate the
321       // greatest Y coordinate for the balloon.
322       int maxY = dbScreenHeight() * 0.66;
323
324       // Get a random value for the Y coordinate.
325       int y = dbRND(maxY);
326
327       // Display the balloon at its new location
328       // along the left edge of the screen.
329       balloon.display( 0, y );
330
331       // Generate a random value for the balloon's
332       // moving distance.
333       int dist = dbRND(MAX_BALLOON_DIST) + 1;
334
335       // Set the balloon's moving distance.
336       balloon.setDistance(dist);
337   }
338
```

The `restartBalloon` function accepts the `balloon` object as an argument, by reference. When we reposition the balloon, we want it to appear somewhere in the top two-thirds of the screen. The statement in line 322 calculates the maximum Y coordinate for the balloon, and assigns it to the local variable `maxY`. Line 325 gets a random number in the range of 0 through `maxY` and assigns that value to the local variable `y`. Line 329 displays the balloon at its new position. (We always want the balloon to appear at the left edge of the screen, so 0 is always passed as the X coordinate in this statement.)

Line 333 gets a random value for the balloon's moving distance. The `MAX_BALLOON_DIST` constant is set to 14, so this statement will calculate a random number in the range of 1 through 15. Line 336 uses this value to set the moving distance.

The definition of the `restartDart` function is shown in lines 344 through 366, as follows:

Program 12-13   (**BalloonTarget.cpp** *continued*)

```
339   //*****************************************************
340   // The restartDart function restarts the dart at    *
341   // bottom of the screen. It accepts the dart's      *
342   // MoveableSprite object by reference.              *
343   //*****************************************************
344   void restartDart(MoveableSprite &dart)
345   {
346       // We need to make sure the dart sprite has been
347       // created, so we can calculate its position based
348       // on the sprite's width and height.
349       if ( !dbSpriteExist( dart.getSpriteNumber() ) )
350       {
351           dart.display( 0, 0 );
352       }
353
354       // Calculate the dart's X coordinate so it is
355       // centered horizontally on the screen.
356       int x = ( dbScreenWidth() / 2 ) -
357               ( dbSpriteWidth( dart.getSpriteNumber() ) / 2);
358
359       // Set the dart's Y coordinate so it is at the
360       // bottom of the screen.
361       int y = dbScreenHeight() -
362               dbSpriteHeight( dart.getSpriteNumber() );
363
364       // Display the dart at its new location.
365       dart.display( x, y );
366   }
367
```

The `restartDart` function accepts the `dart` object as an argument, by reference. The `if` statement in line 349 determines whether the `dart` sprite has been created yet. We perform this test because a `MoveableSprite` object doesn't actually create the sprite until the `display` member function is called the first time. This function needs to get the size of the sprite, so if it doesn't exist yet, we call the `dart` object's `display` member function in line 351 to create it. The arguments (0,0) that we pass to the `display` member function in line 351 are unimportant at this point because in a moment we are going to calculate the proper coordinates for the sprite.

We want to display the dart sprite horizontally centered at the bottom of the screen. In lines 356 and 357 we calculate the X coordinate, and in lines 361 and 362 we calculate the Y coordinate. In line 365 we call the `display` member function to display the dart at these coordinates.

The definition of the `moveBalloon` function is shown in lines 374 through 384, as follows:

Program 12-13   (`BalloonTarget.cpp` *continued*)

```
368  //****************************************************
369  // The moveBalloon function accepts the balloon      *
370  // object by reference. It moves the balloon to      *
371  // the right. If the balloon is at the right edge    *
372  // of the screen, it restarts the balloon.           *
373  //****************************************************
374  void moveBalloon(MoveableSprite &balloon)
375  {
376      if ( balloon.getX() < dbScreenWidth() )
377      {
378          balloon.moveRight();
379      }
380      else
381      {
382          restartBalloon(balloon);
383      }
384  }
385
```

The `moveBalloon` function accepts the `balloon` object as an argument, by reference. The `if` statement in line 376 determines whether the balloon sprite is at the right edge of the screen. If the balloon sprite has not reached the screen's right edge, line 378 calls the `balloon` object's `moveRight` member function. Otherwise, line 382 calls the `restartBalloon` function to restart the balloon sprite at the left side of the screen.

The definition of the `moveDart` function is shown in lines 419 through 440, as follows:

Program 12-13   (`BalloonTarget.cpp` *continued*)

```
386  //****************************************************
387  // The moveDart function accepts by reference the    *
388  // dart object and the dartLaunched flag variable.   *
389  // If the dart has been launched, it is moved up.    *
390  // If the dart has reached the top of the screen,    *
391  // it is restarted and the dartLaunched flag is      *
392  // set to false.                                     *
```

```
393   //***************************************************
394   void moveDart(MoveableSprite &dart, bool &dartLaunched)
395   {
396       // If the dart has been launched, move it up.
397       if (dartLaunched)
398       {
399           dart.moveUp();
400       }
401
402       // If the dart has reached the top of the screen,
403       // restart it.
404       if ( dart.getY() < 0 )
405       {
406           // Restart the dart.
407           restartDart(dart);
408
409           // Reset the dartLaunched flag.
410           dartLaunched = false;
411       }
412   }
413
```

The `moveDart` function accepts the `dart` object and the `dartLaunched` variable as arguments, by reference. The `if` statement in line 397 tests the `dartLaunched` variable. If it is `true`, then the dart has been launched, so line 399 moves the dart up. The `if` statement in line 404 determines whether the dart has reached the top of the screen. If it has, line 407 calls `restartDart` to reposition the dart, and line 410 sets the `dartLaunched` variable to `false`.

The definition of the `spacebarPressed` function is shown in lines 419 through 440, as follows:

Program 12-13   (**BalloonTarget.cpp** *continued*)

```
414   //***************************************************
415   // The spacebarPressed function returns true if the  *
416   // spacebar has been pressed and released. It         *
417   // returns false otherwise.                           *
418   //***************************************************
419   bool spacebarPressed()
420   {
421       // Boolean flag to indicate whether the
422       // spacebar has been pressed.
423       bool pressed = false;
424
425       // See if the spacebar is being pressed.
426       if ( dbSpaceKey() )
427       {
428           // Do nothing as long as the spacebar
429           // is being held down.
430           while ( dbSpaceKey() )
```

```
431            {
432            }
433
434         // Update the pressed flag.
435         pressed = true;
436      }
437
438      // Return the pressed flag.
439      return pressed;
440   }
441
```

The `spacebarPressed` function returns `true` if the user has pressed and released the spacebar, or `false` if the user is not pressing the spacebar. Line 423 declares a local `bool` variable named `pressed`, initialized to the value `false`. The `if` statement in line 426 determines whether the spacebar is being pressed. If so, the `while` loop in lines 430 through 432 executes. The purpose of the loop is to do nothing as long as the spacebar is held down. When the user releases the spacebar, the `pressed` variable is set to `true` in line 435. Line 439 returns the value of the `pressed` variable.

The definition of the `checkForCollision` function is shown in lines 449 through 475, as follows:

Program 12-13   (`BalloonTarget.cpp` *continued*)

```
442   //****************************************************
443   // The checkForCollision function accepts the dart   *
444   // object, the balloon object, and the dartLaunched   *
445   // flag variable by reference. If the dart and the    *
446   // balloon have collided, a pop sound is played and   *
447   // then the objects are reset.                        *
448   //****************************************************
449   void checkForCollision(MoveableSprite &dart, MoveableSprite &balloon,
450                     bool &dartLaunched)
451   {
452      // Determine whether the dart and the balloon have collided.
453      if ( dbSpriteCollision( dart.getSpriteNumber(),
454                         balloon.getSpriteNumber() ) )
455      {
456         // If the pop sound has not been loaded,
457         // then load it.
458         if ( !dbSoundExist(POP_SOUND) )
459         {
460            dbLoadSound( "pop.wav", POP_SOUND );
461         }
462
463         // Play the pop sound.
464         dbPlaySound(POP_SOUND);
465
466         // Restart the balloon.
467         restartBalloon(balloon);
```

```
468
469              // Restart the dart.
470              restartDart(dart);
471
472              // Reset the dartLaunched flag.
473              dartLaunched = false;
474         }
475    }
```

The `checkForCollision` function accepts the `dart` object, the `balloon` object, and the `dartLaunched` variable as arguments, by reference. The `if` statement that begins in line 453 determines whether the `dart` and the `balloon` sprites have collided. If the sprites have collided, the `if` statement in line 458 determines whether the pop sound has been loaded. If it hasn't, line 460 loads it into memory. Then, line 464 plays the pop sound. Line 467 calls `restartBalloon` to restart the balloon at the left side of the screen, and line 470 calls the `restartDart` function to restart the dart at the bottom of the screen. Line 473 sets `dartLaunched` to `false`.

Review Questions

Multiple Choice

1. A programming practice centered on creating functions that are separate from the data that they work on is called _____.
   a. modular programming
   b. procedural programming
   c. functional programming
   d. object-oriented programming

2. A programming practice centered on creating objects is called _____.
   a. object-centric programming
   b. objective programming
   c. procedural programming
   d. object-oriented programming

3. A member of a class that holds data is called a(n) _____.
   a. method, or member function
   b. instance
   c. field, or member variable
   d. constructor

4. A class's member variables are commonly declared in the _____ section of a class.
   a. private
   b. public
   c. read only
   d. hidden

5. A(n) _____ gets a value from a class's member variable but does not change it.
   a. retriever
   b. constructor
   c. mutator
   d. accessor

6. A(n) _____ stores a value in a member variable or changes the value of a member variable in some other way.
   a. modifier
   b. constructor
   c. mutator
   d. accessor

7. A(n) _____ is automatically called when an object is created.
   a. accessor
   b. constructor
   c. setter
   d. mutator

8. In an inheritance relationship, the _____ is the general class.
   a. derived class
   b. base class
   c. slave class
   d. child class

9. In an inheritance relationship, the _____ is the specialized class.
   a. base class
   b. master class
   c. derived class
   d. parent class

10. If a derived class constructor does not explicitly call a base class constructor, _____ will be automatically called.
    a. the base class's default constructor
    b. the base class's first parameterized constructor
    c. nothing
    d. an error

True or False

1. The base class inherits member variables and member functions from the derived class.

2. The practice of procedural programming is centered on the creation of objects.

3. Object reusability has been a factor in the increased use of object-oriented programming.

4. It is a common practice in object-oriented programming to make all of a class's member variables public.

5. If a derived class constructor does not explicitly call a base class constructor, none of the base class's constructors will be called.

Short Answer

1. What is encapsulation?

2. Why is an object's internal data usually hidden from outside code?

3. What is the difference between a class and an instance of a class?

4. The following statement calls an object's member function. What is the name of the member function? What is the name of the object?

```
wallet.getDollar();
```

5. What is a destructor?

6. What is a constructor?

7. What is an "is a" relationship between classes?

8. What does a derived class inherit from its base class?

9. Look at the following class header. What is the name of the base class? What is the name of the derived class?

```
class Tiger : public Felis
```

10. Which executes first, the derived class constructor or the base class constructor?

Algorithm Workbench

1. Suppose myCar is the name of an object, and go is the name of a member function. (The go function does not take any arguments.) Write a statement that uses the myCar object to call the member function.

2. Look at the following partial class definition, and then respond to the questions that follow it:

```
class Point
{
private:
    int x;
    int y;
};
```

   a. Write a constructor for this class. The constructor should accept an argument for each of the member variables.
   b. Write accessor and mutator member functions for each member variable.

3. Write the class header for a Poodle class. The class should be derived from the Dog class.

Programming Exercises

1. Coin Class
   Write a program with a class named Coin that can simulate the tossing of a coin. When an object of the class is created, it should display the image of a coin that is face up. The class should have a member function named toss that randomly determines whether the coin is face up or face down, and displays the appropri-

ate coin image. (You can create your own coin images, or use the ones provided in the book's online resources, downloadable from www.aw.com/gaddis.)

In the program, create a `Coin` object. Each time the user presses the spacebar, the program should simulate the tossing of the coin.

2. **Dice Simulator**
Write a program with a class named `Die` that can simulate the rolling of a die. The class should have a member function named `toss` that randomly determines which side of the die is facing up (a value in the range of 1 through 6). When the `toss` member function is called, it should display an image of the die side that is facing up. (You can create your own die images, or use the ones provided in the book's online resources, downloadable from www.aw.com/gaddis.)

In the program, create two `Die` objects to simulate a pair of dice. Each time the user presses the spacebar, the program should simulate the rolling of the dice.

3. **`PointKeeper` Class**
Modify the Balloon Target game so it reports the number of points earned by the user. (Each balloon that is popped earns one point.) To keep track of the points, you will write a `PointKeeper` class that has one member variable named `points`. This member variable will hold the number of points earned by the user. The class will also have a constructor and the appropriate mutator and accessor functions.

In the Balloon Target game, create an instance of the `PointKeeper` class. Each time the user pops a balloon, the program should update the `PointKeeper` object. At the end of the game, the program should report the number of points earned.

4. **Floating Asteroids, Part 1**
Write a program that creates an array of at least five `MoveableSprite` objects. Each of the objects in the array should display an image of an asteroid. (You can create your own image, or use the one provided in the book's online resources at www.aw.com/gaddis.)

As the program runs, the asteroids should slowly move across the screen, from right to left. When each asteroid reaches the screen's left edge, it should be repositioned at a random location along the screen's right edge.

5. **Floating Asteroids, Part 2**
Modify the program that you wrote for Programming Exercise 4 to include a spaceship that the user can control with the arrow keys. As the program runs, the user should maneuver the spaceship to avoid colliding with any of the floating asteroids. If the spaceship collides with an asteroid, play an appropriate sound and then regenerate the spaceship at a random location. In the program, create a `MoveableSprite` object to represent the spaceship.

6. **Object-Oriented Catch the Boulder Game**
In Chapter 8, Programming Exercise 5 asks you to design and create a game named Catch the Boulder. The object of the game is to catch falling boulders in a cart that can be moved back and forth on a railroad track. Create an object-oriented version of the game. The program should create objects to represent the boulders and the cart.

A Downloading and Installing the Required Software

To use this book you will need the following software and files:

- Microsoft Visual C++ 2008
- The Dark GDK (Game Development Kit)
- Sample Source Code, Media Files, and Game Case Studies

This appendix serves as a guide for installing these items in the correct order.

To see a video demonstrating the software installation, go to the book's Web page at www.aw.com/gaddis.

VideoNote

Step 1: **Install Microsoft Visual C++ 2008.** When purchased new, this book includes Visual Studio 2008 Express Edition on a DVD. This DVD provides a suite of software development tools. You will need to insert the DVD and install Visual C++ 2008 Express Edition. (If your book does not come with the DVD, skip to the section titled *If You Do Not Have the DVD: Downloading Visual C++ 2008 Express Edition.*)

The DVD has a setup program that should automatically run when you insert the DVD. You might see an Autoplay dialog box similar to the one shown on the left in Figure A-1. If so, select *Run setup.hta.* This will run the setup program. When the setup program runs, you should see the screen shown on the right in Figure A-1. Select *Visual C++ 2008 Express Edition* in this screen. If you are using Windows Vista, at this point you will probably see another dialog asking for permission to run the program. Click *Continue* in that dialog box.

The setup program is very simple. Follow the instructions in the next few screens and in a few minutes Visual C++ 2008 Express Edition will be installed on your system. You can now continue to Step 2, Start Visual C++.

Figure A-1 Visual Studio 2008 Express Edition Setup screen

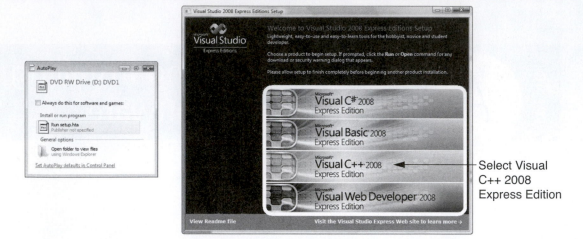

Select Visual
C++ 2008
Express Edition

If You Do Not Have the DVD:
Downloading Visual C++ 2008 Express Edition

If your book does not have the Visual Studio 2008 Express Edition DVD, you can download and install Visual C++ 2008 Express Edition from the following Microsoft Web site:

```
www.microsoft.com/express/download
```

Scroll down the Web page until you see the download area for Visual C++ 2008 Express Edition, as shown in Figure A-2. Click the download link.

Figure A-2 Visual Studio 2008 Express Edition download page

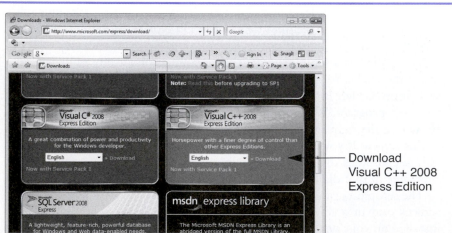

Download
Visual C++ 2008
Express Edition

Next, you should see the *File Download* dialog box, as shown in Figure A-3.

Figure A-3 File Download dialog box

Click *Run*. Some files will be downloaded to your system and then the installation will begin.

The installation is very simple. Follow the instructions in the next few screens. The time required to install the software will depend on the speed of your Internet connection. Once the installation is complete you can proceed to Step 2, Start Visual C++.

Step 2: **Start Visual C++ 2008.** Before installing the Dark GDK, you must start Visual C++ 2008 Express Edition at least once so it can create some initialization files. Follow these steps to start Visual C++ 2008 Express Edition:

- Click the Windows *Start* button.
- Select *All Programs*.
- Click *Visual C++ 9.0 Express Edition*.
- Click *Microsoft Visual C++ 2008 Express Edition*.

After Visual C++ has started, you can exit the program. Click *File* on the menu bar, and then click *Exit*.

Step 3: **Download and Install the Dark GDK.** Now you can download and install the Dark GDK from The Game Creators Web site. Go to the following address:

http://gdk.thegamecreators.com/?f=downloads

The Web page is shown in Figure A-4. As shown in the figure, click the link to install the August 2007 DirectX 9.0c SDK. A *File Download* dialog box will appear next. Click *Run* to download and run this part of the installation. (The file that is downloaded in this step is large, and might take some time to install.)

Once the file has downloaded, the WinZip dialog box shown in Figure A-5 will appear. Make sure the "Overwrite files without prompting" and "When done unzipping open: Setup.exe" boxes are checked, and then click the *Unzip* button.

Figure A-4 Dark GDK Download page

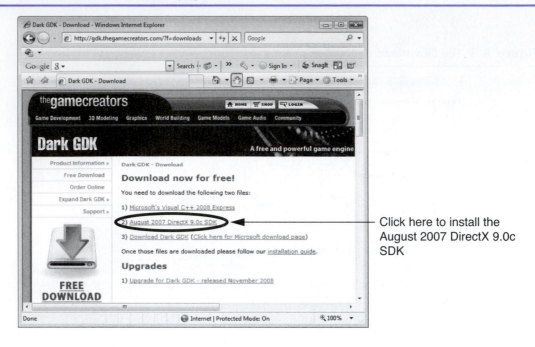

Click here to install the August 2007 DirectX 9.0c SDK

Figure A-5 WinZip dialog box

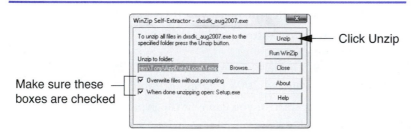

Make sure these boxes are checked

Click Unzip

The program will begin unzipping files to your system, and then you will see a dialog box indicating that the files were unzipped successfully. Click *OK* to dismiss the dialog box.

The setup program for the August 2007 DirectX 9.0c SDK will begin next, with the screen shown in Figure A-6. Click the *Next* button to continue with the setup. Read and accept the license agreement on the next screen, and simply click the *Next* button to accept the default options on each of the screens that you see. The installation will take a few minutes. When it is finished you will see a screen with the message "InstallShield Wizard Completed."

Figure A-6 DirectX SDK setup

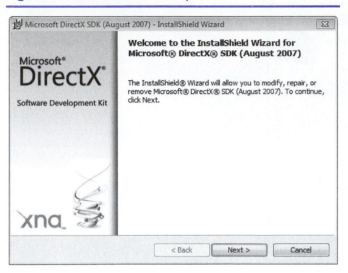

After the August 2007 DirectX 9.0c SDK is installed, go back to the Dark GDK download page and click the link to download the Dark GDK, as shown in Figure A-7. A File Download dialog box will appear next. Click *Run* to install the Dark GDK. (The file that is downloaded in this step is also large, and might take some time to install.)

Figure A-7 Dark GDK Download page

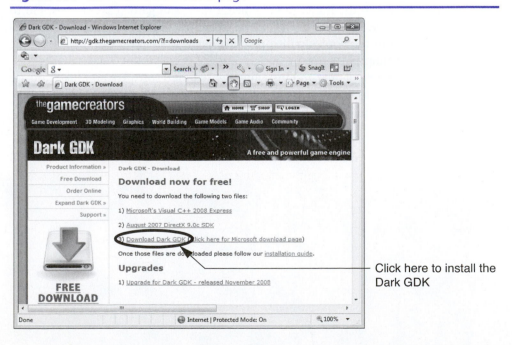

Figure A-8 Dark GDK setup

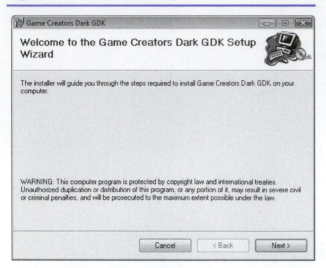

When the Dark GDK setup program executes, you will see the screen shown in Figure A-8. Click the *Next* button to continue with the setup. Read and accept the license agreement on the next screen, and simply click the *Next* button to accept the default options on each of the screens that you see. The installation will take a few minutes. When it is finished you will see a screen with the message "Installation Complete."

Step 4: **Download the Sample Source Code, Media Files, and Game Case Studies.** The last step is to download the sample source code for the examples shown in the book, sample media files, and game case studies. Go to www.aw.com/gaddis and click the image of this book's cover. This will take you to the book's online resource page where you can download the supplementary files for the book.

After downloading and installing the required software and files, you are ready to begin working through this book. In Chapter 1, you will find tutorials for using Visual C++ and the Dark GDK.

B The ASCII Character Set

The following table lists the ASCII (American Standard Code for Information Interchange) character set, which is the same as the first 127 Unicode character codes. This group of character codes is also known as the *Latin Subset of Unicode*. The code columns show character codes and the character columns show the corresponding characters. For example, the code 65 represents the letter A. Note that the first 31 codes, and code 127, represent control characters that are not printable.

Code	Character	Code	Character	Code	Character	Code	Character	Code	Character
0	NUL	26	SUB	52	4	78	N	104	h
1	SOH	27	Escape	53	5	79	O	105	i
2	STX	28	FS	54	6	80	P	106	j
3	ETX	29	GS	55	7	81	Q	107	k
4	EOT	30	RS	56	8	82	R	108	l
5	ENQ	31	US	57	9	83	S	109	m
6	ACK	32	(*Space*)	58	:	84	T	110	n
7	BEL	33	!	59	;	85	U	111	o
8	Backspace	34	"	60	<	86	V	112	p
9	HTab	35	#	61	=	87	W	113	q
10	Line Feed	36	$	62	>	88	X	114	r
11	VTab	37	%	63	?	89	Y	115	s
12	Form Feed	38	&	64	@	90	Z	116	t
13	CR	39	'	65	A	91	[	117	u
14	SO	40	(	66	B	92	\	118	v
15	SI	41	)	67	C	93	]	119	w
16	DLE	42	*	68	D	94	^	120	x
17	DC1	43	+	69	E	95	_	121	y
18	DC2	44	,	70	F	96	`	122	z
19	DC3	45	–	71	G	97	a	123	{
20	DC4	46	.	72	H	98	b	124	|
21	NAK	47	/	73	I	99	c	125	}
22	SYN	48	0	74	J	100	d	126	~
23	ETB	49	1	75	K	101	e	127	DEL
24	CAN	50	2	76	L	102	f		
25	EM	51	3	77	M	103	g		

Index

Symbols and Numbers

<= (less than or equal to) relational operators, 218–219

>= (greater than or equal to) relational operators, 218–219

! (NOT) logical operators
  in Boolean expressions, 218–219
  in compound Boolean expressions, 261, 263–264

&& (AND) logical operators
  Boolean expressions and, 261–262
  precedence of, 264–265
  in short-circuit evaluation, 263

!= (not-equal-to) relational operators, 219

|| (OR) logical operators, 261–262

< (less than) relational operators, 218–219

== (equal to) relational operators
  in Boolean expressions, 218, 219
  in compound Boolean expressions, 261

> (greater than) relational operators, 218–219

2D shapes
  dbCircle function and, 56–58
  dbEllipse function and, 58–60
  dbLine function (city skyline) and, 50–53
  dbLine function (triangle) and, 49–50
  drawn outside the Dark GDK window, 60–61

A

Acceleration, in simulating falling objects, 364

Accessor function, 619

Ada programming language, 15

Alec sprite, 540

Algorithm
  definition of, 53

flowcharts and, 214
  selection sort, 511, 514–516
  shuffling. See Shuffling an array
  sorting, 511

Alpha channel, for storing color, 124

Alpha value, to change sprite opacity, 311–312

American Standard Code for Information Interchange. See ASCII (American Standard Code for Information Interchange)

AND (&&) logical operators
  Boolean expressions and, 261–262
  precedence of, 264–265
  in short-circuit evaluation, 263

Animated sprite, 327. See also Sprite animations

Animation. See also Graphics programming
  cel. See Cel animation
  the game loop and, 281–286
  simple, 286–289
  sprite sheets and, 325–327

Appending a string, 563–564

Arguments
  arrays passed as, 485–487
  in the dbDot function, 44
  definition of, 155
  passing objects to functions as, 642–644
  passing to the base class constructor, 658–660

Arguments, passing to functions
  multiple arguments, 160–163
  overview, 155–156
  parameter variable scope and, 159
  programs illustrating, 156–159
  by reference, 165–169
  by value, 163–165

Arrays
  assigning values to elements, 475–478
  bounds checking, 478
  comparing two, 490
  copying, 485
  dealing cards with. See Dealing cards, with partially filled arrays
  definition of, 474
  drawing polylines with, 487–489
  DWORD color, 483–484
  elements and subscripts, 474
  implicit sizing, 484
  initialization, 481–483
  introduction to, 473–475
  Memory Match game and. See Memory Match game
  of objects, 638–642
  partially filled, 503–504
  passing as an argument to a function, 485–487
  shuffling. See Shuffling an array
  sorting. See Sorting arrays
  of strings, 574–577
  two-dimensional. See Two-dimensional arrays
  using a loop to step through, 478–481

Arrow keys, detecting, 290

Ascending order, 511

ASCII (American Standard Code for Information Interchange)
  character set table, 687
  description of, 9–10
  for string storage, 567

Assembler, 14

Assembly language
  as a low-level language, 15
  machine language and, 14

Assignment operators
  assigning values to variables, 87
  combined, 100–102

atof function, 117–120

atoi function, 117–120
Attributes dialogue box, 200
Audio files. *See* Sound files

B
Back saving features
    for displaying sprites with images
        and graphics, 312–313
    programs demonstrating,
        313–317
    saving sprites, 311
Background images
    bitmaps as, 182–185
    color key transparency and. *See*
        Color key transparency
    with tiles. *See* Tile maps
Ball sprite
    in falling simulation, 367–370
    illustrations, 369, 373
    in motion in two directions
        simulation, 371–373
Balloon Ace game, 407
Balloon Target object-oriented
    game
    checkForCollision function
        and, 675–676
    DarkGDK function and, 669–670
    global constants declarations and,
        668–669
    illustration, 668
    introduction to, 667–668
    moveBalloon function and, 673
    moveDart function and, 673–674
    restartBalloon function and,
        671–672
    restartDart function and,
        672–673
    spacebarPressed function and,
        674–675
Bar charts
    drawing of, 103
    program demonstrating, 104–107
Base class, 653
Base class constructor, passing
    arguments to, 658–660
Basic 2D shapes
    dbBox function and, 53–56
    dbCircle function and, 56–58
    dbEllipse function and, 58–60
    dbLine function (city skyline)
        and, 50–53
    dbLine function (triangle) and,
        49–50
    drawn outside the Dark GDK
        window, 60–61

BASIC programming language, 15
Binary digits, 6–9
Binary format, for data storage,
    10–11
Binary numbering system, 7
Bitmap number, 187
Bitmaps
    as background images, 182–185
    creating slide show program
        with, 188–190
    definition and function of, 179
    deleting from memory, 191
    file locations, 181–182
    flipping, mirroring, fading and
        blurring of, 191–194
    getting file name from user,
        185–187
    getting size and color depth, 191
    loading multiple, 187–188
    loading of, 180–181
    path entered by user, 187
Bits, for data storage, 6–9
Blue screen technology. *See* Color
    key technology
Blueprint illustration, 615
Blurred images, 193–194
bmp file format, for saving images,
    203, 205
bool variables
    returning values and, 420–422
    for storing values, 272–273
Boolean expressions
    compound, 261
    definition of, 217
    do-while loops and, 246–247
    if-else-if statements and, 235
    if-else statements and,
        223–225
    logical operators and. *See* Logical
        operators
    relational operators and,
        217–219
    while loops and, 238–240
Boulder sprite, 407
Bounding rectangle
    clicking sprites and, 448–450,
        452
    sprites and, 329–330
Bounds checking, array, 478
Bowling ball sprites
    collision detection and, 330–333
    collision detection with sound,
        347–350
    illustrations, 333, 350
Broken egg sprite, 399

Buffer overflow, 563, 564
Bug Zapper game
    DarkGDK function and, 456–459
    displayBugsZapped function
        and, 464
    displayIntro function and,
        459–460
    elapsedTime function and, 463
    generateNewBug function and,
        462–463
    global constants declarations and,
        455–456
    initBug function and, 461
    initMouse function and,
        460–461
    introduction to, 455
    mouseFullClick function and,
        464–465
    onSprite function and,
        465–466
    setUp function and, 459
    updateBug function and, 462
    updateMouse function and,
        461–462
Bug Zapper game (version 2)
    checkForHighScore function
        and, 601
    DarkGDK function and, 596–597
    discussion of, 604
    displayBugsZapped function
        and, 600–601
    displayIntro function and,
        598
    elapsedTime function and, 600
    generateNewBug function and,
        600
    initBug function and, 599
    initMouse function and,
        598–599
    introduction to, 595
    mouseFullClick function and,
        602–603
    newHighScore file and, 601–602
    onSprite function and, 603
    setUp function and, 597–598
    updateBug function and,
        599–600
    updateMouse function and, 599
Bumblebees, and specialization,
    652
Button clicks. *See also* Mouse,
    working with
    detecting, 441–442
    processing full, 444–447
Bytes, for data storage, 6–9

C

C++/Dark GDK program
  code file creation, 23–24
  compilation and execution of, 25–27
  graphics programming in. *See* Basic 2D shapes; Graphics programming
  overview, 19–20
  program demonstrating, 27–29
  project creation, 21–22
  Start Page for, 21
  text editing in, 24–25
C# programming language, 15
C programming language, 15
C++ programming language
  array bounds checking in, 478
  the Dark GDK library and, 19–20. *See also* C++/Dark GDK program
  description of, 16
  graphics programming with. *See* Graphics programming
  New Project dialogue box, 181–182
  table of key words, 16–17
  to work with strings, 562
  writing value-returning functions in, 411–413
Calculations
  of a box's coordinates, 93–94
  combined assignment operators, 100–102
  grouping with parentheses, 97–99
  of a line's midpoint, 98
  order of operations in, 96–97
  overview, 92
  program demonstrating, 95–96, 99–100
camelCase convention, 86
canMoveDown function, 426–427, 435
canMoveLeft function, 429, 435
canMoveRight function, 431–432, 436
canMoveUp function, 424–425, 434
Cards
  dealing. *See* Dealing cards, with partially filled arrays
  illustrations, 509, 521
Catch the Boulder game, 407–408
CD (compact disc)
  for data storage, 5
  loading music from, 360–363

Cel animation
  overview, 323
  playing sprite animations, 327–329
  program demonstrating, 324–325
  simplifying with sprite sheets, 325–327
Central processing unit (CPU)
  overview, 2–3
  programming and, 11–13
char arrays
  appending a string to, 563–564
  copying a string to, 562–563
  displaying a string stored in, 562
  for string storage, 559–560, 561
  two-dimensional, 574
  using strcpy to copy a string to, 562–563
Characters
  ACSII character set, 9–10, 687
  invalid, 120
  null, 560–561
  storing, 561
Chroma key, 195
Circle class
  array of objects program, 639–642
  instance of, 622
  overloaded constructors program and, 635–638
  overloaded draw functions and, 632–634
  passing objects program, 642–644
  program description, 623–626
  programs demonstrating, 617–618, 619–621
Circle class constructor
  introduction to, 626
  program demonstrating, 626–629
Circles
  array elements and, 476–478
  button clicks and, 441–443
  with dbCircle function, 56–57
  full mouse clicks and, 444–447
  generation of random, 113–114
  illustrations, 414, 443, 444, 477
  program for bull's eye, 57–58
  value-returning functions and, 412–413
City skyline
  with dbLine/dbBox functions, 55–56
  with dbLine function, 50–53

Class
  blueprint/cookie cutter metaphors, 615
  definition of, 614–615
  instance of, 616
  private/public sections, 617
Class declarations
  introduction to, 616–617
  program demonstrating, 617–619
Class header
  definition of, 617
  inheritance notation in, 654
Classes and objects
  class declarations, 616–619
  constructors, 626–629
  creating an object, 622–626
  creating arrays of objects, 638–642
  creating multiple objects from the same class, 629–631
  defining member functions, 619–621
  destructors, 644
  introduction to, 614–616
  mutators and accessors, 619
  overloaded constructors, 635–638
  passing objects as arguments to functions, 642–644
  sprite class. *See* Sprite class
clearToBlack function, 485–487
Cloning
  sounds, 354
  sprites, 319–322
COBOL programming language, 15
Code
  definition of, 18
  in graphics programming, 74
  simplified with functions, 140
Code reuse, 140–141
Coins and Snakes game, 557
Collision detection
  PizzaBot game and, 333–337
  PizzaBot game with sound and, 347–350
  program demonstrating, 330–333
  sprites and, 329–330
Color arrays, 483–484
Color channels, 122
Color key technology, 195–196
Color key transparency
  adding a key color, 204–207
  changing the key color, 196–199
  dbLoadImage function and, 196

deleting images from memory, 207

displaying images with `dbPasteImage`, 196

Microsoft Paint and. *See* Microsoft Paint

overview, 195–196

Colors

clearing the window, 128

decision structures for testing, 222–223

drawing in, 124–126

drawing the Italian flag, 126–128

generating in Dark GDK, 122

getting depth in bitmaps, 191

key. *See* Key color

program demonstrating, 123

saving program, 593–595

storing RGB colors in memory, 123–124

Combined assignment operators

definition and function of, 100–101

program demonstrating, 101–102

Comments, 40–41

compact disc (CD)

for data storage, 5

loading music from, 360–363

Comparing strings

introduction to, 565–566

program demonstrating, 566–568

Compilers, 17–18

Components. *See* Hardware

Compound Boolean expressions, 261

Computers

data storage, 6–11

hardware, 2–6

introduction to, 1

Condition-controlled loop, 238

Conditional execution, in if-else statements, 225

Constructors

default, 637

definition of, 626

overloaded, 635–638

program demonstrating, 626–629

sprite class and, 646

Control key, detecting, 290

Control structures

with `if-else` statements, 223–225

increment and decrement operators in, 248

introduction to, 213–215

logical operators and. *See* Logical operators

nested decision structures as. *See* Nested decision structures

for a number guessing game, 226–227, 232–234

numeric truth, flags, `bool` variables and, 271–273

processing pixels in images, 255–260

repetition structures as. *See* Repetition structures, `for` loops; Repetition structures, `while` and `do-while` loops

the `switch` statement, 266–270

writing a decision structure. *See* Decision structures, writing with the `if` statement

Controlling objects, with the keyboard

additional keyboard operations, 294–295

introduction to, 289–290

key detection for, 290

letting the user move an object, 292–294

program demonstrating, 291–293

Cookie cutter illustration, 615

Coordinates. *See also* X coordinate; Y coordinate

clicking sprites and, 448–452

drawing polylines and, 488–489

of the mouse, 439–440

Copying a string, 562–563

Count-controlled loop

definition of, 238

the `for` loop as, 249–251

Counter variable

in the body of the loop, 253

declaring in the initialization expression, 252

decrementing of, 254–255

definition and function of, 249–251

program demonstrating, 253–254

CPU (central processing unit)

overview, 2–3

programming and, 11–13

Ctrl key, detecting, 290

Cursor, 379–381

Custom mouse pointer

illustration, 454

program demonstrating, 452–453

D

Dark BASIC language, 46

`DarkGDK` function, 38–40

Dark GDK library

audio effects in. *See* Sound files

C++ programming language and, 19–20. *See also* C++/Dark GDK program

downloading and installing, 683–685

example program execution, 27–29

graphics programming and. *See* Graphics programming

math functions list, 116

playing sprite animations with, 327–329

refreshing the screen in, 281–283

Dark GDK window

changing size of, 131–133

clearing, 128

default, 43

drawing outside of, 60–61

drawing within. *See specific shapes/functions*

empty, 39–41

pixel locations in, 44

program demonstrating, 39–40

`.dat` extension file names, 580

Data hiding, 612

Data storage

additional data, 10–11

characters, 9–10

numbers, 7–9, 10

overview, 6–7

real numbers, 10

Data types

`char`, 559–560

`double`, 85

`DWORD`, 85

`float`, 85

`int`, 85

variables, 85

`dbABS` math function, 116

`dbACOS` math function, 116

`dbASIN` math function, 116

`dbATAN` math function, 116

`dbBitmapDepth` function, 191

`dbBitmapHeight` function, 191

`dbBitmapWidth` function, 191

`dbBlurBitmap` function, 193–194

`dbBox` function

for checkerboard drawing, 54–55

for city skyline drawing, 55–56

to draw graphics over bitmap image, 182–185
for rectangle drawing, 53–54
dbCenterText function
  displaying a string stored in a char array, 562
  displaying text with, 64–65
dbChangeMouse function, 443
dbCircle function
  in the Dark GDK library, 56–58
  to draw graphics over bitmap image, 182–185
  program for bull's eye, 57–58
dbClear function, 122–123, 128
dbCloneSound function, 354
dbCloneSprite function, 319–320
dbCloseFile function, 582–583, 584
dbControlKey function, 290
dbCOS math function, 116
dbCreateAnimatedSprite function
  PizzaBot game and, 338
  sprite animations and, 327–329
  Vulture Trouble game and, 390
dbDeleteBitmap function, 191
dbDeleteImage function, 207
dbDeleteMusic function, 359
dbDeleteSound function, 353
dbDeleteSprite function
  for deleting sprites from memory, 312
  Vulture Trouble game and, 403
dbDot function
  drawing dots with, 44–46
  drawing stars with, 50–51, 71, 150, 184
  in hierarchy chart, 151
  programs illustrating, 45, 47
  repetition structures and, 37–238
dbDownKey function, 290
dbEllipse function, 58–60
dbEscapeKey function, 290
dbFadeBitmap function, 192–193
dbFileEnd function, 592–593
dbfileExist function, 271–272, 569–570
dbFileOpen function, 584–585
dbFlipBitmap function, 192
dbFlipSprite function, 310–311
dbHideAllSprites function, 307
dbHideMouse function, 441
dbHideSprite function
  for hiding sprites, 307
  for sprite collisions, 330

dbInk function, 124–125
dbInput function
  for getting file name from user, 185–187
  for reading numeric input, 117–118
dbLeftKey function, 290
dbLine function
  for city skyline drawing, 50–53
  to draw graphics over bitmap image, 182–185
  overview, 48–49
  for triangle drawing, 49–50
dbLoadCDMusic function, 360–363
dbLoadImage function
  overview of, 196
  for creating sprites, 296–298
dbLoadMusic function, 357–358
dbLoadSound function, 346
dbLoopMusic function, 358
dbLoopSound function, 350–351
dbMirrorBitmap function, 192
dbMirrorSprite function, 310–311
dbMouseClick function, 441–443
dbMouseMoveX function, 443–444
dbMouseMoveY function, 443–444
dbMouseX function, 439–440
dbMouseY function, 439–440
dbMusicExist function, 359
dbMusicLooping function, 358–359
dbMusicPlaying function, 358–359
dbOffsetSprite function, 304–307
dbOpenToRead function, 583
dbOpenToWrite function
  opening output files, 581
  writing data to output files, 582
dbPasteImage function, 196
dbPasteSprite function, 317
dbPauseMusic function, 359
dbPauseSound function, 353–354
dbPlayMusic function, 358, 360
dbPlaySound function
  playing/looping sound file and, 352
  sound files and, 347–350
dbPositionMouse function, 441
dbPrint function
  displaying a string stored in a char array, 562

displaying text with, 61–62
setting the cursor position and, 379–381
dbRandomize function, 113–115
dbReadFile function, 584
dbReadFloat function, 584
dbReadString function, 584
dbResumeMusic function, 359
dbResumeSound function, 353–354
dbReturnKey function, 290
dbRGB function, 124
dbRightKey function, 290
dbRND function
  for getting random numbers, 110–112
  in seeding the random number generator, 113–114
  value-returning functions and, 410
dbRotateSprite function, 302–304
dbScreenHeight function, 108–110
dbScreenWidth function, 108–110
dbSetBackgroundType function, 378
dbSetCursor function, 379–381
dbSetImageColorKey function
  color key transparency and, 196–198
  program demonstrating, 198–199
dbSetMusicSpeed function, 360
dbSetMusicVolume function, 360
dbSetSoundPan function, 355–357
dbSetSoundSpeed function, 355
dbSetSoundVolume function, 354
dbSetSprite function, 311
dbSetSpriteAlpha function, 311–312
dbSetSpriteImage function, 309
dbSetSpritePriority function, 308–309
dbSetTextFont function, 374–375
dbSetTextOpaque function, 377–378
dbSetTextSize function, 374
dbSetTextToBold function, 375–376
dbSetTextToBoldItalic function, 375–376
dbSetTextToItalic function, 375–376
dbSetTextToNormal function, 375–376

dbSetTextTransparent function, 378

dbSetWindowTitle function, 65–67

dbShiftKey function, 290

dbShowAllSprites function, 307

dbShowMouse function, 441

dbShowSprite function, 307

dbSIN math function, 116

dbSizeSprite function, 307–308

dbSoundExist function, 353

dbSoundLooping function, 352

dbSoundPlaying function, 352

dbSpaceKey function, 290

dbSprite function, 296–298

dbSpriteCollision function, 330

dbSpriteExist function, 309

dbSpriteFlipped function, 311

dbSpriteHeight function, 302

dbSpriteMirrored function, 311

dbSpriteWidth function, 302

dbSQRT math function, 116

dbStopMusic function, 358

dbStopSound function, 352

dbStretchSprite function, 308

dbSync function, 283–285

dbSyncOn function, 283–285

dbSyncRate function, 283–285

dbTAN math function, 116

dbText function
   displaying a string stored in a char array, 562
   displaying text with, 63–64

dbTextHeight function, 378–379

dbTextWidth function, 378–379

dbTimer function, 113–115

dbUpKey function, 290

dbWait function, 46–47

dbWaitKey function, 40–42, 46

dbWriteFile function, 582

dbWriteFloat function, 582

dbWriteString function, 582

Dealing cards, with partially filled arrays
   analyzing the program code, 508–510
   introduction to, 504
   program demonstrating, 505–508

Decision structures
   combining sequence structures with, 229
   definition of, 215
   examples of, 220
   nested. *See* Nested decision structures

sequence structure nested inside, 230
   simple (single alternative), 215–216

Decision structures, writing with the if statement
   with Boolean expressions and relational operators, 217–219
   overview, 215–217
   program demonstrating, 221–222
   putting it together, 219–221
   with testing colors, 222–223

Deck of cards. *See* Dealing cards, with partially filled arrays

Decrement operators
   the counter variable and, 254–255
   definition and function of, 248

Default constructors, 637

Derived class, 653

Descending order, 511

Destructors
   in a class, 644
   sprite class and, 646–647

Dialogue box
   Attributes, 200
   Edit Colors, 201
   File Download, 683
   WinZip, 684

Digital data, 10–11

Digital devices, 10

DirectX SDK setup, 685

Disk drive, 5

Displaying text, in the Dark GDK window
   with dbCenterText function, 64–65
   with dbPrint function, 61–62
   with dbText function, 63–64
   Orion Constellation program. *See* Orion Constellation program
   in title bar, 65–67

Divide and conquer approach, 140–141

do-while loops
   overview, 246–247
   as repetition structures, 238–240

.doc extension file names, 580

Domination Card game, 556–557

Dot notation, 622

Dots
   with dbDot function, 44–46
   illustrations, 416
   programs illustrating, 45, 47
   value-returning functions and, 415–417

double data type, 85

Down arrow key, detecting, 290

Download page
   Dark GDK library, 684, 685
   Visual Studio 2008 Express Edition, 682

Downloading and installing software
   download and install the Dark GDK, 683–686
   download the sample source code, media files and game case studies, 686
   downloading Visual C++ 2008 Express Edition, 682–683
   install Microsoft Visual C++ 2008 DVD, 681–682

Drawing
   bar charts, 103–107
   in color, 124–126
   in the Dark GDK library. *See* *specific shapes/functions*
   the Italian flag, 126–128

Dual alternative decision structures, 223–225

DWORD data type
   color arrays and, 483–484
   description of, 85
   for storing color, 124–125

E

Edit Colors dialogue box, 201

Egg sprites
   illustrations, 390, 391, 395, 398, 399
   in Vulture Trouble game. *See* Vulture Trouble game

elapsedTime function
   Bug Zapper game and, 463
   Bug Zapper game (version 2) and, 600

Elements, array
   accessing in two-dimensional arrays, 523–524
   assigning values, 475–478
   definition of, 475
   swapping, 502–503
   two-dimensional arrays and, 522–523

Ellipse, 58–60

else clauses, 234–236, 510

Empty window. *See* Dark GDK window, empty

Encapsulation, 612

ENIAC computer, 3

Enter key, detecting, 290
Equal to (==) relational operators
  in Boolean expressions,
    218, 219
  in compound Boolean
    expressions, 261
Escape key, detecting, 290
ESP, 556
Existence, of sprites, 309

F
Faded images, 192–193
Falling brick, speed, 364–366
Falling objects, simulating. *See*
    Simulating falling objects
Fetch-decode-execute cycle, 13
Fields, in object-oriented
    programming, 612–613, 614
File Download dialogue box, 683
File input and output
  closing an output file, 582–583,
    584
  detecting the end of a file,
    592–593
  determining if a file is open,
    584–585
  file names, 580
  file numbers, 580
  opening an input file, 583
  opening an output file, 580
  overview, 578–580
  reading data from an input file,
    584
  reading data program, 588–590
  reading data program,
    description of, 590–592
  saving colors program, 593–595
  using loops to process files, 592
  writing data program, 585–588
  writing data to an output file,
    582
File number, 580
`FileRead` program
  program description, 590–592
  for reading data from a file,
    588–590
Files
  copying bitmap to project folder,
    181–182
  getting file name from user,
    185–187
  input and output of. *See* File
    input and output
  specifying bitmap file path, 182
  using loops to process, 592

writing/reading data on, 579
`FileWrite` program
  program description, 587–588
  for writing data to a file,
    585–587
Fill with Color tool, 201, 204
Flags, 272
Flash drives. *See* USB drives
Flipped images
  bitmaps and, 192
  sprites and, 310–311
`float` data type, 85
Floating-point notation, 10
Floating-point truncation
  in simulating falling objects,
    367–370
  in variable declaration, 91
Floppy disk drives, 5
Flowcharts
  for combining sequence
    structures with a decision
    structure, 229
  for dual alternative decision
    structures, 224
  for example decision structures,
    220
  for the logic of a `do-while` loop,
    246
  for the logic of a `while` loop,
    239
  for a nested decision structure,
    232–234
  for nested `if` statements, 231
  for a sequence structure nested
    inside a decision structure, 230
  for sequence structures, 214
  for simple decision structures,
    216
  for a `switch` statement, 266
Fonts
  changing size, 374–375
  illustration, 377
`for` loops
  basic definition, 215
  counting backward by
    decrementing, 254–255
  declaring the counter variable,
    252
  functions of, 249–251
  incrementing by values other
    than 1, 254
  processing pixels, 255–256,
    258–259
  program demonstrating,
    251–252

programs illustrating pixel
    processing in images, 256–257,
    259–260
  to step through an array,
    478–481
  using the counter variable in,
    253–254
FORTRAN programming language,
    15
Friendly spider program, 197–199
Full mouse clicks
  definition of, 445
  processing, 444–446
  program demonstrating,
    446–447
Function body, 142
Function call, 40, 143–145
Function definition, 141–143
Function header, 142
Function names, 141–142
Function prototypes, 145–147
Functions
  arrays passed as an argument to,
    485–487
  definition of, 38
  passing objects as arguments to,
    642–644
  two-dimensional arrays passed
    to, 526–528

G
Game Case Studies, downloading,
    686
The Game Creators, 20, 683
Game loop
  clearing the screen in, 289
  code, 285
  definition, 281
  formatting steps, 284–285
  introduction to, 281–283
  key detection in, 291–293
  program demonstrating, 283–284
  returning control to the Dark
    GDK, 285
  shuffling an array and, 501–502
  simple animation and, 286–288
  sprites and. *See* Sprites
Games
  Balloon Ace game, 407
  Balloon Target. *See* Balloon
    Target object-oriented game
  Bug Zapper. *See* Bug Zapper
    game
  Bug Zapper (version 2). *See* Bug
    Zapper game (version 2)

Catch the Boulder, 407–408
Coins and Snakes, 557
data stored in files with, 578
Domination Card, 556–557
ESP, 556
Mad Libs, 571–574
Matching Card, 556
Memory Match. *See* Memory
  Match game
Number guessing game,
  226–227, 232–234, 240–242
PizzaBot, 333–337
PizzaBot with sound, 347–350
Tic-Tac-Toe, 557
Vulture Trouble. *See* Vulture
  Trouble game
Generalization, 652
`getMaximumX` function, 414–416,
  417–419
`getMaximumY` function, 414–416,
  417–419
Global constants
  Balloon Target game and,
    668–669
  Bug Zapper game and, 455–456
  Layered Maps program and,
    543–544, 550
  overview of, 171–173
  PizzaBot game and, 334, 338
  in the Vulture Trouble game,
    383–384
  Walking Alec program and,
    534–535, 540–541
Global variables, 169–171
Graphics programming
  basic 2D shapes in. *See* Basic 2D
    shapes
  comments, 40–41
  displaying text. *See* Displaying
    text, in the Dark GDK window
  program development cycle,
    74–75
  screen coordinate system in. *See*
    Screen coordinate system
  skeleton program for, 39–40
  style in, 41–42
Grasshoppers, and specialization,
  652
Gravity, 364
Greater than or equal to (>=)
  relational operators, 218–219
Greater than (>) relational
  operators, 218–219
Green screen technology. *See* Color
  key technology

H
Hardware
  CPU, 2, 3, 11–13
  definition of, 2
  input/output devices, 2, 5
  main memory, 2, 3–4
  secondary storage devices, 2, 4–5
Height
  of a sprite, 302
  text effects and, 378–379
Hiding, sprites, 307
Hierarchy charts, 150–151
High-level languages
  executing and compiling with, 18
  programming and, 14–16
High score message, 604
Hit basket sprite, 398
Hourglass pointer, 443

I
`if` clauses, 234
`if-else-if` statements
  nested decision structures and,
    228–231
  program demonstrating, 235–236
`if-else` statements
  conditional execution in, 225
  as control structures, 223–225
`if` statements
  in decision structures. *See*
    Decision structures, writing
    with the `if` statement
  nested, 231
Image editors, 578
`ImageNumber`, 196
Images
  bitmap. *See* Bitmaps
  cel animation, 323
  changing of sprite, 309
  with color key transparency. *See*
    Color key transparency
  displaying sprites and, 313–317
  introduction to, 179
Implicit sizing, of arrays, 484
Include directive, 38
Increment expression
  the `for` loop and, 249–252
  by values other than 1, 254
Increment operators
  definition and function of, 248
  using values other than 1, 254
Infinite loops
  program demonstrating, 282
  repetition structures and,
    245–246

Inheritance
  generalization and specialization,
    652
  the "Is a" relationship and,
    652–653
  `MoveableSprite` class. *See*
    `MoveableSprite` class
  passing arguments to the base
    class constructor, 658–660
  `ThickCircle` class and. *See*
    `ThickCircle` class program
Inheritance notation, 654
Initialization
  array, 481–483
  of member variables, 626
  of two-dimensional arrays,
    524–526
Initialization expression
  declaring the counter variable in,
    252
  the `for` loop and, 249–251
Initialization list, 481
Initializing, of variables, 87–88
Input, 5
Input devices, 2, 5
Input file, 578. *See also* File input
  and output
Input/output. *See* File input and
  output
Insertion point
  offsetting of, 304–307
  for rotating a sprite, 302
Installing software. *See*
  Downloading and installing
  software
Instance
  of the `Circle` class, 622
  of a class, 616
`int` data type, 85
Integer literals, 82–83
Interpreters, 17–18
Invalid characters, 120
"Is a" relationships, and
  inheritance, 652–653
Italian flag
  drawing in color, 126
  program demonstrating, 127–128

J
Java programming language, 16
JavaScript programming language,
  16
Jet image, in `StealthJet` program,
  312
`.jpg` extension file names, 580

K

Key color
  adding to digital photos,
    204–207
  changing of, 196–199
  definition of, 195
Key detection functions, 290
Key words, C++, 16–17
Keyboard. *See* Controlling objects,
  with the keyboard

L

Latin Subset of Unicode, 687
Layered Maps program
  `arrowKeyPressed` function and,
    547
  `checkCollisions` function and,
    549, 551
  `DarkGDK` function and, 544–545,
    550
  `displayObstacles` function and,
    546–547, 551
  `displayTiles` function and, 546
  global constants declarations and,
    543–544, 550
  introduction to, 542
  `moveAlec` function and,
    548–549, 551
  `setUp` function and, 545–546
  `switch` statement and, 549, 552
  `updateDirection` function and,
    547–548, 551
less than or equal to (<=) relational
  operators, 218–219
Left arrow key, detecting, 290
Less than (<) relational operators,
  218–219
Library, 20. *See also* Dark GDK
  library
Line arrays
  illustration, 483
  program demonstrating, 481–482
Line comment, 40
Line midpoint, 98–100
Literal data
  definition and function of, 81
  programs illustrating, 82–84
Local variables
  definition and function of,
    151–152
  programs illustrating, 152–154
  scope and, 154–155
Logic errors, 75
Logical operators, 264–265
  AND (&&), 261–263

list of operators and Boolean
  expressions, 261
NOT (!), 263–264
OR (||), 262–263
precedence of, 264–265
short-circuit evaluation by, 263
`LoopGDK` function
  description of, 283
  in the game loop, 284–285
Looping music, 358
Looping sounds, 350–351
Loops
  `do while` loops. *See* `do-while`
    loops
  introduction to, 215
  `for` loop. *See* `for` loops
  to process files, 592–593
  `while` loops. *See* `while` loops
Low-level language. *See* Assembly
  language

M

Machine language
  assembly language and, 14
  programming and, 12
Mad Libs word games
  discussion of, 573–574
  introduction to, 571
  program demonstrating, 571–573
Main memory
  overview of, 3–4
  programming and, 13
Matching Card game, 556
Math expressions
  definition of, 92
  values and, 97–98
Math functions
  function/description of, 116
  as value-returning, 115–116
Math operators, 92
Media files, downloading and
  installing, 686
Member functions
  definition of, 619–621
  in object-oriented programming,
    614
Member variables, in object-
  oriented programming, 614
Memory
  data copied into, 579
  deleting a sound from, 353
  deleting bitmaps from, 191
  deleting images from, 207
  deleting music from, 359
  deleting sprites from, 312

storage of strings in, 560–561
storage of two-dimensional
  arrays in, 528
storing RGB colors in, 123–124
Memory Match game
  `DarkGDK` function in, 492–493
  `displayArray` function in, 498
  `displayRandom` function in, 494
  `displayResults` function in,
    495–497
  `generateRandom` function in,
    493
  `getUserNumbers` function in, 495
  introduction to, 490–491
  `matchingNumbers` function in,
    497
  `setText` function in, 493–494
Memory Match screens, 491
Memory sticks. *See* USB drives
Methods, in object-oriented
  programming, 612–613, 614
Microprocessors, 3, 4
Microsoft Paint
  creating and saving image,
    202–203
  overview of graphics program,
    199
  program demonstrating,
    203–204
  setting image size/background
    color, 200–201
Microsoft Visual C++ 2008 Express
  Edition
  downloading and installing (from
    Web site), 682–683
  installation (with DVD), 681–682
  introduction to, 20
  programming language. *See* C++
    programming language
Microsoft Web site, 682
Mirrored images
  bitmaps and, 192
  sprites and, 310–311
Mnemonics, 14
Motion, in two directions
  program demonstrating, 371–373
  simulation of, 370
Mouse crosshairs, 470
Mouse, working with
  Bug Zapper game using. *See* Bug
    Zapper game
  clicking sprites with, 448–452
  creating a custom mouse pointer,
    452–454
  detecting button clicks, 441–443

displaying the hourglass pointer, 443

getting coordinates of, 439–440

getting movement distances, 441–443

introduction to, 439

processing full mouse clicks, 444–447

showing, hiding and positioning of, 441

`mouseFullClick` function

Bug Zapper game and, 464–465

Bug Zapper game (version 2) and, 602–603

for working with the mouse, 445–447, 451–452

`MoveableSprite` class

constructor definition and, 662

`DarkGDK` function and, 665–666

declaration for, 661

final output, 667

`getDistance` member function and, 662

introduction to, 661

`moveDown` member function and, 663

`moveRight` member function and, 664–665

`moveUp` member function and, 663

`setDistance` member function and, 662

`MoveableSprite` objects, 670

Moving an object on the screen, 292–294

Multiple alternative decision structure. *See* `switch` statement

Multiple objects

creating from the same class, 629–631

overloaded member functions, 631–634

Music files

deleting from memory, 359

determining existence of, 359

introduction to, 357

loading from a CD, 360–363

loading of, 357–358

pausing and resuming, 359

playing, looping, and stopping, 358

playing or looping determination, 358–359

volume and speed of, 360

Mutator function, 619

N

Named constants

definition and function of, 129

program demonstrating, 130–131

Names

of functions, 141–142

of variables, 86

Negative coordinates, 60

Negative integers, 10

Nested decision structures

combining sequence structures with a decision structure, 229

`if-else-if` statements in, 235–236

introduction to, 228

nested `if` statements, 231

for a number guessing game, 232–234

programming style and, 234

sequence structure nested inside a decision structure, 230–231

Nesting function calls, 115

Not-equal-to operator, 219

NOT (`!`) logical operators

in Boolean expressions, 218–219

in compound Boolean expressions, 261, 263–264

Null character, 560–561

Number guessing game

introduction to, 226

program demonstrating, 226–227

program enhancing, with a `while` loop, 240–242

program for enhancing, with feedback, 232–234

Number storage, 7–9

Numeric input, keyboard reading of

`atoi` and `atof` for invalid characters, 120

converting numeric values to strings, 120–121

overview, 117–118

program demonstrating, 118–120

Numeric values

converting to strings, 120–121

representing true or false conditions, 271–273

O

Object-oriented game. *See* Balloon Target object-oriented game

Object-oriented programming (OOP)

example of an object, 613–614

object reusability in, 613

overview, 612–613

terminology, 613–614

Objects. *See also* Classes and objects

controlling with keyboard. *See* Controlling objects, with the keyboard

creating, 622–626

creating arrays of, 638–642

creating multiple objects from the same class, 629–631

illustrations, 612–613

passing as arguments to functions, 642–644

reusability of, 613

One-dimensional arrays, 521

`onSprite` function

Bug Zapper game and, 465–466

Bug Zapper game (version 2) and, 603

for working with the mouse, 452

OOP. *See* Object-oriented programming (OOP)

Opacity, of sprites, 311–312

Operands, 92

Operators

logical, 261–264

overview, 16–17

relational, 217–219

OR (`||`) logical operators, 261–262

Order of operations, 96–97

Orion constellation program

hand sketches of, 69–70

overview of graphic programming for, 67–68

pseudocode and program demonstrating, 71–73

using bitmap as background, 182–185

Output, 5

Output devices, 2, 5

Output file, 578. *See also* File input and output

Output/input. *See* File input and output

Overloaded constructors

overview, 635

program demonstrating, 635–638

`ThickCircle` class program and, 655

Overloaded draw functions, 632–634

Overriding, of a member function, 656

P

Panning sounds
   overview, 355
   programs demonstrating,
      356–357
Parameter variable
   definition of, 155
   scope of, 159
Parameterized constructor, 628
Parentheses, 97–99
Partially filled arrays
   dealing cards with. *See* Dealing
      cards, with partially filled
      arrays
   program demonstrating,
      503–504
Pascal programming language, 15
Passing by reference, 165–169
Passing by value, 163–165
Pasting, of sprites, 317–319
Picket fence program, 137
Pixels
   in bounding rectangles, 329
   changing the window size and,
      131–132
   data storage with, 10–11
   for loops for processing,
      255–256, 258–259
   programs illustrating pixel
      processing in images, 256–257,
      259–260
   resizing sprites and, 307–308
   in the screen coordinate system,
      43–44
   in sprite sheets, 326
   transparency of. *See* Color key
      transparency
PizzaBot game
   with sound, 347–350
   without sound, 333–337
Playing sound effects and music.
   See Music files; Sound files
Points, 374
Polylines
   illustrations, 488, 489
   program demonstrating,
      487–489
Postfix mode, 248
Posttest loops, 246–247
pow function, 115
Prefix mode, 248
Pretest loops, 242–245
Primitive graphics, 313–317. *See
   also* Graphics programming
Priority, of a sprite, 308–309

Private section, of the class, 617
Procedural programming
   overview, 611–612
Procedures, 611
Program testing, 141
Programmer, 1
Programming
   C++ and. *See* C++ programming
      language
   compilers and interpreters in,
      17–18
   Dark GDK library and. *See* Dark
      GDK library
   graphics programming, 74–75
   high-level languages, 14–16
   key words, operators and syntax
      in, 16–17
   languages, 15–16
   from machine language to
      assembly language, 14
   overview, 11–13
Programming style
   introduction to, 41–42
   nested decision structures and,
      234
Programs
   benefits of modularizing with
      functions, 139–141
   breaking down into functions,
      148–151
   definition of, 1
   designing, 74
   testing, 75
Project folder, for bitmap, 181–182
Prompt, 120
Pseudocode, 51–53
Pseudorandom numbers, 112
Public section, of the class, 617
Python programming language, 16

R

Radius array
   contents of, 478
   program demonstrating, 476–477
radius member function, 623
RAM (random-access memory), 4
random function, 410
Random numbers
   generation of, 110–111
   program demonstrating, 111–114
   seeding the generator, 112–113
randomColor function, 417–419
Read position, 590–592
Reading data illustrations, 579,
   591–592

Real numbers, 10
Redefinition, of a member function,
   656
Reference variables, 165–169
Relational operators
   Boolean expressions and,
      217–219
   list of, 218
Repetition structures, for loops
   basic definition, 215
   counting backward by
      decrementing, 254–255
   declaring the counter variable,
      252
   functions of, 249–251
   incrementing by values other
      than 1, 254
   program demonstrating,
      251–252
   using the counter variable in,
      253–254
Repetition structures, while and
   do-while loops
   basic definition, 215
   condition-controlled/count-
      controlled loops, 238
   definition and function of,
      237–238
   the do-while loop, 246–247
   for enhancing the number
      guessing game, 240–242
   infinite loops and, 245–246
   the while loop, 238–240
   the while loop as a pretest loop,
      242–245
Reserved words, 16–17
Resolution, 43
Return key, detecting, 290
return statement
   program demonstrating,
      415–417
   value-returning functions and,
      411, 413–414
Return type, 411
RGB color system
   definition and function of, 122
   storing in memory, 123–124
Right arrow key, detecting, 290
RotateSpriteWithOffset project,
   306
Rotation, of a sprite
   overview, 302
   program demonstrating,
      302–304, 305
Ruby programming language, 16

S

Sample Source Code, downloading and installing, 686
Samples, digital, 11
Saving a Game's High Score. *See* Bug Zapper game (version 2)
Scope
  local variables and, 154–155
  parameter variable's, 159
Screen coordinate system
  dbDot function in, 44–46
  dbWait function in, 46–47
  overview, 43–44
Secondary storage devices, 2, 4–5
Seed value, 112–113
Selection sort algorithm
  program demonstrating, 514–516
  for sorting arrays, 511
selectionSort function, 514–516, 517–520
Sequence structures
  combining with a decision structure, 229
  definition of, 213–214
  nested inside a decision structure, 230
Setup, Dark GDK, 685
Setup screen, Visual Studio 2008 Express Edition, 682
shapes, 2D
  dbCircle function and, 56–58
  dbEllipse function and, 58–60
  dbLine function (city skyline) and, 50–53
  dbLine function (triangle) and, 49–50
  drawn outside the Dark GDK window, 60–61
Short-circuit evaluation, 263
Showing, sprites, 307
Shuffled images, 502, 521
Shuffling an array
  introduction to, 498
  programs demonstrating, 499–501, 517–520
  swapping elements, 502–503
Simple animation
  game loops and, 286–289
Simulating falling objects
  calculating distance of a falling brick, 366–367
  calculating speed of a falling brick, 364–365
  motion in two directions and, 370–373

program simulating a falling ball, 367–370
Single alternative decision structure, 215–216
Size
  for bitmaps, 191
  of text, 374
Size declarators
  definition of, 474
  for two-dimensional arrays, 522–523
Skeleton program, 39–40
Slide show programs, 188–190
Software
  for C++/Dark GDK program, 20
  definition of, 1
  downloading and installing of. *See* Downloading and installing software
Software developer, 1
Sorted images, 521
Sorting algorithm, 511
Sorting arrays
  introduction to, 511
  program demonstrating selection sort algorithm, 514–516
  program demonstrating shuffling and, 517–520
  using a selection sort algorithm, 512–514
Sound files
  cloning of, 354
  deleting from memory, 353
  determining existence of, 353
  determining playing or looping in, 352
  introduction to, 345–346
  loading, 346
  looping, 350–351
  panning, 355–357
  pausing and resuming, 353–354
  playing, 347–350
  playing/looping part of, 352–353
  speed of, 355
  stopping, 352
  volume of, 354
Source code, 18
Space bar, detecting, 290
Special effects, with bitmaps images, 191–194
Specialization, and inheritance, 652
Speed
  of music files, 360
  of sound files, 355
Spreadsheets, 578

Sprite animations. *See also* Sprite sheets
  playing with the Dark GDK, 327
  program demonstrating, 328–329
Sprite class, 616
  class declarations, 645–646
  constructor in, 646
  destructor in, 646–647
  display member function and, 647
  getImageNumber member function and, 648
  getSpriteNumber member function and, 648–649
  getX member function and, 649
  getY member function and, 649
  hide member function and, 648
  introduction to, 645
  Moveable. *See* MoveableSprite class
  show member function and, 647–648
Sprite collision detection
  overview, 329–330
  PizzaBot game and, 333–337
  program adding sound, 347–350
  program demonstrating, 330–333
Sprite constraint
  introduction to, 422–423
  moving down, 425–427
  moving left, 427–429
  moving right, 430–432
  moving up, 423–425
  program demonstrating, 432–438
Sprite sheets
  illustration, 326
  playing animation and, 327–329
  simplifying animation with, 325–327
Sprites
  animation using. *See* Sprite animations; Sprite sheets
  changing the image, 309
  class. *See* Sprite class
  clicking, 448–452
  cloning of, 319–322
  collisions of. *See* Sprite collision detection
  constraining to visible area. *See* Sprite constraint
  creating a custom mouse pointer and, 452–454
  creation of, 296–298
  definition of, 296

deleting from memory, 312
determining existence of, 309
displaying with images and graphics, 312–317
flipping and mirroring of, 310–311
getting the width and height, 302
getting *X* and *Y* coordinates, 301
Layered Maps program and. *See* Layered Maps program
moving of, 298–301
offsetting insertion point, 304–307
pasting of, 317–319
resizing of, 307–308
rotating, 302–304, 305
setting a priority of, 308–309
setting back save and transparency features, 311
showing and hiding, 307
simulating falling objects and, 367–370
simulating motion in two directions, 371–373
using alpha value of, 311–312
Vulture Trouble game and, 388–391
Walking Alec program and. *See* Walking Alec program
XY coordinates, 448
Starting value, 112–113
Statements, 17
StealthJet program, 312
strcat function, to append a string, 563–564
strcmp function, to comparing strings, 565–568
strcpy function, to copy a string, 562–563
String concatenation, 563–564
String literals
  char variables and, 560, 561
  in literal data, 82–83
Strings
  arrays of strings, 574–577
  char data type, 559–560
  comparing, 565–568
  converting numeric values to, 120–121
  copying to char arrays, 562–563
  definition of, 61–62
  displaying a string stored in a char array, 562
  introduction to, 559
  Mad Libs word games, 571–574

reading, as input, 564–565
storing strings in memory, 560–561
strstr function and, 569
testing for a file's existence, 569–570
using char arrays for string storage, 561
using standard C++ library functions, 562
using strcat function to append to array, 563–564
using strlen function to get string length, 564
strlen function, to get string length, 564
strstr function, to search for strings, 569
Structure charts. *See* Hierarchy charts
Subscripts, array
  definition of, 475
  two-dimensional arrays and, 522–523
swap function, 517–520
Swapping
  array elements, 502–503
  sorting arrays and, 511–514
switch statement
  definition of, 266
  format of, 267–268
  Layered Maps program and, 549, 552
  program demonstrating, 269–271
  Walking Alec program and, 539, 542
Syntax, 16–17
Syntax errors
  correcting, in graphics programming, 74
  definition of, 18

T

Teamwork, 141
Terminals, in flow charts, 214
Test expression, and the for loop, 249–252
testExpression, in switch statements, 267–268
Text, displaying in the Dark GDK window
  with dbCenterText function, 64–65
  with dbPrint function, 61–62
  with dbText function, 63–64

Orion constellation program. *See* Orion constellation program
in title bar, 65–67
Text effects
  background transparency, 377–378
  changing the font, 374–375
  changing the size of, 374
  getting width and height, 378–379
  introduction to, 374
  program demonstrating, 376–377
  setting the cursor position, 379–381
  using bold and italic styles, 375–376
ThickCircle class program
  declaration and, 654
  inheritance notation in, 654
  introduction to, 653–654
  overloaded constructors and, 655
  setThickness member function and, 655
ThickCircle class program, version 2
  constructors in, 659–660
  declaration and, 659
  introduction to, 658–659
Tic-Tac-Toe screen, 557
Tile-based images, 529, 555
Tile maps
  displaying layered sets of tiles. *See* Layered Maps program
  introduction to, 529–530
  program adding action to tile maps. *See* Walking Alec program
  program demonstrating, 532–534
  steps in constructing, 530–532
Tiles
  definition of, 529
  illustrations, 530
Top-down-design
  program demonstrating, 149–151
  for using functions, 148–149
Transparency. *See also* Color key transparency
  saving sprites, 311
  for text background, 377–378
Traveling dog program
  background images and, 205–207
  illustrations, 205
Travelling dog program
  illustrations, 207
Triangle, 49–50

Truncation
in the `dbDot` function, 46
floating-point, 91
Truth tables
for the `!` operator, 264
for the `&&` operator, 262
for the `||` operator, 262
Two-dimensional (2D) graphics.
See Basic 2D shapes
Two-dimensional arrays
accessing the elements in,
523–524
declaring, 522–523
definition and function of,
521–522
illustrations, 522, 523, 525, 526,
528
initializing, 524–526
passing to a function, 526–528
Two-dimensional game character, 48
`.txt` extension file names, 580

U
Unicode, 10
Uninitialized variables, 90–91
USB drives, 5
User, 41

V
Value-returning functions
definition and function of,
108–109, 409–410
getting random numbers,
110–112
math functions, 115–116
nesting function calls, 115
program demonstrating, 109–110
Value-returning functions, writing
constraining a sprite and. *See*
Sprite constraint
format for, 410–412
overview, 409–410
program demonstrating, 412–413
to return a color, 417–419
returning Boolean values and,
420–422
using the `return` statement,
413–416
Values
assigning to variables, 87
sorting arrays and, 511–514
Variable declaration
assigning values, 87
floating-point truncation in, 91

initializing, 87–88
location for, 90
programs illustrating, 88–90
uninitialized variables in, 90–91
Variables
counter variables. *See* Counter
variable
data types, 85
declaration. *See* Variable
declaration
limitations of, 473–474
local. *See* Local variables
names, 86, 154–155
overview, 84–85
Visual Basic programming
language, 16
Visual C++ programming language.
See C++ programming language
void functions
calling, 143–145
definition of, 142–143. *See also*
Function names; Function
prototypes
designing a program for use of,
148–151
global constants and, 171–173
global variables and, 169–171
local variables, 151–155
passing arguments to. *See*
Arguments, passing to
functions
program modularization with,
139–141
value-returning functions and,
409
Volume
of music files, 360
of sound files, 354
Vulture Trouble game
`checkCollisions` function and,
396–397
`createSprites` function and,
388–391
`DarkGDK` function and, 384–386
`deleteSprites` function and,
403
global constants declarations and,
383–384
`intro` function and, 387–388
introduction to, 382
`loadResources` function and,
386–387
`moveBasket` function and,
391–392

`moveEgg` function and, 394–395
`moveVulture` function and,
392–393
`render` function and, 400–401
`resetEgg` function and, 399–400
`showBrokenEgg` function and,
398–399
`showHitBasket` function and,
397–398
`summaryScreen` function and,
401–403

W
Walking Alec program
`arrowKeyPressed` function and,
538, 542
`DarkGDK` function and, 536, 541
`displayTiles` function and,
537, 541
game loops and, 536, 541
global constants declarations and,
534–535, 540–541
illustrations, 540
`moveAlec` function and,
538–539, 542
`setUp` function and, 536–537,
541
switch statement and, 539, 542
`updateDirection` function and,
538, 542
WAV format. *See* Sound files
Web browsers, 578
Web sites
The Game Creators, 683
Microsoft, 682
while loops
basic definition, 215
for comparing two arrays, 490
condition-controlled/count-
controlled loops, 238
definition and function of,
237–238
`do-while` loop, 246–247
enhancing the number guessing
game with, 240–242
the game loop as, 285
infinite loops and, 245–246
logic of, 239
overview, 238–240
as a pretest loop, 242–245
as repetition structures, 238–240
Width
of a sprite, 302
text effects and, 378–379